Living by Vow

When life comes we just face life
Don't be used by it.

Why is it that so much in
Buddhism is numbered??

Webster dictionary
def. of English word
empty - containing nothing,
not filled or occupied
synonym: vacant, unoccupied
uninhabited, clear, free
— lacking meaning or sincerity
emptiness - the state of
containing nothing
void, vacuum, lack,
gap

~~as a human condition~~ is a
sense of boredom, social alienation
and apathy

Buddhist term emptiness - refers
specifically to the idea that
everything is dependently originated
including the causes + conditions
Taoism - state of emptiness - state
of stillness + placidity
"mirror of the universe"
a ~~state~~ of "vacancy, stillness,
placidity, tastelessness, quietude
silence + non-action

LIVING BY VOW

A PRACTICAL INTRODUCTION TO EIGHT ESSENTIAL ZEN CHANTS AND TEXTS

Shohaku Okumura

EDITED BY DAVE ELLISON

Wisdom Publications
199 Elm Street
Somerville MA 02144 USA
wisdompubs.org

Library of Congress Cataloging-in-Publication Data
Okumura, Shohaku, 1948–
Living by vow : a practical introduction to eight essential Zen chants and texts / Shohaku Okumura ; edited by Dave Ellison.
pages cm
Includes bibliographical references and index.
ISBN 1-61429-010-5 (p : alk. paper)
1. Zen literature—History and criticism. 2. Zen Buddhism—Rituals. 3. Buddhist chants. I. Title.
BQ9273.O58 2012
294.3'438—dc23
2011048873

ISBN 978-1-61429-010-0 eBook ISBN 978-1-61429-021-6

19 18 17 16 15
6 5 4 3 2

Cover art by Eiji Imao: www.eonet.ne.jp/~eijin/index.html. Cover design by JBTL. Interior design by Gopa&Ted2. Set in Diacritical Garamond 11.9/11.5.

Wisdom Publications' books are printed on acid-free paper and meet the guidelines for permanence and durability of the Production Guidelines for Book Longevity of the Council on Library Resources.

This book was produced with environmental mindfulness. For more information, please visit wisdompubs.org/wisdom-environment.

Printed in the United States of America.

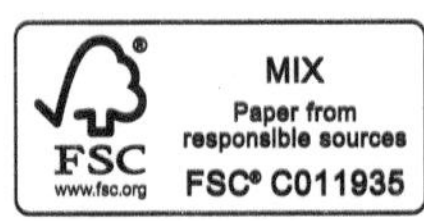

Please visit fscus.org.

CONTENTS

Empty space - allows all beings to exist and it doesn't disappear even when beings disappear.
never changes, never appears, never disappears. Never defiled, never pure
Emptiness - without self-nature or substance, impermanent and always changing.

Put your mind in neutral —

* Zen Buddhism is a mixture of Indian Buddhism & Taoism.

Editor's Preface

On their first encounter with the sutras many Zen beginners are perplexed. A few words might look familiar from other reading. Perhaps the overall gist seems apparent. But on first reading many sutras are an impenetrable mixture of meaningless foreign phrases and illogical paradoxes. To the experienced student, sutras can present another sort of problem. After years of study and practice, many of us fall into narrow, knee-jerk interpretations of the sutras we've recited so often. This book is aimed directly at both problems. As an experienced practitioner of Zen, Shohaku Okumura speaks clearly and directly of the personal meaning and implications of Zen practice. He uses his own life experiences to illustrate the practical significance of the sutras to the beginning student. As a scholar of Buddhist literature he reveals the subtle, intricate web of culture and history that surrounds the words so familiar to the longtime student. The net effect is of a sympathetic friend who has practiced Zen for decades (and also happens to be a Buddhist scholar) patiently explaining, annotating, and illuminating eight of the most important sutras. Esoteric Sanskrit terms take on vivid, personal meaning. Worn-out, empty phrases gain rich new poetic resonance. Both the neophyte and the experienced practitioner will come away with a richer appreciation of these sutras.

For instance, take the word "vow." Many modern readers, scientists, skeptics, and secular humanists might find this concept distinctly uncomfortable. Some may feel it carries the taint of ancient dogma draped in musty, jewel-encrusted robes. It hints of rigid rules for diet, sexual practices, clothing, and social hierarchies. Okumura Roshi uses the teachings and poetry of the Buddha, Dōgen, Katagiri Roshi, Uchiyama Roshi, and others to elucidate the central role of vow in Zen practice. In the process he gives fresh meaning to the word. Instead of a static pledge, vow is shown to be a dynamic, day-to-day expression of the most fundamental aspect of our true nature. He shows how our sitting practice, our Zen community, and our livelihood can all be animated and illuminated by vow.

Emptiness, or *śūnyatā*, like many concepts in Zen, is slippery and paradoxical. In his chapter on the *Heart Sutra*, Okumura Roshi uses the words of masters selected from the twenty-five-hundred-year tradition of Zen to elucidate this challenging but crucial reality. The result is multilayered, cross-cultural, philosophical, and at the same time personal. His interpretation of the five *skandhas* can be read as a paraphrase of a modern neuroscience text. He quotes Nāgārjuna, who lived nearly two thousand years ago, to demonstrate how awareness of emptiness leads naturally to a more peaceful, stable life in our modern world. Impermanence and interdependence are not merely philosophical abstractions. They are fundamental aspects of our daily existence. Ongoing recognition of this reality leads naturally to generosity, egolessness, and inner calm. The appreciation and application of this concept is a very practical antidote to the pervasive angst of our modern consumer society.

This book offers the thoughtful reader an opportunity to apply the cumulative insights of twenty-five hundred years of disciplined spiritual research to their own everyday existence. It is neither a quick, effortless panacea nor an abstract metaphysical treatise, but rather a series of signposts to guide and inspire the determined seeker.

Dave Ellison

Author's Preface

This book is based on a series of lectures I gave as the interim head teacher at the Minnesota Zen Meditation Center (MZMC) in Minneapolis from September 1993 to August 1996. The center was founded by Dainin Katagiri Roshi. He originally came to the United States in 1963 to serve at Zenshū Sōtōji, the Sōtō Zen temple for the Japanese-American community in Los Angeles. A few years later, he moved to Sōkōji to assist Shunryū Suzuki Roshi, the resident priest at Sōkōji and the founding teacher of the San Francisco Zen Center. He practiced and taught there as the assistant teacher until Suzuki Roshi's death in 1971. The next year he moved to Minneapolis and founded the MZMC, where he served as abbot until his death in March 1990 at the age of sixty-three.

The MZMC is located on the eastern shore of Lake Calhoun in South Minneapolis near the Uptown neighborhood. The center was named Kōun-zan Ganshōji by Katagiri Roshi. The mountain (*zan*) name Kōun means "cultivating the clouds" and is taken from one of Dōgen's well-known poems.[1] The temple name Gansho means "living by vow" and alludes to one of the definitions of a bodhisattva: "Ordinary people are those who live being pulled by their karma (*gosshō no bonpu*); bodhisattvas are those who live led by their vows (*ganshō no bosatsu*)."

I had the opportunity to practice with Katagiri Roshi for one month at Daijōji monastery in Kanazawa, Japan, in 1988. He was the head teacher of the one-month special training period sponsored by Sōtōshū Shūmuchō for Western Sōtō Zen teachers. I was one of the assistants during the training period. Katagiri Roshi gave lectures on the *Shōbōgenzō* chapter Kūge (Flower of Emptiness) in English to the Western teachers. When I listened to his lectures, I was astonished and very inspired. I already had some experience giving dharma talks in English to Westerners, but until then I did not think I could give lectures on *Shōbōgenzō*. Later I had several opportunities to visit the MZMC to lecture his students while he was sick with cancer. That was why I was invited to be the interim head teacher three years after Katagiri Roshi's death.

When I accepted the invitation from the MZMC I resolved to continue Katagiri Roshi's style of practice and transmit the same essential spirit of bodhisattva practice, or living by vow (*ganshō*), to his students. Therefore, when I started to teach, my first seven talks were on the bodhisattva vows.

Some of the differences and similarities between Katagiri Roshi's style of practice and my own can be understood in terms of the history of our lineages. From Shakyamuni Buddha until the seventy-fifth ancestor, Gangoku Kankei Daiosho̅ (1683–1767), our lineage is exactly the same. Katagiri Roshi was the sixth generation and I am the eighth generation from Gangoku Kankei Daioshō. Soon after he was ordained as a Sōtō Zen priest, Katagiri Roshi practiced for three years with Hashimoto Ekō Roshi, who was the *godō* (instructor for training monks) at Eiheiji monastery. Hashimoto Roshi was a close friend of Sawaki Kōdō Roshi, and my teacher, Uchiyama Kōshō Roshi, was a disciple of Sawaki Roshi. They both emphasized *nyohō-e*, traditional sewing of the *okesa* and the *rakusu* worn by priests and laypeople who receive the Buddha's precepts. Hashimoto Roshi and Sawaki Roshi practiced together under Oka Sōtan Roshi's guidance at Shuzenji monastery. Another student of Oka Roshi was Kishizawa Ian Roshi, with whom Shunryū Suzuki Roshi studied in Japan. The lineages of Kishizawa Roshi, Hashimoto

Roshi, and Sawaki Roshi are thus closely related. In the United States the influence of these three roshis continues through the lineages of Suzuki Roshi, Katagiri Roshi, and Uchiyama Roshi.

Although Hashimoto Roshi and Sawaki Roshi were good friends, their styles of practice were quite different. Hashimoto Roshi emphasized the importance of maintaining the details of Dōgen Zenji's monastic practice. Narasaki Ikkō Roshi and Tsūgen Roshi, the abbots of Zuiōji, retained Hashimoto Roshi's style in Japan. Narasaki Roshi and Katagiri Roshi were very close. Katagiri Roshi also adhered to Hashimoto Roshi's very traditional monastic practice and sent some of his disciples to Zuiōji. Together, Narasaki Roshi and Katagiri Roshi planned to create an international monastery at Shōgoji, in Kumamoto Prefecture in Kyūshū. Katagiri Roshi was going to lead the international summer practice period when the construction of the monks' hall (*sodo*) was completed. Unfortunately he passed away before that happened.

Sawaki Roshi never had his own temple or monastery. He was a professor at Komazawa University for more than thirty years. He also traveled throughout Japan to teach. Many laypeople started to practice zazen because of his efforts. Sawaki Roshi was called "homeless" Kōdō because he did not have a monastery or temple but instead traveled all over Japan. He called his teaching style a moving monastery. My teacher Kōshō Uchiyama Roshi was ordained by Sawaki Roshi and practiced only with him. After Sawaki Roshi passed away, Uchiyama Roshi became the abbot of Antaiji. He focused on zazen practice with minimal ceremony, ritual, and formality. Uchiyama Roshi started five-day "sesshins without toys," during which we simply sat fourteen fifty-minute periods of zazen. I was ordained by Uchiyama Roshi and practiced at Antaiji until he retired in 1975.

After Uchiyama Roshi's retirement I practiced at Zuiōji, where Narasaki Ikkō Roshi was abbot. There, for a short period of time, I experienced Hashimoto Roshi's style of practice. I learned firsthand that Katagiri Roshi's style of practice and the style taught by Uchiyama Roshi were quite different.

Recently Arthur Braverman, a friend of mine from Antaiji, wrote an article about Uchiyama Roshi in *Buddhadharma* magazine. In it he said:

> While Shunryū Suzuki was igniting a Zen revolution in San Francisco in the late sixties, Kōshō Uchiyama was trying to foster a Zen reformation in Japan. It was perhaps an even more imposing challenge when one considers the power of the traditional Sōtō Zen sect in Japan.
>
> Both masters believed greatly in the power of meditation, and both did a masterful job of transmitting the importance of zazen to their students. While Suzuki Roshi was attempting to get his American students to see the importance of many of the Japanese forms, Uchiyama was trying to teach his Japanese students not to be attached to the forms, but to let the forms grow out of the practice.[2]

This is a very clear explanation of both the difference and the underlying unity of Uchiyama Roshi's style and that of Suzuki Roshi and Katagiri Roshi. Katagiri Roshi also put emphasis on traditional formal Sōtō Zen monastic practice. For me, the decision to follow Katagiri Roshi's style was a big one. For all Dōgen Zenji's descendants, of course, the basic spirit of the bodhisattva practice is the same. I feel that the essence of bodhisattva practice and the common ground of various styles of practice is living by vow.

Katagiri Roshi often spoke about living by vow. In his book *Each Moment Is the Universe*, he says that wholehearted practice of zazen is itself living by vow.

> In zazen many things come up: thoughts, emotions, sometimes anger and hatred. But all you have to do is take care of zazen in eternal possibility. It's completely beyond good or bad, right or wrong, so put aside all kinds of imagination fabricated by your consciousness. Don't attach to thoughts

> and emotions, just let them return to emptiness. Just be present there and swim in buddha-nature. This is living the bodhisattva vow to help all beings. Then the great energy of the universe supports you and you take one step toward the future with all beings.[3]

Katagiri Roshi wrote his *yuige* (bequeathed verse) a few weeks before his death:

> Living in Vow, silently sitting
> Sixty-three years
> Plum blossoms begin to bloom
> The jeweled mirror reflects truth as it is.[4]

While my practice and understanding were greatly enriched by my study of Katagiri Roshi's style of practice, I also learned from him how to teach Americans. For that I am very grateful. For twenty years I practiced Uchiyama Roshi's style of sesshin with no activities other than zazen. At MZMC I gave lectures and had dokusan (private interviews) during sesshins. It was a challenge, but I learned a great deal.

After lecturing on "living by vow," I spoke on the verses and sutras in the MZMC sutra book. Since these are chanted regularly, they are the Buddhist literature most familiar to Sōtō Zen practitioners, both in Japan and in the West. Many people memorize them. But the meaning of these verses and sutras is rarely explained. That is why I gave lectures on them. I talked about them on Saturday mornings for about three years until 1996, when I finished my term as the interim head teacher at MZMC.

Most of the lectures included in this book were transcribed by José Escobar and Dave Ellison. Some lectures were not recorded and a few tapes were missing. I rewrote these sections to fill the gaps. My talks on the *Heart Sutra* were transcribed and edited by Dave and printed in the MZMC newsletter. Tom Goodell, one of the practitioners at MZMC, was the first person who worked on this project. Since both Tom and

I were very busy, especially after I moved to California to work for Sōtōshū North America Education Center (currently Sōtōshū International Center), the project could not be completed. A few years later, Dave kindly took over the project and patiently continued to work on it for more than ten years. I gave these lectures more than fifteen years ago, right after I moved to Minneapolis from Japan. Even though I had lived in the United States for five years, my English was not fluent. I had a limited vocabulary with which to express my thoughts. I am sure that it was difficult for Dave to understand what I wanted to say. I deeply appreciate his hard work, which "translated" my very Japanese English into readable English.

I would like to express my appreciation to Jōkei Molly Whitehead, a disciple of mine at Sanshinji. While she was busy for preparing for her ordination ceremony, she worked hard on the final stages of this book and gave us many helpful suggestions. I also express my gratitude to Andrea Martin, who allowed me to read a draft of her book *Ceaseless Effort: The Life of Dainin Katagiri* and gave me permission to quote Katagiri Roshi's *yuige*. Finally I am extremely delighted to have Eiji Imao's beautiful painting "Tsukinohikari (Moonlight)" on the cover of this book. I appreciate his generous permission to use a painting of his again, as we did on *Realizing Genjokoan*.

Katagiri Roshi's dharma heirs and their students fulfilled his vow to transmit Dōgen Zenji's teaching and practice to America. The tree of Dharma transplanted by Katagiri Roshi continues to grow as its roots spread and deepen in the soil of American spiritual culture in the Twin Cities and elsewhere. I deeply appreciate their continuous efforts and their friendship.

Gassho,
Shohaku Okumura

INTRODUCTION

ALL BUDDHIST SCHOOLS have rituals, services, and ceremonies. At almost all such formal activities we chant verses, poems, or sutras and dedication of merit (*ekō*). Each Buddhist school has a collection of these writings, often called a sutra book (*kyōhon* in Japanese), used in daily practice. This book presents my lectures on some of the verses and sutras in the sutra book.

In the Sōtō Zen tradition, the official sutra book published by the administrative headquarters (Shūmuchō) is *Sōtōshū Nikka Gongyō Seiten*. This collection was translated into English and published by Shūmuchō in 2002 with the title *Sōtō School Scriptures for Daily Service and Practice*. Before the publication of this sutra book, each Zen center in the United States created its own book, sometimes using different translations. Many centers still use their own versions. The text I used for the lectures in this book is MZMC's sutra book.

As is often said, there is no perfect translation, especially in the case of religious scriptures. A translation optimized for meaning is often difficult to read and chant. But to create a beautiful verse we may have to sacrifice the exact meaning of the original texts. Each teacher and translator has a different interpretation and mode of expression. The translations in the MZMC version, which I use except for the meal chants, are no exception. Sometimes I offer an understanding of certain words that differs from the meaning expressed in the MZMC translations. My interpretation is based on my study and practice, but it is not the only correct one. My hope is that this book will help practitioners understand the meaning of the verses and sutras in the context of their own practice. Perhaps my commentary will be a foundation for better translations in the future.

I believe that all verses and scriptures in the Sōtō Zen tradition are based on the Mahāyāna teaching of the bodhisattva vow. That is why I titled this book *Living by Vow*. It is meant to be a practical introduction not only to Sōtō Zen practice but also to Mahāyāna teaching in general.

Sōtō Zen Buddhism is part of the Mahāyāna Buddhist tradition in which practitioners are called *bodhisattvas*. We receive bodhisattva precepts and take bodhisattva vows. The historical origin of Mahāyāna Buddhism is not yet clear. In Japan, until the nineteenth century, all Mahāyāna sutras were considered the recorded sayings of Shakyamuni Buddha. When modern historical and critical Buddhist study was established, scholars found that Mahāyāna sutras were created at least several hundred years after Shakyamuni Buddha's death. When they began to study the origin of the Mahāyāna Buddhist movement, some scholars thought Mahāyāna developed from Mahāsāṃghika, one of the early Buddhist sects. Later, scholars such as Akira Hirakawa (1915–2002) proposed that Mahāyāna Buddhism grew from lay Buddhist movements in various areas of India, a claim derived from the study of stūpa worship and biographical literature praising Shakyamuni Buddha's bodhisattva practice. Examples are texts such as *Mahāvastu*, Aśvaghoṣa's *Buddha-carita*, and the Jātaka tales. When I was a university student this was a new and exciting hypothesis. Many Japanese Buddhist scholars accepted the theory, although opinions differed on details. Scholars hypothesized that there were bodhisattva *gaṇa*s (i.e., sanghas) that existed independently from monastic sanghas. Today, some Western scholars criticize this hypothesis and suggest that Mahāyāna began as a movement of a small number of elite monks who aspired to live and practice in the forest like Shakyamuni Buddha when he was a bodhisattva in his previous lives.

Either way, one of the fundamental ideas of Mahāyāna Buddhism is to take the bodhisattva vow and practice like Shakyamuni to attain buddhahood. The story that Shakyamuni Buddha took the bodhisattva vow appears not only in biographies of the Buddha but also in accounts of his past lives. I think that Shakyamuni's vow originated when he rose from his seat under the bodhi tree and decided to teach. This story, which probably came into existence several hundred years after the Buddha's death, was the original inspiration for bodhisattva practice. I would like to introduce a story from the Pāli canon. Although it is not a Mahāyāna text, all the essential points of the bodhisattva ideal are already there. One important difference is that in the Pāli tradition the term *bodhisattva* refers only to Shakyamuni himself before he attained buddhahood. Only later did tradition create past buddhas such as Vipaśyin Buddha and the future buddha Maitreya. But Mahāyāna Buddhists believed that any one of us could become a bodhisattva if we aroused *bodhi-citta* (bodhi-mind), took bodhisattva vows, and practiced the six *pāramitās*, or perfections.

This story comes from the Khuddaka Nikāya of the Pāli canon. One part of this Nikāya, the Jātakas, comprises 547 tales of Shakyamuni Buddha's previous lives. One of these stories is of Sumedha (the Buddha in a previous life). When he took a vow to become a buddha the Buddha Dīpaṃkara predicted that Sumedha would successfully attain buddhahood in a future life. This story illustrates the origin of the bodhisattva vow and many of the important points of bodhisattva practice. It is interesting that the archetypal image of the bodhisattva already existed in the Pāli Nikāyas.[5]

This story took place countless eons ago. In a city called Amaravatī lived a Brāhmin named Sumedha, who was an outstanding person from a prestigious family. When Sumedha was still young his parents died. A minister of the state, who was steward of the family's property, showed Sumedha the wealth accumulated for seven generations that he inherited from his parents. The family treasury was filled with gold and silver, gems and pearls, and other valuables.

When he saw the treasure he thought, "After amassing all this wealth, none of my parents and ancestors were able to take even a penny with them when they passed away. Can it be right that I should seek to take my wealth with me when I go?" Then he told the king that he would give all this wealth to the poor and leave home to become a spiritual practitioner.

He saw that a life transmigrating within samsara—the cycle of birth, sickness, aging, and death—was suffering and he wanted to find the path of deliverance into nirvana. Sumedha thought, "Suppose a man, after falling into a heap of filth, hears about a distant pond covered with lotuses of five colors. That man ought to search for that pond. If he does not, that's not the pond's fault. In the same way, there is a lake—the great, deathless nirvana—in which to wash off the defilements of my harmful karma. If I do not seek it that will not be the lake's fault." So he left home and entered a forest in the Himalayas to practice as a hermit. Because he was a person of great capability, he attained superhuman knowledge and supernatural power.

While he was practicing thus, Dīpaṃkara Buddha appeared in the world and started to teach. Dīpaṃkara Buddha visited a city not far from where Sumedha was living. The people of that city invited the Buddha and his assembly of followers for a meal. In preparation they began to fix the road, which was flooded, and decorate it with flowers. Sumedha flew there by means of his supernatural power. He asked why they were working so hard and were so excited. They explained that Dīpaṃkara Buddha was coming. Sumedha was delighted and offered his help. Because people knew that Sumedha had supernatural powers, they asked him to fill the muddy part of the road with soil. But Sumedha, although he could easily have filled the muddy road using his supernatural power, wanted to use his own hands instead. He started to carry soil by hand. Unfortunately, Dīpaṃkara Buddha and his assembly arrived before his work was completed.

Sumedha did not want the Buddha to walk through the mud, so

he loosened his matted hair, lay down on the ground, and asked the Buddha to walk on him—a dramatic expression of his commitment to take refuge in the Buddha, the Dharma, and the Sangha. Even today, some Buddhists make prostrations by laying their bodies full length on the ground. When we make prostrations in the Sōtō Zen tradition, we place five parts of our bodies—both knees, both elbows, and forehead—on the ground. We place our hands palm up at the level of our ears as if to accept the Buddha's feet on our hands. This is the form we use to express our respect and gratitude to the Buddha.

When Sumedha, lying in the mire, looked up at Dīpaṃkara Buddha, he made a vow: "If I want I could now enter the Buddhist sangha and by practicing meditation free myself from deluded human desires and become an arhat. Then at death I would at once attain nirvana and cease to be reborn. But this would be a selfish course to pursue, for thus I should benefit myself only. I want to help all beings as Dīpaṃkara Buddha is doing now. I am determined. I vow to attain what Dīpaṃkara Buddha attained and benefit all beings." Upon seeing Dīpaṃkara Buddha, Sumedha abandoned his earlier intention to escape from samsara. Now he aspired to live like the Buddha, staying in samsara to help all living beings.

Dīpaṃkara Buddha, seeing Sumedha lying in the mud, understood that the young man had vowed to become a buddha. He told his assembly that in the distant future Sumedha would become a buddha named Gautama. Hearing this prediction, Sumedha was delighted and believed his vow would be realized. Having praised Sumedha for his vow, Dīpaṃkara Buddha and his assembly departed. Thus Sumedha became "the Bodhisattva," which in this case means "the Buddha-to-be." This is an early example of the path called bodhisattva practice chosen by Shakyamuni Buddha.

Sumedha then realized that to become a buddha he should practice the ten pāramitās: the perfection of giving (*dāna*), the perfection of moral practice (*śīla*), the perfection of renunciation (*nekkhamma*), the perfection of wisdom (*paññā*, known more commonly by the Sanskrit *prajñā*), the perfection of diligence (*viriya*), the perfection of patience (*khanti*), the perfection of truthfulness (*sacca*), the perfection of determination (*adhitthāna*), the perfection of loving-kindness (*mettā*), and the perfection of equanimity (*upekkhā*). This list of ten pāramitās is found in the Pāli canon. It is interesting to note that five of them (giving, moral practice, patience, diligence, and wisdom) are present in the Mahāyāna list of six pāramitās. The sixth pāramitā, missing in the Pāli version, is meditation (*dhyāna*). But in some Mahāyāna sutras, for instance the *Ten Stages Sutra*, ten pāramitās are mentioned: the six pāramitās just mentioned and these four: skillful means (*upāya*); vow, resolution, or determination (*pranidhāna*); spiritual power (*bala*); and knowledge (*jñāna*).

The image of Shakyamuni as a bodhisattva is broadly similar in early Buddhism and Mahāyāna. One significant difference is that Mahāyāna Buddhists have always held that anyone, even ordinary people like us, can be a bodhisattva if they arouse bodhichitta, take the bodhisattva vow, and practice the six pāramitās. None of us can expect to receive a prophecy assuring us of attaining buddhahood, but since all beings intrinsically have buddha-nature, it is certain that we will complete our vow and attain buddhahood.

The archetypal image of the bodhisattva in this story suggests that all Mahāyāna Buddhist practice is based on the bodhisattva vow. The vow has two aspects: becoming a buddha and helping all beings become buddhas. These two cannot be separated. We vow to become buddhas together with all beings. That is, we vow not to become a buddha until all beings become buddhas. We vow to stay in samsara on purpose to walk with all beings. This explains why the Zen master Guishan Lingyou (Isan Reiyū) said he would be reborn as a water buffalo, for the water buffalo, which walks in muddy water to help farmers grow rice, symbolizes bodhisattva practice. The bodhisattva vow is an essential point in Mahāyāna teachings and practice. All the verses and sutras discussed in this book are based on or relate to this concept.

Repentance, or atonement, is intimately connected to vow. My teacher Uchiyama Kōshō Roshi always emphasized that vow and repentance are two sides of one practice. Because our vow is endless, our practice is never complete. This awareness of incompleteness is repentance. In *The Hungry Tigress* Rafe Martin tells the story of the beginning of Shakyamuni Buddha's search for truth.[6] In this story Shakyamuni was a king named Suprabhasa. One day the king asked his elephant trainer to bring his great white elephant for him to ride. The trainer said that the elephant had escaped to the jungle but it would return because he had trained it well. The king did not believe him, grew angry, lost all self-control, yelled at him, and told him to leave. Next morning, the trainer reported that the elephant had returned. "The training was good," he said. "We have conquered his old, wild ways." When he heard this the king thought, "Though I am a king holding great power over others, I have as yet failed to conquer what is closest—myself. I was unable to control my own anger. This will not do."

Such a reflection and realization of one's own incompleteness is repentance. It is the origin of Shakyamuni Buddha's search for the Way. This same realization gives us the energy to study and practice diligently.

The verse of the Triple Treasure clearly states the connection between refuge and vow. When Sumedha, lying on the muddy road, asked Dīpaṃkara Buddha to walk on him, he took refuge in the Buddha, the Dharma, and the Sangha. Dīpaṃkara noticed Sumedha's gesture and vow and predicted that he would be a buddha. By taking refuge, we make clear the direction we intend to follow. Taking refuge in the Buddha, we vow together with all beings to walk his path of wisdom and compassion; taking refuge in the Dharma, we vow to share the teachings and wisdom as boundless as the ocean; taking refuge in the Sangha, we vow to create harmony without hindrance.

In the Mahāyāna tradition, people become Buddhists when they take the bodhisattva vow, repent their previous way of life, and take refuge in the Triple Treasure. Some of them choose to leave home and practice at monasteries. In the traditional Sōtō Zen monasteries, monks in training live in the monks' hall where they share their entire time and space with other practitioners. Their practice of vow includes not just the study of Dharma teachings and meditation practice but all the activities of daily life, including sleeping, eating, working, washing the face, and shaving the head. In addition to shelter, food and clothing are the most important elements of the monks' lives. The robe chant and the meal chants originate from this way of life dedicated to the bodhisattva vow.

In the robe chant verse, sometimes called the "Verse of the Kesa," we affirm our aim to practice with the same vow that Shakyamuni Buddha and all other bodhisattvas including Dōgen Zenji took—to save all beings. Dōgen Zenji himself took a vow when he first saw Chinese monks venerate the robe (okesa/kesa) by putting it on their heads and chanting. His vow was to introduce the okesa and encourage Japanese people to venerate it as a part of bodhisattva practice.

In *Shōbōgenzō* "Kesakudoku" (Virtue of the Kesa) Dōgen Zenji quotes a Mahāyāna sutra, the *Sutra of Compassion Flower* (*Hige-kyō*), in which Shakyamuni Buddha, when he was a bodhisattva in one of his past lives, took five vows regarding the okesa (or *kaṣāya*). One of his vows was that he would help students put on the okesa with respect and veneration. Then Dōgen Zenji commented on these vows:

> Truly, the kaṣāya is the buddha robe of all the buddhas in the past, present, and future. Although the virtues of the kaṣāya [from any buddha] are boundless, attaining the kaṣāya within the Dharma of Shakyamuni Buddha must be superior to getting it from other buddhas.
>
> This is because when Shakyamuni Buddha was in the causal stage [of practice] as the Great Compassion Bodhisattva, he took five hundred vows in front of the Jewel-Treasury Buddha. He particularly took vows regarding the virtues of the kaṣāya.

Even mundane daily activities like eating are related to vow. In the Zen tradition, monks sleep, meditate, and eat in a building called a *sōdō* (monks' hall). When we have formal meals in this hall, we chant verses to remind ourselves that eating is also a bodhisattva practice. We remember Shakyamuni Buddha's life and give praise. Then we vow to receive the food that comes to us from the network of interdependent origination, share it with all beings, and fulfill the bodhisattva vow to attain buddhahood together with all beings.

The *Heart Sutra* explains the practice necessary to achieve this vow. After Sumedha received Dīpaṃkara Buddha's prediction, he decided to practice the ten pāramitās. In Mahāyāna Buddhism the sixth pāramitā, the pāramitā of meditation (*dhyāna*), should be practiced by all bodhisattvas. The *Heart Sutra*, one of the early Mahāyāna *Prajñāpāramitā Sutras*, emphasizes the pāramitā of *prajñā*, or wisdom, as the most essential of the six. Without prajñā, the other five practices cannot be pāramitās (perfections). Although a relatively recent sutra, the *Heart Sutra* is considered the essence of the large collection of *Prajñāpāramitā Sutras*. It points to the essential role of prajñā in our efforts to fulfill our vows. To follow the bodhisattva path, we study and practice prajñāpāramitā, the wisdom that sees impermanence, no-self, emptiness, and interdependent origination. When we clearly see this reality; that we and other things exist together without fixed independent entities, our practice is strengthened. We understand that to live by vow is not to accept a particular fixed doctrine but is a natural expression of our life force.

Zen Buddhism originated in China. "Sandōkai," a poem written in the ninth century by the Zen master Shitou Xiqian, is a Chinese expression of Buddhist wisdom that sees emptiness. In the very beginning of "Sandōkai," the author clearly states that the mind of the Buddha has been intimately transmitted through ancestors in the Zen tradition. "Intimately" means from person to person, not through written words and concepts. When the first ancestor of Chinese Zen, Bodhidharma, traveled from India to China, he was practicing his bodhisattva vow: to transmit and share the true Dharma, the mind of the Buddha, with Chinese people. Dōgen Zenji commented on Bodhidharma's practice in *Shōbōgenzō* "Gyōji" (Continuous Practice), "This way of protecting and maintaining practice [*gyōji*] stemmed from his great compassion and his vow to transmit the Dharma and save deluded living beings. He was able to do it because he himself was the dharma-self of transmission and for him the whole universe was the world of transmitting Dharma." In the same way, transmission of Buddha Dharma from Asian Buddhist countries to the West is the result of many Buddhist monks and laypeople who live by vow. Shitou, the eighth-generation ancestor from Bodhidharma expresses prajñā as the merging of the two truths, ultimate (*ri*) and conventional (*ji*). At the end of "Sandōkai" he encourages us to practice wholeheartedly and not waste time.

The "Verse for Opening the Sutra" explicitly points to the importance of vow. When we chant it before a dharma talk (open the sutra), we vow to listen, understand, digest, and apply the teaching to our practice. This is another expression of the third bodhisattva vow. Not only written texts and Dharma lectures but everything we encounter is a sutra that shows us, day by day and moment by moment, the true reality of all beings, continuously deepening our understanding and practice.

In the Sōtō Zen tradition, our practice is based on Dōgen Zenji's teaching of continuous practice and the identity of practice and verification. The bodhisattva Way is not linear. It's not a path that we move along from a starting point to a finish, as in a board game. In *Shōbōgenzō* "Gyōji," Dōgen explained that we practice together with all buddhas, bodhisattvas, and ancestors.

> In the great Way of the buddhas and ancestors, there is always unsurpassable continuous practice which is the Way like a circle without interruption. Between the arousing of awakening-mind, practice, awakening, and nirvana, there is not the slightest break. Continuous practice is the circle of the Way. Therefore, [this continuous practice] is not [activities that we are] forced to do by ourselves or by others [buddhas and ancestors]. It is the continuous practice that has never been defiled [by our three poisonous minds]. The virtue of this continuous practice sustains ourselves and others. The essential point is that, in the entire earth and throughout

> heaven in the ten directions, all beings receive the merit of our continuous practice. Although neither others nor ourselves know it, that is the way it is. Therefore, because of the buddhas' and ancestors' continuous practice, our continuous practice is actualized, and our own great Way is penetrated. Because of our own continuous practice, the continuous practice of all buddhas is actualized, and the great Way of buddhas is presented. Because of our own continuous practice, there is the virtue of the circle of the Way. Because of this, each and every one of the buddhas and ancestors dwells as a buddha, goes beyond Buddha, upholds Buddha mind, and completes buddhahood without interruption. Because of continuous practice, there are the sun, moon, and stars; because of continuous practice, there is the great earth and empty space. Because of continuous practice, there is the self and its environment, and body and mind; because of continuous practice, there are the four great elements and the five aggregates. Although continuous practice is not something worldly people love, nevertheless it is the true place to return for all people. Because of the continuous practice of all buddhas in the past, present, and future, all buddhas in the past, present, and future are actualized....Therefore, the continuous practice of one day is nothing other than the seed of all buddhas and [is itself] the continuous practice of all buddhas.

All aspects of our practice—zazen in the monks' hall, chanting of verses and sutras during services, ceremonies in the Dharma hall—and all our other activities in daily life are the practice of the bodhisattva vow actualized moment by moment. We chant these verses and sutras as an expression of this interpenetrating reality with all beings throughout endless time and boundless space.

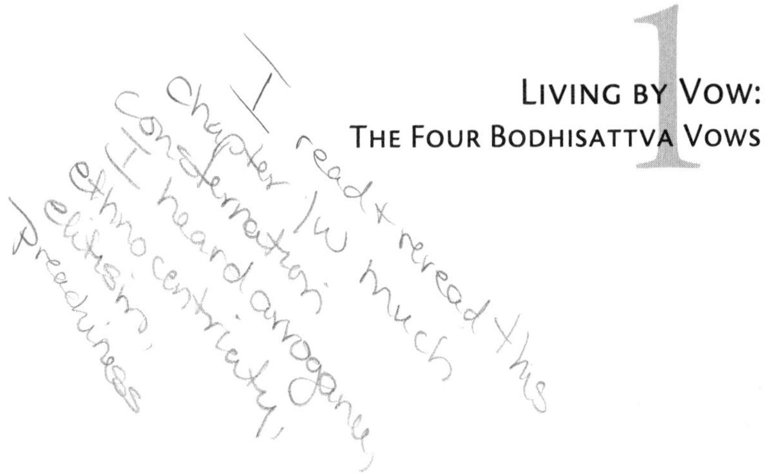

1 Living by Vow: The Four Bodhisattva Vows

Sentient beings are numberless; I vow to save them.
Desires are inexhaustible; I vow to put an end to them.
The dharmas are boundless; I vow to master them.
The Buddha's Way is unsurpassable; I vow to attain it.[7]

THIS VERSE, which states the four bodhisattva vows (*shigu-seigan-mon*), is one of the shortest we recite. It is also one of the most important and challenging to understand. It is difficult in part because the meaning of *vow* in this verse departs from the usual English meaning of "solemn promise" or "personal commitment." In Buddhism *vow* has a much larger and more complex meaning. To understand it we need to consider Japanese Buddhist culture.

One of my experiences with the difficulties involved in translating from one cultural tradition to another took place in Kyoto, where I lived for a year in a Catholic convent. Although we were not part of the community, my family and I were given a small house inside the monastery. One day the abbess of the convent, Sister Cleria, visited our house. She was a very elegant old woman, an American. She had been in Japan for more than thirty years as a missionary and spoke fluent Japanese. She asked me to speak on the role of prayer in Buddhism at a gathering of the nuns in the convent. Because they had been so generous to us I couldn't refuse. I began to think about prayer in Buddhism and realized that there is no prayer in Buddhism.[8] That was how I started my talk for the Christian nuns. We don't have prayer in Buddhism, but vow holds the same importance for Buddhists as prayer for Christians. So I talked about the four bodhisattva vows.

Prayer, *inori* in Japanese, is a Christian term that means communion, communication, or oneness with God. Today there are many Catholic priests who practice zazen. Before becoming a Catholic priest, Ichirō Okumura (no relation to me) practiced with the famous Rinzai master Sōen Nakagawa Roshi. Nakagawa Roshi encouraged him to become a Catholic priest, and he has continued to practice zazen. At sixty he was the head of a Carmelite order in Japan. He traveled the world giving meditation instruction to Catholic communities and wrote a book about meditation practice in the Catholic faith. The title of his book is *Inori* (Prayer). An English translation (*Awakening to Prayer*) has been published.[9]

Father Okumura uses an expression from the Old Testament, "to be quiet in front of God," to describe silent sitting practice. This communion with God without language is, he believes, the purest form of prayer. I think this is true in a Christian context, but for me, zazen is not a communication with God or with anything else. I don't think of zazen as a form of prayer. This is a major difference between Buddhism and Christianity. There is no object in our zazen. We just sit.

When I looked in a dictionary of Japanese Buddhist terms, there is no entry for prayer (*inori*). There is a word, *kitō*, which can be translated into English as "prayer" but is actually quite different. Kitō is a Buddhist practice of the Shingon school, a Japanese Vajrayāna school. In India, Vajrayāna Buddhists adopted the practice of kitō under the influence of Hinduism. Hindu gods have an interesting habit. When priests recite special mantras and perform certain rituals, the gods are obliged to grant their requests. In Vajrayāna or Shingonshū there is a similar practice. Believers sit in lotus posture, chant mantras, and enact rituals. The practitioner can then become one with the buddha or bodhisattva enshrined in front of him and his requests will be granted. This is the Shingon practice of kitō. Many Japanese temples practice kitō to insure traffic safety, success in school entrance examinations, easy childbirth, recovery from sickness, or success in business. This is one of the ways Japanese Buddhist temples make money. Sōtō temples are no exception.

Originally, Buddhism had no such practice. From the beginning, however, especially in Mahāyāna Buddhism, vow is essential for all bodhisattvas. In fact, part of the definition of a bodhisattva is a person who lives by vow instead of by karma. Karma means habit, preferences, or a ready-made system of values. As we grow up, we learn a system of values from the culture around us, which we use to evaluate the world and choose actions. This is karma, and living by karma. In contrast, a bodhisattva lives by vow. Vow is like a magnet or compass that shows us the direction toward the Buddha. There are two kinds of vow: general vows, taken by all bodhisattvas, and particular vows for each person. Each bodhisattva makes specific vows unique to his or her personality and capabilities. The four bodhisattva vows are general vows that should be taken by all Mahāyāna Buddhist practitioners. We must live by these vows. That is our direction. Our sitting practice should also be based on these vows.

When I explained the four bodhisattva vows to the Christian nuns, I told them that I see a basic contradiction between the first and second half of each sentence. "Sentient beings are numberless; I vow to save them": but if sentient beings are numberless, we cannot possibly save them all—this is a contradiction. "Desires are inexhaustible; I vow to put an end to them": if they are inexhaustible, how can I put an end to them? That's logically impossible. "The dharmas are boundless; I vow to master them": if they are boundless, then we cannot completely master them. The "contradiction" in the fourth vow is subtler: "The Buddha's Way is unsurpassable; I vow to attain it": if it's so transcendent, can we really expect to realize it? These contradictions are very important and have a profound practical and also religious meaning. But before I discuss them, I will explain each sentence of the verse.

Originally these four vows were connected to the four noble truths. The older version of the verse of four vows is as follows.

> I vow to enable people to be released from the truth of suffering.
> I vow to enable people to understand the truth of the origin of suffering.
> I vow to enable people to peacefully settle down in the truth of the path leading to the cessation of suffering.
> I vow to enable people to enter the cessation of suffering, that is, nirvana.[10]

The four noble truths are the basic teachings of Shakyamuni Buddha. The first is the truth of suffering or dissatisfaction (*duḥkha* in Sanskrit; *dukkha* in Pāli). Human life is full of duḥkha. The second is the truth of the cause of suffering: thirst or delusive desires. The third is the truth of the cessation of suffering: nirvana. The fourth is the truth of the path that leads us to nirvana.

The first bodhisattva vow is related to the first noble truth: "I vow to enable people to be released from the truth of suffering." Perhaps "truth" is unnecessary. "I vow to enable people to be released from suffering." "Suffering" here is the specific kind of suffering mentioned in the four noble truths. The Buddha said that our life is full of suffering, and so his teaching is often interpreted as being pessimistic. The suffering referred to here is not limited to the pain, suffering, unhappiness, or sadness brought about by the circumstances of our lives. The deeper meaning of duḥkha or suffering is related to impermanence or egolessness. Everything is impermanent and always changing. As a result there is nothing substantial that we can grasp. And yet we continue to try. But since everything continues to change, we suffer. This suffering arises because we cannot possess or control anything. As long as we try to do so, we suffer and feel dissatisfaction. The fact that we cannot control the reality of our lives is the root of the suffering described by the Buddha, which is based on our delusions about and attachment to the ego. This is the second of the four noble truths.

The second bodhisattva vow is "I vow to enable people to understand the truth of the origin of suffering." The origin of suffering is our delusive desire, which in this context is called *bonnō*. This Japanese word is a Chinese translation of the Sanskrit *kleśa*, often rendered in English as "delusion," although it actually refers to the hindrances, troubles, defilements, or passions that drive us to unwholesome action. According to the Yogacāra school, there are four fundamental bonnō or delusive ideas that defile our minds and our lives. The first, *gachi*, is ignorance of the Dharma, of the reality of impermanence and egolessness. The second is *gaken*, or egocentric views based on ignorance. We cling to established views of things around us. The third one is *gaman*, or arrogance. When we justify ourselves or try to be righteous we become arrogant. We put ourselves above others. The fourth is *ga-ai*, or self-attachment. *Ai* in Japanese is often used as a translation for "love," with a positive meaning. But in Buddhism *ai* is more often a kind of attachment and carries a negative connotation. *Gachi*, *gaken*, *gaman*, *ga-ai*—ignorance, egocentric view, arrogance, and self-attachment—are the four basic desires (*kleśa*). Perhaps "desire" isn't the best word to characterize these things, but they are the cause of suffering and unwholesome karma. The second vow relates to this truth. Bodhisattvas vow to help people understand the truth of the origin of suffering. This is what the second vow means when it says, "Desires are inexhaustible; I vow to put an end to them."

The third vow in the older verse is "I vow to enable people to peacefully settle down in the truth of the path leading to the cessation of suffering." This is about the fourth noble truth, the truth of *mārga*, the path leading to nirvana. (The order of truths is different in the two versions.) The path referred to is our practice of the eightfold noble path: right view, right thinking, right speech, right action, right livelihood, right effort, right mindfulness, and right meditation. The third vow has to do with the fourth noble truth, to enable people to settle in the way of practice. It begins with "The dharmas are boundless." Here the original word for "dharmas" is *hōmon* (dharma gate), which means teachings about reality and about reality-based practice. "The dharmas are boundless; I vow to master them" means that we vow to study and settle down in the way of practice. That is the fourth noble truth and the third vow.

An older version of the fourth vow, "The Buddha's Way is unsurpassable; I vow to attain it," is "I vow to enable people to attain nirvana." This vow is related to the third noble truth. In this context, "Way" is a translation of *bodhi*, or awakening, not of *mārga*, or path. "The Buddha's Way" refers to the Buddha's awakening or nirvana. So this vow says, "The Buddha's awakening is unsurpassable, but I vow to attain it."

This is the meaning of the four vows. It is important to understand that they are directly connected with the four noble truths, the fundamental teaching of Shakyamuni Buddha.

It is interesting to compare the older version of the four vows with the version we usually recite. Again, the older version is:

> I vow to enable people to be released from the truth of suffering.
> I vow to enable people to understand the truth of the origin of suffering.
> I vow to enable people to peacefully settle down in the truth of the path leading to the cessation of suffering.
> I vow to enable people to attain nirvana.

In this version of the four bodhisattva vows, "I" refers to a bodhisattva who has taken vows, been released from suffering, and understood the truth of the origin of suffering. This is someone who has already settled down in practice, in the four noble truths: someone who is already in nirvana. These vows are for someone who is already enlightened. However, the verse we usually recite is, once again:

> Sentient beings are numberless; I vow to save them.
> Desires are inexhaustible; I vow to put an end to them.
> The dharmas are boundless; I vow to master them.
> The Buddha's Way is unsurpassable; I vow to attain it.

This person still has inexhaustible desires or delusions, and so still has something to study, something to learn. The person has not yet attained the Way. The person him/herself still has inexhaustible delusive desires, and therefore the person vows to eliminate them. This is not a vow to help others to be released from inexhaustible desires. The older version is the vow made by an already enlightened bodhisattva, someone who is above all deluded sentient beings, making a vow to help all people.

In the newer version, the one we now chant, we still suffer but vow to save all beings. We have inexhaustible desires but vow to put an end to them. "The dharmas are boundless...." There are so many things to learn, and yet we vow to master them. We must make an effort to study the dharmas, the teachings, and practice, but we realize that practice is endless and so we resolve to practice endlessly. "The Buddha's Way is unsurpassable." We are not yet enlightened, but we vow to attain it. We are ordinary human beings and yet, if we take these four vows, we are bodhisattvas. In reality, we are ordinary human beings with inexhaustible desires. We have to study the teachings and practice endlessly, day by day, moment by moment, to attain the Buddha's enlightenment. That is our vow. In making these four vows, we are bodhisattvas.

As we said, there is a contradiction inherent in these vows: we vow to do things that are impossible. This means that our practice is endless and that we cannot completely fulfill the four vows. Our practice and study are like trying to empty the ocean with a spoon, one spoonful at a time. It is certainly a stupid way of life, not a clever one. A clever person cannot be a bodhisattva. We are aiming at something eternal, infinite, and absolute. No matter how hard we practice, study, and help other people, there is no end to it all. When we compare our achievement with something infinite, absolute, and eternal, it's like nothing.

We shouldn't compare our practice, our understanding, or our achievements with those of other people. When we do, we become competitive. We think, "I'm better than them" or "I'm practicing harder." Our practice becomes a competition based on egocentricity, something totally meaningless as a practice of the Buddha's Way. We cannot peacefully settle down in such a competitive practice. No matter how hard or long we practice, if our practice is based on ego, we are totally deluded. Such practice leads to a selfish view, arrogance, and self-attachment. Even though we think we are practicing the Dharma, we are against the Dharma completely. When we understand that our goal is eternal, infinite, and absolute, no matter how hard we practice, no matter how many things we master, no matter how deep our understanding of Buddha's teaching, compared to the infinite, we are zero. We cannot afford to be arrogant.

There is another side to this. Even if we cannot practice as hard, sit as long, study as much, or understand as deeply as others, we don't need to feel guilty or inferior. Compared to the eternal, the absolute, or the infinite, we are all equal to zero. There is something deeply meaningful in our comparison with the absolute. Understanding ourselves in this way frees our practice from competition based on selfishness. This is a most important point. We cannot be proud of our practice, and we don't need to be too humble about our lack of practice or understanding. We are just as we are. Our practice is to take one more step toward the infinite, the absolute, moment by moment, one step at a time.

According to Dōgen Zenji this one step, or even a half-step, in our practice is the manifestation of absolute enlightenment. This is what he meant when he spoke of "just sitting," or *shikantaza*. When we sit, we just sit. That doesn't mean we don't need to do anything else. It doesn't mean we are all right only when we are sitting. It means that when we sit, there is no comparison. We are right now, right here, with this body and mind, awakening to reality. This is the complete manifestation of absolute, infinite, eternal enlightenment. Even a short period of sitting is bodhisattva practice. And our practice is not only sitting. All of our day-to-day activities should be based on the four vows and the four noble truths, which are the basic teaching of Shakyamuni Buddha.

When I explained all this to the Christian nuns, they liked it! They felt that the teachings of Catholicism are the same as those of Buddhism. In Christianity the absolute, the infinite, is God. Being in front of God, no one can be proud of their achievement. Therefore, believers have to be still in front of God. The philosophical or doctrinal basis is different, but the attitude toward our everyday lives is the same. When we talk to people of other religions, we don't need to discuss the differences in theory. Of course, it is important to understand the differences, but we don't need to argue about which are true.

The four bodhisattva vows are an essential point, not just in our practice of zazen but also in our day-to-day lives. Each of us has a job or a family and in each situation we try to practice the four noble truths and the four bodhisattva vows. Our practice is the whole of our life, not something special that we do only in the monastery or at a sesshin or retreat. Those are important parts of our practice, but the Buddha taught us to just awaken to the reality of our lives and live on the basis of that reality. We have to live right now, right here, with this body and mind, and in the company of others. The guiding force, the compass that leads us to live out this reality, is the bodhisattva vows.

Shakyamuni Buddha's Vow

According to the Sanskrit literature, Shakyamuni sat alone under the bodhi tree and was enlightened. He saw that beings suffer in samsara—in the six realms of the world: the realms of hell, hungry ghosts, animals, asuras, human beings, and heavenly beings. This is the meaning of suffering as the first noble truth. The Indian folk belief was that we are born into one of these six realms, and when we die we are reborn into another realm according to our deeds in this life. The transmigration continues endlessly until we are free from twisted knots of karma created by the three poisonous minds of grasping, aversion, and ignorance.

I don't know if these realms actually exist after death, but I see that they exist in human society and inside each of us. *Hell* is when people live together and make each other suffer. Everything each one does irritates the others. This sort of thing often happens even within ourselves: two conflicting parts of us argue and fight. We have a constant internal struggle. That's hell.

Hungry ghosts are beings consumed by unsatisfied craving. In this realm we always feel something is lacking. We consume or try to obtain things we desire but are never satisfied.

Animals are happy when they are fed; they feel content and go to sleep. Some animals, like cows or elephants, work from birth to death; they just work, work, work. Many Japanese people live like this. Some of my friends who work in Tokyo leave their homes at seven in the morning and start work at eight thirty or nine. It may take them two hours to get to their jobs. They work until nine in the evening and then return home and go to bed around eleven or twelve. That's their life. When I heard this, I was amazed. Their lives are much harder than intensive sitting practice during sesshin! I can't imagine how a person could live that way. It's living in the realm of animals.

Asuras are fighting spirits. Asura was a mythical Indian god of justice. When we believe we are right, we criticize others based on our own concept of justice. If necessary we fight with others until we win. Exterminating people who oppose us becomes the purpose of our lives. Such people cannot be satisfied without enemies. They can't live without something against which they can struggle. We all have this sort of attitude sometimes. When we have someone to criticize, we feel safe, righteous, and good.

Human beings seek fame and profit. Animals are satisfied when their stomachs are full, but we with our human minds are never full, because we think of our future. I want to make sure I will be fulfilled tomorrow, the day after tomorrow, and for the rest of my life, and that my children will live long, happy lives. Even if we don't have any problems at this moment, we are not satisfied because we worry about the future. Animals don't worry about safety or security in the future. Only human beings save something extra for tomorrow.

Heavenly beings are those whose desires are completely met. They need nothing; they seem happy, and yet they are not. Since they have everything, they don't need to seek anything and are unable to find motivation to do anything. These people become lazy and also worry about losing what they already possess. It can be difficult for them to find truly intimate friends because they think others befriend them only to take something. Even if they live successful lives, they lose everything when they die. When such people face death, they might question the meaning of their hard work and achievements. Even someone who has it all cannot be happy in an absolute way as long as the goal in life is to satisfy ego-centered desires. This is the insight the Buddha attained under the bodhi tree.

The Buddha contemplated the causes of these forms of suffering and tried to find their root cause. Later in Buddhist history people assumed that the Buddha contemplated the twelve links of causation—the way our lives become suffering and how we can be liberated from suffering. He found that the ultimate cause of suffering is ignorance and delusive desires based on that ignorance. This ignorance is *mumyō* in Japanese, *avidyā* in Sanskrit. *Myō* means "brightness" or "wisdom," and *mu* means "no." *Mumyō* means that we cannot see the reality of life. As we try to fulfill our desires, we do things that are good or bad. As a result of our deeds, we transmigrate through the various realms of samsara and we suffer. This is the teaching of causality based on our karmic deeds. Our desires and the actions that arise from them are based on our ignorance. The consequences of our deeds cause suffering. When we clearly see our ignorance it disappears. When we see with the eye of wisdom that ignorance causes our suffering, we are free from both ignorance and suffering. This is called nirvana or enlightenment.

Shakyamuni Buddha remained sitting for several weeks to savor his enlightenment. He was released from all ignorance and suffering and he enjoyed it. He felt that what he now saw, the causes of suffering, was very difficult to understand. He feared that if he tried to teach others what he had discovered, no one would understand. He thought, "The content of my enlightenment, the concept of interdependent origination, is extremely difficult to comprehend. Those who enjoy clinging take pleasure in attachment and are fond of their ties of dependence, and they will never be able to understand it." He expressed this thought in verse:

> That enlightenment which I have attained through
>   many hardships
> Should I now teach to others?
> Those who hold fast to greed and hatred

> Cannot easily understand this Truth.
> Against the common stream,
> Subtle, profound, fine, and difficult to perceive,
> It cannot be seen by those
> Who are lost in desire, cloaked in darkness.[11]

Pondering thus, he was not inclined to teach the Dharma.

Here "the common stream" refers to the cycle of birth and death within samsara. The Buddha initially thought that people would find it too difficult to understand what he had discovered. In the Sanskrit story Brahmā Sahāmpati, a god, divined what the Buddha was thinking. (Perhaps this is not a description of real events but an account of what was happening in the Buddha's mind.) When he saw that the Buddha had decided not to teach, he asked him to reconsider. "In this world there are some people who bear only a small amount of hindrance and whose wisdom is outstanding," he said. "Please preach your Dharma to them." Still the Buddha hesitated. Brahma repeated his request, and again the Buddha did not consent. After the third request he accepted. Then he said, "The gateway of ambrosia (deathlessness) is thrown open for those who have ears to hear."

The Buddha's hesitation to teach is understandable. When I first studied the Buddha's teaching I had difficulty accepting it. It was not so hard to understand it intellectually. It's easy to understand as an abstract theory that the cause of suffering is ignorance and desire, or to see examples in other people. But it's difficult to see when we ourselves suffer and are ignorant. It's also hard to accept that we are deluded. We believe that we are special, important, and valuable. It's really not a matter of intellectual understanding, not a set of abstract hypotheses. If we agree with the Buddha's teaching, we need to practice it and make an effort to transform our lives.

Because of Brahma's request, the Buddha went to Benares and taught a group of ascetic monks who had practiced with him. These monks accepted his teaching. The Buddha's determination to start teaching was the origin of the vow in Buddhism. After that the Buddha traveled all over India by foot and continued teaching for over forty-five ye He lived by his vow from his enlightenment until his death at the age of eighty.

The Buddha's vow was to help people awaken to reality and save them from suffering. This is the vow we take as a bodhisattva: "Beings are numberless, we vow to free them." A bodhisattva is a disciple or a child of the Buddha, a person who aspires to learn the Buddha's teaching and follow his example. Vow is essential for us as Buddhist practitioners. It is a concrete and practical form of wisdom and compassion. This is the important point to understand when we think about vow.

Katagiri Roshi's Poem on Vow

Katagiri Roshi, the founding teacher and abbot of the Minnesota Zen Meditation Center until his death in 1990, named the center Ganshōji, which means "temple born of vow." After I became the head teacher there, I used his office. In it was a cabinet holding his writings. Since I wanted to understand his goals, attitude, and teaching, I read much of his work. I found a poem he wrote in 1988 that is quite wonderful.

Peaceful Life

Being told that it's impossible,
One believes, in despair, "Is that so?"
Being told that it is possible,
One believes, in excitement, "That's right."
But whichever is chosen,
It does not fit one's heart neatly.

Being asked, "What is unfitting?"
I don't know what it is.
But my heart knows somehow.
I feel an irresistible desire to know.
What a mystery "human" is!

As to this mystery:
Clarifying
Knowing how to live
Knowing how to walk with people
Demonstrating and teaching,
This is the Buddha.

From my human eyes
I feel it's really impossible to become a Buddha.
But this "I," regarding what the Buddha does,
Vows to practice
To aspire
To be resolute,
And tells me, "Yes, I will."
Just practice right here, now
And achieve continuity
Endlessly
Forever.
This is living in vow.
Herein is one's peaceful life found.[12]

This is a poem about vow. I also found his original poem in Japanese. When I read it closely, I saw that it is a lucid explanation of the four noble truths. The first stanza expresses the truth of suffering. "One believes in despair ... one believes in excitement ... whichever is chosen; it does not fit one's heart neatly." This is the reality of our lives. In Japanese this stanza reads, *Hito ga dame da to ieba / gakkarishite so dana to omoi / Hito ga iinda to ieba hashaide so o nanda to omou.* The phrases he used for "possible" and "impossible" are *dame da* and *iinda. Dame da* means both "impossible" and "not good." *Iinda* can be interpreted as "good." We encounter many such judgments in our lives. Sometimes people say you are good, sometimes not good. Each time we are judged we feel despair or excitement. We live based on opinions, not just other people's but also our own. When we are successful, we think, "Yeah, this is great." When we've had a hard time, we feel small. We may even feel that life is not worth living. This up and down is samsara, the reality of our life that is described as transmigration through the six realms.

This is our life as human beings. We always feel somewhat unsatisfied. "Whichever is chosen; it does not fit one's heart neatly." Happy or sad, there is some dissatisfaction. We feel that there is something unsettled in ourselves and in our way of life. We are moved by others' expectations, by the situation, or even by our own self-image. We can't find a peaceful, steady, absolute foundation for our life. As we move in samsara. We always feel somewhat unsafe, somewhat unsettled. Something is lacking even if we are in the heavenly realm and all our desires are fulfilled. Of course, if we are in hell, we really suffer. This is our life. So we start to question: What's wrong? What's the problem? What causes this feeling of emptiness? We want to understand this feeling. In the second stanza Katagiri says, "Being asked what is unfitting; I don't know what it is." Our motivation to question and understand is called bodhi-mind. Katagiri writes, "My heart knows somehow. / I feel an irresistible desire to know." We want to know the real cause of the problem. This is unique to human beings. We alone ask who we are and how we should live. Other animals don't have this problem.

Dōgen Zenji said that "to study the Buddha Way is to study the self." I think a human is a being that has to study the self. Other living things do not have to do this; they have no questions. But for us, this self is a big question. We humans are troublesome, mysterious creatures. We need to understand this mystery. This questioning, this need to understand, is our bodhi-mind—a mind that awakens to the reality of our life.

Katagiri continues, "As to this mystery: / Clarifying / Knowing how to live / Knowing how to walk with people / Demonstrating and teaching, / This is the Buddha." The Buddha understood or clarified this mystery. He saw the answer to the questions: What are human beings? What is the cause of human suffering? He awakened and understood how we can live in a wholesome way with peace.

The reality that the Buddha found in his enlightenment is

interdependent origination. Katagiri's phrase "knowing how to walk with people" refers to this interdependence. It means that we can't live without other people and things. For Buddhists, studying the self means studying how to walk with others. That's why the Buddha emphasized the importance of the sangha, a place where people live and practice together.

Katagiri's comment in the last stanza, "From my human eyes / I feel it's really impossible to become a Buddha," reminds us that even though we study the Buddha's teaching we are still human. The Buddha's achievement is so great that it's almost impossible for us as humans to follow his Way. Even so, one "vows to practice." In the Japanese version, the word for "vow" is *negau*, which means "to wish." We wish to practice and aspire to become buddhas. Katagiri uses the word "aspire" as the translation for *inori*. *Inori*, we've seen, is usually translated as "prayer," but here it means "deeply wish for something that doesn't seem possible." Even though we know that it is impossible to follow the Buddha's Way, we deeply wish to make it possible. Then Katagiri says he vows "to be resolute." Here the Japanese version has *kesshin*, which means "to make up one's mind, to be fixed and determined." Next, he says he tells himself, "Yes, I will." Even though he feels it's impossible, he cannot help but say this. That vow comes from the deepest part of the self. Intellectually it seems impossible. But from our deep life force we can't help but say, "Yes, I will." That is vow. A vow should not be made by our intellect or an emotional impulse. It should come from the deepest part of us.

"Just practice right here, now" means that we start practicing immediately. We can't postpone it because the wish is so deep. Somehow we have to start searching for our own self. There is no time to wait. "And achieve continuity" means to practice continuously. Because it's impossible to achieve what Buddha did, we have to practice forever. There is no end, no goal, and yet we take small steps one by one, moment by moment. We try to walk along the Buddha's Way one step or just half a step in all situations. Sometimes we are happy because we feel we are good practitioners and doing the right thing. Sometimes sitting in this posture every morning is boring or painful, and yet we do it. In any situation we try to adopt the attitude Katagiri describes. "Being told that it's impossible / One believes, in despair, 'Is that so?' / Being told that it is possible, / One believes, in excitement, 'That's right.'" Even in our practice we need to work with this attitude of up and down. Sometimes sitting in our zazen we feel great; we feel that we are enlightened. Sometimes we feel we are in hell. In either situation we just go through it endlessly, forever.

Katagiri Roshi said, "This is living in vow." It means to sit, to try to help others, to live and work with others each day of our lives. When we are living in vow, in our emotion, in our human sentiment, there are good times and hard times. Like all people in samsara, we are still in the six realms. And yet, we can find a peaceful basis, a foundation for our life which is never moved by human sentiment. That is vow. That is the reality of our life.

The last line of his poem is "Herein is one's peaceful life found." When we vow, we feel we have a duty. Usually, taking a vow is like making a promise: if we don't keep it, we feel bad or fear that we might be punished. But vow in Buddhism is not like that. It's not something we do with our intellect or shallow emotion. We vow toward the Buddha, toward something absolute and infinite. As a bodhisattva, we can never say, "I have achieved all vows." We cannot be proud of our achievements, because in comparison with the infinite anything we achieve is insignificant. Each of us has different capabilities, of course. If we cannot do very much, we practice just a little. There is no reason for us to feel small or to say we're sorry. We just try to be right here with this body and mind and move forward one step or just half a step. This is our practice in a concrete sense.

Katagiri Roshi used the expression "living in vow" because it sounds natural in English. I like "living *by* vow," perhaps because D. T. Suzuki has this expression in his book *Living by Zen*.[13] In the Japanese translation of this book he says something like "All living beings are living in Zen but only human beings can live by Zen." Saying that all living beings—dogs, cats, plants, flowers—are living in Zen doesn't mean they abide in meditation or samādhi, but rather that they are living the reality of life as it is, or *tathātā* in Sanskrit. Everything lives in the reality of life, in Zen; but only human beings have to make a conscious effort to do so. We devote ourselves to the study and practice of Zen and consciously live *by* Zen. As Suzuki says, only human beings do this, but that doesn't mean that we are superior to other beings. Because of our doubts and delusions we cannot *simply* live in reality. We have to consciously return to reality and make an effort to live on that basis. That, according to Suzuki, is living by Zen.

A life led by vow is a life animated or inspired by vow, not one that is watched, scolded, or consoled by vow. These verbs create a separation between the person and the vow. The simple phrase "living by vow" emphasizes that the person and the vow are one. Our life is itself a vow.

D. T. Suzuki's Vow

The Japanese translator of *Living by Zen*, Sōhaku Kobori, wrote about a conversation he had with Suzuki when he was young. Kobori asked a question that had popped into his mind: "What is your kenshō?" In Rinzai Zen, *kenshō* means enlightenment. Suzuki replied, "Well, my kenshō is *shujō mu hen sei gan do*."[14] The Japanese expression means "Living beings are numberless; I vow to save them." That was his enlightenment. I was surprised when I first read this conversation, but I now believe Suzuki was a real bodhisattva. His many books in English have introduced Zen around the world. He worked continuously until he died at the age of ninety-six. The basis of his effort was the vow "Sentient beings are numberless; I vow to save them." In this respect there is no distinction between Rinzai and Sōtō. We are all Buddhists or bodhisattvas. Zen in the West began with D. T. Suzuki's bodhisattva vow, just as Buddhism began with the Buddha's vow.

In his writings Suzuki elaborated on the bodhisattva vow:

> Let me remark ... that "vow" is not a very appropriate term to express the meaning of the Sanskrit *pranidhāna*. Pranidhāna is a strong wish, aspiration, prayer, or an inflexible determination to carry out one's will even through an infinite series of rebirths. Buddhists have such a supreme belief in the power of will or spirit that, whatever material limitations, the will is sure to triumph over them and gain its final aim. So, every Bodhisattva is considered to have his own share in the work of universal salvation.[15]

Suzuki's kenshō was his strong determination and vow to help liberate all living beings from a delusive way of life. He carried out this vow till death.

Uchiyama Roshi and Vow

Uchiyama Roshi placed great emphasis on living by vow. Although we didn't chant much at Antaiji, before and after each of his lectures we chanted the four bodhisattva vows verse instead of the "Verse for Opening the Sutra." In fact, the bodhisattva vows verse was the only verse we regularly chanted in our practice life at Antaiji. Uchiyama Roshi felt that the vows were essential to our practice. He writes:

> A classic Mahāyāna text says, "The true mind of every sentient being itself teaches and leads each sentient being. This is the vow of Buddha." Vow is not a special speculative approach to something outside us. The true mind of sentient beings—that is, universal self—itself is vow. Thus, when we consider universal self from the vantage point of the personal self, we realize that we cannot live without vow.[16]

As human beings living at the intersection of the universal self and the ego-centered self, we cannot live without being led by vow as the direction of our lives. Uchiyama Roshi took two personal vows based on the four general bodhisattva vows. One was to study the truth of life from not only Zen or Buddhism but also other spiritual traditions, to digest it through his own way of life, and to share it through his writings with Japanese and Westerners alike. His other vow was to produce determined practitioners of zazen who are thoroughly settled in the life of zazen practice.

Uchiyama Roshi often used the expression *ichiza nigyō sanshin*. The first word, *ichiza*, means "one sitting," referring, of course, to our practice of zazen. *Nigyō* means "two practices," vow and repentance. *Sanshin*, "three minds," refers to three mental attitudes described by Dōgen Zenji: joyful mind, parental mind, and magnanimous mind. "One sitting," Uchiyama Roshi says, is the center of our zazen practice. By "one sitting" he doesn't mean one of many. In this context "one" means absolute. In the chapter of *Shōbōgenzō* titled "Zammai ō zammai," Dōgen Zenji writes:

> That which directly goes beyond the whole world is *kekkafuza* (full-lotus sitting). It is what is most venerable in the house of the buddhas and ancestors. That which kicks away the heads of non-Buddhists and demons and enables us to be inhabitants of the innermost room of the house of the buddhas and ancestors is kekkafuza. Only this practice transcends the pinnacle of the buddhas and ancestors. Therefore, the buddhas and ancestors have been practicing zazen alone, without pursuing anything else.[17]

This is the meaning of "one sitting."

According to Dōgen Zenji, our sitting is not part of our practice, but rather other activities are part of our zazen. This is what is meant by the phrase "our zazen is absolute." This is a very important point. In *Bendōwa*, Dōgen Zenji said, "Even if only one person sits for a short time, because this zazen is one with all existence and completely permeates all time, it performs everlasting Buddha guidance within the inexhaustible dharma world in the past, present, and future."[18] In this sense, sitting is absolute. This means that we become awakened to the reality that we are one with all beings, all times, and all space. This too is the meaning of "one sitting."

According to Uchiyama Roshi zazen has two aspects. One is vow and the other is repentance. In this context "aspect" doesn't mean that there are two parts to our zazen. It means that the whole of sitting is the practice of vow and, at the same time, the practice of repentance. Whether or not we aware of it, we are living out the reality of life. Unfortunately, we lose sight of this reality. Our life is like a hand. When we see it as a hand, there is no distinction between the fingers. But when we see it as a collection of fingers, each finger is independent and has its own name and characteristics. Each has a unique shape and function. They can act independently and are not interchangeable.

In the same way, human beings are individuals. If we cut off a finger, it can't function as a finger anymore. A finger always works with other fingers. This is the reality of human life as well, but we often forget and think of ourselves only as individuals. This is a fundamental delusion for us. We have to wake up to the reality that we can be a finger only in relationship to other fingers working as one hand. The hand can be a family, a sangha, a society, or the whole universe. Yet if we think of this community as an entity in itself, it can become just another, bigger ego. We shouldn't consider either the hand or the finger to be a separate, independent thing. Both are like a bubble. The bubble doesn't exist as a separate thing, but only as a condition of water and air: it is air trapped inside a film of water. But we can't deny that the bubble exists. The bubble is there. "Bubble" is just a name for a condition of air trapped in water. So we can say neither that the bubble doesn't exist nor that the bubble exists independently. Air and water are themselves the same in that they are merely collections of atoms. In the same way, atoms are aggregates of even smaller particles.

Although this is the reality of our life, we are almost always unaware of it. We think of this person which is ourself as most important, as the center of the universe. We need to return to the reality that exists before egocentricity arises, before the separation of this body and mind from the rest of the world. This is what Uchiyama Roshi meant when he said we are living at the intersection of the universal self and the ego-centered self.

To vow to save all beings doesn't mean that we believe that we have the power to help all those who are in trouble. Imagining that were so would truly be quite arrogant. To save all beings means to *be one with* all beings. We cannot become one with others by means of our individual efforts. But we can wake up to the reality that from the beginning we are one with all beings. That is why we study the obstacles that prevent us from seeing this reality. That is how we become free from delusion. To become free from delusion, we have to study the Buddha's teachings. Reality itself is also a teaching. All beings in this universe—trees, leaves, and animals—teach us to awaken to the reality that is impermanent and egoless. We are not sensitive enough to hear this teaching without effort, so we must actively listen and study. In our practice together, we vow to attain the Buddha's Way, the Buddha's enlightenment, and to be one with all beings. As the Buddha said in the *Lotus Sutra*, "But now this threefold world is all my domain, and the living beings in it are all my children."[19] That is the Buddha's attitude, and we vow to attain such an attitude. We know it's almost impossible, but we vow to do so.

Each of the four bodhisattva vows is a kind of a paradox or contradiction. It is impossible to accomplish or completely achieve the vows. Since we are working at something infinite and absolute, it's important to reflect on the fact that we can never accomplish it. We cannot be perfect. This awakening to our own imperfection is repentance.

In Buddhism repentance does not mean saying "I'm sorry" because of some mistake I have made. That kind of repentance is relevant, but as Buddhists repentance means awareness of our imperfections and limitations. Vow and repentance are two kinds of energy that enable us to continue our practice. Zazen is itself the practice of vow. Zazen is itself the practice of repentance.

When we sit, we face the absolute, the infinite, and we let go of thought. This means that we don't judge things by our own yardsticks, but instead we are measured against the absolute. That is our practice of vow and repentance. Facing the infinite or absolute, we are really nothing. No matter how long we practice zazen, we cannot be proud of what we have accomplished. At the same time, we don't need to feel guilty or inadequate because we cannot practice enough, or because we cannot help others so much. No matter how great or small our accomplishments, they are all the same compared to the infinite. The important point is that even if it is only a small thing, we just do it. We don't need a fancy way to attain perfect enlightenment or a means to help all living beings. Just sit a little more, or help others a little more. We should be down to earth. This is our practice.

The Three Minds

As we have seen, our practice of zazen has two aspects. One is vow, to resolve to take one more step ahead. The other is repentance, to be aware of our imperfection. This zazen has to be applied to our day-to-day lives. According to Dōgen Zenji, the attitude we should maintain toward the things we encounter in our everyday lives is "three minds." He discusses this in "Tenzokyōkun" (Instructions to the Cook). In this text, he talks about the attitude the person who is in charge of cooking in the monastery must have. Of course, he is recommending this for all people who are working as a community. Three kinds of mind are mentioned in the final part of "Tenzokyōkun."

Joyful Mind

> On all occasions when the temple administrators, heads of monastic departments, and the tenzo are engaged in their work, they should maintain joyful mind, nurturing mind, and magnanimous mind. What I call joyful mind is the happy heart. You must reflect that if you were born in heaven you would cling to ceaseless bliss and not give rise to Way-seeking mind.[20]

Heaven is the realm in samsara in which people's desires are all fulfilled; only pleasure and happiness remain. There is no suffering. But if we don't encounter some hardship or difficulty, we don't arouse bodhimind. We won't seek after the Way when our life is full of happiness and joy. Heaven is not a good place to practice.

> This would not be conducive to practice. What's more, how could you prepare food to offer to the three jewels? Among the ten thousand dharmas, the most honored are the three jewels. Most excellent are the three jewels. Neither the lord of heaven nor a wheel-turning king can compare to them. The Zen'en Shingi says, "Respected by society, though peacefully apart, the sangha is most pure and unfabricated."[21]

The *Zen'en Shingi* is a collection of regulations for monastic life in the Chinese Zen tradition. It recommends that the community of Buddhist practitioners should be pure and unfabricated. Here "unfabricated" is a translation of *mui*, which can mean "nondoing," or "nonaction." In this context it means free of artifice. The Buddhist sangha or community is a place where people can escape from artificial ways of thinking and return to reality. This passage means that the sangha should be pure and free from attachment, delusion, and egocentricity.

The great importance of the Buddhist sangha isn't of course restricted to the Zen center as an institution. If we think of "sangha" as referring to a specific group of Buddhists, it becomes a sort of group ego. We should see sangha as more inclusive. The community of people living in this area is a sangha. This country, the community of all countries, and the society of all human beings should also be considered sanghas. Anywhere we go to return to reality or live according to reality is a sangha and is therefore most precious.

Dōgen remarks further, "Now I have the fortune to be born a human being and prepare food to be received by the three jewels. Is this not a great karmic affinity? We must be very happy about this." His expression "great karmic affinity" is a translation of *dai innen*. Here *innen* means the causes and conditions that enable us to practice and participate in a sangha. The conditions cannot be taken for granted:

> Consider that if you were born in the realms of hell, hungry ghosts, animals, fighting gods, or others of the eight difficult births, even if you desired refuge within the sangha's power, you would never actually be able to prepare pure food to offer the Three Treasures. Because of suffering in these painful circumstances your body and mind would be fettered. However, in the present life you have already done this [cooking], so you should enjoy this life and this body resulting from incalculable ages of worthy activity. This merit can never fade.[22]

The sangha has power because in community we encourage one another to practice in the Buddha's Way. When we can work as a tenzo or in any other position to support others' practice we should appreciate this good fortune.

Furthermore, "You should engage in and carry out this work with the vow to include one thousand or ten thousand lives in one day or one time." Here he is alluding to the oneness of this moment, this day, and all eternity. As far as our attitude is concerned, eternity and this moment are one. This means that what we do this moment is not a step to the next stage. We cook not to feed people but to cook. When we cook, cooking itself should be our practice. It should not be preparation for something else. Cooking is in itself a perfect action if it is cooking just for the sake of cooking. When the food is ready, just offer it. Offering is not the result of cooking as preparation. Offering is just offering. Eating is just eating. Each moment is perfect in itself, not a step to the next one. Each moment is one with eternity. This is the attitude we should maintain.

The same is true of zazen. When we sit in this posture, we are one with all beings, all time, and all space. It's all very dynamic, not limited to one single person or one moment of work. Even though we and our work are small, they are connected with the whole universe. When we are without a limited attitude or purpose, our work has no limits.

"This will allow you to unite with these virtuous karmic causes for ten million lives," says Dōgen Zenji. "The mind that has fully contemplated such fortune is joyful mind." This positive attitude we can sustain even in hard times. As a tenzo, if we don't have fancy ingredients, we just work with what we have. Dōgen Zenji uses the expression "Pick a single blade of grass and erect a sanctuary for the jewel king; enter a single atom and turn the great wheel of the teaching."[23] We pick up just one small piece of bread and build the loftiest of the Buddha's temples. That's our practice.

Whatever we accomplish, it cannot be just for ourselves. "Truly, even if you become a virtuous wheel-turning king but do not make food to offer the Three Treasures, after all there is no benefit. It would only be like a splash of water, a bubble, or a flickering flame." If we do things for our private gain or personal benefit, then no matter how hard we work, no matter how much we achieve, it will come to an end. Instead we dedicate our work to all beings. That is our attitude toward work and toward other people. That is joyful mind.

Parental Mind

The second aspect of sanshin is nurturing or parental mind. "As for what is called nurturing mind," Dōgen continues, "it is the mind of mothers and fathers. For example, it is considering the Three Treasures in the way that a mother and father think of their only child." We try to care for the Three Treasures, the Buddha, Dharma, and Sangha, as if they were our only child. It is especially important to have this attitude when we practice in a community. The attitude of parents is to take care of others. When we live together, caring and being cared for are the same. The reality of what is happening is the same. The inner attitude of the caregiver, however, is very different from that of the one who expects to be cared for. This difference determines the quality of the community. A place where people want to be taken care of is very different from a place where people care for others. We should understand that this small difference in our inner attitude has very large effects on the world around us.

> Even impoverished, destitute people firmly love and raise an only child. What kind of determination is this? Other people cannot know it until they actually become mothers and fathers. Parents earnestly consider their child's growth without concern for their own wealth or poverty. They do not care if they are cold or hot but give their child covering or shade. In parents' thoughtfulness there is this intensity. People who have aroused this mind comprehended it well. Only people who are familiar with this mind are truly awake to it.[24]

When we are small, we are not capable. We can't survive without being taken care of by our parents or society. We should be grateful for the support and help we receive from our parents and others. When we become mature enough, we should take care of things around us, the way parents take care of their children. When you have this attitude you understand what it is.

For Dōgen this attitude is one of "watching over water and over grain." Here he is talking about the tenzo's work. When the tenzo cooks, he must take care of water, grain, fire, everything that happens in the kitchen. We have to pay careful attention to everything. When we prepare meals, many things are going on at the same time. As we cook the rice, we have to prepare soup and other side dishes. It's even more difficult when you cook with firewood. It's very easy to forget about the fire when you're doing something else. You have to be very careful, attentive to each thing. Even when we are caught up with several different things, we must remember the fire.

This attitude, concentrating on a particular thing while remaining aware of everything else, is the same as in our zazen. We don't concentrate our mind on a certain object in our zazen. Our mind is nowhere and at the same time everywhere. It's the same as when we are driving.

We don't focus our attention on a particular object like the steering wheel but are just awake. Our mind is really nowhere, which means everywhere. When our mind is nowhere and everywhere, we can react very naturally to whatever happens. That is our zazen. Our minds should not be fixed in one place but rather be nowhere and everywhere. That is our awakening. That is parental mind. Dōgen Zenji continues:

> Therefore, watching over water and over grain, shouldn't everyone maintain the affection and kindness of nourishing children? Great Teacher Sakyamuni even gave up twenty years of a buddha's allotted life span to protect us all alike in these later times. What was his intention? It was simply to confer parental mind. Tathāgatas could never wish for rewards or riches.[25]

According to Buddhist scriptures, the Buddha could have lived one hundred years, and yet he died when he was eighty in order to donate twenty years of his life span to all beings. This is how the Buddha manifests parental mind, the attitude of caring for things and other people.

Magnanimous Mind

The third aspect of the attitude advocated by Dōgen Zenji is magnanimous mind. "As for what is called magnanimous mind," he said, "this mind is like the great mountains or like the great ocean; it is not a biased or contentious mind."

We must try to avoid bias or a one-sided perspective and instead strive to see the whole situation. If we say, "This is me and that is them," our community is divided and our minds become one-sided. This leads to internal conflict and struggle and our group cannot be called a community or sangha. A sangha is a peaceful community of people, a mixture of water and milk, not water and oil. The attitude of magnanimous mind is no separation.

"Carrying half a pound, do not take it lightly; lifting forty pounds should not seem heavy." Here again Dōgen is talking about cooking. Sometimes we cook for one or two people. Sometimes we have to cook for one or two hundred people. We should not think that to prepare a meal for one or two people is easy or that to prepare a meal for many people is heavy or difficult. We take the same careful, attentive attitude in either case.

"Although drawn by the voices of spring, do not wander over spring meadows; viewing the fall colors, do not allow your heart to fall." Here spring and fall are used to represent favorable conditions and adversity. In spring we are happy and we wander around and forget reality. During the fall we become sorrowful and forget about reality. Too often we are moved by emotions, by circumstances, by good times and bad. Magnanimous mind, according to Dōgen, means that "the four seasons cooperate in a single scene." Spring, summer, autumn, and winter are one season. We should accept them as one reality of life. That is magnanimous mind.

"Regard light and heavy with a single eye," he goes on to say. "On this single occasion you must write the word 'great.' You must know the word 'great.' You must learn the word 'great.'" The attitude of magnanimous mind is the same as that of our zazen. Let go of thought, resist the pull of discrimination, and accept the situation as one.

These are the three attitudes or three minds with which we want to practice as a community, as a sangha. Our vow functions as the three minds, to nurture the Dharma, to practice with others, to create a situation or place to practice with other people. To do this we have to maintain these three attitudes, especially magnanimous mind. We must not be fettered by circumstance. We try to keep practicing steadily. That is the attitude we learn from our sitting practice. Whatever happens, whatever the situation, we just keep sitting. Sometimes we are busy, sometimes we are tired, sometimes we are involved in things. But we always come back to the zendo and sit down quietly. This is our practice.

Vow as Sangha

Sangha, or community, is an important manifestation of the concept of vow. We see this in the life of Guishan Lingyou, a famous Chinese Zen master who established a large and influential sangha in China.[26] How he accomplished this is instructive.

Guishan was instrumental in the establishment of Zen monasteries. Before his time there were no formal Zen Buddhist orders. People simply came together to practice. But then Zen monks started to create their own unique form of monastic practice. It was the beginning of Zen as a distinct school of Chinese Buddhism. This at least is the traditional view of the history of Chinese Zen.

Guishan was tenzo, the chief cook in the monastery where he practiced with his teacher, Baizhang Huihai. One day Guishan was standing near the abbot's room where Baizhang was staying.

Baizhang asked Guishan, "Who is it?" and Guishan replied, "It's me, Lingyou" (Guishan's dharma name). Baizhang said, "Would you dig in the firepot and see if there is fire or not?" It was winter and the firepot was their source of heat. Guishan stirred the firepot and said, "No fire." Then Baizhang got up and came over, dug deep into the ashes, and found a tiny ember. He showed it to Lingyou and said, "What is this? Isn't this fire?" Guishan was enlightened.

The fire in this story refers to the buddha-nature. Buddha-nature is not something solid or immovable, but rather an energy that motivates us to practice—and not just zazen or Buddhist practice. Buddha-nature is the fire of the life force that enables us to aspire to be better persons, to be more helpful to others, to settle into a healthy way of life, and to practice the Way. It's difficult to find the fire of buddha-nature inside ourselves, but we must. It's there. We are alive, so we have this force that drives us to practice and wake up to the reality of life. It may be only an ember, but all of us without exception have it. When we practice with other people, we gather together small fires. If we try to build a fire in a hibachi or firepot with a single piece of charcoal, it soon dies out. But even one tiny ember, if fed with charcoal, becomes a big fire. This is the meaning of sangha. We practice together with other people in a sangha. Each one of us has a small fire, which alone will die out sooner or later. Together we become bigger than ourselves. This was Guishan Lingyou's enlightenment.

Baizhang sent Guishan to Mount Gui, an isolated, precipitous, and awe-inspiring mountain suitable for a great monastery. He practiced there alone for several years. Dōgen Zenji comments on Guishan's practice, which he greatly admired, in a chapter of *Shōbōgenzō* titled "Gyōji." *Gyōji* means continuous or ceaseless practice. Here Dōgen talks about many Chinese Zen masters and their practice, Guishan being one of them. For Dōgen, Guishan's practice offered an important example of how to establish a monastery or sangha. He remarks:

> After the bestowal of the prophecy (Dharma transmission), Zen master Dayuan (Daien) of Mount Gui [i.e., Guishan Lingyou] went directly to the steep Gui Shan. There he made friends with bears and animals, lived at a thatched hermitage, and kept practicing. He didn't avoid hardships with wind and snow. He ate only chestnuts or horse chestnuts. There were neither temple buildings nor temple provisions. However, he ceaselessly devoted himself to continuous practice for more than forty years. Later, his temple became well known throughout the country and many excellent practitioners gathered there.[27]

People came to practice with him, and eventually his sangha grew huge. It is said that he had fifteen hundred students and forty-one dharma successors. Even though in the beginning he practiced alone, his practice was not for himself. He vowed to create a monastery or sangha to practice with others.

Dōgen Zenji discusses the inner attitude we should maintain when we vow to create a sangha or practice place. He continues, "When we make a vow to found a temple (a sangha or a monastery) we should not be motivated by human sentiment, but we should strengthen our aspiration for the continuous practice of Buddha Dharma." Our vow, then, should not be based on the human tendency to undertake things that we see as good, useful, or beneficial for ourselves alone—things we expect to bring us fame, profit, or self-satisfaction. This human sentiment isn't necessarily bad, but when we practice Buddha Dharma with others it is a hindrance. If each person seeks his or her own happiness and holds his or her own views, opinions, values, and ways of thinking, then there will be conflict. If we practice with other people on the basis of human sentiment, it may work for a while, but eventually it will fail. So our practice should be based not on human sentiment but on an aspiration for the continuous practice of Buddha Dharma.

Dōgen Zenji continues, "Even if we don't have lofty temple buildings, if we practice, the place can be called a *dōjō* of ancient buddhas." *Dōjō* means a place for practice. We now use the word *dōjō* for martial arts like karate or aikido, but originally this term referred to the place where the Buddha was enlightened under the bodhi tree. *Dōjō* is both a place for practice and a place of enlightenment because practice and enlightenment are one.

"We hear that ancient people practiced on the ground or under a tree. Such places are sacred forever. A single person's continuous practice creates a dōjō for many buddhas." This is the basic point of Dōgen Zenji's practice. We don't need lofty temple buildings for our practice. We don't need a formal zazen hall. When we vow to establish a dōjō, monastery, or sangha, we should not forget this. The number of buildings or people is not essential. The critical points are practice and aspiration. Dōgen said:

> Foolish people in this degenerate age should not be vainly engaged in construction of temple buildings. The buddhas and ancestors never had desires for buildings. Many people today meaninglessly construct a Buddha hall or other temple buildings although they haven't yet clarified the eye of their own self. Such people build temples, not in order to

> offer the buildings to buddhas, but to make them their own homes of fame and profit.

They don't understand Buddha Dharma, but they construct lofty buildings. That's why there are so many temples in Japan now. They are monuments to their founders. Today, Japan is prosperous. Even Buddhist priests have money. They construct gorgeous buildings, huge Buddha halls, and beautiful zendos. I was surprised when I visited a big temple in Japan. They had just built a huge two-story building. The first story had a spacious hall for giving lectures. On the second floor, there was a zendo with a big Mañjuśrī statue. But there were no monks practicing there. They used the building only once a month to have *zazen-kai*, day-long meditation retreats, and retreats for laypeople a few times a year. To me this is a waste of wealth. It has no meaning as Buddha Dharma. Dōgen Zenji made this same criticism. My teacher, Uchiyama Roshi, was also very critical of this kind of activity. Many people, sincere practitioners who would like to practice as Dōgen Zenji did, try to have a formal sōdō and a statue of Mañjuśrī, and everything Dōgen Zenji described. These people build a zendō for the sake of human sentiment. They think that buildings are essential and that they cannot practice without formal monastic buildings. Uchiyama Roshi said that we can practice zazen with only three square feet for each person, a *zafu* (round cushion) and *zabuton* (square mat) to sit on, and our aspiration to practice. That's all we need. This is a very important point.

Dōgen Zenji continues:

> We have to quietly contemplate Guishan's continuous practice in ancient times. To contemplate means to think of it as if we were living on Mount Gui right now. Listen to the sound of rain at midnight. The raindrops have power to pierce not only moss but also a rock. On a snowy night in winter, even birds and animals don't come to us. Unless we devote ourselves to continuous practice, valuing Dharma more than our own lives, we cannot stand such a life.

Guishan practiced alone, but I think this is not just a description of his solitary lifestyle. This is a description of our zazen. When we sit in zazen, even if we are with other people in a busy city, we are totally alone. The sound of raindrops and the sounds of the birds and animals are the sounds of our life. The snow is the scenery of our life. We just see it. We don't need to worry about what we should do today or tomorrow. Of course, we have a schedules, goals, and projects. But we just sit, right now, right here. We try to see that this is the only reality and everything else is the scenery of our life. We don't consider this practice as a step to something else. This practice right now, right here, brings about the next step. We don't need to worry about the next step. We should be fully right here, right now, in this situation, and awake to the reality of this self. That is an essential point.

> So Guishan didn't hurry to cut the grass to prepare the land, or engage in constructing temple buildings. He only continued to practice and put his whole energy into cultivating the Way. We cannot help but have sympathy for the authentic ancestor who transmitted the true Dharma and who had to undergo such hardships in a secluded steep mountain. I heard that on Mount Gui there was a pond and a brook which might be covered with layers of ice and mist. Although it was too solitary for a human being to tolerate, practice of the Buddha Way and the innermost truth vigorously came together there through his continuous practice.

This is the most important point in this chapter. Practice of the Buddha's Way is not something abstract but rather our concrete practice of the innermost truth of Buddha Dharma. This is the Buddha's teaching of the reality of our life. Even though our practice is very small, it merges with the innermost truth—Buddha's teaching of the reality of this universal life. This is an important aspect of our practice. Dōgen Zenji frequently talks about our concrete practice with our body and mind and that our personal practice actualizes the boundless, universal truth. Without our small, individual practice with this body and mind, the Buddha's teaching, or universal reality, is just an abstraction, something written in scriptures that we read and try to imagine. The universal truth or life force can only be manifested through our practice. If no one practices, Buddhist texts remain only words. If no one lives the teaching, it's just another part of our library; it's not alive. Even if our bodhi-mind or aspiration is weak, our practice is the manifestation of the universal truth taught by the Buddha.

Without the practice of this limited body and mind, temple buildings and zendos are meaningless. According to Dōgen Zenji, the meaning of our practice is practice at this moment, right now, right here, actualizing the Buddha's teaching. Without our practice there is no Buddha's teaching.

Katagiri Roshi's Vow

In 1988 Katagiri Roshi gave a lecture titled "Twenty-five Years of Dharma Transmission in North America" in which he spoke about his experiences in the United States and his vow and vision of his activities.[28] One of his experiences in his early time at the San Francisco Zen Center made him question the attitude of some American practitioners in the 1960s. At that time there were many young hippies living in the San Francisco area. Katagiri Roshi invited them to participate in practice at the center. One of them came to all the activities there. Katagiri Roshi said to him, "You come so often. What do you do? What's your job?" He answered, "I get unemployment." After he worked for six months or so, he could collect unemployment and meanwhile participate in activities at the center. After his unemployment payments expired, he would find another job. Katagiri Roshi was surprised by this reply. He had thought that this person was a good Zen student, but in fact the young man was engaging in an irresponsible way of life—irresponsible to his work, his society, and himself. According to Katagiri Roshi, taking advantage of the social welfare system to fulfill one's desire, even a desire to study Dharma, didn't have anything to do with the Dharma and was inconsistent with the bodhisattva practice of vow. Katagiri Roshi felt that a vow entails responsibility to one's own life, to other people, and to the whole of society. The most important point was always to walk together with all living beings.

In the lecture Katagiri Roshi also talked about his plans for the Zen community of MZMC. He mentioned four projects. I was surprised that he was so ambitious. First, he wanted to establish a monastery at Hokyōji,[29] where people could practice together as a sangha in an intimate setting. For Katagiri Roshi, Dharma means living beyond our egocentricity, individuality, and distinctions based on nationality and culture. It means living together as practitioners. This is the essence of Buddhism. Second, to educate and train his priest-disciples, he planned to establish a place where people could practice with experienced teachers. Finally, within Hokyōji's compound Katagiri Roshi wanted to build a separate facility as a retreat center, not just for monks but for anyone who wanted to experience a quiet life in nature. Fourth was Ganshōji, the Zen center in Minneapolis. This center is meant to have a function in the larger community, not just for the members of this sangha. Katagiri Roshi established a Buddhist study program that would appeal to a broad group of laypeople.

The Power of Raindrops

In his comments about Guishan Lingyou's practice, Dōgen Zenji talks about raindrops. He asks us to contemplate Guishan's practice in the mountains. We should try to feel as if we were in Guishan's place. "Listen to the sound of raindrops at midnight. The raindrops have the power to pierce not only moss but also rock." Guishan sat by himself in the deep mountain. Our practice of zazen, like his, resembles a raindrop. We are small and can sit for only a short time. Each drop alone has little power, but still we continue to practice. As raindrops eventually pierce not only moss but also rock, continuous practice of zazen has the power to make a hole in even a rock. This is an essential point. Our practice doesn't have a mystical, mysterious, or magical power to clear away all delusions. But like the raindrops, we sit moment by moment, day after day, year after year, and this sitting generates the power to erode a rock. When we think of our plans to establish a monastery, it's the same. Our effort is like raindrops; it doesn't create change in one day, or a few days, or a few years. But if we just keep doing it, when conditions are ripe, it happens.

We should remember Guishan Lingyou's example. Our actual practice is most important. We need time to work toward our goals, but to accomplish any project the appropriate cause and conditions are essential. The cause may be compared to the seed of a plant, and the conditions to temperature, humidity, and sunshine. If we put a seed on a desk, it won't sprout. It needs the right conditions. But even when conditions are perfect, if the seed isn't healthy it won't sprout. So we must be careful to keep our practice healthy and deeply rooted. We should keep the root of our practice wholesome.

The changing of the seasons is similar. When I came to Minneapolis in August, all the trees had green leaves. It was very beautiful. After a few weeks, the trees turned many different colors, and this too was beautiful. If we tried to paint each leaf by hand, it would take forever. But when autumn comes, all the leaves change color suddenly, almost at once, because there is a cause inside of the tree. That's how things happen. If we don't have the right conditions, not even a single leaf will change color. This is important to consider in the context of vow. Vow is kind of a long-range project or plan. We don't need to be in a hurry. Just practice and recharge our energy in the sangha. Practice, sit, keep the seed alive, and when conditions ripen, it will grow.

Katagiri Roshi's vow was huge. This is the same as practice. Buddha Dharma is something universal, infinite, and absolute. As individual human beings, we are small and limited. But when we sit in this posture and let go of individuality, we are one with everything. We are infinite, absolute, part of the universe. When we give up our limited attitudes, there is no separation between this small individual self and the boundless universe. The smallness of individuals and universality of reality is a main point in Dōgen Zenji's teaching. It can also be described as the merging of difference and unity. Difference is individuality; each person is different. Unity means that everything is one; there is no separation. This is our reality. We are independent, small, and limited. Yet when we sit in this posture and let go of thought and of our limited desires, we are moved by a vow that comes from the very core of our being, and there is no separation between us and the whole universe.

Dōgen Zenji often referred to this merging of individuality and universality. For example, in *Eihei Kōroku* he quotes Hongzhi Zhengjue (Wanshi Shōkaku), a famous Chinese Zen master and the Dharma brother of Changlu Qingliao (Chōro Seiryō). Hongzhi was asked, "What is the self before discrimination?" He answered, "A toad in a well swallows the moon."[30] A tiny being in a small well swallowed the moon, a symbol of universality, the reality of our life.

In *Eihei Kōroku* Dōgen Zenji changed the expression to "A toad in the bottom of the ocean eats gruel." This is a strange image, since there are no toads in the ocean. Here's how we can understand it. The toad in the bottom of the ocean symbolizes a practitioner in a monastery; the gruel is what practitioners eat almost every day for breakfast, and the ocean represents the sangha. So we are all toads in the ocean. A well refers to narrow egocentricity, or individuality. When we practice in a sangha, we are still toads, although we no longer live in a well but in the ocean.

Dōgen continues, "A jewel rabbit in the sky washes the bowl."[31] As a child in Japan, I was taught that there was a rabbit in the moon, because the pattern of the moon's craters resembles a rabbit, at least for the Japanese. So "jewel rabbit" refers to the moon. What does Dōgen mean when he says that a toad in the ocean eats gruel and a jewel rabbit washes the bowl? I think he means that we are very limited beings, but when we practice with the sangha and eat gruel for breakfast, the rabbit, meaning the moon, comes to this person and washes the bowl. So this practitioner is not a toad anymore, but the jewel rabbit in the moon. There is a transformation here. Hongzhi's expression is poetic, not about day-to-day activity. But Dōgen Zenji expresses very well the reality of our practice. We are small living beings like toads, and yet, when we practice with the sangha, we are not just individuals but part of the ocean of beings, of all existence. Eating gruel for breakfast is a very concrete activity. Even a small act by a small person manifests the universal reality, which is the reality of our life. Any effort, however small, is enough. We do what we can in this moment, and then in the next moment, and then tomorrow; one moment at a time. It is the same as our practice of zazen, and our practice in our daily activities.

Meanings of Living by Vow

Vow is one of the most important aspects of practice as a bodhisattva. It can be understood from three different perspectives. First, a vow is a direction for an individual. We live the reality of life whether we are deluded or enlightened. This reality is called as-it-is-ness, or *tathātā*. It is also true that we frequently deviate from this reality of life because we are deceived by our egocentricity. The reality of our life is not so simple for us human beings. Enlightened or deluded, we are living out our as-it-is-ness, and yet we are always blind to it. This is our life as human beings. First we have to realize that we are deluded. Then we have to go back to the reality of life through the practice of this reality. As-it-is-ness for human beings is dynamic. We live in the reality of life, yet always lose sight of it, so we must return to it. These three points are the movement, the actual reality of our lives. To go back to the reality of life in the midst of this reality is our practice. This practice is based on vow. This vow is not a special promise we make to the Buddha but rather a manifestation of the foundation of our being. This is the most fundamental meaning of taking a vow. We go back to the reality of life within that reality.

The second aspect of living by vow is to live within a sangha and practice with other people, that is, to walk together with all living beings. We do this with the three minds—joyful mind, parental mind, and magnanimous mind. Our vow is manifest in our day-to-day lives as these three minds. Finally, we practice as a sangha, not simply as an individual but as one whole body. The sangha itself needs to have a direction to grow. That is the meaning of living by vow as a sangha. By working on the vow as a sangha little by little, one thing at a time, like raindrops, we meet the challenges and create a new stage in the history of Buddhism in the West.

2 Awakening to Incompleteness: The Verse of Repentance

All the karma ever created by me since of old
Through greed, anger, and self-delusion
Which has no beginning, born of my body, speech, and thought
I now make full repentance of it[32]

TRADITIONALLY in Chinese and Japanese Buddhism, there are two kinds of repentance. One is formal and concrete repentance, called *ji-sange*, in which we repent concrete offenses by means of rituals conducted with the help of a particular buddha, teacher, or sangha member. Another kind of repentance is called *ri-sange*. *Ji* and *ri* are important concepts in Chinese Buddhism. *Ji* refers to the relative, conventional, phenomenal, and formal level, whereas *ri* refers to the absolute, supreme, total, and formless level. A verse different from the one quoted above is used for ri-sange.

Sitting in zazen and letting go of thoughts is formless repentance. This kind of repentance has been emphasized in the Sōtō tradition since the Edo period (seventeenth–ninteenth centuries). But in Dōgen Zenji's writings, as far as I know, only the verse of ji-sange is recorded. I think both are important. Formal repentance is for our misdeeds that break the bodhisattva precepts we receive when we become the

Buddha's students. Formless repentance is to awaken to the total interpenetrating reality beyond separation of subject and object, self and others. This is zazen.

The original Buddhist repentance was ji-sange, or formal repentance. In the original Buddhist sangha in India, when someone made a mistake the Buddha admonished the person not to repeat the deed. These admonitions were memorized and compiled in a category of Buddhist scripture called Vinaya by one of the ten great disciples, Upāli, at the first council after the Buddha's death. Since then, people receiving ordination as monks and nuns took these precepts as guidelines and vowed to uphold them. Sangha members held meetings for repentance called *uposatha* (Jap., *fusatsu*) twice a month on new and full moon days. A leader of the sangha recited the precepts text, called the Prātimokṣa, and people who had transgressed against the precepts made confession and repentance. They incurred penalties depending upon the severity of their violations. Lay Buddhists received five precepts and could participate in uposatha gatherings.

So the original meaning of repentance is to reflect on one's misdeeds and confess them to the sangha. This is a concrete, formal repentance. In order to make repentance, we first have to receive the precepts. The precepts are guidelines for our day-to-day lives. When we become aware of our deviation from these guidelines, we repent and go back to the precepts. This is the meaning of receiving the precepts as standards for our lives and making repentance.

Since Mahāyāna Buddhism was initially a lay movement, practitioners didn't have their own Vinaya. They received only the bodhisattva precepts. Later Mahāyāna monks lived in monasteries and practiced based on the Vinaya.[33] In China, Mahāyāna Buddhist monks received both the Vinaya and Mahāyāna precepts: the ten major precepts and the forty-eight minor precepts. However, in almost all schools of Japanese Buddhism except the Ritsu (Vinaya) school, both monks and laypeople receive only the bodhisattva precepts. This tradition originated with the founder of the Japanese Tendai school, Saichō (767–822). In the Sōtō Zen tradition founded by Dōgen, both priests and laypeople receive only sixteen bodhisattva precepts: the three refuges, the threefold pure precepts, and the ten major precepts.

In our *jukai* (precepts-receiving) ceremony, we recite this verse of repentance before accepting the precepts. Repentance is like washing a cloth before dying it a certain color. By repenting the way we have been living, we cleanse our body and mind. This is a decisive turning point in our lives. We change our direction from the pursuit of wealth, fame, and success to the bodhisattva Way of living at one with all beings.

Many recite this verse not just once in a lifetime at the jukai ceremony but also at bimonthly repentance ceremonies called *ryaku-fusatsu*. Katagiri Roshi's practice at MZMC was to recite it at the beginning of the morning service together with the verses of the three refuges and the four bodhisattva vows. Even though we have received the precepts, we often forget them and lose our direction as bodhisattvas. So we remember that the precepts are the guidelines of our lives and renew our aspiration and commitment. This is the meaning of the recitation of repentance in our daily practice.

There is another, deeper meaning of repentance. We live in the reality of our life whether or not we observe the precepts. No one can escape from this reality. Even when we are deluded, we live in reality as deluded human beings. Ultimately there is no separation between reality and delusion. In other words, reality includes delusions. Even though we live in the reality that is beyond discrimination, we have to discriminate in our day-to-day lives. We have to decide what is good or bad. Without discrimination we can do nothing. Even as we practice the Buddha's teachings, we have to make choices. This is the unavoidable reality of our concrete lives.

Zazen is the only exception. When we sit in this posture and open the hand of thought, we are truly free from discrimination. Whenever thoughts come up, we just let them go. In our daily activities, however, we have to make choices based on discrimination even though we practice the reality that is beyond discrimination. For instance, right now I am thinking, "How can I express the Buddha's teachings in the most understandable way in English?" This is my intention. Even when we try to manifest the reality beyond discrimination, we have to discriminate and make choices about the best way to do so. Repentance means that although I think this is the best thing to do in this situation, I recognize that it might be a mistake. It might even be harmful to others and to me—I don't know.

When I was at Pioneer Valley Zendo in Massachusetts, I had to cut many trees to clear the land and plant a garden. I killed many small animals, insects, and worms. Once, for example, after I dug a well the hole filled with rainwater and a skunk drowned. My intention was to work for the Buddha Dharma and to create a place for practice. To do so, I harmed other creatures. Even when we try to work for the benefit of all beings, we may harm others. We cannot predict the consequences of our actions. All of us have to eat to live. Even if we don't eat meat, we have to eat vegetables. This means we have to kill vegetables. To live as a human being is to be supported by others' lives and deaths. Even if we are not conscious of it, we may create evil karma that can injure ourselves and others. As bodhisattvas we cannot live without repentance.

"All the karma ever created by me since of old": This translation does not specify bad karma, but the original does. *Shoakugō* means "bad karma." Some other translations use words such as "unwholesome," "twisted," or "harmful" to avoid the duality between good and bad. We practice repentance on the basis of total interpenetrating reality. We live only with the support of all beings but recognize that we may harm some. Even when we live as well as we possibly can, we still need to repent because from our limited viewpoint we can't know which acts might result in harm.

"Through greed, anger, and self-delusion": In Buddhism these are the three poisons. Self-delusion or ignorance is the cause of the other two. In this case it refers to ignorance of the reality of impermanence and ego.[34] The *Heart Sutra* tells us that all five skandhas are empty. The five skandhas make up our body and mind. This means that we are empty, and yet we don't often see the emptiness of our body and mind. It feels as if we have a body and mind. We assume there is something called an "ego" that owns and operates our body in the same way a person owns and drives a car. In reality there is no driver but only this body and mind. There is no driver, but somehow the car runs. This is really an "auto-mobile."

When we are unaware of impermanence and egolessness, the ego appears to be the center of the world. Anger and greed arise because the ego tries to protect itself. Greed prompts us to accumulate more and more to satisfy egocentric desires. Anger is caused by the ego's need to stay secure and powerful. These three poisons are the basic causes of our bad karma.

Body, speech, and thought create our good and bad karma. "No beginning" means we cannot see the origin of our karma. Our body and mind are influenced even by things that have happened before we were born. Everything that has happened in the whole universe since the Big Bang influences our ways of thinking and behaving. It is all really without beginning.

"I now make full repentance of it": The original word was *sange*, which as we've seen means "repentance." Repentance includes confession but is not necessarily limited to confession. As the Buddha's students, we receive the precepts and vow to live by them. This is why we have to repent deeds against our vow. In the first line the Japanese word *issai* ("all") means all the misdeeds or mistakes we have made, even if we are not conscious of them. Vow and repentance are inseparable. When we closely look at our past deeds, we cannot help but repent. When we awaken to the total interpenetrating reality of our being and look to the future, we cannot refrain from making the vow to live with all beings and to practice according to the Buddha's teachings. Vow and repentance are two sides of the single practice of zazen.

Another important verse of repentance is from the *Samantabhadra Sutra*. It addresses formless repentance (*ri-sange*) and repentance of true reality (*jissō-sange*).

> The ocean of all karmic hindrances
> arises solely from delusive thoughts.

> If you wish to make repentance,
> sit in upright posture and be mindful of the true reality.
> All misdemeanors, like frost and dew,
> are melted away in the sun of wisdom.[35]

In this repentance we do not actually say something like, "I'm sorry because of this or that specific mistake." Rather, our zazen is itself repentance.

"The ocean of all karmic hindrances / arises solely from delusive thoughts": Here "karma" means all of our activities—not just our mistakes or misconduct. Even when we do good things we may create karmic hindrance. Almost all of our actions, good or bad, are based on self-centeredness. Therefore they are not in accord with the reality of oneness, impermanence, and interdependent origination. Any actions (karma) caused by our ignorance of the reality of life are a hindrance because they prevent us from awakening to reality and liberating ourselves from self-clinging. Any activity we do solely for ourselves, for our family, community, or nation—including Buddhist practices—can be a hindrance to actualizing total interpenetrating reality.

Even our charitable acts often have egocentric motivations. We seek satisfaction by trying to be better or more important. To gain respect from others, we try to be seen as compassionate. When there is the slightest deviation between our actions and our true mind, we create karmic hindrances. When we do something evil or make a mistake, we find it easy to repent. We have no difficulty in seeing it's our own fault, and if we don't recognize our misdeeds, others will help us by showing their anger. But when we are doing good things, it is really difficult to notice our karmic hindrances because people praise us and we feel good. Our good deeds that generate karmic hindrance make us arrogant and careless. We become blind to the fact that we are still limited, ordinary, self-centered human beings.

"If you wish to make repentance, / sit in upright posture and be mindful of the true reality": To be bodhisattvas, we have to be free from the hindrance of even our good deeds. To do that, we just sit and try to be mindful of the reality of our life. To be mindful of true reality does not mean *thinking* about reality. When we sit in the zazen posture, we keep our body straight and breathe quietly through our nose, smoothly and deeply, feeling the air as it fills our chest. We let go of thoughts. Whatever comes up in our mind, we just let it go. We don't hide anything, even negative feelings or stupid thoughts, even thoughts about the Buddha's teaching. We just let them come up and go away. Repeatedly we return to zazen, to our posture and breathing.

In this practice we are mindful of true reality that exists independent of our thoughts. To be mindful means to settle down right now, right here, without seeking after or escaping from anything. We refrain from either affirming or negating anything. We accept everything as it is, as the reality of our own life. In this sitting and letting go, true reality manifests itself. We can become intimate with ourselves as a whole. In this way we can be free from the egocentricity that makes us do "good" things. In other words, we do not become attached to what we think is good, meaningful, or important according to our own system of values.

"All misdemeanors, like frost and dew, / are melted away in the sun of wisdom": This is true formless repentance, in which we liberate ourselves even from Buddhist teachings. This is what Linji (Rinzai) meant when he said that if you meet the Buddha you should kill the Buddha. Dōgen Zenji said that sitting Buddha is killing Buddha. We see the reality of things with ever-fresh eyes, unclouded by even our good will. We are not caught in one particular place. We don't rely on anything inside or outside ourselves.

If we did something good yesterday, we should forget it and face what confronts us today. What we did yesterday is no longer real. We cannot be proud of what we did in the past or think we are a great person because we did such and such. Nor should we be caught up in our mistakes. We let go of them and start again. We start right from this posture in silence, from the ever-fresh life force that is free from any defilement. Moment by moment, we start again and again. This is not where our human evaluation and discrimination works. This is true repentance.

A Japanese Sōtō Zen master, Banjin Dōtan (1698–1775), comments on this verse in his *Zenkai-shō* (Comments on Zen Precepts):

> The essence of repentance is that delusion and enlightenment, or living beings and buddhas, are one. Because of this, a person who practices repentance is endowed with all virtue. We usually think that delusive thoughts and true reality are separate and distinct, as an owner and that which is owned. When we are completely liberated, we see that there is no person who possesses delusions nor are there delusions that are possessed. This is the true path of Buddha Dharma. We should not understand this verse to mean that we have to get rid of delusive thoughts by sitting upright and being mindful of the true reality. Repentance is another name for the Three Treasures. To repent is to take refuge in the Three Treasures. When the dharma of repentance is carried out, it completely includes the three refuges and the threefold pure precepts. Repentance, the three refuges, and the threefold pure precepts are not apart from falsehood caused by delusions. We are, however, able to attain liberation within delusions. We could say that before delusions leave, true reality has arrived. This is what is meant by the expression "Before the donkey leaves, the horse has arrived." We should learn that repentance is nothing other than the Dharma, the practice of the Buddha's awakening.[36]

Banjin Dōtan says that to awaken to the reality that exists prior to the separation between delusion and enlightenment, between living beings and buddhas, is the essence of repentance. Because of awakening, a person who practices the repentance of sitting in upright posture in zazen is endowed with all virtues of the Buddha, the reality of life.

We usually think that delusive thoughts or desires are incompatible with the enlightenment of true reality. We believe that in order to attain enlightenment, we have to eliminate delusions. Banjin Dōtan, however, says that when we are completely liberated, we see that there is no one who possesses delusions, nor are there any delusions that are possessed. When we are sitting in zazen and letting go of thoughts, we are completely liberated. We see that both persons and delusions are without substance. This is the emptiness of reality, the true path of Buddha Dharma.

Our practice is not a means to get rid of delusive thoughts. Being mindful of true reality is not a method to eliminate delusions. In fact, when we sit in zazen, we sit squarely within the reality before the separation of delusion and enlightenment. We usually think of ourselves as deluded human beings and of buddhas as enlightened beings. We imagine that our practice is a method to transform a deluded being into an enlightened one by removing delusion. This idea is itself dualistic and contrary to the reality before separation.

So should we give up practice and pursue our delusions? No, what we must do is sit in zazen and let go of all dualistic ideas. In doing so, true reality manifests itself. Delusion and enlightenment are both here. Neither is negated or affirmed; neither is grasped. We sit on the ground of letting go. This is the meaning of Dōgen Zenji's expression "Practice and enlightenment are one." There is no state to be attained other than our practice of letting go. We practice within delusions and manifest enlightenment through sitting practice and day-to-day activities based on zazen. These practices enable us to settle our whole existence on that ground.

Banjin Dōtan also said that repentance is itself the Three Treasures. When we really repent in zazen and let go of thoughts, we take refuge in the Buddha, Dharma, and Sangha. Repentance in Buddhism is not something negative. It is a very positive activity through which we become true Buddhists. Our practice doesn't make us perfect or holy people. In a sense, practice means giving up trying to become perfect; it means realizing our imperfect nature. We accept even our delusions and take care of them as if they were as precious as our children. If we ignore our delusions (or our children), they can do great harm. When we take good care of them, they can be quieted. We can be liberated within delusions only if we face and care for them. If we don't, they become an impregnable barrier. There is a path of liberation within delusions and suffering. When we see reality clearly, we can see delusions as just delusion.

"We could say that before delusions leave, true reality has arrived. This is what is meant by the expression 'Before the donkey leaves, the horse has arrived,'" writes Banjin Dōtan. Donkeys do not run fast, and we usually consider them lazy and foolish. We think a horse is better than a donkey. But this expression says that before the donkey (a deluded human being) leaves, the horse (true reality) has arrived. This means that right within this moment, our life force, this body and mind, both donkey and horse, are present, and we don't need to hit the donkey to force it to go. We should not, however, mistake the donkey for the horse. Taking good care of the donkey is our practice. Within this practice is the horse. We can find egocentricity deep inside our good deeds. But this doesn't mean we should carry out good deeds until we have completely eliminated our egocentricity. We strive to practice good and keep awakening to delusions, even those in our benevolent deeds. If we practice in this way we cannot avoid repentance. This formless, true repentance is in fact our zazen.

I think this repentance is essential for modern human beings because we have such powerful technologies. We can kill all the living beings on the earth. Most of the major problems we face today are a result of human activities. They are not caused by bad, foolish, or cruel people. Wars, ecological destruction, and so on have been caused by sincere, brilliant people under the banners of justice, liberty, human welfare, and national prosperity. These people are often respected as great leaders. Many religions cause problems by encouraging us to cling to doctrines and beliefs. We have to become aware of our self-delusion and clinging even while we try to accomplish good. Only in this way can we become free from the defilements caused by performing good deeds with imperfect motives. This is the true meaning of repentance.

3

Final Shelter: The Verse of the Three Refuges

The English translation of the verse of the Triple Treasure in the MZMC sutra book is:

> I take refuge in the Buddha, vowing with all sentient beings, acquiring the Great Way, awakening the unsurpassable mind.
>
> I take refuge in the Dharma, vowing with all sentient beings, deeply entering the teaching, wisdom like the sea.
>
> I take refuge in the Sangha, vowing with all sentient beings, bringing harmony to all, completely, without hindrance.[37]

When we become Buddhists, we first make repentance and take refuge in the Three Treasures of Buddhism: the Buddha, Dharma, and Sangha. These refuges are the first three of the sixteen precepts we receive in the Japanese Sōtō Zen tradition established by Dōgen Zenji. Without these three there is no Buddhism. Shakyamuni Buddha, born in India about twenty-five hundred years ago, is our original teacher. He awakened to the reality of our life. Both his teachings about this reality and the reality itself are called Dharma. Sangha is the community of people who study the Buddha's teaching and follow his way of life. His first students were the five monks who had practiced with him before his enlightenment. They understood, became his disciples, and established the first sangha. That was the birth of Buddhism. From the very beginning, the Buddha as teacher, the Dharma as teaching, and the Sangha as community have been the essential elements of Buddhism.

Taking Refuge in the Buddha

When we become Buddhists, we vow to take refuge in the Buddha, the Dharma, and the Sangha. When we accept the Buddha's teaching as a student of the Buddha, we make this vow with all sentient beings. It would be better to translate this as "all living beings." The original word in Japanese is *shujō*. *Shu* means "many" or "various"; *jō* means "life" or "living beings." The next phrase, *taige taidō*, or "acquiring the Great Way," is an interesting expression. *Tai* means "body" and *ge* means "to understand," so this can be translated as "understanding with the body." We have to understand the Great Way with our bodies. The Buddha's teaching is not something we can understand merely with our intellects; we have to practice it in our day-to-day lives. To understand and agree with his teaching is not enough. If we agree with his teaching, we have to carry it out, to live it. *Taige* means to embody, study, learn, or incorporate into our everyday lives. *Taidō*, or "Great Way," means "awakening." Here the "Way" is a translation of the Sanskrit word *bodhi*. This phrase means we have to embody the Great Awakening of the Buddha in our daily lives.

The first refuge includes the phrase "awakening the unsurpassable mind." Unsurpassable mind (*mujō-shin*) is the same as bodhi-mind (*bodai-shin*). Both are abbreviations of the Sanskrit *anuttarā-samyaksambodhi-ciṭta*. *Anuttarā* means "unsurpassable," "supreme," or "highest." *Bodhi* means "awakening." *Mujō* is the translation of *anuttarā* and *bodai* is the transliteration of *bodhi*. When we embody the Great Awakening, we awaken to the awakening mind. It's a strange expression, but that is the reality. We awaken the awakening mind in order to wake up. We usually think we are awake except when we are asleep at night or napping, but actually we are usually asleep and dreaming. We imagine this world, our lives, and ourselves. We create dream-worlds and then believe that they are reality. And yet, they are only constructs of our mind. We create a story in which we are the hero or heroine. We think we are the center of the world, and all other people and things are resources to make a happy ending for our story. This is how we live in a dream. To awaken means to drop off body and mind, become free from dreaming and encounter reality. We try to act based on the reality that exists before we process the world through the intellect. Our intellection is based on our education and all our experiences since birth. But these experiences are a limited way of viewing the world, so we must wake up to reality.

Another aspect of "unsurpassable mind" is compassion for all beings. When we awake to the reality that has not yet been processed by our ego-centered mind, we cannot help having compassion for all beings. We realize that we live together with all beings, supported by networks of interconnection. We share air, water, and life by offering ourselves to each other. We live supported by all beings. In turn, we must support all other beings. This is compassion. We have to awaken to the reality that we live together as knots within Indra's net. We do not and cannot live independently, as limited and conditioned individuals. This is the meaning of taking refuge in the Buddha.

Taking Refuge in Dharma

The next section begins, "I take refuge in the Dharma." The Sanskrit word *dharma* has many meanings, but two are important here—the Buddha's teaching and the reality of all beings. It continues, "Vowing with all sentient beings, deeply entering the teaching." The original word for "the teaching" is *kyō zō*. *Kyō* means "sutra," and *zō* means "warehouse," "storehouse," or "treasury." Buildings in Buddhist temples where sutras or texts are stored called *kyō zō*. *Jin nyū kyō zō* means "deeply entering into the storehouse of sutras." Another possible interpretation of this word *kyō zō* is "sutra *piṭaka*," that is, one of the three "baskets" (*piṭaka*) of Buddhist scriptures: sutras, commentaries on the sutras (*Abhidharma*), and precepts (*Vinaya*). Either way, we vow to study the sutras thoroughly. In a chapter of *Shōbōgenzō* titled "Sansuikyō" (Mountains and Waters Sutra), Dōgen Zenji wrote, "These mountains and waters of the present are the manifestation of the Way of the ancient buddhas." This implies that the reality of all beings is itself a sutra. Not only the mountains and waters but also the birds singing, the sun shining, and everything happening around us are sutras teaching us the reality of being. They teach impermanence and interdependence. Nothing lasts forever, everything is always changing, and there is no fixed ego or substance. All beings in the universe teach this reality, but we don't listen; we don't really see it. We think, "I want to do this" or "I wish to do that," and we are blind to the reality of impermanence and interdependence. The phrase "deeply entering the teaching" doesn't require that we read all the Buddhist texts. Although reading is an important part of entering the teaching, the deeper meaning is really to awaken to the reality before our eyes, the reality that we actually live.

The phrase "wisdom like the sea" refers to an unlimited and boundless perspective. We are like a frog in a well that can see only a small patch of sky. Our view is limited, yet we think we are the center of the world and know everything. We base our actions on our conditioned understanding, perceptions, and opinions. The beginning of wisdom is to see that our view is limited. The view we have at sea is wider than in a well. There is no limitation to something so vast and boundless. By studying the Buddha's teaching we become free from our limited views and open ourselves to boundless reality. The meaning of taking refuge in the Dharma is that we value Dharma more than our own limited opinions and views based on our personal karma.

Taking Refuge in Sangha

The third vow begins, "I take refuge in the Sangha." *Sangha* is a Sanskrit word meaning an association or union of people. In India at the time of the Buddha, cities were forming, and some people were freed from the daily labor of agriculture. Classes of merchants, craftsmen, warriors, and nobles arose. People established unions or associations called sanghas (or *gaṇas*). A sangha is a democratic community of members who share the same interests and status. The vow continues with "vowing with all sentient beings, bringing harmony to all." The phrase "bringing harmony" is a translation of the Japanese word *tori*, which means "unify." Buddhist sangha members are unified by the Dharma. To have a community instead of a collection of individuals, to have harmony, we need something that unifies. To make soup we chop the ingredients and put them in a pot, then add seasoning and cook it until the individual flavors blend to make one taste. Similarly, we need to cook ourselves and make these individuals into one community with one taste—the taste of Dharma. Harmony unifies a collection of individuals into a community in which we can take refuge.

The next phrase is "completely, without hindrance." With harmony and unity, there is no hindrance. When individuals think "me first," endless problems and obstacles arise. But when we wake up to impermanence and egolessness, and share the life of this moment, there is no hindrance. Of course, there are still difficulties to overcome, but with harmony we can work on them. If we have discord, we cannot. This is the meaning of sangha and of taking refuge in the Three Treasures.

The Reason for Taking Refuge

Shōbōgenzō is a collection of about ninety-five of Dōgen Zenji's independent writings. One of the chapters is called "Taking Refuge in Buddha, Dharma, and Sangha" (Kie-buppōsōbō). Here he quotes a section from *Kusharon* (*Abhidharmakośa bhāṣya*), chapter 14, about why we take refuge in the Three Treasures. This text was originally written in India and translated into Chinese. The Indian text says, "Many people out of fear take refuge in the deities of mountains, forests, trees, gardens, shrines, and so on."[38] We take refuge in gods because of fear. We need shelter—in this case spiritual shelter—because we are weak and afraid. Human beings are not necessarily the strongest animals. We are not as big as elephants, as fast as cheetahs, or as strong as gorillas. All phenomenal elements, such as too much or too little rain, cause suffering in our lives. Full of fear and uncertainty, primitive people needed something to worship, to rely on. Even in civilized society it's dangerous to rely on things outside of ourselves. Everything outside of us is uncertain, always changing and unreliable. We worship, pray to, or rely on this thing that we believe to be eternal and unchanging. This is one of the reasons we need religion. Buddhism, of course, is one of the religions. But the Buddha didn't teach us to take refuge in a deity beyond this phenomenal world. He taught us to find refuge within this world, within ourselves. This is the basic teaching of the Buddha and a difference between Buddhism and other religions.

The Indian text continues, "Taking refuge in such deities, however, is not excellent and worthwhile. It is not possible to be released from various pains or sufferings by means of taking refuge in such kinds of deities." So we cannot find security through worship of things in nature or beyond nature. "If people take refuge in the Buddha and take refuge in the Dharma and the Sangha, they will, in keeping with the four noble truths, constantly contemplate with wisdom: they know suffering, they know the cause of suffering, they know eternally going beyond suffering, and they know the eightfold noble path." Shakyamuni Buddha taught that people who take refuge in the Buddha, Dharma, and Sangha are able to see with the wisdom expressed in the four noble truths. Wisdom is important in Buddhism, together with compassion and faith. In other religions, we can't understand, so we believe. But in Buddhism we have faith because we have the wisdom to see. This is an important point. By taking refuge in the Buddha, the Dharma, and the Sangha, we learn to find stability, peace, and liberation from fear by examining what's happening. We see that the cause of fear is inside us.

With the four noble truths, the Buddha taught the reality of suffering or duḥkha. In Buddhism it said that there are four kinds of suffering: birth, aging, sickness, and death. All of us are born crying with pain. Life is filled with suffering, as is death. Another four kinds of suffering are often mentioned: separating from beloved people, meeting with people we don't like, not being able to gain what we want, and not being able to control the five *skandhas*. The first three are the painful experiences all of us often experience in our social lives. Sometimes we have to separate from people we love, and at other times we have to associate with people we don't like. That is the reality of our life. Often we cannot acquire something we really want, and so we suffer. The most fundamental form of suffering is the last one, which is inherent in human nature. We are collections of five skandhas or aggregates: form, sensation, perception, mental formations, and consciousness. These elements, of which we and all other beings are formed, are impermanent and always changing. They cannot be controlled because there is nothing to control them. We cannot control our lives. This body and mind is not a possession that can be mastered. Therefore, human existence itself is always unsatisfactory and we feel suffering. This is the meaning of suffering in Buddhist teachings.

The second of the four noble truths is the cause of suffering. The Buddha taught that delusive desires and attachments based on fundamental ignorance are the cause of all suffering. We are always thirsty and hungry and chase after things to fill our empty stomachs, and when we can't find anything we suffer. When we are successful, we want more, or we fear losing what we have.

Third is the truth of the cessation of suffering, or nirvana. When we first hear that Buddhism teaches that life is full of suffering, we think it must be very pessimistic or nihilistic. But the Buddha taught that it's possible to be in nirvana, to become free from suffering. This is because suffering has causes and conditions. If we work on changing those causes and conditions, we can release ourselves from suffering. Shakyamuni Buddha's teaching is not at all pessimistic.

The fourth noble truth, the way to eradicate the causes of suffering, is the eightfold noble path. To follow this path we must view things correctly, base our thinking on reality instead of egocentricity, speak truthfully, act in accord with the right view, engage in a wholesome livelihood, make diligent efforts, and practice right mindfulness and meditation. The Buddha gave us these eight guidelines for our practice.

He taught that we can find the real foundation for a peaceful life within ourselves, within this phenomenal world, without relying on a deity. This teaching and practice of the Middle Way to which the Buddha awakened are the shelter and foundation of our life.

The *Abhidharmakośa* text continues, "Therefore, taking refuge in the Three Treasures is supreme and most venerable." We take refuge in various things in this world. In a financial context, taking refuge might mean trusting money or insurance. We rely on insurance to provide security when we are unable to work. We do this to be free from fear, but when life insurance is actually paid you are no longer there. So it's really no benefit to you at all. We rely on many different things, but nothing is really certain; nothing has a truly stable foundation. The only stable foundation for our life, according to the Buddha, is the Dharma and the self. In the *Dhammapada* the Buddha said:

> Your own self is
> your own mainstay,
> for who else could your mainstay be?
> With you yourself well-trained
> you obtain the mainstay
> hard to obtain.[39]

In another old scripture, the *Suttanipāta*, the Buddha said:

> The independent man does not tremble or get confused. But a man who is dependent on something is clutching, grasping at existence in one form or another, and he cannot escape from existences.[40]

The Buddha's advice to us is not to count on others but depend on the Dharma and rely on our own self. Neither the Dharma nor the self is eternal, and everything is changing. We can't really rely on anything, yet this reality of egolessness (no-self) and impermanence is itself the foundation of our life. We can find peace and liberation by seeing deeply the impermanence and egolessness of life itself. This is the only possible stable, peaceful foundation of us because it is the only reality that is here and now. Nothing in the past, nothing in the future, nothing beyond this reality is reliable. Reality is ever changing and therefore ever fresh and new. My teacher, Uchiyama Roshi, urged us to open the hand of thought and awaken to the reality that is always changing. This is the most reliable foundation of our life. This refuge is supreme and most venerable.

In *Abhidharmakośa* the final reason to take refuge in the Triple Treasure is that "By taking refuge, people are surely released from various sufferings." This is why the Buddha and other masters encourage us to take refuge in the Buddha, the Dharma, and the Sangha. I think that of these three, the sangha is most significant to us today. Of course, the Buddha and the Dharma are the basis of Sangha. However, without Sangha, a living community of people, the Buddha is someone who lived in the past, and his teaching is something printed in a textbook. Because there is a community of practitioners who follow his teaching and manifest reality in their daily activities, the Buddha and the Dharma come alive right now, right here. I have been a monk-priest for about twenty-five years. I don't think that I could have lived the Buddha's teaching and practiced by myself for so long. With the help of my teacher, my dharma brothers, and the people who practice with me, I can practice. A sangha of practitioners is most important. We really have to take refuge there. This vow brings Sangha vividly alive.

Three Meanings of the Triple Treasure

The basic original meaning of the Buddha, the Dharma, and the Sangha is straightforward. "Buddha" refers to Shakyamuni Buddha, who was born in India about twenty-five hundred years ago. "Dharma" is both the reality to which he awakened and his teachings about that reality. "Sangha" is the community of the Buddha's students. As Buddhism evolved, the understanding of the Three Treasures became more complex. The death of Shakyamuni Buddha was a great loss for his students.

He was not only their teacher, he was the only teacher. None of his disciples could become a second Buddha and assume his position in the sangha. They were sad and also confused as to who could be their teacher. Then they remembered that Shakyamuni said that people who see the Dharma see the Buddha. For them, Shakyamuni Buddha was not just a person who had a physical body and had died. The Buddha was still there as the teaching and as the reality. They called this the dharma-body (*dharmakāya*) of the Buddha, as opposed to the material body (*rūpakāya*) that perished with Shakyamuni's passing away. They believed that the Dharma, the Buddha's teaching, was the Buddha himself.

The Buddha said, "Monks should not take care of the Buddha's dead body." Monks were supposed to concentrate on practice not the past. Consequently, Shakyamuni Buddha's funeral was left to lay students. They performed the funeral, separating his ashes or relics into eight sections, which were enshrined at eight different sites in India. Lay followers built stūpas and made pilgrimages to them to pay homage to the Buddha. The Buddha's statue or relics enshrined in a stūpa symbolized Shakyamuni Buddha. So there are three meanings of Buddha: the historical Buddha, the Buddha as dharma-body, and the Buddha as a statue, image, or relic.

People also started to think that there were three kinds of Triple Treasure. Historically "Dharma" meant the Buddha's teachings, but in "dharma-body" it refers to reality itself. This reality was there before Shakyamuni awakened to it. He said, "I didn't invent the truth, teaching, or reality. I was like a person who finds an old castle hidden in a forest." This reality is the original meaning of *dharma*. All beings and all things in this universe are the manifestation of this original reality. Since all beings manifest this reality, they are always awakened because they are reality itself. All beings in the universe can be called members of the universal sangha. Ultimately speaking, the dharma-body is the Buddha Treasure; the Dharma, the true way of things as they are, is the Dharma Treasure; and all beings as an expression of Dharma are called the Sangha Treasure. This very idealistic interpretation of the Three

Treasures is known as Ittai Sanbō. *Sanbō* means "three treasures"; *ittai* means "one body." In this context *one* means "absolute." So the Three Treasures are one body, one reality. The Buddha, the Dharma, and the Sangha are just one reality. Ittai Sanbō is referred to as the Absolute Three Treasures or the Unified Three Treasures.

The historical Three Treasures—Shakyamuni Buddha, his teaching, and his community of students—are called Genzen Sanbō (Manifesting Three Treasures) because they are historical, real-world manifestations of the Absolute Three Treasures. After the Buddha's death, his followers continued to practice his teaching. For several centuries the sutras were transmitted as an oral tradition. Eventually they were written down in Sanskrit or Pāli. In India the sutras were written on the leaves of *tala* trees. The Buddha's teaching was recorded as a kind of a scripture and called the Dharma Treasure. The Buddha's images or relics were considered symbols of the Buddha, or the Buddha Treasure, and the sangha was called the Sangha Treasure. These were called *Jūji Sanbō*. *Jūji* means "maintaining." In order to maintain the Buddha's teaching after he died, the Buddha's image, sutras, and the communities of practitioners were considered to be Three Treasures. When we become Buddhists, we take refuge in the Buddha, the Dharma, and the Sangha. There are three kinds of Three Treasures and we take refuge in all of them. There are sanghas, or communities of the Buddha's students, throughout the world. The Buddha's teachings have been translated into many different languages, and each translation is a dharma treasure and should be respected.

The Triple Treasure as Teacher, Medicine, and Friends

In the chapter of *Shōbōgenzō* entitled "Taking Refuge in Buddha, Dharma, and Sangha," Dōgen Zenji mentions the reason why we take refuge in those three. He says, "We take refuge in the Buddha because the Buddha is our great teacher, we take refuge in the Dharma because the Dharma is good medicine for us, and we take refuge in the Sangha because the people in the Sangha are excellent friends for us."

Dōgen's word for "excellent friends" is *shōyū*. *Shō* means "excellent," "superior," or "good." We have three kinds of good friends in Buddhism: teachers, fellow practitioners, and people who support our practice. According to Dōgen Zenji, the Buddha is a great teacher, the Dharma is good medicine, and the Sangha is a community of good friends. Another text says that the Buddha is like a doctor, the Dharma is good medicine, and the people of the Sangha are our nurses. The doctor makes a diagnosis and gives a prescription. To study the Dharma and practice according to the teaching is taking the medicine. Sangha is the community of co-practitioners—people who like nurses take care of the practice with each other. In modern society nurses are professional people, but in ancient times there were no nurses. Family or friends took care of the sick. So here "nurse" doesn't mean a professional but rather a member of the sangha. The people of the sangha should care for one another.

To say that the Buddha is a doctor, the Dharma is medicine, and Sangha members are nurses implies that we are sick. According to the Buddha's teaching, all people are indeed sick. We may be sick physically and are usually sick spiritually. What kind of sickness do we have? Before Shakyamuni Buddha left home and started to seek the Way, he was a prince. He was healthy and wealthy, certainly not sick in the common sense. But he needed something, and so started to practice. He came to see all sentient beings as sick and practiced to find a way to release them from sickness. Eventually he realized that the cause of our sickness is ignorant egocentricity and the desires that arise from it.

Many religions originate in our weaknesses and fears. Before civilization conditions of life were very severe. There were many dangers and people needed something to pray to. In many primal religions people worshiped natural phenomena: the ocean, mountains, thunder, or ancient trees. They worshiped things larger, more powerful, and longer lasting than themselves. Gradually civilization developed and human beings became better at survival. We then became each other's enemies. We started to fight, and at the time of Shakyamuni, about the fifth century BCE, people had enough wealth to fight over territory. They fought each other to establish countries and kingdoms. Stronger nations conquered weaker ones. We needed some principle to live together in harmony. This is the second reason for religion: to teach us to live together with other people. I think this is the point of all religions and philosophies in the history of humanity. We live in civilizations that have developed over twenty centuries in America, Japan, and Europe, and yet we are still spiritually sick. We still don't know how to live in peace with people from different national, racial, religious, or cultural backgrounds. The Buddha's teaching is a prescription for curing this sickness.

Final Place to Return

Dōgen Zenji quotes another phrase from an old Buddhist scripture titled *Daijō-gi-shō* about why we take refuge in the Three Treasures. It says, "We take refuge in these Three Treasures because they are the final place to return."[41]

Dōgen's word for "final place to return" is *hikkyō-kisho*. *Sho* means "place," *ki* means "to go back or return," and *hikkyō* means "finally," "final place," and "to go back." Our life is a journey. Childhood is like our home, where we are born. We don't need to go anywhere. We are happy simply to be there. When we grow up, we become travelers. We search here and there for treasure—something valuable or meaningful. We yearn for something better. We seek happiness and satisfaction. Sometimes we are happy, sometimes sad. Finally, at the end of our lives we face death. Regardless of our success or failure, each of us has to face it. When we do, we are afraid. Wealth, fame, and social position don't help us then. We face death alone.

Where, then, is the final place to which we return? This is, I think, the fundamental question we have to keep in mind. In modern society it's easy to forget. In the past people were born, lived, got sick, and died, all at home. Life and death were right there in front of everyone. But in our modern society people are born at the hospital. When they are sick, they go to the hospital, and when they die, it's usually in the hospital. Life and death are hidden from us. While we are young and healthy, we can forget about life and death. Suddenly we are aging or sick; the matter of life and death is in front of our eyes, and we are afraid. This is the reality of our life. Before we have to face death, we should try to think about life and death, to awaken from the dream of success even while dreaming it. We must wake up to the reality of the impermanence of our lives. Because of impermanence, our death is inevitable. We must find the best and most peaceful way of life. Success, wealth, and fame are not significant in the final stage of our lives. The important point is to return to the matter of life and death, to wake up to the reality of this body and mind, and on that basis create a way of life. This, I think, is the meaning of taking refuge in the Buddha, the Dharma, and the Sangha.

You don't have to become a Buddhist and take refuge. Buddhism is only one of many paths, one way to wake to the reality of our life. When we become a Buddhist due to various causes and conditions, we follow the path of the Buddha. We seek to manifest the universal life force which we have been given. We live on this earth with everything we need as a gift from nature. It seems that our society doesn't live in accordance with nature. It acts like a cancer, independently, in its own way. When a cancer becomes too strong, the body dies. When the body dies, the cancer also must die. Cancer is paradoxical. Modern civilization is similar. We have no direction. We just try to live in an ever more convenient way. We chase after prosperity. We live separate from nature and build an artificial world around us. As we get stronger and stronger, we destroy more of the environment. When nature dies, we die.

How can we go back to nature, to the vital life force? This is the essential koan for us, the question we have to work on. In a sense this whole universe is like a hospital. We are all sick. How can we recover from this human sickness? The Buddha's teaching and the Buddhist Way can be one of the paths to recovery. The Buddha is the doctor who guides the healing process; dharma practice is the medicine he prescribes; the sangha, and all living beings in this universe, are nurses to aid our recovery. This is what the text means by "These three treasures are the final place to return." They release us from the suffering of a life based on egocentricity and return us to the original, wholesome way of life.

4 Cultivating the Virtuous Field: The Robe Chant

Verse on the Kesa

Great robe of liberation.
Virtuous field far beyond form and emptiness.
Wearing the Tathāgata's teaching
I vow to save all beings.[42]

Dai sai gedappuku
Musō fukuden e
Hibu nyorai kyō
Kōdo shoshu jō

When Dōgen Zenji went to China and began to practice at Tiangtong monastery in 1223, he found that in the sōdō (monks' hall), the monks rested their folded okesas (the formal term for the *kesa*, or monk's robe) atop their heads with veneration and chanted this verse after early morning zazen each day. He had read of this practice in the *Āgama Sutra* but had never seen it. When he experienced the traditional chanting of this verse and saw the monks put on their okesas, he was deeply impressed. Dōgen Zenji wrote about this experience in the chapter *Shōbōgenzō* "Kesakudoku" (Virtue of the Kesa): "At that time, I felt that I had never before seen such a gracious thing. My body was filled with delight, and tears of joy silently fell and moistened the lapel of my robe."[43] The young Dōgen vowed to transmit this practice to Japan. As a result, for the last eight hundred years in Dōgen Zenji's lineage we have chanted this verse every morning after zazen when we put on our okesas or rakusus.

The Buddha himself decided the kesa's design. A king who was a lay student of Shakyamuni Buddha went to visit the Buddha one day. On the way he saw a religious practitioner walking across the road. He thought this person was a disciple of the Buddha and got off his cart to greet him. When he found that he was not a Buddhist monk he felt a little embarrassed. He asked Shakyamuni Buddha to make a special robe for his disciples so they could easily be recognized as Buddhist monks.

One day the Buddha, walking in the countryside with his attendant Ānanda, noticed the beautiful patterns of rice paddies newly planted with green seedlings and surrounded by footpaths. They are especially beautiful in the rainy season when the rice is new. The Buddha remarked to Ānanda, "These are so beautiful. Could you make a robe like this?" Ānanda agreed. The Buddha conceived the pattern and Ānanda created the design. Since then, Buddhists have worn the okesa in all traditions and in all countries.[44]

In Japanese the first words of the verse of the kesa is *dai sai*. *Dai* means "to be great" or "magnificent." *Sai* has no meaning by itself but functions as an exclamation mark: "How great!" The next part of the verse gives three different names for the okesa. In the chapter "Virtue of the Kesa" Dōgen Zenji introduced many names for the okesa. He said, "We should understand that the kesa is what all buddhas have respected and taken refuge in. The kesa is the Buddha's body and the Buddha's mind. The kesa is called the robe of liberation, the robe of the field of virtue, and the robe of formlessness. It is also called the robe of supremacy, the robe of patience, the robe of the Tathāgata, the robe of great compassion, the robe of the victory banner (against delusion), and the robe of unsurpassable enlightenment. Truly, we should receive and maintain it gratefully and respectfully."[45] These are all different names for the okesa used in various Buddhist scriptures. In this verse, the first three names are mentioned: the robe of liberation, the robe of formlessness, and the robe of the field of virtue.

The first name for the okesa is the robe of liberation. The Sanskrit word *kaṣāya* refers to a muted or broken color (*ejiki*). To make okesas, Indian monks collected abandoned rags from graveyards and refuse heaps, so that they would have no attachment to the material. They cut the rags into pieces and washed, dyed, and sewed them together. They didn't dye them pure colors—blue, yellow, red, black, or white—but instead mixed different colors together to darken the cloth, rendering it valueless by ordinary standards. The okesa was made out of materials that had no value and were not attractive to people. Even today if we have new material from which to make an okesa, we cut it into pieces so that the material loses its value. No one would want to steal it. This is why the okesa is free from attachment. In Buddhism, things free from attachment are immaculate. When we become Buddhists, we receive the okesa as a symbol of our faith in the Buddha's teachings. This means we also become free from ego attachment.

The construction of the okesa symbolizes the emptiness of the five skandhas. The pieces come from all over, are sewed together, and stay for a while in the shape of a robe. The okesa is an example of emptiness or egolessness (*anātman*), impermanence, and interdependent origination. So the robe is much more than a uniform; it embodies the basic teachings of the Buddha.

When I first studied "Kesakudoku" (Virtue of the Kesa), I was confused because Dōgen discussed the virtue of the okesa in various ways. He wrote that the okesa had been transmitted from Vipaśyin Buddha, the first of the seven buddhas. It is said that each buddha's life span was shorter than the last. Their bodies also became smaller and smaller. And yet the okesa transmitted from the previous buddha perfectly fit all of the following buddhas. I wondered how Dōgen could say such a thing, since he knew that the okesa was designed by Shakyamuni Buddha and his disciple Ānanda. How could all the buddhas before Shakyamuni have worn and transmitted it?

Dōgen also discusses the fact that Shakyamuni's okesa was transmitted to Mahākāśyapa, and then from Mahākāśyapa to the next ancestor. It was then transmitted through each subsequent ancestor to Bodhidharma. Bodhidharma brought it from India to China, and then the okesa was transmitted through six generations to the sixth ancestor, Huineng. The okesa was used as the symbol of the Dharma and also of the authenticity of the Dharma's transmission.

Dōgen Zenji encourages us to sew our own okesa and venerate it as the symbol of the Buddha's vow to save all living beings, the symbol of the Dharma itself, and the symbol of the authenticity of transmission in his lineage.

Later I realized that this corresponds to the Three Treasures he mentions in *Kyōjukaimon* (Comments on Teaching and Conferring the Precepts). Here he comments on the precepts of taking refuge in the Buddha, the Dharma, and the Sangha and on the Absolute Three Treasures, the Manifesting Three Treasures, and the Maintaining Three Treasures.[46]

The okesa used by all buddhas in the past, present, and future—and which perfectly fits all of them despite their differences in size—corresponds to the Absolute Three Treasures. The okesa designed by Shakyamuni and Ānanda corresponds to the Manifesting Three Treasures. And the okesa used as a symbol of transmission and the okesa Dōgen encourages us to sew, wear, and venerate correspond to the Maintaining Three Treasures. When Dōgen discusses the virtue of the okesa, he freely switches among these three meanings of the word. This is why I was confused. The okesa is the symbol of the Dharma itself in its various facets.

The second name of the okesa is the robe of formlessness (*musō*). In our sutra book, *musō* is translated as "far beyond form and emptiness." This is a questionable translation. It seems to me that "far beyond form and emptiness" refers to a line in the *Heart Sutra*: "That which is form is emptiness and that which is emptiness, form." In this case "form" is a translation of the Sanskrit word *rūpa*, one of the five aggregates, which means materials that have physical form and color. The Chinese translation of rūpa is *se*, and the Japanese pronunciation is *shiki*. The *Heart Sutra* says that material beings are emptiness and emptiness is material beings. But here the word used is not *shiki* but *sō*, a translation of the Sanskrit *nimitta*, which means "appearance," as opposed to *shō*, "nature" or "essence." Other possible translations of *nimitta* are "mark" or "attribution." *Musō* is *animitta* in Sanskrit. This use of "form" does not imply material beings. Instead, it means temporal form or appearance. The reality of emptiness has no fixed form. The robe of formlessness (*musō-e*) means that this robe has no form (*animitta*), not that it is beyond form and emptiness.

In this English translation, the phrase "far beyond form and emptiness" modifies "virtuous field" (*fukuden*). This is not a correct interpretation of the line because *musō-e* and *fukuden-e* are the two different names of the okesa.

The *Diamond Sutra* says, "To see all forms as no-form is to see the true form." What is beyond form and emptiness? Form is emptiness and emptiness is form. There is nothing beyond form and emptiness. And in this verse there is no word that refers to emptiness. Here "formless" means that the okesa has a form and yet the form itself is formless or empty. Emptiness means moving and changing moment by moment. In this moment, this robe exists in the form of the okesa but has no fixed, permanent form. *Musō* also means free from attachment. Because it is formless, we cannot attach ourselves; we cannot grasp it. If we grasp this as the Buddha's teaching, as something important and hold on to it, we miss the point of the Buddha's teaching. Instead we open our hands. This is the meaning of formlessness.

It is the same with our lives. Our body and mind are collections of many different elements that exist in this moment. Because they are always changing, we cannot grasp them as "my" body, "my" mind, or "my" property. And yet we attach ourselves to the present, transient form. But since nothing is substantial, we cannot actually grasp it. When we try to control it, we diminish our life force. Instead, we open our hands. This is what we practice in our zazen. The okesa and our body and mind are the same. This subtle difference in attitude can change our lives completely. When we grasp something, we lose it. When we open our hands, we see that everything we need is an offering from nature. If we have something extra, we offer it to others. This is the life attitude of a bodhisattva. Just open our hands. The okesa is a symbol of this attitude.

As noted just now, the third name of the okesa in this verse is the robe of the field of virtues (*fukuden-e*). *Fuku* means "happiness," "blessing," "fortune," or "virtue," while *den* means "rice paddy." In Asian countries people consider rice paddies the foundation of everything good. Rice is the most important product and the basis of the whole economy. When rice grows we are blessed by nature. The Buddha's teachings, the Buddha-mind, and the practice of Dharma are often compared to a rice paddy.

The *Suttanipāta* is one of the oldest collections of short suttas in Pāli. In it we find the *Kasībhāradvāja Sutta* (The Farmer Bharadvaja), which records the Buddha's conversation with an Indian farmer. When the Buddha was staying in a farming village, he woke up one morning, put on the okesa, and went out to the village for *takuhatsu* (begging for food). The Buddha came across a rich farmer's house. The farmer was giving food to his workers. The Buddha was standing in front of the farmer to receive food.

The farmer said, "I eat after cultivating fields and planting seeds. I eat after working. Why don't you work? Why do you beg for food?" The Buddha replied, "I am a farmer, too. I also work." The farmer asked further, "You say you are also a farmer. But I never saw you farming. I ask you, what do you mean when you say you are a farmer? Tell me so that I can understand." Then the Buddha answered, "Faith is a seed. Practice is rain. Wisdom is my yoke and plow. Repentance (having a sense of shame) is my plow bar. Aspiration is a rope to tie a yoke to an ox. Mindfulness is a plow-blade and digging bar. I behave prudently. I am discreet in speech. I eat moderately. Truth is my sickle to mow grass. Gentleness is untying the yoke from an ox when finished working.

Diligence is my ox which takes me to peacefulness (nirvana). I go forth without backsliding. Once I reach peacefulness, I have no anxiety. My farming is done in this way. Its result is sweet dew. If you engage in this farming, you will be released from all kinds of suffering."[47]

The farmer left home and became the Buddha's disciple. In the Buddha's simile, farming is a practice aimed at freedom from ego-attachment and a peaceful life. When we wear the okesa, we are also farming. This is the meaning of "robe of virtuous field" (*fukuden-e*). This body and mind is the field we work. It is not a field of fortune from which we can expect to receive blessings without practice. We have to cultivate our life.

The third line of the verse is "Wearing the Tathāgata's teaching" (*hibu nyorai kyō*). *Hi* means "to open," "unfold," or "uncover," so I translate this line as "I unfold and wear the Tathāgata's teaching." First we have to unfold the Buddha's teaching and cover ourselves with it. *Bu* means "humble," "thankful," or "respectful." Then what is meant by "the Tathāgata's teaching" (*nyorai-kyō*)? The Buddha taught the interdependent origination of all beings. Since no beings have self-nature, we should not attach ourselves to anything. We should be free from ego-attachment, transform our way of life, and choose a path to peacefulness. We unfold this teaching through practice. We receive the teaching of the Tathāgata, unfold it, wear it, and are covered by it. This is the meaning of wearing the okesa and practicing zazen.

Formlessness means the same as emptiness, egolessness, and interdependent origination. Since we are not substantial, we cannot live alone without being supported by other beings. We have to live together with others. This is another essential point of the Buddha's teaching. We cannot be completely peaceful unless all living beings are in peace. We cannot be completely happy if we are aware of someone who is unhappy. When we awaken to this reality, the bodhisattva vows arise naturally. The vow to save all beings is not a duty or a promise to the Buddha. The vow does not mean that we are great people and we have to save all others, like millionaires who give money to the poor. When we open our eyes to the reality of our lives, we simply cannot help but share happiness and sadness, pleasure and pain with all beings. To be peaceful, we have to do something for other beings. We live within the Buddha's vow to save all beings.

Zen Master Dongshan Liangjie (Tōzan Ryōkai, 802–869) was the founder of the Chinese Caodon (Sōtō) school. Dongshan asked a monk, "What is most painful?" The monk replied, "To be in hell is most painful." Dongshan said, "No, it isn't." Then the monk asked, "What do you think, then, is most painful?" Dongshan replied, "Wearing the okesa yet not having clarified the great matter is most painful." Hell is the worst part of samsara and is considered the most agonizing. But Dongshan said that there is a more painful condition. When we wear the okesa, we are in nirvana. We are apart from samsara, and yet when we chase after something, even enlightenment, our practice becomes an activity within samsara. When we look for something better through zazen, that striving is more painful than hell. If you suffer in samsara because you don't know the Buddha's teachings, you can be saved by studying the Buddha Dharma and practicing zazen. But if you already know the Buddha Dharma, receive the precepts, wear the okesa, practice zazen, and *still* chase after something, there is no way to be saved. One of the most famous sayings of Kōdō Sawaki Roshi is, "Wear the okesa and sit in zazen: that's all." That's it. There is nothing else to search for. There's nowhere to go. Still, we look for something more valuable. Even when we sit in the zendo we are often hungry ghosts in samsara.

Whenever we deviate from where we are now, we immediately return to what's right here, right now, by letting go. This is our zazen. This is the meaning of wearing the okesa after reciting this verse.

5 Continuous Circle of Offering: The Meal Chants

Dōgen's Comments on the Significance of Taking Food

Meal chants are the verses we recite during formal *ōryōki* meals at Sōtō Zen monasteries and Zen centers during sesshin. Dōgen Zenji's comments at the beginning of "Fushukuhanpō" (The Dharma for Taking Meals) are a good introduction to these verses. He describes how to eat, use the bowls, and comport ourselves during an ōryōki meal. "The Dharma for Taking Meals" is a section of *Eihei Shingi*. The word *shingi* means regulations or standards, and Eiheiji is the monastery founded by Dōgen Zenji. "The Dharma for Taking Meals" is one of the six sections of *Eihei Shingi*; another is "Tenzokyōkun" (Instructions for the Cook). Dōgen Zenji teaches that cooking and receiving food are both important parts of our practice. Eating is an essential part of our practice because it's a necessary part of our life. We eat three times every day of our lives but rarely think about the significance of eating. Both "Tenzokyōkun" and "Fushukuhanpō" show us how activities in our daily lives can become spiritual practice.

In "Tenzokyōkun," Dōgen Zenji describes the attitude we should maintain toward foods, fire, water, and utensils when we cook. "When steaming rice, regard the pot as your own head; when washing rice, know that the water is your own life."[48] Everything is part of our life. As tenzo we should think about the people who eat, who receive the food, and who practice. According to Dōgen Zenji, practice itself is enlightenment, so people who practice are enlightened, and therefore as tenzo we prepare meals to offer to the Buddha. Through work with food in the kitchen, the tenzo's energy becomes part of the Buddha, so the tenzo should be sincere and careful. This is an important point. Since the tenzo doesn't sit in the zendō all the time, the kitchen is the tenzo's place of practice. When the tenzo cooks, the food is the Buddha and the cooking is the tenzo's zazen. We should receive the food gratefully and with the same attitude with which it was cooked. That's the meaning of this ritual.

It's difficult when we begin to study the rituals of ōryōki and memorize the chants because many of us don't like formality. I myself don't like it much, but I try to follow it because it's our practice. If we think of the meaning or significance of this practice, we can appreciate this formality on a deeper level. That is the point of this section of "Fushukuhanpō" (The Dharma of Taking Meals):

> A sutra says, "If you can remain the same with food, all dharmas also remain the same; if all dharmas are the same, then also with food you will remain the same." Just let dharma be the same as food, and let food be the same as dharma. For this reason, if dharmas are the dharma-nature, then food also is the dharma-nature. If the dharma is suchness, food also is suchness. If the dharma is the single mind, food also is the single mind. If the dharma is bodhi, food also is bodhi. They are named the same and their significance is the same, so it is said that they are the same. A sutra says, "Named the same and significance the same, each and every one is the same, consistent with nothing extra." Mazu said, "If the dharma realm is established, everything is entirely dharma realm. If suchness is established, everything is entirely suchness. If the principle is established, everything is entirely

> the principle. If phenomena are established, all dharmas are entirely phenomena." Therefore this "same" is not the sameness of parity or equality, but the sameness of awakening to the true sameness [*anuttarā-samyaksambodhi*]. Awakening to the true sameness is the ultimate identity [of all the suchnesses] from beginning to end. The suchness of the ultimate identity from beginning to end is the genuine form of all dharmas, which only a buddha together with a buddha can exhaustively penetrate. Therefore, food is the dharma of all dharmas, which only a buddha together with a buddha can exhaustively penetrate. Just at such a time, there are the genuine marks, nature, substance, power, functions, causes, and conditions. For this reason, dharma is itself food; food is itself dharma. This dharma is what is received and used by all buddhas in the past and future. This food is the fulfillment that is the joy of dharma and the delight of meditation.[49]

The quote at the beginning, "If you can remain the same with food, all dharmas also remain the same; if all dharmas are the same, then also with food you will remain the same," comes from the *Vimalakīrti Sutra*.[50] Dōgen Zenji comments on this passage, "Just let dharma be the same as food, and let food be the same as dharma." This sutra says that as practitioners of Mahāyāna Buddhism we should maintain the same attitude toward everything we encounter. We should not discriminate between things as valuable or worthless on the basis of conventions. We should not discriminate between good times and hard times, delusion and enlightenment, samsara and nirvana, or deluded human beings and buddhas. This is the basis of the Mahāyāna teaching of śūnyatā. We must go beyond discrimination and keep the same attitude toward all things because everything we encounter is the Buddha's life. The *Vimalakīrti Sutra* says that as a practitioner of Mahāyāna Buddhism, we should have the same attitude toward all food and not discriminate between something expensive or delicious and something cheap or not so tasty on the basis of preferences or worldly values.

Subhūti, one of the ten greatest disciples of Shakyamuni Buddha, was doing takuhatsu, begging for food. Vimalakīrti offered him some delicious food, saying he could eat it if he didn't discriminate between delicacies and the food of the poor. In his comment Dōgen Zenji twisted the meaning slightly. He said: "Just let dharma be the same as food, and let food be the same as dharma." Dōgen Zenji says that dharma and food are the same. He doesn't discriminate between good and bad food. He simply says that dharma and food are the same.

We have to be careful here about the meaning of the word *dharma*. It can be used to mean the Buddha's teaching. A second meaning is the truth about which the Buddha taught, the reality of our life. A third meaning of *dharma* is all beings or things. The phrase often used to express this, "myriad dharmas," means all beings, everything. In this usage, Dōgen is saying that food, as one of the "myriad dharmas," reveals the reality of all beings, and therefore the food itself is the teaching (Dharma) of the Buddha. The Buddha awakened to and taught this reality, so his teaching is called Dharma. His teaching became a kind of law, principle, or basic standard of morality. In "The Dharma for Taking Meals," "dharma" means an etiquette or standard of behavior that we should follow when we eat meals. In his commentary Dōgen is playing with words. He uses "dharma" not to designate a kind of ritual but as reality itself as well as the teachings about that reality. He says that our practice and the food we eat is dharma, reality, or truth itself. We should receive our food as we receive the Buddha's teaching and reality itself.

He continues, "For this reason, if dharmas are the dharma-nature, then food also is the dharma-nature." Dharma-nature is almost synonymous with buddha-nature. For human beings the term "buddha-nature" is used. For other beings or inanimate objects, all of reality, the phrase "dharma-nature" is used. Our food is dharma-nature. Dharma-nature and food are really one, so "if the dharma is suchness [reality or truth], food also is suchness." Suchness means the way all beings, all dharmas, are. So food is nothing but suchness itself. In the same way, "If the dharma is the single mind," another name for Buddha mind, "food also is the single mind," the One Mind, or Buddha mind. So we should receive food with the same attitude we receive the Buddha and his teachings. Dōgen says, "If the dharma is bodhi, food also is bodhi." Bodhi means enlightenment or awakening to the reality of all beings. So dharma is awakening. We usually think of awakening as something subjective that happens inside a person, and dharma as the object of awakening. In the teachings of Mahāyāna Buddhism, there is no separation between subject and object, between the person who sees reality and the reality that is seen. When we separate the two, wisdom becomes delusion. Awakening, beings, and reality are one. The dharma is bodhi, awakening itself. Awakening is not some special psychological state or stage of development. When we are one with all beings we are awake. When we are mindful, right now, right here, our body and mind completely present in this moment and engaged with what we are doing, we are awake and enlightened. The dharma is bodhi, and food is also bodhi. Food and dharma are both dharma-nature, buddha-nature, and suchness.

Dōgen continues, "They [dharma and food] are named the same and their significance is the same, so it is said that they are the same. A sutra says, 'Named the same and significance the same, each and every one is the same, consistent with nothing extra.'" This means that when we receive this body and mind and the things we encounter in our daily lives as self, we are connected with all beings in the whole universe. This whole universe is one reality. We should receive the rituals of meals and universe with the same attitude. Dōgen quotes Mazu (Baso), "If the dharma realm is established, everything is entirely dharma realm." "Dharma realm" is a translation of *dharmadhātu*, this dharma universe. This whole universe is dharma universe; there is nothing extra. Everything is entirely the dharma world; nothing is outside it. He continues, "If suchness is established, everything is entirely suchness." If we see this whole reality as suchness, everything is entirely suchness. There is nothing that is not suchness. Within delusion there is suchness as delusion. The fact that we are deluded is reality. When we see delusion as delusion, delusion is part of reality and there is nothing to be eliminated, nothing to be negated. We should accept everything as the

Buddha's life. Mazu continues, "If the principle is established, everything is entirely the principle," and "If phenomena are established, all dharmas are entirely phenomena." These two concepts, principle and phenomena, or *ri* and *ji*, are important in the "Merging of Difference and Unity," the title of a text by Shitou discussed below. *Ri* means reality as a whole regardless of differences among individuals. A hand has five fingers. If we see it as one hand it is actually one thing. We cannot separate it into parts. But we can also see it as five fingers, each with a different shape, function, and name. So *ri* refers to the entire totality of a being, and so does *ji*. There is nothing that is half-and-half. *Ri* means all of this one hand, and so does *ji*, the five fingers. When we see this as one hand, there are no separate fingers. When we see it as five fingers, there is no single hand. This is the way we see reality. We call principles "absolute" and phenomena "relative." The absolute and relative ways of seeing things are reality at work.

Dōgen Zenji continues, "Therefore, this 'same' is not the sameness of parity or equality, but the sameness of awakening to the true sameness." "Awakening to the true sameness" is a translation of the phrase *anuttarā-samyaksambodhi*. A common Chinese translation of this phrase is *shōtōgaku*. *Shō* means "true," "correct," or "absolute"; *tō* means "sameness" or "equality"; and *gaku* is "awakening." This "sameness" is a difficult concept. We cannot use the word "equality" here because Dōgen Zenji said, "Therefore this 'same' is not the sameness of parity or equality." This is not a matter of comparing two things and finding them to be the same or equal, as in one hand and five fingers. This is one thing with two names. Food and dharma really are the same thing. This sameness, Dōgen says, is sameness within *anuttarā-samyaksambodhi*. *Samyak* means "sameness," "equality," or "identity." This sameness is not a matter of comparison: good versus bad food, or like versus dislike. This sameness means that we should encounter each thing as an absolute reality, as a whole, as the Buddha. When I drink water, water is the Buddha. This means that this water is connected with all beings. Someone brings a glass of water for me. The water came from a river or lake, and before that from the sky. The water in the sky came from the ocean. Everything really is connected. This interpenetrating, connected reality is the Buddha, and we are part of it. There is no separation between myself and the water. The water becomes part of me when I drink it. This glass, this body and mind, and the water are all Buddha. When we see them as Buddha we are part of the whole universe. When we see them as separate entities, each of them and each of us is a small, individual thing or ego.

Dōgen Zenji goes on to say, "Awakening to the true sameness is the ultimate identity [of all the suchnesses] from beginning to end." Awakening to the true sameness means accepting all beings as our own life, as the Buddha's life. A quote from the *Lotus Sutra* helps explain the meaning of the following: "The suchness of the ultimate identity from beginning to end is the genuine form of all dharmas [the reality of all beings], which only a buddha together with a buddha can exhaustively penetrate." In the second chapter of the *Lotus Sutra* the Buddha said, "Concerning the prime, rare, hard-to-understand dharmas, which the Buddha has perfected, only a Buddha and a Buddha can exhaust their reality, namely, the suchness of the dharmas."[51] "The suchness of the dharmas" in the *Lotus Sutra* and "the genuine form of all dharmas" in "Fushukuhanpō" are the same word. The reality of all beings can be understood or seen only by buddhas.

The sutra continues by listing the ten suchnesses: "The suchness of their marks (form), the suchness of their nature, the suchness of their substance (body), the suchness of their powers (energy), the suchness of their functions, the suchness of their causes, the suchness of their conditions, the suchness of their effects, the suchness of their retributions, and the absolute identity of their beginning and end."[52] "Ultimate identity from beginning to end" is another translation for the ending of this quote. In Japanese the phrase is *nyoze honmatsu kukyō tō*. *Hon* (beginning) and *matsu* (end) refer to the nine points of reality: form, nature, body, energy, function, cause, condition (secondary cause), effect, and retribution. Each being has its own unique form, nature, body, energy, and function. For example, this glass has a form, round and transparent. This being has a nature as a glass and as a body that is different from other glasses. The Japanese word translated here as "body" is sometimes translated as "substance" or "embodiment," but "body" is better. Each being has its own power and energy. Even this glass has chemical, potential, kinetic, and nuclear energy. Essentially there is no difference between energy and being. "Being" is nothing other than various forms of energy in certain conditions. The function of this glass is to contain liquid. Each being has a different combination of these five characteristics: a different form, nature, body, energy, and function. Each being has a cause and a secondary cause as its conditions. "Secondary cause" refers to the way this glass was made. Someone works with materials to form glass into this shape. That person is a secondary cause. In addition to the person who makes the glass there is electricity, water, and raw materials. The person who makes the glass eats food, which is also a secondary cause of this glass. Everything is connected with everything else. Each being has causes, secondary causes, and effects. This being has effects because of its function. Because this glass functions to contain water, I can drink the water. That is an effect of this being we call a glass. The last of the nine points is "retribution." This could also be translated as "secondary effect." Because this glass can contain the water, it allows me to drink the water, and the water can become part of my body, which enables me to continue to talk. That's a secondary effect. The first five suchnesses describe the unique characteristics of each being, each dharma; and the next four are the interconnections between beings throughout time and space. A secondary cause is the relationship between this being and its function and other beings within space at the present moment. Secondary effect is the connection with other beings in the future within time.

Each thing also has its own unique characteristics. In this sense, it is independent. This glass is different from all other glasses. All beings, including this body and mind, have unique characteristics, and yet we are interconnected. We live together with each other. All beings have two aspects: independence and connectedness. This is the same concept as seeing one hand or five fingers. The tenth suchness, "absolute identity of their beginning and end," means that the other nine—from the first, form, up to the ninth, retribution—are one. Within this one being, all are included. The universal interconnection within Indra's net is manifested in this one being, in each and every being. It's really hard to comprehend this reality of our life, the way we live with both individuality (independence) and connection (interdependence) at the same time. I have to take responsibility for whatever I do because I am I, not you or another person. And yet my personal action influences the entire world.

Without this being, there are no other beings. This is called wondrous dharma or true dharma. We cannot grasp it with our concepts, and yet, as a reality, it's right in front of us. It means: This is one, this is Shohaku Okumura; and yet, at the same time: This is not Shohaku Okumura, this is not an individual. When we use the principles of logic we avoid contradiction, and so we cannot see reality as a whole. We see only one side of reality, either the individuality of all beings or their identity. When we think about ourselves and the reality of our lives, we cannot see both aspects at once. Sometimes we see five fingers: I am not you, and you are not me. But at the same time, this is one hand and there is no separation. If we think logically, it's contradictory. If we can set our logic aside, we can see reality as it is, five fingers and one hand at the same time. That's the reality of the network of interdependent origination. And so, getting back to Dōgen's text, we should accept food as a part of this reality. There is no separation between the person eating and the food eaten. Both are part of this wondrous dharma.

Dōgen Zenji continues, "Therefore, food is the dharma of all dharmas, which only a buddha together with a buddha can exhaustively penetrate." The phrase "only a buddha together with a buddha" means that no human being can penetrate this dharma. By human beings Dōgen means individuals. When we see this total reality, we are Buddha. The words "I see" are not really adequate because they imply a separation between the person who sees and the reality which is seen. Because we are born, live, and die within the network, we can only see the network from inside. We cannot be an objective observer from the outside. "Accept" is a better word than "see." We should accept this reality and make it manifest through our practice. When we accept food and dharma in this way, Dōgen Zenji says, "Just at such a time, there are the genuine marks, nature, substance, power, functions, causes, and conditions." He lists seven of the ten suchnesses described in the *Lotus Sutra*. I think the other three—effects, retributions, and absolute identity—should be included. All of them are manifested within the one action of eating.

He concludes, "For this reason, dharma is itself food; food is itself dharma. This dharma is what is received and used by all buddhas in the past and future." In this context "dharma" means reality itself. This reality is accepted and used by all buddhas in the past and future. He said, "This food is the fulfillment that is the joy of dharma and the delight of meditation." This joy of dharma and delight of meditation is part of the verse we chant before informal meals. We say, "As we take food and drink, we vow with all beings to rejoice in zazen, being filled with delight in the dharma (*Nyaku onjiki ji tōgan shujō, zennetsu ijiki, hōki jūman*)." When we eat, we should be happy. This happiness is the enjoyment of dharma. We consider the taste of food to be the taste of dharma. When we receive or eat a meal, we shouldn't grasp the taste. Usually when we eat, we encounter our food with our desires. These desires are the cause of delusion or samsara. The Buddha and Dōgen Zenji teach us to become free from the desires caused by objects. This is Dōgen's teaching of *shinjin datsuraku* (dropping off body and mind). Our joy when we receive food is not the fulfillment of our desire. It is the joy of dharma and zazen. I think this is the most essential teaching about food and eating. When we can see this reality that Dōgen Zenji describes in "Fushukuhanpō," not only eating but everything we do becomes our spiritual practice.

Ludwig Feuerbach, a nineteenth-century German philosopher, once said, "We are what we eat." In fact, we are not only what we eat, but what we see, hear, think, and do. When we accept everything that we encounter as it is, and accept all things and beings as ourselves, that is *jijuyū zammai*—samādhi that is self-receiving and self-employing. The most important thing taught by Dōgen Zenji is to accept this body and mind and everything we encounter as our life. Then the self and the entire dharma world become one seamless reality. We should accept and use everything we encounter as samādhi, not as a kind of business. Our life as a whole is samādhi. This means that each and every thing we do in our daily lives becomes a manifestation of our zazen.

Formal Meal Verses

Verse upon Hearing the Meal Signal

> Buddha was born in Kapilavastu,
> enlightened in Magadha,
> taught in Vārāṇasī,
> entered nirvana in Kuśinagara.

At the beginning of each ōryōki meal we chant this verse and remember the most important events in the life of the Buddha Shakyamuni.[53] The Buddha was born at Lumbinī Park, not far from the palace of his father, King Śuddhodana, at Kapilavastu. The Buddha attained supreme awakening under a bodhi tree at Uruvelā, later called Bodhgayā, in the kingdom of Magadha. The Buddha taught the Dharma for the first time to the five monks at Deer Park (Mṛgadāva) in Sārnāth near Vārāṇasī (Benares). After that, he continued to teach for more than forty years, until he was about eighty years old, when he entered the great nirvana under twin *sāla* trees in Kuśinagara. These places have been considered the four most sacred sites in Buddhism. Following the Buddha's death, Buddhists built stūpas at these places to enshrine his relics, and pilgrimaging there became a common Buddhist practice. People from all over the world still visit these four places even today.

In the *Mahāparinibbāna Sutta*, the Buddha's attendant Ānanda says, "Lord, formerly monks who had spent the rains in various places used to come to see the Tathāgata, and we used to welcome them so that such well-trained monks might see you and pay their respects. But with the Lord's passing, we shall no longer have a chance to do this." The Buddha answered, "Ānanda, there are four places the sight of which should arouse emotion in the faithful. Which are they? 'Here the Tathāgata was born' is the first. 'Here the Tathāgata attained supreme enlightenment' is the second. 'Here the Tathāgata set in motion the Wheel of Dharma' is the third. 'Here the Tathāgata attained the nibbāna-element without remainder' is the fourth. And Ānanda, the faithful monks and nuns, [and] male and female lay-followers will visit those places. And any who die while making the pilgrimage to these shrines with a devout heart will, at the breaking-up of the body after death, be reborn in a heavenly world."[54]

It is difficult for me to imagine that the Buddha called himself Tathāgata, encouraged people to worship his relics, and promised that if they made pilgrimages they would be born in heaven. But it seems certain that such a belief and practice was there when the Nikāyas were written down using the Pāli language several hundred years after the Buddha's death.

One of the four bodhisattva vows is "The Buddha's Way is unsurpassable; we vow to realize it." Even though we are in a very immature stage of the bodhisattva path, because a bodhisattva is a child of the Buddha, the direction of our practice is to live like the Buddha. When we receive food, we are reminded why we are here and why we eat. It is not to satisfy our desire for food but to continue to practice and walk the path taught by the Buddha. In our minds, we make a pilgrimage to those four sacred places.

Verse for Setting Out Bowls

To begin the meal we unwrap our bowls and arrange them on the table before us. As we open the ōryōki bowls we recite this verse:

> Now we set out Buddha's bowls;
> may we, with all living beings,
> realize the emptiness of the three wheels:
> giver, receiver, and gift.

The initial *ō* in *ōryōki* means "in proportion to," *ryō* means "amount" or "quality," and *ki* means "container." *Ōryōki* thus means a container with which we receive a food offering depending on our need to maintain our life for practice. We receive only the amount of food we need. So we have to eat everything we receive without wasting even one grain of rice. To do so, we need to know how much is enough.

In Zen Buddhist tradition, around the eighth century, after the story in which the sixth ancestor, Huineng, received the robe and ōryōki bowl as evidence of his dharma transmission from the fifth ancestor, the bowl was considered the symbol of continuity of Dharma from teacher to disciple. We receive a set of ōryōki bowls from our teacher when we participate in the *shukke tokudo* ceremony to become a monk/priest. Our ōryōki is the Buddha's bowl.

The verse says, "May we ... realize the emptiness of the three wheels." The emptiness of the three wheels is a crucial teaching from the *Prajñāpāramitā Sutra*. The three wheels are the giver, receiver, and gift; these wheels turn the dāna-pāramitā, the perfection of generosity. To practice dāna-pāramitā, there should be no attachment to any wheel.

The *Diamond Sutra*, one of the earliest Mahāyāna sutras, says, "When bodhisattvas give a gift, they should not be attached to ... anything at all. They should not be attached to a sight when they give a gift. Nor should they be attached to a sound, a smell, a taste, a touch, or a dharma when they give a gift."[55]

The famous story of the Bodhidharma's meeting with Emperor Wu makes the same point. The emperor had put on the robes of a monk and gave lectures on one of the group of *Prajñāpāramitā Sutras*. It is said that when he lectured, people saw heavenly flowers falling and the earth turning to gold. He studied extensively and supported Buddhism generously. He issued orders throughout his country to build temples and ordain monks. People called him the Buddha Heart Emperor. When Bodhidharma first met him, the emperor asked, "I have built many temples and allowed many monks to be ordained; what merit is there in this?"

Bodhidharma answered, "There is no merit."[56] "Merit" is a positive effect of certain actions. Even when doing good actions, if we expect to receive merit for ourselves, it is off the mark from the ultimate point of view because it is defiled by our selfish desire.

Ten Buddha Names

After we open the bowls, the *inō* (director of the zendō) recites:

> In the midst of the Three Treasures
> which verify our understanding,
> entrusting ourselves to the sangha,
> we recall: ...

Then everyone recites the ten names of the Buddha. This is an invitation for all buddhas and bodhisattvas to share this offering with us. And this is also an expression of our awareness that we are practicing together with all buddhas and bodhisattvas in the past, present, and future in the ten directions.

> ... Vairocana Buddha, pure dharmakāya;
> Locana Buddha, complete sambhogakāya;
> Shakyamuni Buddha, myriad nirmāṇakāya;
> Maitreya Buddha, of future birth;
> All buddhas throughout space and time;
> Lotus of the Wondrous Dharma, Mahāyāna sutra.
> Mañjuśrī Bodhisattva, great wisdom;
> Samantabhadra Bodhisattva, great activity;
> Avalokiteśvara Bodhisattva, great compassion;
> All honored ones, bodhisattvas, mahāsattvas;
> Wisdom beyond wisdom, mahā prajñā-pāramitā.

These are called the ten Buddha names, but actually there are eleven. Dōgen Zenji added "Lotus of the Wondrous Dharma, Mahāyāna sutra."

The first three names refer to the three bodies of Buddha. Different masters use Vairocana to refer to either dharmakāya or sambhogakāya depending upon the context. Here, Vairocana means the dharmakāya, the Buddha's body, identical with the entirety of Dharma and everything existing. Vairocana as the dharmakāya appears as the main buddha in the *Mahāvairocana Sutra* (Sutra of the Great Radiant One; *Dainichikyō* in Japanese). This is one of the most important sutras in Vajrayāna (Shingon) Buddhism. Vairocana literally means the universal illumination of the radiant light and refers to the light of the sun which illuminates entire world.

Vairocana also appears as the main buddha in the *Avataṃsaka Sutra* (Flower Ornament Sutra) and the *Brahma Net Sutra* (*Bonmōkyō*). Here it is sometimes considered to be the sambhogakāya, the retribution body that is produced upon entering buddhahood as a result of the vows and practice undertaken while the buddha was a bodhisattva. The Chinese transliteration of Vairocana is Pilushena. Locana is another spelling for the shortened form Lushena. In the *Brahma Net Sutra*, the shortened form Locana Buddha is used.

In his commentary on the *Lotus Sutra*, Tientai Zhiyi said that Vairocana is dharmakāya, Locana (Lushena) is sambhogakāya, and Shakyamuni is nirmāṇakāya.[57] "Myriad nirmāṇakāya" refers to the Buddha Shakyamuni, the manifestation of the dharmakāya with a human body in a particular time and space. This expression also comes from the *Brahma Net Sutra*:

> "I have cultivated this Mind-Ground Dharma Gate for hundred of eons. My name is Locana. I request all buddhas to transmit my words to all sentient beings, so as to open this path of cultivation to all." At that time, from Lion's Throne in the Lotus Treasury World, Locana Buddha emitted rays of light. A voice among the rays is heard telling the buddhas seated on thousands of lotus petals, "You should practice and uphold the Mind-Ground Dharma Gate and transmit it to the innumerable Shakyamuni Buddhas, one after another, as well as to all sentient beings. Everyone should

uphold, read, recite, and single-mindedly put its teachings into practice."[58]

Modern Buddhist scholars think the *Brahma Net Sutra* was not translated from an Indian text but composed in Chinese. In the original Chinese text, the *Vai* in *Vairocana* is dropped and *Vairocana* is written as *Locana*. It is said that there are innumerable Shakyamuni Buddhas sitting on the lotus flowers. It seems these ten Buddha names are created within the tradition based on the teachings of the *Avataṃsaka Sutra* (Flower Ornament Sutra) and *Brahma Net Sutra*.

Maitreya Buddha is considered to be the future Buddha. He is now abiding in the Tuṣita heaven, as did Shakyamuni Buddha before he was born in this world. It is believed that Maitreya Buddha will be born 5.6 billion years after Shakyamuni's death.

Dōgen Zenji added the *Lotus Sutra* to the list of ten Buddha names because he thought this sutra was very important. In *Shōbōgenzō* "Kie-buppōsōbō" (Taking Refuge in Buddha, Dharma, and Sangha), he wrote, "The *Dharma Flower Sutra* is the causes and conditions of the one great matter of the Buddha Tathāgata. Of all the sutras expounded by the great teacher Shakyamuni, the *Dharma Flower Sutra* is the great king and is the great teacher. Other sutras and other teachings are all the retainers and people or the family dependents of the *Dharma Flower Sutra*."[59]

The next three names are the most well-known bodhisattvas. Mañjuśrī is the symbol of the Buddha's wisdom to see the reality of all beings. Samantabhadra is the symbol of the Buddha's vow and practice of skillful means to help all beings. Avalokiteśvara is the symbol of the Buddha's boundless compassion toward all beings. In addition to these three great bodhisattvas, all living beings throughout time and space who have aroused bodhicitta (Way-seeking mind) are also bodhisattvas. We are connected with all of them and we practice together with all of them.

The final name is *mahā prajñā-pāramitā*, the Buddha's wisdom that sees the emptiness of all beings. Prajñā-pāramitā is called the mother of all buddhas.

Food Offering Verses

After the ten names of the Buddha are chanted, the head monk (*shuso*) chants the following verses to praise the virtue of the meal offering.

> (*at breakfast*)
> This morning meal of ten benefits
> nourishes us in our practice.
> Its rewards are boundless,
> filling us with ease and joy.

The ten benefits of rice gruel, the traditional morning meal in Zen Buddhist monasteries, are mentioned in the Vinaya of Mahāsāṃghika. They are: making one's complexion healthy and lively, maintaining one's strength, prolonging one's longevity, allowing one to feel ease, keeping one's tongue clean, not upsetting one's stomach, preventing one from catching cold, satisfying one's hunger, keeping one's mouth from thirst, and keeping one's bowels regular.

> (*at lunch*)
> The three virtues and six tastes of this meal
> are offered to the Buddha and the sangha.
> May all sentient beings in the universe
> be equally nourished.

The three virtues of the meal are softness, cleanness, and accordance with dharma (proper preparation). The six tastes are sweetness, spiciness, saltiness, bitterness, sourness, and simplicity. The previous verse is about benefiting the self who eats the food. This verse is about benefiting others: buddhas, sangha members, and all living beings.

Verse of Five Contemplations

When the preceding verses have been chanted, the food is served. Prior to eating, the following verses of five contemplations are chanted.

We reflect on the effort that brought us this food and consider how it comes to us.
We reflect on our virtue and practice, and whether we are worthy of this offering.
We regard greed as the obstacle to freedom of mind.
We regard this meal as medicine to sustain our life.
For the sake of enlightenment we now receive this food.[60]

We chant this verse to remind ourselves that eating is a spiritual practice, not just a way to fill our stomachs and satisfy our desires. We acknowledge that we eat "to support our life," but also affirm the important spiritual meaning of the meal. We eat to keep this body in good shape and also to renew our bodhi-mind, our aspiration to practice according to Buddha's teaching.

"We reflect on the effort that brought us this food and consider how it comes to us." The first of the five contemplations is to appreciate the immeasurable work of those who produce the food and prepare the meal. Basically the meal chant is about the practice of dāna-pāramitā. In India, Buddhist monks neither produced food nor prepared meals. Every day after morning meditation practice they went to town to beg for food. Farming was prohibited for monks because farmers have to kill living beings while cultivating the land. Monks simply received the food offered by laypeople.

In China it is said that Zen monks began to cultivate grains and vegetables to support their practice. There are many koan stories in the Zen tradition about masters and monks working in the fields. One of these is the story of Guishan Lingyou (Isan Reiyū, 771–853) and his disciple Yangshan Huiji (Gyōsan Ejaku, 807–883), the founders of the Guiyang (Igyō) school. One day Yangshan was digging on a hillside to make a rice paddy. Yangshan said, "This place is so low, that place is so high." Guishan said, "Water makes things equal. Why don't you level it with water?" Yangshan said, "Water is not reliable, teacher. A high place is high level. A low place is low level." Guishan agreed.

Guishan's teacher Baizhang Huihai (Hyakujō Ekai, 749–814) was also famous for his diligent practice of community work. His saying "A day without work is a day without eating" has been one of the most popular Zen mottos. In the traditional Zen monastery, the monks who grew grains and vegetables and prepared the meals were givers, and the rest of the monks received their offerings. Of course, none of these monks sustained themselves completely by their own labor. Zen monasteries became large institutions supported by the emperor, the government, and the aristocracy, and laypeople donated food. Many monasteries also owned manors cultivated by lay farmers.

Today at American Zen centers, practitioners pay to participate in sesshins and retreats. Food provided during the retreat is purchased with this money, so participants may not consider the food they eat as a gift or think of themselves as recipients. Rather, they may think they are purchasing a service. And yet, if we think carefully about this matter, we realize that we cannot buy food if farmers do not work. And if the weather does not support growing plants, farmers cannot produce crops. Plants need water, air, fertilizer, earthworms, and microorganisms, etc. All the elements in the network of interdependent origination support the farmers' work. All food we receive is a gift from nature.

After the food is grown, we need people to transport it to the marketplace and then to factories to be processed and the various places where consumers shop. On highways we see countless trucks carrying commercial products. Without all these people's work, we could not eat even a single grain of rice.

There are also factors beyond those we can see on the earth. Because of the distance between the sun and the earth, we receive just the right amount of heat. If we had more or less, we could not live the way we live now. This distance is a result of the balance among the planets in the solar system working together.

When we consider these interconnections, we see that our existence itself is a gift from the network of all beings. The totality of this network that enables everything to exist is called the dharma body of the Buddha, the Buddha's life, or the Buddha's compassion. When we awaken to this reality of interconnection, we cannot help but express our appreciation and gratitude.

"We reflect on our virtue and practice, and whether we are worthy of this offering." When we realize that we are supported by this network of interdependent origination, we need to reflect on whether we are worthy of this gift. Since our lives are supported by all beings, we need to appreciate and support them instead of harming them. The first of the four bodhisattva vows, "Beings are numberless, we vow to save them," arises from this awakening to interconnection.

"We regard greed as the obstacle to freedom of mind." In Japanese this line of the original Chinese verse reads as "*Shin wo fusegi, toga wo hanaruru koto wa, ton tō wo shū tosu." Shin wo fusegu* means "to protect our mind." *Toga wo hanaru* means "to keep away from misdeeds." *Ton tō* means "greed," but here it also means the three poisonous minds—not only greed but anger/hatred and ignorance as well. *Shū tosu* means "it is essential." So this line says: to protect our mind, avoid unwholesome deeds, and keep ourselves in healthy shape, it is essential to be free from the three poisonous minds.

Shakyamuni Buddha taught that our six sense organs (eye, ear, nose, tongue, body, and mind), the six corresponding sense objects (forms, sounds, smells, tastes, tactile objects, and objects of mind), and the six kinds of consciousness caused by the contact between these sense organs and their objects (eye consciousness, ear consciousness, nose consciousness, tongue consciousness, body consciousness, and mind consciousness) are the elements of our lives. He taught that these eighteen elements of our lives all burn with the flames of greed, anger/hatred, and ignorance.

The Buddha taught us to extinguish the flames of the three poisonous minds with the fire of wisdom. It is said in the teaching of the four noble truths that the three poisonous minds are the cause of suffering in samsara. Buddhist practice is the path that leads to the cessation of suffering. Our practice protects us from the flames of greed, anger/hatred, and ignorance and so nurtures our virtue.

Because we receive food as part of our Buddhist practice, we need to free ourselves from the three poisonous minds. And yet, food can easily be the object of our greed and anger or hatred.

When I practiced at Antaiji, most of the monks and lay practitioners were young people in their twenties. We were always hungry. Especially during sesshin, because there is no entertainment at all except for the three meals a day, I often ate a lot even though the food was not particularly fancy.

When we have fancy food, we often eat more than we need and suffer later. When the taste of the food is not what we expect, we often dislike it, and we may get angry with the person who prepared it. During a single meal it is possible for us to transmigrate through all six realms of samsara. When I have to eat something I dislike, I feel like a hell dweller. When I am hungry, I feel like a hungry ghost. Sometimes when I eat and become sleepy, I am like an animal. Sometimes, I am as angry as an asura (fighting spirit) with the person who cooked the food. Sometimes when I eat fine food I feel like a heavenly being. These likes and dislikes and transmigration within my mind are caused by ignorance. The taste of food exists only while the food is in my mouth. After I swallow it, whether I love or hate it, it's all the same. It all becomes nutrition that sustains our body and mind in practice.

Receiving food in the zendō during ōryōki meals is a very powerful practice. We cannot complain about the taste, and we receive only the amount of food we can use. There is no way for us to be pulled by the three poisonous minds. We simply receive what is offered to us. This attitude should be maintained throughout our lives.

In the last discourse of Shakyamuni Buddha, recorded in *Butsuyuikyōgyō*, the Buddha taught the eight awakenings of the great being (Jap., *hachidainingaku*). These are the eight important points of our practice. The first two are to have modest desires (*shōyoku*) and to know how much is enough (*chisoku*). Dōgen Zenji writes:

> The first is having few desires. (Not pursuing too intensively the things we have not yet gained among the objects of the five senses is called "having few desires.") The Buddha said,

> "Monks, you should know that people who have many desires avariciously seek after fame and wealth; therefore they experience great suffering and anguish. Those who have few desires, because they have nothing to pursue and desire, are free from such troubles. Having few desires is itself worth learning and practicing. All the more so, as it gives birth to various virtues. Those who have few desires do not flatter to gain others' favor. Also, they are not pulled by their desire for gain. The mind of those who practice having few desires is peaceful, without any worries or fears. They are always affluent with whatever they have and never have a sense of insufficiency. Those who have few desires experience nirvana. This is called 'few desires.'"
>
> The second is to know satisfaction. Even among things which have already been given, you set a limit for taking them. This is called "knowing satisfaction." The Buddha said, "Monks, if you want to be free from suffering and anguish, you should contemplate knowing how much is enough. The dharma of knowing satisfaction is the place of richness, joy, peace, and calm. Those who know satisfaction, even when they lie down on the bare ground, still consider it comfortable and joyful. Those who don't know satisfaction are discontented even when they live in a heavenly palace. Those who do not know satisfaction are poor even if they have much wealth. Those who know satisfaction are rich even if they are poor. Those who don't know satisfaction are constantly pulled by the five sense desires and pitied by those who know satisfaction. This is called 'knowing satisfaction.'"[61]

A meal is an opportunity to practice the Buddha's teachings about having few desires and knowing how much is enough.

"We regard this meal as medicine to sustain our life." Buddhism is not an ascetic practice. Before he attained final awakening the Buddha

practiced austerities for six years, engaging in extremely harsh practices such as holding his breath until almost he died or eating only one grain of sesame or rice a day. It is said that having nearly died, he realized that this kind of practice is not wholesome or meaningful for the purpose of awakening. He received some milk porridge from a young woman named Sujātā, and he bathed in the river. He gave up ascetic practice and sat down under the bodhi tree. When he taught the five monks at Deer Park, the very first thing he said was that he had found the Middle Way.

The Buddha said, "One who has gone forth from worldly life should not indulge in these two extremes. What are the two? There is indulgence in desirable sense objects, which is low, vulgar, worldly, ignoble, unworthy, and unprofitable, and there is devotion to self-mortification, which is painful, unworthy, and unprofitable. Avoiding both these extremes, the Tathāgata has realized the middle path. It produces vision, it produces knowledge, it leads to calm, to higher knowledge, to enlightenment, to nirvana."[62]

An ōryōki meal is a practice of the Middle Way. We become free from the three poisonous minds that lead to indulgence in sensual pleasures. And yet we receive food to keep our body and mind healthy and functional.

"For the sake of enlightenment we now receive this food." The final contemplation is to confirm our determination to receive and eat the food in order to attain the Way. This is the same determination the Buddha made when he received the milk porridge from Sujātā.

Verse of Food for Spirits

> O spirits, we now give you an offering;
> This food is for all of you in the ten directions.

After we recite the five contemplations at the lunch meal, we offer a small piece of food on the *setsu*, the wooden scraper we use for cleaning ōryōki bowls. This practice is called *saba* in Japanese. We leave this small amount of food for all living beings. When we take food, we are receivers. Before the tenzo obtains the food he will cook, many people work to produce it. The tenzo collects the ingredients, cooks them, and makes them into a meal. To a practitioner who receives, who eats in the zendō, food is an offering from the tenzo and the many other people and living things involved in its production. The idea of saba is that we are donors as well as receivers. We give a small piece of what we have received. This is temporarily our food, but from this food we take a small piece and offer it to all beings.

The original Japanese expression for "O spirits" is *jiten ki jin shū*. This means "many demons and gods." *Ji* is "you," *ten* makes *ji* (you) into plural, and *ki jin* is Japanese or Chinese for unseen beings such as demons and gods. A *ki* is a demon and a *jin* is a god. This phrase refers to two kinds of unseen beings, some harmful and some beneficial. *Shū* means "group" or "assembly."

These unseen beings have vanished from our modern society. Perhaps they live only for a day on Halloween, or in comic books or horror movies. I grew up in a small town named Ibaraki between Kyoto and Osaka. I was surprised to learn that Ibaraki is a sister city of Minneapolis. I lived there from 1952 to 1968. I went to elementary school, middle school, and high school there. When I was a kid, it was a small town of maybe thirty thousand people. Today it has grown tenfold to more than three hundred thousand and has become a part of the metropolis of Osaka. When I lived in Ibaraki there were many Shintō shrines. Each block had its own small shrine that felt like a sacred place, separate from the outside world. When we played in the precincts of the shrines we felt different from the way we did outside. We felt something sacred. We felt that we were protected. In 1970, shortly after I left, they had a World Expo near Ibaraki. In preparation for it, the town was completely changed. We call it development, but in a sense it is a destruction of the living environment. The Shintō shrines were surrounded by houses, shops, and big apartment buildings instead of woods. I've gone back to Ibaraki several times to visit the shrines, but I didn't feel any spirits there or anything spiritually alive. There are just buildings. Today belief in spirits is called animism and is considered to be left over from primitive religion. We don't appreciate it anymore. But we still have a psychological need for this belief. Natural phenomena still influence our mentality or spirituality. Without demons, gods, and natural forces our lives become materialistic, and something is lost. The Buddha's teaching doesn't rely on animistic beliefs; it is rational. The Buddha taught that our life is full of suffering caused by our desires and greed. The essence of Buddhism doesn't rely on demons or gods. And yet Buddhism never opposed folk religions. In fact, in many countries Buddhism accepted and assimilated them. In Japan, for example, Buddhism and Shintoism have coexisted for centuries. Shintō is an animistic folk religion that worships nature, yet nature has been nearly eliminated from modern society. This makes me sad. I don't worship Shintō's demons and gods, and I don't even believe in them as beings. But I think that as symbols of nature—symbols of forces that can become very fearsome or harmful—these spirits can be a kind of blessing. Nature can be frightening and dangerous, certainly, but it also gives us everything we need: food, water, and air. Everything we have is given to us by nature, and yet nature can kill us. Many people believe that beings more powerful than humans control these natural phenomena. They pray to these gods or demons to protect them; they make offerings to insure a good harvest and avoid disasters. Not originally part of Buddhism, these gods and demons became part of people's everyday lives.

Early Buddhist scripture abounds with stories, legends, and myths that mention food offerings to unseen beings. Three are especially well known. The first is about a demon king's wife named Hārītī (Kishimojin in Japanese, which means "mother of demons"). According to the scripture she had ten thousand offspring, whom she fed with human children. The Buddha saw what Hārītī was doing, so he hid her youngest child in the ōryōki. Hārītī was very upset, and she searched all over the world but couldn't find the baby. Finally she came to the Buddha and asked where the child was. He told her, "You have ten thousand children and still, when you lose just one of them, you are sad and you suffer. You are in pain. Human beings have only one child or two. You should consider the parents' sadness when they lose their children." After being taught in this way, Hārītī accepted Buddha's teaching and received the precepts. She said that she would not kill human children anymore, but then she asked how she could feed her own children. The Buddha said, "From now on I will tell my disciples to offer a small amount of food for you at each meal so that your children will never starve." This is the origin of the offering we make to unseen beings. After this, Hārītī became the guardian of children and mothers.

The second story, which appears in the Mahāyāna *Parinirvana Sutra*, involves a demon who ate one person a day. The Buddha taught the demon and instructed him in the precept of not killing. The demon asked the same question as Hārītī and the Buddha gave almost the same answer.

The third story, in the Vinaya, may be more realistic. When the Buddha was still alive monks went to town to do takuhatsu—this is, to beg for food—and returned before noon to have their meal. Dogs came hoping to find some food to eat, but some disciples didn't give them anything. The Buddha taught them that monks should always offer some of the alms food they received to animals.

These stories convey the original spirit of food offerings made to birds, animals, and unseen beings. When we receive an offering from all beings, we should not be the end of this cycle of offering. We cannot live without the offerings we receive, but we should not keep them all for ourselves. We should offer a small amount to other beings. This practice makes the offering a circle. We take from nature and we also give back.

There is a story about the Chinese Zen master Tianhuang Daowu (Ten'nō Dōgo, 748–807) and his dharma heir, Longtan Chongxin (Ryūtan Sōshin, ninth century). Before he became a monk, Chongxin was a cake seller. Every day he offered ten cakes to the master. Each time, the master returned one cake to him saying, "I offer this to you. This is for the sake of your descendants." One day Chongxin asked the master, "I brought these cakes to offer to you. Why do you return one cake to me? Does it have any special meaning?" The master said, "You bring the cakes, so what harm is there in returning one to you?" At these words, Chongxin grasped the deeper meaning. Because of this, he left home and became a monk.

Bowl-Raising Verse

After chanting the Verse of Five Contemplations and the Verse of Food for Spirits, we put our spoon in the ōryōki bowl and chopsticks across the second bowl. We return to gasshō and chant the following verse.

> First, this is for the Three Treasures;
> next, for the four benefactors;
> finally, for the beings in the six realms.
> May all be equally nourished.

Then we pick up the ōryōki, hold it with both hands at eye level, and chant the following:

> The first portion is to end all evil;
> the second is to cultivate every good;
> the third is to free all beings.
> May everyone realize the Buddha's Way.

The Japanese reading of the first Chinese verse is *"Jōbun sanbō / Chubun shi on / Gekyū roku dō / Kai dō kuyō." Jōbun sanbō* means that the upper portion is for the Three Treasures. *Chūbun shion* means that the middle portion is for the four benefactors. *Gekyū roku dō* means the lower portion is for all living beings in the six realms. *Kai dō kuyō* means to offer this food to support all of them equally.

The expressions *jō* (upper), *chū* (middle), and *ge* (lower) are a reflection of the vertical social structure in ancient China and other East Asian countries influenced by Chinese culture. A correspondence is implied between the upper portion of food and the Three Treasures, the middle portion of food and the four benefactors, and the lower portion of food and living beings in the six realms. Because this vertical idea is not suitable in the modern society, all English translations of this verse avoid using "upper," "middle," and "lower." One translation uses "first," "next," and "finally." Another one has "first," "second," and "third." There is also a translation which avoids even specifying an order: "This food is for the Three Treasures, / For our parents, teachers, leaders, and homeland / And for all beings in the six worlds."

I think there is no problem with using the phrase "to offer the food to the Three Treasures and all living beings in the six realms." But the use of the phrase "to offer" for *kuyō* in relation to the four benefactors needs some explanation.

"Four benefactors" is a translation of *shi on* (Chi., *si en*). *Shi* means four. As for *on* (*en*), this is a difficult word to translate. In a Chinese-English dictionary it is translated as kindness, favor, grace. Another dictionary has: kindness, goodness, favor, mercy, blessing, benefit. In Chinese and Japanese morality, this word also connotes a "debt of kindness." If we receive a kindness from someone when we are in need, we have a debt of kindness to that person. It is very important to repay the debt of kindness with our appreciation and gratitude. We are indebted toward people who did us favors, and we have an obligation to return the debt. This is called *hōon* or *ongaeshi* (repaying the debt of kindness). If we fail to repay this debt we are called *onshirazu* (ungrateful, thankless), that is, someone who doesn't know the importance of repaying the debt of kindness.

According to a Buddhist dictionary, the concept of *on* as a debt of kindness is not emphasized in Indian Buddhism. But in Chinese Buddhism this notion became very important. In Buddhist teachings all of us have four benefactors to whom we have a debt of kindness. There are several different sets of four. According to a sutra titled *Daijōhonshō shinchi kankyō* (Mahāyāna Original-Life Mind-Ground Contemplation Sutra), "four benefactors" refers to one's parents, all sentient beings, rulers of the country, and the Three Treasures. According to another sutra, *Shōbō Nenjo kyō* (True Dharma Mindfulness Foundation Sutra), the four benefactors are one's mother, one's father, the Tathāgata, and one's dharma teacher. The first set is more general, applying to any human being in any society, while the second is limited to the context of Buddhism.

In both cases parents are included. All living beings have parents. We have a unique, intimate connection with them. Parents give birth to us and take care of us until we become independent. In ancient times parents taught their children all the skills necessary to live. Farmers learned how to grow grains and vegetables from their parents. So we all owe much to our parents. We should appreciate their love and kindness. In East Asian countries a very important responsibility of children is to take over the family's work, maintain the family's wealth, and care for their aging parents.

As human beings we are supported not only by our parents but by many other people in society—teachers, friends, and colleagues. We are also supported by many other things—air, water, food, clothes, and houses. We have a debt of kindness toward all beings. This is the second benefactor in the first set of four.

The third benefactor is rulers, kings, or emperors. In these modern times we don't think that presidents or prime ministers have helped us much, so we have no debt of kindness to them. In ancient times, however, people thought that a king or emperor owned the whole country. The king governed people, protected the country from enemies, and kept it peaceful.

The third line of the Bowl-Raising Verse is *gekyū roku dō*, "for all beings in the six realms." This refers to all living beings transmigrating in the six realms of samsara: the realms of hell, hungry ghosts, animals, asuras or fighting spirits, human beings, and heavenly beings.

We express our gratitude to the Three Treasures and to all beings that support our life. This eating of food is not an individual action but rather something we do together with all beings. We can live because we eat food. When eaten, food becomes our energy and part of our body. This body and mind is supported by all beings. We in turn should nurture all beings. That is the idea of *on*, repaying the debt of kindness.

The word *kuyō* is important in Buddhist practice. Unfortunately, in this translation of the meal chant the final line is rendered as "May all be equally nourished." *Kuyō* has disappeared. This word is usually translated as "to make an offering." *Ku* means "offering" and *yō* means "nourish" ot "sustain." The offering here is not limited to offering monks something material such as food, drink, medicine, clothing, shelter, and so forth. The second chapter of the *Lotus Sutra* presents a wide range of offerings:

> If anyone goes to stūpas or mausoleums,
> To jeweled or painted images,
> With flowers, incense, flags, or canopies
> And reverently makes offerings;
>
> Or if they have others perform music,
> By beating drums or blowing horns or conch shells,
> Or playing pipes, flutes, lutes, harps,
> Mandolins, cymbals, or gongs,
> Producing fine sounds and presenting them as offerings;
>
> Or if they joyfully praise
> The Buddha's virtues in song,
> Even with just a tiny sound,
> They have fulfilled the Buddha way.
>
> If anyone, even while distracted,
> With even a single flower,
> Makes an offering to a painted image,
> They will progressively see countless buddhas.
>
> There are those who worship by prostrating themselves,
> Some merely by putting palms together,
> Others only by raising a hand,
> And others by a slight nod of the head.

All of these,
Honoring images in various ways,
Will progressively see countless buddhas,
Fulfill the unexcelled way themselves.

Save countless beings everywhere,
And enter into nirvana without residue,
As a fire dies out
When the firewood is all consumed.

If anyone, even while distracted,
Enters a stūpa or mausoleum
And even once exclaims, "Hail to the Buddha,"
They have fulfilled the Buddha way.[63]

In *Shōbōgenzō* "Kuyō-Shobutsu" (Making Offering to Buddhas), Dōgen Zenji introduced ten kinds of offerings and said:

> Such service of offerings we should perform unfailingly with sincere mind. It has been performed without fail by the buddhas. Stories about it are evident throughout the sutras and Vinaya. At the same time, the Buddhist ancestors themselves have personally handed down its authentic transmission. Days and months of waiting in attendance and doing work are just times of serving offerings.[64]

There are many ways to make offerings. Our practice of zazen is one offering. Acting for the sake of the Three Treasures instead of fulfilling one's desires is an offering. Because we exist within a network of support, we need to support others. This is what "repaying the debt of kindness" and "making offering and sustaining" (*kuyō*) mean. How do we practice this? How can we pay our debt to all beings? The next verse, quoted earlier, explains:

> The first portion is to end all evil;
> the second is to cultivate every good;
> the third is to free all beings.
> May everyone realize the Buddha's Way.

At the end of this verse, we bow with our ōryōki bowls and begin to eat.

The Japanese interpretation of the Chinese original is "*Ikku i dan issai aku / Niku i shu issai zen / San ku i do sho shu jō / Kaigu jō butsudō*." *Ikku*, *niku*, and *sanku* mean first, second, and third bites. The first bite is to end all evil, to stop unwholesome deeds. The second bite is for the practice of all good things, and the third is for *do sho shu jō*. This is usually translated as "to save all sentient beings," but the literal meaning of *do* is "to go across." So it means to help all beings to cross the river from this shore to the other. This shore is samsara, in which all beings transmigrate through the six realms. The Buddha taught that we should cross the river to the other shore, nirvana. "To help people" means, in this case, to help all beings cross over to nirvana. This is the first of the four bodhisattva vows. These three points are the same as the threefold pure precepts, one category of the sixteen precepts we receive at the *jukai* (precepts-receiving) ceremony. The first is the precept of embracing moral codes, the second is embracing all good actions, and the third is embracing all living beings. We receive the threefold pure precepts to become Buddha's children or bodhisattvas. These precepts become our vow. We vow to live with this guidance, to refrain from unwholesome deeds by embracing moral codes, to practice only wholesome deeds, and to live together with all living things, doing no harm to any.

A question we should ask now is, What is good or wholesome, and what is bad or unwholesome? The definition of good and bad in Buddhism is clear. Any action we take (or karma we make) that causes suffering to self or others is bad (unwholesome). Actions that reduce suffering or bring joy or happiness to self and others are good (wholesome). The original Sanskrit word for pain or suffering is *duḥkha*, while joy or happiness is *sukha*. So the definition of good and bad in Buddhism has to do with the relation between cause and effect. It is difficult to tell whether one action is good or bad by observing it in isolation. We need to look at the consequences of many related actions. Depending on its results, an action can be good or bad. We can never be entirely certain whether an action is good or bad. An action with good intentions may cause either a beneficial or harmful result. The best we can do is try to do good. This aim to do good is our vow. If our action based on good intentions causes an unwholesome effect, we have to make repentance and try to avoid repeating the mistake. This is our practice of vow and repentance. Vow and repentance together with the precepts are very important aspects of bodhisattva practice. The precepts we receive are the guidelines for our life as the Buddha's children.

The final line is "May everyone realize the Buddha's Way," or in Japanese "Kai gu jō butsu dō." *Kai gu* means "together with all beings." We should not accomplish or complete Buddha's Way alone but with all beings. It's not possible for one person alone to attain buddhahood. When we recite or chant these verses during meals, we renew our vows and reflect on our deeds, our incompleteness, and try to be better. Our practice is to see reality as prajñā, the wisdom that sees the impermanence and egolessness of all beings. In Mahāyāna Buddhism this is called emptiness. We may practice zazen to pacify or calm ourselves, but that is not enough. We have to engage in the activity of our day-to-day lives. Precepts supply guidance for these activities outside of the meditation hall. Precepts, meditation, and wisdom are called the three basic studies of Buddhism. All our activities, all the parts of our lives, should become our practice to accomplish the Buddha's Way with all beings.

Verse of the Rinse Water

When the preceding verses have been chanted, we begin eating. When finished, we wash our bowls. After washing, we offer water and chant the following verse.

> The water with which we wash our bowls
> Tastes like ambrosia.

We offer it to the many spirits;
May they be satisfied.
On ma ku ra sai so wa ka.

After we eat food, we clean the ōryōki bowl and other small bowls with a *setsu*, or scraper. To avoid wasting any food, we clean the bowls with water that we then offer to the various spirits. The meaning of this verse is almost the same as the verse of offering the food before eating, discussed above: "O spirits, we now give you an offering; / This food is for all of you in the ten directions." Here the verse says, "The water with which we wash our bowls / Tastes like ambrosia." I don't know what ambrosia tastes like. The original word, however, is *kanro*, which literally means "sweet dew." Often this word is used as a symbol of Buddha's teachings, the Dharma. Food is Dharma, and Dharma is food. When we offer food, we offer Dharma; and this water tasting like sweet dew is Dharma too.

"We offer it to the many spirits; / May they be satisfied." The original word for spirits is *ki jin*, the same word we saw in the Verse of Offering Food. Although Buddhist philosophy claims there is no soul, Buddhism never negates unseen beings or "spirits." The Buddha never denied reincarnation or transmigration, according to which there is something that never dies and transmigrates when this body dies. Philosophically, reincarnation and the Buddha's teaching of no soul, no ego, or anātman appear contradictory. This contradiction has been an important issue in many philosophical arguments within Buddhism and between Buddhism and other philosophies in India as well as in China.

But since a majority of common people believed in ghosts, spirits, demons, and gods, Buddhism didn't try to eliminate these beliefs but rather accepted them as part of the Buddha's teaching. Many Indian gods, like Indra, were accepted within Buddhism as guardians or protectors of the Dharma. If you think logically, this may strike you as strange. However, when traditional peoples accept the existence of souls and gods, this is not a philosophical concept for them, but rather a feeling, which we share, that we live together with all beings in nature.

We feel an intimacy with nature and we can communicate with it. If we negate these beings, all nature becomes merely a collection of matter, and there is no way to communicate or live together with immaterial things. And if we think of material things as nothing more than objects of our desire, we will use and misuse them in any way to satisfy ourselves.

The next line is a mantra. In Japanese we pronounce this as *On, makurasai, sowaka*. In Sanskrit it goes *Om mahorase svāhā*. We don't know much about this mantra. *Om* and *svāhā* appear in almost all mantras. *Om* is a word that begins the mantra. It is a holy word in India. Vajrayāna Buddhism, in particular, accepted many practices of this kind from Hinduism. According to a commentary on *Chanyuan Qinggui* (*Zen'en Shingi*), *mahorase* is a compound of *mahā* (big) and *urase* (abdomen). Probably this refers to hungry ghosts.

Verse of Purity While Abiding in the World

> Abiding in this ephemeral world
> Like a lotus in muddy water,
> the mind is pure and goes beyond.
> Thus we bow to Buddha.

In "The Dharma for Taking Meals" (Fushukuhanpō) Dōgen Zenji wrote that, in Eiheiji, "hearing the tsui chin, the ino chants the 'Existing in the world' verse. This is the traditional ritual of Sōjō (Bishop) Yōjō [Eisai], so we are following it for now."[65] Dōgen Zenji basically followed the procedure of formal ōryōki meals described in *Chanyuan Qinggui* (*Zen'en Shingi*), but he added this verse, chanted at the end of the meal, from the tradition of Eisai, who was the first Japanese master to introduce Zen to Japan. Eisai was a Rinzai Zen master. Dōgen Zenji first practiced Zen in Japan with Eisai's disciple Myōzen at Keninji, which was founded by Eisai. However, the verse itself is much older than Eisai. It appears in the precepts-receiving ceremony in fascicle 9 of *Chanyuan Qinggui*.

The meaning of this verse is important for us as the Buddha's children. The English translation is a bit different from the original. This is a verse praising the Buddha's virtue. My literal translation of this verse is "Dwelling in this world like empty space, and like a lotus flower without being stained by muddy water. Purity of the mind goes beyond. Therefore we make prostration to the most venerable one." In the English translation, *kokū* (empty space) is an adjective modifying "world," yielding the meaning "this ephemeral world." In the original, however, empty space modifies "abiding." The way the Buddha abides in the world is like empty space and also like a lotus flower.

Like empty space, the Buddha dwells in this world. Empty space or kokū is a symbol of perfect interpenetration. In Buddhism it has three meanings. In a cup, there is a certain amount of water, and above the water there is empty space as a conditioned phenomenal thing. This is a very common meaning of empty space—the space where nothing exists. And yet this space is not really empty. It is filled with air. Empty space in the common sense is not really empty.

Another meaning of empty space in Buddhism is the space that does not disappear even when it is occupied by something. This is considered unconditioned; it never arises or perishes. If a glass is here, the space the glass is occupying doesn't actually disappear. This space allows all beings to exist, and it doesn't disappear even when beings disappear. This space never changes, never appears, and never disappears. It's always there. And this empty space is never defiled or pure. If the space is occupied by dirty things, it is not defiled.

The third meaning of the word *kokū* is empty space as a metaphor for prajñā or wisdom, the emptiness of all beings. Emptiness means the way the Buddha sees all beings—without self-nature or substance, impermanent, and always changing. This way of being is different from the empty space in the cup, which is a lack of being. It is also different from the space that allows all things to exist. This third kind of emptiness is the way all beings exist without self-nature. Since everything is connected with everything else, the reality of all beings, which is emptiness, pervades and penetrates the whole universe. There is no discrimination, no attachment, and nothing to grasp. This meaning of *kokū* is used as a metaphor for the emptiness that is the reality of our life. In this verse, *kokū* means the emptiness of all beings. The Buddha dwells in this world of the five skandhas as emptiness.

Kokū appears in the Verse of the Wind Bell, composed by Dōgen Zenji's teacher, Tiantong Rujing.

> The whole body is like a mouth hanging in empty space.
> Not questioning the winds from east, west, south, or north,
> Equally with all of them, speaking of prajñā:
> Ding-dong-a-ling ding-dong.

Dōgen's teacher wrote this poem about a wind bell hanging under the temple roof. In the *Hōkyōki*, Dōgen recorded his conversation with Rujing about this poem.

> Dōgen made one hundred prostrations and said, "In your poem about the wind bell, I read in the first line, 'The whole body [of the wind bell] is like a mouth hanging in empty space' and in the third line, 'Together expressing prajñā equally to all beings.' Is the empty space referred to one of the form [*rūpa*] elements? Skeptical people may think empty space is one of the form elements. Students today don't understand Buddha Dharma clearly and consider the blue sky as the empty space. I am sorry for them."
>
> Rujing replied with compassion, "This empty space is prajñā. It is not one of the form elements. The empty space neither obstructs nor not-obstructs. Therefore this is neither simple emptiness nor truth relative to falsehood. Various masters haven't understood even what the form is, much less emptiness. This is due to the decline of Buddha Dharma in this country." Dōgen remarked, "This poem is the utmost in excellence. Even if they practice forever, the masters in all corners of the world would not be able to match it. Every

> one of the monks appreciates it. Having come from a far-off land and being inexperienced, as I unroll the sayings of other masters in various texts, I have not yet come across anything like this poem. How fortunate I am to be able to learn it! As I read it, I am filled with joy, and tears moisten my robe, and I am moved to prostration because this poem is direct and also lyrical."
>
> When my teacher was about to ride on a sedan-chair, he said with a smile, "What you say is profound and has the mark of greatness. I composed this poem while I was at Chingliang monastery. Although people praised it, no one has ever penetrated it as you do. I grant that you have the Eye. You must compose poems in this way."[66]

Rujing said that this kokū is not the empty space that disappears when it is occupied by something, which is one of the rūpa elements. Neither is it the second meaning. He clearly says this is prajñā itself. Therefore, I am sure that Dōgen Zenji interprets this kokū in the meal chant as meaning prajñā.

The Buddha dwells in this world with prajñā, which sees the true emptiness of all things as neither having form nor being without form. This line echoes the line in the verse for setting out the bowls:

> Now we set out Buddha's bowls;
> may we, with all living beings,
> realize the emptiness of the three wheels:
> giver, receiver, and gift.

The Buddha dwells in this world like a lotus flower. The lotus flower emerges from muddy water. It is a beautiful flower which mud does not defile. It symbolizes the Buddha's virtue, compassion, and wisdom. It is a sacred flower and an important symbol in Buddhism and Hinduism.

According to a Hindu creation myth, when the god Vishnu was

asleep in water a lotus flower grew from his navel. Another god, Brahma, was sleeping on this lotus. Brahma created this world while Vishnu was asleep. The yogic cross-legged posture is called the lotus position because of this myth.

In Buddhism many Buddha statues are sitting or standing on lotus petals. This is for a reason. Right after the Buddha attained awakening, he hesitated to teach because he thought the truth he found was too deep and subtle for anyone to understand. Then Brahma asked the Buddha to teach. Then the Buddha, out of compassion for living beings, surveyed the world. He saw that there are many different kinds of people.

> Just as in a pond of blue or red or white lotuses, some lotuses might be born in the water, grow up in the water, and thrive while submerged in the water, without rising up from the water; some lotuses might be born in the water, grow up in the water, and stand at even level with the water; some lotuses might be born in the water and grow up in the water, but would rise up from the water and stand without being soiled by the water—so too, surveying the world with the eye of a Buddha, the Blessed One saw beings with little dust in their eyes and with much dust in their eyes, with keen faculties and with dull faculties, with good qualities and with bad qualities, easy to teach and hard to teach, and a few who dwelt seeing blame and fear in the other world.[67]

After this survey, the Buddha made up his mind to teach the five monks at Deer Park. In this example, the lotus flower signifies the different capacities of living beings. In another sutra, however, it also represents the Buddha himself. In this sutra the Buddha elucidates the nature of dharma teachings. He said, "I do not dispute with the world; rather, it is the world that disputes with me. A proponent of the Dharma does not dispute with anyone in the world. Of that which the wise in the world agree upon as not existing, I too say that it does not exist. And of that which the wise in the world agree upon as existing, I too say that it exists."

The Buddha did not teach some fabricated dogmatic theory with which wise people did not agree. He taught the truth everyone can see if their eyes are open. In another sutra, the Buddha said:

> And what is it, bhikkhus, that the wise in the world agree upon as not existing, of which I too say that it does not exist? Form that is permanent, stable, eternal, and not subject to change: this the wise in the world agree upon as not existing, and I too say that it does not exist. Feeling—Perception—Volitional formation—Consciousness that is permanent, stable, eternal, and not subject to change: this the wise in the world agree upon as not existing, and I too say that it does not exist.
>
> And what is it, bhikkhus, that the wise in the world agree upon as existing, of which I too say that it exists? Form that is impermanent, suffering, and subject to change; this the wise in the world agree upon as existing, and I too say that it exists. Feeling, perception, volitional formations, consciousness—that is impermanent, suffering, and subject to change: this the wise in the world agree upon as existing, and I too say that it exists.

Here the Buddha talks about the reality of the emptiness of all phenomenal things emphasized in Mahāyāna teachings. Nothing is substantial or permanent; therefore everything is subject to change. If we think that this body is permanent, we attach to it, and from this attachment spring our desires. This mistaken idea comes from ignorance, and from ignorance greed, anger, and hatred arise. According to the Buddha, this is the source of suffering in samsara. Not only the body, but feelings, perceptions, formations, and consciousness—all five skandhas—are impermanent and without any fixed self-nature. To see the five skandhas (our body and mind) as impermanent and unstable, subject to change and decay, is the way we free ourselves from attachments and liberate ourselves from the three poisonous minds.

According to the Buddha, to see all beings as fixed is the delusion that causes suffering. On this point there is no difference between early Buddhism and Mahāyāna Buddhism. So we should see the reality of all beings as impermanence, the way the Buddha sees all beings.

Then the Buddha goes on: "Bhikkhus, just as a blue, red, or white lotus is born in the water and grows up in the water but having risen up above the water, it stands unsullied by the water, so too the Tathāgata was born in the world and grew up in the world, but having overcome the world, he dwells unsullied by the world."[68]

The Buddha was born in this world as the lotus was born in the muddy water and grew in this world as the lotus grows in the water. But the Buddha "rises to the surface." This is a metaphor of the Buddha's teaching and way of life. The Buddha was never separated from the muddy water, from this world, and yet he was not defiled by the worldly way of doing things or mundane, selfish desires.

The verse we are discussing says, "The mind is pure and goes beyond." The mind goes beyond the muddy water of the dusty world. The Buddha does not escape the world, but the purity of the Buddha's mind goes beyond the world. It is said that the Buddha and bodhisattvas do not stay in this world because of wisdom and never leave this world because of compassion. The Buddha is here and at the same time not here because of wisdom and compassion. So we venerate the most venerable one.

One of the basic teachings of the *Avataṃsaka Sutra* is that there are no differences between the Buddha, the mind, and living beings. These three are one, and there can be no discriminating between them. This is a verse of praise for Buddha. In this verse "the mind" also refers to the nature of bodhisattvas. In the not-yet-matured stages, bodhisattvas are, like us, ordinary human beings. Even though we have aroused bodhicitta, received the bodhisattva precepts, and taken the four bodhisattva vows, we live in the muddy water. We harbor many delusions and fundamental ignorance, and we are not yet completely free of greed, anger, and hatred. We are still defiled in many ways. Our perception is defiled and conditioned. Each of us usually thinks, "I am most important." We judge things to be good, useful, or valuable to the extent that we find them important, useful, or attractive to us. This is the worldly, conditioned way of viewing things, which is contrary to the Buddha's teaching. Our individual perspective is empty, so we cannot use it as a yardstick to measure the value or meaning of things. But we do. This is our basic delusion, and we cannot live without it.

Because all of us measure things with our own yardsticks, we get into arguments. If I think something is important, and you don't, we have to argue about who is right. If both of us think an object is important, we might fight about who owns it. When we live based on our own yardstick, this becomes a world of competition and argument.

If we cannot depend on anything man-made or conditioned, how can we live within this society with other people and their yardsticks? One way is to see that my own yardstick is limited. When I recognize my limitations, I create the space to consider that other people have other yardsticks and measure things differently. I can open my heart to them. This is how we can live in muddy water with other people in peace and harmony. This is our practice of letting go of self-centered thoughts. When we live in this way without attachment to objects or to our conditioned way of viewing and judging things, the lotus flower can bloom in our lives.

For me, this is the meaning of our practice of zazen: letting go of thought. Letting go of thought is letting go of my yardstick. But this doesn't mean I should discard this yardstick, because it's all I can use. Letting go doesn't mean it disappears; it is still there, but we know that it is relative and limited. That is the way we can see things in a broader perspective. Our minds become more flexible. The Buddha is the model for us bodhisattvas, children of the Buddha, and we make prostrations to this Buddha. This means we give up clinging to our own personal yardsticks. To make prostrations to the Buddha means to let go of our system of values and to trust in the reality of all beings.

The verse ends with "Thus we bow to Buddha." The original

expression is "Ki shu rin bujōson." *Ki shu rin* is the deepest bow or prostration, called *gotai-tōchi* (*lit: gotai*, five parts of the body; *tōchi*, are cast on the ground) We place our forehead and both knees and elbows on the floor. We hold our hands upward at the height of our ears. This means we receive the Buddha's feet on our hands. This is a most humble way to show respect to the Buddha. Our head is the highest point of ourselves, and the Buddha's foot is the lowest point of the Buddha, *bujōson*, the most venerable one. We make prostrations to the Buddha to become free from our egocentricity, our clinging, and our selves. We open our hands and venerate the reality of all beings that is the Dharmakāya Buddha.

When we understand the meaning of these verses in the meal chants and wholeheartedly practice, our meals become an essential practice of the Buddha's teaching.

6 Sound of Emptiness: The Heart Sutra

Mahāprajñāpāramita Hṛdaya Sutra

Avalokiteśvara Bodhisattva
When practicing deeply the prajñā-pāramitā
Perceived that all five skandhas are empty
And was saved from all suffering and distress.

"O Śāriputra, form does not differ from emptiness;
Emptiness does not differ from form.
That which is form is emptiness;
That which is emptiness, form.
The same is true of feelings, perceptions, impulses, and consciousness.

"O Śāriputra, all dharmas are marked with emptiness;
They do not appear or disappear,
Are neither tainted nor pure,
Do not increase or decrease.

"Therefore in emptiness, no form,
No feelings, no perceptions, no impulses, no consciousness;

No eyes, no ears, no nose, no tongue, no body, no mind;
No color, no sound, no smell, no taste, no touch, no object of mind;
No realm of eyes and so forth until no realm of mind consciousness;
No ignorance and also no extinction of it, and so forth until no old age and death and also no extinction of them;
No suffering, no origination, no stopping, no path;
No cognition, no attainment.
With nothing to attain
The bodhisattva depends on prajñā-pāramitā
And the mind is no hindrance.
Without any hindrance no fears exist;
Far apart from every perverted view the bodhisattva dwells in nirvana.

"In the three worlds all buddhas depend on prajñā-pāramitā
And attain unsurpassed, complete, perfect enlightenment.

"Therefore know the prajñā-pāramitā
Is the great transcendent mantra,
Is the great bright mantra,
Is the utmost mantra,
Is the supreme mantra,
Which is able to relieve all suffering
And is true, not false.
So proclaim the prajñā-pāramitā mantra,
Proclaim the mantra that says:
Gate, gate, pāragate, pārasamgate! Bodhi, svāha!"

THE *Mahāprajñāpāramita Hṛdaya Sutra*, one of the most well known sutras, is commonly called the *Heart Sutra*. Most people who are interested in Buddhism have heard of it and many recite or chant it regularly. More than a hundred commentaries have been published, and many are available in any Japanese bookstore. Despite its popularity, I think the *Heart Sutra* is very difficult to understand.

I first read this sutra when I was sixteen years old. I was interested in everything related to religion, philosophy, and literature, and so I was interested in Buddhism. One of my uncles, a Shingon Buddhist priest, lent me a commentary on the *Heart Sutra* from his library. I read it but couldn't understand it. Even so, I found it very attractive, so I learned it by heart, memorizing all 268 Chinese characters. School didn't interest me, so during class I would write out the sutra although I didn't really understand what it meant. When I took a walk, I enjoyed chanting this sutra without thinking about the meaning. That was my first encounter with the *Heart Sutra*.

When I studied the teachings of early Buddhism at Komazawa University, I was surprised by what I learned about this sutra. It says that Avalokiteśvara saw that the five skandhas—the five mental and material elements of which we are composed—are empty and do not exist. It also says that the eighteen elements of our consciousness do not exist. This refers to the six sense organs, their six objects (color and shape, smell, sound, taste, touch, and objects of mind), and the six perceptions that arise when the six sense organs interact with their objects.

The sutra continues, "No ignorance and also no extinction of it, and so forth until no old age and death." Ignorance is the first of the twelve causes of suffering, and old age and death is the last. The sutra denies the existence of all twelve. Next it says, "No suffering, no origination, no stopping, no path." It claims that these four noble truths, the basic teachings of the Buddha, do not exist. The *Heart Sutra* denies the existence of the five skandhas, the eighteen elements of our experience, the twelve links of dependent origination, and the four noble truths. Yet it claims to be the true teaching of the Buddha. I was amazed and confused. How could the author of this sutra negate the Buddha's teachings and still call himself a student of the Buddha? After studying Mahāyāna Buddhism as a philosophy I understood the meaning of this sutra in an abstract sense. Only in the last few years have I understood its significance for my own practice. This question of why the *Heart Sutra* negates the teachings of the Buddha is essential to its understanding.

While I was in Japan, I had a chance to give a series of lectures on Dōgen's *Shōbōgenzō* to a group of Japanese Catholic laymen. I intended to talk first on "Genjōkōan" (Actualization of Reality), the first and most popular chapter of *Shōbōgenzō*. The second chapter of the seventy-five-volume version of *Shōbōgenzō* is "Maka Hannya Haramitsu" (Mahā Prajñā Pāramitā), a commentary by Dōgen Zenji on the *Heart Sutra*. Since my audience knew nothing about Buddhism, I needed to talk about the *Heart Sutra* before discussing Dōgen's commentary. While preparing these lectures I studied "Genjōkōan," "Maka Hannya Haramitsu," and the *Heart Sutra* together. It was then that I first realized that the *Heart Sutra* is very important to an understanding of Dōgen Zenji's "Maka Hannya Haramitsu" and "Genjōkōan." If we have a deep understanding of the *Heart Sutra* and "Maka Hannya Haramitsu," we can see that "Genjōkōan" is a clear and practical expression of prajñā-pāramitā.

The sutra's full title is *Mahāprajñāpāramita Hṛdaya Sutra. Mahā* means "great" or "vast." It also means "absolute" in the sense of beyond comparison or discrimination. *Mahāyāna* means "great vehicle," which can transport not just one person but many. Mahāyāna is also used as a synonym of "one vehicle" (*eka yāna*), which includes the three vehicles (*śrāvaka-yāna*, *pratyekabuddha-yāna*, and *bodhisattva-yāna*).[69] *Prajñā* means "wisdom." Wisdom and compassion are the two main aspects of Buddhism and must always go together. Without wisdom, compassion doesn't work, and without compassion wisdom has no meaning; it's not alive. This sutra is about the wisdom that sees emptiness.

Hṛdaya means "heart." In this context it means a part of our body and also the essence or most important point. The heart is the most important part of our body. If it stops, everything stops, and the whole body dies. Today many consider the brain to be more important. They believe that when the brain stops a person is dead, and their organs can be transplanted. But historically for Buddhists the heart is the basis for judging whether a person is alive or not. In Japan brain death is not recognized, and so heart transplants are still very uncommon. To remove a heart before it has stopped has been considered murder. There is a serious controversy among Japanese doctors over the proper way to determine death.[70] Since "heart" means the most important or essential point, the *Heart Sutra* is very short. The *Prajñāpāramitā Sutra* cycle is a six-hundred-volume collection of sutras. It's said that the *Heart Sutra* is the essence of those six hundred volumes.

Sutra means scripture or written expression of the Buddha's teachings. *Pāramitā*, usually translated as "perfection," is a word that is vital to an understanding of Mahāyāna Buddhism. The title of this sutra is usually translated as "Perfection of Great Wisdom." According to Chinese Buddhist philosophers, perfection or pāramitā means to cross the river to the other shore. It implies that we are living on this shore of samsara, and there is a river we must cross to reach nirvana. On this shore we transmigrate through the six realms of samsara: the realms of hell, hungry ghosts, animals, asuras (fighting spirits), human beings, and heavenly beings. We transmigrate according to our deeds. Nirvana is beyond these realms. Pāramitā, reaching the other shore, is a transformation of our way of life. The six pāramitās are commonly considered to be the method for transformation, but sometimes they are considered to be the transformed way of life instead of the means to reach there.

In samsara, our lives are based on desires. We chase after happiness. We want satisfaction, so we pursue our desires. We run after things we want and away from things we dislike. Sometimes we succeed and we are happy. Sometimes we fail and we are unhappy. This constant up-and-down is samsara.

Many people believe in transmigration from one lifetime to another. I don't believe in this, but I know we transmigrate within this life. Sometimes we feel like heavenly beings, sometimes like hell dwellers. Often we are like hungry ghosts, craving satisfaction, constantly searching for more. When our stomachs are full and we have nothing to do, we become sleepy and lazy like animals. Sometimes we are like asuras or fighting spirits. As human beings we work to acquire fame and profit. Even when our stomachs are full, we are not satisfied. We need something more, such as fame or wealth. Heavenly beings are like millionaires whose desires are completely fulfilled. They look happy but I think such people are rather bored. There's no challenge for them because all their desires are fulfilled.

Within this constant transmigration there is no peaceful basis for our lives. This way of life is a vain attempt to satisfy our egos. A life based on this constant search for satisfaction is filled with meaningless suffering. Suffering means not just physical or mental pain but also meaningless effort. This is what the Buddha meant when he said, "Everything is suffering." This is the first of the four noble truths.

According to the Buddha, the reality of our life is impermanence and egolessness. Nothing is fixed, and there is nothing that doesn't change. In Buddhism, ego refers to the idea that there is something that is changeless. Our bodies and minds change continually from birth, and yet we believe there is something that doesn't change. When I was born in 1948, I was a tiny baby; since then I have gone through many different stages of human life: a boy, a teenager, a young adult, a middle-aged person, and then a senior citizen. The conditions of my body and mind have changed in each stage and yet I think, "That was me and this is me. There is something that doesn't change." For Buddhists, the ego as an unchanging entity that is the owner and operator of the body and mind is an illusion. The Buddha taught that there is no such thing, that ego is an abstract fabrication.

Buddhism is not pessimistic nihilism, because the Buddha also taught that there is a way to become free from this kind of life. There is a path that leads to liberation from this continual transmigration through samsara. We can make a peaceful, stable foundation for our lives. It's called nirvana. It is not a particular state or condition of our minds but rather a way of life based on impermanence and egolessness. In every moment we must awaken again to the impermanent reality of our lives. Everything is always changing, and there is no substance. In Mahāyāna Buddhism, this is called emptiness. The Buddha taught that there are two different ways of living. If we are blind to the reality of egolessness and impermanence, our life becomes suffering. If we waken to this reality and live accordingly, our life becomes nirvana. This awakening is called bodhi or enlightenment. The way of transformation from the life of suffering in samsara to the life of nirvana is the eightfold noble path. This path is our practice. It is a change in the basis of our life from egocentricity to egolessness. This transformation is called pāramitā, or "reaching the other shore." This eightfold path taught by Shakyamuni Buddha consists of right understanding, right thinking, right speech, right action, right livelihood, right effort (diligence), mindfulness, and samādhi (meditation). Instead of the eightfold path, the Mahāyāna practice for bodhisattvas emphasizes the six pāramitās or perfections. The first of the six is generosity (*dāna*). We are generous because we understand there is no one who can possess and nothing to be possessed. Generosity should be based on the realization of emptiness, egolessness, and impermanence. The second pāramitā, the precepts (*śīla*), is the same as right livelihood in the eightfold path. We base our day-to-day lives on the Buddha's precepts or teaching. When we become Buddhists we accept the precepts as guidelines for our lives. We regulate our activities with the Buddha's precepts—no killing, lying, stealing, and so forth. The third, patience (*kṣānti*), is emphasized in Mahāyāna Buddhism because it is a practice designed for laypeople. In a monastery patience is not considered so important because monks are assumed to have similar values and aspirations. Laypeople are in greater contact with people who have different philosophies and ways of thinking. For this they need patience. For a bodhisattva, patience is one of the most important practices.[71] The last three pāramitās are diligence (*vīrya*), meditation (*samādhi*), and wisdom (*prajñā*). The *Heart Sutra* and all the other *Prajñāpāramitā Sutras* say that prajñā is the most important of the six pāramitās to the practice of bodhisattvas.

Without prajñā the other five pāramitās don't work. For example, generosity without wisdom can be harmful. We must understand what is really needed before we can help someone. If we give money or assistance without wisdom, the person may become dependent and have more difficulty as a result. This is also true of raising children. Too much protection will spoil a child. We need prajñā or wisdom to really help people grow. Without prajñā the precepts become no more than a lifeless set of rules. We may even discriminate between people on the basis of a particular set of precepts or customs. Each nation or religion has its own set of precepts and taboos. It's easy to see people who follow our precepts as friends and to believe that all the others will go to hell. This is an example of precepts without wisdom, a type of egocentricity of a group instead of an individual.

We need a deep understanding of a situation to see what is most helpful to everyone involved. Dōgen Zenji said in *Shōbōgenzō* "Bodaisatta Shishōbō" (Bodhisattva's Four Embracing Dharmas) that as bodhisattvas we should aim at activities that benefit both others and ourselves. We should try to see the whole situation and do what is best for everyone. If we aim only for patience, we may harm ourselves or others. Patience alone can be a kind of poison. It can make the situation worse.

The same is true of diligence. If diligence is misdirected, the harder we work, the farther we deviate from the correct path. Without the wisdom to see which way to go, our diligence is meaningless effort.

Wisdom is also essential to meditation. If we don't understand the significance or meaning of meditation, our practice of zazen becomes no more than an escape from a noisy society. It becomes a meaningless method to simply calm our minds and reduce our stress. If our life is harmful to others and we practice meditation to relax and gain more energy for self-centered activities, our practice has nothing to do with Buddhist teachings. So wisdom, real wisdom, is essential. This is the meaning of pāramitā. According to the *Heart Sutra*, prajñā-pāramitā is the essence of Buddhist teaching. It is necessary to the transformation of our life from samsara to nirvana.

The Situation in Which the *Heart Sutra* Is Expounded

One reason the *Heart Sutra* is difficult to understand is that it's not clear who is speaking. There are two versions of the sutra. The one we usually chant, which is printed at the beginning of this chapter, is the shorter of the two. The longer version describes the situation more completely. The opening lines of this version, translated from Sanskrit by Edward Conze, are:

> Thus have I heard at one time. The Lord dwelled at Rājagṛha, on the Vulture Peak, together with a large gathering of both monks and bodhisattvas. At that time, the Lord, after he had taught the discourse on dharma called "deep splendor," had entered into concentration. At that time also the Holy Lord Avalokita, the Bodhisattva, the great being, coursed in the course of the deep perfection of wisdom; he looked down from on high, and he saw the five skandhas, and he surveyed them as empty in their own-being.
>
> Thereupon the Venerable Śāriputra through the Buddha's might said to the holy Lord Avalokita, the Bodhisattva, the great being: "How should a son or daughter of good family train themselves if they want to course in the course of this deep perfection of wisdom?"[72]

"Thus have I heard," is the traditional beginning of a Buddhist sutra. The "I" is Ānanda, a longtime attendant of Shakyamuni Buddha who memorized all of his sutras.

> The Lord dwelled at Rājagriha, on the Vulture Peak, together with a large gathering of both monks and bodhisattvas. At that time, the Lord, after he had taught the discourse on dharma called "deep splendor," had entered into concentration.

"Lord" refers to the Buddha. I question the use of this word. The Buddha never called himself Lord. In fact, he said that he owned nothing. The original word used in the sutra is "Bhagavat," which is usually translated into English as World-Honored One. "Concentration" means zazen or samādhi. After he gave a talk on "deep splendor," he stopped speaking and started to sit zazen. This sutra takes place within the Buddha's zazen. This is a very important point.

> At that time also the Holy Lord Avalokita, the bodhisattva, the Great Being, coursed in the course of the deep perfection of wisdom; he looked down from on high, and he saw the five skandhas, and he surveyed them as empty in their own-being.

In this translation the name Avalokiteśvara is divided into two parts, "Avalokita" and "īśvara." *Avalokita* means "to see." *Īśvara* is usually translated as "freely." This is what the Chinese translation *Kanjizai* means. Here *īśvara* is translated as "lord," a free person who does not belong to anyone. "Great Being" is a translation of Mahāsattva, another word for bodhisattva. To "course in the course" is a Sanskrit expression for practice. So Avalokiteśvara was practicing deep prajñā-pāramitā. And from within his practice of deep wisdom, he looked down on this world in which all sentient beings are living.

"Looked down" is a translation from Sanskrit. In Japanese this is *shōken*. *Shō* means "to illuminate," and *ken* "to see" or "view." So *shōken* means "see very clearly," as if a scene were illumined with a bright light. The Sanskrit expression is "he looked down from on high." When we are on the same level as all other human beings we can't see distinctly, but from a high place like a mountain, one can see the whole clearly.

"And he saw the five skandhas": From his practice of deep prajñā, that is, zazen, he saw that all beings are collections of the five skandhas and nothing but the five skandhas. The skandhas are the elements that comprise all beings. The first, form or *rūpa*, refers to all material things. For human beings, this means our bodies. The other four are the functions of our mind. So Avalokiteśvara saw that everything in this world is an accumulation of the five skandhas.

"And he surveyed them as empty in their own-being": The bodhisattva further saw that these skandhas are empty.

"Thereupon the Venerable Śāriputra through the Buddha's might said to the holy Lord Avalokita, the Bodhisattva, the great being": Śāriputra was one of the ten greatest of the Buddha's disciples. It is said he was the most sharp-witted. Śāriputra asked Avalokiteśvara through the Buddha's might, so it's really the Buddha, not Śāriputra, who is speaking. Śāriputra's question was "How should a son or daughter of good family train themselves if they want to course in the course of this deep perfection of wisdom?" His question was how people should practice if they aspire to prajñā-pāramitā. Avalokiteśvara's answer to Śāriputra's question is the teaching of the *Heart Sutra*. The person who gives this speech is Avalokiteśvara, but this question and answer both take place within the Buddha's samādhi, that is, zazen. This is a description of the Buddha's zazen and of ours. This teaching in the *Heart Sutra* is not a philosophical discussion between the Buddha's disciple Śāriputra and a bodhisattva about the philosophy of emptiness in Mahāyāna Buddhism. It is about our practice of zazen.

This description of how the conversation begins helps us to understand what Avalokiteśvara says in this sutra.

Who Is Avalokiteśvara?

When I first visited MZMC in 1989 I attended morning service and we chanted the translation of the shorter version of the *Heart Sutra*. I was surprised by the translation of the last line of the following paragraph.

> Avalokiteśvara Bodhisattva
> When practicing deeply the prajñā-pāramitā
> Perceived that all five skandhas are empty
> And was saved from all suffering and distress.

This line was completely different from my understanding. The translation implies that Avalokiteśvara was suffering and distressed, but through the practice of prajñā-pāramitā he was saved and released.

It is important to understand who Avalokiteśvara is. According to Mahāyāna Buddhism there are two kinds of bodhisattvas. We ordinary humans, who aspire to study, practice, and follow the Buddha's teaching are one kind. We are all called bodhisattvas. The other kind of bodhisattva is not an ordinary human being. Great bodhisattvas like Avalokiteśvara, Samantabhadra, or Mañjuśrī are the symbol of some part of the Buddha's virtue. They choose not to enter nirvana, or not to stay there, in order to help other beings cross over to the far shore.

In the chapter of *Shōbōgenzō* titled "Kannon," Dōgen Zenji said that Avalokiteśvara is the father and mother of buddhas. In a past life Avalokiteśvara was a buddha called Shōbōmyō Nyorai (True Dharma Wisdom Tathāgata). *Shōbō* means "true dharma." *Myō* is "light," the symbol of wisdom. So he was a buddha called "the light of true dharma." But because of his vow to save all beings, he became a bodhisattva and appeared in this world. He wasn't in trouble. So I don't think the translation quoted above is accurate. I found Katagiri Roshi's translation of the *Heart Sutra* in a magazine. He translates this paragraph: "Avalokiteśvara Bodhisattva, when practicing the profound prajñā-pāramitā, by virtue of illuminated vision, saw the five skandhas as empty and passed beyond all sufferings."[73] He wasn't saved from suffering but rather passed beyond it. The original Chinese words are *Do issai ku yaku*. *Do* is a verb and is sometimes translated as "to save." Another meaning of the Chinese character *do* is "to cross over from this shore." This *do* is not passive. So he wasn't saved, but rather he saved (others) or crossed over. He saved all beings in trouble, all who are suffering and in distress. This meaning is quite different. In the Sanskrit version we have today, this final part of the sentence is missing. In that version the point is that Avalokiteśvara came to the realization of emptiness, and that was it. There's no statement as to whether this realization relieved his suffering or that of others. This sentence may have been added by the Chinese translator, Xuanzang (Jap., Genjō), who lived in the seventh century. He may have been working from a different Sanskrit version from the one we have. In any case, the text seems to me clearer and simpler without the last phrase. Avalokiteśvara saw the five skandhas are empty. This is prajñā-pāramitā, the perfection of wisdom.

As noted above, in the Chinese translation of the *Heart Sutra*, "Avalokiteśvara" is translated as Kanjizai Bosatsu. Avalokiteśvara is also called Kanzeon Bosatsu in Chinese. Kanjizai and Kanzeon have different meanings. *Kan* means "to see" or "observe." *Jizai* is the translation of the Sanskrit word *īśvara*, a person who can see freely without obstruction. This means one who is free from egocentricity and ignorance, one who sees things as they are without distortion by intellect, desire, or expectation. This is the meaning of Avalokiteśvara.

Kanzeon Bosatsu as a translation appears in the twenty-fifth chapter of the *Lotus Sutra*, "The Universal Gateway of the Bodhisattva Perceiver of the World's Sounds," translated by Kumārajīva. In this case the name "Avalokiteśvara" is interpreted as "Avalokita" (to see) and "svara" (sound). The name Kanzeon means "one who hears the sound of the world." Human beings make sounds when they suffer. Avalokiteśvara hears these sounds of suffering and appears in various ways and tries to help. Kanzeon Bosatsu represents the aspect of compassion and the work of helping others. Kanjizai Bosatsu emphasizes the aspect of wisdom or prajñā—seeing things exactly as they are, free of distortion. In the *Heart Sutra* the bodhisattva is called Kanjizai Bosatsu. As a symbol of the wisdom of seeing the reality of our life clearly, he/she is, of course, a creation of the imagination of Mahāyāna Buddhists, not a historical being.

This bodhisattva, although a buddha, yet came back to this world of delusion and suffering in order to help people, vowing not to become Buddha until all sentient beings are saved and become Buddha together. So Avalokiteśvara will remain in this world, on this shore, as long as there are deluded human beings. To the extent that we are deluded Avalokiteśvara is here now. This is a very important point. Avalokiteśvara is not a person but rather a force that reminds us to awaken.

Today you have come to the Zen Center to sit and to listen to my talk. It's not necessarily fun. But you're here. You could have gone anywhere. This is a beautiful morning and you could be having fun, but you decided to come here and sit in this posture. It's not necessarily a comfortable posture and my talk is not necessarily interesting. But you made a decision to come here. What made you decide to come to the Zen Center and sit zazen? Avalokiteśvara. This is the power that keeps us practicing and tells us to awaken. Avalokiteśvara is a power not just inside us but all around us, which leads us to awaken to the impermanence and egolessness that is the reality of our lives.

New leaves are coming out on the trees. They show us that time passes and everything changes; now winter to spring and soon spring to summer. Life always changes, is always new and always fresh. We see everything around us change and yet we believe that we do not. We believe that "I am": "I am the same person I was forty years ago, twenty years ago, or yesterday." "I will be the same person tomorrow." But the reality is that we are always changing. Our bodies and minds constantly change. So in the spring the leaves appear and birds sing to tell us, "Awake, awake to this reality. Everything is moving and changing." Everything is ever fresh each moment. That is Avalokiteśvara helping us see things clearly as they are.

Everyone we encounter is Avalokiteśvara. Our parents who took care of us, our friends, our competitors, or even enemies can be Avalokiteśvara. They are here to show us the reality of life. We should be thankful. We should appreciate ourselves, all people we encounter, and all things in this universe. All of this is Avalokiteśvara telling us to wake up and not be caught in egocentric delusion, encouraging us to become free from illusion and see our life force straight on. That is Avalokiteśvara. This sutra is speaking from our life force.

In "Kannon," a chapter of *Shōbōgenzō*, Dōgen Zenji wrote about Avalokiteśvara.[74] He quotes a very interesting koan, or question and answer between two Chinese Zen masters, Yunyan (Ungan) and Daowu (Dōgo).[75] The two practiced together for forty years with various teachers at different monasteries. Many of their conversations have been recorded. This koan begins with Yunyan asking Daowu, "What does the Great Compassion Bodhisattva do with so many hands and eyes?" (Yunyan refers to Avalokiteśvara or Kanzeon Bosatsu. It is said that Avalokiteśvara had one thousand eyes and one thousand hands. Eyes symbolize wisdom, and the hands work with compassion to help others.) In answer to Yunyan's question Daowu replied, "It is like a person groping behind his head for his pillow at night."

We all turn over during the night as we sleep. Sometimes we lose our pillows. Daowu describes looking for his pillow in the dark with his hands behind his back. Complete darkness is rare these days. Even if we switch off all the lights there is usually some artificial light from outside. But in ancient times nighttime was completely dark. Once I had the experience of walking in complete darkness. There is a famous mountain outside of Kyoto called Mount Hiei, where Dōgen Zenji was ordained. There is a huge Tendai monastery there. I was staying at Antaiji in the northwest part of Kyoto. We had a party after a five-day sesshin and drank lots of sake and beer. After the party I had a lot of energy and decided to hike up the mountain to see the sun rise from the top. It took me three or four hours to walk up to the top. Since it is near the city of Kyoto most of the path was dimly lit by the lights of the city. But there was one stretch of several hundred meters covered by evergreens that was completely dark. I couldn't even see my hand. It was very frightening. My feet and hands became my eyes. I took each step very slowly and carefully because at the edge of the path was a cliff.

Perhaps blind people have this experience frequently. It's amazing to me to see blind people walking with a white cane. Their feet, hands, and even their canes are their eyes. Their whole body is their eyes. At night our entire body serves as our eyes. When we try to find a lost pillow our whole being, our whole body and mind, becomes our eyes and hands. Darkness has a special meaning in Buddhism. It means nondiscrimination. In the dark we can't see anything, and so we can't discriminate between things. We see only one darkness.

This is a metaphor for our zazen. In complete darkness there is no discrimination. Our body and mind work together as one. The *Heart Sutra* says there are no eyes, no ears, no nose, no tongue, no anything. Because they are not independent, they work together as one, and there is no distinction between eye or nose or tongue. The whole body becomes an eye in the darkness. The whole body becomes a tongue when we eat. We don't eat and taste with our mouths and tongues alone. We see the food with our eyes, we smell it with our noses, we touch it with our hands. The whole body functions together as one in all our actions. So there are no eyes or ears independent of other organs—all work together. That is the reality of life. This is how our life functions like a person groping for a pillow in the night.

> Yunyan said, "I get it, I get it. I understand what you mean."
> "How do you understand it?" asked Daowu.
> "The entire body is hands and eyes."

Since eyes don't work in the darkness of nondiscrimination, the whole body becomes eyes and hands.

> Daowu answered, "Good, you expressed reality almost completely. But only 80 to 90 percent. There is something lacking."
> Yunyan asked, "That is my understanding. What about you?"
> Daowu replied, "The whole body is hands and eyes."

Yunyan used the Chinese "hen shin." *Hen* means "entire." Daowu's wording was "tsū shin." *Tsū* means "whole." "Entire body" and "whole body" mean the same thing. Their answers were exactly the same. This is Avalokiteśvara. We have many hands and eyes besides our own. Our hands and eyes are universal. Our hands and eyes, our entire body, is part of the whole universe. The whole universe works as one, just like our whole body. There are innumerable hands and eyes. What is this whole universe doing for us? It's telling us to awaken from our dream of egocentricity and open our eyes. Whether Yunyan's and Daowu's expressions are the same or not and why Daowu said Yunyan's answer was only 80 to 90 percent complete are the points of this koan.[76]

Avalokiteśvara is like a person groping for a pillow in the darkness, with body and mind working as one. There is no distinction between eyes, hands, tongue, ear, or nose. The universe functions as one. This is the meaning of egolessness and impermanence. Everything is always changing, but we are blind to all of this. We dream that "I" am here, and unless my desires are fulfilled, my life is meaningless. We try to be successful. We build a fence between our body and mind and other beings in the universe. We say, "This is me. This is my territory. This is my house." We try to keep things we value inside our territories and things we dislike outside. If we own a lot of valuable things, we consider our lives successful. Our lives are a constant struggle to increase our income and decrease our expenses. This is our way of life. It works because human society is based on artificial conventions to which we all agree in order to make our lives more convenient.

But outside social conventions this framework doesn't apply. When we face our death, strategies of accumulation and avoidance don't work. No matter how successful your life, when you face death, you have to leave everything. Your property, your fame, and all your accomplishments disappear. Avalokiteśvara helps us awaken. Until we wake up to reality our life is like a building without a foundation. The *Heart Sutra* is about transforming our way of life. It is about waking up to reality and creating a life based on the reality that exists before convention. For us, the practice of zazen is the turning point of this transformation. According to Dōgen Zenji, zazen itself is enlightenment or awakening. Of course, even in our zazen we have delusive thoughts, desires, and emotions. And so we let go of them. This letting go is transformation. Our life is no longer personal, and we live out the universal life force. This is the meaning of zazen.

Both Sides

Avalokiteśvara Bodhisattva
When practicing deeply the prajñā-pāramitā
Perceived that all five skandhas are empty
And was saved from all suffering and distress.

Avalokiteśvara was practicing prajñā-pāramitā. We must be careful to remember that prajñā-pāramitā is something to be practiced. Prajñā (wisdom) is not simply a matter of how our brain works. In *Shōbōgenzō* "Maka Hannya Haramitsu," Dōgen Zenji refers to the "whole body's clear seeing."[77] He is reminding us that this wisdom should be practiced with our whole body and mind. Seeing with the whole body and mind means we become one with the emptiness of the five skandhas. These five skandhas are nothing other than our body and mind. When we sit zazen our whole body and mind becomes nothing other than the whole body and mind that is empty. The five skandhas become five skandhas that are completely empty. Zazen is itself prajñā. The five skandhas (whole body and mind) clearly see the five skandhas (whole body and mind). There is no separation between subject and object.

In early Buddhism body and mind are described as being made up of the five skandhas (aggregates) to emphasize that there is no fixed ego. The five skandhas are form (Skt., *rūpa*; Jap., *shiki*), sensation (*vedanā*, *ju*), perception (*saṃjñā*, *so*), impulse or formation (*saṃskāra*, *gyo*), and consciousness (*vijñāna*, *shiki*). The first, form, refers to material things that have shape and color. In the case of human beings, form is body. The other four skandhas are mental functions. When we encounter an object we receive sensory stimulation, which may be pleasant, unpleasant, or neutral. This stimulation caused by objects we call sensation. The Chinese character for *ju* means "reception." This received sensation creates images or representations in our mind. We call this perception. Impulse (*saṃskāra*) is the power of mental formation, that is, will or volition. Based on sensation, perception, and impulse, the object is recognized and judgments are formed. This is the function of the fifth skandha, consciousness.

The Buddha taught that since we are made up of these five constantly changing skandhas, there is no fixed ego, and we are impermanent. Later, in Abhidharma philosophy, Buddhist scholars believed that we are egoless but that these five skandhas exist in an independent, fixed way. Mahāyāna Buddhists criticized this theory. The *Prajñāpāramitā*

Sutras said that these five skandhas are also empty. This emptiness is another way of describing impermanence and egolessness.

We can be saved from suffering because the cause of suffering is our selfish desire based on an ignorance of impermanence and egolessness. We cling to our body and mind and try to control everything, but we cannot. When we truly see the emptiness (impermanence and egolessness) of the five skandhas of our body and mind, we see that there is nothing to cling to. So we open our hands. This is liberation from the ego-attachment that causes suffering.

The sutra continues:

> "O Śāriputra, form does not differ from emptiness;
> Emptiness does not differ from form.
> That which is form is emptiness;
> That which is emptiness, form.
> The same is true of feelings, perceptions, impulses, and
> consciousness."

The five elements of our life are all empty, and emptiness is those five skandhas. The phrases "form is emptiness" and "emptiness, form" say that "since *A* is not different from *B*, and *B* is not different from *A*, then *A* is *B*, and *B* is *A*." This is very simple. But this sutra has a more complex meaning. The longer version of the *Heart Sutra* reads:

> "There are the five skandhas, and those he sees in their own-
> beings as empty.
> Hear, O Śāriputra, form is emptiness and the very emptiness
> is form;
> emptiness is no other than form, form is no other than
> emptiness;
> whatever is form, that is emptiness, whatever is emptiness,
> that is form."[78]

The first sentence says that there are five skandhas, and they are empty. This sentence is very important to our understanding of the *Heart Sutra*. The *Āgama Sutras*, a collection of early Buddhist discourses similar to the Pāli Nikāyas, say that all phenomenal beings are aggregates of causes and conditions without any fixed entity. According to the *Āgama Sutras*, the Buddha affirmed that there is no ego, and we are merely collections of five skandhas. "Ego" means something unchanging and singular that owns and operates this body and mind. The Buddha taught there is no such thing. In Sanskrit "ego" is called *ātman*. To express the reality of no-ātman (*anātman*) he stated that only the five skandhas exist, and these various elements form the temporal being that is a person. Later, Abhidharma philosophers believed that the ego or ātman doesn't exist but that the five skandhas exist as substance. They analyzed these five skandhas into seventy-five elements. A particular combination of elements enables this being to exist as a unique person, and when one of the elements changes, this body and mind changes or even disappears. It's like atomic theory. Science says this body, desk, or notebook can be divided into smaller and smaller pieces until we eventually come to something that cannot be divided. Greek philosophers called this the atom. The conventional concept of the individual is analogous to the Greek concept of the atom. In the last century we learned that the atom can be split. It is no longer the ultimate particle. The *Heart Sutra* says the same thing about people. It says that each being is made up of five skandhas, five categories of elements, and these are empty. This line in the sutra is a criticism of the Abidharma philosophy that maintained the five skandhas exist as fixed substance.

Mahāyāna Buddhists criticized the Abhidharma idea of the self-nature of the skandhas. They believed the five skandhas or elements are empty, that they don't really exist. The skandhas are dependent on cause and conditions and have no existence independent from other things. In fact, nothing exists except in relationship with all other beings. This fundamental teaching of the Buddha is called interdependent origination.

Nāgārjuna was one of the greatest Mahāyāna philosophers. His Examination of the Four-Fold Noble Truth in *Mūlamadhyamakakārikā*

Nagarjuna - Mahayanna philosopher

is helpful in understanding these lines. He identified two levels of truth. The Dharma as taught by the Buddha is not some kind of objective reality. It is the reality of our own lives based on two truths, relative and absolute. He said, "Those who don't know the distinction between the two truths cannot understand the profound nature of the Buddha's teaching" (24:9).[79] The profound nature of the Buddha's teaching is prajñā, the Buddha's wisdom. In order to understand the Buddha's wisdom, we have to clearly understand this distinction between absolute and relative truth.

Nāgārjuna continues, "Without relying on everyday common practices (i.e., relative truths), the absolute truth cannot be expressed. Without approaching the absolute truth, nirvana cannot be attained" (24:10). Here "common practices" means relative truth, the way we usually think in our day-to-day lives. For instance, "I am a man. My name is Shohaku Okumura. I am a Buddhist priest. I was born in Japan and came to America. I have two children." This is our everyday way of explaining who we are. As a teacher, I have responsibilities and now I'm giving a talk. This is common practice, a relative truth. When I say I am Japanese that means I'm not an American. "My name is Shohaku Okumura" means I'm not someone else. "I'm a man" means I'm not a woman. These definitions are relative.

Nāgārjuna says that the absolute truth cannot be expressed without relying on relative truth. The absolute truth is beyond words, which are relative. That is śūnyatā or emptiness. That is prajñā. Without approaching the absolute truth, nirvana cannot be attained. As long as we stay only in the relative truth, in conventional ways of thinking, we cannot move toward nirvana. Nirvana is the most peaceful foundation of our life. In the realm of relative thinking, this body and mind change with each new encounter or situation. We are always thinking about how to behave in this situation, always adjusting ourselves. Often a situation is competitive, and we have to be careful, either to defend ourselves or become aggressive. It's a restless way of life. Nirvana is beyond the relativity of subject and object, teacher and student, customer and shop clerk.

Nāgārjuna continues, "We declare that whatever is relational origination is śūnyatā. It is a provisional name [i.e., thought construction] for the mutuality [of being] and, indeed, it is the middle path" (24:18). "Relational origination" is a synonym for interdependent origination. Everything is interconnected, and because of certain linked causes and conditions this person or this thing exists for awhile. This is not a substance; it is called śūnyatā or emptiness. Because of relational origination, nothing exists independently. The elements of this provisional existence are called the five skandhas. The idea of the five skandhas as fixed and the idea of emptiness contradict each other. If the five skandhas exist independently and permanently, there is no emptiness; if all is really emptiness, there are no fixed five skandhas. This simple sentence in the *Heart Sutra* is important to understand.

Form, as we've seen, is one of the five skandhas. In the case of human beings, it means our bodies. To say this body is empty means it doesn't actually exist. In a sense, "form is emptiness" means that form is not form. "Emptiness" means there is no form, and "form" means there is form. So this is not a simple logic at all. Nāgārjuna says that whatever is relational origination is śūnyatā. Emptiness, like all words, is a provisional name without substance that can exist and has validity only in relation to other words.

Form, feelings, perceptions, impulses, and consciousness—all five skandhas—are provisional names: names without substance. They are thought-constructions created by our minds. Everything is simply a provisional name. "Shohaku" is a provisional name. "Priest" is a provisional name. "Japanese" is also a provisional name. All of these are simply provisional names for "the mutuality of beings." This mutuality of beings means that nothing can exist by itself, but only in relationship with other elements. This means everything is empty; everything is merely a provisional name that exists temporarily as a collection of the five skandhas. This way of viewing things, beyond the duality of "independent being" and "nonbeing," is the middle path.

Nāgārjuna stated there are two levels of truth: absolute truth (śūnyatā) and conventional truth (provisional being). He said we must see reality from both sides. We must see it as śūnyatā and as a provisional name. This is the middle path. By seeing reality from both sides we can see without being caught up in either side. The *Heart Sutra* says, "Form is not different from emptiness." This means form is a tentative or a provisional name. This person Shohaku Okumura is just a provisional name and doesn't actually exist. That means emptiness. So form is not different from emptiness. This is one way of seeing. This is negation of form, negation of this being. This being looks like existence but isn't.

By negating independent being, we become free from attachment to this body and mind. This is a most important point. If we don't see the reality of emptiness, we cannot become free from clinging to this tentative being that is defined by relative concepts. Through the wisdom of seeing this being as empty and impermanent, we can free ourselves from clinging. This is the meaning of "form is emptiness." To see that form is emptiness means to negate attachment to this collection of five skandhas. Even though we cling to this body and mind, sooner or later it is scattered. If we really see the reality of emptiness, we are free from ego attachment. This is the meaning of the sentence "Form does not differ from emptiness." This is the way to negate our relative perceptions and open our eyes to absolute reality.

However, freedom from attachment to this body and mind is not enough. Once we see the absolute reality that is emptiness, we must return to tentative reality. This is the meaning of "Emptiness does not differ from form." When we really see the emptiness, we become free from this body and mind. That's okay, but then how shall we live? We cannot live within the absolute truth because without distinctions there is no way to choose. Without making choices we cannot live. To choose a path, we have to define who we are and what we want to do. To accomplish things, to go somewhere, we have to make distinctions. If we have no direction, there is no way to go. So to live out our daily lives we have to return to relative truth.

Nāgārjuna also said, "A wrongly conceived śūnyatā can ruin a slow-witted person. It is like a badly seized snake or a wrongly executed incantation" (24:11). If we don't understand emptiness as the middle path, we can become irresponsible. Freedom and irresponsibility can be the same thing. But the Buddha's compassion means to be free and yet responsible to everything. It is compassion without attachment. Through wisdom we see that everything is empty. Through compassion we return to relative truth. We must think, "How can I take care of this body and mind to keep them healthy so I can help others?" This is what the Buddha taught. To be responsible to whatever situation surrounds us, we have to become free from emptiness. We have to come back to the relative truth of everyday activities and take care of things. So this is not just a formal, simple logic, *A* is *B* and *B* is *A*. When we say form is emptiness, we negate this body and mind. When we understand that emptiness is form, we negate emptiness. Negate means to let go. To let go of thought means to become free from both sides. Then we can see reality from both perspectives without being attached to either. The wisdom of Avalokiteśvara is the Middle Way that includes both sides. It is not something in between this side and that. From the middle path we see reality from both views, relative and absolute. We simultaneously negate and affirm both sides. To let go of thought means to become free from both perspectives and simply be in the middle (reality).

According to Dōgen Zenji, sitting in zazen posture and letting go of thought is itself the Buddha's wisdom, prajñā. So prajñā is not a particular state of mind or way of thinking. To express this Middle Way, Dōgen Zenji paraphrased the *Heart Sutra* in the chapter of *Shōbōgenzō* called Mahāprajñāpāramita. He said, "Form is emptiness, emptiness is form. Form is form, emptiness is emptiness." When we say, "Form is emptiness," there is still separation between form and emptiness, between relative and absolute. When we really see the middle path we don't need to say, "Form is emptiness" or "Emptiness is form." When we see form, emptiness is already there. We don't need to say, "Form and emptiness are the same." When we say so, we are still comparing form and emptiness and thinking these two are one. This is still a relative way of thinking. So Dōgen Zenji said, "Form is form and emptiness is emptiness." This is our practice of zazen based on Mahāyāna philosophy.

For us as practitioners, a mere understanding of this philosophy is not enough. We must apply this understanding in our everyday activities. We see that we cannot do anything completely by ourselves. We cannot live alone; we are always living with other people and other beings. To work together and live together with other people and beings, we have to negate ourselves. We have to negate this person to see what other people are doing or thinking. This means that we negate the five skandhas and see śūnyatā as it is. When we interact with our environment, we have to express the things happening inside us through our lives. We have to do something. We have to respond to situations and make choices. As Dōgen Zenji said in "Genjōkōan," "To study the Buddha's Way is to study the self. To study the self is to forget the self." To forget the self means to negate this one. By negating this one we see others more clearly. When we negate our egocentricity or personal point of view, we can see things more objectively. We can see the situation as a part of ourselves, and at the same time we see ourselves as a part of the situation. We can choose what to do right now, right here, as this person who is a part of the total situation. That's how we can be responsible to the situation.

This attitude applies to more than our daily lives. Dōgen Zenji said in *Shōbōgenzō* "Shōji" (Life and Death), "To clarify life and death is the most significant point of practice of the Buddha's students." We see our life and death from both sides and see reality as the Middle Way. Our body and mind is just a collection of five skandhas that is empty and will someday disappear. Sooner or later we will die. To negate the five skandhas is to see emptiness, egolessness, and impermanence. And yet if we see only in this way we may become nihilistic, pessimistic, or irresponsible. We will not live with compassionate hearts. We might think that if sooner or later it will all disappear, why should we strive to accomplish anything? That is the sickness of emptiness.

Then we must return to the relative truth. Although we are empty and sooner or later we disappear, right here and now we are living as reality. We exist right now as a tentative collection of five skandhas. We choose to be responsible to this life at this moment. So there must be some way to live. There must be some direction to follow. This is an important point of our practice. We see reality, the middle path, from both sides and become free from attachment to either. Therefore Dōgen Zenji said in *Shōbōgenzō* "Shōji,"

> When we speak of life, there is nothing other than life; when we speak of death, there is nothing other than death. Therefore, when life comes we just face life. When death comes we just face death. We should not be used by them or desire them. This present life-and-death is the Life of buddha. If we dislike it and try to get rid of it, we would lose the Life of buddha. If we desire to remain [in life-and-death] and attach ourselves to it, we would also lose the Life of buddha.[80]

This is almost impossible for an ordinary person. But that is the path the Buddha or Avalokiteśvara saw and tried to show us. It is very difficult simply to become free from ego attachment. To become free from emptiness is even more difficult. Yet to follow this way of life is our direction as Buddhist practitioners. This is our vow. Somehow I cannot help but follow this way of life. It is my practice. And when I see another person living this way I feel encouraged. If even one person is inspired or encouraged by my practice, I am really happy.

Emptiness in Theory

The third paragraph of the *Heart Sutra* says:

> "O Śāriputra, all dharmas are marked with emptiness;
> They do not appear or disappear,
> Are neither tainted nor pure,
> Do not increase or decrease."

First I will discuss the philosophical aspects of this passage and then its practical meaning. This passage is very important to Mahāyāna

Buddhism. If we read it superficially, we might think there is something that neither appears nor disappears, is neither tainted nor pure, and neither increases nor decreases. We might think that this passage refers to something that exists beyond the phenomena we see. We think the purpose of our practice is to realize this something beyond phenomena. But this is not Buddhism. There is nothing beyond this phenomenal world in which things are always changing, appearing and disappearing. There is nothing that never appears or disappears. That is the Buddha's teaching.

What does this mean? To understand these lines I think it's helpful to look at Nāgārjuna's dedicating verse in the *Mūlamadhyamakakārikā*. Here he elaborated and refined the philosophy of emptiness. At the very beginning of this piece he wrote:

> I pay homage to the Fully Awakened One,
> the supreme teacher who has taught
> the doctrine of relational origination,
> the blissful cessation of all phenomenal thought
> constructions.
> (Therein, every event is "marked" by):
> non-origination, non-extinction,
> non-destruction, non-permanence,
> non-identity, non-differentiation,
> non-coming (into being), non-going (out-of-being).[81]

The fully awakened one, the supreme teacher, refers to Shakyamuni Buddha. "Buddha" literally means "awakened one." Relational origination, we've seen, is the same as interdependent origination. It means nothing exists independently, but only in relationship with other things, causes, and conditions. Nothing has substance, self-nature, or independent being. Everything is impermanent, egoless, and always changing. These teachings of Buddha are the same in early Buddhism and Mahāyāna Buddhism.

"Thought constructions" means idle discussion or argument about metaphysical philosophy, the meaning of life, or of this world. The teaching of relational origination, according to Nāgārjuna, puts an end to all idle arguments. "Non-origination" has the same meaning as "not appear" (*fushō*) in Chinese. "Non-extinction" is the same as "not disappear" or, for human beings, birth and death. Nothing can be destroyed and nothing is permanent. Nāgārjuna lists five pairs of dichotomies: birth and death, one and many, identity and differentiation, coming and going, delusion and enlightenment. We could add any dichotomy to the list, and Nāgārjuna would put a "no" in front of it.

This is because we can only think about one side of things. When we think about something we take a point of the view. We form an opinion. We think, "This exists," or "This doesn't exist." We may think, "I am deluded" or "I am enlightened" or "There must be something eternal" or "There is nothing eternal." These are opinions. To form our way of thinking we have to take a side. We cannot function in society without a point of view. If we adopt different points of view at the same time, we are seen as inconsistent and untrustworthy. But according to Nāgārjuna these are all phenomenal thought constructions, idle or meaningless arguments. Whichever side you take it's only a half of reality. Reality is there before taking a view.

According to Nāgārjuna things do not appear or disappear, are neither tainted nor pure, do not increase or decrease. This means we should not think that these things appear at a certain time in the past and stay in this moment and then disappear sometime in the future. For instance, I was born on June 22, 1948. Before that day I didn't exist. On that day I started to exist. I will exist for a certain period of time and then I will disappear. This is a very common way of thinking. It's not a mistake on a conceptual level. But in reality if we look closely at this being, there is nothing that can be called Shohaku. I am no more than a collection of five skandhas, different elements.

This body and mind is like a waterfall. A river flows past a place where there is a change of height, and a waterfall is formed. Yet there is no such thing as a waterfall, only a continuous flow of water. A waterfall is not a thing but rather a name for a process of happening. This body and mind is like a waterfall. We cannot distinguish where the waterfall starts and ends because it is a continuous process. Since there is no "I," no substance called Shohaku Okumura, I cannot say "I" will disappear. This is the meaning of "do not appear or disappear." It refers to this body and mind and to all beings. It is not about mysterious beings beyond the phenomenal world. This is very clear, ordinary reality, and yet we cannot define it, so it is strange and wondrous. We see things happening every moment, and yet we cannot grasp them. That is the meaning of wondrous dharma. We cannot grasp it, and yet it is not mysterious. It is ordinary things happening every day. For instance, this is a book, this is a desk, this is my robe, and this is Shohaku Okumura. These are like definitions we can find in the dictionary. We think these things exist in a fixed way because they are defined in the dictionary, but it's not true.

In another part of *Mūlamadhyamakakārikā* Nāgārjuna says, "Those of low intelligence [i.e., inferior insight], who see only the existence and nonexistence of things, cannot perceive the wonderful quiescence of things."[82] By "low intelligence people" he means people who lack wisdom. Existence and nonexistence is the same kind of dichotomy he referred to in the dedicatory verse and in the *Heart Sutra*. This is our usual way of thinking: good or bad, right or wrong, rich or poor. But wonderful quiescence is the reality of all beings before being processed by our conceptual thinking.

Pingala, a late third- or early fourth-century Indian scholar, wrote a commentary on *Mūlamadhyamakakārikā*. We know nothing about who Pingala was, but Kumārajīva translated Nāgārjuna's *Mūlamadhyamakakārikā* together with Pingala's commentary and gave it the title "Zhonglun" (Jap., Chūron, The Thesis of the Middle). In it he says, "When people have not yet attained the way, they don't see the true form of all beings. Because of causes and conditions of attachment to their own limited views, they engage in various meaningless arguments."[83] Our views are always shaped and limited by our experiences, and we are very attached to them. For example, if we have an experience with someone that leads us to believe this person is not honest or trustworthy, we make a judgment and decide this is not a good person. We then cling to this definition or preconception. We form stereotypes about people, countries, everything. These stereotypes are the basis of our usual way of seeing things. Nāgārjuna believed that these phenomenal thought constructions were the basis for meaningless arguments.

Pingala continues, "When they see something appear they call it 'being' and take it as existence. When they see something disappear they think it perishes and call it nonexistence." When we encounter something we form a view, idea, or conception. This is our usual way of life. It is not a matter of good or bad, but rather the way we are. So it follows that "When a wise person sees something appear, he extinguishes the view of nonexistence. When a wise person sees something disappear he extinguishes the view of existence." We usually form a view when we experience something. But Pingala says that when a wise person meets someone or experiences something he extinguishes, or lets go of, his preconceptions. So each encounter becomes an opportunity to transform our preexisting ideas and to set aside our biases and preconceptions. Each experience becomes an opportunity to see a fresh new world. This is an important point. The difference between ordinary and wise is not a difference in the quality of a person's intelligence. It's a difference in the attitude with which they meet things in their daily lives. We form ideas that become fixed as the basis of our identity. This identity, this way of thinking or system of values, becomes a limitation and we are imprisoned by it. It's difficult to open our perception again because it becomes very stiff, and we become very stubborn. To be a wise person, according to this commentary, we must negate, break, or open up our premade system of values every time we experience something. This is not something mysterious. It's very clear.

"Therefore, although a wise person sees all beings, the person sees them as phantoms or dreams," says Pingala. Ordinary beings and wise people see things in the same way, but their attitude is different. Nothing is fixed. No one is necessarily a bad person (always bad) or a good one (always good). There is no fixed nature because we are always changing. In a sense, each time we meet a person, we meet a different person. Because I am changing, and the other person is also changing, we can appreciate each meeting as a fresh new one.

An important phrase that conveys the spirit of having tea together in the tea ceremony is "Ichi go ichi ye." The phrase *ichi go* means "one time," "one occasion," or "one life." *Ichi ye* means "one meeting." Each meeting or encounter happens only once. We cannot meet with the same person twice. Each meeting, each moment, is very significant and precious because it is unique. To see things as phantoms or dreams doesn't mean they are not important. Because reality is like a phantom or dream, we have to appreciate it. Since everything is changing, since nothing stays forever, this is the only time we can meet. We have to savor each moment.

Pingala says, "A wise person extinguishes even a view of the undefiled way." "Undefiled way" refers to the Buddha's teaching. A wise person extinguishes, negates, and goes beyond any view, opinion, or understanding of the Buddha's teaching. This point is crucial to an understanding of the next part of the *Heart Sutra*, which appears to negate almost all of the Buddha's teaching. To negate means to free oneself from any view, even a Buddhist one. If we take the Buddha's teaching as an opinion or view, it's no different from the preconceptions we have about other things. In Buddhism it's said that ordinary people are bound by iron chains. If we liberate ourselves from these iron chains, we are still bound by the gold chain of Buddhism. We are still not free. We have to become free even of the Buddha's teaching, even of enlightenment. That is the Buddha's teaching.

This is the reason Dōgen Zenji says we shouldn't seek after enlightenment. In "Fukanzazengi" (Universal Recommendation of Zazen) he says that when we sit, we should give up even our aspiration to become a buddha. This is important. It's not a matter of delusion or enlightenment but attitude. It's a matter of whether we are caught by our desires, expectations, and fixed ideas. To become free from these things is our zazen. To extinguish our views is to let go of thought.

Pingala's conclusion is that "unless one sees the Buddha's peaceful dharma by extinguishing views, we see being and nonbeing." The Buddha's peaceful dharma is reality itself free of all dichotomies. This reality is blissful and precious. We don't usually see reality itself but only our preconceptions: things we like or dislike, something useful or useless, something desirable or undesirable. We divide reality into categories, running after things we desire and trying to avoid those we detest. Our life becomes a matter of chasing and escaping. That is our usual way of life. In this kind of life there is no stable foundation, no peace, because we are always escaping from or chasing after something. There's no time to rest, to just calm down and be right here. Letting go of thought in zazen for ten minutes or for a day or for five days is very precious. The blissful dharma, true reality, is revealed when we let go and become free from our fixed views. When the *Prajñāpāramitā Sutra* says things do not appear or disappear, are neither tainted nor pure, do not increase or decrease, the sutra doesn't refer to things outside us. It means that when we refrain from viewing and judging things in dualistic ways, our attitudes toward external things are transformed. The relation between things inside of us and our perception of the world is changed. The perceptions of the external things cease to be the objects of our desires and self-centered views. We are released from the habitual association between subject and object. Then things begin to reveal themselves as they are. When our attitude toward each thing in the world is shifted as Pingala described, our way of life is transformed. The *Heart Sutra* does not say that there is something mysterious which neither appears nor disappears, is neither tainted nor pure, neither increases nor decreases.

My teacher, Uchiyama Roshi, wrote a poem about life and death when he was about seventy years old and very sick. For fifty years he had tuberculosis. He'd been living with sickness almost all of his life. Several times a year he bled from his lung. He was facing death. He felt that was his practice. Facing life and death is the most important challenge for the Buddhist practitioner. This is one of his poems.

Samādhi of the Treasure of Radiant Light

Though poor, never poor.
Though sick, never sick.
Though aging, never aging.
Though dying, never dying.
Reality prior to division.
Herein lies unlimited depth.

Radiant light is a metaphor or symbol of the Buddha's life. Uchiyama Roshi was poor. He never worked just to earn money. He contrasts dichotomies—life and death, poverty and wealth, sickness and health—with the unlimited depth of reality prior to division. Our practice is to deepen our understanding and experience. This is what we do in zazen by letting go of thought. Our sitting practice is the practice of prajñā-pāramitā, which enables us to actually transform our way of life. If our lives are based on dichotomies like good and bad, we chase after good things and run from bad things. We are concerned about whether we are good or not. If we think we are good, then life is worth living. If we think we are bad, then life is just a mistake. This dualistic thinking makes our life rigid and narrow.

No matter what mistakes we make, we can start over because everything is impermanent. We can change. We can change the direction of our life. That is the way we transform our life, our thinking, and our views. According to Dōgen Zenji, sitting in zazen and letting go of everything is the key to shifting the basis of our life. By sitting and letting go we become free, even from the Buddha's doctrine. We are not deluded, and we are not enlightened. So we just keep practicing. That is the meaning of shikantaza, or just sitting. If you feel good or enlightened in certain conditions, and you cling to this experience, you are deluded. You are already stagnating in enlightenment. So we open our hands and keep practicing. This is the meaning of just sitting, of continuous practice. There is no one who is deluded or enlightened.

Sitting is itself enlightenment. This is why Dōgen Zenji said that we need to arouse bodhi-mind, moment by moment, billions of times.

Emptiness in Practice

> "O Śāriputra, all dharmas are marked with emptiness;
> They do not appear or disappear,
> Are neither tainted nor pure,
> Do not increase or decrease."

This paragraph was discussed above in relation to Nāgārjuna's sayings in *Mūlamadhyamakakārikā*. It refers not to something outside ourselves but rather to the way we see things, the way we grasp things using our intellect. Nāgārjuna says that our usual way of seeing and thinking is based on mental formations or thought constructions that he describes as meaningless argument. This is an important point in Mahāyāna philosophy that is difficult to understand. I will discuss it from the perspective of my own experience.

Buddhist teachers from Shakyamuni Buddha to Nāgārjuna to Dōgen Zenji address the reality of our life, the true form of all beings. The problem is that when we think about this reality, when we try to grasp it, we lose it. We live inside reality. We are never apart from it, and yet we almost always lose sight of it. To discuss something we have to take a particular point of view. This is the problem.

A long time ago I read a book on logic that included many famous paradoxes. One of the most interesting was a story about a king who told his retainers that no liars should be allowed into his kingdom. He built a barrier at the border. The guard asked everyone who wanted to enter the kingdom whether he was a liar or an honest person. Since everyone wanted to get into the country, they all said they were not liars, except for one who admitted, "I am a liar." The guard didn't know what to do. If this person really was a liar, then his statement was true; he was telling the truth and therefore he was not a liar. If he was not a liar, his statement was false, which meant he was a liar. Either way there could be no conclusion. Our usual way of thought presents a similar paradox. It doesn't really fit reality, so we often make poor decisions.

This story is an example of emptiness. Before we decide whether someone is a liar or an honest person, we have to define these terms. A liar is a person who tells lies, of course, and yet this is not enough. A liar is a person who *always* lies, and an honest person *always* tells the truth. This is the basic definition of a liar and an honest person. When we use these definitions, we should be consistent. A liar always lies. If a liar tells the truth, "liar" doesn't apply. But in reality there is no one who always tells lies. We tell lies to deceive other people but if we speak only lies, we cannot deceive anyone. If someone always lies, I'll know that the opposite of what he says is true. In fact, there is no one so honest he never tells a lie. If we think someone is weird, we don't say, "You are weird." We might say instead, "You are unique." No one speaks only lies or only the truth.

In reality there are no liars and no completely honest people. Thinking based on such definitions is an example of a thought construction, or meaningless argument. Such thinking misses the reality that we all lie to some degree. And yet there are some really honest people, and there are some liars. As Buddhists, we have to try to avoid lying because it is one of our precepts. If we interpret the precept of not lying with strict logic, we cannot be Buddhists. We can never completely follow the Buddha's precept. So we have to inquire deeply into reality. This is not a matter of pure logic but of our attitude. This is our way of life, the Buddha's truth, and the true form of human beings. In Buddhism the true form of all beings, the reality of our lives, is not based on simple logic. The wisdom of seeing emptiness is to see both sides. There are no liars and no honest people, and yet we try to avoid lying. There are two sides, and to see things from both is prajñā.

Our thoughts, values, and attitudes are based on our work, education, and experiences. We must have some yardstick to live in society. But this yardstick is not absolute. I was born in Japan and grew up in Japanese society and cannot be completely free of a Japanese way of thinking and behaving. I don't think that I have to become American, or that you should become Japanese. We have to understand that neither the American nor the Japanese way of thought is absolutely right. There is another way of thinking, of acting, of valuing things. It is the way of letting go of thought.

This is what we do in our zazen. We become flexible. We have to let go of our evaluations and discriminations, or we cannot really connect with people from other traditions or cultures. In the past there were separate cultures that didn't meet on a daily basis. Our modern world is becoming one society. Here in the United States many different kinds of people live together. If we hold on to our yardsticks and negate other people's ways of doing things, we will fight. We will feel that we have to eliminate those who don't agree with us. But when we let go of our way of thinking and become even a little bit free of our yardsticks, we have room to accept other ways of thinking. Our lives become broader and richer.

The United States is the only foreign country I have lived in so far. Japan and America are special countries for me. My ideas about America have changed many times. I was born three years after World War II. My first memory of America is when I was about four or five years old and was told that my family lost all its wealth when the Americans bombed Osaka in March 1945. My family had lived in the center of Osaka for three hundred years, and they had accumulated some wealth. In one night we lost everything. I remember the only thing we had after the bombing was a statue of the Buddha, quite a large one for a lay family to own. I heard that my family had a shrine for this statue. I never saw it, but it must have been a large building. I also knew that my uncle was killed during the war. In my mind these memories created anger, hatred, and fear. In elementary school I heard that Japan was very poor and survived only because of help from America. America was a very prosperous country, while ours was very poor. America seemed like paradise, and we hoped to follow the American way. I then had two completely different, almost opposite views of America. America became something very positive, something we had to study as an ideal of democracy, science, technology, and materialistic consumer culture.

My generation studied the American way of life, production, and system of values. Japan became much too American, almost more American than America. When I was a high school student during the Vietnam War, the Japanese mass media presented American imperialism as the enemy of humanity. This was another completely different idea. Later, when I studied history, I learned that the Japanese army did terrible things in China, Korea, Taiwan, and other Asian countries during World War II. My understanding deepened. Anger, hatred, and fear turned into a kind of sadness about humanity. All human beings have the same problems. America, Japan, all nations, and all individuals have the potential to do terrible things. To see things from different points of view is good. Finally I came to America to live in 1975. I lived in Massachusetts for about five years and experienced the American way of life. I found that there are many kind people and some who are not so kind, just as in Japan. People smile, laugh, cry, and scream the same ways in Japan and America. I think there is no big difference.

To deepen our understanding we must negate our concepts. When we negate our beliefs and preconceptions we can see things from other points of view or a wider perspective. We should try to avoid grasping with our ready-made preconceptions or prejudices. If we open our hands and perceive things carefully, closely, then we can see other perspectives. This is opening the hand of thought. This is what we do in our zazen.

This practice of letting go of thought enables us to see people and things with fresh eyes. Right now we have many flowers outside. When we see them we think they are beautiful. But when we look closely at a flower, it's more than beautiful, it's something really wondrous. Why is this flower so beautiful? Why does this flower bloom like this? Why is it that I can appreciate this beauty? There is surprise when we encounter things with fresh eyes. When we see the flower without thinking "This is beautiful" or "What is this flower called?" we really meet the flower itself. When we see the flower without thinking, we find that our life, this body and mind, and the life of the flower are the same life. There's no separation. We can say, "I am blooming there as a flower." To extinguish our views, to let go of thought, or to negate our own way of thinking is not negative. It makes our life very vivid and dynamic.

To return to the passage:

> "O Śāriputra, all dharmas are marked with emptiness;
> They do not appear or disappear,
> Are neither tainted nor pure,
> Do not increase or decrease."

If we read this carelessly, we may think dharma is somehow beyond appearance and disappearance, beyond taint and purity, or increase and decrease. We might assume there is something formless beyond phenomena. But the passage shouldn't be understood in this way. For example, this bookstand was made in the past by someone using pieces of wood and today it exists as a bookstand. Someday it will break and disappear. This is a temporal form, a phenomenon. When we hear "since all dharmas are marked with emptiness, they do not appear or disappear," we might imagine there is "something" beyond the phenomenon, in this case, the bookstand. We might believe this something is a noumenon which does not either appear or disappear, something that is permanent. We imagine this something beyond form is the true nature of this tentative phenomenon, and that to see this true nature of emptiness is enlightenment. In other words, we think emptiness is separate from form. This is not what is meant by the *Heart Sutra*. Emptiness is simply how form is. This bookstand is itself emptiness. We should not seek emptiness beyond this concrete bookstand.

"Neither tainted nor pure, do not increase or decrease" should be understood in the same way. This bookstand is neither tainted nor pure. We should not think that there is something neither tainted nor pure that exists beyond this bookstand. Some people think that enlightenment is to see and become one with something formless and permanent beyond concrete things which have form and are impermanent. But the *Heart Sutra* says, "Form is emptiness, emptiness is form." We should not look for emptiness beyond form. There is nothing beyond phenomena. Phenomena are emptiness.

In "Genjōkōan," Dōgen Zenji says, "Conveying oneself toward all things to carry out practice-enlightenment is delusion. All things coming and carrying out practice-enlightenment through the self is realization."[84] Delusion and enlightenment depend on the relationship between ourselves and other beings. We cannot say this individual person is either enlightened or deluded because there is no person without relationship to others. Practice-enlightenment is not some mysterious experience. It is as clear and obvious as everyday reality.

"Genjōkōan" continues, "When the Dharma has not yet fully penetrated body and mind, one thinks one is already filled with it. When the Dharma fills body and mind, one thinks something is [still] lacking."[85] When we are not filled completely with Dharma we grasp our self as the center of the world. We think this self is an absolute person who can see things objectively and understand them as they are. This belief occupies some part of our being, so the Dharma cannot completely permeate this body and mind. Therefore, we have to empty ourselves. Then the Dharma suffuses us and starts to fill the Dharma itself. When the Dharma completely pervades this body and mind, we feel something is lacking. Our way of thinking, our yardstick, is not complete or absolute, so we feel inadequate. We search more deeply. This is prajñā, to become free from our own yardstick and see things from a broader or deeper perspective. This is the wisdom that sees emptiness. There is nothing we can hold on to, nothing we can grasp. We open our hearts.

Dōgen Zenji used an analogy: "For example, when we sail a boat into the ocean beyond sight of land and our eyes scan [the horizon in] the four directions, it simply looks like a circle. No other shape appears. This great ocean, however, is neither round nor square. It has inexhaustible characteristics. [To a fish] it looks like a palace; [to a heavenly being] a jeweled necklace. [To us] as far as our eyes can see, it looks like a circle. All the myriad things are like this. Within the dusty world and beyond, there are innumerable aspects and characteristics; we only see or grasp as far as the power of our eye of study and practice can see.

When we listen to the reality of myriad things, we must know that there are inexhaustible characteristics in both ocean and mountains, and there are many other worlds in the four directions."[86]

The ocean is not merely round. It has many other characteristics and aspects. In Buddhism it is said that the heavenly beings see water as jewels. There are many ways to perceive a single thing. The ocean is just one example of the myriad things we encounter in our lives. All people and things exist in ways other than how we see them. The phrase Dōgen Zenji uses is *san gaku gen riki*, meaning the power of the eye attained through practice. We develop the ability to see things clearly, closely, and deeply through the practice of letting go of thought. In Dōgen Zenji's writing, practice means zazen.

This is a very concrete description of emptiness in our practice. According to Dōgen Zenji our practice of zazen is the practice of prajñā that sees emptiness. Empty means ungraspable. We open our hand and see things from other perspectives by letting go of our own personal yardsticks. The Mahāyāna Buddhists who wrote the *Prajñāpāramitā Sutras* considered the *Heart Sutra* to be a sutra of transformation of the self. This is the way we transform ourselves, transform our way of life, enabling us to be flexible and see things without attachment. It is not mere insight or wisdom but rather a practice. Practice in the form of zazen is the foundation of our life. But since we cannot sit twenty-four hours a day, we have to learn how to encounter all things in our daily lives. We have to learn about the self, about our body and mind. We have to practice together with others. To live and practice together with all beings is the bodhisattva Way. This practice enriches our lives.

Dongshan's Nose

"Therefore in emptiness, no form,
No feelings, no perceptions, no impulses, no consciousness;
No eyes, no ears, no nose, no tongue, no body, no mind;
No color, no sound, no smell, no taste, no touch, no object
of mind;

> No realm of eyes and so forth until no realm of mind consciousness."

This is one of the most popular parts of the *Heart Sutra*. It says there is nothing. I started to study Buddhism when I entered Komazawa University. The first thing we had to do was to memorize the dharma numbers. For instance, there are the five skandhas: form, sensation, perception, impulse, and consciousness (in Japanese, *shiki ju sō gyō shiki*). Also, there are six sense organs—eyes, ears, nose, tongue, body, and mind. The eye senses shape and color; the ear hears sound; the nose smells; the tongue tastes; with our skin we touch. Each of these six sense organs has sense objects, and these two sets of six are called the twelve sense fields.

When sense organs encounter objects, something happens within our mind. These interactions are called the six consciousnesses, *roku shiki*. The sutra uses the word "realm." For instance, the realm of the eyes is eye-consciousness, or *genshiki*. I think "realm" is not a good word here. The word used is *dhātu*, which in this case means element, not realm. When the eye encounters shape or color, eye-consciousness arises but initially no judgment is made. It's just a sensation, which then becomes a perception. Impulse or formation is a process of making definitions, conceptions, and judgments, which finally become consciousness. Each sense organ and object gives rise to a corresponding consciousness. These are called the eighteen dhātu, the eighteen elements of our lives. So there are five skandhas, twelve sense fields, and eighteen dhātu.

In the next sentence the *Heart Sutra* says, "No ignorance and also no extinction of it, and so forth until no old age and death and also no extinction of them." These are the twelve links of causation. "Ignorance" is the first link, "old age and death" is the twelfth, and the phrase "and so forth until" simply means that all the intervening links are likewise negated. Next, "No suffering, no origination, no stopping, no path." This refers to the four noble truths.

These dharma numbers were the first things I learned when I began studying Buddhist teachings at the age of nineteen. But the *Heart Sutra* seemed to contradict what I had learned. It said there are no such things. I was surprised and confused. What did this mean? If the people who wrote the *Heart Sutra* wanted to negate the Buddha's teaching, they should have said they were not Buddhists. But they claimed to be true Buddhists. Now I realize that this was a childish opinion. If you study the history of Buddhism, especially Mahāyāna Buddhism, you see that this really is the Buddha's teaching. But as a nineteen-year-old I didn't understand at all.

Later I read the biography of a Chinese Zen master, Dongshan Liangjie (Tōzan Ryōkai). Dongshan was the founder of the Caodong (Sōtō) school in China. This is a translation from *Denkōroku* (*The Record of Transmitting the Light*) by Keizan Jōkin.

> While still young, [Dongshan] read the *Heart Sutra* with a teacher. When he reached the place where it said, "There is no eye, ear, nose, tongue, body, or mind," he suddenly felt his face with his hand. He asked his teacher, "I have eyes, ears, nose, tongue, and the rest. Why does the scripture say that they do not exist?"[87]

That was Dongshan's original question. His biography says that Dongshan's first teacher was amazed by his question and knew immediately that he was an unusual person. The teacher knew he couldn't be this boy's teacher and sent him to a better instructor. I was happy to know that Dongshan had the same question that I did. It's true we have a nose, eyes, and so forth. Why does the *Heart Sutra* say we have no such things? This is a very simple, childish question, but if you don't understand this point the *Heart Sutra* is incomprehensible.

The longer version of the *Heart Sutra* I introduced above begins:

> At that time also the Holy Lord Avalokita, the Bodhisattva, the great being, coursed in the course of the deep perfection of wisdom; he looked down from on high, and he saw

the five skandhas, and he surveyed them as empty in their own-being.[88]

So the five skandhas exist. Avalokiteśvara saw them. But he didn't see the self or ego. In our everyday lives we think, "I have a body and mind." But what is this "I"? Where is this "I" that thinks it is the owner and operator of this body and mind? Avalokiteśvara saw that there is no "I," only the five skandhas. When the *Heart Sutra* says Avalokiteśvara saw only the five skandhas it means there is no ego, no "I," no self. Only the body and the functions of mind exist.

The *Heart Sutra* also said that Avalokiteśvara saw that the five skandhas are empty. To understand this statement we have to understand something about the history of Buddhism. Three or four hundred years passed between the life of Shakyamuni Buddha and the beginning of Mahāyāna. During this period Buddhist monks studied Buddhist philosophy and established the system called Abhidharma. In Abhidharma philosophy there is no ego, no "I," only the five skandhas and the other elements. There are several ways to categorize these elements. One way is into twelve sense fields, another is into eighteen dhātu. The system of Abhidharma philosophy established in the school known as Sarvāstivādin categorizes dharma into seventy-five elements. As a student of Buddhism, I had to memorize this system. There is another system called Yogācāra that analyzes the dharma into one hundred elements. I tried to memorize them all, with their definitions. Traditionally that's how we studied Buddhist philosophy in Japan.

In the Abhidharma philosophy there is no ego, no substance. Only the dharmas or elements exist, and they never change. The ego or self is just a collection of elements. Abhidharma philosophers believed that the seventy-five dharmas, which cannot be further divided, have existed in the past, exist in the present, and will exist in the future. In the *Heart Sutra* or *Prajñāpāramitā Sutra*, Mahāyāna Buddhists said that even those elements are empty. That is a philosophical way of understanding this passage. There are no eyes because eyes are empty. The objects of eyes, such as color and shape, are empty. Empty means they cannot be grasped. There is no self-being or self-nature, so we cannot grasp the self.

For instance, we think there is something in front of our eyes when we see a notebook. But our eyes are limited. We can see light waves only between ultraviolet and infrared lengths. This is a small part of the spectrum, but other animals can see a broader range. To them this world looks totally different. Our ears can hear only sounds of certain frequencies; dogs hear higher ones. What we think is quiet could be very noisy for dogs. What we see and hear really depends on our capabilities. We believe that what we see exists just the way we see it, but this is an illusion.

Our picture of the world is our reality, but we should understand that it is distorted. This is the meaning of emptiness. Our mind is emptiness. Our sense organs are emptiness. Things outside us are also emptiness. Everything is just illusion. The fact that we live with illusion is our reality. When we really understand this and see how illusion is caused, we can see reality through the illusion. Whatever we see, whatever we grasp with our sense organs and consciousness, is illusion. When we see this we are released from attachment to our limited view, to what we have, to what we think we own. We may not become completely free, but we become less restricted by our limitations.

In our zazen we sit in an upright posture and breathe quietly, smoothly, and deeply into our abdomen. We let go of whatever comes up in our mind. In front of our eyes is nothing but a white wall. This letting go of thought means to become free from what we are grasping, from the objects to which we attach ourselves. This letting go is prajñā or wisdom. It means to become free of our picture of the world caused by our karma. In this way our view becomes a bit broader and deeper. We keep practicing this zazen, sitting and letting go of thought, trying to see things in the most flexible way. This doesn't mean we negate our delusions. We can never negate them; they are our life. But so long as we fail to see that they are illusory and grasp them as reality, we cannot be free. When we really see the emptiness of subject and object, we can be free from grasping, clinging, and greed.

Dōgen Zenji described zazen as *shin jin datsuraku*, or dropping off body and mind. He recorded his conversation with his teacher, the Zen master Rujing (Nyojō), about *shin jin datsuraku* since it was originally Rujing's expression. Rujing explained that "dropping off body and mind" means to become free from the five desires caused by the five objects (eyes, ears, nose, tongue, and body)—he didn't mention mind.

When the five senses encounter an object, desire arises to grasp or hate it. We think, "I want this," "I don't like this," or "I don't care." These are all desires caused by an object contacted through the five sense organs. We are like kids. We see something good, something attractive, and we want it. We try to grasp it. When I go to the supermarket with my kids they run to the toys and take whatever they want and just put it in the cart. When I try to take it back to the shelf, they scream. They are very honest.

We are not so honest. We pretend that we are not attached to things, but deep in our hearts we cling to what we encounter. We are still childish. We cling not to toys but to wealth, reputation, or to very subtle things in our minds. We want to get these things. Sawaki Roshi called this grasping our thief-nature. We also have buddha-nature. All human beings have both buddha-nature and thief-nature. Depending on our actions, we become a thief or a buddha. When we let go of thought and become free from the five desires, we are buddhas.

We must see the emptiness of the subject, of things outside us, of our sense organs, our minds, and the delusions or desires caused by the encounter between the sense organs and objects. When we really truly see the emptiness of all this, we become free from the five desires. We don't get rid of delusion or illusion, but we understand that illusion is illusion and delusion is delusion. We see that we don't have to satisfy all our desires.

Even if we are dissatisfied, that's okay. Just let it go. We can still live. We don't need to satisfy all our desires. We think that when all our desires are satisfied we will be happy, but if not, we can still be happy if we feel oneness with other people and other beings. Other people's happiness then becomes my happiness, other people's pleasure my pleasure, other people's sadness my sadness. Together we can feel a synthesis called in Japanese *hōraku*, joy or delight in the Dharma. It is not a pleasure caused by fulfillment of our individual desires.

Dharma embraces the reality that we are living together with all beings. We are all connected, so there is nothing to gain and nothing to lose. Everything is coming and going in a natural circulation. But human beings create fences or walls between themselves. We calculate how much we gain for our side and how much we lose. When income is greater than expenses, we feel happy. This is a fiction, but in human society it works. We don't need to break or destroy these rules. They're okay. In human society each person should be independent. But in reality all beings are interdependent. Our life has two layers.

We usually see only the surface, where we appear independent. We should keep our record of income and expenses. That's all right. But if we see only this level, our life is no more than a calculation of how much we acquire, how much we lose, and whether we get more or less than others. On a deeper level we are all living together. There are no walls that separate us from other beings. This is seeing emptiness, no separation. The wall is a useful illusion in human society, so we shouldn't negate or destroy it. Still, we should see that this barrier is just a useful fiction, a means to live together with other people. I think this is a practical definition of seeing emptiness.

In his "Maka Hannya Haramitsu" (Mahā Prajñā Pāramitā) commentary on the *Heart Sutra*, Dōgen Zenji quotes his teacher Rujing's poem about a wind bell hung in a Japanese or Chinese temple. I included it in chapter 5, but here it is again:

> The whole body is like a mouth hanging in empty space.
> Not questioning the winds from east, west, south, or north,
> Equally with all of them, speaking of prajñā:
> Ding-dong-a-ling ding-dong.[89]

This whole body of the wind bell is ourselves. The winds come from all directions, yet the wind bell never discriminates among them. There are many kinds of wind. Spring brings pleasant breezes. In winter a cold north wind blows. In summer the wind is hot. Wind has a different meaning in each situation, each season. All different kinds of wind come to the wind bell, yet the wind bell never discriminates. It abides "Equally with all of them, speaking of prajñā." The wind bell expresses the prajñā or wisdom that sees the reality of our life. The empty wind bell is hanging in emptiness. When wind comes it makes sound that is prajñā. The last line of the poem, "Ding dong a ling ding dong," is the sound of the bell. This is our practice of zazen. We are empty, but when we encounter others we make a sound that is prajñā. Together with all beings we express prajñā. This poem is an expression of the reality of our zazen and our lives.

No Buddhism

> "No ignorance and also no extinction of it, and so forth until
> no old age and death and also no extinction of them;
> No suffering, no origination, no stopping, no path."

As we saw above, these lines refer to the twelve links of dependent origination, the four noble truths, and the eightfold noble path. Dependent origination is one of the essential teachings of the Buddha. It can be expressed as follows:

> All things arise from a cause.
> He who has realized the truth has explained the cause,
> And also how they cease to be:
> This is what the great samana has taught.[90]

The twelve links of dependent origination are the final and most complete form of the teaching of dependent origination. This teaching does not refer to objective beings in the phenomenal world around us, but rather to the causes and extinction of suffering in our lives. In early Buddhism, it is called dependent origination, but in Mahāyāna Buddhism after Nāgārjuna, it is called interdependent origination. This is for a reason. In the early Buddhist teachings cause and result flow in one direction only. Ignorance is the cause of action, action is the cause of consciousness, and birth is the cause of old age and death. Old age and death depend on birth, but birth does not depend on old age and death. In Nāgārjuna's and other Mahāyāna teachings, however, all things are interdependent on each other.

This teaching does not refer to the objective beings in the phenomenal world around us but rather to the causes of suffering in our own lives and the extinction of them. In the *Heart Sutra* only the first cause (ignorance) and the last condition (old age and death) are mentioned. The other ten causes and conditions are referred to by the words "and so forth until," as we saw above. The phrase "No ignorance and so forth until no old-age and death" is therefore a negation of all twelve causes and conditions. They are listed in an order that parallels transmigration through samsara. The sutra also negates the extinction of all twelve causes from ignorance to old age and death, a progression that parallels movement toward nirvana. In one phrase, "No suffering, no origination, no stopping, no path," the *Heart Sutra* denies the causes and conditions of both samsara and nirvana!

The *Heart Sutra* thus appears to deny the core of the Buddha's teaching. This negation of Buddhism points beyond Buddhism. In other words, Buddhism negating Buddhism is still Buddhism. The *Heart Sutra* says that to truly live the Buddha's teaching, we must negate it. A true student of the Buddha must go beyond the study of his teachings as recorded in the scriptures. When we directly see and experience the Buddha's truth in our own lives, his teachings and the scriptures are irrelevant. The truth becomes a vivid reality. Seeing the reality of our lives with our own eyes through our practice is the wisdom that sees emptiness. This is the wisdom that is called prajñā. This is why prajñā is called the mother of buddhas.

What did the Buddha teach with the twelve links of dependent origination and the four noble truths? Why does the *Heart Sutra* negate all of them? We will start with the four noble truths. The first truth is that everything in samsara is suffering. Suffering (Skt., *duḥkha*) is categorized into eight kinds. The first four are birth, aging, sickness, and death. The fifth is the suffering we feel when we meet someone we don't like. The sixth is what we feel when we are separated from people we like. The seventh results when we can't get what we want. These don't need explanation because we all experience them often in our daily lives. The last kind of suffering is a result of the fact that our life, a collection of the five skandhas, is itself suffering. This is different from the usual sorts of suffering which are the opposites of pleasure, joy, and happiness. It occurs because we can never make the world completely conform to our desires. Because of continually changing causes and conditions, the world around us must change. These constant changes in the world and our lives are not designed to fulfill our desires. Reality is impermanent and egoless, but we are blind to this and strive to satisfy our egocentric desires. Often reality doesn't cooperate with our plans. We cannot really control even our own bodies and minds. Even if we are very lucky and successful, eventually we die and lose everything. This is simple reality.

The second truth is that the basic cause of suffering is desire or "thirst" (Skt., *tṛṣṇā*). It's as if we are thirsty and looking for water. There is always a feeling that something is lacking, and we try to fill that emptiness. We believe that if we get the right thing, we will be satisfied. We constantly search for and run after the things we desire. There is no end to our desires. Even when they are temporarily fulfilled, we suffer because we are afraid of losing what we have. The Buddha's teaching doesn't make sense until we realize that this constant search for satisfaction is itself suffering. When we see that a life spent in pursuit of something better is empty and meaningless, we begin to seek a spiritual path; we begin to practice.

For those who have begun this search, the Buddha taught a third truth—the cessation of suffering. We can live without being pulled about by egocentric desires. How? The fourth truth is the path that leads to cessation of suffering, or nirvana. It is called the eightfold noble path and consists of right view, right thinking, right speech, right action, right livelihood, right effort, right mindfulness, and right meditation.

The lessons of the four noble truths are straightforward. We spend our lives trying to fill the emptiness we feel. When we succeed we are happy and feel as if we are in heaven. When we fail we are miserable as if we are in hell. Our life is a continuous transmigration through the six realms of samsara. The Way leading to release from this suffering is the eightfold noble path.

The twelve links of dependent origination explain the first two of the four noble truths in more detail. In short, our lives become suffering because we act (create karma) based on ignorance and desires. This is the teaching of the four noble truths and the twelve links of dependent origination. Why does the *Heart Sutra* seem to negate all of them? A serious Buddhist practitioner might be offended by this. I don't think the early Mahāyāna Buddhists wrote this to insult other Buddhists. They felt they had to negate these things to sincerely practice the teachings of the Buddha.

There are two reasons for this. First, this negation is a criticism of the Buddhist monastic orders of the first century CE, when Mahāyāna Buddhism emerged. These monks believed that to eliminate ignorance and desire, they had to study and practice in quiet monasteries. In ordinary society they would encounter difficult situations that could cause anger, hatred, or competition. This could lead to transmigration through samsara. To become emancipated from ignorance and desire, monks primarily lived apart from the rest of society. They made no great effort to help laypeople who needed their spiritual guidance. To Mahāyāna Buddhists these monks who studied and practiced the Buddha's teachings only for their own liberation may seem somehow selfish because they appeared to do little for others who were seeking the Way. Mahāyāna Buddhists felt this selfish attitude contradicted the spirit of Shakyamuni Buddha's practice. Many of the Jātaka stories say Shakyamuni Buddha practiced as a bodhisattva for many lifetimes for the sake of all living beings. And the historical Shakyamuni Buddha walked all over India for forty years teaching.

Mahāyāna Buddhists referred to the monks who practiced for their own sake as *Hīnayāna* (the smaller vehicle). Mahāyāna Buddhists believed that practice for the sake of others was more important than eliminating one's own desires. The theoretical basis for this belief is the prajñā of emptiness. "No ignorance and no extinction of it" means the same as "Ignorance is emptiness and emptiness is ignorance." The latter expression is used to negate the five skandhas. Since ignorance and other causes are empty from the beginning, there is no possibility of eliminating them. We should not think of them as enemies and spend our lives trying to kill them. The bodhisattva vow to save all beings is more important. Eliminating the negative is less important than nurturing the positive. We can be free from selfish desires without fighting against them when we are trying to help others. This is a more joyful way to practice.

The second reason is more existential. If we seriously practice the four noble truths and the twelve links of dependent origination, we are faced with a self-contradiction. We begin to study and practice Buddhism when we realize that a life spent pursuing our desires is meaningless. We set forth with an aspiration to find a better way of life and achieve emancipation from the suffering of samsara. This aspiration is called bodhi-mind. When we practice with this Way-seeking mind we are confronted with a terrible contradiction. The aspiration that motivates us to find a way of life free of suffering is merely another selfish desire. We substitute a desire for emancipation or enlightenment for the desire for fame and wealth. The object of desire is different but what is happening inside us is the same. We feel dissatisfaction and are driven to find something to remedy it. Spiritual ambition may be a more sophisticated form of desire, but it's the same principle. When we seriously devote ourselves to practice this becomes a crucial question: Isn't the desire to eliminate ignorance caused by ignorance? In the practice of zazen we have to ask ourselves, "Isn't this practice like pulling the cushion on which we sit from under us?" We can't quit practice and go back to our earlier life of chasing worldly desires because now we know it's useless and hollow. We can go neither forward nor backward. We are at a dead end.

I faced this problem when I returned to Japan in 1981 from the Valley Zendo in Massachusetts. I was thirty-three years old. I had been ordained by Uchiyama Roshi when I was a university student in 1970. After graduation I had practiced with Uchiyama Roshi at Antaiji until 1975 when he retired. There our practice was focused on sitting. We sat nine periods daily for more than a year. We had a five-day sesshin each month except February and August. During sesshin we sat fourteen periods a day for five days. We had no ceremony, no chanting, and no lecture. We just sat.

In 1975 I went to Massachusetts. We bought about six acres of land to establish a small practice center in the woods of western Massachusetts. We built a house and zendo by ourselves. When I first went there the house was still incomplete. We survived the winter with a wood stove but had no electricity on the second floor. We sat and studied by the light of a kerosene lamp. For the first three years three Japanese monks from Antaiji lived there together. We sat four periods daily. We had a one-day sesshin every Sunday and a five-day sesshin each month. We cut trees, pulled out stumps, and made a green garden, all with hand tools. We dug a well with shovels. We used a huge amount of firewood for cooking and heating. Since we had no financial support from Japan, we harvested blueberries and potatoes for local farmers. Later we worked in a tofu factory to support our practice. After five years, I had pain in my neck, shoulders, elbows, and knees from the hard physical labor. I couldn't work, and sitting sesshin was very difficult. I had no health insurance or money for medical treatment. I had to return to Japan.

When I got back I was completely alone. My body was half broken. I had no money, no job, and no place to live or practice. I stayed at my brother's apartment in Osaka for several months while he traveled in the United States. Then I moved to Seitai-an, a small temple in Kyoto, where I lived as a caretaker for three years. Seitai-an is near Antaiji's original site. There I had a monthly five-day sesshin with one of my dharma brothers and cotranslator, Rev. Daitsu Tom Wright, and a few other people. I couldn't practice as I had before because of my physical condition. This was the first time I had lived and practiced alone after ten years at Antaiji and Valley Zendo. I had to give up medical treatments. Initially I did takuhatsu (begging) to raise money for them. But during takuhatsu we hang a *zudabukuro* (a bag) from our necks. This aggravated my neck injury, and my chiropractor said it wouldn't get better if I continued to do takuhatsu. It was a vicious circle. Finally I gave up both takuhatsu and the treatments. I did takuhatsu only a few times a month to survive. When I had extra income I spent it on books.

I had a hard time for several months while I was staying at my brother's apartment before moving to Seitai-an. I was bewildered and didn't know what to do. My biggest problem was that I couldn't practice as I had for the last ten years because of my physical condition. In my twenties I had committed my entire life-energy to practice. Nothing else had seemed important to me. I didn't know how to live outside that way of practice.

While in this situation I read a Japanese translation of *Buddha-carita*, a biography of the Buddha written by the famous Indian Buddhist poet Aśvaghoṣa. When describing the Buddha's experience of seeing the old, sick, and dead outside the gates of his palace, the author refers to the "arrogance of youth and health." This expression hit me. I realized that my belief that practice was the best and most meaningful way of life was nothing more than the "arrogance of youth and health." That's why I was at a loss when I could no longer practice that way because of my health. My previous practice had been an attempt to satisfy a need for status and benefit. I wanted to live a better life than ordinary people. Ever since I read Uchiyama Roshi's book as a high school student and began practicing according to Dōgen Zenji's teachings, I knew that I should not practice zazen for gain. Sawaki Roshi, Uchiyama Roshi's teacher, said that zazen is good for nothing. Dōgen Zenji says that we should practice Buddha Dharma only for the sake of Buddha Dharma, with no expectations. That is shikantaza, or just sitting. I knew all of this and thought I had been practicing with the correct attitude.

Now, when I found myself unable to continue that practice, I was perplexed and depressed. I didn't know what to do. I discovered that I had relied on a practice that was possible only for the young and healthy. I used the teachings of the Buddha, Dōgen Zenji, Sawaki Roshi, and Uchiyama Roshi to fulfill my own desires. This discovery completely broke my "arrogance of youth and health." I saw clearly that my practice had not been for the sake of Buddha Dharma but for my own self-satisfaction. I knew I couldn't continue to practice with this attitude. Nor could I stop practicing and go back to an ordinary life. I was stuck in this situation for some time.

One day something made me sit on a cushion. I had no desire, no reason, no need to sit, but found myself sitting at the apartment by myself. It was very peaceful. I didn't sit because of the Buddha's teaching. I didn't need a reason to sit; I just sat. There was no need to compete with others or with myself. Thereafter I didn't need to sit as often as I had before. I could sit just as much as my physical condition allowed. Finally I felt free of my understanding of the Buddha's teachings and my desire to be a good monk. I felt free to be myself and nothing more. I was still a deluded, ordinary human being with ignorance and desires. But when I just sat and let go of thoughts, I was—or more precisely, my zazen was—free of ignorance and selfish desires.

Even though we may understand all this intellectually, we cannot sit without hope for gain unless our "arrogance of youth and health" is completely broken. This is what Dōgen Zenji meant when he said in "Genjōkōan," "Conveying oneself toward all things to carry out practice-enlightenment is delusion. All things coming and carrying out practice-enlightenment through the self is realization."

Was my previous practice meaningless? I don't think so. In "Sesshin-sesshō" (Expounding Mind, Expounding Nature), a chapter of *Shōbōgenzō*, Dōgen Zenji wrote:

> After we arouse bodhi-mind and wholeheartedly practice the difficult practice, even though we practice, we cannot hit the mark even once out of one hundred times. And yet, we can hit the mark while we practice with our teachers and with scriptures. Hitting the mark at this present moment is enabled by the strength of the one hundred attempts which were off the mark. One hundred practices which were off the mark enable us to become mature.[91]

As we continue to practice wholeheartedly, even with a shallow understanding, we become mature enough to see our own shallowness and stupidity. As we see our shallowness, we go deeper into the dharma. To the extent that we struggle to eliminate our ignorance and desires, we are still within our karmic self based on ignorance and desire. We create an endless feud between two sides of ourselves. If we think we can become completely free from ignorance and desire as a result of an enlightenment experience, we have not yet thoroughly seen ourselves. As we awake to the reality of ourselves, we see more clearly that we are deeply deluded.

"No ignorance and also no extinction of it, and so forth until no old age and death and also no extinction of them," the *Heart Sutra* tells us. From the beginning, ignorance does not exist as a fixed entity, and yet it will never die out. This expression arises from a profound understanding of the reality of ourselves and the dharma.

And then: "No suffering, no origination, no stopping, no path." This denial of the fundamental beliefs of Buddhism is the expression of a truth that can be seen only by those who actually practice these teachings, instead of merely understanding them intellectually.

No Attainment

> "No ignorance and also no extinction of it, and so forth
> until no old age and death and also no extinction
> of them;

> No suffering, no origination, no stopping, no path;
> No cognition, no attainment."

After listing the twelve links of dependent origination and the four noble truths, the *Heart Sutra* negates each of them. It then concludes, "No cognition, no attainment." No cognition means no person. No attainment means there is nothing to attain. There is no one to realize or understand the dharma. There is no dharma or enlightenment we can attain. This is the meaning of "No cognition and no attainment."

When we start to practice we almost always have a problem. Something is bothering us. We want to find a better way of life. We feel something is lacking or not quite right. That's why Shakyamuni Buddha left his home. He was a crown prince, and yet he left his palace and became a beggar to search for the truth of life. When we start to practice or study we have the same problem. We are looking for the truth. This is good. This is called bodhi-mind or Way-seeking mind. We are seeking after the truth or reality of our life. We are trying to find the best way of living. Without this bodhi-mind, the mind that seeks the Way, we cannot practice.

Shakyamuni Buddha found that the cause of suffering, of the trouble we have in our worldly lives, is clinging or thirst. He found that thirst, clinging, greed, and hatred resulted from ignorance of the reality of our lives. This is what the Buddha discovered and what he taught. He showed us the way to become free from clinging, greed, hatred, and ignorance. He showed us the four noble truths. The Buddha's students devote themselves to this very difficult practice.

We have to see deeply inside of ourselves, both the positive and negative sides of our psyches. We have to control our desires and delusions. This is the Buddha's practice. It is called nirvana. We practice to become free of self-delusion and ego. For many hundreds of years the first Buddhists practiced in this way. But Mahāyāna Buddhists felt there was a problem with this type of practice. Our usual way of life based on delusion, likes and dislikes, is samsara. We transmigrate in the six realms from hell to heaven, always moving up and down, up and down. This is our usual way of life. We want to find a more peaceful, stable way of life. The four noble truths are the way to transform our life in samsara to a life of nirvana. And yet if we really practice in this way we discover a deep, basic contradiction. Without bodhi-mind or a desire to practice, we cannot practice. But this desire is itself a cause of suffering.

The desire for truth and the desire for fame or profit are not so different. We feel something is lacking, so we try to get it. When we are poor we want more money. We want to become famous, and we want to become free from desire. These are different goals but the inner thirst is the same. We feel emptiness and we try to fill it with something. Life in samsara is characterized by the first two noble truths: suffering and desire (the cause of suffering). The Buddha taught the third and fourth noble truths: transformation is possible through practice. We try to transform our lives from samsara to nirvana, a life based on the Buddha's teaching. This is our practice. Yet if we separate samsara and nirvana, we miss the path. If we imagine that we are here in samsara and desire to get over there to the path or the Buddha's Way, this desire or aspiration itself creates another type of samsara. It is almost impossible to become completely free from our desires, so we have to put our whole energy into practice. We have to pay attention to each of our activities. We have to examine our motives. Even when we help other people, we have some egocentricity. If we really practice hard and sincerely, we cannot ignore this egocentricity. Even in our practice, even in our good deeds, we have some delusion and self-clinging.

To the extent that we try to negate life in samsara and live in nirvana we create a deep separation. We perceive a chasm between samsara and nirvana, and no way to cross it. Mahāyāna Buddhists felt that because of emptiness, the division between samsara and nirvana is a dream. The five skandhas have no self-nature. Suffering is caused by the five skandhas, so suffering, ignorance, clinging, greed, and hatred are all delusions. They don't exist as substance. Mahāyāna Buddhists found that egocentricity itself is illusion.

There's no separation between samsara and nirvana, or between delusion and enlightenment. "No ignorance and no extinction of it" means that ignorance and extinction are both without substance. Ignorance is always there, but it's an illusion. This means there is no separation between samsara and nirvana. It's a contradiction, and yet that is our life. We have to practice life within samsara. Samsara and nirvana are one. There are no steps, no separation between our usual, ordinary, deluded, material life and an enlightened, Buddhist, sacred, holy life. We are living in a single reality, and within this one reality, many things are happening. The continuous interaction between the self and the conditions surrounding the self creates our life and our karma.

Our practice is not to escape from delusion or samsara but to practice right in the middle of them. We try to manifest nirvana within samsara. Ignorance, greed, hatred, all negative emotions, intellection, and misunderstanding exist. We want to be free of all this. But to become free of something and to eliminate it are two different things. Our bodhisattva practice is not to eliminate delusion or the three poisons of ignorance, greed, and hatred. We shouldn't negate anything. We should accept everything and try to work with it. This is how to make our world nirvana.

Our world always has the potential for both samsara and nirvana. We are responsible for what we create. It all depends on our attitude toward life. There's no objective samsara and no objective nirvana. We create our own world. Delusion never disappears. Delusion is delusion; it never exists as substance, and it never disappears. Delusion is like a movie. Different scenes appear on the screen, but they are not reality. Seeing the scenes as a movie is reality. Delusion remains delusion, and yet the fact that we are deluded, that we are living in delusion, is reality. Our brain is always producing something, perhaps a totally deluded projection or maybe a very pure, lofty, peaceful illusion of the Buddha land or enlightenment. These are all delusions or illusions. We don't need to destroy them. What we have to do is see them as illusions. This is the meaning of letting go of thought. Thought is delusion, but it is a necessary part of the reality of our lives.

When we sit we let go of all illusions, good and bad, all emotions, and all philosophical understanding. We just let them go. We just open our hands. This is the way we accept reality without separating it into negative or undesirable parts and positive or desirable parts. When we stop this escaping and seeking, reality is right there. We are living in reality. We never left. This is what we do in our zazen. This is the basis upon which we have to create our way of life. We must be free from the illusions that arise from both sides, samsara and nirvana, and just work right here and now.

In bodhisattva practice we try to see the reality before separation. When we see the reality of our life, we find that we are not living as an individual substance but are more like a phantom, a bubble, or a flash of lightning, as the *Diamond Sutra* says. We are phenomena caused by many different elements and factors. We live with the support of all beings. This dynamic interpenetration works constantly. Nothing exists independently. We live together in this universal movement. Our existence is movement. We have to accept this ever-changing reality as our self.

When we see this reality it's very natural to try to be kind, friendly, and helpful to others. This is the bodhisattva vow. It's not something special. This way of life arises spontaneously from a realization of the reality of our life. It's not an order from the Buddha or God. When we see this reality we cannot avoid taking the bodhisattva vow.

Mahāyāna Buddhism identifies three kinds of nirvana. In Japanese, the first is *uyo-nehan*. An example of uyo-nehan is Shakyamuni Buddha. After he became enlightened and attained nirvana he lived forty years. He still had his physical body and mind and could suffer. The second type of nirvana is *muyo-nehan*. *Muyo* means "without anything extra," specifically, without body or mind. *Muyo-nehan* means that at the moment of his death, Shakyamuni became free of his physical body. This is called *parinirvana*, or perfect nirvana.

Lastly, Mahāyāna Buddhism names a nirvana called *mujūsho-nehan* for bodhisattvas. *Mu*, again, means "no." *Jūsho* means "place to live or stay." *Mujūsho* thus means "no dwelling" or "no place to stay" and refers to nirvana. This means that a bodhisattva doesn't stay in samsara because of wisdom and doesn't remain in nirvana because of compassion for others. A bodhisattva always practices in this world of desires and helps others but never dwells on either side. It is said there is a river between this shore of samsara and the other shore of nirvana, and a bodhisattva operates the ferry, traveling freely between shores but not abiding on either.

This third kind of nirvana is the basis of our practice. We don't practice to reach the other shore. We always practice on this shore. In fact, we don't separate this shore from the other. Both shores are right now, right here. If we separate this shore from the other, we generate dualism and contradiction. There's no way to escape this shore and attain the other. In reality there is no separation. We practice in this world, in this society; to carry out the bodhisattva vow, to walk with all living beings, to help and support each other. Then we can find nirvana right here within samsara. We vow eventually to transform samsara into nirvana without escape.

Our practice is not an escape from a worldly life of desire and delusion. It is not a method to "attain" enlightenment or wisdom. We just sit in the absolute reality that is before separation into enlightenment and delusion. They are both here. We negate nothing. We accept everything as reality and work together with it. There is no one to attain enlightenment and no enlightenment to be attained. The *Heart Sutra* says this is wisdom or prajñā. To see that there is no separation between delusion and enlightenment or between ignorance and wisdom is true enlightenment, true wisdom. This prajñā is often called the wisdom of nondiscrimination. It means to see both sides as a whole and create our own way of life based on this absolute reality. This is what Dōgen Zenji called shikantaza, just sitting.

Shikantaza doesn't mean that we are okay as long as we are sitting or that we don't need to do anything else. Just sitting really means just sitting, with no attempt to escape from or chase after anything. Just settle down right now, right here. This is just sitting. It doesn't mean we should sit exclusively, without doing anything else. Just sitting means just settling down right now, right here, and working on the ground of this absolute reality before the separation of samsara and nirvana.

Samsara and nirvana are one. That is prajñā. That is wisdom before separation or discrimination. It's easy to talk about but very difficult to practice.

I first studied Buddhism at Komazawa University. I liked studying, but studying books about Buddhism is like studying recipes without cooking or tasting. When I decided that was not what I wanted to do, I visited Uchiyama Roshi and asked to become his student. Since I had studied hard in school, I knew a lot about Buddhism. When I started to practice at Antaiji we sat a lot. We sat three fifty-minute periods in the morning and two in the evening. We had five-day sesshins every month. During these sesshins we sat fourteen periods each day. We did nothing but sit—no chanting, no lecture, no working, nothing but sitting. I believed that this practice of just sitting, taught by Dōgen Zenji, was the Way. I kept up this practice for many years until eventually I was unable to continue. Zazen became very painful for me. I had no money. I was thirty-one years old. I had no place to live. My body was broken so I couldn't work. I had no group to practice with. I was completely alone.

It was a really good situation in which to see myself. It was a very hard time, and I thought a lot about what I had been doing. I could no longer devote myself to practice as before. Dōgen Zenji taught there's nothing to attain. Sawaki Roshi said our practice of zazen is good for nothing. I knew that I shouldn't expect anything from practice. I had thought I was practicing without expectation, but when I couldn't practice in the way I had, I felt I was good for nothing. I thought I had been doing things without desire, but when I was unable to continue I felt useless and empty. I finally realized that I felt worthless because I was unable to fulfill my desire to practice in a certain way. I finally understood that the purpose of our practice is not to fulfill our desires, even our desire for the dharma.

If we practice in order to fulfill our desires, sooner or later we lose those things that fulfill our desire. We all lose our youth and eventually our health. If we believe that a certain style of practice is the Buddha's true practice and makes a person a real Buddhist, we are not good

Buddhists. This is samsara. Sometimes we are good, sometimes we are not. I realized that to the extent my practice was based on a distinction between good and bad, there was no nirvana for me. The way I practiced before I was thirty really was good for nothing. I was practicing in samsara, not nirvana. I was unable to continue practicing, but if I stopped and started doing something else, I would create another samsara. So I tried to just stop everything. I started doing takuhatsu to survive. I lived on about three hundred dollars a month, just enough for food. I had to give up any treatment for my body. I quit everything. I also quit practice based on desire, on my idea of what practice should be. I practiced as much as my physical and financial situation allowed. I found that I didn't need to compete with other people or with myself. I didn't need to compete with who I was or who I thought I should be. I had to accept reality with a half-broken body in a very hard situation. When I did, there was nothing to seek after, nothing to escape from. I didn't need to sit fourteen periods a day for five days. I simply had to settle down in the present moment.

This was the turning point of my practice. I became free of my own practice. I became free of my teacher's teaching and the Buddha's teaching. I just settled down in the reality where I was and practiced as much as possible. This is a really peaceful practice. You don't need to compete. Just settle down. If I hadn't had physical problems, I don't think my practice would have changed. I thought I was a great Zen master, but fortunately or unfortunately that didn't happen. Adverse experience gave me a broader perspective on the dharma. I am really grateful for that. This is bodhisattva practice. Although our capability is sometimes severely limited, we can find the compassionate Buddha that allows us to practice, even if only a little. That is enough. I think this is real nirvana. We don't need to find nirvana in a special place or state of mind. Nirvana is right now, right here.

This nirvana is not something special, just an ordinary way of life. I think the *Heart Sutra* is trying to show us this way of life. Just accept the reality of this body, mind, and world as it is and practice as much as possible. This is bodhisattva practice.

No Hindrance

"The bodhisattva depends on prajñā-pāramitā
And the mind is no hindrance.
Without any hindrance no fears exist;
Far apart from every perverted view the bodhisattva dwells
in nirvana.

"In the three worlds all buddhas depend on prajñā-pāramitā
And attain unsurpassed, complete, perfect enlightenment."

The sutra up to this point has talked about the emptiness of all beings. Emptiness means everything is impermanent, so there is no unchanging self-nature. Seeing impermanence and egolessness is the wisdom called prajñā-pāramitā. A consequence of this prajñā is there is no one to see reality. No one is there. There is nothing we can gain through wisdom. Actually there is no wisdom. If wisdom existed, our practice wouldn't be really empty. The conclusion of wisdom, of prajñā, is that there is no one who gains and nothing to be gained.

This section of the *Heart Sutra* talks about our wisdom and the practice of that wisdom. It says, "With nothing to attain, the bodhisattva depends on prajñā-pāramitā." The present translation says "the bodhisattva" but doesn't specify a particular bodhisattva. Rather, it refers to each one of us as a bodhisattva. As we see in the longer version of the *Heart Sutra*, Avalokiteśvara here is responding to Śāriputra's question about how people who wish to practice profound prajñā-pāramitā should train themselves. And this sutra is Avalokiteśvara's answer. Therefore, "the bodhisattva" refers to any person who has aroused bodhi-mind, including ourselves. Originally, "the Bodhisattva" referred to Shakyamuni before he became the Buddha. Shakyamuni aroused bodhi-mind, Way-seeking mind, or aspiration to find the truth. When he attained the Way or enlightenment, he was called the Buddha. Before he became the Buddha he was called the Bodhisattva, the person who is seeking the truth. Later in the Buddhist literature, especially in Mahāyāna Buddhism, there are many bodhisattvas, such as Mañjuśrī and Avalokiteśvara. They are very great bodhisattvas. Avalokiteśvara, who is preaching this *Heart Sutra*, is not seeking to attain enlightenment, and not choosing to become a buddha. Out of compassion for others Avalokiteśvara stays in this world as a bodhisattva and yet is considered the teacher of buddhas. So in Mahāyāna Buddhism "bodhisattva" doesn't necessarily mean a person who is practicing to become a buddha. There are bodhisattvas who vow not to become buddhas because of their compassion.

The important point in Mahāyāna Buddhism is that all of us, not just great bodhisattvas like Mañjushrī, Avalokiteśvara, or Maitreya, are bodhisattvas if we awaken the bodhi-mind that seeks the Way or reality. As bodhisattvas we try to see the emptiness in which there is no one who sees reality and nothing to be seen. No wisdom: this is the meaning of "nothing to attain, no one who attains, and nothing which is attained." The Japanese for "with nothing to attain" is *mushotoku*. Mu means "no" or "nothing" and *shotoku* means "income," so *mushotoku* means "no income." We have no income. This is prajñā—no gain and no loss. There's nothing coming in or going out because there is no place where anything can come to or go from. There is no border, no separation, just a flow of energy. This is reality beyond our conceptual and calculating way of thinking.

We are born as human beings and we gain nothing. We will die sooner or later and lose nothing. We are born with nothing but this body and mind. While we are living we think we attain, gain, or accomplish something. But when we die we leave everything behind, so only this body and mind die. We really attain nothing and lose nothing. This is the reality of our life. But we don't see this because we are always calculating our income and expenditures. When we have more coming in than going out we think our life is secure and successful. But if we understand that nothing comes in and nothing goes out, we actually have a much more secure foundation for our lives. We don't need to worry so much about income and expense, success and failure, poverty and wealth. It's not a real problem. As bodhisattvas we rely on this wisdom.

A bodhisattva's mind has no hindrance. "Hindrance" here means something that covers our mind, or an obstacle that prevents us from seeing reality as it is. A hindrance is something that makes it impossible for our mind to be natural. The Chinese expression is *keige*. *Kei* and *ge* both mean difficulties through which we can pass. These impediments are within us. Something covers or constrains our mind so we cannot be free. We are limited and made rigid by our knowledge and ways of thinking. Life is always moving. It's soft and flexible. When you put a big rock on a plant it tries to move through or around the obstruction and continue to grow. This is the flexibility of the life force. If we have an idea that we have to be this way or that, we have something very heavy sitting on our life. We cannot grow. We think our life is a failure and that we're in trouble. But the life force is flexible. There is always some other way to live, to grow, and to manifest our life force.

We should try to see the hindrances in our minds, the obstacles that block our free growth. As bodhisattvas we are freed from hindrances by seeing emptiness. We see that nothing exists as substance, so there is nothing to prevent our growth. Obstacles are illusions, delusions, and creations of our thought. We fear because of our desires. We think they must be fulfilled, and we're afraid that's impossible. We think there is only one way to live even though there are many ways. So our desires, our ideas, our values become hindrances, and we are not free. This is the meaning of fears. But if we remove our imagined obstacles we can grow in many different ways.

The sutra tells us that the bodhisattva dwells "far apart from every perverted view." The expression in Japanese is *ten dō musō*. Here *mu* means "dream" and *sō* means "thinking." *Musō* then literally means "thought in dream." *Tendō* means "upside-down." Our attitude, or understanding of our thought, is upside-down. We cannot wake up. We are thinking in a dream. We create our own picture of the world depending on our karma or experience. Our experience is very limited, and yet we think it is the whole world. So we are like the frog in the well. We can see only a small circle of sky, but we think we are seeing the whole universe. Even seeing emptiness doesn't allow us to see the whole universe, but it enables us to realize that our view is limited.

In our zazen we see that we are deluded. This is enlightenment. We see that we are deluded and limited, so we let go of thought. We become free from our limited views. This doesn't mean we can see the whole universe. That's impossible because we always have a particular position or point of view. When I look in this direction I can see this side of the world. I cannot see the half behind me. I know it's there because of my memory. But it's just a memory. We are seeing only half the world, but because of our assumptions and memory we think we can see the whole. We even think that we can see how other people see the world. But since we each have a unique perspective, we can never see the world in the same way. In fact, each of us has a different perspective, a unique way of seeing, thinking, feeling, and valuing things. We become flexible when we free ourselves from our fixed views. This is prajñā.

"Perverted" literally means "upside-down." We usually assume that our thoughts operate our body and mind. Our body and mind serve the emperor, thought. This is really upside-down. Thought is just one part of our life, but we so often live on the basis of our thinking. This is really an upside-down way of seeing things. If we turn it over, then we are living. We all have life force. Part of it is our power of thought. We don't need to discard this power, but we should realize that what we think is not reality. Once we really accept that thought is only a part of our life, most of the fear and other problems caused by our thoughts will disappear. We want to be secure. If we can't support ourselves we are afraid. It's very natural. But we can think too much. We can think about ten, twenty, or thirty years in the future. We even worry about the world after our death. It's okay to think about the future, but if worrying about it prevents us from living in this present moment, it's too much. Bodhisattva practice is about this present moment.

Within this present moment there is a direction to the future. We usually think what we are doing right now is a preparation for the future or a step to accomplish something. But this is an upside-down way of seeing things. Our effort, work, or study at this present moment brings about the future. We can think about it but we don't need to worry. Worry dilutes our effort and it's not healthy. So just be right now, right here, and put your whole energy into what you are doing. This is prajñā. It is very difficult. Moment by moment we have to let go of worry and fear and return to this moment. That is our practice of mindfulness, sitting in zazen, letting go, and coming back to this moment. This letting go is the practice of prajñā.

The next two lines of the sutra are:

> "In the three worlds all buddhas depend on prajñā-pāramitā
> And attain unsurpassed, complete, perfect enlightenment."

The three worlds here are the past, present, and future. The Japanese for "three worlds" is *sanze*. *San* is "three" and *ze* means "generation" or "time." "Unsurpassed, complete, perfect" means "absolute." There is nothing relative. There is no separation between self and others or between self and all beings. That is enlightenment. Here the *Heart Sutra* tells us that through prajñā-pāramitā we can liberate ourselves. We can transform ourselves from slaves of thought, slaves of the ego, into bodhisattvas. We use our thoughts, delusions, and desires as the seeds of prajñā, which we nurture with our practice. We make them function as the Buddha's work. Prajñā is called the Buddha's mother. This is the way of life the *Heart Sutra* and Mahāyāna Buddhism encourage us to follow.

To become free from all perverted views or upside-down ways of seeing things means to turn the foundation of our life over, to see reality and live based on it. Reality means impermanence and egolessness. Nothing stays forever unchanged. There is nothing substantial. Everything is changing, and everything is supported by everything else. We are all connected, one universal life force.

As we've seen, in Dōgen's teaching mushotoku—no income, no attainment—is essential. In *Shōbōgenzō* "Zuimonki," a record of his informal talks, he says:

> Now if you wish to practice the way of the buddhas and ancestors, you should practice the way of the previous sages, as well as the conduct of the ancestors with no (expectation of) profit; expect nothing, seek nothing, gain nothing. Although you should quit seeking and give up expectations of buddhahood, if you stop practicing and continue engaging in your former evil deeds, you will still be guilty of seeking and will fall back into the old nest.
>
> Without having the slightest expectation, maintain the prescribed manner of conduct. Think of acting to save and benefit living beings, earnestly carry out all good deeds, and give up former evil ones. Do this solely for the sake of becoming the foundation of happiness for human and heavenly beings. Without stagnating in good deeds of the present, continue practicing your whole lifetime. An ancient called this practice "breaking the bottom of the lacquer pail." The way of the life of the buddhas and ancestors is like this.[92]

Here Dōgen admonishes us to be mushotoku, without expectation of income. It's very strict. Our zazen, study, work, all the activities of our daily lives are our practice. We should do them as the practice of this moment without expectation of result or reward in the future. Just put our whole energy into this moment and results or fruits will grow naturally. We simply need to trust the life force itself.

When we hear this teaching we might think to practice is to seek after enlightenment. If so, it sounds like Dōgen Zenji is saying you shouldn't practice. He, however, continues, "*Although you should quit seeking and give up expectations of buddhahood, if you stop practicing and continue engaging in your former evil deeds, you will still be guilty of seeking and will fall back into the old nest.*" Evil deeds mean karmic deeds, activities based on our personal desires. So if we stop practice to avoid seeking buddhahood, we are still seeking. We become just ordinary human beings. So we have to continue practicing without expectation. It's really difficult.

"*Without having the slightest expectation, maintain the prescribed manner of conduct.*" Here he's talking about monks living in a monastery. They should follow the schedule and devote their whole energy to daily practice. In the case of laypeople, taking care of our families, living in communities, and working is what we do.

"*Think of acting to save and benefit living beings, earnestly carry out all good deeds, and give up former evil ones. Do this solely for the sake of becoming the foundation of happiness for human and heavenly beings.*" In each activity we should think of how we can benefit all living beings. That is our vow. We try to practice skillfully to create a foundation of happiness for all beings. That means we try to make this world better, even if only in small ways. We have many problems in this world today. We should do what we can to make it a better place for those who follow us. That too is our vow. Each of us has different capabilities and each of us can do something, even something small to improve this world. That is true bodhisattva practice.

"*Without stagnating in good deeds of the present, continue practicing your whole lifetime.*" *If we think we are doing good, we already have a problem. If we think we are good people because we try to make the world better, we have a problem. This is a judgment. We think that we are good and that those who don't follow us are bad. This is a problem. If we think in this way we ignore emptiness. Even though we are doing good deeds, we should not think of ourselves as good people. We are doing what we choose to do or feel we should. It's just a natural function. This is a subtle point. Our good deeds can make us arrogant. Fighting is often caused by this kind of arrogance. We think, "We are doing good and they are not, so they are our enemy. We have to eliminate them to make the world a better place."* Then we really have a problem. Many wars are caused this way. The wisdom of emptiness is a way to avoid conflict based on concepts of justice.

Just keep doing. This is the meaning of *shikan*. Dōgen Zenji's most famous phrase is "just sitting," or shikantaza. We may think that just sitting means it's okay if we merely sit, that we don't need to do anything else. But shikantaza doesn't mean that. It means just sit for now, without any expectation for the future, without thinking that we are doing good or practicing well. Just sit.

"*An ancient called this practice 'breaking the bottom of the lacquer pail.'*" This is a common expression for becoming enlightened. For Dōgen Zenji enlightenment means just sitting or just doing good. Just keep practicing without any expectation.

"*The way of the life of the buddhas and ancestors is like this.*" This is the way buddhas and ancestors practiced. When he mentions just sitting, Dōgen Zenji is talking about the practice of prajñā. He's talking about becoming free of even the Buddha's teaching. This is the Buddha's practice, or prajñā-pāramitā.

Nāgārjuna says something very similar in *Mūlamadhyamakakārikā*: "Those who delight in maintaining, 'Without the grasping, I will realize nirvana; nirvana is in me,' are the very ones with the greatest grasping" (16:9).[93] We believe that we are letting go of thought, opening our hands, and grasping at nothing; we think that we are completely free from self-clinging and that we are in nirvana or nirvana is within us. Nāgārjuna says that those who think this way are the very ones with the greatest grasping. We must open our hand even concerning our practice, even about opening our hand. Nāgārjuna continues, "Where nirvana is not (subject to) establishment and samsara not (subject to) disengagement, how will there be any conception of nirvana and samsara?" (16:10). We don't have to establish nirvana or eliminate samsara. There is no separation between them. This is a koan. There is no answer, so we have to keep opening our hands. If we think we are okay because we open our hands, then we are grasping. So what? This is our practice.

Great Bright Mantra

"Therefore know the prajñā-pāramitā
Is the great transcendent mantra,
Is the great bright mantra,
Is the utmost mantra,

Is the supreme mantra,
Which is able to relieve all suffering
And is true, not false."

In this section the sutra says that prajñā-pāramitā is the wisdom to see impermanence and interdependence. This body and mind exist as a result of many factors. When these elements change, we change. Consequently, there is no fixed self-nature within us, nothing substantial. To see this reality is prajñā-pāramitā. It is a difficult reality to face moment by moment. We often forget about it because our way of thought in daily life is very different.

In our usual thinking we use concepts and words. Each word has a certain meaning or definition that doesn't change. A word should always mean the same thing. If the meaning changes, we have no basis for consistent communication. I'm always Shohaku Okumura, always Japanese, always a man, always a Buddhist priest. But in reality my body and mind are always changing. On a conceptual level, however, I'm always Shohaku Okumura, and it's difficult to see these changes. When the two levels of our life, conceptual thought and life force, harmonize, we have no serious problems. But sometime our thinking contradicts reality.

For instance, I still think of myself as a young man when in fact I am getting older every day. One of my son's favorite games was to sit on my shoulders and beat my head like a drum. He did this often.[94] One day I was sitting on the sofa when he jumped onto the back of my neck. I had no pain that day but the next morning I couldn't move my neck. I was in bed for two days and missed Thanksgiving dinner. Pain is so realistic, always fresh. It's very difficult to accept the reality that I am getting older and unable to do some things and that my son is getting bigger every day. If I try to move something too heavy, it's difficult. These are examples of how our conceptual thinking and self-image often diverge from the reality of our lives. When there is too great a gap between reality and our thinking we run into trouble. Prajñā-pāramitā is the wisdom to see both sides. It's not simply a negation of our thought or a particular way of thinking. It is seeing the limitations of our usual logic. Our day-to-day thought is unable to see the reality of constant change.

The *Heart Sutra* says that this prajñā or wisdom which sees the reality of impermanence, egolessness, and interdependence is a mantra. *Mantra* was originally a term used in the Vedic tradition of ancient India commonly called Brahmanism, and later it became an essential part of Hinduism. The practice of chanting mantras was much older than Buddhism. One of the oldest of the many sacred scriptures of ancient India is called the *Rig Veda*. In the Vedas there are many gods much more powerful than human beings. The basic idea of a mantra was that if Brahman priests uttered the proper words and conducted the right rituals, the gods would comply with their requests. These mantras supposedly had the supernatural power to move the gods. Originally Indian Buddhist monks didn't use mantras. But Mahāyāna Buddhism was strongly influenced by Hinduism and began to use them. The word "mantra" is used commonly in Vajrayāna Buddhism, which arose around the seventh century as the final development of Indian Buddhism. In the Vajrayāna school (such as the Shingon school in Japan), prayers serve a particular purpose. For example, on certain occasions the priest builds a fire inside the temple, sits in full lotus, makes a particular mudra, and chants mantras. Then Vairocana, the main Buddha in Vajrayāna, is supposed to help them. This is the basic idea of the Vajrayāna or Shingon school of Buddhism.

On Shikoku, one of the major Japanese islands, there are eighty-eight destinations for pilgrims. As Shingon practitioners visit each temple, they often chant the *Heart Sutra*. This sutra is also used as a mantra in Vajrayāna Buddhism. For Zen Buddhists, however, reciting the *Heart Sutra* doesn't mean that we believe it's a mantra that can influence the gods. For instance, right now I have pain in my neck, but I don't believe that reciting the *Heart Sutra* will relieve it. Although the sutra has the phrase "relieve all suffering," I don't believe it works as a kind of pain-killer. Instead it enables us to change the way we view our lives and ourselves. It allows us to see the deeper meaning and broader reality of our life. Our way of thinking is limited by our experience, education, culture, and values. Our picture of the world is narrow. This wisdom of prajñā-pāramitā enables us to break through these fixed systems of value and see reality from a wider perspective.

The *Heart Sutra* concludes:

> "So proclaim the prajñā-pāramitā mantra,
> Proclaim the mantra that says:
> Gate, gate, pāragate, pārasamgate! Bodhi, svāha!"

Since this is a mantra, the words themselves are believed by some to have divine power and so are not translated. Depending on the translator, the meaning is, "Gone, gone, gone beyond" or "Gone altogether beyond. Oh, what an awakening!" *Bodhi* means "awakening" and *svāhā* means "all hail." "Gone" points to a reality beyond our system of values, beyond the boundary of our ready-made picture of the world and ourselves. This mantra enables us to break through our internal limitations and see a deeper reality inside us. The Buddha taught us to wake up to this deeper meaning in our daily lives.

Some of my time in Japan I lived on takuhatsu, religious begging. Usually I walked the street and stopped in front of each shop. I would stand there and say, "Hō." In Japanese this literally means "bowl," and figuratively it means "dharma." In Osaka there is a large temple called Shitennōji.[95] Here, on the twenty-first of each month, people observe *en'nichi*, a kind of a memorial day for Kōbō Daishi, the founder of the Japanese Shingon school. Thousands of people visit the temple. Whenever possible I went to that temple on the twenty-first and did standing takuhatsu. I stood from about ten o'clock in the morning until about four in the afternoon. For six hours I didn't move. I just stood with a begging bowl and recited the *Heart Sutra*. It takes about three or four minutes to recite the whole sutra, so I would chant it more than a hundred times. Usually when people do takuhatsu they chant *Enmei-jukku-kannon-gyō*. This is a very short sutra, too short to repeat for six hours, so I recited the *Heart Sutra* instead. Chanting kept my mind from darting here and there in distracted thinking.

The people who visit the temple are mostly older people who are very religious in the traditional sense. They are very sincere Buddhists and give generous donations, sometimes a small amount of money, sometimes ten yen or a hundred yen, about one dollar. When they made a donation they did gasshō and bowed to me. I also bowed while I was chanting. I saw many people who were poor but more generous than the rich. It was apparent to me that they were suffering. Some were in wheelchairs. Chanting the *Heart Sutra* was a very powerful practice. I could see people's suffering. It's not something mysterious, but there was a special realm in which we were living together, sharing our suffering. Although we didn't talk we communicated on a profound level. I felt dharma joy. The *Heart Sutra* was a mantra that enabled us to relieve suffering.

Suffering is more than just pain. Suffering is pain plus something mental. Pain alone is not such a big problem because it will end sometime. For example, I had pain this morning and knew I had to give a talk. That made my pain suffering. Still, I was able to come and speak. Chanting this mantra, this *Heart Sutra*, enables us to communicate with each other deeply without speaking. For this reason chanting is a really good practice.

At some Zen centers in the United States, we chant in both Japanese and English. Some ask me why we chant in Japanese. They think it doesn't make sense. Chanting is first of all a practice of breathing. When you chant you use your *hara*. In a Japanese monastery one is taught, "Chant with your hara, your abdomen, not with your mouth." Chanting is a practice of deep breathing with your abdomen. Next we are taught, "Chant with your ear, not with your mouth." That means we should listen to what other people are chanting. We should be together with all beings when we chant. We shouldn't chant alone. When we chant with others, the chanting of all people should be one, like a chorus or orchestra. Chanting enables us to be right now, right here at this moment. We have to put our whole body and mind into chanting and let go of other things. When we are chanting we should not think about sitting or eating or errands we have to do. Just be right now, right here,

100 percent. In this way chanting is a mantra. The meaning is not so important. Of course, it's better to understand the meaning, but the meaning is not really the point. Chanting can be prajñā-pāramitā if we put our whole time and being into it. It can open our eyes to reality, not to an intellectual reality but rather to our life energy. When we chant wholeheartedly, our voice is the sound of emptiness, exactly like the sound of the wind bell in Rujing's poem. It is the sound of the wind, the bell, our ears, our mind, the entire universe.

7 All Is One, One Is All: Merging of Difference and Unity

Sandōkai

The mind of the great sage of India
Is intimately communicated between east and west.
People's faculties may be keen or dull,
But in the path there are no "southern" or "northern"
 ancestors.
The spiritual source shines clearly in the light;
The branching streams flow in the darkness.
Grasping things is basically delusion;
Merging with principle is still not enlightenment.
Each sense and every field
Interact and do not interact;
When interacting, they also merge—
Otherwise, they remain in their own states.
Forms are basically different in material and appearance,
Sounds are fundamentally different in pleasant or harsh quality.
"Darkness" is a word for merging upper and lower;
"Light" is an expression for distinguishing pure and defiled.
The four gross elements return to their own natures
Like a baby taking to its mother;

Fire heats, wind moves,
Water wets, earth is solid.
Eye and form, ear and sound;
Nose and smell, tongue and taste—
Thus in all things
The leaves spread from the root;
The whole process must return to the source;
"Noble" and "base" are only manners of speaking.
Right in light there is darkness, but don't confront it
as darkness;
Right in darkness there is light, but don't see it as light.
Light and dark are relative to one another
Like forward and backward steps.
All things have their function—
It is a matter of use in the appropriate situation.
Phenomena exist like box and cover joining;
Principle accords like arrow points meeting.
Hearing the words, you should understand the source;
Don't make up standards on your own.
If you don't understand the path as it meets your eyes,
How can you know the way as you walk?
Progress is not a matter of far or near,
But if you are confused, mountains and rivers block the way.
I humbly say to those who study the mystery,
Don't waste time.[96]

THE TITLE of this poem, "Sandōkai," is composed of three characters. The first, *san* (*cen* in Chinese) means "difference," "diversity," "variety." In this poem it is used as a synonym for *ji*, which indicates the concrete, phenomenal aspect of our life. The second character, *dō* (*tong* in Chinese), means "sameness," "equality," "commonality." Here it is used as a synonym of *ri*, the absolute or ultimate reality of emptiness beyond discrimination. *Kai* (*qi* in Chinese) means "promise," "agreement," or "tally." In ancient times when merchants made a contract, they wrote it on a tally (a wooden board), which they then broke into halves. When they actually exchanged goods, they put the two halves of the tally together to confirm the agreement. *San-dō-kai* refers to both aspects of our lives: the concrete, comprised of many specific situations, ideas, evaluations, and things; and the absolute, based on universality, emptiness, and nondiscrimination. These are like the halves of a tally. These aspects work together as one seamless reality. Hence, "Sandōkai" can be translated as the "Merging of Difference and Unity."[97]

The Mind of the Great Sage of India

> The mind of the great sage of India
> Is intimately communicated between east and west.
> People's faculties may be keen or dull,
> But in the path there are no "southern" or "northern"
> ancestors.

The first four lines of this poem by the Zen master Shitou Xiqian (Sekitō Kisen) are an introduction to what follows. To understand this, we need to know the situation in Shitou's time.

"Southern" and "Northern" Ancestors

Shitou lived in eighth century China, from 700 to 790. He practiced with the sixth ancestor, Dajan Huineng (Daikan Enō, 638–713) when he was young, perhaps as a teenager. After Huineng died he practiced with one of Huineng's disciples, Qingyuan Xingsi (Seigen Gyōshi, 660–740). Shitou became Qingyuan's dharma successor, thus a second-generation disciple of the sixth ancestor. It is said that earlier, under the fifth ancestor Daman Hongren (Daiman Kōnin, 602–675), Zen had divided into two schools, Southern and Northern. Huineng's lineage was called the Southern school, while the Northern school was founded by Yuquan Shenxiu (Gyokusen Jinshū, 606–706), one of Huineng's dharma brothers. There is a famous story about the dharma transmission from the fifth ancestor Hongren to Huineng.

According to the *Platform Sutra* of the sixth ancestor, Huineng was practicing at the fifth ancestor's monastery. He had not yet been ordained and was still a lay practitioner working at the monastery. Shenxiu, the founder of the Northern school, was the head monk and a very experienced practitioner. He was the oldest student of the fifth ancestor. The fifth ancestor was getting old and looking for a successor. He assembled his students and asked them to write a poem to show their understanding of the dharma. All the other monks, convinced that Shenxiu would be chosen as the fifth ancestor's successor, declined to compose poems. Shenxiu alone wrote one, as follows:

> The body is the bodhi tree,
> The mind is like a bright mirror's stand.
> At all times we must strive to polish it
> And must not let dust collect.[98]

This body, our human body, is the bodhi tree. *Bodhi*, as we've seen, means "awakening," so this body is the tree of awakening or enlightenment. Original wisdom is like a clear mirror. But there is usually dust on the mirror, so it doesn't reflect things as they are. We have to continually polish the mirror of our mind to keep it clean. This was Shenxiu's understanding of the dharma, human beings, and the meaning of practice. Our body and mind is original enlightened reality itself, but the dust of desire and ignorance cover it. When we polish it, the mirror becomes bright and functions as wisdom.

Huineng couldn't read or write. Even though he was not well educated, when he heard people reciting Shenxiu's poem he must have thought, "That is not deep enough." So Huineng asked one of the students to transcribe a poem for him, which he posted next to Shenxiu's poem. His poem was:

> Bodhi originally has no tree.
> The bright mirror also has no stand.

Fundamentally there is not a single thing.
Where could dust arise?[99]

Huineng said that enlightenment has no tree and the mirror no shape or form. Nothing exists. Since everything is completely empty, there is no place for dust to land. There is nothing that can be called desire or delusion. Our enlightenment or reality is always clear. There is nothing we have to polish and nothing we have to eliminate. That was Huineng's understanding.

The fifth ancestor secretly gave dharma transmission to Huineng in the night and let him leave the monastery. Shenxiu's teaching, the Northern school, was called "gradual" enlightenment because Shenxiu held that we become enlightened after a long period of practice, polishing the mirror. In this school people practice to eliminate delusion based on ignorance. Huineng's teaching was called "sudden" enlightenment. According to the Southern or "sudden" school realization is attained suddenly, without any stages of gradual practice. People realize reality beyond the discrimination between delusion and enlightenment. For example, the story of Huineng's first realization experience—which happened before he began to study Zen when he heard someone chanting the *Diamond Sutra*—was taken to illustrate the idea of sudden enlightenment.

The two schools separated under the fifth ancestor, and Shitou was a dharma grandson of Huineng. This is what Shitou refers to when he says that in the path, the Buddha's Way, there are no "southern" or "northern" ancestors. Even though he was a dharma grandson of Huineng, the founder of the Southern school, he says that there is no distinction between southern or northern, which means between sudden or gradual enlightenment. Shitou wrote this poem to show the fundamental reality and go beyond the distinction between the factions of schools. This is a traditional understanding of the history of Chinese Zen in the eighth and ninth centuries.

Historical Reality

To understand Shitou's position in the history of Chinese Zen Buddhism and also what he wrote in "Merging of Difference and Unity," it might be helpful to understand the historical background of Zen in the eighth and ninth centuries. The actual reality was probably much more complex than we usually imagine. Guifeng Zongmi (Keihō Shumitsu, 780–841) was a famous Zen master and Buddhist philosopher who was born eighty years after Shitou. He was a scholar of the Kegon School, a Buddhist philosophical school based on the *Kegon Sutra* (*Avataṃsaka Sutra* or *Flower Ornament Sutra*). Feixiu (Haikyū, 797–870), a government minister, was very interested in Zen but was confused because there were so many different Zen groups at that time. He couldn't understand how such diverse groups could have a common origin. When he questioned Zen practitioners, their answers were paradoxical. They said nothing logical. Since Zongmi was a scholar as well as a Zen practitioner, the minister asked him to explain the origin, tradition, and history of Zen, and how the many different methods of teaching related to this tradition. Zongmi explained the lineages of Zen from Bodhidharma in a short treatise. He wrote that at the time there were six schools of Zen, not just the Southern and Northern.

The first one was called Niutou (Gozu, or Oxhead) school, named for the mountain where the founder lived. This school was headed by Niutou Farong (Gozu Hōyū, 594–657), who is said to have been a disciple of the fourth ancestor. So there was a division in Zen even before the fifth ancestor.

The second, the Northern school, was Shenxiu's school. It was particularly popular in the imperial court. Shenxiu himself and a few of his disciples became teachers of the emperors. This school was attacked by Heze Shenhui (Kataku Jinne, 668–760) in the first half of the eighth century and lost popularity within a few generations.

The third and fourth were two smaller groups, the Jingzhong (Jōshū) school founded by Jingzhong Wuxiang (Jōshū Musō, 684–762) and Baotang (Hotō) school started by Baotang Wuzhu (Hotō Mujū,

714–774). Those were the streams that branched from the fifth ancestor. Zongmi did not say much about these two minor schools.

The fifth and sixth were "Southern" schools derived from Huineng's lineage. The fifth was called the Hongzhou (Kōshū) school founded by Mazu Daoyi (Baso Dōitsu, 709–788). Nanyue Huairang (Nangaku Ejō, 677–744) was a disciple of Huineng, and Mazu was Nanyue's disciple and of the same generation as Shitou. Mazu was also Huineng's dharma grandson.

The last school, the Heze (Kataku), was founded by one of Huineng's disciples named Heze Shenhui, who attacked the Northern school and claimed that his teacher, Huineng, was the legitimate dharma heir of the fifth ancestor.

Zongmi didn't talk about Shitou's group at all, probably because it wasn't big enough. He did discuss the similarities and differences between the Niutou school, the Northern school, and the two divisions of the Southern school, Hongzhou and Heze. Zongmi himself claimed that he belonged to the Heze school, whose teaching he considered the highest of all. However, modern scholars think Zongmi had no connection with this lineage. Shenhui was one of the most active of Huineng's disciples and probably created the story of the dharma transmission from the fifth ancestor to Huineng. As Huineng's disciple, Shenhui wanted him to be seen as greater than Shenxiu and recognized as the sixth ancestor. Shenxiu's Northern school was more powerful and popular in the capital, in the north of China, whereas Huineng came from the southern countryside, was not well known, and may have lacked credibility because of his youth.

In a sense, the history of different groups of Zen before Zen became established in Chinese Buddhism shows the meaning of "merging of difference and unity." The groups were different and yet they were all considered as Zen practitioners.

One Mind

Zongmi compared the four schools on the basis of their understanding of difference and unity. Difference is a translation of *ji* and refers to the phenomenal or relative aspect of our life. Unity refers to the absolute aspect. Originally these two concepts, difference and unity, the phenomenal and absolute aspects of our life, are discussed as the two aspects of the One Mind.

Shitou uses the phrase "the mind of the great sage of India." The idea of a One Mind originated in the *Awakening of Faith in Mahāyāna*, one of the most important texts on the theory of *tathāgata-garbha*, or buddha-nature. It begins:

> The revelation of the true meaning [of the principle of Mahāyāna can be achieved] by [unfolding the doctrine] that the principle of One Mind has two aspects. One is the aspect of Mind in terms of the absolute (*tathātā*, suchness), and the other is the aspect of Mind in terms of phenomena (*samsara*, birth and death).[100]

Samsara is the aspect of life into which we are born, live for a while, and die. It refers not only to the psychological mind but also to the functions of our lives. During the period between birth and death, our minds and lives constantly change, and we are limited by our particular time and place. We are conditioned by our unique experiences, education, and culture. Delusive desires function within this aspect because we can't perceive reality as a whole. We have to make choices based on our limited perspectives.

The *Awakening of Faith* continues, "Each of these two aspects embraces all states of existence. Why? Because these two aspects are mutually inclusive." They completely interpenetrate each other. According to the text, we live a universal, eternal life as the absolute aspect of the Mind, and yet, as the phenomenal aspect of the same Mind, our life is individual and limited by that individuality. The Buddha addressed the relationship between these two aspects. He taught that life is suffering and the cause of this suffering is our desire, which arises out of ignorance. He taught that we have to transform our way of life into nirvana. This is the Buddha's basic teaching. To realize nirvana we have to practice, to walk the eightfold noble path leading out of samsara. In the *Awakening of Faith*, samsara and nirvana are really two aspects of One Mind. The basic idea here is that both are embodied in the reality of our individual lives. Even though the reality of one life is beyond discrimination and delusion, from a relative or phenomenal perspective we are deluded and egocentric. We have delusive desires that bring suffering to our lives. So what should we do? How can we live in nirvana? The various answers to this question are the basis of the many different teachings and schools.

Zongmi's Comments on the Four Schools

Zongmi discussed the four schools, although he wasn't completely objective because he felt that his was the best form of practice. He used the interesting analogy of a *mani* jewel, the bright, transparent gem that symbolizes buddha-nature or One Mind. He explained that this jewel has no color, so when it is illuminated by light of a particular color, it takes on that color. A transparent jewel placed on a black sheet of paper becomes black. On a red sheet it appears red. These apparent changes were used as an analogy for individual or relative aspects of situations in our lives. If our life becomes really black, full of delusion and desire, the jewel of One Mind appears black. The bright jewel takes on the color of each situation. Yet the jewel itself is transparent and does not change.

Zongmi said the Northern school taught that the black color is false. To become enlightened, to reveal the bright jewel, we have to remove the black. Our practice is to erase the darkness of our delusions. We have to polish the bright jewel to remove the colors that arise from particular situations. This requires constant practice.

Mazu's Hongzhou school maintained that everything we do, whether we are enlightened or deluded, is the function of the bright jewel. They taught that without color—black, white, or red—there is no bright jewel. We don't need to eliminate a particular color to reveal the jewel. Buddha-nature doesn't exist independently of particular situations. Even deluded actions are nothing other than the function of buddha-nature. So we don't need to polish anything or engage in any particular practice. We just accept everything as reality, as a function or movement of buddha-nature.

Zongmi made another analogy to explain Mazu's beliefs. He compared buddha-nature to the flour used in cakes and bread. One can bake many types of bread and cake with different shapes and tastes, but the same flour is used to make them all. So it is with buddha-nature in the myriad situations of our lives. Mazu believed that there is nothing other than buddha-nature and that we need to realize that everything is buddha-nature. Zongmi may have exaggerated Mazu's beliefs, as a way of criticizing Mazu. We cannot be sure whether this is what Mazu and his students really thought. But according to Zongmi, those who followed this form of practice/enlightenment felt that it is enough to believe that everything is a manifestation of the absolute. They believed that we don't need any particular form of practice and can live freely.

Zongmi explained that while Mazu's school taught that everything is a manifestation of buddha-nature, Niutou's teaching maintained that everything is empty. Not only the jewel's color, but even the transparent jewel itself is empty, like a dream. So we should not grasp anything. Delusion is empty and without substance, as is the bright jewel. Our practice then is not to attach ourselves to anything. This is a complete penetration of emptiness. There is nothing we can achieve, nothing we have to eliminate. We must see both delusion and buddha-nature as empty. We have to realize the emptiness of all things. Zongmi criticized the Niutou school for its failure to recognize the permanent essence of One Mind and its mistaken belief that the One Mind is also empty.[101]

Finally, the Heze school, as interpreted by Zongmi, believed that each of the other schools was partially correct. They asserted that the individual colors caused by various conditions are false, an imperfect reflection of reality. This means our discriminations are false, empty delusions. At the same time, they believed that the One Mind is not empty. We cannot grasp it, but it is here, clear and bright, and it is not empty. We must realize this oneness and see this bright jewel covered with delusions and then practice to free ourselves from delusions through sudden enlightenment. Thus this school combined the elements of gradual practice and sudden enlightenment.[102]

Shitou's Lineage

Our lineage, the Sōtō school, was also transmitted by the sixth ancestor, Huineng. Qingyuan Xingsi was Huineng's dharma heir and Shitou's teacher. Shitou transmitted the dharma to Yaoshan Weiyan (Yakusan Igen, 751–834). Yaoshan taught Yunyan Tansheng (Ungan Donjō, 780–841). The founder of the Chinese Sōtō school, Dongshan Liangjie (Tōzan Ryōkai, 807–869), was Yunyan's disciple. This lineage was not well known by the other Zen schools at the time of Zongmi, who was a contemporary of Dongshan. This was perhaps because Mazu's Hongzhou school was overwhelmingly larger and more popular. It was called the "one-stop shop," like a supermarket that had something for everyone. Shitou was a contemporary of Mazu. In comparison with Mazu's style of practice, Shitou's school was called the "real-gold shop." His form of practice was considered very pure, and since the school offered only real gold, it was small. Yaoshan's sangha was in fact very small, fewer than twenty people. Yunyan was a very quiet person. He didn't think of himself as enlightened. After the time of Dongshan and his disciples, this lineage finally became popular and the sayings of these five masters were recorded.

"Sandōkai" is Shitou's attempt to record his understanding of the relationship between buddha-nature—the absolute aspect of our life—and the relative or phenomenal aspect of our life, in other words, between enlightenment and delusion. He does this by contrasting the beliefs of the various schools. The Northern school emphasized difference and tried to transcend it through unity. In Mazu's Hongzhou school, unity is found only in difference. Since there is no unity outside of difference, they believed we must accept difference. In the Niutou school difference and unity are both empty, and we are taught to strive to become free from such distinctions. Finally, the Heze school focused on recognizing that differences are empty, while unity is not. Shitou suggested that we must try to see the relationship between difference and unity clearly. He emphasized neither, but instead tried to see reality as a merging of difference and unity. I think this is what "Sandōkai" (Merging of Difference and Unity) expresses.

Shitou says, "People's faculties may be keen or dull, but in the path there are no 'southern' or 'northern' ancestors." He means there is no difference between sudden and gradual enlightenment. People have different capabilities. Some understand suddenly and some more gradually, but in reality there is no such distinction. For Shitou, any division of the dharma or discussion of which approach to it is superior is senseless. Instead he tries to show us the One Mind, "the mind of the great sage of India" before separation. This One Mind embraces two aspects: a spiritual source and branching streams.

Spiritual Source and Branching Streams

> The spiritual source shines clearly in the light;
> The branching streams flow in the darkness.
> Grasping things is basically delusion;
> Merging with principle is still not enlightenment.

As we've learned, in Shitou's time Buddhism was separated into schools that argued about basic issues like the nature of enlightenment and the best method of practice. Shitou's response was to describe the mind of the great sage of India. He wasn't talking about psychology, but rather about the reality of life that includes both the absolute and phenomenal aspects in terms of the relation between the self and other things as objects.

As Dōgen Zenji said in *Shōbōgenzō* "Genjōkōan," "To study the Buddha's Way is to study the self. To study the self is to forget the self. To forget the self is to be verified by all things. To be verified by all things is to let the body and mind of the self and the body and mind of others drop off."[103] The study of the Buddha's teaching is the study of this body and mind, of who we are. Shitou's teachings on difference and unity, two different understandings of the Buddha Way, are really about seeing our lives from two different perspectives as one seamless reality.

In Buddhism the concept of seeing one reality from two angles originated in Nāgārjuna's teaching. In *Madhyamikakarika* Nāgārjuna said, "Without relying on everyday common practices (i.e., relative truths), the absolute truth cannot be expressed. Without approaching the absolute truth, nirvana cannot be attained" (24:10).[104] Here he distinguishes between relative truth, our day-to-day way of thinking, and absolute truth. In this way he introduces the idea of seeing one reality in two ways, which is the origin of the idea of difference and unity. The *Awakening of Faith* says, "The revelation of the true meaning of the principle of Mahāyāna can be achieved by unfolding the doctrine that the principle of One Mind has two aspects."[105] Here "One Mind" is the same as one reality, or "the mind of the great sage of India." This One Mind has two aspects, absolute truth and relativity or phenomena. One Mind can be seen from two perspectives. This is the origin of the idea of difference and unity called *ji* and *ri* in Chinese Buddhism. As we've seen, *ji* literally means "event" or "thing," something very particular and concrete. It can also mean phenomenon, material, or something individual and independent. *Ri* means "principle" or "law," something abstract that has no shape or form, something universal. These two aspects are not two parts of one thing. Both aspects are included in reality, the One Mind. From one side, One Mind is a collection of individual things, and from another side, this whole reality is simply one. There is no distinction or separation within this one reality. And yet, individuality does not disappear. Individuality is there without separation. This means we don't discriminate between individuals.

One Hand and Five Fingers

For example, if I hold up my hand you might see it as a hand. And yet you can also see it as five fingers. One hand has five fingers, and there is no hand beyond these five fingers. Five fingers and one hand are the same thing: two aspects of one reality. Within this collection of five fingers, each finger is different and even has a different name. In Japanese the thumb is called *oyayubi*, or "parent." The index finger is called *hitosashiyubi*, the finger to point at something. The middle finger is called *nakayubi*, which literally means the finger in the middle. The ring finger is called *kusuriyubi* because sometimes a doctor would use this finger to check medicine. The fifth finger is called *koyubi*, "child." Each finger differs in name, function, and shape. Each is independent, and yet when we call them a hand, the individuality of each finger disappears. *Ji* and *ri* are two ways of viewing things—as independent beings and as a whole. In the same way, the hand is a part of our body, which has many more parts. Each part—hand, head, foot, and billions of cells—is different, and yet this body works as one thing, a body.

Form and Emptiness

The phrase "the spiritual source" refers to unity or *ri*; "branching streams" refers to plurality or *ji*. The spiritual source is one and the branching streams are many. In "Sandōkai" *ji* is first translated as "things." Later the same word is translated as "phenomena." In the phrase "merging with principle," principle is a translation of *ri*. So "things" is *ji* and "principle" is *ri*.

In the *Heart Sutra* the terms "form" and "emptiness" correspond to *ji* and *ri*. "Form" refers to an individual being with a beginning and end; it is born, stays for a while, and disappears. Transient beings or entities without permanent self are said to have form. The *Heart Sutra* tells us that form is emptiness. This means that nothing exists as a truly independent being with a fixed self-nature. We appear to be independent but in reality are supported by all beings. I cannot survive as a human body or mind without the support of air, water, food, and so forth. The *Heart Sutra* also says that emptiness is form. Emptiness does not exist outside of form. We are a merging of difference and unity. From one perspective we are independent, but at the same time we are completely interdependent. As Buddhists we try to understand this contradiction by seeing it as two perspectives on a single reality. This is the basic idea of difference and unity, or ji and ri.

Light and Darkness

In the sentence "The spiritual source shines clearly in the light," light symbolizes ji or difference. The original word for "shines clearly" is *kōketzu*. *Kō* means "white," and *ketzu* means "clear and undefiled." This evokes an image of a full moon. But the moon shines in the darkness, not in the light. This sentence confuses us by saying the moon or the spiritual source shines in the light.

In the phrase "branching streams flow in the darkness," darkness represents ri. I didn't understand these two sentences for a long time because the spiritual source is ri, unity, and light is ji, or difference. This sentence means that the spiritual source (or unity) shines clearly in the light (or difference). Similarly the "branching streams," a symbol of ji or difference, "flow in the darkness," a symbol of ri or unity. The statement that unity shines in difference and difference flows in the unity is a paradox. It points out the dynamic interpenetration of discrimination and nondiscrimination.

We Are Separate but Together

We should try to understand this as a whole. Unity and difference are not two different things; they merge. From the perspective of ji or difference, we are independent people, separate individuals. I am not you; you are not me. Yet we cannot live completely alone. We live with other people and things; they are part of the reality of our life. Even so, I can't feel your pain, and you can't feel mine. My wife has pain in her teeth, but I have never had pain in my teeth. I have never even been to the dentist. I can't feel her pains, but I have different pains of my own. I have pain in my lower back that she cannot feel. The reality is that we are completely separate individuals. We can't even share pain. We are born alone, and we die alone. No one can be born for me, no one can live for me, and no one can die for me. From birth we are alone: we live alone, completely independent, and when we die we are really alone.

And yet we can never be completely alone. We cannot be born without a mother and father. We cannot grow up without support from our parents, family, and society. There are two aspects of our lives:

independent and interdependent. This is not a matter of separate parts of our life. Our whole life is individual, and at the same time our whole life is 100 percent interdependent. There is no separation of the two. This is an important point. We should see both aspects of our life at the same time. This is how we wake up to the reality of our life. This seems contradictory, and it causes problems when we think about it. These two aspects become separate things, two principles: individualism and socialism. If we don't understand, if we are unable to awake to reality, we become unhealthy. If we cling to the principle of individuality, we live on the basis of "I am I, I am not you, and you are not me." We live in isolation from the rest of the world. On the other hand, if we cling to the aspect of unity or wholeness, individuality is ignored. Then the individual lives only to serve society, and that's not healthy either.

In American society, individualism is a problem. In Japan, however, until recently the family was most important, and each person lived for the sake of the family. Either extreme is unhealthy.

Just Sitting Is Itself Merging of Difference and Unity

Often the practice or study of Zen or Buddhism involves an attempt to negate or go beyond individuality. We try to become one with universality, or buddha-nature. I disagree with this approach. For example, the Chinese master Sheng-yen wrote in a commentary on "Merging of Difference and Unity," "The first line of this couplet refers to light or brightness. The second line refers to darkness. Lightness represents enlightenment, and darkness represents vexation, or the condition of sentient beings before enlightenment."[106] In his interpretation, darkness is delusion, and we are deluded human beings because we don't see the unity. He says that enlightenment is to perceive the unity. However, Shitou is saying that delusion is grasping ji, that is, grasping independent things. I believe this is true. Shitou goes on to say, "Merging with principle is still not enlightenment." To merge with principle means to transcend individuality and become one with unity. It means to see the emptiness of all things. But Shitou says, "Merging with principle is still not enlightenment." Neither individuality nor unity is enlightenment.

Zen is often understood as a series of steps. We start out egocentric, completely deluded, clinging to ourselves. Through study and practice we try to become free from egocentricity. To be free from ego-clinging, we have to see the emptiness of all beings. This is called kensho or satori. But this is not final enlightenment. We have to return to individuality. This is a common way of explaining the steps of practice, but it is not consistent with my understanding of dharma or practice based on Dōgen Zenji's teachings.

Dōgen taught that there are no steps in practice. He said that practice and enlightenment are actually one. If there were steps, there would be deluded people and enlightened people, and there would be a step from the deluded to the enlightened stage of mind. There would be a separation between delusion and enlightenment, and between deluded and enlightened people. This separation is itself delusion, because in the absolute realm there is no such step, no discrimination between delusion and enlightenment. Discrimination between enlightenment and delusion only exists in ji; there is no distinction in ri. In unity or emptiness, delusion and enlightenment are not different, nor are samsara and nirvana, or deluded human beings and buddhas. That's the teaching of emptiness. Our practice does not proceed step by step. With this body and mind we sit in both individuality and universality. We are often pulled by our egocentricity. When we sit in this posture and let go of thought in our zazen, we have no technique. We have no object of meditation or contemplation. We don't concentrate our mind on anything particular. We don't even pay special attention to our breathing. We don't count breaths. We don't visualize anything. We just sit in this upright posture, breathe through the nose, quietly, deeply, and smoothly, and let go of thought. To let go of thought means to allow whatever comes in to go out. We let any idea, desire, or imagination come up and then go free. Nothing stays forever. We don't try to control our mind. We simply keep our body straight, breathe quietly, and let go of thought. This is our zazen based on Dōgen Zenji's teachings.

Within this zazen individuality is not lost. This is my practice; no one else can sit for me. My sitting is mine alone. And yet within this sitting practice we let go of our egocentricity. To let go of thought means to let go of our egocentricity. This body and mind is really part of buddha-nature, not something separate. Within this zazen, both ji and ri are manifested; neither is negated, neither affirmed. Both sides arise naturally in this simple practice. That's the meaning of Dōgen Zenji's expression "practice and enlightenment are one." Practice is my own individual practice, and enlightenment is universal. There is no separation between my enlightenment and your enlightenment, but practice is individual. I cannot practice for you. Practice is my personal activity, which manifests the universal reality of life. This zazen is itself the merging of difference and unity, not a step-by-step meditation practice. When we sit, we just sit. We express completely difference and unity, individuality and universality. To let go of thought is, I think, the most important point of our practice of zazen.

Practice in Day-to-Day Activities

We cannot let go of thought in our day-to-day activities. For example, when we prepare a meal we have to read the recipe. We have to use the correct ingredients in the proper way. Since we cannot let go of thought, we have to practice with our thoughts, with what we are doing now. We have to be clear about what we are cooking. We need to discriminate. Salt and sugar look very similar but are completely different, so we must discriminate between them. We need discrimination, and yet, as a practice when we are cooking, we let go of thought. In this case to let go of thought means to let go of all thought that is not needed for cooking. This means we are completely mindful of what we are doing right now, right here, at this moment. We use our whole mind to concentrate on our day-to-day activities.

Cooking also involves serving others. To prepare a meal for others is to make an offering. Our life becomes part of another person's life. This is the concrete meaning of interdependent existence. Through our activities we can become one with other beings. Oneness of subject and object is not a matter of philosophy, contemplation, or belief but a result of concrete action. Through an activity like cooking for others, our energy becomes the meal, and the meal becomes other people's energy. Our day-to-day activity, not only at the zendo but also at home and work, should be based on our zazen, on a merging of difference and unity. Our practice is not to kill our individuality. Of course, our practice is not to become more egoistic, but neither is it to simply become one with unity, with all beings. Our practice is to manifest the merging of difference and unity completely in every activity, including zazen. We try to live and act on this basis. We don't rely on others and yet we practice together with others. This is difficult but it is the healthiest way of life. We can be independent and not rely on others but still help them. Yet we often go astray. To be natural is the most difficult thing for us human beings.

Subject-Object: Interact and Not Interact

> Each sense and every field
> Interact and do not interact;
> When interacting, they also merge—
> Otherwise, they remain in their own states.

Each line in the original Chinese poem consists of five Chinese characters. In these four lines Shitou uses only fifteen different Chinese characters, fifteen words to express the whole of reality. This is incredible to me. I could write a whole book about these four lines.

Six Sense Organs and the Six Objects

The first phrase, "each sense," is a translation of the Chinese expression *monmon*. *Mon* means "gate," "entrance," or "exit." This expression refers to each of the six sense organs. These are called gates because stimulation from outside comes to us through them, and we express our thoughts and emotions through them to the outside. The next phrase, "every field," is a translation of *issai no kyō*. *Issai* means "all," and *kyō* in a Buddhist context means "objects or things outside of ourselves." This refers to the six objects of the sense organs. The object of the sixth sense organ, the mind, is something that we cannot touch, see, hear, smell, or taste but can imagine. Abstract concepts like love, numbers, and things that do not exist such as "the hair of a turtle" or "the horn of a rabbit" can be objects of mind. We cannot perceive these things, and yet we can think about them.

The sense organs and their objects are the totality of our life. Our life consists of subject (self, body, and mind) and objects (all beings as the objects of our sense organs). The objects of our sense organs are outside of our body and do not belong to us. Common sense tells us that there is a separation between the six sense organs and their objects. We, with our bodies and minds, relate to the objects outside us. We consider some things valuable or useful, others we don't. So we judge and evaluate, discriminate and categorize. When we encounter an object, we put it into a category and think we understand it. That's our usual way of seeing.

The six sense organs and their six objects appear in the *Heart Sutra*: "No eyes, no ears, no nose, no tongue, no body, no mind; / No color, no sound, no smell, no taste, no touch, no object of mind." The sutra says that such categories are not real. In fact, it says there is no independent thing called "I" to establish these categories. There are no independent entities called eyes, ears, nose, tongue, body, or mind. Nor are there independent entities called color, sound, smell, taste, touch, or objects of mind. In reality there are no independent entities at all, either inside or outside us. Instead, eyes, ears, nose, tongue, body, and mind work together as one body and mind, as one self. Color, sound, smell, touch, taste, and objects of mind also work together. This is the meaning of emptiness or dependent origination. Everything supports everything else; nothing has independent self-nature. As a result everything permeates everything else.

We Exist Supported by All Things

Without food, water, and air, we cannot live. We cannot maintain our bodies and minds. Food is made of other beings; when we digest, we incorporate them into ourselves, into our bodies. Our life is supported by all beings. This is the meaning of dependent origination. We are also supported by things from the past. I can use this glass to drink water today because someone made it and someone put water in it and served it to me. Everything in this present moment, in the past, and also in the future, supports everything else. It all works together as one function. This is the meaning of śūnyatā, emptiness, or dependent origination.

Sense Organs Work Together

In the sentence "Each sense and every field interact and do not interact," "field" refers to the object of each sense working together with the sense organ. There is no separation from the universal view. And yet we cannot say that the eye and ear are the same. Eye is eye, ear is ear, and nose is nose. They have different functions and shapes. They cannot replace each other. If we lose our eyes, we can't see. If we lose our nose, we can't smell. But in a universal sense they are not independent; none of them have self-nature. They are really interdependent. And yet in our common sense way of seeing the world, eye is eye, nose is nose, tongue is tongue. Individuality and universality always coexist, and neither side should be negated or ignored. We should always try to see reality, all beings, and our lives from both perspectives.

Interact and Not Interact

In the phrase "interact and do not interact," the Japanese for "interact" is *e-go*. *E* means "turn around," and *go* means "each other" or "mutually." So *e-go* means mutually to turn, to influence, to work together, or to penetrate each other. Interaction is the aspect of unity—eye, ear, nose, tongue, body, and mind working together with no separation. The second half of the phrase, *fu e-go*, means "do not interact"; eye is eye, ear is ear, nose is nose, tongue is tongue. Everything is independent in its own function. This refers to individuality, independence, and difference, as in the title "Merging of Difference and Unity."

Consider an orchestra: Each person plays a different instrument. A violin is not a piano, and a piano is not a drum. They all make different sounds. They are independent and cannot replace each other. Yet when they work together, they make one musical whole. But even as we listen to an orchestra as one sound, there are still many independent musicians all playing their own parts. Both sides are always present. This is true of any community. For example, in this sangha there are different positions, each filled by a different person who carries out his or her own duties. But this sangha also exists as a whole, as one sangha, and in this sense there is no separation among us. "Interact" refers to everything working together and "not interact" describes everything having its own individual shape, function, and practice.

Harmony in Community

Community always includes both aspects. If we ignore either, the sangha, family, or body becomes sick and functions poorly. If we think only of one individual and lose sight of the community as a whole, the community doesn't work. But it's not healthy to put too much emphasis on the community and ignore individuals. When we go too far toward either extreme, we become sick. We have to try to find the Middle Way. This is one of the most important concepts in Buddhism. We find the Middle Way when we sacrifice neither the individual nor the community. In *Shōbōgenzō* "Bodaisatta Shishōbō" (Bodhisattva's Four Embracing Dharmas), Dōgen Zenji said, "Identity-action means not to be different—neither different from self nor from others."[107] This means we have to find a way for both self and others to be peaceful, harmonious, and beneficial as a whole. This is called compassion. It doesn't mean that I sacrifice myself for the sake of the community but that the community should include this self. We have to find a way that this community can include this individual self and be healthy. This is the bodhisattva Way.

Interacting and Not Interacting Interact

The next line of "Sandōkai" says, "When interacting, they also merge." "When interacting" as a translation of *e-go* is not quite accurate because it implies that things interact only at particular times. Actually all things are always interacting. The Japanese word for "merge" here is *wataru*.

The Chinese character for this word has two parts; one means "water" or "river," and the other means "to walk." Together, the two mean to cross the river, in this case to cross on foot a river with no bridge. Often Chinese or Japanese villages are separated by a small river. The river is a boundary that is crossed only when there is a problem to be resolved. This character thus means to negotiate, to meet in order to solve problems. It also means to see around the world, or to walk around the world and see things. So *wataru* means to cross borders and work together.

At the same time, it implies some independence, since people don't cross the boundaries between villages very often. Especially in ancient times, people who were born in a village died in the same village. One family might live in the same village for many generations. When I lived in a small farming village in Kyoto, Japan, there were about seventy families, most of whom had lived there more than five hundred years. In the temple there was a family grave that dated back to the sixteenth century. The villagers didn't get out much. But when there were problems they had to cross the boundary and meet, negotiate, and work together. That's the meaning of wataru. This kanji, or Chinese character, shows both individuality and collaboration. The interaction it describes is not tied to a special time or occasion but ongoing, among all beings and things. And yet at the same time all things have independence.

Not Interacting Within Interacting

The next line, "Otherwise, they remain in their own states," refers to noninteraction, which is also an ongoing aspect of reality rather than a specific time or circumstance. Eye is always eye, nose is nose. I am I, you are you. The Chinese character translated here as "state" has two parts. One means "human being or person," the other "standing." Together they describe a person standing in a certain place, meaning that each person has his or her own place or position. This refers not only to individuals but to the functions of each individual. All the senses and their objects are independent. Each has its own place, stage, rank, and function. They cannot combine. Both aspects, individuality and interaction, are always present. This seems contradictory but is in fact the nature of reality.

Wondrous Dharma

Dōgen Zenji's major work is *Shōbōgenzō*. *Shō* means "true," "right," or "correct." *Bō* is "dharma." *Gen* means "eyes." A *zō* is a storehouse or treasury. *Shōbōgenzō* thus means "treasury of the true dharma eye." This means that this reality, the reality of our life, is a treasury of the eye. In this case, "eye" stands for the wisdom that sees the true dharma. The Sanskrit for "true dharma" is *saddharma*. It is part of the title of the *Lotus Sutra*, *Saddharmapuṇḍarīka Sutra*, where it means "true reality or true teaching." The Chinese translation of this Sanskrit word is *myōhō*. *Myō* is an interesting character with two parts: one means *woman* and the other *young*. Literally, *myō* refers to the beauty of a young woman. It means beautiful, excellent, wonderful, strange, and always changing—something we can't grasp. *Myō* is sometimes translated into English as "wondrous," meaning excellent and ungraspable. We can't understand it with logic. So the reality of our life is excellent, wonderful, and yet strange and hard to understand. As explained above *hō* means dharma.

Reality itself is a question for us. There is no way to reduce the reality of our life to any logical system and completely understand it, because our life is so complex. Reality is always asking us, "What is this life? Who are we? What am I doing?" Somehow we have to answer with our practice. Practice doesn't necessarily mean sitting or studying the Buddha's teaching. Practice can mean the activities of our day-to-day lives. Even when we try to avoid answering reality's questions, that avoidance itself is an answer. If we try to deny reality, that's also an answer. So we can't avoid it. Each one of us has to engage this reality, including our self, body, mind, and situation. Our self and our situation work together. We have to accept this total reality as our self. Self is not a separate part of reality. Our life is the sum of all the things happening inside and outside us. We try to be peaceful, not only inside ourselves but throughout the whole universe. There may be no war within this country, but if there is fighting somewhere else this country cannot be peaceful, because everything is connected. We have to work together with things inside and outside ourselves. This attitude is bodhisattva practice.

These four sentences express the wondrous reality of our life; a life that has two aspects, interacting and not interacting, that also interact with each other. And yet each and every thing stays in its own dharma position. This expression "dharma position" is originally from the *Lotus Sutra*. Dōgen Zenji uses it in *Shōbōgenzō* "Genjōkōan," where he says that firewood stays at the dharma position of firewood, and ash stays at the dharma position of ash, and yet "before and after is cut off" by the fire. It's difficult to understand, but we have to work through this as a koan. *Genjō* refers to whatever is happening in this present moment as the dharma position. *Koan* means both "reality" and also "question." Reality asks a question, "What is this?" and we must try to answer. The answer is our practice.

Darkness and Light

> Forms are basically different in material and appearance,
> Sounds are fundamentally different in pleasant or harsh
> quality.
> "Darkness" is a word for merging upper and lower;
> "Light" is an expression for distinguishing pure and defiled.

Differences of the Objects

Here "forms" means the material objects of our sense field. Although this poem only mentions forms and sounds, it means all six objects of our sense organs (including mind, which senses mental formations). All things have varied natures and characteristics. We are all human beings and yet each of us looks different. Although we share a common nature or essence, we vary in appearance. All things have some aspects in common and also some unique qualities.

Shitou continues, "Sounds are fundamentally different in pleasant or harsh quality." There are many different kinds of sound, some pleasing, some terrible. We feel good when we listen to beautiful music, but if we are sitting in the zendo and someone turns on loud rock-and-roll, it's disturbing. The same song might make us feel good or bad depending on the situation. The effect of a song depends not only on the nature of the sound itself but also on the condition of this body and mind.

The same is true of taste. Delicious food and awful food might have very similar nutritional value. But we have likes and dislikes. Each thing has its own unique character, and we also respond to it in different ways. Sometimes we feel good, sometimes we feel bad. Even when we have delicious food in front of us, if we are not hungry the delicious food is the same as junk food. When we are really hungry, even junk food seems a feast. The appearance, quality, meaning, and value of things around us all depend on the properties of each thing and on the condition of our body and mind. Nothing has a fixed nature or value.

Darkness and Light: Nondiscrimination and Discrimination

Shitou goes on to say, "'Darkness' is a word for merging upper and lower; 'Light' is an expression for distinguishing pure and defiled." This is the same principle as *ji* and *ri*. *Ji*, it will be recalled, is the aspect of independence; each thing has its own characteristics. *Ri* is the aspect of universality or unity. For example, a hand is made up of five independent fingers, each with a different shape, function, and name. We cannot separate the fingers from the hand, and we cannot separate the fingers from the billions of cells that make them up. A cell is a collection of billions of atoms that cannot be separated. Each atom is also a collection of smaller particles. This one hand is a part of my body, which is a part of the human society, which is a part of the larger ecology of the earth. Earth is a small part of the whole universe. Nothing is fixed and yet each thing is really independent. This is really a wondrous way of being. This is what is meant in the *Heart Sutra* when it says, "form is emptiness and emptiness is form." Nothing is fixed, yet this hand is this hand. I am I, but this "I" doesn't exist independently. I can exist as a part of something or as a collection of things. Darkness, or *ri*, is the universal aspect of our life. Light, *ji*, is the individual, independent aspect of our life. In the dark, colors are indistinguishable. In the light, everything becomes clear. We can distinguish between red and blue, north and south, grass and water. We should see our life and world from both perspectives, light and darkness, differentiation and non-differentiation. We usually see ourselves as individuals, distinct from other people. I say this is me, and this is my opinion. I like this, I hate that. If someone else has a different opinion we may feel angry or sad. Many conflicts and problems arise from this difference. Yet when we see oneness or universality, we understand that we are living out the same life, supported by all beings. We realize that without others we cannot live. When we clearly, deeply understand this, many problems disappear naturally.

Nondiscrimination Is Not Enlightenment

Because of our upbringing, we can easily see our individuality. So the first thing we have to learn is to see the universality of our life. We need to be able to see that we share our life with other people, with all beings in the whole universe. That is the meaning of interdependence, one of the main teachings of the Buddha. But if we cling to that perspective and call it enlightenment, it's a mistake. The Buddha taught that we must see the reality of our life from both sides.

Our zazen practice is to awaken to the reality prior to separation. Ordinarily we see things from one perspective or the other. When we sit, we let go of thoughts and all particular perspectives. We don't grasp anything. That doesn't mean that we have to extinguish thought. Thought is always there as we experience our life, even when sitting in this posture. Our mind often seems busier than usual when we sit in a quiet place. In fact, our body and mind are busier and noisier in everyday life, but since our environment is also noisy, we don't notice the commotion inside ourselves. When we come to a quiet place, however, we hear even the smallest noise. When we sit in the zendo, we can hear the sound of the clock. The sounds our bodies make, coming from within us, become more noticeable, and it seems that our mind is noisier than usual. I think that's a good sign of our practice. We hear this noise because our mind is beginning to calm down. Of course, we should let go of the internal noise. We should neither cling to nor try to escape from the noise. We should just be awake and let it go. Let all thoughts, feelings, and daydreams simply come and go freely. Everything is moving; nothing stays forever. Just let everything be with you.

In zazen you should keep this upright posture, breathe quietly through your nose, and let go of everything. We don't try to control anything, just keep this posture and let go. That is how darkness and light manifest. Thought is still there. Yet we don't think. It's a difficult point to explain. It's like when you are driving a car and shift into neutral. The engine is moving but the car doesn't go anywhere. In our zazen we put our mind into neutral. Thought is there but we are not moved by it. My teacher Uchiyama Roshi said, "Thought is just a secretion from our brain." Thought is not a poison. But if you grasp and are controlled by it, it becomes poisonous. We actualize both darkness and light when we open our hand of thought and are not moved. That is sitting practice. Our zazen is not a method to contemplate reality which has lightness and dark. It is a way to manifest both darkness and light. We are not the observer but rather the reality itself.

Four Gross Elements

The four gross elements return to their own natures
Like a baby taking to its mother;
Fire heats, wind moves,
Water wets, earth is solid.
Eye and form, ear and sound;
Nose and smell, tongue and taste—

The four gross elements are fire, wind, water, and earth. Here these four words refer not to the literal elements but to the elements of our life. For example, fire represents body heat; wind symbolizes breathing and moving; water denotes blood, tears, or other bodily liquids; and earth suggests bones, nails, hair, and other solids. In addition to these four, Mahāyāna Buddhism considers *ku*, which means "emptiness" or "space," the fifth gross element. In Chinese, space and emptiness are represented by the same character, which means "sky." Everything occupies space, so space is, in a sense, another element.

Each element has its own nature: fire heats, wind moves, water is wet, earth is solid. These elements cannot be confused. But at the same time the five elements combine to form one body, one mind, one person. Not only this one person but everything in this universe is composed of these five elements. Everything is just a collection of those elements, and yet each being, each thing, maintains its independence. It's really wondrous and yet this is reality.

Shitou continues, "Eye and form, ear and sound; nose and smell, tongue and taste." This is a list of some of the sense organs of the body and mind and their objects. They are independent and yet work together to create the world. When we sit in this space, the space and my sitting become one. When I cook in the kitchen, this body, my self, the ingredients, the water, the fire, the utensils, and the space called the kitchen become one being working together. When we play baseball, this whole universe becomes the world of playing baseball. Our activity and the universe become one. It all works together. If we become angry, this whole world becomes the world of anger. Everything around us makes us crazy, angry. When we have a competitive mind, this entire world becomes the world of competition. All other beings, all other people, become competitors. Our body and mind work together with our environment to create one world. In this sense our mind is very important. A change in our mind could change the whole world. Our practice is important because it is not just the practice of our mind; it influences the whole universe.

Root and Leaves Return to the Source

> Thus in all things
> The leaves spread from the root;

The whole process must return to the source;
"Noble" and "base" are only manners of speaking.

The Source Gives Birth to the Root and the Leaves

Here Shitou uses the expression "leaves and root" in the same way as "spiritual source and branching streams." This too is a symbol of individuality and universality. The leaves represent individuality and the root symbolizes oneness. I question the translation of the next phrase, "The whole process must return to the source." The Japanese word used for "whole process" is *hon matsu*. *Hon* means "original" or "foundation," and *matsu* means "twigs and leaves." *Hon* can also mean "root." From the root or foundation all individual beings arise. And this sentence says that both *hon* (root) and *matsu* (twigs) must return to the source. A better translation would be, "Unity and individuality must return to the source."

This "source" is different from the "spiritual source" mentioned near the beginning of the poem. "Spiritual source" refers to the root (oneness). In contrast, this "source" is a translation of the Chinese word *zong* (Jap., *shū*), which means "essence" or "origin." This is a very Chinese expression of reality. In Chinese thought, individuality emerges from oneness. It is often said that Zen Buddhism is a mixture of Indian Buddhism and Chinese philosophy—in this case Taoism. The idea that individual beings spring from oneness is a typically Taoist way of thinking. Lao Tzu said, "Return is the movement of the Tao. Yielding is the way of the Tao. All things are born of being. Being is born of nonbeing. The Tao is nowhere to be found. Yet it nourishes and completes all things. The Tao gives birth to One. One gives birth to Two. Two gives birth to Three. Three gives birth to all things."[108] This means that myriad independent things flow from oneness. This oneness in turn derives from the Tao of nothingness, or *mu*. Ultimately both difference and unity return to the source (*shū*), which is nothingness (*mu*).

Unlike the Chinese, Indian Buddhists didn't believe that emptiness is the source of form. They believed that form is emptiness and emptiness is form but not that emptiness is the source of form. In this poem, we can see a mixture of Indian and Chinese philosophy. Some modern Buddhist scholars conclude that because Zen is a mixture of Chinese and Indian thought, it is not true Buddhism. I think the situation is more complex. Chinese Buddhism is Buddhism influenced by Chinese culture. Japanese Buddhism is Buddhism influenced by Japanese culture. We could also say that Japanese Buddhism is Japanese culture influenced by Buddhism. In the same way, we can say that Chinese Buddhism is Chinese culture influenced by Buddhism. We can look at either from two different directions. We can think of American Buddhism as American culture influenced by Buddhism or as Buddhism influenced by American culture. To judge a practice as true Buddhism or not based on the national and cultural background of the practitioner's understanding does not make much sense to me. We need to find our own expression of the dharma, of reality. This is a simple but at the same time complex and interesting reality.

Another example of this contrast between Indian and Chinese thought is the "two truths" in Nāgārjuna's teaching versus the "three truths" in the philosophy of Tientai Zhiyi (Tendai Chigi, 538–597), the most important master in the Chinese Tientai (Tendai) school. To review, Nāgārjuna's two truths are absolute truth and conventional truth. In chapter 24 of the *Mūlamadhyamakakārikā*, "Examination of the Fourfold Noble Truth," Nāgārjuna said:

> The teaching of the Dharma by the various Buddhas is based on the two truths, namely, the relative (worldly) truth and the absolute (supreme) truth. Those who do not know the distinction between the two truths cannot understand the profound nature of the Buddha's teaching. Without relying on everyday common practice (i.e., relative truths), the absolute truth cannot be expressed. Without approaching the absolute truth, nirvana cannot be attained. We declare that whatever is relational origination is śūnyatā (emptiness). It is a provisional name (i.e., thought construction) for the mutuality (of being) and indeed, it is the middle path (24:8–10).[109]

In these passages, according to Hajime Nakamura, a Japanese Buddhist scholar, Nāgārjuna only says that relational (interdependent) origination, śūnyatā (emptiness), provisional names, and the middle path are all the same thing.

In his interpretation of Nāgārjuna's passages, Zhiyi creates three truths. The first is the conventional truth of all beings as provisional names, the second is the truth of śūnyatā (emptiness), and the third is the truth of the middle. First we need to negate the conventional truth and see emptiness. Next, we need to negate śūnyatā and enter the truth of the middle, because śūnyatā is also a provisional name. To be free from provisional names including śūnyatā is the truth of the middle. In this interpretation, provisional names and śūnyatā oppose each other and yet are the same. Freedom from and transcendence of both is the truth of the middle. To me, Zhiyi's interpretation of the three truths and Shitou's saying the root (unity) and twigs (difference) must return to the source show the same pattern of Chinese thought.

The symbol of yin and yang echoes this pattern. Yin (black) and yang (white) oppose each other, and yet yin is included in yang and vice versa. The opposite movements of each are integrated into one circle. This circle is called the "great ultimate" (Chi., *taiji*; Jap., *taikyoku*). It is the source in "Sandōkai."

"Sandōkai" as a Buddhist Text

When we read "Sandōkai" as a Buddhist text, we need to understand it from a Buddhist rather than Taoist perspective. Forms are not derived from emptiness. Unity does not give birth to difference. Five fingers are not born from one hand. Rather, one hand and five fingers are exactly the same thing.

When Shitou says, "'Noble' and 'base' are only manners of speaking," he is referring to buddhas as noble and other humans as base. We can substitute any other dichotomy—enlightenment and delusion, or universality and individuality—for noble and base. He refers here to our dualistic way of thinking and expression as "only manners of speaking." The reality before thought or explanation can only be experienced. We cannot discuss it. As soon as we try, we have already missed it. This is an important point. We can talk about our life or our zazen; but when we talk about our life, our life itself is already somewhere else. When we talk about zazen, zazen itself is somewhere else. So when we sit zazen, we should forget about what zazen is, because we are already doing it. When we think about zazen, we are not doing it; we are thinking. When we sit, we should forget what we are doing. We should forget what zazen is and just sit. That is the meaning of "just sit" or shikantaza.

How Avalokiteśvara Works with Thousands of Eyes and Hands

There is a koan that illustrates this relationship between independence and interdependence. It is a question and answer between Yunyan Tansheng and Daowu Yuanzhi (Dōgo Enchi, 769–835).[110] The brothers Yunyan and Daowu were disciples of Yaoshan Weiyan, who was one of Shitou's disciples. Yunyan was the younger brother and became a monk at an early age. Daowu was an official and became a monk twenty years later. Daowu attained the Way quickly, while Yunyan was never enlightened. Yunyan's main disciple was Dongshan, the founder of the Caodong (Sōtō) school in China. The relationship between two brothers, actual as well as dharma brothers, was very interesting.

Master Yunyan asked Daowu, "How does the Bodhisattva of Great Compassion use his manifold hands and eyes?" The Bodhisattva of Great Compassion is Avalokiteśvara or Kanzeon Bosatsu. He is a symbol of the Buddha's compassion. Some statues of Avalokiteśvara have a thousand hands and a thousand eyes, one on each hand. Eyes are a symbol of wisdom. So this bodhisattva has many eyes to see the differences between beings and many hands to save them. Yunyan's question is, how does Avalokiteśvara use so many hands and eyes?

Daowu replied, "It's like a man reaching behind himself in the night searching for a pillow." Sometimes in the night we lose our pillow, and have to find it in the darkness. Before electricity the night was really dark. Somehow we can find the pillow even though we cannot see it with our eyes. In a way our whole body is our eyes.

Yunyan said, "I understand."

"What do you understand?" Daowu asked.

Yunyan answered, "There are a thousand eyes all over the body."

Daowu said "That's very good, but you express only 80 or 90 percent of it." He was saying that Yunyan's understanding was not yet perfect. This is a very important point in our lineage. If you really become perfect, there is nothing more to do. Our understanding should always be 80 or 90 percent, and we need to keep inquiring.

Yunyan said, "That's my answer, how about you, elder brother?" Daowu replied, "The whole body is hands and eyes." In the chapter on the *Heart Sutra* I explained that one of the points of this koan is whether Yunyan's and Daowu's expressions are exactly the same or not. If we think they are different, we could interpret them as follows. Yunyan said there are a thousand eyes all over the body, and Daowu said the whole body is hands and eyes. In the original Chinese only two characters are different, *hen* and *tsū*, and they both mean "whole" or "entire." It might seem as though Yunyan and Daowu are saying the same thing. But *hen* means that there are hands and eyes all over the body, and in Daowu's expression, *tsū* means this whole body functions as eyes and hands. It's a subtle difference, but Daowu's statement is much more dynamic. He refers to an action or activity. Yunyan's expression is more static.

Daowu is saying that our practice, not just our zazen, but our whole life, should be lived like Avalokiteśvara. We have only two hands and eyes, and yet when we do something our whole body should become eyes. When we see something, for instance a painting in a museum, our whole body should become our eyes. We appreciate the painting with the whole body and mind, not just our eyes. When we eat, we taste not only with our tongue but with our whole body. The color and shape of food is important. The circumstances or environment of the place where we eat is also important. The taste of food depends very much on the situation. When we do something we do it with our whole body. The eye is the eye. It really is independent. Yet when we actually do something, we do it with our whole body and mind. All individual sense organs and parts of our body work together as one body and mind, as one person. This is a very practical meaning of emptiness. Everything works together to create each situation. It is our practice to awaken to this entire reality, which includes the self and all beings, creating together.

Right in Light There Is Darkness

> Right in light there is darkness, but don't confront it as
> darkness;
> Right in darkness there is light, but don't see it as light.
> Light and dark are relative to one another
> Like forward and backward steps.

Light and Darkness Interpenetrate

In the beginning of "Sandōkai," Shitou says, "The spiritual source shines clearly in the light; the branching streams flow in the darkness." This is the way he expresses the interpenetration of difference and unity, ji and ri, the absolute truth and relative truth. Here he uses light and darkness again to describe the attitude we should use to encounter and see the interpenetrating reality.

"Right in light there is darkness, but ..." This translation has "but," but I think "therefore" is better: "therefore don't confront it as darkness." Light and darkness are always together. We cannot understand our life through only one aspect. We often see darkness, unity, or nondiscrimination as enlightenment and discrimination as delusion. From this perspective, enlightenment means to give up light, differentiation, and discrimination and to live in the realm of nondiscrimination. Shitou conveys a more complex understanding. In the phrase "light and dark," light refers to samsara and dark to nirvana or nondiscrimination. But these are inseparable aspects of reality. In Mahāyāna Buddhism, our practice is not to escape samsara for nirvana. Nirvana is within samsara, which is within nirvana. We cannot make this life all nirvana or all samsara because samsara and nirvana always exist together. Right in samsara there is nirvana.

The next sentence repeats the same idea. "Right in darkness there is light, therefore don't see it as light." We cannot define this light using only one concept. Delusion and enlightenment always exist together. Delusion is a product of our mind. The fact that our brain has the power to produce delusion is reality. We cannot remove this capability from our brain. Somehow we must live with our delusions as the reality of our life. But if we forget that our delusions are created by our own minds and mistake them for reality, then we are completely caught and our life becomes a mess. We can't see where to go. We have to find a way to live with delusion without being pulled around by it.

Shitou continues, "Light and dark are relative to one another like forward and backward steps." There is no light without darkness and no darkness without light. But what do forward and backward steps mean? In walking, when the right foot is forward, the left foot is backward. When the right foot is backward, the left foot is forward. In this sense, light and darkness are like right and left feet. They are always together but sometimes we see only light and sometimes only darkness. Sometimes darkness is forward, sometimes light. But light and darkness are always together just like our feet when we are walking.

Darkness Is Negative, Light Is Positive

There are two meanings each for light and darkness. We can combine them to make three different pairs of meanings. Darkness is usually used in a negative sense, as ignorance, absence of discrimination, lack of intellection, or the inability to distinguish good from evil. Without knowledge we cannot understand what is happening. This meaning of darkness is negative because it's defined as a lack of discrimination. One meaning of light is the opposite of this first meaning of darkness; light can mean intellection. We study how to analyze, categorize, and conceptualize things. In this way we can see things outside ourselves in more detail, more clearly. This way of interacting with the things around us is called rationalism. The use of reason to understand our world is the original English meaning of enlightenment. In eighteenth-century Europe enlightenment emphasized the accumulation of knowledge.

Our suffering is caused by ignorance, so we must study more and use our reason. This is still an underlying assumption in education, not only in the West but also in the rest of the world.

Light Is Negative, Darkness Is Positive

The first meaning of light is the use of our intellect to see things not only outside of ourselves but inside as well. We call this discrimination. Abhidharma was a Buddhist form of rationalism, an attempt to understand things through reason and analysis. Abhidharma was the mainstream of Buddhist philosophy before Mahāyāna. The Abhidharma text *Abhidharmakośa bhāṣya* categorized all things into seventy-five dharmas or elements. These philosophers believed that there is no ātman or ego, no body and mind beyond a collection of elements, and that self has no substance. That's the meaning of emptiness or selflessness. They believed that the seventy-five elements really did exist and that all beings are collections of those seventy-five elements. They wrote clear definitions of each element. The five skandhas is another way to analyze a being into categories.

Mahāyāna Buddhism transcends this rationalism and conceptualization with the philosophy of emptiness. Mahāyāna Buddhism taught that the elements themselves are without substance, that they are empty. That is the meaning of the statement that the five skandhas are empty. Even the fundamental elements are empty. This means that eye, ear, nose, and tongue don't function separately, but only as a whole. They are all connected with each other. That is one meaning of emptiness. Nothing can exist as an independent entity and everything functions as part of a larger system. This perspective is called nondiscriminating mind or nondiscriminating wisdom. It is also referred to as darkness in this poem.

Going Beyond Negative and Positive

If darkness as lack of discrimination or intellection and light as rational discrimination are paired, darkness is negative and light is positive. However, we can also make a second pair with light as negative (discrimination from a limited view) and darkness as positive (a nondiscriminatory way of seeing).

In Buddhism we commonly think that nondiscrimination is the answer; that we should try to set aside discrimination and enter the realm of nondiscrimination, which is enlightenment. That's true but it's not the end of the story. There is another meaning of light called the Buddha's wisdom or "later obtained discriminating wisdom," which is also based on nondiscrimination. In our daily lives we have to discriminate to practice and to help others. In this case, nondiscrimination means nonattachment. This light is called prajñā and is described in the *Heart Sutra* as the bright mantra. It's very important that we go beyond nondiscrimination. In Zen there are some people who attain so-called enlightenment and stay in a condition of nondiscrimination. Sometimes such people cling to that condition with a kind of greed. These practitioners are called *an shō no zenji*. *An* means "darkness" and *shō* is "enlightenment." So the phrase means "enlightenment in darkness," a negative condition. Buddhism and our life itself have many dimensions. We should not stagnate in one condition. In this poem, it appears that Shitou discusses only the relationship between light and darkness, between differentiation and nondifferentiation. But the insight Shitou uses to describe the relationship between light and darkness is an example of the Buddha's wisdom, this third meaning of light. He shows us that differentiation between darkness and light is just another kind of discrimination. He discriminates between these two and then integrates them. This is a very practical wisdom, free from both discrimination and nondiscrimination. It is a more natural function of our life.

Box and Cover Joining

All things have their function—
It is a matter of use in the appropriate situation.
Phenomena exist like box and cover joining;
Principle accords like arrow points meeting.

Each Thing Has Its Own Place and Function

"All things have their function." Everything and everybody has a unique function. We all have different capabilities, talents, characteristics, personalities, bodies, and languages. All things have a function appropriate to some situation. The word in Japanese for "appropriate situation" is *sho*, meaning "place." Each one of us has to find the best place to use this body and mind. This unique body and mind exists as an intersection of difference and unity. That is the place where we can create our own unique way of life. That is our practice. Our practice doesn't mean we have to make ourselves into a particular shape. We are not like cars with certain standard shapes and qualities. We have a responsibility to accept this unique body and mind and put it to use. To fulfill the potential of this body and mind, we have to find an appropriate situation and embrace it as our own life, as our own work.

Phenomena and Principle Are Like Box and Lid

Next Shitou says, "Phenomena exist like box and cover joining; principle accords like arrow points meeting." "Phenomena" is a translation for *ji*, meaning particular things or beings. "Principle" is a translation of *ri*, the unity or universality of all beings. Shitou says that phenomena exist in accord with principle, and principle exists in accord with phenomena. "Phenomena exist like box and cover joining; principle accords like arrow points meeting" is actually just one sentence. This is rhetoric used in Chinese poetry to avoid repetition of the same two subjects. Each of the two clauses is about the way phenomena and principle exist and work together. We should read, "Phenomena and principle exist like box and cover joining; principle accords with phenomena like arrow points meeting." Phenomena and principle, ji and ri, difference and unity, exist like box and cover joining. Each box is a different size with a lid that fits exactly. So there is no principle other than phenomena. Phenomena and principle are like box and cover, completely joined.

Arrow Points Meeting in the Air

"Arrow points meeting" is a reference to a classic Chinese story about two archery masters.[111] One was the teacher and the other his excellent disciple. When the student felt his skill had surpassed his teacher's, he challenged him. When they took aim at each other and shot, the arrows met in midair and fell to the ground. Both lived because they had equal skill. Shitou says that phenomena and principle, difference and unity, should meet like the arrows. Our practice is to actualize this relationship between difference and unity in each situation. For example, we cannot live by ourselves. We are part of a community, and yet no matter where I live, I am I. I cannot be another person, and yet to be a member of a community I have to transcend "I am I" and see the situation of the whole community. We have a point of view as an individual and also as a member of the sangha or community. We also have another "I" who sees the situation from both perspectives. The viewpoint of an individual person is in this case an example of difference. It's very natural that I have an opinion different from other people. We shouldn't negate our individual opinions, but as a member of a community, we have to see things as a whole. The most desirable condition is when both ways of seeing meet each other like the arrows shot by the masters. If we can perceive a situation like that, we can be really peaceful. It doesn't happen very often because it's really difficult. Our way of life is always like arrows missing each other. That's why we have pain in our social lives. There is no way another person or a god can make these arrows meet. Our practice is to find the "appropriate situation" in which this person as an individual and this person as a member of the sangha can meet like a box and cover joining, or like two arrows in midair.

Do Not Waste Time

> Hearing the words, you should understand the source;
> Don't make up standards on your own.
> If you don't understand the path as it meets your eyes,
> How can you know the way as you walk?

Progress is not a matter of far or near,
But if you are confused, mountains and rivers block the way.
I humbly say to those who study the mystery,
Don't waste time.

Words and Reality

This is the final message from Shitou to us. "Hearing the words, you should understand the source." We have been reading and studying his words in this wonderful poem. He gives us the final advice that if we grasp what he has written as a theory, memorize his words, and build a system of concepts from his teaching, we will totally miss his point. All words and concepts are discriminatory. The basic function of words and concepts is to separate one thing from all other things. Even when we use the word "absolute," we have already slipped into the opposite concept, "relative." "Nondiscrimination" has meaning only in a dichotomy with "discrimination." How can we go beyond the discrimination between "absolute" and "relative," or "discrimination" and "nondiscrimination"? The only way is to see the source, the reality as it exists before being processed by our thinking mind. To do so, we need practice. Any theoretical system of concepts or thoughts is a distorted copy of reality. We can only practice it, experience it, and nod our head.

All doctrines, theories, and descriptions using words and concepts are distorted images of reality from our own point of view. When we realize this, even a distorted copy can be useful. However, if we mistake the distorted map for the true reality, we stray, making up our own standards of judgment.

Just Sitting on the Ground of Reality

Shitou asks, "If you don't understand the path as it meets your eyes, how can you know the way as you walk?" When we wake up to reality, the Way is always in front of our eyes. We are born, live, and die within this reality. We never fall out of reality. And yet, we almost always lose sight of it. By just sitting and letting go of thought, we can be within reality. Just sitting allows us to put our entire being on the ground of reality. But usually, we make up our own standards and create our distorted version of reality. Therefore, we need to constantly practice letting go. When we place ourselves on the ground of reality, we will find the path we need to walk. Otherwise, we will be lost in the map made by our minds.

Practice Is Moment by Moment

"Progress is not a matter of far or near, but if you are confused, mountains and rivers block the way." Our practice is not a race with others, a competition run from the starting point to the goal. It is not a matter of far or near. Our practice is moment by moment. When we awake, we are right in the middle of the Way. At the next moment, when we lose sight of reality, we are 100 percent off the mark. If we walk within a distorted map, no matter how long we practice, we wander far from the Way even though we are always right within the Way. We are blocked by mountains and rivers within our mind.

"I humbly say to those who study the mystery, don't waste time." No matter how hard we practice, if our practice is not based on true reality, we are wasting our time.

8 Endless Practice Here and Now: The Verse for Opening the Sutra

An unsurpassed, penetrating, and perfect Dharma
is rarely met with even in a hundred thousand million kalpas.
Having it to see and listen to, to remember and accept,
I vow to taste the truth of the Tathāgata's words.[112]

This is a reasonably accurate English translation of the verse chanted before dharma talks at many American Zen centers. A more literal translation from the original Japanese is:

An unsurpassed, most profound, subtle, and wondrous
Dharma,
even in a hundred thousand ten thousand kalpas, it is diffi-
cult to encounter.
I now see and listen, and I am able to accept and uphold it;
I vow (or wish) to understand the true meaning of the
Tathāgata.

This seems to be a very simple verse. It says that since the Dharma, the Buddha's teaching, is rarely encountered, now that I have met it, I want to deeply understand it. I think, however, that it takes some time to taste and really appreciate this verse.

In Japanese the first line is "Mujō jin jin mimyō no hō wa." *Mujō* means "unsurpassed." The first *jin* means "very" or "extremely," and the second means "deep" or "profound." So *mujō jin jin* means "highest and also deepest." *Mi* means "very small" or "subtle," something we cannot see with our unaided eyes. So the first line means that the Dharma or the Buddha's teaching is the highest or ultimate, and also the deepest and most subtle.

Dharma has two meanings: the Buddha's teachings, and the truth to which he awakened. So *Dharma* means both teachings about reality and the reality itself. This first line says that the Buddha's teaching is the highest, deepest, and most subtle and wondrous of teachings. It also says that the reality to which Shakyamuni Buddha awakened is the highest, deepest, and most subtle and wondrous. "Highest" implies upward movement; "deepest" implies downward. In Buddhism this pair has special meaning. To go up means to see reality with wisdom or prajñā. To go down means to use skillful means with compassion for all beings. The Buddha sees reality from the peak of wisdom and descends to help all beings awaken to and practice this reality. *Mujō jin jin* refers at the same time to the highest and deepest qualities of the Buddha's wisdom and compassion. "Subtle and wondrous" describe something we can't see with our eyes or our usual way of thinking.

The expression *jin jin mimyō no hō* is from the *Lotus Sutra*, one of the most important sources of Dōgen Zenji's teachings. For Dōgen Zenji the *Lotus Sutra* was essential because it describes the Mahāyāna Way of the bodhisattva. The expression "most profound, subtle, and wondrous dharma" is from the second chapter, titled "Expedient Devices." The first verse of the chapter in which this expression appears begins:

> The Hero of the World is incalculable.
> Among gods, worldlings,
> And all varieties of living beings,
> None can know the Buddha.
> As to the Buddha's strengths (*bala*), his sorts of
> fearlessness (*vaiśāradya*),

> His deliverances (*vimokṣa*), and his samādhis,
> As well as the other dharmas of a Buddha,
> None can fathom them.[113]

This passage says that none can know the Buddha; no human being can understand who the Buddha is. "Fathom" means to measure the size of something. The English unit of length is the foot, which was originally based on the length of a human foot. We measure by comparison to familiar things. To measure means to understand or grasp. Without something familiar for comparison we cannot measure anything. When we measure the size of the universe, we use a unit like the light-year. Since we can't experience a light-year, it is an abstraction, something meaningful only to scientists. To make meaningful measurements we must use our own experience as a yardstick. The Buddha and the Dharma are limitless and boundless and therefore cannot be measured. To comprehend something boundless, something infinite, we have to open our hand and become free of our yardsticks. We do this in zazen. When we stop measuring, we can understand something limitless. That is what the phrase "none can fathom them" means. This doesn't mean that 99 percent of human beings are unable but that some very superior people, sages or enlightened ones, can fathom the boundless with their special yardsticks. No one can measure something limitless because all yardsticks are limited. We can't measure without concepts based on our limited experience. When we open our hand and stop using our yardsticks, we can encounter something boundless. That's our practice. That is the quality of this Dharma.

The *Lotus Sutra* continues with the passage that is the source of the expression "profound, subtle, and wondrous Dharma."

> Formerly, following numberless Buddhas,
> He fully trod the various paths,
> Those dharmas profound and subtle,
> Hard to see and hard to understand.
> Throughout countless millions of kalpas

He trod these various paths; [then]
On the platform of the Path, he was able to achieve the fruit.
This I fully know.[114]

"Kalpa" is an interesting expression. It is a unit of time, something like a light-year, which is defined in an unusual way. Imagine that a storehouse with a capacity of ten cubic miles is filled with poppy seeds. Once every century someone removes a single poppy seed. A kalpa is defined as the time it would take to empty the storehouse. The sutra says millions of kalpas, which effectively means never. The expression "is difficult to encounter even in a hundred thousand million kalpas" means we can never encounter the Dharma. But then it contradicts itself and says, "I now see and listen, and I am able to accept and uphold or maintain it." The translation in the MZMC sutra book is "having it to see and listen to, remember and accept." The word "having" is not strong enough. We have to uphold, maintain, and nurture it. It's not enough to merely have the Dharma; we also have to cultivate it.

In this translation the important word "now" is omitted. When we merely *think* about the Dharma and try to "get it," we are unable to. As long as we try to grasp it with our intellect, we are unsuccessful because it's impossible. The word "now" means at this present moment, the only reality. The past is already gone and the future has yet to come. Neither is reality. Only this moment, *now*, is reality. And yet this *now* is strange and wondrous. We cannot grasp it because it has no length. If it did, we could cut it in half. Suppose I want to speak the word "now." When I make the initial sound *na-*, the rest of the sound, *ow*, still lies in the future; and when I do the *ow*, the *na-* is already past. So when is the present? The present is nothing. It is empty. So the past and future are never here, and the present is empty. It's really wondrous, and we cannot understand it. We experience reality, actually live our lives and do things, and yet everything is empty. When we try to grasp it there is no substance.

Reality is empty like a phantom. This is the meaning of "form is emptiness and emptiness is form." This is reality. This present moment, which is zero or empty, is the only reality. It is the only time we can meet the Dharma by letting go of our limited measurement, our conventional ways of seeing and judging. To see the Dharma, the reality, we must open our hand and just accept that reality. There is no sound, and yet we have to listen for and accept this boundless Dharma. We cannot discuss the absolute. Argument doesn't work. When we discuss the nature of the Dharma, we discuss our insight, our understanding of reality. Each of us has a different life experience and different ways of seeing things. Our opinions or expressions of this reality can differ. We can discuss or argue, and yet reality itself cannot be the object of meaningful argument.

All we can do is simply accept, maintain, and uphold it. "Maintain" means to use it. "Use" doesn't mean I use the Dharma, in the sense that the Dharma is the object of my activity. Instead it means we are the Dharma itself. There is no truth or reality outside ourselves. We cannot be outside reality. We are born into and live in this reality, this Dharma. Since we are part of the Dharma, we can't observe it from outside. Everything we do in our day-to-day lives is a manifestation of this boundless Dharma. The limitless, unsurpassed, most profound Dharma should be manifested through practice with our small, limited, impermanent body and mind. Practice means more than sitting zazen in the zendō. It includes practice outside of the zendō. Our practice, our life, is the only way to manifest this infinite Dharma. The only time we can see, listen, accept, and maintain this Dharma is right now.

The *Lotus Sutra* continues:

> As to such great fruit and retribution as these,
> Such varied doctrines of nature and marks,
> I and the Buddhas of the ten directions
> Are the only ones who can know these things.
> These dharmas cannot be demonstrated;
> Words, which are only signs, are quiescent in them.
> Among the remaining kinds of living beings
> None can understand them,

Except for the multitude of bodhisattvas,
Whose power of faith is firm.

The phrase "nature and marks," which refers back to what Shakyamuni Buddha says in the prose section preceding this verse, is essential to an understanding of Mahāyāna Buddhism. The Buddha is speaking to Śāriputra, one of his ten great disciples: "Śāriputra, we need speak no more. Why is this? Concerning the prime, rare, hard-to-understand dharmas, which the Buddha has perfected, only a Buddha and a Buddha can exhaust their reality, namely, the suchness of the dharmas."[115] "Suchness of the dharmas" is a translation for *shohō jissō*. *Shohō* means "myriad dharmas" or "all beings." *Ji* means "true or real," and *ssō* is "form." So *jissō* means "reality" and "all dharmas or beings." This Dharma is the reality of all beings, not something abstract that exists outside the phenomenal world. It is the reality of all phenomenal things, including ourselves.

The sutra continues, "the suchness of their marks, the suchness of their nature, the suchness of their substance." "Marks" is translation of *sō*, which means "form." "Nature" is the characteristics of each thing. The original word translated here as "substance" is *tai*. It means "body," not substance—something impermanent or egoless. Each thing has its own body: a book, clothing, water, grass, a person—all have bodies. The list continues with "the suchness of their powers, the suchness of their functions." Each being has its own power or energy. It's not a dead thing. And anything with power or energy has function. Even though it doesn't move visibly, a mountain has functions. Dōgen Zenji says that mountains are always moving, always walking.

Finally, "the suchness of their causes, the suchness of their conditions, the suchness of their effects, the suchness of their retributions, and the absolute identity of their beginning and end."

These "ten suchnesses" were discussed in the beginning of the chapter 5. As we saw there, the first five suchnesses of all beings refer to the uniqueness of each being. And the next four imply that each and every unique being can exist only within relation with others within the network of interdependent origination throughout entire time and space.

The tenth suchness is the "absolute identity of their beginning and end." "Beginning" refers to the first suchness and "end" to the ninth, the retributions. These nine points are not independent aspects of our being but rather only one, because we cannot separate them. This last, tenth suchness is difficult to understand. Each being is unique and yet is connected with all beings, from the beginningless beginning to the endless end. When we take one being, we take all beings and all times. Nothing is substantial. Everything is empty. When we try to grasp with our intellect, using concepts, we become neurotic. When we grasp one aspect, we miss another. When we try to understand the difference between beings we differentiate and miss the connections between them. When we focus on the relationships between all beings, we miss the uniqueness of this being. These two basically contradictory aspects of the true reality of all beings are expressed in the *Heart Sutra* as "form is emptiness and emptiness is form." In "Sandōkai" the same reality is expressed as merging of difference (*ji*) and unity (*ri*).

Because it is difficult to fathom and grasp both sides of reality at once using concepts and intellect, as the *Lotus Sutra* says, we need the power of faith. Through our practice based on faith, we can experience the true reality even though we cannot see and measure it as an object.

The faith of power derives from taking refuge in the Triple Treasure. We take refuge, we take the precepts, and we take the four bodhisattva vows and continue to practice, wearing a buddha's robe and receiving offerings with gratitude from the network of interdependent origination, gifts such as air, water, food, and many more things. We keep up our effort to hear, understand, and uphold the teachings of the sutras—through texts, talks, and instructions from teachers and others—and of reality itself.

Our practice includes all activities of this body and mind—including our thoughts, which are one way to understand this wondrous Dharma. We don't need to cut off our thoughts. Thinking is, in fact, a function of the Dharma. But we should understand that thought cannot grasp reality. So we have to open our hands and work with the reality we encounter daily. When we think about each part in isolation it's really difficult to see reality as a whole and explain it. But the Buddha's teaching is really simple. It is the reality we always experience, not something mysterious or mystical beyond the phenomenal world. It's not something esoteric. Even so, it is difficult to fathom the ways all beings exist in this phenomenal world in which we live. The way we live is actually mysterious. The truth is not hidden but always here, always manifested. The goal of our practice is not to experience something different from our day-to-day lives. It is to see deep into the reality of each being, including this one. This is really wondrous and difficult to grasp. To appreciate this is to meet with the Dharma. When we really see, listen to, accept, and maintain that Dharma, we can't help but vow to understand it more deeply. That's the meaning of the last line of this verse, "I vow to understand the true meaning of the Tathāgata." We vow to deeply understand the dharmakāya into which we are born; the reality that is itself the Buddha's body, in which we live and die together with all beings.

Notes

1. "The ancestral way come from the west I transmit east.
   Fishing the moon, cultivating clouds,
   I long for the ancient wind.
   How could red dusts from the mundane world fly up to here?
   Snowy night in the deep mountains in my grass hut."
   Dōgen, *Dōgen's Extensive Record: A Translation of Eihei Koroku*,
   trans. Leighton and Okumura (Wisdom Publications, 1995), p. 638.
2. *Buddhadharma*, Spring 2011, p. 25.
3. Dainin Katagiri, *Each Moment Is the Universe: Zen and the Way of Being Time* (Boston: Shambhala, 2007), p. 216.
4. I found this poem in the draft of *Ceaseless Effort: The Life of Dainin Katagiri*, by Andrea Martin (Minnesota Zen Meditation Center).
5. The story is based on the translation by Thomas William Rhys Davids, *Buddhist Birth-Stories: Jataka Tales* (1880) (repr., Calcutta: Srishti Publishers, 1998). Another version is found in Rafe Martin, *The Hungry Tigress: Buddhist Legends and Jataka Tales* (Berkeley: Parallax Press, 1990).
6. Martin, *Hungry Tigress.*
7. This is the translation of the verse of four bodhisattva vows in the sutra book used at Minnesota Zen Meditation Center. The translation in *Sōtō School Scriptures for Daily Services and Practice* published by Sōtōshū Shūmuchō is as follows: "Beings are numberless; I vow to free them. / Delusions are inexhaustible; I vow to end them. / Dharma gates are boundless, I vow to enter them. / The Buddha way is unsurpassable; I vow to realize it." In Japanese: "Shujō mu hen sei gan do, / Bonnō mu jin sei gan dan, / Hō mon mu ryō sei gan gaku, / Butsu dō mujō seigan gan jō."
8. This does not mean Buddhists do not pray. Originally Buddhism did not have sacred beings to pray to; but later, in Mahāyāna and Vajrayāna Buddhism, buddhas, bodhisattvas, and some guardian gods came to be considered objects of prayer.
9. Augustine Ichirō Okumura, *Awakening to Prayer*, trans. Theresa Kazue Hiraki and Albert Masaru Yamato (Washington, D.C.: ICS, 1994).

10. This is the translation of the verse from *Bosatsu-yōraku-hongōkyō* (*Bodhisattva Jewel Necklace Sutra*), Taisho, vol. 24, p. 1013.
11. This verse appears in the Mahavāgga of the Pāli Vinaya. This English translation is from Hajime Nakamura, *Gotama Buddha: A Biography Based on the Most Reliable Texts*, trans. Gaynor Sekimori (Tokyo: Kosei, 2000), p. 228.
12. This poem was published in the MZMC newsletter, Spring 1991, on the occasion of the first anniversary of Katagiri Roshi's death.
13. D. T. Suzuki, *Living by Zen: A Synthesis of the Historical and Practical Aspects of Zen Buddhism* (London: Samuel Weiser, 1972).
14. D. T. Suzuki, *Zen ni yoru Seikatu*, trans. Kobori Sōhaku, Suzuki Daisetsu Zen senshu, vol. 3 (Tokyo: Shunjūsha, 1975), p. 173.
15. D. T. Suzuki, *Outlines of Mahayana Buddhism* (New York: Schocken Books, 1963), p. 307.
16. Kōshō Uchiyama, *Opening the Hand of Thought* (Boston: Wisdom, 2004), p. 157.
17. Shohaku Okumura, *Shikantaza: An Introduction to Zazen* (Kyoto: Kyoto Sōtō Zen Center, 1985), p. 63.
18. Shohaku Okumura and Taigen Dan Leighton, trans., *The Wholehearted Way: A Translation of Eihei Dōgen's Bendōwa with Commentary by Kōshō Uchiyama Roshi* (Boston: Tuttle, 1997), p. 23.
19. This saying appears in the third chapter of the *Lotus Sutra*, "Simile and Parable." Burton Watson, trans., *The Lotus Sutra* (New York: Columbia University Press, 1993), p. 69.
20. Taigen Dan Leighton and Shohaku Okumura, trans., *Dōgen's Pure Standards for the Zen Community: A Translation of Eihei Shingi* (Albany: State University of New York Press, 1996), pp. 47–49.
21. Ibid.
22. Ibid. p. 48.
23. Ibid. p. 37.
24. Ibid. p. 48.
25. Ibid. pp. 48–49.
26. Guishan Lingyou (Isan Reiyū) lived from 771 to 853 CE during the golden age of Chinese Zen. He founded the Guiyang (Igyō) school, one of the five schools of Zen in China. Guishan was a dharma successor of Baizhang Huihai (Hyakujō Ekai). Baizhang is known for his *Baizhang Qingguei* (*Hyakujō Shingi*), a compilation of the regulations for a Zen monastery. With Baizhang's regulations, Zen monastic practice was formally established.
27. This is my translation. Another can be found in Gudo Nishijima and Chodo Cross, trans., *Master Dōgen's Shōbōgenzō, bk. 2* (BookSurge, 2006), p. 170. Zen Master Dayuan is the honorific title given by the emperor to Guishan.
28. This lecture at the Sōtōshu Kyōka Kenshūsho (Sōtō School Propagation and Research Institute) was translated by Rev. Rosan Yoshida and appeared in the MZMC newsletter in three parts: Fall 1990, Spring 1991, and Summer 1991.
29. Hōkyōji is a country practice center in Southeastern Minnesota established in 1978. In 2007 it became independent from the MZMC and is currently named Hōkyōji Zen Practice Community.
30. This is a part of a conversation between Hongzhi and his teacher Donxia Zichun (Tanka Shijun, 1074–1117), which appeared in Hongzhi's biography in *The Record of Hongzhi* (Chi., Hongzhi-lu; Jap., Wanshi-roku). Originally this saying was by Baima

Xingai (Hakuba Gyōai) and appeared in *The Record of the Transmission of the Dharma Lamp* (Chi., *Jingde chuandeng lu*; Jap., *Keitoku Dentōroku*), vol. 23.

31. This expression by Dōgen Zenji appears in Dharma discourse no. 2 in *Eihei Kōroku*. See Taigen Dan Leighton and Shohaku Okumura, trans., *Dōgen's Extensive Record: A Translation of the Eihei Kōroku* (Boston: Wisdom, 2004), p. 76.
32. The translation in the *Sōtō School Scriptures for Daily Services and Practice* is "All my past and harmful karma, / born from beginningless greed, hate, and delusion, / through body, speech, and mind, / I now fully avow."
33. This is based on the theory of the origin of Mahāyāna Buddhism held by Japanese scholars such as Akira Hirakawa. When I lectured on these matters in 1993 I did not know about Western scholars' criticism of the hypothesis that Mahāyāna Buddhism was originally a lay Buddhist movement. Today few scholars support this hypothesis.
34. Here "ego" is used as a translation of the Sanskrit *ātman*, which is usually translated as "self" or "soul." "Egolessness" is a translation of *anātman*, "no-self." According to *The Shambhala Dictionary of Buddhism and Zen* (Boston: Shambhala, 1991), *ātman* means "the real immortal self of human beings, known in the West as the soul." In Mahāyāna Buddhism, not only the "soul" of human beings, but also the substance of material things is negated.
35. This is my translation from *Busso-shōden Zenkaishō (Essence of Buddha Ancestors' Authentically Transmitted Zen Precepts)*, Taisho, vol. 82, no. 2601.
36. This is my translation from Sōtan Oka, *Kaitei Busso-shōden Zenkaishō Kōwa* (*Lecture on the revised Busso-shōden Zenkaishō*) (Tokyo: Kōmeisha, 1931), pp. 44–48.
37. The translation in *Sōtō School Scriptures for Daily Services and Practice* is "I take refuge in buddha. / May all beings / embody the great way, / resolving to awaken. / I take refuge in dharma. / May all living beings / deeply enter the sutras, wisdom like an ocean. / I take refuge in sangha. / May all beings / support harmony in the community, / free from hindrance." This verse was originally a part of the longer verse in chapter 11 of the *Avataṃsaka Sutra*, titled "Purifying Practice." The English translation is as follows. "Taking refuge in the Buddha, / They should wish that all beings / Continue the lineage of Buddhas, / Conceiving the unexcelled aspiration. / Taking refuge in the Teaching, / They should wish that all beings / Enter deeply into the scriptures / And their wisdom be deep as the sea. / Taking refuge in the Community, / They should wish that all beings / Order the masses, / All becoming free from obstruction." Thomas Cleary, trans., *The Flower Ornament Scripture: A Translation of The Avatamsaka Sutra* (Boston: Shambhala, 1993), pp. 315–16.
38. This is my translation. Another translation is in Nishijima and Cross, *Master Dōgen's Shōbōgenzō*, bk. 4, p. 178.
39. Thanissaro Bhikkhu, trans., *Dhammapada: A Translation* (Barre, Mass.: Dhamma Dana, 1998), v. 160, p. 46.
40. H. Saddhatissa, trans., *The Sutta-Nipata* (London: Curzon, 1994), p. 88.
41. *Dasheng-yi-zhang (Jap., Daijō-gi-shō, The meanings of Mahāyāna Teaching)*, written by Huiyuan (Eon) in the Sui dynasty (589–618), Taisho, vol. 44, no. 1851, p. 654.
42. This is the translation in the MZMC sutra book, p. 1. The translation in *Sōtō School Scriptures for Daily Services and Practice* is "How great, the robe of liberation, / a formless field of merit. / Wrapping ourselves in Buddha's teaching, / We free all living beings." This verse also appears in *Chanyuan Qinggui (Rules of Purity for the Chan Monastery)*, vol. 8, in the section describing the precepts-receiving ceremony for novices (*shami*).

There is one character different from the version we chant. The third line reads, "Wearing the Tathāgata's precepts."

43. This is my translation. Another translation appears in Nishijima and Cross, *Master Dōgen's Shōbōgenzō*, bk. 1, p. 146.
44. This story appears in Vinaya texts. See, for example, I. B. Horner, trans., *The Book of the Discipline (Vinaya-piṭaka)*, vol. IV (London: Luzac, 1951), p. 407.
45. This is my translation. See also Nishijima and Cross, *Master Dōgen's Shōbōgenzō*, bk. 1, p. 127.
46. As far as I know, an English translation of *Kyōjukaimon* has not yet been published. In *Shōbōgenzō Kie-sanbō (Taking Refuge in the Three Treasures)*, Dōgen introduces four kinds of Three Treasures, including the three mentioned here. See Nishijima and Cross, *Master Dōgen's Shōbōgenzō*, bk. 4, p. 177.
47. This is a free translation from Japanese. The English translation from Pāli is in H. Saddhatissa, *The Sutta-Nipata*, p. 8.
48. Leighton and Okumura, *Dōgen's Pure Standards*, p. 36.
49. Ibid., pp. 83–84.
50. Robert A. F. Thurman, trans., *The Holy Teaching of Vimalakīrti: A Mahāyāna Scripture* (College Park: Pennsylvania State University Press, 1988), p. 27.
51. Leon Hurvitz, trans., *Scripture of the Lotus Blossom of the Fine Dharma* (New York: Columbia University Press, 1976), p. 22.
52. Ibid., p. 23.
53. The texts of meal chants in chapter 5 are from *Sōtō School Scriptures for Daily Services and Practice*, p. 75, not from the sutra book of the Minnesota Zen Meditation Center.
54. Maurice Walshe, trans., *The Long Discourses of the Buddha: A Translation of the Dīgha Nikāya* (Boston: Wisdom, 1987), p. 263.
55. Red Pine, trans., *The Diamond Sutra: The Perfection of Wisdom: Text and Commentaries translated from Sanskrit and Chinese* (Washington, D.C.: Counterpoint, 2001), p. 3.
56. Thomas Cleary, trans. *The Blue Cliff Record* (Boulder, Colo.: Shambhala, 1977), case 1, p. 3.
57. *Fahuawengou*, Taisho, vol. 34, #1718, p. 0128a16.
58. Translation by the Buddhist Text Translation Society with a few minor changes by Okumura. http://www.purifymind.com/BrahmaNetSutra.htm.
59. My translation. See also Nishijima and Cross, *Master Dōgen's Shōbōgenzō*, bk. 4, p. 178.
60. Menzan Zuihō (1683–1769), one of the greatest Sōtō Zen monk-scholars of the Tokugawa period, wrote a commentary on this "Verse of Five Contemplations" titled *Jujikigokan-kunmo* (Instruction on the Five Contemplations for Receiving Food) in 1720. He said that these five contemplations were first mentioned in a Vinaya text by Nanshan Daoxuan (Nanzan Dōsen), the founder of the Chinese Ritsu (Vinaya) School. Later the verse was rewritten by one of the famous Chinese literati of the Song dynasty who was also a Zen practitioner, Huang Tingjian (Kō Teiken, 1045–1105). It also appears in *Chanyuan Qinggui* (*Zen'en Shingi, Rules of Purity for the Chan Monastery*) by Changlu Zongze (Chōro Sōsaku, ?–1107). Dōgen Zenji took the verse from the Chinese Standards. However, modern scholars doubt Huang's authorship because the same verse is found in a text that precedes his birth.
61. These are parts of my unpublished translation of *Shōbōgenzō* "Hachidainingaku" (Eight Points of Awakening of Great Beings). Another translation is found in Nishijima and Cross, *Master Dōgen's Shōbōgenzō*, bk. 4, pp. 233–34.

62. Rewata Dhamma, *The First Discourse of The Buddha* (Boston: Wisdom, 1997), p. 17.
63. Gene Reeves, trans.*The Lotus Sutra: A Contemporary Translation of a Buddhist Classic* (Boston, Wisdom Publications, 2008), pp. 93–94.
64. Nishijima and Cross, *Master Dōgen's Shōbōgenzō*, bk. 4, p. 173.
65. Leighton and Okumura, *Dōgen's Pure Standards*, p. 98.
66. This is my translation. Another is in Kazuaki Tanahashi, ed., *Enlightenment Unfolds: The Essential Teachings of Zen Master Dōgen* (Boston: Shambhala, 1999), p. 23.
67. Bhikkhu Bodhi, trans., *The Connected Discourses of the Buddha*, vol. 1 (Boston: Wisdom, 2000), p. 233.
68. Ibid., p. 950.
69. Three vehicles are the Mahāyāna categorization of Buddhism. *Śrāvaka* means "hearer" and refers to the disciples of the Buddha. *Pratyekabuddha* means "solitary awakened one" and refers to the practitioners who attain awakening without a teacher and do not teach others. From the Mahāyāna point of view, both were *Hīnayāna*, "lesser vehicles."
70. When I gave this talk in 1993, heart transplants were not yet legal in Japan. In 1997 the procedure was legalized, but it is still very rarely performed.
71. I live in America as a foreigner and need a great deal of patience. Katagiri Roshi's name Dainin means Great Patience. I think it was a very suitable name for him as a teacher in the United States, where the spiritual and cultural backgrounds are very different from Japan. American Buddhist practitioners who practice with teachers from Japan or other Asian Buddhist countries must need the same sort of patience. Actually, any two people who live or work together will sometimes have conflicts and need to practice patience.
72. Edward Conze, trans., *Perfect Wisdom: The Short Prajñāpāramitā Texts* (Devon: Buddhist Publishing Group, 1973), p. 140.
73. Katagiri Roshi's translation appeared in *Zen no Kaze* (Wind of Zen), a magazine published by Sōtōshū Shūmuchō. The translation of this sentence in *Sōtō School Scriptures for Daily Services and Practice* is "Avalokiteśvara Bodhisattva, when deeply practicing prajñā pāramitā, clearly saw that all five aggregates are empty and thus relieved all suffering."
74. *Shōbōgenzō* "Kannon" is included in Nishijima and Cross, *Master Dōgen's Shōbōgenzō*, bk. 2, p. 211.
75. Yunyan was the teacher of Dongshan (Tōzan), the founder of Chinese Caodon (Sōtō) Zen. He is mentioned below.
76. If you are interested in the discussion of this koan, study case 54 in the *Book of Serenity* and case 89 in the *Blue Cliff Record*. Thomas Cleary, trans., *Book of Serenity: One Hundred Zen Dialogues* (New York: Lindisfarne Press, 1990), p. 229. Cleary, *Blue Cliff Record*, p. 489.
77. Shohaku Okumura, trans., *Realizing Genjōkōan: The Key to Dōgen's Shōbōgenzō* (Boston: Wisdom, 2010), app. 2, p. 207.
78. Conze, *Perfect Wisdom*, p. 140.
79. Kenneth K. Inada, trans., *Nāgārjuna: A Translation of His Mūlamadhyamakakārikā with an Introductory Essay* (Tokyo: Hokuseidō Press, 1970), p. 146. (Chapter and verse numbers are cited in the text.)
80. This is my translation. Another translation is in Nishijima and Cross, *Master Dōgen's Shōbōgenzō*, bk. 4, p. 221.
81. Inada, *Nāgārjuna*, p. 39.
82. Ibid., p. 59.

83. This is my translation from the Chinese, which Kumārajīva translated with Pingala's commentary, Taisho, vol. 30, no. 1564, p. 8a07.
84. Okumura, *Realizing Genjōkōan*, p. 1.
85. Ibid., p. 3.
86. Ibid.
87. Francis Cook, trans., *The Record of Transmitting the Light: Zen Master Keizan's Denkōroku* (Boston: Wisdom, 1996), pp. 193–94.
88. Conze, *Perfect Wisdom*, p. 140.
89. Okumura, *Realizing Genjōkōan*, p. 209.
90. Nakamura, *Gotama Buddha*, p. 319.
91. My translation. Another is found in Nishijima and Cross, *Master Dōgen's Shōbōgenzō*, bk. 3, p. 55.
92. Shohaku Okumura, trans., *Shōbōgenzō-zuimonki: Sayings of Eihei Dōgen Zenji* (Tokyo: Sōtōshū Shūmucho, 1987), p. 124.
93. Inada, *Nāgārjuna*, p. 103.
94. When I gave this talk in 1994 my son was three years old and I was forty-five. That was the first time I felt I was aging.
95. One of the oldest temples in Japan, Shitennōji was built by Prince Shōtoku in the sixth century at the very beginning of Japanese Buddhism. At that time Osaka and Nara were the two main cities. Nara was the capital, and Osaka was a port for travel to Korea and China. The prince also built a temple in Nara called Hōryūji. Hōryūji has the world's oldest wooden structure, almost fifteen hundred years old.
96. This translation, in the MZMC sutra book, p. 8, is by Thomas Cleary and is included in Cleary, *Timeless Spring: A Sōtō Zen Anthology* (Tokyo and New York: Weatherhill, 1980), p. 36. In the sutra book the word "patriarch" in the original translation was changed to "ancestor."
97. The word *Sandōkai* derives from the title of a Daoist text on the *Yijing* (Book of Changes) written during the Han dynasty (206 BCE–220 CE).
98. John McRae, *Seeing Through Zen: Encounter, Transformation, and Genealogy in Chinese Chan Buddhism* (Berkeley: University of California Press, 2003), p. 61.
99. Ibid., p. 62.
100. Yoshito S. Hakeda, trans., *The Awakening of Faith* (New York: Columbia University Press, 1967), p. 31. This is one of the most important texts on the theory of *tathāgata-garbha*, or buddha-nature, which is an essential part of Zen teachings.
101. Hakeda says, "Since it has been made clear that the essence of all things is empty, i.e., devoid of illusion, the true Mind is eternal, permanent, immutable, pure, and self-sufficient; therefore, it is called 'nonempty'" (ibid., p. 35).
102. Zongmi's discussion about the differences among the four schools appears in "Chart of the Master-Disciple Succession of the Chan Gate That Transmits the Mind Ground in China." See Jeffrey Lyle Broughton, trans., *Zongmi on Chan* (New York: Columbia University Press, 2009), pp. 69–100.
103. Okumura, *Realizing Genjōkōan*, p. 2.
104. Inada, *Nāgārjuna*, p. 146.
105. Hakeda, *Awakening of Faith*, p. 31.
106. Sheng-yen, *The Infinite Mirror: Commentaries on Two Chan Classics* (Boston: Shambhala, 1990), p. 25. Sheng-yen translates *Sandōkai* as "inquiry into matching halves." "Inquiry" is *san*, "matching" is *dō*, "halves" is *kai*. This is very different from the Japanese interpretation.

107. Translation by Shohaku Okumura and Hozan Alan Senauke, in *The Bodhisattva's Embrace: Dispatches from Engaged Buddhism's Front Lines*, by Alan Senauke (Berkeley: Clear View Press, 2010), p. 215.
108. Stephen Mitchell, trans., *Tao Te Ching* (New York: HarperCollins, 1988), pp. 40–42.
109. Inada, *Nāgārjuna*, pp. 146–48.
110. This kōan is called Yunyan's "Great Compassion" in *Congronglu* (Shōyōroku), case 54. Cleary, *Book of Serenity*, p. 229.
111. This story appears in the Chinese Daoist classic *Liezi*, vol. 5.
112. This verse in the *Sōtō School Scriptures for Daily Services and Practice* is: "The unsurpassed, profound, and wondrous dharma / is rarely met with, even in a hundred, thousand, million kalpas. / Now we can see and hear it, accept and maintain it. / May we unfold the meaning of the Tathāgata's truth."
113. Hurvitz, *Scripture of the Lotus Blossom*, p. 23.
114. Ibid.
115. Ibid., p. 22.

Glossary of Names

Note: Sources for this glossary include *Bukkyōgo Daijiten* (Nakamura Hajime, Tokyo Shoseki), *Zengaku Daijiten* (Taishūkan Shoten), *Bukkyō Daijiten* (Shōgakkan), and *The Shambhala Dictionary of Buddhism and Zen* (Shambhala).

Ānanda: One of the ten great disciples of the Buddha. He was the personal attendant of the Buddha for twenty years and memorized all the teachings of the Buddha. His exposition of the Buddha's discourses formed the basis for the sutras at the first council.

Aśvaghoṣa: Indian monk-poet who lived in the first to second centuries CE. He wrote *Buddha-carita: Life of the Buddha.* Another work, *Awakening of Faith in Mahāyāna*, was attributed to Aśvaghoṣa, but some scholars today think the text was written in China.

Avalokiteśvara: One of the most important bodhisattvas of Mahāyāna Buddhism, considered to be the symbol of the Buddha's compassion.

Baizhang Huihai (Hyakujō Ekai, 749–814): An important Zen master of the Tang dynasty in China. He was a dharma successor of Mazu Daoyi and master of Guishan Lingyou and Huangbo Xiyun.

Traditionally he was considered to be the author of the first rules of purity (*Qinggui*, *Shingi*).

Baotang Wuzhu (Hotō Mujū, 714–774): The founder of the Baotang school of Zen in the Tang dynasty.

Bodhidharma (Bodaidaruma): The twenty-eighth ancestor after Shakyamuni Buddha in the Indian lineage, who came from India to China and became the first ancestor of the Zen tradition.

Butsuju Myōzen (1184–1225): A disciple of Myōan Eisai who transmitted Rinzai Zen tradition to Japan and was Dōgen's first Zen teacher in Japan. Myōzen and Dōgen went to China together, but Myōzen died while practicing at Tiantong monastery.

Changlu Qingliao (Chōro Seiryō): A Chinese Caodong (Sōtō) Zen master, a dharma heir of Danxia Zichun (Tanka Shijun), and the elder dharma brother of Hongzhi Zhengjue.

Changlu Zongze (Chōro Sōsaku, ?–1107): The Chinese Zen master who compiled *Chanyuan Qinggui* (*Zen'en Shingi*, Rules of Purity for the Chan Monastery).

Dai Daoxin (Daii Dōshin, 580–651): The fourth ancestor of Chinese Zen and the master of Doman Hongren. Dai and Doman's assemblies were later called East Mountain Dharma Gates.

Dainin Katagiri Roshi (1928–1990): The founder of Minnesota Zen Meditation Center. He came to the United States in 1963 and assisted Shunryū Suzuki Roshi at the San Francisco Zen Center until Suzuki Roshi's death in 1971. He moved to Minneapolis to establish the MZMC in 1972.

Dajan Huineng (Daikan Enō, 638–713): The sixth ancestor of Chinese Zen and dharma heir of the fifth ancestor, Daman Hongren. He is considered the founder of the Southern school of Chinese Zen.

Daman Hongren (Daiman Kōnin, 602–675): The fifth ancestor in the Chinese Zen tradition, from whom the Northern and Southern schools were derived.

Daowu Yuanzhi (Dōgo Enchi, 769–835): A dharma heir of Yaoshan Weiyan and dharma brother of Yunyan Tansheng.

Dongshan Liangjie (Tōzan Ryokai, 802–869): The dharma heir of Yunyan Tansheng. Dongshan was the founder of the Chinese Caodong school.

Edward Conze (1904–1979): A British Buddhist scholar who taught in England and the United Sates. The author of many books on the *Prajñāpāramitā Sutras.*

Eihei Dōgen (1200–1253): A dharma heir of Tiantong Rujing, Dōgen is the founder of Japanese Sōtō Zen Buddhism.

Emperor Wu (464–549): The first emperor of the Rian dynasty. He supported Buddhism and himself lectured on Buddhist sutras such as the *Parinirvana Sutra*. In the Zen tradition it is said that he met with Bodhidharma.

Feixiu (Haikyū, 797–870): A government official of the Tang dynasty. He studied Fayen (Kegon) Buddhism with Guifeng Zongmi and Zen with Huangbo Xiyun.

Guifeng Zongmi (Keihō Shūmitsu, 780–841): A scholar-monk of the Fayen school and also a Zen master in the Tang dynasty. He wrote *The Chart of the Master-Disciple Succession of the Chan Gate That Transmits the Mind Ground in China*, *Prolegomenon to the Collection of Expressions of the Chan Source*, and many other texts.

Guishan Lingyou (Isan Reiyū, 771–853): A dharma heir of Baizhang Huihai. Together with his disciple Yangshan Huiji, he is considered the founder of one of the five schools of Chinese Zen, the Guiyang school.

Hārītī (Kishimojin): The daughter of a demonic being (*yaksa*) in Rājagriha. She had five hundred (or one thousand or ten thousand) children to whom she fed the babies of others. When she heard the Dharma from the Buddha, she repented her misdeeds and vowed to protect Buddhism. In Japan she is invoked for an easy delivery and the health of children.

Heze Shenhui (Kataku Jinne, 668–760): A disciple of the sixth ancestor, Huineng. He attacked the Northern school and insisted that Huineng was the legitimate successor of the fifth ancestor. He is considered to be the founder of Heze school.

Hongzhi Zhengjue (Wanshi Shōkaku, 1091–1157): A famous Chinese Caodong (Sōtō) Zen master who served as abbot of Tiangtong monastery. Hongzhi was well known for the excellence of his poetry, and he composed verses to supplement a hundred koans. Wansong Xingxie later wrote commentaries on these verses and created the *Congronglu* (Shōyōroku).

Huang Tingjian (Kō Teiken, 1045–1105): A famous poet and calligrapher of the Song dynasty in China. He was a lay disciple of the Linji Zen master Huanglong Zuxin.

Ichirō Okumura (1923–): Father Ichiro Okumura entered the Catholic Church in 1948 and was ordained to the priesthood within the Order of Discalced Carmelites in 1957.

Jingzhong Wuxiang (Jōshu Musō, 684–762): A Tang dynasty Zen master from Korea and the teacher of Baotang Wuzhu.

Kōdō Sawaki (1880–1965): A modern Sōtō Zen master, and Kōshō Uchiyama's teacher. He was a professor at Komazawa University but never had his own temple or monastery. He was called "homeless Kōdō" because he traveled throughout Japan to teach.

Kōshō Uchiyama (1912–1998): Kōdō Sawaki's dharma heir who succeeded Sawaki at Antaiji. He wrote many books, several of which have been translated into English and other languages.

Kumārajīva (344–413): One of the most important translators of Buddhist texts from Sanskrit to Chinese. He translated many Mahāyāna texts including the *Lotus Sutra*, *Vimalakīrtinirdeśa Sutra*, *Mūlamadhyamakakārikā*, and *Mahāprajñāpāramita-Śāstra*.

Longtan Chongxin (Ryūtan Sōshin): A Tang dynasty Zen master in Shitou Xiqian's lineage. Shitou's disciple Tianhuang Daowu was his teacher and Deshan Xuanjian his disciple.

Mahākāśyapa: One of the ten major disciples of Shakyamuni Buddha. He was famous for his strict discipline living in the forest even after the Buddha founded monasteries. After the Buddha's death he became the leader of the sangha and took the leadership for the first council of five hundred arahats. In the Zen tradition he is considered the first ancestor in the Indian lineage, since he received dharma transmission from the Buddha.

Maitreya Buddha: The next buddha. Maitreya is in Tuṣita heaven now as a bodhisattva and is expected to come to this world in the future.

Mañjushrī: The bodhisattva of wisdom. In Zen, Mañjushrī is enshrined in the center of the monks' hall.

Mazu Daoyi (Baso Dōitsu, 709–788): One of the most important Tang dynasty Zen masters. Mazu was a disciple of Nanyue Huairang. He had many disciples, including Baizhang Huihai and Nanyuan Puyuan.

Menzan Zuihō (1683–1769): One of the important Sōtō Zen monk-scholars in the Tokugawa period. Dharma heir of Sonnō Shūeki, he studied Dōgen extensively and wrote many commentaries on *Shōbōgenzō* and other writings of Dōgen.

Myōan Eisai (1141–1215): The first Japanese master, who transmitted the Rinzai Zen tradition to Japan. He established several Zen monasteries including Kenninji Kyoto, where Dōgen practiced Zen with Eisai's disciple Myōzen.

Nāgārjuna: One of the most important philosophers of Buddhism and the founder of Mādhyamika school of Mahāyāna Buddhism. His most important work is *Mūlamadhyamakakārikā*. In the Zen tradition he is considered to be the fourteenth ancestor.

Nanshan Daoxuan (Nanzan Dōsen, 596–667): A Buddhist master in Tang dynasty China. He was the founder of the Nanshan (Nanzan) Ritsu-shū (Vinaya school).

Nanyue Huairang (Nangaku Ejō, 677–744): A Tang dynasty Zen master. He was dharma heir of the sixth ancestor, Huineng, and the master of Mazu Daoyi.

Niutou Farong (Gozu Hōyū, 594–657): A Tang dynasty Zen master. He was considered the disciple of the fourth ancestor, Daoxin, and the founder of the Niutou (Ox Head) school of Zen.

Qingyuan Xingsi (Seigen Gyōshi, 660?–740): A Tang dynasty Zen master. One of the dharma heirs of the sixth ancestor, Huineng, he was the master of Shitou Xiqian.

Samantabhadra: One of the most important bodhisattvas in Mahāyāna Buddhism, who is venerated as the protector of all those who teach the Dharma.

Shakyamuni Buddha: The founder of Buddhism. Shakyamuni means "sage from the Shākya clan."

Śāriputra: One of the ten great disciples of Shakyamuni Buddha. He is considered to be the person with the deepest wisdom in the Buddha's assembly.

Shitou Xiqian (Sekitō Kisen, 700–790): A Tang dynasty Zen master. The dharma heir of Quingyuan Xingsi and the master of Yaoshan Weiyan, he is famous for his poems "Merging of Difference and Unity" (Sandōkai), and "Song of the Grass Hut."

Shōtoku Taishi (574–622): Prince of Emperor Yōmei. He served as prince regent for his aunt, Empress Suiko. He played a key role in establishing Buddhism in Japan. He founded Hōryūji in Nara and Shitennōji in Osaka.

Sōen Nakagawa (1907–1984): A modern Japanese Rinzai Zen master. He was the abbot of Ryūtakuji temple.

Subhūti: One of the ten great disciples of Shakyamuni Buddha, considered to have the deepest understanding of emptiness.

Śuddhodana: King of the Shākya clan and Shakyamuni Buddha's father.

Tianhuang Daowu (Ten'nō Dōgo, 748–807): A Tang dynasty Zen master, one of Shitou Xiqian's disciples.

Tientai Zhiyi (Tendai Chigi, 538–597): One of the most important Chinese Buddhist masters. The Chinese Tientai (Tendai) school is based on his teachings.

Tiantong Rujing (Tendō Nyojō, 1163–1227): A Song dynasty Zen master who was the abbot of Tiantong monastery when Dōgen practiced in China. Dōgen received dharma transmission from Rujing.

Vairocana Buddha: The main Buddha of the *Avataṃsaka Sutra* is the sambhogakāya buddha. Maha Vairocana (Dainichi Nyorai) is the dharmakāya buddha and the main Buddha in Vajrayāna Buddhism.

Vimalakīrti: The principal character of *Vimalakīrtinirdeśa Sutra*. He was a rich lay student of the Buddha who had better understanding of emptiness than the Buddha's disciples.

Vipaśyin Buddha: The first of the seven buddhas in the past. The seventh is Shakyamuni.

Xuanzang (Genjō, 600–664): One of the most important translators in the history of Chinese Buddhism. He traveled to India by himself and stayed there for seventeen years and transmitted the teaching of the Yogācāra school and established the Faxiang (Hossō) school.

Yangshan Huiji (Gyōsan Ejaku, 807–883): A Tang dynasty Zen master, dharma heir of Guishan Lingyou, and considered as the cofounder of the Guiyang (Igyō) school of Zen.

Yunyan Tansheng (Ungan Donjō, 780–841): A Tang dynasty Zen master, dharma heir of Yaoshan Weiyan, and the teacher of Dongshan Liangjie.

Yuquan Shenxiu (Gyokusen Jinshū, 606–706): A Tang dynasty Zen master, a disciple of the fifth ancestor, Daman Hongren, and the founder of the Northern school of Zen.

Glossary of Terms and Texts

Abhidharma: The earliest compilation of Buddhist philosophy and psychology. It took form in the period between the third century BCE and the third century CE. Its interpretations and explanations of concepts in the sutras reflect the views of individual Buddhist schools.

Absolute Three Treasures (*ittai sanbō*): One of the three categories of the Three Treasures mentioned in Dōgen's comments on the sixteen precepts. See *ittai sanbō.*

Āgama Sutra: The name used in China for collections of early Buddhist sutras, comparable to the Pāli Nikāya.

aggregate (Skt., *skandha*): A bundle, pile, or collection.

ambrosia: An English translation for the Sanskrit word *amṛta*, in Japanese *kanro*. This is a drink for heavenly beings. When one drinks it one attains immortality. It symbolizes nirvana and the Buddha's teachings.

anātman: Nonself, nonessentiality; one of the three marks of everything that exists. The anātman doctrine is one of the central teachings of Buddhism; it says that no self exists in the sense of a permanent, eternal, integral, and independent entity within an individual. Thus, in Buddhism, the ego (self) is no more than a transitory, fluid process that is a result of the interaction of the five aggregates. In early Buddhism this analysis is limited to the personality. In Mahāyāna it is applied to all conditionally arising beings. This freedom from self-nature is called emptiness.

ancient buddha (*kobutsu*): Dōgen used this expression as a title of the Zen masters who truly attained the Dharma, such as Zhaozhou, Hongzhi, and his teacher Tiantong Rujing.

Antaiji: A Sōtō Zen temple located in Kyoto, Japan, where Kōdō Sawaki Roshi and Kōshō Uchiyama Roshi taught. It moved to Hyōgo Prefecture in 1976.

asura: One of the six realms of samsara. English translations are "fighting spirit," "demon," "evil spirit," and "titan."

ātman: According to Brahmanism, the real immortal self of human beings, corresponding to what is known in the West as the soul. It is the nonparticipating witness of the *jīva* (unchanging essence) beyond body and thought, and, as absolute consciousness, is identical with *brāhman*, the underpinning of all reality. By virtue of its identity with *brāhman*, its characteristic marks (*ātmakara*) are identical: eternal absolute being, absolute consciousness, and absolute bliss. In Buddhism the existence of an *ātman* is denied: neither within nor outside of physical and mental manifestations is there anything that can be designated as an independent, imperishable essence.

Avataṃsaka Sutra (Flower Ornament Sutra): A Mahāyāna sutra that is the basis of the teachings of the Chinese Huayen (Kegon) school, which emphasize "mutual interpenetration."

Awakening of Faith in Mahāyāna (Daijōkishinron): One of the most important Mahāyāna Buddhist texts, which advocates tathāgata-garbha theory (see *buddha-nature*). This text greatly influenced many Chinese and Japanese Buddhist teachings.

Bhagavat: One of the ten epithets of the Buddha, World-Honored One.

Bodhgayā: One of the four sacred places of Buddhism, where Shakyamuni Buddha attained complete enlightenment.

bodhi tree: The fig tree under which Shakyamuni Buddha attained complete enlightenment.

bodhi-mind (Skt., *bodhi-citta*): awakened mind, the mind of enlightenment; Way-seeking mind.

bodhisattva: In early Buddhism, Bodhisattva refers to Shakyamuni Buddha before he attained buddhahood. In Mahāyāna Buddhism, a bodhisattva is a person who has aroused bodhi-mind, taken the bodhisattva vows, and walks the bodhisattva path.

bonnō: A Japanese word for the Sanskrit *kleśa*. Although usually translated as delusion, illusion, or passion, this word has much wider connotations, including worldly care, sensual desire, suffering, and pain.

Brahma Net Sutra (Brahmajāla Sūtra; Jap., *Bonmōkyō*): A Mahāyāna Buddhist sutra that contains the ten major precepts and forty-eight minor precepts of bodhisattvas.

Brahma: Brahma was originally one of the gods in Indian mythology. In Buddhism, Brahma is considered to be one of the guardian gods of Dharma.

buddha-nature (Skt., *buddhata*): The same concept as *tathāgata-garbha*; tathāgata's embryo or womb. The true, immutable, and eternal nature of all beings.

Caodong school: Caodong (Jap., Sōtō) is one of the five schools of the Chinese Chan (Zen) tradition founded by Dongshan Liangjie and his disciple Caoshan Benji. This lineage was transmitted from China to Japan by Eihei Dōgen and continues today.

causality: The principle of cause and result. The Buddha said that without cause, nothing exists. It can be expressed as "If this exists, that exists; if this comes into being, that comes into being; if this is not, that is not; if this ceases to be, that ceases to be."

Chanyuan Qinggui (*Zen'en Shingi*, Rules of Purity for the Chan Monastery): The earliest Chan (Zen) monastic code, compiled by Changlu Zongze in 1103.

"Chiji Shingi" (Pure Standards for the Temple Administrators): One part of Dōgen's *Eihei Shingi*. *Chiji* refers to the six monastic administrators: director (*tsūsu*), assistant director (*kansu*), treasurer (*fūsu*), supervisor of the monks' conduct (*inō*), chief cook (*tenzo*), and work leader (*shissui*).

consciousness (Skt., *vijñāna*): The fifth of the five aggregates (*skandhas*). When the six sense organs encounter their objects, six consciousnesses arise: eye consciousness, ear consciousness, nose consciousness, tongue consciousness, body consciousness, and mind consciousness. In Yogācāra teaching, two deeper consciousnesses are added: *manas vijñāna* (ego-consciousness) and *ālaya vijñāna* (storehouse consciousness).

dāna-pāramitā: One of the six *pāramitā*s, it is the practice of giving or generosity. There are two kinds of *dāna*: offering Dharma and offering material things.

Deer Park (Mṛgadāva): One of the four sacred places in Indian Buddhism. After attaining enlightenment Shakyamuni Buddha went to the Deer Park in Sārnāth, on the outskirts of Vārāṇasī, and taught the five monks. This is called the first turning the dharma wheel.

dependent origination: see *interdependent origination*.

Dhammapada: One of the oldest and most well-known Buddhist scriptures, included in the Khuddaka Nikāya.

Dharma gate (Skt., *dharma mukha*): The teachings of the truth; the gate to the truth.

Dharma/dharmas: A term with various meanings. *Dharma*, with a capital *D*, refers to the truth or reality to which the Buddha awoke and the teachings of the Buddha as expressions or explanations of this truth. With a lowercase *d*, and in the plural, *dharma* refers to phenomenal beings, norms of behavior and ethical rules, objects of thought, ideas, and reflections of things in the mind.

dharma-nature (Skt., *dharmatā*; Jap., *hosshō*): The true nature of all beings; thusness or emptiness.

dharmadhātu (dharma-realm): In Mahāyāna Buddhism, the notion of a true nature that permeates and encompasses all phenomena. As a space or realm, the realm of dharmas is the uncaused and immutable totality in which all phenomena arise, dwell, and perish.

dharmakāya: One of the three bodies of a buddha in Mahāyāna Buddhism. Dharmakāya is the true nature of the Buddha, which is identical with ultimate reality, the essence of the universe. The dharmakāya is the unity of the Buddha with all beings in the universe. At the same time it represents the dharma, the teaching expounded by the Buddha. The other two bodies are sambhogakāya (reward body) and nirmāṇakāya (transformation body).

Diamond Sutra (Skt., *Vajracchedikā-prajñāpāramitā Sūtra*). Sutra of the Diamond-Cutter of Supreme Wisdom. One of the sutras in the group of *Prajñāpāramitā Sutras*. It shows that all the forms of phenomenal beings are not ultimate reality but rather illusions, projections of one's own mind.

duḥkha: Sanskrit word usually translated as "suffering." It is the first of the four noble truths. Duḥkha not only signifies suffering in the sense of unpleasant sensations, it also refers to everything, both material and mental, that is conditioned, subject to arising and perishing, comprised of the five aggregates, and not in a state of liberation. Thus everything that is temporarily pleasant is suffering, since it is subject to change and must end. Duḥkha arises because of delusive desire and craving and can be transformed by the elimination of desire through practicing the eightfold noble path.

eightfold noble path (Skt., *aṣṭāṅgika-mārga*): The fourth of the four noble truths; the path leading to cessation of suffering, comprising right view, right thinking, right speech, right action, right livelihood, right effort, right mindfulness, and right concentration.

Eihei Kōroku: *Dōgen's Extensive Record*, a collection of Eihei Dōgen's dharma hall discourses at Kōshōji, Daibutsuji, and Eiheiji, including dharma words and Chinese poems compiled by his disciples Ejō, Senne, and Gien.

Eihei Shingi: The collection of Dōgen's writings regarding monastic regulations: "Instructions for the Cook" (Tenzokyōkun), "The Model for Engaging the Way" (Bendōhō), "The Dharma for Taking Meals" (Fushukuhanpō), "Regulations for the Study Hall" (Shuryō Shingi), "The Dharma when Meeting Senior Instructors of Five Summer Practice Periods" (Taitaiko Gogejarihō), and "Pure Standards for the Temple Administrators" (Chiji Shingi).

ejiki (Skt., *durvarṇī-karaṇa*): Muted color of the *okesa*, or square robe. In ancient India Buddhist monks picked up discarded pieces of cloth, washed and dyed them an ochre color, and sewed them into a robe.

emptiness (Skt., *śūnyatā*): An expression used in Mahāyāna Buddhism, such as in the *Prajñāpāramitā Sutra*, for the nonexistence of the permanent self (*anātman*) and interdependent origination.

Enmei-jukku-kannon-gyō: A very short sutra with only forty-two Chinese characters on Kanzeon Bosatsu (Avalokiteśvara Bodhisattva) originating in China.

fearlessness (Skt., *abhayadāna*; Jap., *muise*): Freedom from anxiety. One of the three kinds of offering (*dāna*). The other two are offering of material and offering of the Dharma.

feeling or sensation (Skt., *vedanā*): The second of the five aggregates. When each of the six sense organs contacts its objects, we receive pleasant, unpleasant, or neutral sensations.

form (Skt., *rūpa*): The first of the five aggregates: material elements. In the case of human beings, the body is *rūpa*, whereas the other four aggregates are functions of mind.

formations (Skt., *saṃskāra*; Jap., *gyō*): The fourth of the five aggregates. Formations include all volitional impulses or intentions that precede an action.

four benefactors (Jap., *shion*): There are different sets of the four benefactors in various texts. The most common set is (1) father and mother, (2) all living beings, (3) king of the country, and (4) the Three Treasures.

four gross elements: The constituents of all living beings and things: the earth element, occurring in solid things such as bones; the water element, such as blood and other body liquids; the fire element, as in body heat; and the wind element, or movement.

four noble truths (Skt., *ārya-satya*): The most basic teaching of Buddhism. The noble truths are suffering (*duḥkha*), the origin of suffering, the cessation of suffering, and the path that leads to the cessation of suffering.

fukuden (Skt., *puṇya-kṣetra*): The field (rice paddy) which brings about the harvest of happiness or merit (*puṇya*). *Puṇya* refers to the karmic merit gained through good actions such as generosity and reciting sutras. Offerings to the Three Treasures, especially to the Buddha and monks, bring merit. Therefore the sangha of monks was considered to be a field of happiness.

"Fushukuhanpō" (The Dharma for Taking Meals): A section of *Eihei Shingi*, written by Eihei Dōgen. It describes the procedure of formal morning and noon meals at the monks' hall.

genzen sanbō: One of the three alternative ways to define the Three Treasures, in terms of the historical origins of Buddhism: Shakyamuni Buddha is the Buddha Treasure; the Buddha's teachings are the Dharma Treasure; and the Buddha's disciples and lay students are the Sangha Treasure. The other two definitions are the Absolute Three Treasures (*ittai sanbō*) and the Maintaining Three Treasures (*jūji sanbō*). See also *Three Treasures*.

great ultimate (Chi., *taiji*; Jap., *taikyoku*): A Chinese cosmological term for the supreme, ultimate state of undifferentiated absolute and infinite potentiality, contrasted with the *wuji* (without ultimate). The great ultimate is the source of the two opposing powers, yin and yang, that produce all things.

hachidainingaku (eight points of awakening of great beings): The eight points to watch in practice appear in the *Sutra of the Last Discourse of the Buddha* (*Butsu-yuikyōgyō*). This is also the title of the final chapter of Dōgen's *Shōbōgenzō*, written in the year he died.

head monk (*shuso*): The head monk of a practice period, who, as an exemplary monk, shares teaching responsibilities with the abbot and leads and encourages other monks' practice. He is one of the six heads of the different monastic departments.

hikkyo-kisho: The place to which we ultimately return. Dōgen says that we should take refuge in the Three Treasures because they are the place to which we finally return.

Hongzhou school: Hongzhou (Jap., Kōshū) is the school of Chinese Zen founded by Mazu Daoyi. Hongzhou is the name of the province where many of his disciples lived.

hṛdaya: A Sanskrit word translated into Chinese as *xin* (mind/heart). The original meaning is the heart as a part of the body. It also means "essence," as in the title of the *Prajñāpāramitā-hṛdaya Sutra*.

impermanence (Skt., *anitya*): One of the three marks of all beings. The other two are suffering (*duḥkha*) and no-self (*anātman*).

Indra's net: A metaphor used to illustrate the concepts of emptiness, interdependent origination, and interpenetration, found in the *Avataṃsaka Sutra*. The metaphor shows that all phenomenal beings are intimately connected. Indra's net has a multifaceted jewel at each vertex, and each jewel is reflected in all of the other jewels.

interdependent origination (Skt., *pratītya-samutpāda*; Jap., *engi*): A cardinal Buddhist teaching about causality. Other translations are "dependent origination" and "dependent arising."

ittai sanbō: One of the three categorizations of the Three Treasures, the Absolute Three Treasures. *Ittai* literally means "one body." The Buddha Treasure is the dharmakāya Buddha; the Dharma Treasure is the way all beings are; and the Sangha Treasure is the interconnection of all beings within the Indra's net of the universe. See also *Three Treasures*.

Jātaka: Part of the Khuddaka Nikāya, a collection of the stories regarding the Buddha's previous lives. In these stories the Buddha is called a bodhisattva.

ji: phenomenal, concrete things, as opposed to principles; the relative, as opposed to and the absolute. See also *ri*.

jijuyū zammai: Self-receiving and self-employing samādhi. This term, used by Dōgen as a foundation for his teachings on zazen, points to the dropping off of conceptual boundaries such as "self," "other," "myriad beings," and "practice" in zazen or any wholehearted practice.

joyful mind: One of the three minds discussed in Dōgen's "Tenzo-kyōkun." The other two are the magnanimous mind and the nurturing mind.

jūji sanbō: The Maintaining Three Treasures, one of the three categorizations of the Three Treasures. The Buddha symbolized by Buddha images is the Buddha Treasure; the printed Buddhist texts are the Dharma Treasure, and the sangha members in each Buddhist sangha is the Sangha Treasure. These have maintained Buddhist tradition since Shakyamuni Buddha's death. See also *Three Treasures*.

jukai ceremony: We become a Buddhist through this ceremony in which we receive the Buddhist precepts as the guideline of our lives.

kalpa: An exceedingly long period of time. To express the length of a kalpa two similes are used. In the first, a kalpa is how long it would take to empty a ten-cubic-mile container of poppy seeds by removing a single seed once every one hundred years. In the second, if once every one hundred years a heavenly woman brushes a solid one-cubic-mile rock with her silk sleeve, a kalpa is the time it would take for the rock to wear away.

Kapilavastu: The name of the city where Shakyamuni Buddha's father Śuddhodana was king. The Buddha was born in the Lumbinī Park near the city. One of the four sacred places of Indian Buddhism.

karma: A deed that is produced by the action of the mind, body, or speech, and which will produce an effect in the future.

kaṣāya (Jap., *kesa*): The square robe for Buddhist monks. This word refers to the color of the robe, usually muted black, blue, or red. Monks were allowed to own three kinds of *kaṣāya*: *saṃghāṭī*, *uttarāsaṃgha*, and *antarvāsa*.

kesa (okesa): Traditional monk's robe sewn by hand and originally pieced together with discarded fabric. Okesa is a polite form of kesa.

kitō: Praying to buddhas, bodhisattvas, or other guardian gods of Buddhism for some specific purpose. This was originally a practice in esoteric Buddhism, but later it was practiced in other Buddhist schools including Zen.

Kuśinagara: Place where Shakyamuni Buddha entered nirvana. One of the four sacred places in Indian Buddhism.

kuyō: A Japanese word for making an offering to the Buddha, the Dharma, and the Sangha, or to deceased persons through actions of body, speech, and mind.

Kyōjukaimon: Eihei Dōgen's comments on the sixteen precepts recorded by his dharma heir, Koun Ejō. This short text is the basis of the teaching on morality in Sōtō Zen tradition.

kyōzō (Skt., Sūtra Piṭaka): One of the three divisions of the Buddhist scriptures, a collection of the Buddha's discourses. The other two are the Abhidharma Piṭaka (psychological compilations of his teachings) and the Vinaya Piṭaka, the collection of the Buddha's admonitions regarding monk's misdeeds. Later in China and Japan *kyōzō* came to refer to the building in which Buddhist scriptures are stored.

lotus posture: Cross-legged posture used in sitting meditation. Originally in esoteric Buddhism this term referred to the Hindu yoga posture known as *padmāsana*. In Zen Buddhism the terms *kekkafuza* (full lotus) and *hankafuza* (half lotus) have been used.

Lotus Sutra (Skt., *Saddharmapuṇḍarīka Sūtra*; Jap., *Myōhō-renge-kyō*): One of the most important sutras in Mahāyāna Buddhism, especially popular in China and Japan. The Tientai (Tendai) and Nichiren schools are based on its teachings. Since Dōgen was originally ordained and trained in the Tendai tradition before starting to practice Zen, he valued the *Lotus Sutra* as the king of all sutras.

Lumbinī Park: One of the four sacred places in Indian Buddhism. Shakyamuni Buddha was born in this park near Kapilavastu, the capital of the Shākya clan.

Magadha: North Indian kingdom at the time of Shakyamuni Buddha. Rājagriha was the capital of the kingdom where the first Buddhist monastery, Veluvana (Bamboo Grove) Vihāra, was founded. The king of Magadha, Bimbisāra, and his son Ajātasatru supported Shakyamuni and his sangha.

magnanimous mind: One of the three mental attitudes all Zen practitioners need to maintain, mentioned in Dōgen's "Instructions to the Cook" (Tenzokyōkun). The other two attitudes are nurturing mind and joyful mind. A magnanimous mind is like a mountain or ocean, immovable and without discrimination.

mahāsattva: Literally, "great being"; a term for bodhisattvas.

Mahāyāna Buddhism: Literally means "great vehicle." Mahāyāna is one of the two main branches of Buddhism that originated in India, the other being Theravāda. In the Mahāyāna tradition one aims to attain buddhahood together with all living beings.

mantra: A syllable or series of syllables that is believed to have special power and to manifest cosmic forces and aspects of the buddhas. Sometimes a mantra is the name of a buddha. Continuous repetition of mantras, also called dhāranīs, is a meditation practice in many Buddhist schools, particularly in esoteric Buddhism. In the Zen tradition the use of mantras shows the influence of esoteric Chinese Buddhism.

mārga: The Buddhist path, specifically the fourth of the four noble truths: the eightfold noble path that leads to the cessation of suffering.

"Merging of Difference and Unity": A translation of the title of the poem "Sandōkai," composed by Shitou Xiqian.

Middle Way (Skt., *madhyama-pratipad*): A term for the practice of the eightfold noble path taught by Shakyamuni Buddha, who said that the two extremes, self-indulgence and self-mortification, should be avoided. Later in the Mahāyāna, Nāgārjuna described the Middle Way as refraining from choosing between opposing positions in relation to the existence or nonexistence of all things. Therefore his school was called Mādhyamika.

mind-ground: A translation of the Japanese word *shinchi*, synonymous with expressions such as mind-nature and mind-source. *Mind* here refers to a mind of absolute suchness. This mind is like a ground from which all different plants, grasses, grains, trees, and so forth arise and grow.

Mount Hiei: The mountain east of Kyoto and the site of the main monastery of the Japanese Tendai school, Enryakuji. Eihei Dōgen became a monk at this monastery.

mui (Skt., *asaṃskṛta*): "Unconditioned" or "unproduced." Things that are beyond conditioned existence, beyond arising, dwelling, changing, and perishing. In the original teaching, only nirvana was regarded as unconditioned. The Sarvāstivāda school had three kinds of unconditioned space and two kinds of dissolution (*nirodha*).

mujūsho-nehan: One of the three kinds of nirvana, the nirvana of nonabiding. This is the nirvana of bodhisattvas who, because of their wisdom, do not stay on the shore of samsara and because of their compassion do not dwell on the far shore of nirvana.

mumyō (Skt., *avidyā*): Ignorance, one of the three poisonous minds. Ignorance of the four noble truths and the reality of all beings is the primary cause of suffering within samsara.

mushotoku: Without gaining. Freedom from the desires to gain any desirable result form Buddhist practice. This expression appears in the *Prajñāpāramitā Sutras*, such as the *Diamond Sutra* and the *Heart Sutra*. Eihei Dōgen put emphasis on practice without gaining mind in "Gakudōyōjinshū" (Points to Watch in Practicing the Way).

nirvana (Jap., *nehan*): Literally *nirvana* means "extinction" or "blowing out" of the fires of greed, anger/hatred, and ignorance; it is the state of perfect peace of mind. In early Buddhism it meant departure from the cycle of rebirth in samsara and entry into an entirely different mode of existence. Nirvana is unconditioned, beyond arising, abiding, changing, and perishing. In Mahāyāna, nirvana is not different from samsara or from the ultimate nature of the dharmakāya. The duality of samsara and nirvana exists only from a conventional viewpoint.

Niutou school: Niutou (Oxhead; Jap., Gozu) is one of the schools of Chinese Zen founded by Niutou Farong, a disciple of the fourth ancestor, Daoxin.

Northern school: One of the schools of Chinese Zen. The Northern and Southern schools separated after the time of the fifth ancestor, Daman Hongren. The founder of the Northern school was Yuquan Shenxiu, a senior dharma brother of Huineng.

nurturing mind (Jap., *rōshin*): One of the three minds mentioned in Dōgen's "Tenzokyōkun." Another possible translation is "parental mind": the mind that takes care of others the way parents nurture their children.

okesa: see *kesa*.

One Mind (Jap., *isshin*): This expression can refer both to the mind in the aspect of phenomena (*jishin*) and to the mind in the aspect of the absolute (*rishin*). The former is the discriminating mind, the latter the mind beyond discrimination.

ōryōki (Skt., *pātra*): A set of eating bowls that Zen monks receive at their ordination. In a narrower sense *ōryōki* refers to the largest of these bowls. In India, Buddhist monks used only one bowl for begging and eating, a bowl much larger than the ōryōki of the Zen tradition today.

pāramitā: Literally means "perfection" of certain virtues. In Mahāyāna Buddhism the six pāramitās—giving, morality, patience, diligence, concentration, and wisdom—are considered to be the bodhisattva practice.

perception (Skt., *saṃjñā*): The third of the five aggregates. Perception denotes not only the construction of mental images and the formation of concepts but also the concepts themselves.

phenomenal beings (Skt., *saṃskṛta*; Jap., *ui-hō*): Conditioned beings. All interdependent and conditioned phenomenal beings which arise, abide, change, and perish. Everything conditioned is empty, impermanent, without substance.

prajñā (Jap., *hannya*): Wisdom, a central concept of Mahāyāna Buddhism and one of the six pāramitās of bodhisattva practice. This wisdom sees emptiness, the true reality of all things.

precept (Skt., *śīla*): One of the six pāramitās of bodhisattva practice: perfection of morality, ethics, virtue, proper conduct. Guidelines for conduct may be further specified as explicit precepts for the various types of practioners.

prophecy (Skt., *vyākaraṇa*; Jap., *juki*): Prophecy given by a buddha regarding someone's attainment of buddhahood in a future life.

repentance (Skt., *kṣamā*; Jap., *sange*): An important part of Buddhism from its beginning. Twice a month each sangha gathered for a ceremony known as *uposatha* (Jap., *fusatsu*). During the gathering, the leader of the sangha recited the Vinaya precepts and monks who violated the precepts made repentance.

ri: principles, as opposed to phenomenal, concrete things; the absolute, as opposed to the relative. See also *ji*.

Rig Veda: The oldest collection of the verses of wisdom called Vedas in Indian thought.

saba: Small pieces of food offered by practitioners to unseen beings such as hungry ghosts during ōryōki meals at Zen monasteries.

samādhi (Jap., *zammai*): Concentration of the mind, one of the three foundations of the study of Buddhism, the other two being morality (*śīla*) and wisdom (*prajñā*). Dōgen called his practice of zazen *jijuyū-zammai*.

samsara: Literally *samsara* means "continuous flow," that is, the cycle of birth, life, death, and rebirth within the six realms. This cycle ends in the attainment of liberation and entrance into nirvana.

sangha: The Buddhist community. In a narrow sense the sangha consists of monks, nuns, and novices. In a wider sense the sangha also includes lay followers.

sanshin: Three minds or mental attitudes for practitioners in a Zen monastery, mentioned in Dōgen's "Tenzokyōkun": joyful mind, nurturing mind, and magnanimous mind.

sentient beings: The mass of living beings subject to illusion, suffering, and transmigration within samsara.

sesshin: Literally, "touching or embracing the mind/heart." This refers to the intensive practice periods in Zen monasteries during which monks focus on sitting meditation practice.

shikantaza: "Just sitting." Originally this expression was used by Tiantong Rujing, Eihei Dōgen's teacher. Dōgen also taught a practice of wholehearted sitting without any special meditation technique.

Shingon school: Japanese esoteric Buddhist school founded by Kūkai (774–835).

Shitennōji: One of the oldest Buddhist temples, founded by prince Shōtoku in Osaka in the seventh century.

Shōbōgenzō: True Dharma Eye Treasury. The title of the collection of Eihei Dōgen's essays. The *Shōbōgenzō* is considered the most profound work in Zen literature and the most outstanding work of Buddhist literature of Japan.

śramaṇa (Jap., *shamon*): Wandering ascetic monk. Another name for a Buddhist monk.

skillful means (Skt., *upāya*; Jap., *hōben*): A skillful method or expedient device used by buddhas and bodhisattvas to guide beings. This is also the title of the second chapter of the *Lotus Sutra*.

sōdō (monks' hall): One of the seven basic buildings of Zen monasteries in which monks sleep, practice meditation, and eat meals.

Sōtō Zen tradition: Sōtō or Caodong is one of the five schools of Chinese Zen, founded by Dongshan Liangjie and his disciple Caoshan Benji. This tradition was transmitted from China to Japan by Eihei Dōgen and continues today.

Southern school: One of the schools of Chinese Zen founded by the sixth ancestor, Huineng. The central teaching of this school is sudden enlightenment.

stūpa: Originally stūpas were memorial monuments for Shakyamuni Buddha built at various sacred places such as Lumbinī Park, where the Buddha was born; Bodhgayā, where the Buddha attained enlightenment; Sārnāth, where the Buddha gave his first discourse to five monks; and Kuśinagara, where the Buddha entered nirvana.

suchness: "Suchness," "thusness," and "as-it-is-ness" are translations for the Sanskrit word *tathātā* and the Japanese word *shinnyo*, which refer to the reality of all beings as it is. Suchness is a synonym for *dharmatā*.

suffering: see *duḥkha*.

śūnyatā: see *emptiness*.

Suttanipāta: A collection of short sutras. One of the oldest scriptures of Buddhism, included in the Khuddaka Nikāya.

takuhatsu (Skt., *piṇḍapāta*): Traditional religious begging practiced by Buddhist monks from the Buddha's time in India. This is still practiced in the Theravāda tradition and by Zen monks in Japan. In Japan today the monks receive mainly monetary donations instead of food.

Tathāgata: One of the ten epithets for the Buddha, literally the "thus-come one" or "thus-gone one."

tathātā: "Suchness," "thusness," "as-it-is-ness." One of the central concepts of Mahāyāna Buddhism, which refers to the true reality of all beings.

"Tenzokyōkun" (Instructions for the Cook): The first section of *Eihei Shingi*. Eihei Dōgen wrote this text to teach the importance of communal work as a practice, using the example of cooking.

thought construction (Skt., *prapañca*; Jap., *keron*): One of the important expressions in Nāgārjuna's teachings on emptiness. It refers to the deluded conceptualization of the world through the use of ever-expanding language and concepts, all rooted in the delusion of self. Other translations are conceptual proliferation or self-reflexive thinking.

three poisonous minds: The three destructive, deeply rooted human tendencies—greed, hatred, and delusion—that are the source of all suffering. All result from ignorance of our true nature.

Three Treasures: Same as the Three Jewels, or the Triple Gem: three things in which a Buddhist takes refuge and looks to for guidance—the Buddha, the Dharma, and the Sangha. Can be defined in three complementary ways. See also *ittai sanbō*, *genzen sanbō*, and *jūji sanbō*.

transmigration: Transmigration, or reincarnation, is believed to occur after death when the soul or spirit comes back to life in a newborn body. This doctrine is a central tenet within the majority of Indian religious traditions, such as Hinduism, Jainism, and Sikhism. The Buddhist concept of rebirth is also often referred to as reincarnation.

Tripiṭaka: The three baskets (of Buddhist scriptures): the Sutra Piṭaka, Abhidharma Piṭaka, and Vinaya Piṭaka.

Tuṣita heaven: The heaven where Shakyamuni Buddha stayed before he was born. It is believed that Maitreya is residing there and will be born in this world several billions of years from now.

twelve links of dependent origination: see *interdependent origination*.

Two Truths: conventional truth and ultimate truth. Nāgārjuna is the first Buddhist master who clearly mentioned the two truths, in his *Mūlamadhyamakakārikā*.

unsurpassable mind: A translation of the Japanese word *mujōshin*, a synonym for *bodaishin* (Skt., *bodhi-citta*). *Bodhi-citta* is considered to be a shortened form of *anuttarā-samyaksambodhi-citta*. "Unsurpassable" is a translation of *anuttarā*.

Vajrayāna: A school of Buddhism that emerged in sixth- or seventh-century India. This school is also called esoteric Buddhism or Tantric Buddhism. It developed out of Mahāyāna Buddhist teachings strongly influenced by Hinduism. It reached into China, Japan, and Tibet. The Shingon school founded by Kūkai is a Japanese form of Vajrayāna Buddhism.

Vinaya: One of the three *piṭaka* (baskets) of Buddhist scriptures. Vinaya is a collection of the rules and regulations for the communal life of monks and nuns.

Vishnu: The Supreme God in the Vaishnava tradition of Hinduism.

Vow (Skt., *pranidhāna*): In Mahāyāna Buddhism, bodhisattvas take a vow stating that they will strive to liberate all sentient beings from samsara and lead them to enlightenment. Bodhisattvas do not seek to awaken solely for themselves, but rather endeavor to free all beings and help them reach nirvana.

Vulture Peak (Skt., Gṛdhrakūṭa): A mountain near the city of Rājagṛha. Shakyamuni Buddha often gave discourses on this mountain. It is said that the *Lotus Sutra* was expounded on this mountain. In Zen the transmission from the Buddha to Mahākāśyapa took place there when the Buddha held up a flower and smiled.

wheel-turning king (Skt., *cakravarti-rāja*): In the Indian tradition, an ideal king who rules the world by rolling the wheel he receives from heaven at his enthronement. The wheel of his chariot rolls everywhere without obstruction.

Yogācāra school: One of the two Mahāyāna schools in India, founded by Maitreyanātha, Asaṅga, and Vasubandhu.

zendō: An abbreviation of *zazendō*, a hall for zazen practice; meditation hall in Zen tradition.

Index

T

About the Author

Shohaku Okumura was born in Osaka, Japan in 1948. He is an ordained priest and Dharma successor of Kōshō Uchiyama Roshi in the lineage of Kōdō Sawaki Roshi. He is a graduate of Komazawa University and has practiced at Antaiji with Kōshō Uchiyama Roshi, Zuioji with Narasaki Ikkō Roshi in Japan, and Pioneer Valley Zendo in Massachusetts. He taught at Kyoto Sōtō Zen Center in Japan and Minnesota Zen Meditation Center in Minneapolis. He was the director of the Soto Zen Buddhism International Center (previously called Soto Zen Education Center) in San Francisco from 1997 to 2010.

His previously published books of translation include *Dōgen's Extensive Record: A Translation of the Eihei Kōroku*; *Shikantaza: An Introduction to Zazen*; *Shōbōgenzō Zuimonki: Sayings of Eihei Dōgen Zenji*; *Heart of Zen: Practice without Gaining-mind* (previously titled *Dōgen Zen*); *Zen Teachings of "Homeless" Kōdō*; *Opening the Hand of Thought*; *The Whole Hearted Way: A Translation of Eihei Dōgen's Bendōwa with Commentary by Kōshō Uchiyama Roshi*; and *Dōgen's Pure Standards for the Zen Community: A Translation of Eihei Shingi.* Okumura is also the editor of *Dōgen Zen and Its Relevance for Our Time*; *Soto Zen: An Introduction to Zazen*; and *Nothing is Hidden: Essays on Zen Master Dōgen's*

Instructions for the Cook. He is the author of *Realizing Genjōkōan: The Key to Dōgen's Shōbōgenzō*.

He is the founding teacher of the Sanshin Zen Commuinity, based in Bloomington, Indiana, where he lives with his family.

Also Available by the Author from Wisdom Publications

Realizing Genjokoan
The Key to Dōgen's Shobogenzo
Shohaku Okumura
Foreword byTaigen Dan Leighton

The Zen Teaching Of Homeless Kodo
Shohaku Okumura and Kosho Uchiyama

Dōgen's Extensive Record
A Translation of the Eihei Kōroku
Eihei Dōgen
Taigen Dan Leighton, Shohaku Okumura, John Daido Loori, and Steven Heine
Foreword byTenshin Reb Anderson

Opening The Hand Of Thought
Foundations of Zen Buddhist Practice
Kosho Uchiyama, Tom Wright, Jisho Warner, and Shohaku Okumura

About Wisdom Publications

Wisdom Publications is the leading publisher of classic and contemporary Buddhist books and practical works on mindfulness. To learn more about us or to explore our other books, please visit our website at wisdompubs.org or contact us at the address below.

Wisdom Publications
199 Elm Street
Somerville, MA 02144 USA

We are a 501(c)(3) organization, and donations in support of our mission are tax deductible.

Wisdom Publications is affiliated with the Foundation for the Preservation of the Mahayana Tradition (FPMT).

Contenido

Prefacio

Aprende a distinguir

Uno de los grandes proyectos financieros de padres e hijos, además de la compra de una vivienda, puede ser la planificación de los gastos universitarios. Si eres como la mayoría de los padres ante la perspectiva de un hijo que inicia sus estudios universitarios, te sentirás lleno de entusiasmo por las oportunidades que depara el futuro, pero al mismo te preocupará cómo encontrar financiación para su educación. Sin embargo, el proceso es más fácil de lo que parece, y con ayuda financiera, prácticamente todos pueden acceder a la universidad.

Como director ejecutivo de la National College Scholarship Foundation, Inc., (Fundación Nacional de Becas Universitarias, Inc.) organización sin fines de lucro que ofrece seminarios y programas promocionales de ayuda financiera en Montgomery County Maryland Public High Schools (Escuelas públicas de secundaria del Condado de Maryland, Montgomery), llevo más de diez años trabajando con la comunidad hispana asistiendo a padres e hijos con la planificación de ayuda financiera. Adicionalmente, como director de ayuda financiera de Montgomery Community College en Maryland, que atiende a más de 20,000 estudiantes, entre los cuales se cuenta un gran número de hispanos, he tenido la oportunidad de otorgar ayuda financiera a estudiantes en la universidad, y también de aconsejar familias sobre el proceso de ayuda financiera.

Aprovechando esta experiencia única, se ha creado este libro, *El libro de respuestas para la ayuda financiera*, para estudiantes hispanos y sus padres. Se incluyen instrucciones línea por línea para llenar los formularios gratuitos de solicitud de ayuda financiera federal, Free Application for Federal Student Aid (FAFSA), y proporciona también ideas, sugerencias y consejos para que tú y tu familia logren el éxito en la obtención de ayuda financiera.

Puesto que conozco especialmente los problemas que enfrentan las familias hispanas para manejar los gastos educativos universitarios, he enfocado este libro en las siguientes áreas:

- Comprensión del sistema de ayuda financiera
- Identificación de recursos de ayuda financiera disponibles
- Preparación para llenar los formularios correctamente
- Cumplimiento de las fechas límite de solicitud importantes

Es esencial que entiendas que literalmente estás compitiendo contra miles de familias en busca de ayuda financiera y, como en cualquier competencia, debes jugar a ganar. *El libro de respuestas para la ayuda financiera* te ofrece el conocimiento sólido que necesitas para ser un ganador y, por consiguiente, obtener el dinero para la universidad.

He observado que muchos estudiantes de bajos ingresos y estudiantes que pertenecen a minorías no se presentan a las universidades académicamente más competentes, porque asumen que nunca podrían asistir debido a los altos costos de la institución. Voy a acabar este mito y a comprobar que, con la ayuda financiera, los estudiantes pueden asistir a la universidad que escojan.

Puesto que generalmente, son los padres quienes asumen la responsabilidad de pagar la universidad, este libro va dirigido a ellos. Sin embargo, también deben leerlo los estudiantes, de manera que puedan participar en las conversaciones familiares para determinar cómo financiar su educación. El pago de los gastos universitarios es un asunto de toda la familia. Gracias a *El libro de respuestas para la ayuda financiera*, podrán encontrar la forma de costear la universidad. ¡Buena suerte!

—Dr. Herm Davis

Director Ejecutivo

National College Scholarship Fund, Inc.

Introducción

Asume los gastos universitarios

Asumir los gastos universitarios puede generar mucho estrés, especialmente si tienes en cuenta los costos actuales de las universidades. Consecuentemente, muchas familias no estimulan a sus hijos a iniciar sus estudios universitarios, pues creen que no podrán costearlos. Igualmente, no contemplan las universidades de más altos costos porque se asustan con el monto de la matrícula. Otras familias ni siquiera solicitan ayuda financiera porque piensan que sus ingresos son demasiado altos o porque tienen mucho dinero ahorrado. Sin embargo, no sólo todas las familias pueden enviar a sus hijos a la universidad, sino que incluso las universidades más costosas son asequibles. Te sorprendería saber que:

- $ 7 de cada 10 estudiantes a tiempo completo reciben alguna forma de ayuda financiera.
- $ La ayuda financiera cubre el 40 por ciento o más del presupuesto de estudiantes a tiempo completo.
- $ Las subvenciones y los préstamos son las formas más comunes de ayuda financiera.
- $ Más de la mitad de los estudiantes universitarios a tiempo completo recibían ayuda en forma de subvención a finales del siglo veinte.
- $ 1 de cada 5 estudiantes universitarios proviene de familias con un ingreso por debajo de $20,000 al año.

El libro de respuestas para la ayuda financiera fue creado para aliviar tu estrés y tus preocupaciones y brindarte la información necesaria para obtener la mejor ayuda financiera posible para tu hijo. Este libro también devela el misterio del proceso de ayuda financiera. En pocas palabras, la ayuda financiera es dinero proveniente de fuentes externas para ayudarte a pagar los gastos educativos de tus hijos después de la secundaria, conocidos como estudios de educación superior. La educación superior incluye universidades, escuelas universitarias vocacionales y técnicas, escuelas universitarias de oficios y escuelas de negocios. Es importante distinguir dos categorías básicas de ayuda:

1. **Ayuda basada en la necesidad**
2. **Ayuda no basada en la necesidad**

La ayuda no basada en la necesidad es también conocida como ayuda por mérito, y generalmente se otorga a estudiantes como reconocimiento a sus destrezas o talentos especiales, o su habilidad académica. Este tipo de ayuda también se puede otorgar con otros criterios, tales como campo de estudio, servicio comunitario o capacidad de liderazgo.

No obstante, la ayuda basada en la necesidad conforma la mayoría de ayuda disponible para educación superior. Si no cuentas con recursos suficientes para pagar los estudios de educación superior, se considera que tienes necesidad financiera. Este es el primer requisito para recibir ayuda financiera basada en la necesidad; sin embargo, es necesario que tú y tu hijo cumplan con otros requisitos que explicamos más detalladamente en el Capítulo 5. Tu elegibilidad para ayuda financiera generalmente se determina en función de la información financiera de tu familia, que se analiza de acuerdo a una serie de cálculos estándar. Esta evaluación de necesidad o análisis de necesidad, como generalmente se le conoce, da origen al Expected Family Contribution, EFC (Aporte Esperado de la Familia). Tu EFC indica precisamente el monto que se espera que tu familia aporte para sufragar los gastos educativos de un año de educación superior.

Existen tres tipos básicos de ayuda financiera:

- $ **Préstamos.** Constituyen la fuente de ayuda financiera más disponible. Tendrás que reembolsar el préstamo, pero las tasas de interés son frecuentemente más bajas que las de préstamos comerciales. Los pagos generalmente se aplazan hasta después de que tu hijo termine sus estudios universitarios.
- $ **Subvenciones y becas.** No necesitas reembolsar este tipo de ayuda ni respaldarla trabajando en el campus. Las subvenciones generalmente se basan sólo en la necesidad financiera, mientras que las becas se otorgan a estudiantes según criterios específicos, tales como mérito académico o deportivo, sin importar si el estudiante necesita el dinero para ayudar pagar la universidad.

- $ **Trabajo y estudio.** Esta opción permite a los estudiantes trabajar de 10 a 15 horas semanales durante el año académico y tiempo completo durante el verano, a fin de obtener dinero para pagar la universidad.

Cada tipo de ayuda cuenta con cuatro posibles fuentes:

1. **Federal**
2. **Estatal**
3. **Institucional**
4. **Privada**

El gobierno federal es la mayor fuente de ayuda de acuerdo a la necesidad. A decir verdad, sólo el gobierno federal provee más de $60 mil millones para ayuda estudiantil cada año. La mayoría de la ayuda federal se encuentra disponible a través del Departamento de Educación de Estados Unidos y el Departamento de Salud y Servicios Humanos de Estados Unidos. La ayuda respaldada por el estado varía de un estado a otro y puede tener restricciones en cuanto a residencia dentro del estado o asistencia a una universidad dentro del estado.

Muchas universidades ofrecen a sus estudiantes ayuda basada en la necesidad y ayuda no basada en la necesidad. Este tipo de ayuda se conoce como ayuda institucional y varía según la universidad. La ayuda institucional es más importante ahora para las familias debido al incremento en los costos educativos. La ayuda privada proviene de patrocinadores no institucionales y no gubernamentales. Puede constituir una ayuda significativa para asumir los gastos educativos y reducir la deuda, pero generalmente requiere de más esfuerzo, ya que primero es necesario ubicar las fuentes de financiación y luego solicitar ayuda.

El paquete de ayuda se negociará con el funcionario de ayuda financiera de la universidad que tu hijo escoja. El paquete reúne todos los tipos de ayuda para los que calificas y, muy probablemente, tendrá una combinación de los tipos de ayuda antes mencionados. Encontrarás mayor información sobre los paquetes de ayuda financiera en el Capítulo 4.

¿POR QUÉ DEBES SOLICITAR AYUDA FINANCIERA?

A continuación, encontrarás algunas de las preocupaciones e inquietudes más comunes de los padres respecto de la ayuda financiera, junto con las razones por las cuales no debes desanimarte para solicitar la ayuda que necesitas:

- $ ***El formulario de solicitud requiere demasiada información personal.*** La cantidad de páginas para llenar en los formularios puede hacer que el proceso de ayuda financiera parezca indiscreto e intimidante. Probablemente, no quieras dar a conocer información financiera que consideras privada. No obstante, verás que los formularios no son tan complicados como parecen y que la información requerida es la misma que debes presentar al Internal Revenue Service, IRS (Servicio de Impuestos Internos) cada año. Tu información personal es necesaria para determinar el monto de ayuda financiera que puedes recibir.
- $ ***La ayuda financiera es caridad; debo ser capaz de pagar la educación de mis hijos por mi mismo.*** Actualmente, es muy rara la familia que puede pagar los altos gastos universitarios. La premisa de la ayuda financiera es que los estudiantes junto con sus padres deben responsabilizarse de su propia educación, pero como no tienen los medios, el gobierno provee ayuda en forma de inversión. Esta inversión es un derecho de cada estudiante; el gobierno provee más de $60 mil millones al año en subvenciones, programas de trabajo y préstamos para hacer la universidad asequible a todo aquel que califique. Un título universitario generalmente significa que el estudiante obtendrá un trabajo mejor pagado, contribuirá más a la sociedad y pagará más impuestos a lo largo de su vida.
- $ ***No quiero adquirir una gran deuda.*** Es cierto que la mayoría de familias debe ahorrar dinero para pagar la universidad. Sin embargo, un préstamo educativo no es igual a prestar dinero para vacaciones, ni a una tarjeta de crédito. Es una sabia inversión que producirá una buena ganancia, una carrera profesional para tu hijo. De manera similar, los préstamos educativos con frecuencia tienen tasas de interés más bajas y menos multas que los

préstamos al consumidor. Finalmente, no olvides que algunos préstamos pueden condonarse, dependiendo de la carrera de tu hijo. Por ejemplo, muchos maestros que enseñan en zonas de bajos ingresos, pueden ser elegibles para que se les condonen los préstamos. Comunícate con la oficina de ayuda financiera para obtener mayor información.

$ ***La ayuda financiera es tan confusa, hay tanto por aprender que temo cometer errores.*** ¡Por eso compraste este libro! Aquí te explicamos de principio a fin el proceso de ayuda financiera, para que puedas entenderlo más fácilmente. Te brindamos detalles sobre los formularios que necesitas e incluso te damos instrucciones renglón por renglón para llenar la FAFSA. Si necesitas más información, comunícate con la oficina de orientación vocacional de la escuela secundaria de tu hijo y la entidad de ayuda financiera de tu estado, y busca a través de recursos confiables de Internet. El mejor recurso para ti y tu hijo son los funcionarios de ayuda financiera de las universidades donde tu hijo postule. Su trabajo es explicarte los requisitos de la universidad y ayudarte con todo el proceso de solicitud. Por consiguiente, asegúrate de obtener una cita con el funcionario de ayuda financiera cuando visites el campus; probablemente te sentirás después más tranquilo para solicitar ayuda.

Nada debe detener a tu hijo en su interés para continuar con sus estudios de educación superior, mucho menos las preocupaciones financieras. Las familias tienen a su disposición una serie de programas y organizaciones para ayudarles a aliviar la carga financiera de la universidad. En las páginas siguientes, *El libro de respuestas para la ayuda financiera* te orienta en el camino para que puedas apropiarte de toda la ayuda financiera a la que tu familia tiene derecho.

[illegible]

La [illegible] se [illegible] por [illegible] [illegible]

[illegible]

[illegible]

[illegible]

Cómo comenzar: Formularios básicos

Este capítulo presenta los formularios principales que necesitas llenar para obtener ayuda financiera. Es importante que tengas en cuenta que el proceso de solicitud de ayuda financiera puede ser bastante prolongado y algunos fondos son limitados, especialmente los destinados para becas. Por esta razón, debes presentar todos los formularios de solicitud y seguimiento en las fechas límites fijadas por la universidad; así puedes estar seguro que tu hijo será tomado en cuenta para todos los fondos disponibles.

No esperes a recibir una oferta de ingreso para solicitar la ayuda financiera. Si esperas, con seguridad perderás el mejor paquete de ayuda financiera.

Con ayuda financiera, prácticamente todos pueden costearse una educación superior. El primer paso es comprender los formularios que debes usar para saber cómo tu hijo puede costearse la universidad. Los formularios básicos son:

- $ Free Application for Federal Student Aid, FAFSA (Solicitud Gratuita de Ayuda Federal para Estudiantes)
- $ College Scholarship Service (CSS) Profile (Servicio de Becas Universitaria (CSS) Profile)
- $ Documentos para ayuda institucional complementaria

FREE APPLICATION FOR FEDERAL STUDENT AID (FAFSA)

Éste es el nombre del formulario de solicitud que todos los estudiantes deben llenar para pedir ayuda financiera. Como lo dice su nombre, es totalmente gratuito y puedes presentarlo en español o inglés, en medio impreso o electrónico. La información que proporcionas en la solicitud FAFSA sobre ingresos, activos y aspectos demográficos de tu familia servirá como base para determinar la elegibilidad de tu hijo para los programas federales de ayuda estudiantil y, en muchos casos, fuentes de ayuda institucional, estatal y privada.

Sólo debes llenar una solicitud FAFSA al año, aunque tu hijo esté solicitando ingreso en más de una universidad. Cada miembro de tu familia que asista a la universidad debe llenar una solicitud FAFSA individual. No olvides que puedes solicitar que la información FAFSA se envíe hasta un máximo de 6 universidades diferentes a la vez. En la solicitud FAFSA debes incluir el nombre completo y la dirección de la universidad, junto con el código universitario federal respectivo, para que se envíe correctamente. Encontrarás la lista de códigos universitarios federales en: www.ed.gov/offices/OSFAP/Students/.

Quienes soliciten ayuda financiera federal por primera vez, deben llenar la solicitud FAFSA regular, que es un formulario de 6 páginas con numerosas preguntas. Este formulario está disponible en la mayoría de las bibliotecas públicas y oficinas universitarias de ayuda financiera o puedes descargarlo desde la página de Internet: www.ed.gov/offices/OSFAP/Students/apply.html. Presenta la solicitud FAFSA tan pronto como te sea posible, después del 1° de enero del año de ingreso de tu hijo a la universidad, y antes de la fecha prioritaria de presentación fijada por la universidad. Por ejemplo, si tu hijo comienza su primer año de universidad en septiembre de 2004, y la universidad que le interesa ha fijado el 15 de marzo como fecha prioritaria de presentación, debes presentar tu formulario lo antes posible, a partir del 1° de enero de 2004. Así lograrás reunir toda la información financiera del año fiscal 2003 antes del 15 de marzo, 2004. Revisa la información de la universidad para conocer la fecha prioritaria de presentación; casi siempre se encuentra en los catálogos, documentos de solicitud de ingreso, folletos o en Internet.

Un formulario de renovación FAFSA se envía automáticamente por correo a los estudiantes que llenaron exitosamente la solicitud FAFSA el año anterior. Este formulario te llegará con información pre-impresa extraída de tu solicitud FAFSA anterior. Si es necesario, simplemente debes actualizar esta información para el nuevo año escolar. Si no recibes el formulario de renovación FAFSA, averigua la razón con un administrador de ayuda financiera o llama al 800-4-FEDAID.

Solicitudes electrónicas FAFSA

Los formularios de solicitud FAFSA regulares y de renovación están disponibles electrónicamente. Actualmente, la mayoría de universidades utilizan servicio de Electronic Data Exchange, EDE (Intercambio Electrónico de Información) del Departamento de Educación. A través del EDE, estas universidades pueden ingresar información FAFSA y transmitirla directamente al Central Processing System, CPS (Sistema Central de Procesamiento) para su análisis. Verifica en las oficinas de ayuda financiera de las universidades donde tu hijo desea ingresar, si pueden transmitir electrónicamente tu información FAFSA.

Las solicitudes electrónicas para ayuda estudiantil federal se pueden presentar en FAFSA en la Web o vía FAFSA Express. En FAFSA en la Web, desarrollada por el Departamento de Educación, puedes llenar electrónicamente una solicitud FAFSA. Para evitar posibles problemas, utiliza un buscador certificado para llenar solicitudes FAFSA por Internet, de manera que puedas completar y enviar tu información de FAFSA directamente al CPS. Para finalizar el proceso de solicitud, después de llenar el formulario por Internet puedes enviar por correo al procesador la página que requiere la firma, o firmar electrónicamente con un Número de Identificación Personal (PIN, por su nombre en inglés) que te suministran en la página Web. Una vez recibida la página firmada, el CPS imprime y te envía por correo un Student Aid Report, SAR (Informe de Ayuda para el Estudiante). La dirección FAFSA en la Web es www.fafsa.ed.gov.

FAFSA Express es una herramienta de aplicación de software independiente que te permite diligenciar electrónicamente tu solicitud, directamente con el Departamento de Educación. El software de FAFSA Express se puede descargar y usar en cualquier computadora con módem que use Windows. Las ventanas del software tienen una presentación similar a una solicitud FAFSA de papel e incluye vínculos de ayuda e instrucciones por Internet. También es posible obtener copias individuales del software FAFSA Express en las universidades para usarlas en tu computadora. Igualmente, puedes descargar el software FAFSA Express desde la página Web, www.ed.gov/offices/OSFAP/students/apply.fexpress.html.

Consulta en www.fafsa.ed.gov/beforebrowser_req.htm la lista más reciente de buscadores aceptados. El Departamento de Educación recomienda usar una "versión doméstica" de buscador (56 bits y 128 bits cifrado) para mayor seguridad de la información en la solicitud.

COLLEGE SCHOLARSHIP SERVICE (CSS) PROFILE

Algunas universidades también pueden exigir que llenes el formulario de solicitud del College Scholarship Service (CSS) PROFILE, que requiere un pago de $7.00 para registrarte, más $17.00 por cada institución a la que decidas enviar los resultados del Profile. El Profile reúne información adicional a la información de FAFSA, como el valor de la vivienda principal de los padres. Las universidades usan esta información para otorgar ayuda institucional financiera, generalmente en forma de donaciones (subvenciones o becas) que no deben reembolsarse al prestamista.

Si deseas recibir un formulario CSS PROFILE, primero debes registrarte para solicitarlo al teléfono 800-778-6888 de lunes a viernes, de 8:00 a.m. a 10 p.m., hora oficial del Este. Recibirás tu formulario dentro de los diez días siguientes a tu llamada. También puedes solicitar tu formulario por Internet en www.collegeboard.com. Puedes presentar el formulario cada año después del 1° de octubre.

DOCUMENTOS COMPLEMENTARIOS DE AYUDA INSTITUCIONAL

Muchas universidades exigen que completes uno o más documentos complementarios con información adicional a la solicitud FAFSA, con el fin de otorgar ayuda financiera institucional. Es posible que una universidad desee saber si tu hijo tiene destrezas que se pueden aplicar a un trabajo o si tiene permiso para trabajar. Por ejemplo, es probable que las universidades necesiten salvavidas, editores de periódicos, consejeros de dormitorios, choferes, operadores de conmutadores o de computadoras.

Estos documentos también se usan para saber la filiación religiosa de tu hijo, discapacidades físicas, atributos personales, o si pertenece a un grupo minoritario. ¿Por qué? Es posible que la oficina de ayuda financiera tenga becas para estudiantes que cumplan requisitos específicos. Si tú eres, por ejemplo, de ascendencia hispana, es posible que existan becas subvencionadas por organizaciones hispanas. Para estar seguro de que se te considerará para todo tipo de ayuda otorgada por una universidad, debes completar todos los documentos complementarios y los formularios de solicitud exigidos.

Toda solicitud CSS se envía con una copia de una declaración sin custodia y un suplemento empresarial/agrario. Por lo general, la declaración sin custodia se solicita a padres divorciados o separados; en tanto que el suplemento empresarial/agrario se le solicita frecuentemente a aquellos padres que tienen un negocio o granja. Si es tu caso, debes diligenciar los documentos correspondientes y presentarlos a cada universidad de la lista que te solicite una copia. Es conveniente que envíes una fotocopia a cada universidad y te quedes con el original para usarlo en el futuro.

Dado que algunos estados también exigen información adicional, y los formularios pueden variar considerablemente de un campus a otro, y de un estado a otro, es mejor trabajar en estrecha colaboración con la oficina de ayuda financiera de cada universidad a la que envíes solicitudes. Así estarás seguro de haber presentado los formularios necesarios para todos los tipos de ayuda disponible. Para saber si la solicitud FAFSA es suficiente, o si es preciso diligenciar solicitudes adicionales, puede ser útil consultar catálogos de universidades, páginas Web o guías completas de universidades, como las publicadas por Peterson's.

CÓMO DILIGENCIAR LA SOLICITUD FAFSA

Con frecuencia, muchas familias cometen errores costosos por apresurarse al llenar la solicitud FAFSA. Los siguientes son tres de los errores más graves y las formas de evitarlos:

1. **No llenar completamente la solicitud FAFSA o hacerlo con inexactitudes.** La información incompleta o inexacta puede generar demoras en el procesamiento de solicitudes. Los errores también pueden originar una reducción en el monto total de la ayuda ofrecida a tu hijo. Debes responder completamente todas las preguntas con exactitud. Una vez que hayas diligenciado completamente la solicitud FAFSA, léela en su totalidad para asegurarte de haber respondido todas las preguntas y de no haber cometido errores.

2. **No presentar todas las solicitudes exigidas para todas las posibles fuentes de ayuda.** Por ejemplo, muchas universidades exigen una solicitud complementaria para ayuda institucional. Confirma y reconfirma, si es necesario, que hayas

entregado todos los formularios exigidos y que éstos hayan sido recibidos por la persona o institución correcta.

3. **No entregar los formularios de solicitud en las fechas prioritarias de presentación publicadas.** La mayoría de universidades exigen que presentes la solicitud FAFSA y otros documentos para solicitar ayuda financiera, en una fecha prioritaria de presentación de documentos. Si no cumples con esta fecha, es posible que te ofrezcan una ayuda financiera menor, o menos deseable, de aquella que, de otra manera, te hubieran ofrecido. Verifica con la oficina de ayuda financiera de cada universidad donde tu hijo solicite ingreso, las fechas límite para presentar la solicitud FAFSA y otros formularios de solicitud de ayuda financiera. Fija estas fechas en un sitio visible para recordarlas.

Preparación de la FAFSA y del CSS Profile

La solicitud FAFSA te pide información sobre todos los ingresos y activos familiares del año calendario anterior al año para el cual el estudiante solicita ayuda financiera. Las oficinas de ayuda financiera se refieren a este período de tiempo como el año impositivo o año base. Para simplificar el trámite de la solicitud FAFSA o PROFILE, debes obtener los siguientes documentos:

- $ Formularios de impuestos federales sobre la renta del año base tuyos y de tu hijo. Quizás te resulte conveniente llenar en borrador un formulario del año pasado para consultarlo al completar la solicitud FAFSA. La información en este borrador puede usarse como estimado aunque no la hayas enviado al IRS (Servicio de Impuestos Internos).
- $ Puedes usar copias de los últimos formularios de impuestos federales sobre la renta a fin de estimar los ingresos del año anterior, en lugar de utilizar el formulario final de impuesto federal sobre la renta (si llenas la solicitud FAFSA con los ingresos estimados).
- $ Los formularios W-2 para ti y tu hijo, así como otros registros de ingresos adquiridos o recibidos durante el año anterior. (Estos registros son necesarios para verificar las casillas de impuestos sobre la renta en la solicitud FAFSA.)

- Una copia del último comprobante de nómina tuyo y de tu hijo para determinar los ingresos recibidos en el año hasta la fecha (year-to-date, YTD). Este dato puede usarse también como ingreso anual estimado, en lugar del formulario final 1040 para impuestos federales sobre la renta.
- Registros de ingresos exentos de impuestos, como pagos para manutención de hijos, seguro social, aportes voluntarios a programas de impuestos diferidos sobre la renta (tales como planes de pensiones, IRA [cuenta de jubilación individual], Keogh, 401(k), y planes de jubilación para maestros), además de subsidios de vivienda para miembros del ejército, clero y otros.
- Créditos impositivos informados en el 1040, que incluye créditos de ingresos ganados, créditos para becas Hope, crédito impositivo o créditos impositivos Lifetime Learning.
- Registros empresariales y agrarios.
- Registros de acciones, bonos y otras inversiones para padres y estudiantes.
- Números de seguro social y licencia de conducir de tu hijo.

Si vas a diligenciar la solicitud FAFSA electrónicamente, el último paso de preparación es solicitar un PIN (Número de Identificación Personal). Como ya te hemos mencionado, puedes firmar electrónicamente tu solicitud electrónica FAFSA, una vez terminada, con un PIN en lugar de detenerte en medio del proceso para solicitar un PIN. Si presentas una solicitud FAFSA en papel y tus datos personales corresponden con los registrados en la Administración del Seguro Social, recibirás un PIN. El PIN no sólo sirve para firmar electrónicamente una solicitud, también puede usarse para:

- Ingresar a tu Student Aid Report (SAR), que contiene tu información FAFSA procesada. Ver Capítulo 4 para mayor información
- Hacer correcciones a tu información de solicitud
- Ingresar a tus registros de solicitud por Internet

Encontrarás mayor información sobre el proceso PIN en la página Web, www.studentaid.ed.gov; también puedes llamar al Federal Student Aid Center (Centro de Información de Ayuda Financiera para el Estudiante) al teléfono 800-4-FED-AID.

[illegible]

[illegible]

[illegible]

[illegible]

[illegible]

[illegible]

[illegible]

[illegible]

[illegible]

[illegible]

[illegible]

[illegible]

Cómo llenar la FAFSA

Ya has reunido el material que necesitas para diligenciar tu FAFSA y estás preparado para completar el formulario. Las siguientes son pautas generales:

- $ Escribe cuidadosamente en letras de molde mayúsculas.
- $ Salta una casilla entre palabras.
- $ Usa un bolígrafo de tinta negra.
- $ Llena los óvalos completamente sin salirte de los bordes (los escáner electrónicos no leen los resultados si hay rastros de tinta fuera de los óvalos).
- $ Escribe un cero antes de los números inferiores a 10 (por ejemplo, 07).
- $ Registra solamente cantidades en dólares completos, omitiendo centavos. ($12,685.39 debe registrarse como $12,685.)
- $ Registra los números negativos como cero (por ejemplo, –500 se debe registrar como 0.)
- $ Usa números o un cero para responder preguntas. No coloques respuestas tales como [N/A] o [–] ni dejes preguntas en blanco.
- $ Coloca las fechas con números (por ejemplo, 11-10-00).
- $ Las preguntas en las páginas amarillas son para las respuestas de los estudiantes; las preguntas en las páginas púrpura son para los padres.
- $ No envíes la FAFSA por un servicio de mensajería, ya que al enviarla a un apartado postal nadie podrá firmar su recepción y demorará el proceso.

$ No adjuntes, pegues, ni engrapes ningún documento a la solicitud FAFSA, puesto que inevitablemente se desechará y sólo retardará el procesamiento de las solicitudes.

Conserva las hojas de trabajo con las anotaciones que usaste para completar tu FAFSA, pues algunas universidades pueden solicitarlas para verificar información. Guarda copias de los documentos que has completado. Si tienes preguntas sobre los formularios, llama a la línea de atención del Departamento de Educación de EE.UU., 800-433-3243.

INSTRUCCIONES LÍNEA POR LÍNEA PARA COMPLETAR LA SOLICITUD FAFSA

En el resto del capítulo encontrarás instrucciones línea por línea para algunas de las respuestas menos obvias, notas para tener en cuenta y una lista de errores comunes al llenar la FAFSA. En las páginas siguientes, encontrarás partes reales de la FAFSA en español para que las consultes. Recuerda que la FAFSA trae una sección de Información para el Estudiante. Las instrucciones en esta sección fueron escritas especialmente para estudiantes. Igualmente, hay una sección de Información para los Padres, con instrucciones para padres o tutores legales.

Primer Paso: Información para el estudiante (a ser completado por tu hijo)

1-3. Nombre completo (tal cual aparece en su tarjeta de Seguro Social)

1. APELLIDO 2. NOMBRE 3. INICIAL

4-7. Dirección postal permanente

4. NÚMERO Y CALLE (INCLUYA NÚMERO DE APTO.)

5. CIUDAD (Y PAÍS SI NO ES EE.UU.) 6. ESTADO 7. CÓDIGO POSTAL

Líneas 1 a 3: **Usa nombres propios y escribe todo en mayúscula.** No uses apodos.

Líneas 4 a 7: **Usa una dirección postal permanente.** Toda correspondencia sobre la FAFSA y otros formularios de ayuda financiera se envían a una dirección permanente.

8. Número de Seguro Social

9. Fecha de nacimiento M D / / 1 9

10. Número de teléfono permanente ( ) –

11-12. Número de licencia de conducir y estado (si corresponde)

11. NÚMERO DE LICENCIA

12. ESTADO

13. ¿Es usted ciudadano de los EE.UU.? Escoja uno. **Véase la página 2.**

a. Sí, soy ciudadano de los EE.UU. **Pase a la pregunta 15**.......... 1

b. No, pero soy extranjero con derecho. **Complete la pregunta 14**... 2

c. No, no soy ciudadano o extranjero con derecho......................... 3

14. NÚMERO DE REGISTRO DE EXTRANJERO A

Línea 8: **Es necesario tener un número de seguro social (SSN) para procesar este formulario.** Si no lo tienes, solicítalo lo antes posible llamando al 800-772-1213 o visita www.ssa.gov. Recuerda que la FAFSA no se puede procesar sin un SSN.

La Línea 8 tiene uno de los registros más elevado de errores y constituye una de las causas de inelegibilidad para recibir ayuda. Si no puedes obtener un número de seguro social por tu documentación de ciudadanía, busca ayuda con tu funcionario de ayuda financiera.

Líneas 9 a 10: **Escribe tu fecha de nacimiento y el número telefónico de tu casa.**

Líneas 11 a 12: **Escribe el número de tu licencia de conducir.** Si no tienes licencia, deja la línea en blanco.

Líneas 13 a 14: **Si eres un no–ciudadano elegible de Estados Unidos (residente permanente), escribe tu número de Registro de Extranjería (8 ó 9 dígitos).** Si no eres un no–ciudadano elegible, llena el óvalo (c); en este caso no eres elegible para ayuda federal financiera ni para la mayor parte de ayuda estatal ofrecida, pero puedes ser elegible para ayuda financiera ofrecida por una universidad.

Los residentes permanentes que se convierten en ciudadanos de Estados Unidos tienen algunas veces problemas con su número de seguro social si no es el mismo registrado en la FAFSA. Esto puede ocurrir si no se notifica el cambio en el estatus de ciudadanía a la Administración del Seguro Social. Notifica a la oficina local o regional cualquier cambio al respecto, como el cambio de residente permanente a ciudadano de Estados Unidos. Si necesitas asesoría adicional llama a la Administración del Seguro Social, al 800-772-1213.

15. ¿Cuál es su estado civil actual?	Soy soltero(a), divorciado(a) o viudo(a) .... ◯ 1 Estoy casado(a)/vuelto a casar .... ◯ 2 Estoy separado(a) .... ◯ 3					**16.** Mes y año en que usted se casó, se separó, se divorció o enviudó	MES __ __ / AÑO __ __ __ __			

Para cada pregunta (17 a 21), por favor indique si usted asistirá a tiempo completo, 3/4 de tiempo, medio tiempo, menos de medio tiempo o si no asistirá. Véase la página 2.

17. Verano 2003	Tiempo completo/indeciso(a) ◯ 1	3/4 de tiempo ◯ 2	Medio tiempo ◯ 3	Menos de medio tiempo ◯ 4	No asistiré ◯ 5
18. Otoño 2003	Tiempo completo/indeciso(a) ◯ 1	3/4 de tiempo ◯ 2	Medio tiempo ◯ 3	Menos de medio tiempo ◯ 4	No asistiré ◯ 5
19. Invierno 2003-2004	Tiempo completo/indeciso(a) ◯ 1	3/4 de tiempo ◯ 2	Medio tiempo ◯ 3	Menos de medio tiempo ◯ 4	No asistiré ◯ 5
20. Primavera 2004	Tiempo completo/indeciso(a) ◯ 1	3/4 de tiempo ◯ 2	Medio tiempo ◯ 3	Menos de medio tiempo ◯ 4	No asistiré ◯ 5
21. Verano 2004	Tiempo completo/indeciso(a) ◯ 1	3/4 de tiempo ◯ 2	Medio tiempo ◯ 3	Menos de medio tiempo ◯ 4	No asistiré ◯ 5

22. ¿Qué nivel escolar alcanzó su padre?	Escuela intermedia ◯ 1	Secundaria ◯ 2	Universidad/posgrado ◯ 3	Otro/lo desconozco ◯ 4
23. ¿Qué nivel escolar alcanzó su madre?	Escuela intermedia ◯ 1	Secundaria ◯ 2	Universidad/posgrado ◯ 3	Otro/lo desconozco ◯ 4

Línea 15: **Responde adecuadamente a la pregunta sobre estado civil.** Esta pregunta es para un estudiante que sea independiente, como un padre o madre, que desee aprovechar programas de ayuda financiera. Recuerda que la ayuda financiera universitaria es tanto para padres como para sus hijos.

Línea 16: **( ) Mes ( ) Año** Escribe la fecha de tu matrimonio, separación, divorcio o de fallecimiento de tu cónyuge.

Líneas 17 a 21: **Marca en cada pregunta tu estatus correcto de inscripción:** 12 o más créditos equivalen a tiempo completo; 9 a 11 créditos, a tres cuartos del tiempo; 6 a 8 créditos, medio tiempo; y 5 o menos créditos, menos de medio tiempo.

Líneas 22 a 23: **Selecciona el nivel más alto de educación logrado por cada uno de tus padres.** Décimo grado se considera secundaria, un semestre de universidad, se considera nivel universitario. Puesto que la FAFSA se usa como solicitud común, algunos estados pueden tener una definición diferente en cuanto a los requisitos de escolaridad.

24. ¿Cuál es el estado en que usted reside legalmente? ESTADO [ ][ ]

25. ¿Se hizo usted residente legal de este estado antes del 1 de enero de 1998? Sí ○ 1 No ○ 2

26. Si su respuesta a la pregunta 25 es "**No**", proporcione el mes y año en que usted se hizo residente legal. MES [ ][ ] / AÑO [ ][ ][ ][ ]

27. ¿Es usted varón? (La mayoría de los estudiantes varones deberán inscribirse con el Servicio Selectivo militar para poder obtener ayuda federal.) Sí ○ 1 No ○ 2

28. Si es varón (entre 18 y 25 años de edad) y no está inscrito, conteste "Sí", y el Servicio Selectivo lo inscribirá. Sí ○ 1 No ○ 2

29. ¿Para qué título universitario o certificado estará estudiando durante 2003-2004? **Consulte la página 2** y escriba el número correcto en la casilla. [ ]

30. ¿Cuál será su nivel de estudio cuando empiece el año escolar 2003-2004? **Consulte la página 2** y escriba el número correcto en la casilla. [ ]

Líneas 24 a 26: **Coloca la abreviatura del estado y la fecha de adquisición de residencia legal.** Residencia legal no es lo mismo que estatus de ciudadanía. Esta pregunta se refiere a la fecha en que te mudaste a tu residencia permanente. Incluye la abreviatura del estado de tu residencia permanente, no la del estado en el que planeas residir en la universidad.

Si tu hijo pretende vivir en el estado donde asiste a la universidad luego de graduarse, es conveniente averiguar cómo calificaría para convertirse en residente del estado en lo relacionado con matrículas y becas estatales.

Líneas 27 a 28: **Registrarse para el servicio selectivo militar es una ley federal que deben cumplir todos los varones entre 18 y 26 años de edad.** Si no te has registrado, no recibirás ninguna ayuda estudiantil federal; éste es un asunto que debes tomar con toda seriedad.

Línea 29: **Los niveles más usados son el No. 1 para título universitario o el No. 8 para especialización o título profesional.** Consulta en las instrucciones FAFSA para otros programas universitarios que llevan a título o certificado.

Línea 30: Nivel de grado es:

0 = 1er año	**5** = 5to año
1 = 1er año de asistencia	**6** = 1er año de estudios de posgrado o profesionales
2 = 2do año	**7** = 2 o más años de estudios de posgrado o profesionales
3 = 3er año	
4 = 4to año	

31.	¿Habrá obtenido su diploma de la escuela secundaria o un GED antes de iniciar el año escolar 2003-2004?	Sí ○ 1	No ○ 2
32.	¿Habrá obtenido su primera licenciatura (*bachillerato* en Puerto Rico) antes del 1 de julio de 2003?	Sí ○ 1	No ○ 2
33.	Además de las becas, ¿le interesan los préstamos para estudiantes (que luego usted tendrá que reembolsar)?	Sí ○ 1	No ○ 2
34.	Además de las becas, ¿le interesa el "trabajo-estudio" (ayuda económica que se gana trabajando)?	Sí ○ 1	No ○ 2

35. **No deje esta pregunta en blanco.** ¿Ha recibido alguna vez una condena por posesión o venta de drogas ilegales? De ser así, conteste "Sí", complete y presente esta solicitud, y le enviaremos una hoja de trabajo por correo para que usted determine si la condena afecta su derecho a recibir ayuda económica. No ○ 1 Sí ○ 3 NO DEJE LA PREGUNTA 35 EN BLANCO

Línea 31: **( ) Sí ( ) No.** Si tienes un GED, diploma de equivalencia de la escuela superior, marca "Sí."

Si tu hijo tiene un certificado de calificaciones universitario que respalde dos años de crédito universitario y que pueda ser válido para la obtención de un grado universitario, dicho certificado se considera como equivalente a un diploma de secundaria.

Línea 32: **( ) Sí ( ) No.** Si aún no tienes título universitario y no lo tendrás para el 07/01/03, marca "No". Marca "Sí" si tienes un título de otro país equivalente a un título universitario.

Las becas Pell no se otorgan a estudiantes que tengan un grado universitario.

Línea 35: **Esta pregunta sobre drogas debe responderse o no se procesará la solicitud FAFSA.** Es muy importante y no debes dejarla sin respuesta. Si marcas "Sí" a una condena por posesión o venta de drogas ilícitas, recibirás otro formulario para que lo completes a fin de determinar si la condena afecta tus posibilidades de recibir ayuda financiera.

Segundo Paso: Estatus independiente

Líneas 39 a 51: Las instrucciones línea por línea para las líneas 39 a 51 (ingresos y activos del estudiante) aparecen en la página 30 porque las líneas 74 a 84 (ingresos y activos de los padres) plantean las mismas preguntas.

Tercer Paso: Estatus Dependiente

Líneas 52 a 58: **Estas líneas permiten determinar la capacidad del estudiante para optar por ayuda como estudiante independiente o dependiente.** Puedes tener elegibilidad para una mayor ayuda si solicitas como estudiante independiente. Sin embargo, la edad es el principal criterio para establecer el estatus de independiente mientras asistes a una universidad. Si tienes 24 años o naciste antes del 1° de enero de 1980, calificarás automáticamente para el estatus de independiente. Algunas universidades pueden exigir otros requisitos para el estatus de independiente, a fin de otorgar su ayuda institucional.

52. ¿Nació usted antes del 1 de enero de 1980?	Sí ○ 1	No ○ 2
53. Durante el año escolar 2003-2004, ¿piensa estudiar para obtener una maestría o doctorado (por ejemplo, MA, MBA, MD, JD, o PhD, EdD, certificado de posgrado, etc.)?	Sí ○ 1	No ○ 2
54. Actualmente, ¿está casado(a)? (Responda "Sí" si está separado[a] pero no divorciado[a].)	Sí ○ 1	No ○ 2

Línea 52: **( ) Sí ( ) No.** ¿Naciste *antes* del 1° de enero de 1980?

Línea 53: **( ) Sí ( ) No.** ¿Trabajarás en un programa de maestría o doctorado durante el año escolar 2003–2004?

Línea 54: **( ) Sí ( ) No.** A la fecha, ¿eres casado? "Sí" implica estar casado o separado. Si eres divorciado, te pueden descalificar como estudiante independiente. Al contestar "Sí" a cualquier otra pregunta de esta sección, se te clasificará como dependiente y debes registrar la información de tus padres. ¿Qué hacer? Te recomendamos especialmente que completes la FAFSA como estudiante independiente y solicites a tu consejero de ayuda financiera una revisión de tu situación para que te asigne estatus de estudiante independiente.

55. ¿Tiene usted hijos que reciben de parte suya más de la mitad del sustento?	Sí ○ 1 No ○ 2
56. ¿Tiene dependientes (además de sus hijos o cónyuge) que viven con usted y que reciben de parte suya más de la mitad del sustento, entre hoy y el 30 de junio de 2004?	Sí ○ 1 No ○ 2
57. ¿Es usted huérfano o está/estuvo bajo custodia/tutela de un tribunal hasta los 18 años?	Sí ○ 1 No ○ 2

Línea 55: ( ) **Sí** ( ) **No.** ¿Tienes hijos a quienes aportas más de la mitad de su manutención? Marca "Sí", cuando:

Otras personas (no tu cónyuge) que vivan contigo, obtengan más de la mitad de su manutención de tu parte, y la sigan obteniendo hasta el 30 de junio de 2004. Estas personas no necesariamente tienen que haber sido declaradas en IRS 1040, pero debes demostrar que respondes al menos por la mitad de su manutención.

Línea 56: ( ) **Sí** ( ) **No.** ¿Tienes personas a cargo que viven contigo y para las cuales responderás por más de la mitad de su manutención hasta el 30 de junio del 2004?

Línea 57: ( ) **Sí** ( ) **No.** ¿Eres huérfano o estás bajo la custodia de un tribunal, o lo estuviste hasta los 18 años? Ten en cuenta lo siguiente antes de dar tu respuesta:

1) Se considera que un estudiante es huérfano cuando sus dos padres están muertos y no tiene un padre adoptivo.
2) Todo estudiante que se declare bajo la custodia de un tribunal antes del fin del año de otorgamiento, sin importar su acuerdo de vivenda, será considerado como estudiante independiente durante dicho año.

58. ¿Es usted veterano de las Fuerzas Armadas de los EE.UU.? **Véase la página 2.**	Sí ◯ 1	No ◯ 2

Línea 58: **( ) Sí ( ) No. ¿Eres veterano de las Fuerzas Armadas de Estados Unidos?**

Responde "No" en caso que:

1. nunca hayas prestado servicio activo en las Fuerzas Armadas de Estados Unidos.
2. seas estudiante ROTC o cadete/guardia marina al servicio de alguna academia.
3. seas miembro de la Guardia Nacional o de las reservas y hayas sido llamado a servicio activo sólo para fines de entrenamiento.
4. prestes servicio actualmente en las Fuerzas Armadas de Estados Unidos:

Responde "Sí" en caso que:

1. hayas prestado servicio activo en las Fuerzas Armadas de Estados Unidos.
2. seas miembro de la Guardia Nacional o de las reservas y hayas sido llamado a servicio activo para fines diferentes a entrenamiento.
3. seas cadete o guardia marina y hayas recibido la baja en condiciones no deshonrosas.
4. no seas veterano en la actualidad pero lo serás el 30 de junio, 2004.

Si respondiste "No" a las preguntas 52 a 58, continúa con las preguntas en el Cuarto Paso.

Si respondiste "Sí" a cualquier pregunta entre la 52 y la 58, salta el Paso cuatro y continúa con el Quinto Paso.

Cuarto Paso: Información para los padres (a ser llenada por padres o tutores legales)

Continúa con este paso sólo si tu hijo respondió "No" a todas las preguntas del Tercer Paso.

59. ¿Cuál es el estado civil actual de sus padres?		60. Mes y año en que sus padres se casaron, se separaron, se divorciaron o enviudaron.	MES / AÑO
Casados/Vuelto a casar... ○ 1	Divorciado(a)/Separado(a)... ○ 3		
Soltero(a)... ○ 2	Viudo(a)... ○ 4		

Línea 59: ( ) **Selecciona el estado civil actual de los padres.**

1) Si ambos padres están vivos y son marido y mujer, responde las preguntas sobre ellos.
2) Si eres divorciado o separado, responde las preguntas que correspondan al padre que haya vivido más tiempo con tu hijo en los últimos doce meses. Si tu hijo no ha vivido más con un padre que con el otro, responde refiriéndote al padre que haya suministrado la mayor parte del soporte financiero durante los últimos doce meses, o durante el año más reciente en que realmente hayas aportado para la manutención de tu hijo.

Definición de padre y estado civil:
Casado: Cuando los padres naturales del niño están casados. También puede significar que uno de los padres naturales se ha vuelto a casar. En cualquier caso, la respuesta a la pregunta 59 será "casado".
Padre adoptivo, de cuidado temporal, o padrastro: Los ingresos y activos de este tipo de padres se tratan como si fueran los padres naturales, aunque no se haya llevado a cabo adopción alguna. Las capitulaciones prematrimoniales no se toman en cuenta para la preparación de la FAFSA.

Si uno de los padres muere y sobrevive un padrastro, tu hijo será considerado independiente a menos que el padrastro lo adopte legalmente.

Tutor legal: El tutor legal ya no se trata como padre bajo ninguna circunstancia. Si ambos padres han muerto, el hijo se considera independiente.

Abuelo: Los abuelos no se consideran como padres. Si tu hijo vive con un abuelo, los ingresos de éste no pueden registrarse en la solicitud FAFSA, a menos que el abuelo lo haya adoptado.

Divorciado: Si como padre/madre natural que vives con tu hijo, te divorciaste del padre/madre natural de tu hijo, y te casaste nuevamente, responde "casado" en la línea 59.

Separado: Una pareja se puede considerar informalmente separada, si uno de ellos ha abandonado el hogar por un período indefinido con el fin de divorciarse.

Viudo: Si eres viudo y te volviste a casar, presenta tu documentación como casado e incluye los ingresos y activos de tu nuevo cónyuge.

El nivel de elegibilidad financiera está determinado en gran medida por tus respuestas a las preguntas 65 y 66.

65. **Pase a la página 7** para determinar cuántas personas forman parte del hogar de sus padres. [ ][ ]	66. **Pase a la página 7** para determinar cuántas personas indicadas en su respuesta a la pregunta 65 **(excluyendo a sus padres)** serán estudiantes postsecundarios entre el 1 de julio de 2003 y el 30 de junio de 2004. [ ]

Línea 65: **( ) Escribe el número de personas que viven en tu casa, incluyendo:**

1. Marido, esposa e hijo, aunque tu hijo no viva contigo.
2. Tus otros hijos si vas a responder por más de la mitad de su manutención desde el 1° de julio, 2003 hasta el 30 de junio, 2004.
3. Todas las personas que vivan en tu casa y que reciban de ti al menos la mitad de su manutención y la seguirán recibiendo desde el 1° de julio, 2003 hasta el 30 de junio, 2004.

Nota especial: Puede haber situaciones en las que un padre mantenga un niño que no viva con él, especialmente en casos en que sea divorciado o separado. Son muchas las familias hispanas separadas y algunos hijos aún viven en el país de origen del padre esperando una visa o fondos para unirse a la familia en Estados Unidos. En estos casos, el padre que proporciona más de la mitad de la manutención puede reclamar el niño como parte de su grupo familiar, aunque éste no viva en el mismo domicilio. Las siguientes personas pueden incluirse como parte del grupo familiar de un estudiante dependiente:

1. El estudiante
2. Los padres del estudiante, excepto el padre que no viva en casa por deceso, separación o divorcio.
3. Los hermanos del estudiante, si recibieron o recibirán más de la mitad de su manutención de los padres del estudiante entre 1° de julio, 2003 y el 30 de junio, 2004.
4. Hijos del estudiante, si recibieron o recibirán más de la mitad de su manutención de los padres del estudiante entre 1° de julio, 2003 y el 30 de junio, 2004.
5. Hijo no nato del padre del estudiante o del propio estudiante, si debiera nacer antes o durante el año de otorgamiento (1° de julio, 2003 hasta el 30 de junio, 2004), y si los padres del estudiante van a proporcionar más de la mitad de la manutención del niño desde la fecha proyectada de nacimiento hasta el final del año de otorgamiento.
6. Otras personas que vivan con los padres del estudiante y reciban de ellos más de la mitad de su manutención en el momento de la solicitud y que continúen recibiéndola durante todo el año de otorgamiento (1° de julio, 2003 al 30 de junio, 2004).
7. Miembros de la familia que permanecen fuera del país por fondos o visas pendientes, o por otras condiciones, y que reciben su manutención del padre con quien el estudiante reside en Estados Unidos, siempre que hayan recibido o continúen recibiendo más de la mitad de su manutención de los padres del estudiante entre el 1° de julio, 2003 y el 30 de junio, 2004.

La necesidad financiera se determina por el tamaño del grupo familiar y no por las exenciones que aparezcan en el formulario IRS 1040. Entre mayor sea el tamaño de la familia, mayor necesidad se podrá demostrar.

65. **Pase a la página 7** para determinar cuántas personas forman parte del hogar de sus padres.	66. **Pase a la página 7** para determinar cuántas personas indicadas en su respuesta a la pregunta 65 **(excluyendo a sus padres)** serán estudiantes postsecundarios entre el 1 de julio de 2003 y el 30 de junio de 2004.

Línea 66: **( ) Registra el número de estudiantes universitarios miembros de tu familia en 2003–2004 (excluidos padres o tutores legales).** A partir de la línea 65, determina el número de personas de tu familia que asistirán un mínimo de 6 horas semestrales al menos durante un período académico. Para que se le considere, un estudiante universitario debe cursar estudios que encaminen a un título o certificado, que otorgue una credencial educativa reconocida por una universidad elegible para participar en cualquiera de los programas federales de ayuda al estudiante. Los estudiantes que deben registrarse para crédito universitario a fin de renovar sus certificados profesionales (como maestros y enfermeros) para poder ser empleados, están exentos de que se les exija estar matriculados en programas que encaminen a certificados o títulos.

Nota especial: La pregunta 66 es una de las más importantes en la solicitud FAFSA y tu respuesta puede aumentar tu elegibilidad para programas de ayuda financiera federal y estatal, así como para la mayoría de programas institucionales, ya que tiene que ver directamente con tu necesidad demostrada de ayuda financiera. La fórmula para determinarla es la llamada "metodología federal", en la que se divide proporcionalmente la contribución de los padres por el número de miembros de la familia que asisten a la universidad durante el mismo año académico. Si, por ejemplo, se calcula con la fórmula, luego de evaluar todas tus respuestas, que tu contribución es de $21,000 por hijo universitario, para dos hijos universitarios sería aproximadamente $10,500, para tres, $7,000, etc.

67. ¿En qué estado residen legalmente sus padres? ESTADO

68. ¿Se hicieron sus padres residentes legales del estado indicado en la respuesta a la pregunta 67 antes del 1 de enero de 1998? Sí 1 No 2

69. Si la respuesta a la pregunta 68 es "No", proporcione el mes y el año del inicio de la residencia legal de aquel padre de familia que haya vivido más tiempo en ese estado. MES / AÑO

70. ¿Qué edad tiene el mayor de sus padres?

Línea 67: ( ) **Estado de residencia legal** (usa la abreviatura estatal). Algunos padres pueden tener doble residencia, como sucede con personal militar. La doble residencia se define algunas veces por el estado donde se paga el impuesto sobre la renta. El documento FAFSA te permite incluir sólo un estado de residencia. Debes entonces analizar las posibilidades de tus estados de residencia, comparar las universidades seleccionadas y evaluar todos los programas estatales de ayuda financiera, así como el valor de matrícula como residente, antes de definir el mejor estado para residencia.

Línea 69: **Registra el mes y el año en que te convertiste en residente estatal.** Igual a la definición en la línea 24.

Línea 70: ( ) **¿Cuál es la edad del mayor de los padres?** Escribe la edad del padre de mayor edad en la casa.

Información sobre ingresos y activos de los padres

Puesto que las instrucciones línea por línea para las líneas 39 a 51 (ingresos y activos del estudiante) y para las líneas 74 a 84 (ingresos y activos de los padres) contienen las mismas preguntas, los agrupamos a continuación.

Líneas 39 a 51: Información sobre ingresos y activos del estudiante. Si estás casado (aunque en 2002, no estuvieras casado), registra tus ingresos y activos, y los de tu cónyuge. Si no eres casado, responde las preguntas sobre ti e ignora las referencias al "cónyuge". Si la pregunta no es aplicable, ingresa 0.

Líneas 74 a 84: Registra sólo información sobre los padres con quienes vive el estudiante.

39. ¿Cuál fue su ingreso bruto ajustado (y el de su cónyuge) en 2002? El ingreso bruto ajustado se encuentra en los siguientes formularios del IRS: 1040 – renglón 35; 1040A – renglón 21; 1040EZ – renglón 4; ó *TeleFile* – renglón I. $ ___ . ___

40. Escriba la cantidad total de su impuesto sobre la renta (y la de su cónyuge) de 2002. La cantidad de impuesto sobre la renta se encuentra en los siguientes formularios del IRS: 1040 – renglón 55; 1040A – renglón 36; 1040EZ – renglón 10; ó *TeleFile* – renglón K(2). $ ___ . ___

41. Escriba sus exenciones (y las de su cónyuge) de 2002. Las exenciones se encuentran en los formularios del IRS 1040 – renglón 6d ó 1040A – renglón 6d. Para el formulario 1040EZ ó *TeleFile*, **véase la página 2.**

42-43. ¿Cuánto ganó usted (y su cónyuge) por su trabajo (sueldos, salarios, propinas, etc.) en 2002? Responda a esta pregunta aun si todavía no ha presentado su declaración de impuesto. Esta información se encuentra en los formularios W-2 ó en los siguientes formularios del IRS: 1040 – renglones 7 + 12 + 18; 1040A – renglón 7 ó 1040EZ – renglón 1. Todos aquellos que presenten su declaración por teléfono *(TeleFile)* deberán usar los formularios W-2.

Usted (42) $ ___ . ___

Su Cónyuge (43) $ ___ . ___

Estudiante	Padre	
		Escribe tu ingreso bruto ajustado para 2002, y el de tu cónyuge.
Línea 39	Línea 74	Encontrarás el ingreso bruto ajustado en la línea 35 del formulario IRS 1040; línea 21 del formulario 1040A o línea 4 del formulario 1040EZ.
Línea 40	Línea 75	Escribe el total de tu impuesto sobre la renta para el 2002, y el de tu cónyuge. Encuentras esta cantidad en la línea 55 del formulario 1040; línea 36 del formulario 1040A o línea 10 del formulario 1040EZ.
Línea 41	Línea 76	Registra tus exenciones. Encuéntralas en la línea 6d del formulario 1040 o en la línea 6d del formulario 1040A.
Línea 42	Línea 77	¿Cuánto ganaron (tú y tu cónyuge) en el trabajo en el 2002?
Línea 43	Línea 78	Responde a esta pregunta aunque no hayas presentado una declaración de renta. Encuentras esta información en tus formularios W-2 o en el formulario IRS 1040, líneas 7, 12, y 18; línea 7 del formulario 1040A o línea 1 del formulario 1040EZ.

Hojas de Trabajo para el estudiante (y su cónyuge) (44-46)

44-46. Pase a la página 8 y complete las columnas a la izquierda en las Hojas de Trabajo A, B y C. Escriba los montos totales del estudiante (y su cónyuge) en las preguntas 44, 45 y 46, respectivamente. Revise cada renglón detenidamente aun cuando le(s) correspondan solamente algunas de las partidas en la Hoja de Trabajo.

Hoja de Trabajo A (44)	$ ____ . ____
Hoja de Trabajo B (45)	$ ____ . ____
Hoja de Trabajo C (46)	$ ____ . ____

Estudiante Padre

Línea 44 Línea 79 Ver Hoja de trabajo A. Incluye crédito de ingreso adquirido, crédito impositivo por hijo adicional, beneficios del programa de bienestar, Temporary Assistance for Needy Families, TANF, (Asistencia temporal para familias necesitadas), sin incluir estampillas para alimentos o vivienda subsidiada y beneficios del Seguro Social (aunque cesen en un futuro próximo).

Notas aclaratorias para la preguntas 44 y 79:

- La información correcta sobre beneficios del Seguro Social puede afectar la elegibilidad de ayuda financiera. Si tu hijo recibe beneficios del Seguro Social, el cheque se gira a su nombre y él puede cobrarlo; entonces debes registrar la cantidad de beneficios del Seguro Social recibida durante el año calendario en la línea 44 (Hoja de trabajo A) de la FAFSA, como ingreso exento de impuestos de tu hijo.
- Si el cheque por beneficios del Seguro Social de tu hijo se gira a tu nombre, por ser el padre, y puedes cobrarlo; debes registrar la cantidad de beneficios del Seguro Social recibida durante el año calendario en la línea 79 (Hoja de trabajo A) de la FAFSA, como ingreso exento de impuestos tuyo.
- Si tu hijo tiene un hermano que recibe beneficios y el cheque sale a nombre de éste, la cantidad en beneficios del Seguro Social recibida durante el año calendario no debe registrarse en la FAFSA si tu hijo puede cobrar el cheque de su hermano.
- Si tu hijo tiene un hermano que recibe beneficios, el cheque se emite a nombre tuyo (como padre) y puedes cobrarlo, entonces la cantidad de beneficios del Seguro Social recibidos para el año

calendario se registra como tu beneficio exento de impuestos del Seguro Social en la línea 79 (Hoja de trabajo A) de la FAFSA. La mayoría de beneficios del Seguro Social cesan a los 18 años de edad, y ésta puede ser la edad de tu hijo cuando llene la FAFSA para el año calendario 2003. Muchos funcionarios de ayuda financiera universitaria no toman en cuenta los beneficios del Seguro Social registrados por el aspirante en las preguntas 44 y 79, ya que éstos cesarán cuando tu hijo esté en la universidad. Puedes contactar la oficina de ayuda financiera para analizar este aspecto y solicitar una Opinión Profesional.

Línea 45 **Línea 80** Ver Hoja de trabajo B. Completa la hoja de trabajo e inserta el total aquí.

Los Child Support Payments, CSP (Pagos para manutención de hijos) recibidos en 2002 deben registrarse en cantidades anuales. La mayoría de CSP cesan a los 18 años, edad que tendrá tu hijo cuando complete la FAFSA para el año calendario 2003. Puedes notificar a la oficina de ayuda financiera en cada universidad y pedir que el CSP de tu hijo no se tome en cuenta, puesto que ya no se recibirá durante el año de solicitud de ayuda.

Línea 46 **Línea 81** Ver Hoja de trabajo C. Incluye créditos educativos, pagos de manutención de hijos, ganancias sujetas a impuestos de programas federales de trabajo y estudio u otros programas de trabajo basados en la necesidad, así como toda ayuda financiera registrada en el formulario 1040.

Notas aclaratorias para las preguntas 46 y 81:

- La definición de Ingreso de exclusión (para ventaja tuya) incluye los cuatro tipos de ingresos familiares de la Hoja de trabajo C. Estos reducen tu ingreso bruto ajustado (IBA) y el Expected Family Contribution, EFC (Aporte Esperado de la Familia), haciendo a tu hijo más elegible para ayuda universitaria; además, aumenta el factor de necesidad para recibir el máximo de ayuda financiera.

47. Actualmente, ¿cuál es el patrimonio neto de sus **inversiones** (y las de su cónyuge)? Incluya los bienes raíces exceptuando la casa en que vive. **Véase la página 2.** $.

48. Actualmente, ¿cuál es el patrimonio neto de sus **negocios o inversiones en fincas** (y los de su cónyuge)? No incluya la finca en que vive y trabaja. **Véase la página 2.** $.

49. Actualmente, ¿cuál es el saldo total actual de su dinero (y el de su cónyuge) en **efectivo, ahorros y cuentas corrientes**? No incluya ayuda económica para estudiantes. $.

Estudiante	Padre	
Línea 47	Línea 82	En la fecha de envío de este formulario, ¿cuál es el valor neto corriente de tus inversiones o cuál es tu patrimonio?

***Nota:* Valor menos Deuda = Patrimonio. Incluye bienes raíces (sin incluir la residencia principal), fondos fiduciarios, fondos de mercado monetario, fondos mutuos, certificados de depósito, acciones y bonos (no incluyas fondos de pensión, anualidades, IRA, ni planes Keogh).**

Línea 48	Línea 83	¿Cuál es el valor neto de tus negocios actuales o granjas de inversión?

Notas aclaratorias para las preguntas 48, 83 y 49, 84:

- Valor neto significa valor actual menos deuda.
- Inversión incluye bienes raíces (diferente a tu residencia), fondos fiduciarios, fondos de mercado monetario, fondos mutuos, certificados de depósito, acciones, bonos, otros títulos valores, contratos de pago por cuotas y de venta de tierras (inclusive hipotecas vigentes) y bienes en general.
- Valor de inversión incluye el valor comercial de estas inversiones. No incluyas el valor de seguros de vida ni planes de jubilación (como fondos de pensiones, anualidades, IRA y planes Keogh) ni el valor de planes de prepago de matrícula. Deuda de inversión se refiere solamente a las deudas relacionadas con la inversión.
- Valor comercial incluye el valor comercial de tierras, edificios, maquinaria, equipos e inventarios.
- Deuda comercial se refiere solamente a las deudas para las cuales un negocio fue usado como garantía.

Línea 49	Línea 84	**¿Cuál es el saldo actual de tus cuentas de caja de ahorros y corriente.** Escribe la última cantidad registrada para cada una de tus cuentas bancarias.

Quinto Paso: Información para los padres

Continúa con este paso sólo si tu hijo respondió "Sí" a cualquier pregunta del Tercer Paso.

85. Pase a la página 7 para determinar cuántas personas forman parte de su hogar (y el de su cónyuge).	**86. Pase a la página 7** para determinar cuántas personas indicadas en la respuesta a la pregunta 85 serán estudiantes postsecundarios matriculados a medio tiempo o más entre el 1 de julio de 2003 y el 30 de junio de 2004.

Línea 85 : ( ) **Escribe el número de personas de tu grupo familiar y de tu cónyuge.** El grupo familiar de un estudiante independiente puede incluir las siguientes personas:

1. Tú y tu cónyuge.
2. Tus hijos, si responderás por más de la mitad de su manutención en el período comprendido entre 1° de julio de 2003 y el 30 de julio de 2004.
3. Cónyuge del estudiante, excepto el cónyuge que no viva con el grupo familiar a consecuencia de deceso, separación o divorcio.
4. Otras personas que vivan ahora con el estudiante y reciban más de la mitad de su sustento del grupo familiar del estudiante en el momento de solicitud y durante todo el año de otorgamiento 2003-2004 (1° de julio, 2003 hasta el 30 de junio, 2004).

Línea 86: ( ) Escribe el número de miembros de tu grupo familiar que registraste en la Línea 85 que asistirán a la universidad por lo menos a tiempo parcial en el año académico 2003–2004. La respuesta aquí debe ser por lo menos uno.

Definiciones

Período de inscripción: **1º de julio, 2003 al 30 de junio, 2004.**

Universidad: **Cualquier institución acreditada de estudios superiores.**

Inscripción: **Registrado, por lo menos a tiempo parcial, en un período mientras el estudiante se encuentre inscrito.**

Tiempo parcial: **6 horas semestrales por período o 12 horas-reloj semanales.**

Un período: **Un trimestre, un semestre, etc.**

Sexto Paso

Ésta es la fase final para completar la FAFSA, pero es de especial importancia. Si no usas los códigos correctos o registras las universidades incorrectamente u olvidas firmar y fechar el formulario, es posible que recibas ayuda con fondos limitados o no recibas nada.

	Código federal				Estado	Planes de alojamiento
87.	1RO CÓDIGO FEDERAL	Ó	INSTITUCIÓN EDUCATIVA / DIRECCIÓN Y CIUDAD		ESTADO	PLANES DE ALOJAMIENTO 88. en recinto 1, fuera de recinto 2, con padres 3
89.	2DO CÓDIGO FEDERAL	Ó	INSTITUCIÓN EDUCATIVA / DIRECCIÓN Y CIUDAD		ESTADO	90. en recinto 1, fuera de recinto 2, con padres 3
91.	3RO CÓDIGO FEDERAL	Ó	INSTITUCIÓN EDUCATIVA / DIRECCIÓN Y CIUDAD		ESTADO	92. en recinto 1, fuera de recinto 2, con padres 3
93.	4TO CÓDIGO FEDERAL	Ó	INSTITUCIÓN EDUCATIVA / DIRECCIÓN Y CIUDAD		ESTADO	94. en recinto 1, fuera de recinto 2, con padres 3
95.	5TO CÓDIGO FEDERAL	Ó	INSTITUCIÓN EDUCATIVA / DIRECCIÓN Y CIUDAD		ESTADO	96. en recinto 1, fuera de recinto 2, con padres 3
97.	6TO CÓDIGO FEDERAL	Ó	INSTITUCIÓN EDUCATIVA / DIRECCIÓN Y CIUDAD		ESTADO	98. en recinto 1, fuera de recinto 2, con padres 3

Líneas 87 a 97: **Lista de universidad(es) preferida(s).** Si envías la FAFSA a más de seis universidades y algunas de ellas utilizan el CSS PROFILE, coloca siempre primero las universidades que no usan este sistema. Lo anterior, debido a que las universidades que lo usan, ya han recibido la Confirmación de Profile, y para toda razón práctica, ya has cumplido con la fecha límite prioritaria. Deja que FAFSA cumpla con la mayoría de las fechas límites prioritarias del resto de las universidades de tu lista. Recuerda que una de las causas más frecuentes por la que no se recibe el máximo de ayuda financiera, es el incumplimiento de las fechas límites.

Errores más comunes en el Sexto Paso:

Error No. 1: No esperes a ser admitido para registrar la(s) universidad(es) que prefieres en la FAFSA. Aunque sólo estés considerando una universidad, regístrala en la solicitud FAFSA; si consideras más de seis y algunas utilizan el PROFILE registra primero las que no usen este sistema. Esto te permite garantizar que cumplirás con las fechas límites prioritarias establecidas por las diferentes instituciones. El PROFILE cobija la fecha límite prioritaria para las universidades que utilizan este sistema, en tanto que la FAFSA cubre las fechas límites prioritarias para las universidades que no utilizan el sistema de PROFILE. No ingreses más de una universidad en una línea, pues esto retrasará el proceso.

Error No. 2: Omisión de universidad en la FAFSA. La información FAFSA sólo será enviada a las universidades registradas en esta sección. La universidad recibirá la información sólo si das el código y nombre de la universidad contemplados en el Título IV. No es necesario registrar la dirección completa, sólo el código. Puedes encontrar los códigos en el centro de consejería de tu secundaria, la oficina de ayuda financiera de la universidad, en bibliotecas públicas de la localidad, por Internet en www.studentaid.ed.gov, o llamando a la línea de atención federal, 800-433-3243. Los usuarios de líneas por tonos pueden llamar al 800-730-8913.

Error No. 3: Omisión de código de vivienda. Este código es muy importante y debes registrarlo en el formulario porque le permite al encargado universitario de ayuda financiera saber qué presupuesto universitario utilizar. Si no registras un plan de alojamiento, probablemente la universidad utilice el presupuesto más bajo y puede que no recibas el máximo otorgamiento. Generalmente, los estudiantes que seleccionan el plan de presupuesto en el campus, reciben más ayuda que los que optan por planes fuera del campus o planes de alojamiento con sus padres.

Error No. 4: Omisión de firma. Es necesario que los estudiantes firmen su FAFSA para que sea procesada. Adicionalmente, si se considera que tu hijo es dependiente, es necesario que también la firmes; sin estas firmas no se procesará la solicitud y no se podrá calcular el EFC. Esto hará que tu hijo pierda la ayuda financiera de los patrocinadores federales, estatales y universitarios. Al entregar correcciones de los datos del SAR, también te pedirán las firmas correspondientes.

Error No. 5: Omisión del PIN de los padres. Cuando son los hijos quienes completan electrónicamente la FAFSA, se les solicita el PIN del estudiante y se les pregunta cómo planean sus padres firmar el formulario. Al responder que "with a PIN" ("con un PIN"), el sistema no les pide el PIN de los padres y pueden continuar registrando la información. Al finalizar, el sistema les confirmará que la FAFSA ha sido aceptada. El problema surge cuando los padres no continúan el proceso, es decir, regresar a la pantalla inicial de la solicitud FAFSA y firmar en la casilla de "Provide Electronic Signature" ("Suministre firma electrónica"). La solicitud FAFSA no se procesará hasta que se reciba el formulario de firma, lo que puede ocasionar el incumplimiento en las fechas límites o la pérdida de ayuda financiera por "donación".

La información FAFSA se enviará a cada una de las seis universidades registradas en la FAFSA y los estudiantes recibirán un Student Aid Report (SAR) aproximadamente al mismo tiempo que las universidades reciben la información FAFSA. Por lo general, los organismos centralizados de becas estatales consideran la primera universidad estatal registrada que se encuentre como opción para adjudicar la ayuda estatal.

En la mayoría de los casos, no puedes usar un otorgamiento de beca estatal en una universidad fuera de tu estado de residencia. Sin embargo, existen programas de becas estatales que tienen reciprocidad con otros organismos estatales y te permiten utilizar el otorgamiento fuera del estado. Verifica con tu agencia de becas estatales los acuerdos de reciprocidad estatal con otros estados. En el Apéndice encontrarás la lista de organismos de becas estatales con sus direcciones y teléfonos.

Envío de información a más de seis universidades

Puedes agregar universidades a la lista después de recibir el Student Aid Report (SAR). Recibirás el SAR aproximadamente cuatro semanas después de presentar la FAFSA al centro de procesamiento. Ten en cuenta que es más rápido si la completas electrónicamente utilizando tu PIN. Las universidades que agregues podrán consultar tu información FAFSA/SAR 48 horas después de agregar los códigos. Aquí tienes tres formas de agregar universidades a tu lista:

1. **Electrónicamente:** Una vez que recibas el SAR, puedes agregar universidades y correcciones actualizando o corrigiendo tu información electrónicamente con tu PIN en Internet en www.fafsa.gov.
2. **Corrección de formulario de información:** Una vez que recibas el SAR, puedes agregar universidades en el formulario de información del SAR y devolverlo a la dirección que aparece en el SAR.

3. **Corrección telefónica:** Puedes llamar al 319-337-5665 y con tu Data Relase Number, DRN (Número de divulgación de información) que aparece en el SAR, el procesador agregará la(s) universidad(es) que desees. Asegúrate de tener a mano los códigos federales de tus nuevas universidades para darle esta información al operador.

Si usted es el estudiante, al firmar esta solicitud, usted certifica que: (1) utilizará la ayuda económica federal o estatal estudiantil solamente para pagar el costo de asistir a una institución educativa postsecundaria, (2) no se encuentra en estado de incumplimiento de pago de un préstamo federal para estudiantes o que ha convenido en reembolsar dicho préstamo de manera satisfactoria, (3) no debe un pago de una beca federal estudiantil o que ha convenido en reembolsarla de manera satisfactoria, (4) le informará a su institución educativa si usted incurre en el incumplimiento de un préstamo federal para estudiantes.

Si usted es el padre, la madre o el estudiante, al firmar esta solicitud, usted accede, si solicitado, a proporcionar información que acredite los datos suministrados en este formulario. Esta información puede incluir su declaración del impuesto sobre la renta, ya sea federal o estatal. Asimismo, usted certifica que entiende que la **Secretaría de Educación tiene la autoridad de comprobar la información contenida en este formulario con el Servicio de Impuestos Internos (IRS) y con otras agencias federales.** Si usted intencionalmente proporciona información falsa o fraudulenta, podrán imponérle una multa de $20.000, podrán enviarlo a la cárcel o ambas penas.

100. Fecha en que se completó este formulario.

MES / DÍA / **2003** ○ ó **2004** ○

101. Firma del **estudiante** (Firme en la casilla)

1

Firma del **padre** o de la **madre** (cuya información aparezca en el Cuarto Paso) (Firme en la casilla)

2

Líneas 100 a 101: Fecha y firma este documento. Como hemos mencionado, asegúrate de firmar todos los documentos para no demorar el proceso de ayuda.

Consejos finales

NO envíes la FAFSA al procesador antes del 1º de enero del año para el cual estás solicitando.

NO incluyas o anexes ningún otro documento a la FAFSA.

NO envíes nada por mensajería especial pues esto retardará el procesamiento.

NO esperes para presentar tus formularios de impuestos de años anteriores ante el IRS.

NO esperes ser admitido en una universidad antes de presentar la FAFSA.

NO incumplas las fechas límites.

Capítulo 3

Cómo funciona el proceso de ayuda financiera

Una vez que hayas llenado la FAFSA, PROFILE, y los demás documentos de ayuda institucional complementaria, se inicia el proceso real de ayuda financiera. A continuación encontrarás una descripción del proceso, de principio a fin.

1. Envía la FAFSA al Central Processing System, CPS, del Departamento de Educación de Estados Unidos, bien sea electrónicamente o por correo postal.
2. La información FAFSA se ingresa a un sistema computarizado y se analiza. El análisis consta de una evaluación de tus ingresos y activos, y los de tu hijo. Se aplica la fórmula de evaluación conocida como Metodología federal, FM (por sus siglas en inglés), que analizaremos en detalle más adelante en este capítulo.
3. El resultado del análisis determina el Expected Family Contribution, EFC, y es igual a la suma que tendrías que pagar para un año de estudios universitarios.
4. El CPS evalúa tu EFC y envía esta información electrónicamente a cada uno de los organismos y universidades de ayuda financiera indicados en la FAFSA. Esto se conoce como el Institutional Student Information Record, ISIR (Registro Institucional de Información Estudiantil).
5. Tu hijo recibe un Student Aid Report, SAR o un formulario de Confirmación de Información SAR, y al mismo tiempo se envía la información de FAFSA a cada universidad enumerada en la FAFSA, de acuerdo al medio que utilizaste para llenarla. Si la enviaste electrónicamente a través de una universidad, recibirás

un formulario de Confirmación de Información SAR de una página; si enviaste la información vía Internet, vía FAFSA Express o en medio impreso, recibirás un SAR de dos páginas.

6. Revisa el SAR tan pronto como lo recibas para identificar errores o hacer cambios.
7. Revisa la FAFSA para asegurarte de haber incluido todas las universidades seleccionadas, como se menciona en el Paso seis. Puedes agregar universidades al SAR impreso vía telefónica llamando al centro de información del Departmento de Educación de EE.UU., 800-433-3243 (para usuarios de teléfonos por tonos, 800-730-8913). También puedes agregar universidades electrónicamente en la página www.fafsa.ed.gov.
8. Una vez que hayas llenado los formularios de impuesto federal sobre la renta del último año, tuyo y de tu hijo, debes actualizar el SAR con la nueva información sobre declaración de impuestos. Ambos deben firmar el SAR y regresarlo a la dirección que aparece registrada.
9. Si devuelves el SAR para actualizar información, recibirás un nuevo SAR por correo, que incluirá los cambios realizados. Si devolviste el SAR para agregar más de seis universidades a tu lista, el nuevo SAR incluirá dichas universidades. Fíjate que en el nuevo SAR no encontrarás las seis universidades que habías registrado en la FAFSA. Esto se debe a que el SAR, al igual que la FAFSA, sólo puede registrar seis universidades a la vez; sin embargo, las seis universidades registradas anteriormente siguen teniendo acceso a tu información. El procesador no las ha borrado.
10. Una vez que recibas el SAR actualizado, te recomendamos llamar a las oficinas de ayuda financiera para verificar si requieren documentos adicionales. Así, podrás asegurarte de estar cumpliendo con todos los requisitos y fechas límite.
11. Luego de que las universidades reciben el ISIR, la oficina de ayuda financiera de la universidad revisa la carpeta de tu hijo para verificar que no falten documentos. Es posible que la oficina tenga que solicitar información adicional. Los documentos adicionales varían de una universidad a otra, lo cual depende del tipo de ayuda que ofrece la institución y si tu hijo ha sido seleccionado

o no para el llamado proceso de verificación con el fin de comprobar la precisión de la información FAFSA. Asegúrate de enviar los documentos requeridos a las universidades dentro del plazo límite. Como hemos señalado anteriormente, es muy importante enviar documentos completos, firmados y en las fechas estipuladas para evitar retrasos en el procesamiento o en la notificación de otorgamiento. Estos contratiempos pueden disminuir considerablemente la ayuda ofrecida.

La verificación es un proceso de aseguramiento de calidad desarrollado por el Departamento de Educación de EE.UU., por el cual cada universidad debe comprobar la información de un porcentaje asignado de beneficiarios de ayuda financiera seleccionados al azar. Si tu hijo ha sido seleccionado, recibirás una Verification Worksheet (Hoja de trabajo de verificación), que debes llenar y devolver con una copia firmada de la declaración federal de renta tuya y de tu hijo, junto con copias de los formularios W-2. Cabe señalar que esto no es una auditoría.

12. Luego de recibir los documentos mencionados arriba, la oficina de ayuda federal, FAO (por sus siglas en inglés) evalúa la elegibilidad de cada estudiante para obtener ayuda y envía una notificación de otorgamiento, llamada también carta de otorgamiento. En terminología de ayuda financiera se denomina "paquete de ayuda financiera". Volveremos a tratar este tema más adelante en este capítulo.
13. Después de recibir la carta de otorgamiento, fírmala y devuélvela inmediatamente a la oficina de ayuda financiera. No esperes que lleguen otras cartas de otorgamiento de otras universidades, ni información sobre admisiones o de otro tipo. Sólo firma la carta de otorgamiento y devuélvela, ya que no te conviene que se pierda, se estropee o se olvide. Además, todo dinero que ofrezca la universidad es mejor que cualquier otra ayuda que vayas a encontrar fuera de la misma o incluso en la cuenta de ahorros de uno de tus padres.
14. Una vez que recibas las cartas de otorgamiento de las universidades seleccionadas, tu hijo debe escoger una y enviar una atenta carta de renuncia a cada una de las universidades a las que no

Recuerda, la principal razón para perder la ayuda financiera es no cumplir con las fechas límites.

asistirá. Se deben enviar estas cartas lo antes posible, de manera que las universidades puedan disponer de los fondos para otros estudiantes. Asegúrate de que las cartas sean amables y estén bien redactadas, puesto que es probable que tu hijo quiera volver a una de esas universidades para solicitarles que reconsideren la ayuda financiera en caso de que no resulten bien las cosas con la universidad escogida.

15. Si un préstamo estudiantil forma parte del paquete de otorgamiento, será necesario que tu hijo suscriba un pagaré de préstamo estudiantil para recibir los fondos. Fíjate que todas las universidades participan en los programas de préstamo estudiantil federal.

16. Una vez que la universidad haya confirmado la inscripción de tu hijo, y haya recibido la carta de otorgamiento de ayuda financiera firmada, la oficina de ayuda financiera procederá a notificar dicho otorgamiento a su Oficina comercial o a la Oficina de Cuentas Estudiantiles.

17. La Oficina comercial acredita la cuenta de tu hijo con la ayuda financiera otorgada. Toda ayuda otorgada se envía siempre a la Oficina comercial para el desembolso correspondiente.

18. Cuando tu hijo se inscriba en las clases, recibirá una factura estudiantil que indica la matrícula, las cuotas, otros cargos y los abonos de la ayuda financiera. Deberás pagar el saldo después de consignada la ayuda. Fíjate que sólo debes pagar el período al que asistes. En una universidad tradicional de estudios de dos o cuatro años, pagas sólo por un período a la vez; sin embargo, algunas universidades privadas con fines de lucro, pueden solicitarte que pagues la totalidad del costo del programa desde el principio.

19. Si tu hijo tiene abonos de ayuda financiera, el desembolso de fondos normalmente se efectúa una vez transcurrido el período de reembolso del ciclo de estudios al que asiste, que normalmente es la tercera semana de estudios. Por ejemplo, si tu hijo vive en el campus y el costo de matrícula, cuotas, alojamiento y alimentación suman $7,500, entonces la ayuda financiera para el período es $8,000. Tu hijo recibirá un reembolso al finalizar la tercera semana por $500. Normalmente, esto ocurre cuando se asignan

ayudas para costos de alojamiento fuera del campus, además de la matrícula y las cuotas. Si la matrícula y las cuotas suman $4,500 y se le ha adjudicado una ayuda de $8,000, tu hijo recibirá un cheque de reembolso para cubrir el alojamiento y comida fuera del campus por $3,500.

20. El último paso en el proceso es verificar con la oficina de ayuda financiera las fechas y documentos para renovar la ayuda el próximo año lectivo.

CÓMO SE DETERMINA CUÁNTO DEBES PAGAR

Aquí, es importante hacer una distinción entre necesidad y análisis de necesidad. Se define necesidad como la diferencia entre los Gastos de asistencia, COA (por sus siglas en inglés) y el Expected Family Contribution (EFC). Según la universidad, tu necesidad representa la cantidad de dinero que se requiere para que tu hijo asista a una universidad en particular. El análisis de necesidad, por otro lado, se centra en determinar el monto razonable que podrías pagar para los gastos educativos de tu hijo en un año académico determinado.

Principios de análisis de necesidad

Ya que la cantidad de dinero disponible a través de los programas estudiantiles de ayuda financiera federal es limitada, el proceso de distribución de fondos debe ser justo y equitativo. Para entender cómo se hace el análisis de necesidad, es importante comprender los siguientes principios básicos:

- $ Todos los estudiantes tienen la responsabilidad de pagar sus estudios en la medida de sus capacidades.
- $ La situación financiera actual de cada estudiante debe tenerse en cuenta al determinar la necesidad.
- $ El análisis de necesidad debe evaluar equitativamente a todos los postulantes de manera justa y adecuada.

En general, la fórmula de análisis de necesidad considera varios factores al determinar la cantidad razonable que una familia puede aportar para los gastos educativos en un año lectivo. Los dos factores más importantes son:

1. Ingreso familiar (padres y estudiante)
2. Patrimonio familiar en activos (padres y estudiante)

Otros elementos que pueden afectar la capacidad familiar de pago son:

$ El número de miembros de la familia

$ El número de miembros de la familia que dependen económicamente de un ingreso fijo (este factor afectará el monto de ingreso discrecional para gastos universitarios)

$ El número de hermanos que asisten a la universidad durante el mismo año lectivo (si más de un miembro de la familia asiste a la universidad, el EFC debe dividirse entre dicho número en lugar de dividirlo por uno)

Proceso de análisis de necesidad

El proceso para determinar el nivel de elegibilidad para recibir cualquier tipo de ayuda financiera en base a la necesidad se define mediante métodos adicionales que permiten analizar tu capacidad de pago para estudios universitarios. Básicamente sólo se aceptan dos métodos de análisis de necesidad:

1. Metodología federal, FM que usa la solicitud FAFSA
2. Metodología institucional, IM (por sus siglas en inglés) que usa el documento de CSS Profile

Visión general de la Metodología federal, FM

La Metodología federal, FM se usa para determinar el EFC para ayuda financiera de fondos federales con base en la necesidad, tales como el programa Federal Pell Grant (Beca Federal Pell), programas con sede en el campus (Federal College Work Study (Becas federales de trabajo y estudio), Supplemental Grant Program (Programa de Becas Suplementarias), Perkins Loan Program (Programas de Préstamos Perkins), y Federal Subsidized Stafford/Direct Subsidized Loan (Programas de Préstamos Federales Stafford Subsidiados/Directos Subsidiados)). El

EFC no se utiliza para determinar la elegibilidad para el Federal Unsubsidized Stafford Loan (Préstamo Federal Stafford No Subsidiado) y los Direct Unsubsidized Loans (Préstamos Directos No Subsidiados), por lo que se usa una variación de la fórmula.

Aunque sólo existe una metodología federal, son tres los modelos computacionales que contempla la metodología.

Puesto que las variables de la fórmula utilizada al determinar la capacidad de cada familia para costear los gastos educativos fueron definidas por ley del Congreso de Estados Unidos, la fórmula se ha denominado correctamente Metodología federal o FM.

1. La fórmula regular

La fórmula regular de análisis de necesidad es la que se usa para la mayoría de los estudiantes. Permite evaluar tu situación patrimonial y determina una contribución a partir de dicho patrimonio. Esta cantidad se combina con el ingreso disponible a fin de ver claramente tu solvencia financiera.

La fórmula funciona así:

- $ Primero, se calcula tu patrimonio neto agregando los activos registrados en la FAFSA (las cantidades negativas se convierten a cero para este cálculo). El patrimonio neto comercial/agrario se ajusta para proteger una porción del patrimonio neto de dichos activos.
- $ Segundo, el patrimonio neto discrecional se calcula sustrayendo un otorgamiento de protección de activos y ahorros para educación de su patrimonio neto. Esto se hace para proteger parte de los activos (patrimonio neto). El patrimonio neto discrecional puede ser menor a cero.
- $ Finalmente, el patrimonio neto discrecional se multiplica por una tasa de conversión al 12 por ciento para obtener su contribución a partir de los activos, lo que representa la porción del valor de tus activos que pueden considerarse disponibles para ayudar a pagar los costos universitarios de tu hijo. Si la contribución en base a tus activos es menor a cero, se aproxima a cero.

El aporte de la familia en base a los activos se agrega al ingreso disponible; este valor se denomina ingreso disponible ajustado. El ingreso disponible ajustado se multiplica por una tasa de evaluación, porcentaje que aumenta a medida que se incrementa el ingreso disponible ajustado.

Esto finalmente nos da el monto anual previsto en un año determinado que una familia puede pagar para los gastos educativos del estudiante.

Si más de un miembro del grupo familiar asiste a la universidad, al menos a tiempo parcial durante el mismo año lectivo, el EFC se divide en partes iguales entre ellos. Por ejemplo, si se calcula que tu EFC es $5,000 y tu hijo e hija piensan asistir a la universidad durante el mismo año, este monto se dividiría por dos. En otras palabras, se esperaría que el aporte de tu familia fuera $2,500 para cada uno de ellos.

2. Fórmula simplificada o prueba simplificada de necesidades

En situaciones específicas, la información sobre los activos de los padres no se tiene en cuenta en la fórmula de análisis de necesidades. El EFC se calcula sólo en base a tu ingreso, sin evaluar la contribución a partir de los activos. Esta fórmula se denomina prueba simplificada de necesidades y puede aplicarse a un estudiante dependiente si se cumplen todos los siguientes requisitos:

- Presentaste o eres elegible para presentar el formulario IRS 1040A ó 1040EZ, o si no es necesario que presentes ninguna declaración de renta.
- Tu hijo presentó o es elegible para presentar el formulario IRS 1040A ó 1040EZ, o si no es necesario que presentes ninguna declaración de renta
- Tu ingreso proveniente de las dos fuentes abajo mencionadas es $49,999 o menos (sin incluir el ingreso de tu hijo).
- Si declaras impuestos y tu ingreso bruto ajustado en el formulario 1040A ó 1040EZ es $49,999 o menos.
- Si no declaras impuestos y el ingreso reportado en los formularios W-2, tanto tuyo como de tu cónyuge, (más cualquier otro ingreso laboral que no se incluya en los formularios W-2) es $49,999 o menos.

Es importante destacar que la clave para calificar para la fórmula simplificada de necesidades no es si has presentado o no un formulario 1040A ó 1040EZ, sino si eres elegible para presentar uno de estos tipos de declaraciones de impuesto sobre la renta. En otras palabras, si tu ingreso combinado es menos de $50,000 y presentaste un formulario 1040, pero eras elegible para presentar un formulario 1040A ó 1040EZ, aún calificarías para la fórmula simplificada de análisis de necesidades.

3. EFC cero automático

Este tercer método para determinar un EFC no involucra ningún cálculo, sino que automáticamente se determina que tu EFC corresponde a cero dólares. Por esta razón, se denomina adecuadamente EFC cero automático.

Ciertos estudiantes son elegibles automáticamente para EFC cero. Si tu hijo se considera dependiente, automáticamente califica para un EFC cero para el año de otorgamiento si cumple con las dos siguientes condiciones:

1. Tanto tú como tu hijo presentaron o son elegibles para presentar un formulario IRS 1040A ó 1040EZ (no tienes que presentar un formulario 1040), o si tú y tu hijo no tienen que presentar una declaración de impuestos sobre la renta.
2. La suma del ingreso bruto ajustado tuyo y de tu cónyuge es de $13,000 o menos, o si tú y tu cónyuge no declaran y la suma de tus ingresos percibidos es $13,000 o menos.

Visión general de metodología institucional (IM)

La solicitud College Scholarship Service, CSS, Profile se utiliza en muchas universidades y programas de becas que prefieren no usar la metodología federal para otorgar sus ayudas institucionales o fondos privados de becas. Estas universidades ofrecen más ayuda por donación (dinero gratis) a través de la información de Profile en lugar de la información de FAFSA. Si la universidad donde se presenta tu hijo solicita el Profile, asegúrate de presentarlo dentro de las fechas límite establecidas para asegurar que se le considere para ayuda por donación.

El CSS se usa para evaluar la necesidad demostrada de tu familia mediante el uso de información adicional que no se requiere en el cálculo FM. Esta información puede incluir datos de las siguientes fuentes, según lo exija la institución:

- $ Patrimonio en la residencia principal
- $ Contribución mínima prevista de los ahorros de verano de tu hijo
- $ Presentación de una declaración no custodial de activos e ingresos
- $ Valor de las cuentas de jubilación tuya y de tu cónyuge
- $ Valor de activos de las cuentas de hermanos
- $ Presentación de información sobre padre sin custodia

Opinión profesional

La opinión profesional se solicita para apelar a la oficina de ayuda financiera de una universidad escogida respecto de circunstancias especiales y para explicar por qué los métodos de evaluación de necesidades (FM o IM) no son justos para la familia del estudiante. En ciertos casos, el ingreso de año base no refleja con precisión la solidez financiera u otros aspectos de la fórmula no muestran razonablemente la capacidad familiar para pagar los gastos universitarios. Según la Metodología federal, el administrador de ayudas puede cambiar los elementos de información FM para casos individuales de manera que arrojen una medición más precisa de tu capacidad familiar para asumir gastos educativos.

Los ajustes por opinión profesional tienen lugar sólo cuando existan circunstancias inusuales y atenuantes y sólo una vez que tú y tu hijo hayan presentado la documentación relevante. Un ejemplo común de una circunstancia atenuante que llevaría al administrador de ayudas a buscar la opinión profesional es cuando tu familia sufre una pérdida significativa de ingresos en el período transcurrido entre el año base y el actual. Este infortunio puede ocurrir por la pérdida de trabajo de un miembro de la familia o por una reducción en las horas de trabajo. Si te ocurre esta situación, o una similar, el administrador de ayuda financiera puede usar tu ingreso proyectado o del año en curso para calcular la fórmula de análisis de necesidad, en lugar de usar el año base, siempre que suministres la documentación correspondiente.

Los funcionarios de ayuda financiera universitaria agradecen cualquier información adicional que el estudiante o la familia suministre para ayudarles a hacer mejores evaluaciones.

Puedes enviar una carta a cada universidad escogida por tu hijo y explicar la necesidad de la opinión profesional. Algunas universidades tienen su propio formulario de opinión profesional y prefieren que lo llenes para la oficina de ayuda financiera.

A continuación, describimos algunas situaciones a las que quisieras que el funcionario de ayuda financiera pusiera especial atención.

Pérdida de empleo: Si tú o tu cónyuge estuvieron desempleados el año pasado, detalla la situación al funcionario universitario para ayuda financiera: en qué fecha quedaste desempleado, cuánto tiempo llevas sin empleo, nota la indemnización por desempleo recibida, si esta situación de desempleo continuará en el futuro. Es conveniente presentar una carta de solicitud con carta adjunta de tu antiguo empleador (con membrete de la empresa) para documentar la solicitud del estudiante/familia.

Gastos por enfermedad, de salud o médicos: Si tu familia ha tenido gastos extraordinarios de salud, infórmale al funcionario de ayuda financiera sobre este gasto adicional de dinero y susténtalo con documentación expedida por tu médico, como cuentas pagadas o declaraciones de seguros que deberán entregarse a la universidad para reforzar tu carta de solicitud.

Divorcio o separación: Si tu matrimonio está en crisis y en el momento tu hijo sólo cuenta con un ingreso para sus gastos universitarios, infórmalo al funcionario de ayuda financiera. Incluso si aún tienes una declaración conjunta de impuesto sobre la renta, el funcionario puede considerar que tu grupo familiar tiene sólo una fuente de ingresos, puesto que uno de los padres ya no reside en la misma dirección.

Pérdida de pago de manutención de hijos: La manutención de hijos normalmente se recibe hasta los 18 años. Puesto que la información de los documentos de ayuda financiera incluye ingresos sujetos a impuestos y exentos de impuestos recibidos en el año base, es muy probable que un padre reporte en la documentación para análisis de necesidad, el la manutención de hijos recibida durante todo el año. Sin embargo, puesto que tu hijo cumplirá los 18 años el próximo año, hazle saber a la universidad cual será la diferencia en pagos de subsidio familiar para el año en que tu hijo asistirá a la institución. Esto aumentará la elegibilidad de tu hijo.

Pérdida de beneficios de seguro social: Ver pérdida de manutención de hijos.

Pérdida de ingresos de inversión: Debido a la drástica reducción en el valor de acciones, bonos y otras inversiones, no es lógico calcular grandes ingresos de intereses y dividendos con base en la declaración de impuesto sobre la renta de un año para tropezar con pérdidas al año siguiente. La oficina de ayuda financiera necesita copias de informes que reflejen dichas pérdidas para tomar una decisión de opinión profesional que disminuya el ingreso bruto ajustado.

Cómo crear un paquete de subvenciones

Una vez establecida la elegibilidad de tu hijo para recibir ayuda financiera, el siguiente paso es acudir a la oficina financiera para planificar la forma de subvención. El *empaque* es el proceso de combinar diferentes tipos de ayuda proveniente de variadas fuentes para satisfacer tus necesidades. Este proceso cubre la diferencia entre el costo de asistir a una universidad determinada y la cantidad que puedes pagar. El empaque es también la manera cómo los administradores de ayuda financiera distribuyen equitativamente los limitados recursos entre estudiantes. Es importante entender que el procesador de las FAFSA no determina la ayuda financiera para un estudiante ni su paquete de ayuda financiera. Cada universidad toma estas decisiones considerando los gastos de asistencia, el EFC, otros recursos, la cantidad de fondos de ayuda financiera disponibles, el número de estudiantes que solicitan ayuda y los objetivos definidos por la universidad.

Cronograma del paquete

La ayuda financiera puede ser un factor de suma importancia en el proceso de selección de la universidad de tu hijo. Bien lo saben las universidades, por lo que tratan de suministrar lo más pronto posible información a los aspirantes para que hagan una selección informada sobre la institución a la que decidan asistir. Algunas universidades brindan un paquete preliminar de ayuda, aun antes de que el estudiante sea admitido, pero la mayoría espera hasta la admisión formal. La oferta de ayuda financiera generalmente se entrega con la notificación de admisión o posteriormente con un cronograma separado.

Las universidades que ofrecen paquetes de ayuda financiera basados en fechas límite de solicitud, por lo general determinan una fecha límite más cercana para estudiantes de primer año que para estudiantes más antiguos. Los solicitantes para ingresar al primer año deben conocer el cronograma de notificaciones de admisión y cuándo pueden recibir notificación de la ayuda financiera. Estas dos informaciones son de gran importancia y en muchos casos, la decisión de asistir a una determinada universidad no puede hacerse hasta que tu hijo sepa el monto de la ayuda financiera que recibirá. Por ejemplo, si la fecha límite de solicitud de ayuda es el 15 de marzo, las notificaciones de otorgamiento podrían enviarse hacia el 1° de abril. Así, la universidad podría establecer el 1° de mayo como fecha límite para responder, fecha en la cual deberás haber notificado a la universidad si tu hijo piensa matricularse (y quizás hacer un depósito para apartar cupo en los cursos correspondientes). Es posible que a tu hijo se le haya notificado su admisión en enero, pero sólo haya recibido una oferta financiera hasta abril, y dado que puedes estar analizando ofertas de admisión de varias universidades, el tipo de paquete puede inclinar la balanza en favor de algunas de ellas.

Es probable que una universidad que generalmente no ofrece ayuda hasta una fecha específica, o hasta que hayas completado la documentación de ayuda financiera, aún esté dispuesta a brindarte un estimado preliminar de la ayuda que puedes recibir. Si no has recibido una oferta de ayuda de una universidad en la que tu hijo esté realmente interesado, no dudes en contactarla de todas maneras, para que te den información.

Antes de empezar el proceso de empaque, el administrador de ayuda debe tener los resultados de su solicitud FAFSA provenientes del CPS. Es responsabilidad de ustedes (padres y estudiante) asegurarse de que la FAFSA se entregue oportunamente al procesador, para cumplir con las fechas límite de las universidades. Debes también averiguar si la universidad exige formularios de solicitud o documentos de soporte adicionales. No es inusual que las universidades tengan sus propias solicitudes de ayuda institucional, o que exijan declaraciones de renta u otros documentos para verificar o explicar la información proporcionada en la FAFSA. El gobierno federal también exige a algunos solicitantes, declaraciones de renta para confirmar la información sobre ingresos contenida en la FAFSA, que se deben entregar a la oficina de ayuda financiera de la universidad.

Si no te exigieron presentar una declaración de renta, te pueden solicitar otras formas de documentación. Debes tener disponible todo tipo de resumen de ingresos, como formularios W-2, declaraciones de Seguro Social, y comprobantes de asistencia social, en caso que la oficina de ayuda financiera de la universidad los solicite.

Es conveniente completar las declaraciones de impuestos sobre la renta tan pronto como sea posible; así, si la universidad o el gobierno las exigen, podrás enviarlas rápidamente. Es muy importante evitar demoras innecesarias en la notificación de otorgamiento.

Gastos de asistencia

Es importante comprender los conceptos de un proceso de empaque. Ya hemos definido el concepto necesidad y has visto en detalle uno de los componentes de la ecuación de necesidad: el EFC. El componente restante corresponde a los Gastos de asistencia, COA (por sus siglas en inglés).

Por lo general, los gastos de asistencia se refieren al presupuesto del estudiante. Este monto en dólares incluye todos los gastos relacionados con los costos de un año de educación universitaria para tu hijo. Dichos costos educativos incluyen:

- $ Matrícula y cuotas
- $ Alojamiento y comida
- $ Libros y materiales
- $ Transporte
- $ Gastos personales varios

Los gastos incluyen también otro tipo de gastos, como cuotas de préstamo, gastos relacionados a discapacidades (si estos gastos son necesarios para asistir y no han sido cubiertos por otros organismos de asistencia financiera), gastos relacionados con un programa de estudios en el extranjero y gastos relacionados con una experiencia laboral en educación cooperativa. Si tu hijo incurre en otros gastos durante el año lectivo, consulta al administrador de ayuda financiera de la universidad tan pronto como te sea posible durante el proceso de solicitud de ayuda.

Se espera que mientras tu hijo asista a la universidad viva con un presupuesto razonable, pero modesto. La mayoría de las universidades tienen presupuestos estándar que reflejan la cantidad promedio que gasta un estudiante en cada categoría del presupuesto. Por ejemplo, en lugar de calcular presupuestos individuales para cada estudiante basado en los estudios que desea seguir, las universidades generalmente determinan un monto promedio para una amplia categoría de estudiantes. Es posible que los gastos reales de tu hijo difieran levemente, pero por lo general la ayuda se basa en los promedios establecidos. Si existe alguna razón documentada de que tu hijo incurrirá en gastos superiores a los promediados, asegúrate de informar al administrador las circunstancias para que ajuste el paquete de ayuda.

Si tu hijo piensa asistir a la universidad menos de medio tiempo, tendrás un gasto de asistencia modificado. Los gastos sujetos a subvención se limitan a matrícula y cuotas, libros y materiales y transporte. Si tu hijo se inscribe en un programa por correspondencia, sólo se considerará ayuda para matrícula y cuotas. Los libros y materiales, gastos de viaje y alojamiento y comida, son gastos que sólo se incluyen en los gastos de asistencia si se requieren para un período de capacitación como residente.

Los gastos de asistencia varían según el tipo de institución y los gastos asociados para asistir a la universidad. Por ejemplo, las universidades independientes (o privadas) no reciben subsidios operativos gubernamentales, por lo que deben cobrar matrículas y cuotas más altas que un instituto de enseñanza para la comunidad subvencionado por el estado u otro tipo de institución pública de educación superior. Generalmente, esto hace que el costo de asistencia a una universidad privada sea más alto que a una universidad pública. Los gastos de asistencia pueden variar también con cada estudiante. Si tu hijo no vive en el campus, puede tener mayores gastos de alojamiento y comida que un estudiante que vive en las residencias universitarias.

Aunque los gastos de asistencia varían según la universidad y el estudiante, el EFC debe permanecer relativamente constante sin importar la universidad que escoja tu hijo. En otras palabras, la necesidad varía porque los costos varían. Este concepto es importante cuando ayudes a tu hijo a decidir en que universidad estudiar. A continuación, se detallan los componentes de los costos educativos universitarios.

Matrícula y cuotas

Corresponde a la cantidad real que debes pagar y no un promedio basado en un grupo de estudiantes. Esta categoría puede incluir otros gastos como costos de laboratorio y equipos según el tipo de programa en que se inscriba tu hijo.

Alojamiento

Incluye los costos de vivienda de cada estudiante. La naturaleza de los gastos de alojamiento varía considerablemente según tu hijo viva en el campus, en un sitio diferente o en casa contigo. Es necesario recordar que sin importar si tu hijo reside fuera del campus o viaja para asistir a clases, tendrá derecho a asignación para vivienda en el presupuesto para gastos de asistencia.

Comida

Al igual que con los gastos de alojamiento, la asignación para alimentación varía según el lugar de residencia de tu hijo. Normalmente, esta asignación se provee para gastos razonables en comidas nutritivas y, como los gastos de alojamiento, tu hijo tiene derecho a esta asignación, ya sea si reside en el campus, fuera del mismo o si debe viajar para asistir a clases.

Transporte

Si tu hijo viaja para asistir a clases, la asignación de transporte incluye el costo diario de transporte hacia y desde la universidad. Esta asignación no cubre la compra de un auto, pero es suficiente para el aparcamiento y manutención general sin incluir el seguro. Si tu hijo asiste a una universidad con buen servicio de transporte público, la asignación se hará generalmente en base al uso de tal servicio.

Gastos personales

Los presupuestos estudiantiles también proveen gastos personales varios. Necesidades diarias, como las de higiene personal y lavandería, también se incluyen en esta categoría al igual que una modesta ayuda para vestuario. Son muchas las universidades que asignan una pequeña suma para una película u otro tipo de entretenimiento ocasional.

El proceso de empaque

El proceso de empaque puede iniciarse una vez que la universidad haya establecido presupuestos estándar razonables de ayuda estudiantil y que se haya seleccionado el más adecuado para un estudiante en particular. El principio básico es que el estudiante tiene como obligación prioritaria el pago de los costos educativos.

Como se dijo anteriormente, la diferencia entre los gastos de asistencia a una universidad específica y la capacidad de tu familia para pagar estos gastos es lo que determina la necesidad de ciertos tipos de asistencia financiera, generalmente conocidos como ayuda basada en la necesidad. Esta es la fórmula para este tipo de ayuda:

Gastos de asistencia (COA)

– Expected Family Contribution, EFC

= Necesidad

Si tu hijo ha recibido otro tipo de ayuda, (por ejemplo, beca académica de alguna organización comunitaria), este recurso debe tenerse en cuenta para conformar tu paquete de asistencia basada en necesidades. Con esto en mente, la siguiente fórmula es la que se utiliza cuando se deben considerar recursos adicionales:

Gastos de asistencia (COA)

– Expected Family Contribution, EFC y otros recursos

= Necesidad

El EFC es el primer recurso que se considera en el proceso de empaque. Si el EFC es igual o mayor que el COA, una universidad puede conceder a tu hijo ayuda basada en sus propios méritos o tendrás la opción de solicitar un Federal Unsubsidized Stafford Loan o un Direct Unsubsidized Loan.

Antes de otorgar cualquier forma de ayuda estudiantil, la universidad debe determinar si tu hijo es elegible para una Federal Pell Grant. Se considera que esta es la base de todo el paquete, puesto que cualquier otro auxilio se centra en ella. El administrador de ayuda debe calcular el monto real de la Federal Pell Grant requerida con base en tu EFC, el COA para un año académico, el tiempo de asistencia comprendido en la inscripción de tu hijo y su estatus de inscripción.

Luego de establecer la elegibilidad de tu hijo para una Federal Pell Grant, la universidad decide si debe además recibir auxilio de fuentes externas que incluyen cualquier subvención estatal, beca privada (por ejemplo, auxilios de clubes de servicios y becas por méritos), y todo auxilio educativo estudiantil, como los beneficios educativos para veteranos. Una vez que todos los recursos educativos se han sustraído del COA junto con el EFC, toda necesidad que persista deberá cubrirse combinando fuentes controladas por la institución, de acuerdo a sus políticas de empaque y filosofía.

Cómo se determina la necesidad para programas federales que no se no basan en las necesidades

La cantidad que puedes recibir de programas federales que no se basan en las necesidades (por ejemplo, Federal Unsubsidized Stafford Loan y Direct Unsubsidized Loan) se determina un poco diferente a la de los otros programas federales. Como sabes, el EFC no se tiene en cuenta cuando se determina tu elegibilidad para auxilio no basado en las necesidades. Sin embargo, el monto que se puede pedir en préstamo se limita a la diferencia entre el costo de asistencia a una universidad y la cantidad estimada de otra ayuda que recibas. La siguiente es la fórmula para ayuda financiera federal que no se basa en las necesidades:

	Gastos de asistencia
–	Estimated Financial Assistance (Asistencia financiera estimada)
=	Necesidad

No olvides entonces que el monto de ayuda que recibas estará directamente relacionado con los gastos de asistencia a las universidades. El EFC debe ser constante entre una universidad y otra, a menos que la tuya sea ajustada de acuerdo a circunstancias individuales inusuales por el administrador de ayuda de una universidad, mas no por el de otra.

El Federal Unsubsidized Stafford Loan y el Direct Unsubsidized Loan pueden reemplazar toda o parte del EFC. Además, también puedes pedir préstamos dentro de estos programas para satisfacer alguna necesidad. Si eres beneficiario de préstamos no subsidiados, debes solicitar primero cualquier estatus de elegibilidad para préstamo con subsidio.

Si tu hijo presenta una solicitud en una universidad costosa y en otra económica, es muy posible que la cantidad de ayuda ofrecida por la primera sea suficiente para cubrir la diferencia en costos entre las dos instituciones. Al ofrecer más ayuda, el costo real para tu hijo será el mismo, sin importar la universidad que escoja. En este caso, se logra uno de los objetivos fundamentales de la ayuda estudiantil, es decir, suministrar acceso y oportunidad de elegir. Puedes entonces contraer una deuda mayor o tu hijo tendrá que dedicar más horas al trabajo en una universidad que en otra. Entonces, quizás decidas que vale la pena asumir esta responsabilidad adicional para que tu hijo asista a la universidad que prefiere. Los métodos para comparar paquetes de ayuda se analizan con más detalle más adelante en este capítulo.

EJEMPLOS DE PAQUETES DE AYUDA FINANCIERA

Los tres siguientes ejemplos de paquetes de ayuda financiera muestran cómo la ayuda se puede combinar de diferentes maneras y según diversas filosofías de empaque para satisfacer la necesidad específica de tu hijo. No olvides que éstos son sólo ejemplos y que los paquetes reales de ayuda financiera ofrecidos por cualquier institución serán diferentes. Al analizar paquetes de muestras, es importante asegurarte de los siguientes puntos clave en su contenido:

1. **Los gastos de asistencia varían considerablemente según el tipo de institución (por ejemplo, universidades públicas o privadas, estudios de 2 años o estudios de 4 años).**
2. **Los montos y fuentes de ayuda varían según la institución.**
3. **La única constante en los diferentes paquetes de ayuda es el EFC.**

Paquete de ayuda de instituto de enseñanza para la comunidad (estudiante de primer año, tiempo completo)	
Presupuesto	$ 7,500
Expected Family Contribution	– 2,000
Necesidad	$ 5,500
Federal Pell Grant	2,100
Federal Supplemental Educational Opportunity Grant, FSEOG	1,000
Beca estatal	500
Federal Perkins Loan	500
Federal Stafford Loan	– 1,400
Necesidad no satisfecha	$ 0

En este ejemplo, los gastos de asistencia a un instituto de enseñanza para la comunidad son relativamente bajos. La necesidad financiera del estudiante queda totalmente cubierta gracias a auxilios y préstamos.

Paquete de ayuda de universidad pública (estudiante de primer año, tiempo completo)	
Presupuesto	$ 12,000
Expected Family Contribution	– 2,000
Necesidad	$ 10,000
Federal Pell Grant	2,100
Federal Supplemental Educational Opportunity Grant (FSEOG)	1,500
Beca estatal	1,500
Federal Perkins Loan	1,000
Federal Work-Study	875
Federal Stafford Loan	– 2,625
Necesidad no satisfecha	$ 400

En este ejemplo los gastos de asistencia a una universidad pública estatal son mayores que para un instituto de enseñanza para la comunidad. Esto se debe básicamente a que las cuotas son mayores. Fíjate que el EFC es el mismo en el caso del instituto de enseñanza para la comunidad.

Aunque los gastos de asistencia se tienen en cuenta al calcular las Federal Pell Grants, el monto que recibe el estudiante sigue siendo el mismo. Puesto que la matrícula y las cuotas son más altas en una universidad estatal que en un instituto de enseñanza para la comunidad, el estudiante es elegible para una beca estatal más completa. En este ejemplo, la universidad estatal incluyó en el paquete un Federal Stafford Loan de $2,625 para brindar una mayor cobertura a la necesidad del estudiante. Si él decide aceptarlo, se debe llenar una solicitud para el Federal Stafford Loan para presentarla directamente a la universidad. Si el estudiante declina este préstamo, quizás la universidad no esté dispuesta o en capacidad de remplazarlo por otra forma de ayuda, y posiblemente tenga que reunir el dinero por su cuenta, de fuentes como un salario o ahorros personales.

Paquete de ayuda de universidad privada (estudiante de tiempo completo y primer año)

Presupuesto	$ 26,000
Expected Family Contribution	– 2,000
Necesidad	$ 24,000
Federal Pell Grant	2,100
Federal Supplemental Educational Opportunity Grant (FSEOG)	1,700
Beca estatal	2,700
Beca externa	3,200
Beca institucional	8,000
Federal Perkins Loan	1,800
Direct Stafford Loan	2,625
Federal Work-Study	–1,875
Necesidad no satisfecha	$0

En este ejemplo, los gastos de asistencia son mucho más altos que en los dos ejemplos anteriores. Como la matrícula y las cuotas son más elevadas, el estudiante es también elegible para una beca estatal mejor que las ofrecidas por el instituto de enseñanza para la comunidad o la universidad estatal. La ayuda ofrecida también incluye un Direct Stafford Loan por $2,625 y, para recibirlo, el estudiante debe firmar un pagaré de Direct Loan (Préstamo Directo). Además, la mayoría de las universidades privadas tienen sus propios programas de ayuda financiera institucionalmente patrocinados. La ayuda institucional suministra auxilio financiero además del proporcionado por programas de ayuda financiera federal y estatal. Dado que este estudiante tiene una gran necesidad, se le ofreció una subvención institucional de $8,000.

CAMBIOS EN EL PAQUETE DE AYUDA

Las políticas de empaque no sólo afectan los montos y tipos de ayuda ofrecida inicialmente; también afectan las maneras de hacer ajustes a tu asignación cuando cambian las circunstancias. En la mayoría de los casos, los ajustes a un paquete de ayuda se realizan porque cambian tus recursos disponibles. Por ejemplo, si después de haber recibido una oferta y conformado un paquete, tu hijo recibe ayuda adicional de fondos privados de subvención de una organización externa, el administrador de ayuda financiera deberá revisar el paquete para verificar si aún es válido. Dado que las normas federales restringen la ayuda que un estudiante puede recibir y puesto que la ayuda institucional es limitada, los administradores de ayuda financiera generalmente deben revisar nuevamente tu elegibilidad cuando se enteran de que tienes recursos adicionales disponibles.

Las universidades determinan la manera de ajuste para un paquete de ayuda financiera. Si la financiación externa de ayuda se hace en forma de subvención, la política de la universidad puede ser reducir la subvención ya ofrecida. Otra universidad puede tener la política de reemplazar préstamos con recursos externos, para reducir la totalidad de tu deuda. Si tu necesidad no fue previamente cubierta, la universidad puede tener una política que permita el uso de recursos externos para necesidades no satisfechas antes de modificar la ayuda ofrecida. Lo que finalmente influye sobre el ajuste de los paquetes, es la necesidad que presenten otros estudiantes y la cantidad de fondos disponibles para cada tipo de programa de ayuda.

Tienes la obligación de notificar a la universidad donde asiste tu hijo cualquier recurso adicional que recibas, incluso después de que la universidad haya hecho una oferta de ayuda. A fin de cumplir con los requisitos federales, las universidades deben asegurarse de que los solicitantes de ayuda financiera no reciban más ayuda federal de la permitida. Si recibes asistencia no basada en las necesidades (como un Federal Stafford Loan o Direct Unsubsidized Loan o una beca), la ayuda total recibida no puede superar los gastos de asistencia.

Si el administrador de ayuda financiera se entera de que hay un gasto educativo que no cubre el presupuesto estándar del estudiante, se puede aumentar los gastos de asistencia para pagar dicho gasto con los recursos adicionales, en lugar de reducir la ayuda ofrecida. El EFC también puede ajustarse para evitar una subvención excesiva en caso que existan circunstancias atenuantes.

EVALUAR LOS PAQUETES DE AYUDA

El proceso de toma de decisión comienza desde que se admite a tu hijo en una universidad y recibe ofertas de ayuda financiera. Si tiene una fuerte preferencia por una universidad en especial, probablemente aceptarás cualquier oferta de ayuda que le permita asistir a esta institución. Sin embargo, es posible que tu hijo tenga más de una preferencia y entonces la elección ya no sería tan fácil. En estos casos, la ayuda financiera es un factor importante en el proceso de toma de decisión.

Cuando estudies ofertas de ayuda financiera de diferentes universidades, debes considerar tanto los objetivos educativos como tu necesidad financiera. Las aspiraciones educativas de tu hijo deben ser, en lo posible, lo más importante al escoger la universidad.

Después de considerar los aspectos educativos, debes tener en cuenta otros aspectos para evaluar las ofertas de ayuda financiera y tomar una buena decisión. En primer lugar, debes saber que el paquete de ayuda más grande no siempre es el mejor. Debido a las diferencias en los gastos de asistencia entre varios tipos de universidades, es posible que la mayor oferta en términos de dólares sea la que presente un mayor desajuste entre gastos y recursos disponibles; si esto no se puede solucionar con otro recurso, la oferta más grande puede ser insuficiente para que tu hijo asista a esa universidad.

Aunque dos ofertas cubran todas tus necesidades, es probable que no sean iguales. Si el presupuesto estimado de gastos usado para calcular la necesidad es realmente bajo, puedes llegar a tener más necesidades reales sin satisfacer de las que sugiere la carta de otorgamiento. No dejes de comparar los costos establecidos con los de universidades parecidas para asegurarte de que los gastos de asistencia a una universidad estimados sean adecuados.

Los paquetes que contienen igual cantidad de dólares y similar necesidad no satisfecha no siempre son lo mismo. Es posible que tengas una mayor ayuda por donación y por consiguiente, un préstamo y una obligación laboral más reducidos. O bien, puede que un paquete ofrezca una mayor proporción en auto-ayuda y menos ayuda de otorgamiento. De un modo similar, no todas las becas son iguales. Algunas se renuevan automáticamente, otras son renovables sólo bajo ciertas condiciones, como tener siempre un buen rendimiento académico. Algunas becas no son renovables y son válidas solamente para el primer año. Entonces, una beca renovable de $500 puede resultar mejor que una beca de $1,000 que tenga muchas condiciones, o que una beca no renovable de $1,500.

Para algunos estudiantes, ciertos paquetes son mejores que otros. Si tu hijo tiene planeado estudiar una profesión de bajos ingresos o cursa un entrenamiento profesional o de posgrado antes de ingresar al mercado laboral, debes considerar cuidadosamente las obligaciones substanciales del préstamo. Montos iguales no implican necesariamente el mismo nivel de obligación. Por otro lado, aunque los términos y condiciones de los programas específicos de préstamo federal son los mismos en las diferentes universidades, existen variaciones entre los tipos de programas de préstamo federal ofrecidos. Incluso si se presta el mismo monto, un préstamo puede resultar más costoso que otro debido a tasas de interés más altas, menos opciones de aplazamiento, requisitos de reembolso más pronto y pagos mínimos más altos.

Si decides solicitar un préstamo, haz cálculos bajos pero realistas del monto que realmente necesitas. El mejor consejo es solicitar sólo la cantidad que necesitas. Además, debes mantener un registro de los préstamos, quién los otorga y cuándo debes pagarlos. Esta información es esencial para evitar el incumplimiento en el pago del préstamo, ya que si incumples, esto puede tener efectos negativos en tus referencias crediticias y afecta tu capacidad para solicitar préstamos en el futuro.

Al evaluar los préstamos, debes entender los términos y condiciones de cada programa. Mientras que los programas de los Federal Perkins Loans, Federal Stafford y Direct Loans tienen tasas de interés relativamente bajas, el Federal Perkins Loan tiene diferentes opciones de aplazamiento y más opciones de cancelación que los Federal Stafford y Direct Loans. Teniendo en cuenta que estos préstamos pueden tener un gran impacto sobre las actividades de tu hijo y su calidad de vida al terminar sus estudios, bien vale la pena dedicar especial atención al proceso de evaluación de préstamos.

Al evaluar los paquetes de ayuda, recuerda que tu hijo es quien debe pagar los préstamos sin importar si ha completado un programa de estudios o no. El abandono de la universidad o el no poder encontrar empleo en la profesión escogida no libera a tu hijo de su obligación.

NOTIFICACIÓN DE OTORGAMIENTO: ¿QUÉ SON TODOS ESOS PAPELES?

Hay dos componentes del proceso de ayuda financiera que debemos analizar:

1. **Notificación de ayuda ofrecida a un estudiante**
2. **Entrega de dicha ayuda**

Para comprender el proceso de ayuda financiera, debes tener claro qué puedes esperar como respuesta a tus solicitudes de ayuda y el tipo de seguimiento necesario después de recibir una oferta. Puesto que existen muchas fuentes posibles de ayuda financiera, debes llenar y presentar numerosos formularios para asegurarte de recibir el máximo de ayuda. No te sorprendas si recibes gran cantidad de papeles, entre los cuales puedes recibir algunos o todos los siguientes de parte de procesadores y universidades:

$ SAR o Confirmación de información del SAR del CPS

$ Notificación de ayuda por parte de una agencia estatal respecto a tu elegibilidad para una beca estatal, subvención o alguna otra forma de ayuda estatal

$ Notificación de ayuda de fuentes privadas, si corresponde

$ Estimado preliminar efectuado por la universidad de las cantidades y tipos de ayuda para los que tu hijo puede ser elegible

- Si es necesario, una carta de la universidad pidiendo documentos adicionales, por ejemplo, una solicitud institucional, declaraciones de renta, y otros documentos para verificación
- Notificación de ayuda financiera (carta de otorgamiento) dada por la universidad
- Solicitudes de préstamo o pagarés

Student Aid Report, SAR

Como respuesta a la presentación de la FAFSA, el CPS envía un SAR o una Confirmación de información SAR. Recibirás un SAR de dos páginas, si entregaste una FAFSA impresa directamente al procesador FAFSA, completaste FAFSA Express, o la FAFSA en la web. Si la enviaste directamente a la universidad para su posterior envío en forma electrónica al CPS, recibirás una Confirmación de Información SAR de una página que no se podrá corregir.

En el SAR encuentras un resumen de la información de FAFSA, el monto que debes pagar para los gastos educativos de tu hijo en el próximo año académico y además, instrucciones sobre lo que debes hacer luego. Por ejemplo, si tienes un problema con tu número de seguro social, el SAR te da instrucciones sobre los pasos que debes seguir para corregir el problema.

En la mayoría de los casos, no tienes que presentar el SAR a la universidad donde tu hijo quiere asistir. Es importante entender que para poder dar ayudas, las universidades deben tener un EFC oficial del Central Processing System, CPS. Generalmente, las universidades pueden obtener tu EFC electrónicamente. Este documento de información electrónico se llama Institutional Student Information Record, ISIR (Registro Institucional de Información Estudiantil).

Notificación de ayuda estatal

Algunos estados pueden solicitarte que presentes documentos adicionales a la FAFSA para considerarte candidato a un otorgamiento estatal. La información que reciben las agencias estatales contiene tu información financiera, así como un cálculo de tu EFC. Por lo general, las agencias estatales determinan tu elegibilidad para ayuda estatal basadas en dicha información; otras adjudican la ayuda a través del administrador de ayudas de la universidad según las regulaciones estatales.

Muchos estados informan a la universidad que te han asignado una ayuda estatal; sin embargo, como no siempre es así, es bueno que lo notifiques directamente a las universidades donde tu hijo desea estudiar. Así, las universidades podrán tener en cuenta el otorgamiento estatal al crear tu paquete de ayuda financiera. De otra forma, es probable que te enteres del impacto de la ayuda estatal en el paquete total, sólo después que tu hijo se haya inscrito.

Esta ayuda por lo general se entrega directamente a la universidad de tu hijo y se considera como un recurso siempre disponible a partir del momento que se crea tu paquete. Mira cuidadosamente los términos y condiciones de la ayuda estatal, puesto que puede estar restringida a su uso en el estado, a componentes específicos de los gastos de asistencia (por ejemplo, sólo matrícula y cuotas), o en casos de otorgamientos especiales, estar restringidos a programas de especialización específicos. Si tu hijo ha recibido una oferta de ayuda estatal, debe entregar la aceptación firmada antes de la fecha límite estipulada. Nuevamente insistimos, debes ser muy estricto con las fechas límites publicadas; de no hacerlo, generalmente pierdes el otorgamiento y, salvo en circunstancias extraordinarias, no se restablece la ayuda estatal.

Notificación de ayuda de fuentes privadas

Tanto el estilo como la fecha pueden variar en la notificación de ayuda privada. En algunos casos recibes cierto tipo de notificación, independientemente de si tu hijo realmente recibe o no algún dinero. En otros casos, sólo se notifica a los candidatos aprobados. Algunas organizaciones te notifican en la primavera, otras en el verano y otras a principios del otoño.

Si tu hijo recibe fondos de una fuente externa a la universidad, es importante informar inmediatamente a la oficina de ayuda financiera. Si no lo haces, es probable que tengas que reembolsar toda o parte de la ayuda recibida y arriesgar tu futura elegibilidad para ayuda estudiantil.

Lo bueno de las becas privadas es que se trata de dinero "gratis" para la universidad y se entrega a los estudiantes a manera de "donación". Lo malo es que los estudiantes se enteran de este tipo de ayuda demasiado tarde como para tenerlo en cuenta a la hora de seleccionar una universidad. Lo mismo sucede con el tiempo que cubre el otorgamiento. Muchas veces, es válida solamente durante un año. Te sugerimos que solicites cualquier ayuda disponible, pues sólo sabrás de dónde vendrá la ayuda cuando te la otorguen.

Cartas de otorgamiento de ayuda financiera institucional

Una vez que el administrador de ayuda financiera tenga toda la información y formularios necesarios, puede diseñar un paquete de ayuda para satisfacer las necesidades demostradas del estudiante. Una vez creado este paquete, la mayoría de universidades te envían una Carta de otorgamiento, también conocida como Notificación de ayuda financiera o Carta de oferta. Cualquier tipo de notificación de ayuda financiera se denomina Carta de otorgamiento.

La Carta de otorgamiento describe las fuentes, tipos y montos de la ayuda financiera ofrecida y es una especie de compromiso o contrato entre tu hijo y la universidad. Recuerda los términos y condiciones del otorgamiento y preocúpate de no hacer nada que arriesgue la ayuda a recibir. Es decir, lee cuidadosa y completamente la información que acompaña la Carta de otorgamiento, y cumple con todas las fechas límite estipuladas. Dado que los recursos son limitados, las universidades con frecuencia cancelan las ayudas a los estudiantes que no devuelven los formularios a tiempo, y la ofrecen a otros estudiantes elegibles que requieren ayuda. Aunque los administradores de ayudas tratan de asegurarse de que los estudiantes que merezcan ayuda la reciban, no pueden prolongarla indefinidamente. Es tu responsabilidad mantenerte en contacto con el funcionario de ayuda financiera de la institución, de lo contrario te arriesgas a perder la ayuda ofrecida.

Las Cartas de otorgamiento de cada universidad difieren en estilo y formato, pero generalmente tienen la misma información. Idealmente, tanto la Carta de otorgamiento como cualquier documento adjunto, contiene información específica y fácil de entender sobre:

- $ Los COA
- $ Cómo se determinó la necesidad de ayuda para tu hijo
- $ Una lista de tipos de ayuda financiera ofrecida
- $ Momento y frecuencia de desembolso: antes, durante o después del comienzo de clases; regularmente durante el período académico; trimestral o semestralmente, o con otra frecuencia según el calendario académico de la universidad

- $ Forma de desembolso de la ayuda (acreditación de la cuenta estudiantil de tu hijo o por pagos directos a ti o a tu hijo)
- $ Todas las condiciones de la oferta (requisitos académicos, carga académica mínima o avance académico satisfactorio)

Con frecuencia, las universidades te piden aceptar o desistir de las ayudas mediante la firma y devolución de la Carta de otorgamiento a la oficina de ayuda financiera. En caso de oferta de un préstamo, debes firmar formularios adicionales, tales como un pagaré. Si se trata de un Federal Family Education Loan, FFEL (Programa Federal de Préstamo Educativo Familiar), es necesario que completes la solicitud y el pagaré antes de que se desembolse dinero.

A continuación, encontrarás dos tipos de Cartas de otorgamiento, una de Princeton University y la otra de Rutgers University, donde podrás familiarizarte con la información que generalmente contienen.

THE STATE UNIVERSITY OF NEW JERSEY

RUTGERS

FINANCIAL AID AWARD LETTER

2003-2004

Date: 03/25/03
ID#:
College: Rutgers College

Award Information

Your awards are based on the information you reported on your Free Application for Federal Student Aid. Your eligibility for these awards may change if new information is received, including information we may receive with regard to your Satisfactory Academic Progress. Rutgers University reserves the right to adjust your awards.

Please read the Award Letter Guide, enclosed with your initial Award Letter. The Guide explains how to complete the financial aid process. Award information, the Guide, and terms and conditions for receiving aid at Rutgers are online at studentaid.rutgers.edu. You are responsible for understanding these terms and eligibility requirements.

Awards

We are pleased to offer you the following assistance for the 2003-2004 academic year.

	Fall	Spring	Summer	Total
FEDERAL PELL GRANT	$1,000	$1,000	$0	$2,000
NJ EDUC OPPORTUNITY FUND (EOF)	$500	$500	$0	$1,000
FEDERAL PERKINS LOAN	$350	$350	$0	$700
FEDERAL WORK STUDY PROGRAM	$500	$500	$0	$1,000
DIRECT LOAN SUBSIDIZED	$1,250	$1,250	$0	$2,500
DIRECT LOAN UNSUBSIDIZED	$500	$500	$0	$1,000
Total:	$4,100	$4,100	$0	$8,200
Term Bill Credit (see Award Letter Guide)	$3,575	$3,575	$0	$7,150

What To Do Next:

- Verify that accurate assumptions (see next page) have been used to determine your awards.
- Carefully review and follow the instructions on the enclosed Data Change Form.
- **To reduce or decline all or part of your loans, you must complete and return the Data Change Form.**
- We will assume you fully accept the awards above unless you submit changes to us immediately.
- Return corrections and required documents promptly.
- **Retain this letter for your records.**

REQUIRED DOCUMENTS

DOCUMENTS NECESSARY TO COMPLETE YOUR AWARD: Please submit the following documents to the Office of Financial Aid as soon as possible. Failure to respond will result in the delay or loss of your aid.

-The verification worksheet
-A signed copy of your parent(s) 2002 Federal income tax return
-Two signed copies of the Perkins Loan Promissory Note*
-A Job Placement Form for work-study

Promissory Note(s) not required if you decline the loan. The Job Placement Form not required if Federal Work Study declined. To decline either, promptly complete and return the Data Change Form.

03/25/03

DATA CHANGE FORM

Return this form only if you change or update the information listed below. REMINDER: When all required documents are received, your Direct Loans automatically disburse to your student account unless you indicate otherwise. Once disbursed, you are responsible for repayment of these loans under the terms of the promissory note.

I. ENROLLMENT ASSUMPTIONS

You will be a full-time student registered for 12 or more credits per term for the 2003-04 academic year.

This is incorrect. I will be enrolled for:

- ☐ 9 to 11.5 credits
- ☐ 6 to 8.5 credits
- ☐ 5.5 or fewer credits

You will be residing off-campus (not in parents' home).

This is incorrect. I will live:

- ☐ On-Campus
- ☐ With my Parents

II. ALL GRADUATE STUDENTS

You are required to report any financial support you will be receiving from your academic department during the 2003-04 academic year. If you are awarded departmental assistance after the receipt of this letter you are required to notify the Office of Financial Aid immediately. Depending upon the amount of your departmental assistance it may be necessary to reduce the amount of federal financial aid shown on this letter. If so, you will be notified.

I will be receiving a:
☐ Teaching Assistantship ☐ Graduate Assistantship ☐ Fellowship ☐ Other ________

III. OPTIONAL: Change Loan or Federal Work-Study Awards

I wish to decline or reduce the amount of my loan(s) or work-study as indicated below.

REMINDER: Once we have all your required documents, your Direct Loans disburse to your student account unless you indicate otherwise and return this document to the address below immediately.

FEDERAL PERKINS LOAN	From: $700	To: ________	Comments: ________
FEDERAL WORK STUDY PROGRAM	From: $1,000	To: ________	Comments: ________
DIRECT LOAN SUBSIDIZED	From: $2,500	To: ________	Comments: ________
DIRECT LOAN UNSUBSIDIZED	From: $1,000	To: ________	Comments: ________

If you have made changes to any of the information above, promptly mail to:

Rutgers University
Office of Financial Aid
620 George Street
New Brunswick, NJ 08901-1175
(732) 932-7057
FAX: (732) 932-7385

Student Signature: ____________________ Date: ____________

Princeton University

Undergraduate Financial Aid
Box 591, 220 West College
Princeton, New Jersey 08544-0591
Telephone: (609) 258-3330
Fax: (609) 258-0336

DATE

NAME
ADDRESS

Dear FIRST NAME:

Congratulations on your admission to Princeton's Class of 2007.

We have carefully reviewed your application for financial aid and have determined that you are eligible for assistance to help with your expenses at Princeton. Your financial need for the 2003-04 academic year is $30870, the difference between the student budget and total family contribution listed below. The combination of financial aid and your family's resources should enable you to cover your costs for the coming year.

PRINCETON GRANT	$28480
STUDENT SELF-HELP AID	
Princeton Job (non-Federal Work-Study)	$2390
TOTAL FINANCIAL AID	**$30870**

As you can see, your total financial aid equals your need. You and your parents are also expected to pay a portion of your cost of attendance. Our estimate of your family's resources is:

Contribution from Parents	$6850
Your Summer Savings	1590
Share of Your Own Assets	330
Other Resources	0
TOTAL FAMILY CONTRIBUTION	**$8770**

Together, your financial aid and family contribution add up to your Princeton expenses. The student budget we have used for you is:

Basic Charges:		**Other Costs:**	
Tuition	$28540	Books & Personal Expenses	$2991
Room	4109		
Board	4000		

TOTAL STUDENT BUDGET **$39640**

Please keep in mind that financial aid from Princeton is awarded on the basis of need. No University aid is granted for academic, athletic, or other special talents and achievements.

In August you will receive a bill from the Student Accounts Office for the basic charges listed in your student budget, as well as for the student government fee, class dues, and the residential college fee which we have included under 'Books and Personal Expenses.' Your grants will be credited to your account, reducing the amount due the University. The total charges on your bill will be less than the student budget, because it includes out-of-pocket expenses such as books and personal items. If a job is part of your award, you will be paid directly. We assume you will use your earnings to help cover these expenses. The Student Employment Office will send you a job assignment in the summer.

Your aid award will not be made final until you submit a signed copy of your parents' 2002 federal income tax return including W-2 forms (or the equivalent if they worked outside the U.S.) by May 16, 2003. We will compare this information to the data submitted on the Princeton Financial Aid Application. It is possible that your aid award will be revised based on our review of actual income figures. If your parents are not required to file an income tax return, they should request a 'Parent Non-Filer Statement' from this office. In addition, U. S. citizens and permanent residents must file the Free Application for Federal Student Aid (FAFSA) by April 15, 2003 (or sooner if 2002 federal income tax information is available).

A 'Financial Aid Award Acceptance and Limited Power of Attorney' form is enclosed for you to sign and return. Also included is a pamphlet, 'Terms of Your Award,' which provides information about how we determined your eligibility for aid and the basic rules of our financial aid program. In addition, it describes both yearly and longer term options for paying the University bill.

If you have questions about any aspect of your aid award, you are encouraged to get in touch with a member of our staff.

Sincerely,

Don M. Betterton, Director
Undergraduate Financial Aid

DMB\ejv
Enclosures

Respuesta a la Carta de otorgamiento

Puedes aceptar, desistir o pedir aclaración cuando recibes una Carta de otorgamiento. Para aceptar el otorgamiento, por lo general, simplemente debes firmar la Carta de otorgamiento, aunque con frecuencia tienes que llenar formularios adicionales de solicitud de fondos específicos o firmar pagarés sobre préstamos. Desistir de un otorgamiento casi siempre es tan importante como aceptarlo; así, las universidades pueden redireccionar los fondos a otros estudiantes elegibles. Los fondos son limitados. Es necesario que desistas de la ayuda por escrito, y generalmente es un procedimiento que simplemente implica marcar una casilla en la Carta de otorgamiento, firmarla y devolverla a la oficina de ayuda financiera de la universidad. Recuerda que algunas universidades podrían redireccionar los fondos si no has contestado para una fecha específica.

Igualmente, puedes rechazar o declinar ciertos tipos de ayuda financiera. Por ejemplo, aceptar un otorgamiento federal de trabajo y estudio, pero desistir del préstamo. O es posible que quieras aceptar sólo una parte de un otorgamiento específico. Por ejemplo, si te han ofrecido un Federal Stafford Loan de $2,625 para tu hijo y después de analizar cuidadosamente tu presupuesto y recursos, decides que puedes satisfacer tu necesidad con menos, puedes solicitar en préstamo sólo $2,000. Es importante que pienses bien antes de desistir de una subvención, pues se trata de dinero "gratis" que no requiere de reembolso. Sin importar la situación, debes responder a todas las ayudas que te ofrezcan y, si es posible, explica brevemente la razón para desistir de una ayuda.

Una vez recibida la Carta de otorgamiento, es posible que la ayuda ofrecida te parezca insuficiente o que la quieras cambiar (por ejemplo, reemplazar un préstamo por trabajo); o que quieras analizar los términos de una beca privada o notificarle al administrador de ayuda financiera circunstancias familiares especiales, que pueden afectar el otorgamiento. En cualquiera de estos casos, debes consultar con el administrador de ayuda financiera. Si no te sientes contento o satisfecho, o sencillamente estás confundido sobre la ayuda que se le ofrece a tu hijo, ponte en contacto con el

Es importante que tú y tu hijo analicen y entiendan completamente todos los tipos de ayuda ofrecida, junto con las estipulaciones del otorgamiento. Si tienes preguntas o dudas sobre el contenido de la Carta de otorgamiento, comunícate sin demora con el funcionario de ayuda financiera.

funcionario de ayuda financiera de la universidad. Si te ves en una situación delicada o complicada, has una cita con el administrador de ayuda, y en lo posible, lleva toda la documentación o información del caso.

Nunca rechaces una de las universidades que preferías; peor aún, no interrumpas la educación de tu hijo afirmando que la ayuda financiera es insuficiente. En lugar de ello, consulta y estudia otras alternativas con un administrador de ayuda. Ellos tratan de asegurar que los estudiantes que merezcan ayuda no sean rechazados por razones económicas y son solidarios en circunstancias especiales, si tienen claridad de que realmente son circunstancias especiales.

AYUDA FINANCIERA DESPUÉS DEL PRIMER AÑO

Nunca asumas que el otorgamiento concedido a tu hijo será igual para cada año siguiente, incluso si pretende asistir a la misma universidad. Las políticas de otorgamiento varían de una universidad a otra. Algunas ofrecen diferentes tipos de paquetes de ayuda en función del nivel de estudios de tu hijo. Otras asignan mayor subvención y menos auto-ayuda para el primer año. A medida que tu hijo adquiera experiencia y disminuya el riesgo de fracasar en sus estudios, puede aumentar el monto del préstamo o trabajo ofrecido para los años siguientes. Las universidades con fondos institucionales discrecionales pueden premiar a los estudiantes con alto rendimiento, ofreciéndoles mayor subvención o becas de ayuda por mérito para el futuro. Otras universidades tratan de mantener el nivel de ayuda ofrecido a los estudiantes de primer año durante todo el programa de estudios. No dudes en consultar las políticas universitarias de otorgamiento con el administrador de ayuda financiera.

CÓMO Y CUÁNDO SE RECIBE LA AYUDA FINANCIERA

Parte del proceso de notificación de otorgamiento es explicar cómo y cuándo se recibe la ayuda financiera. Puede pagarse por diferentes métodos. La universidad puede acreditar directamente la cuenta estudiantil de tu hijo con los fondos de ayuda financiera, puede pagarle a tu hijo en efectivo por cheque o puede desembolsar los fondos combinando estos dos métodos.

Normalmente, las universidades acreditan los fondos de ayuda financiera a la cuenta universitaria de tu hijo para pagar gastos como matrícula y cuotas. Si sobran fondos de la ayuda financiera, la institución gira un cheque a nombre de tu hijo por el saldo. Este dinero puede utilizarse para otros gastos educativos como libros y materiales, transporte, alojamiento y alimentación fuera del campus (incluso si vive en su casa) y gastos personales misceláneos. Tu hijo no debe presentar recibos para demostrar cómo utiliza este dinero.

Generalmente, la Carta de otorgamiento indica el monto de ayuda que puedes recibir para todo el año académico. Sin embargo, la ayuda se entrega en cuotas y no de una sola vez. Si el sistema de la universidad de tu hijo es trimestral, generalmente se deposita una tercera parte del otorgamiento al principio del trimestre de otoño, otra tercera parte al principio del trimestre de invierno y la última tercera parte al inicio del trimestre de primavera. Si el sistema de la universidad es semestral, se deposita la mitad del otorgamiento al principio del semestre de otoño y la otra mitad al inicio del semestre de primavera.

La mayoría de universidades depositarán todos los fondos estudiantiles de tu hijo para un período de estudios determinado al inicio del mismo período. Sin embargo, para ayudar a los estudiantes a presupuestar sus fondos, algunas universidades hacen pagos menores a lo largo de cada período académico.

Por lo general, las universidades no acreditan los fondos otorgados por medio de un otorgamiento federal universitario de trabajo y estudio. Tu hijo debe ganar ese dinero antes de que se deposite en su cuenta estudiantil.

¿QUÉ SIGUE?

Luego de aceptar la oferta de ayuda financiera de una universidad, debes estar pendiente de ciertos aspectos relacionados con la forma en como la recibirás:

- $ El monto de la ayuda que recibe tu hijo como excedente de los gastos de matrícula, cuotas, y otros gastos relacionados con los cursos, tales como libros y materiales, generalmente se considera ingreso sujeto a impuestos; como tal, debe reportarse en la declaración de impuestos sobre la renta de Estados Unidos que presente tu hijo.

- $ Un otorgamiento de trabajo y estudio se refiere básicamente a que tu hijo es elegible para ganar esa cantidad de dinero durante el año del otorgamiento. Tu hijo debe conseguir un empleo que le permita estudiar antes de recibir el pago, e igualmente trabajar el número de horas necesarias, de manera que gane suficiente para cubrir la totalidad del otorgamiento. El otorgamiento trabajo y estudio no significa que le pagarán a tu hijo por estudiar.
- $ Se requiere una solicitud de préstamo separada para solicitar y recibir dinero del Federal Stafford Loan Program (Programa Federal de Préstamo Stafford) o PLUS Loan Program (Programa de Préstamo PLUS). La oficina de ayuda financiera de la universidad te puede facilitar los formularios y la información sobre los prestamistas participantes. Aunque otros programas de préstamo federal no requieren solicitudes por separado, debes firmar pagarés para cualquier desembolso de fondos.

Capítulo 5

Recursos para ayuda basada en las necesidades

Comencemos por lo básico.

Anualmente, el gobierno federal suministra más de $80 mil millones en subvenciones, préstamos y programas de trabajo que facilitan el ingreso a la universidad a millones de estudiantes elegibles. La clave es saber cómo hacerse elegible. Este capítulo describe los diferentes programas federales de ayuda financiera estudiantil, con énfasis en las ayudas disponibles basadas en las necesidades que ofrece el Departamento de Educación de Estados Unidos, el Departamento de Salud y Servicios Humanos de Estados Unidos y el Departamento del Interior de Estados Unidos. También hay disponible información sobre fuentes de ayuda estatales, institucionales y privadas.

La ayuda basada en las necesidades conforma la mayor parte de las ayudas disponibles para educación superior. Se considera que tienes necesidad financiera si no cuentas con suficientes recursos para seguir pagando la educación de tu hijo cuando termina la secundaria. Aunque la necesidad financiera es el principal requisito para lograr ayuda basada en las necesidades, tienes que cumplir con otras condiciones de elegibilidad. Debes dar tu información financiera para analizarla con fórmulas definidas que determinan si tienes suficientes recursos financieros para cubrir gastos universitarios. Esta evaluación de necesidad, también llamada análisis de necesidad, da como origen a un EFC, que se refiere a la cantidad en dólares que pueden aportar un estudiante y su familia para gastos educativos durante un año determinado.

La ecuación de necesidades

Para fines de ayuda financiera estudiantil, la necesidad se expresa como una ecuación con dos componentes:

Gastos de asistencia, COA

– Expected Family Contribution, EFC

= Necesidad financiera

El EFC se calcula por un proceso llamado análisis de necesidad. Cada universidad determina su COA, de modo que varía de una universidad a otra. Por lo general, los siguientes gastos se incluyen en los gastos de asistencia de cualquier universidad:

- $ Matrícula y cuotas
- $ Alojamiento
- $ Comida
- $ Libros y materiales
- $ Transporte
- $ Gastos personales

Las universidades también pueden incluir los costos asociados con solicitud de préstamos educativos, estudios en el exterior, compra de computadora personal, participación en un programa de educación cooperativa y alguna discapacidad, si corresponde.

Los gastos estimados de asistencia a una universidad son un ejemplo del tipo de información del consumidor estudiantil que la universidad debe dar a la familia.

Las universidades que participan en programas federales de ayuda estudiantil deben tener disponible cierto tipo de información para los aspirantes. Debes examinar cuidadosamente los gastos publicados a fin de asegurarte de que sean reales y razonables para ti en cuanto a las metas profesionales de tu hijo.

El tipo de universidad que escoja tu hijo (pública, privada, vocacional, de oficios o técnica, con estudios a dos o a cuatro años, universidad de posgrado/profesional, instituto de enseñanza para la comunidad local, universidad distante con residencias, en el estado, fuera del estado, o en el exterior) puede tener gran influencia sobre los gastos de asistencia, al igual que sobre los tipos y fuentes de ayuda disponibles para los gastos COA. Los gastos pueden variar de una universidad a otra, pero por lo general, el EFC no varía. En términos generales, la necesidad financiera aumenta cuando aumentan los gastos de asistencia.

PROGRAMAS ADMINISTRADOS POR EL DEPARTAMENTO DE EDUCACIÓN DE ESTADOS UNIDOS

La mayoría de los programas de ayuda federal se iniciaron o consolidaron mediante la Higher Education Act, HEA (Ley de Educación Superior) de 1965 y los administra el Departamento de Educación de Estados Unidos. Los programas más comunes son:

- Federal Pell Grant
- Federal Supplemental Educational Opportunity Grant, FSEOG
- Federal Perkins Loan
- Federal Work-Study, FWS
- Federal Family Education Loan Program, FFEL
- Federal Stafford Loan (subsidiado y no subsidiado)
- Parent Loans for Undergraduate Student, PLUS (Préstamos para Padres de Estudiantes Universitarios)
- William D. Ford Federal Direct Loan Program (Programa de Préstamo Federal Directo Willam D. Ford)
- Direct Subsidized and Direct Unsubsidized Loans

Estos se conocen como programas del Título IV porque están autorizados conforme al Título IV de la Higher Education Act de 1965, según enmienda.

Los programas Federal Pell Grant, FSEOG, Federal Perkins Loan, Federal Work-Study, Federal Subsidized Stafford y Direct Subsidized Loan se basan en las necesidades. Esto quiere decir que al determinar la elegibilidad para recibir fondos de estos programas, se considera el EFC. El William D. Ford Federal Direct Loan Program, conocido como el Direct Loan Program, es relativamente nuevo dentro del escenario de la ayuda financiera. Según el programa adoptado por cada universidad (algunas aplican ambos), podrás solicitar un préstamo al Federal Family Education Loan Program o al Direct Loan Program por un período determinado de inscripciones. Sin embargo, no puedes pedir préstamo a ambos programas al mismo tiempo porque cada universidad sólo puede participar en uno de los dos.

Información general y criterios de elegibilidad

Además de la necesidad, hay otros criterios de elegibilidad para recibir dinero de programas de ayuda estudiantil Título IV. Éstos incluyen:

1. **El estudiante debe ser ciudadano de Estados Unidos o no-ciudadano elegible.**

   Ciudadano de Estados Unidos es un ciudadano de alguno de los cincuenta estados, el distrito de Columbia, Puerto Rico, las Islas Vírgenes, Guam o las Islas Marianas del Norte. Los no-ciudadanos elegibles incluyen ciudadanos naturalizados de Estados Unidos, residentes permanentes de Estados Unidos que tengan tarjeta I-151, I-551 ó I-551C (Alien Registration Receipt Card (Tarjeta de recepción de registro de extranjería)); o personas que tengan un registro de entrada y salida al país (I-94) del Bureau of Citizenship and Immigration Services, BCIS (Oficina de Ciudadanía y Servicios de Inmigración), (anteriormente llamada Immigration and Naturalization Service, INS (Servicio de Inmigración y Naturalización)) bajo una de las siguientes designaciones: refugiado, asilado, libertad indefinida bajo palabra, libertad humanitaria bajo palabra, inmigrante cubano-haitiano o inmigrante condicional (válido sólo si se expide antes del 1° de abril de 1980).

2. **El estudiante debe estar inscrito o aceptado en un programa elegible conducente a título o certificado, u otro programa conducente a una credencial educativa reconocida en una institución superior elegible.**

   No todas las universidades están aprobadas por el Departamento de Educación para participar en programas de ayuda financiera estudiantil, sea por selección o por exclusión.

   Además, tu hijo debe ser admitido a la universidad para obtener un título u otra credencial educativa reconocida. Los estudiantes inscritos en estos programas también pueden recibir Federal Pell Grants, FWS, Federal Perkins o Direct Loans.

3. **El estudiante no puede estar simultáneamente inscrito en una escuela secundaria.**

   Este criterio afecta a estudiantes que están terminando todo o parte de su último año de secundaria en una universidad local.

4. **El estudiante debe tener un diploma de secundaria, su equivalente reconocido o tener la capacidad de beneficiarse del programa de estudios.**

   Si tu hijo no tiene un diploma de secundaria o su equivalente reconocido (generalmente, un diploma con equivalencia del grado de secundaria o un certificado estatal), debe demostrar que puede beneficiarse de la capacitación o educación. Esto lo demuestra si aprueba un examen administrado independientemente y acreditado por el Departamento de Educación de Estados Unidos.

   Tu hijo puede ser elegible para ayuda conforme al Título IV si tuvo excelentes resultados académicos, no terminó la secundaria y quiere ahora inscribirse en un programa educativo para obtener al menos un título asociado o su equivalente. Para la admisión de este tipo de estudiantes, se debe cumplir con la política formalizada y escrita de la universidad y se debe presentar documentación que acredite excelencia académica en secundaria.

   Si tu hijo terminó la secundaria en el marco de una escuela domiciliaria, es posible que obtenga la elegibilidad para ayuda a cosecuencia del Título IV, si la ley estatal considera esta escuela como domiciliaria o privada.

5. **El estudiante debe presentar un número de seguro social válido y verificable.**

   Una parte del proceso de solicitud que hace la Administración del Seguro Social es la verificación por medio de una base de datos de los números de Seguro Social de todos los solicitantes de ayuda financiera federal. Este número, el nombre y apellido, y la fecha de nacimiento de tu hijo se comparan con los archivos de la Administración del Seguro Social. Si la comparación no coincide, tu hijo deberá presentar a la universidad verificación de su número de seguro social para recibir cualquier tipo de ayuda federal estudiantil.

   Para evitar demoras y confusiones innecesarias, si tu hijo usa un nombre diferente al registrado en los archivos del Seguro Social, debes informar el cambio de nombre a la Administración del Seguro Social con bastante anticipación para solicitar ayuda federal estudiantil.

6. **El estudiante debe preguntar en la oficina de ayuda financiera de la universidad si debe presentar un Financial Aid Transcript, FAT (Certificado de ayuda financiera).**

Anteriormente, los solicitantes de ayuda federal estudiantil debían presentar un FAT impreso de cada universidad a la que habían asistido. Los FAT contienen información sobre el historial de ayuda financiera recibida y se usan para verificar ciertos aspectos de elegibilidad para ayuda federal. En la mayoría de los casos, las universidades pueden hoy obtener electrónicamente la información FAT necesaria desde una base de datos del Departamento de Educación, llamada National Student Loan Data System, NSLDS (Sistema Nacional de Información sobre Préstamos Estudiantiles). La universidad debe recibir la información que requiera sobre ayuda financiera y si te solicita la información FAT en papel, debes cumplir con la petición.

Muchas universidades extranjeras, aprobadas para participar en los programas a consecuencia del Título IV, no están registradas en el centro de intercambio de información federal; por lo tanto, pueden pedir el perfil FAT a estudiantes que hayan asistido anteriormente a una universidad.

7. **El estudiante debe firmar una Statement of Educational Purpose (Declaración de Propósito Educativo) que confirme que todos los dineros federales que reciba los utilizará solamente para gastos educativos.**

Todos los beneficiarios de ayuda federal financiera deben firmar una declaración en la que se comprometen a usar todo dinero recibido del programa federal para pagar gastos educativos en las universidades donde estudian. No olvides que cualquier dinero recibido como ayuda federal financiera debes usarlo para pagar matrículas y cuotas, libros y materiales, gastos razonables de manutención y personales, así como otros gastos directamente relacionados con estudios superiores. Este requisito se cumple simplemente al completar y firmar la FAFSA, que contiene la Statement of Educational Purpose en la sección de firmas.

8. **Si es necesario, el estudiante debe registrarse en el Servicio Selectivo.**

   Al cumplir 18 años, todos los varones deben registrarse en el Servicio Selectivo, incluidos ciudadanos de Estados Unidos, residentes permanentes y otros no ciudadanos elegibles.

   Nota: Este registro debe hacerse entre los 18 y 26 años de edad, ya que tu hijo no se puede registrar luego de este límite de edad. No registrarse en el Servicio Selectivo constituye una violación federal y puede traducirse en una multa o encarcelamiento.

9. **Los beneficios federales del estudiante no se pueden haber suspendido o terminado como resultado de una condena por un delito relacionado con drogas.**

   La Reauthorization Act (Ley de Reautorización) de 1998 estipula que se suspenda la elegibilidad para ayuda federal estudiantil en el caso de estudiantes que hayan sido condenados por violar cualquier ley federal o estatal sobre posesión o venta de drogas.

10. **El estudiante debe mantener un avance académico satisfactorio en su programa de estudios.**

    Las normas de avance académico satisfactorio varían de una universidad a otra. Sin embargo, para ser beneficiario de ayuda federal, tu hijo debe mantener un promedio mínimo de calificaciones y cumplir una cantidad mínima de unidades o de horas-reloj en cada período académico.

11. **El estudiante no debe estar en una situación de incumplimiento en el pago de un préstamo federal educativo anterior, ni deber un pago excesivo de una subvención o préstamo educativo federal anterior, ni solicitar préstamos por encima de los límites federales establecidos para préstamos estudiantiles.**

    Si tu hijo se encuentra en una situación de incumplimiento de pago o debe un pago excesivo, puede recobrar su elegibilidad al pagar la deuda o establecer condiciones de pago satisfactorias para el acreedor.

12. El estudiante debe cumplir con los requisitos adicionales específicos al programa.

Las siguientes secciones describen en detalle los programas de ayuda estudiantil administrados por el Departamento de Educación de Estados Unidos. Las páginas 89 y 90 muestran un cuadro que resume tales programas.

Federal Pell Grant Program

En términos de cobertura, el Federal Pell Grant es el segundo programa federal más grande de ayuda estudiantil y proporciona ayuda en subvenciones a estudiantes que aún no han obtenido su diploma universitario, ni un primer título profesional. El objetivo del programa es ayudar a los estudiantes más necesitados. Las Federal Pell Grants pueden obtenerse cuando se está inscrito para tiempo completo, medio tiempo o aún menos de medio tiempo. La Federal Pell Grant tiene características exclusivas y una de ellas es su calidad portátil, lo cual quiere decir que puede usarse en cualquier universidad a la que asista tu hijo. Además, dicha beca no depende de la disponibilidad de fondos en una universidad en particular.

El administrador de ayuda financiera calcula la asignación real con base en tu EFC, los gastos de asistencia y el estatus de inscripción, y puesto que éstos varían de una universidad a otra, también varía la subvención otorgada por la Federal Pell Grant.

Veamos a continuación algunas características notables de la Federal Pell Grant:

- $ **Es una donación (dinero gratis). Es decir, no tienes que reembolsarla ni trabajar para pagarla.**
- $ **La elegibilidad no depende de la disponibilidad de fondos de alguna universidad en particular. Podrás recibir ayuda del programa Federal Pell Grant si la solicitas dentro de las fechas establecidas, demuestras el nivel exigido de necesidades y cumples con todas las condiciones generales y de elegibilidad.**
- $ **Es portátil, lo cual hace que, si eres elegible para una Federal Pell Grant, puedes usarla para estudiar en cualquier programa elegible de cualquier universidad elegible.**
- $ **El monto anual concedido por la Federal Pell Grant depende, en parte, del monto que asigne el Congreso para el programa. Para el año 2003-2004, la máxima subvención basada en las asignaciones fijadas por el Congreso es de $4,050.**

Programas con base en el campus

Los programas con base en el campus son tres:

1. **Federal Supplemental Educational Opportunity Grants**
2. **Federal Work-Study**
3. **Federal Perkins Loans**

El Departamento de Educación asigna estos fondos a universidades participantes a fin de que los concedan a solicitantes elegibles para ayuda financiera. Al contrario del programa de la Federal Pell Grant, ser beneficiario de estos programas con base en el campus depende de la disponibilidad de fondos de una universidad en particular. Esto significa que las subvenciones basadas en el campus no pueden trasladarse de una universidad a otra. Los tipos y montos de los fondos que concede este programa pueden variar entre universidades, aunque no cambie el EFC y los gastos de asistencia continúen siendo similares.

Al igual que con la Federal Pell Grant, tu hijo es elegible para fondos con base en el campus si está inscrito como estudiante de tiempo completo, de tiempo parcial o aún de menos de tiempo parcial, aunque, por lo general, el monto disponible para estudiantes inscritos menos de tiempo parcial es más limitada. No olvides que la cantidad de fondos con base en el campus puede variar, aun después de que tu hijo empiece a asistir a la universidad, especialmente si recibe fondos adicionales externos, como una beca privada.

Federal Supplemental Educational Opportunity Grant (FSEOG) Program

Este programa suministra fondos a estudiantes universitarios con una necesidad excepcional, que no han obtenido un diploma universitario ni un primer título profesional. Se da prioridad a los estudiantes elegibles para una Federal Pell Grant y con un EFC más bajo, según lo determine la universidad. La subvención FSEOG mínima que una universidad puede dar por año es $100 y la máxima es $4,000. La subvención mínima puede prorratearse si tu hijo está inscrito por menos de un año académico completo; si está inscrito en un programa aprobado de estudio en el extranjero, podrá recibir hasta $4,400 al año. Al igual que la Federal Pell Grant, la FSEOG es una donación, lo que significa que no tiene que ganarse trabajando ni ser reembolsada. Sin embargo, al contrario de la Federal Pell Grant, el monto real concedido está sujeto a la disponibilidad de fondos en la universidad escogida por tu hijo.

Federal Work-Study Program, FWS

Este programa proporciona trabajo a estudiantes que necesitan ganar dinero para pagar parte de sus gastos educativos. Tanto los estudiantes universitarios como de posgrado son elegibles para recibir ayuda FWS. El gobierno federal provee los fondos para cubrir hasta el 75 por ciento del salario de los estudiantes; la universidad u otro empleador paga el resto.

El número de horas que tu hijo debe trabajar cada semana varía de una universidad a otra y de un estudiante a otro. Esto depende de la cantidad asignada en la beca de estudio y trabajo, la tarifa de pago por hora o la cantidad de tiempo que tu hijo pueda trabajar.

A diferencia de otros programas de ayuda federal estudiantil, no existen límites sobre el monto que la universidad puede asignar, siempre y cuando la cantidad asignada y tus otros recursos no excedan la necesidad demostrada. Generalmente, las universidades tienen una política que establece montos de asignación razonables en las becas de estudio y trabajo, para asegurarse de que el número de horas trabajado no interfiera con los estudios académicos de tu hijo. Aunque normalmente los estudiantes pueden ganar sus becas FWS trabajando durante el año académico, algunas universidades permiten que obtengas parte del dinero trabajando durante el verano o en los recesos universitarios.

El empleo puede ser en el campus o fuera de él; el empleador puede ser la universidad, el estado, un organismo público local o federal (excepto el Departamento de Educación), o una organización privada sin o con fines de lucro. Los empleados de Federal Work-Study deben recibir un pago por lo menos igual al actual salario mínimo federal. El tipo de trabajo varía. Es común que se ofrezcan empleos en el servicio de comidas o como asistente de oficinas, especialmente para estudiantes sin experiencia previa. También se encuentran disponibles empleos como asistentes de laboratorios, auxiliares de bibliotecas y otros más especializados. Algunas universidades asignan trabajos específicos a los estudiantes FWS, mientras que otras simplemente les permiten participar competitivamente en las ofertas disponibles.

Si tu hijo recibe una beca FWS, debes tener en cuenta lo siguiente:

- $ **Las becas FWS deben pagarse con trabajo y el salario depende del número de horas reales de trabajo.**
- $ **Debes comunicarte con la oficina de ayuda financiera o con la oficina de empleo estudiantil para obtener un trabajo.**

Federal Perkins Loan Program

Éste es el programa de préstamo más antiguo que administra el Departamento de Educación y es una fuente de préstamos a bajo interés (actualmente 5 por ciento) para estudiantes universitarios, de posgrado y profesionales. Si tu hijo está inscrito en una universidad al menos a tiempo parcial, no se cobran intereses. Las universidades deben dar prioridad a los estudiantes que demuestren una gran necesidad financiera, para asignar los Federal Perkins Loans. Los estudiantes universitarios pueden solicitar un préstamo de hasta $4,000 cada año, hasta una suma máxima acumulada de $20,000. Los estudiantes que participen en programas aprobados de estudios en el exterior, pueden también recibir estos préstamos. De hecho, tu hijo puede ser elegible para pedir en préstamo montos anuales y acumulados mayores a los mencionados anteriormente, hasta un 20 por ciento.

El reembolso de estos préstamos comienza nueve meses después de la graduación o cuando tu hijo deje de ser estudiante mínimo a tiempo parcial. Esto se conoce como período de gracia. El plazo máximo de reembolso es 10 años, según el monto prestado. Los beneficiarios que califican por bajos ingresos, pueden tener hasta diez años adicionales para reembolsar la deuda. No hay sanción por pago anticipado de la totalidad o parte de un Federal Perkins Loan.

Además de cumplir con las condiciones generales de elegibilidad, los beneficiarios deben:

- $ **Recibir un aviso de elegibilidad o no elegibilidad para la Federal Pell Grant**
- $ **Estar dispuesto a reembolsar el préstamo**
- $ **Suministrar un número de licencia de conducir (si tu hijo posee una)**

El reembolso puede posponerse o interrumpirse por períodos específicos bajo ciertas condiciones, lo que se conoce como aplazamiento. Todos los préstamos se aplazan mientras tu hijo se encuentre inscrito en una universidad elegible, como mínimo medio tiempo. Algunos aplazamientos tienen condiciones muy específicas, mientras que otros tienen duración limitada. El interés no se acumula durante los períodos de aplazamiento y, al final de cada período, los beneficiarios tienen derecho a otros seis meses de gracia antes de reiniciar el reembolso. En condiciones más limitadas, puedes ser elegible para que se te condone la totalidad o parte del Perkins Loan. Puedes obtener mayor información sobre aplazamientos y condonaciones del administrador universitario de ayuda financiera.

Federal Family Education Loan Program, FFEL

Este programa es una serie de programas de préstamo estudiantil con respaldo federal que incluyen el Federal Subsidized Stafford Loan y Federal Unsubsidized Stafford Loan, a largo plazo y con bajo interés para estudiantes que asisten a universidades elegibles. En circunstancias especiales, estos préstamos pueden utilizarse para asistir a universidades extranjeras elegibles. Este programa incluye también el PLUS Loan, disponible para que puedas pagar la matrícula de tu hijo.

La fuente de fondos para este programa es capital privado de bancos, corporaciones de ahorro y préstamo, cooperativas de crédito y otras instituciones de préstamo. En ciertos casos, las universidades, organismos estatales y agencias privadas sin fines de lucro, también pueden ser prestamistas. El programa FFEL es administrado por agencias de garantía que aseguran contra pérdida a los prestamistas con el respaldo del gobierno federal, en caso de que el beneficiario no reembolse el préstamo o no pueda hacerlo. Puedes obtener información detallada sobre préstamos en la mayoría de centros de consejería de escuelas secundarias, bancos, universidades locales, Internet y en www.petersons.com.

El Federal Stafford Loan Program es la mayor fuente de préstamos estudiantiles de bajo interés, administrado por el Departamento de Educación de Estados Unidos y está disponible para estudiantes universitarios y de posgrado. Los préstamos realizados por este programa pueden ser subsidiados, no subsidiados, o una combinación de ambos. A continuación, describimos en mayor detalle los préstamos con y sin subsidio, conceptos que pueden ser nuevos para ti.

PLUS Loans

Los Parent Loans for Undergraduate Students están destinados a padres de estudiantes dependientes para ayudar a las familias con problemas de flujo de efectivo. No es necesario pasar una prueba para medir tu necesidad y, son otorgados por prestamistas de FFEL o directamente por el Departamento de Educación. El préstamo tiene una tasa de interés variable que no puede exceder el 9 por ciento y no tiene límite específico anual. Puedes pedir prestado un monto que cubra los gastos de asistencia a la universidad, pero debes restarle cualquier monto que recibas de otra ayuda financiera. El reembolso comienza 60 días después de recibir el dinero. De los fondos del préstamo, se sustrae una cuota del 4 por ciento. Generalmente, los padres beneficiarios deben tener un buen historial crediticio para calificar para los préstamos PLUS. Según el tipo de programas de préstamo de cada universidad, el préstamo PLUS se asigna a través del sistema FFEL o del sistema de Direct Loan.

Federal Subsidized Stafford Loans

Un préstamo subsidiado es cuando el gobierno federal paga el interés al prestamista, mientras tu hijo esté estudiando y durante otros períodos en los que no esté obligado a hacer pagos. Como el gobierno paga los intereses mientras él esté asistiendo a la universidad, tu hijo no es responsable de estos intereses y por lo tanto, no se acumulan hasta el momento de reembolso. Sin embargo, cuando se inicia el período de reembolso, tu hijo responde por el pago del préstamo y por los intereses que se originen de ahí en adelante.

Para recibir un Federal Subsidized Stafford Loan, es necesario demostrar necesidad según la fórmula federal de necesidades. Es decir, para que seas elegible para un Federal Subsidized Stafford Loan, se resta tu EFC de los COA y el resultado debe ser mayor a cero. El préstamo también se reduce de acuerdo al monto recibido por otra ayuda otorgada y, por los límites máximos de préstamo anual aplicable al programa. Más adelante, describiremos brevemente estos conceptos.

Federal Unsubsidized Stafford Loans

Los préstamos no subsidiados se asignan a estudiantes que no demuestran necesidad según la fórmula antes mencionada, pero que se beneficiarían al tener acceso a un programa federal de préstamo estudiantil con bajo interés. En un préstamo no subsidiado, el gobierno federal no asume el pago de los intereses por el préstamo efectuado a tu hijo; por lo tanto, todos los intereses acumulados deben pagarse durante el período de duración del préstamo, incluidos los intereses acumulados mientras tu hijo estudia.

Los intereses acumulados mientras tu hijo estudia, se pueden pagar de dos formas:

1. **A medida que se liquidan (cuando se vencen o se acumulan)**
2. **Capitalizándolos (se suman al capital prestado y se deben reembolsar cuando tu hijo deje la universidad)**

La otra gran diferencia con un préstamo no subsidiado es que el EFC no se considera para determinar tu elegibilidad. Por esta razón, se conocen como préstamos no basados en la necesidad. La elegibilidad para un préstamo no subsidiado se determina con una fórmula alterna de necesidad, donde la universidad descuenta de los gastos de asistencia cualquier ayuda financiera estimada, incluso la elegibilidad para un Federal Subsidized Stafford Loan. El resultado de esta fórmula es el monto máximo que puedes solicitar del Federal Unsubsidized Stafford Loan Program. Sin embargo, dicho monto no puede, en ningún caso, exceder la cantidad máxima anual para préstamos, que analizaremos más adelante.

Lo que debes tener en cuenta es que, en este proceso, el interés acumulado se vuelve capital. Si escoges esta opción, terminarás pagando interés sobre interés (es decir, el interés acumulado que se ha capitalizado).

Esta diferencia en la definición de necesidad significa que, al contrario del Federal Subsidized Stafford Loan, el Federal Unsubsidized Stafford Loan se puede usar para remplazar el EFC, siempre que no haya sido reemplazado con otra forma de ayuda.

Son muchos los estudiantes elegibles para solicitar una combinación de Federal Stafford Loans subsidiados y no subsidiados. La elegibilidad para un Federal Subsidized Stafford Loan debe siempre determinarse antes de pedir un Federal Unsubsidized Stafford Loan; así, se asegura que los préstamos menos costosos, por esto los más deseables, se otorguen primero. Si continúas siendo elegible para un Federal Unsubsidized Stafford Loan, puedes solicitarlo, bajo condición de que no excedas tus límites anuales como beneficiario de préstamos.

Además de las condiciones generales de elegibilidad señaladas al comienzo de este capítulo, para que tu hijo sea elegible para un Federal Stafford Loan, debe:

- $ Estar inscrito o aceptado para inscripción al menos medio tiempo
- $ Obtener un aviso de elegibilidad o no elegibilidad para una Federal Pell Grant
- $ Estar inscrito en una universidad que tenga un promedio de incumplimiento de reembolsos aceptable entre los solicitantes anteriores

Recuerda que si la diferencia entre los gastos de asistencia y la ayuda financiera estimada es inferior a los límites anuales establecidos para el Stafford Loan, solamente puedes solicitar el monto que necesitas.

Muchas universidades incluyen automáticamente un Federal Stafford Loan como parte de su paquete de ayuda financiera y te notifican el monto exacto que puedes solicitar con este programa. No olvides que, al contrario de la Federal Pell Grant y de los programas con base en el campus, para ser beneficiario de un Federal Stafford Loan debes llenar el Federal Stafford Loan Master Promissory (Pagaré Maestro), además de la FAFSA. Verifica en la oficina de ayuda financiera de la universidad si es necesario presentar documentos adicionales. Si se aprueba un Federal Stafford Loan, la universidad envía usualmente el pagaré correspondiente, junto con la notificación oficial de asistencia financiera. El Federal Stafford Loan Promissory Note puede también conseguirse con prestamistas participantes en este programa.

En la mayoría de los casos, debes llenar este pagaré y devolverlo a la universidad. Aunque algunas universidades te devuelven la solicitud, de manera que puedas entregarla a un prestamista en particular, la mayoría de ellas envía directamente la solicitud al prestamista indicado en el pagaré.

Límites anuales para el Federal Stafford Loan

Los montos combinados totales que pueden solicitarse en Stafford Loans subsidiados y no subsidiados, no pueden exceder los límites anuales para préstamos establecidos en la ley y los reglamentos. Los montos máximos que se pueden solicitar son:

$2,625 al año para estudiantes universitarios de primer año

$3,500 al año para estudiantes universitarios de segundo año

$5,500 al año para los años restantes de estudios universitarios

$8,500 al año para estudios de posgrado y profesionales

Nota: Estos montos pueden cambiarse con re-autorización de las Enmiendas de Educación Superior para el 2003.

Límites acumulados del Stafford Loan

Todos los estudiantes pueden solicitar un monto total limitado en el Federal Stafford Loan Program durante sus estudios universitarios y de posgrado. Estos límites de préstamo se conocen como máximos acumulados de préstamo y varían dependiendo si tu hijo es un estudiante universitario o de posgrado.

Los estudiantes dependientes universitarios pueden pedir prestado $23,000 en préstamos subsidiados y no subsidiados y, si sus padres no califican para un PLUS Loan, pueden pedir en préstamo $23,000 con el Federal Subsidized Stafford Program y, $46,000 con el Federal Unsubsidized Stafford Loan Program, restando cualquier monto solicitado a través del Federal Subsidized Stafford Loan Program.

Tasa de interés

La tasa de interés para el período de reembolso sobre Federal Subsidized Stafford Loans es variable, se determina el 1° de junio de cada año y no puede exceder del 8.25 por ciento. Los mismos términos y condiciones aplican para los Federal Unsubsidized Stafford Loans, pero tu hijo asume los intereses mientras está estudiando y durante el período de reembolso.

Otros gastos asociados al préstamo

Los prestamistas están autorizados para cobrar cuotas de hasta el 3 por ciento del capital, por sus servicios; adicionalmente, se debe pagar una prima de seguros, que por ley no puede exceder el 1 por ciento del capital. El prestamista puede restar estos cargos de los fondos del préstamo. Se recomienda comparar las tasas y cargos antes de seleccionar un prestamista.

Además de las restricciones antes mencionadas para el Federal Stafford Loan, los estudiantes dependientes con padres que aplicaron y no pudieron conseguir un PLUS Loan, pueden solicitar un préstamo de hasta:

- **$6,625 por año, si eres estudiante de primer año en un programa de estudios que cubra, como mínimo, todo el año académico (por lo menos, $4,000 de este monto debe provenir de préstamos no subsidiados).**
- **$7,500 por año si has terminado tu primer año y el resto del programa de estudios ocupa, como mínimo, todo el año académico (por lo menos, $4,000 de este monto debe provenir de préstamos no subsidiados).**
- **$10,500 por año si has terminado tu segundo año y el resto del programa de estudios ocupa, como mínimo, todo el año académico (por lo menos, $5,000 de este monto debe provenir de préstamos no subsidiados).**

Requisito de consejería sobre préstamos

Antes de recibir fondos de un Federal Stafford Loan, es necesario que tu hijo pase por una consejería sobre préstamos para garantizar que se familiarice con los términos y responsabilidades del préstamo y que entienda perfectamente que debe reembolsar el préstamo. Una vez que se haya cumplido este requisito, la universidad utiliza los fondos del préstamo para gastos de matrícula y cuotas, alojamiento y alimentación, o bien, le entrega el dinero directamente a tu hijo. El dinero puede usarse en libros o para pagar gastos secundarios de asistencia a la universidad.

Reembolso

Pago del capital de un préstamo y, para préstamos subsidiados, de los intereses que se originen después de seis meses de que tu hijo termine estudios o, después de dejar de ser estudiante, como mínimo, de medio tiempo. Los préstamos deben reembolsarse dentro de un período de diez años a partir de la fecha de reembolso, sin incluir los períodos de aplazamiento o por indulgencia de morosidad.

Aplazamiento

Los aplazamientos permiten que los beneficiarios que cumplen con ciertas condiciones pospongan o interrumpan el reembolso. Los aplazamientos disponibles para el Federal Stafford Loan son similares a los del Federal Perkins Loan Program, pero estos tienen un solo período de gracia.

Si deseas mayor información sobre aplazamientos, comunícate con el administrador de ayuda financiera o prestamista. Visita también www.petersons.com en Internet y consulta la sección de ayuda financiera para entrar en la página de Sallie Mae Wired Scholar (disponible en español o inglés).

Además, el Departamento de Educación ofrece opciones de cancelación de préstamo para maestros elegibles:

- **Hasta $5,000 en Stafford Loans para maestros que enseñen en escuelas con bajos ingresos y que hayan recibido su primer Stafford Loan después del 1º de octubre de 1998. Para ser elegible, un maestro debe trabajar cinco años consecutivos en una escuela que haya sido designada como institución de "bajos ingresos".**
- **Hasta 100 por ciento de los Perkins Loans para un maestro que haya recibido su primer préstamo después del 1º de julio de 1987 y que cumpla con cualquiera de las siguientes condiciones:**
  - **Enseñar en un sistema escolar para niños con bajos ingresos**
  - **Enseñar en un sistema escolar con escasez de profesores para una materia en particular**
  - **Enseñar a estudiantes discapacitados en una escuela pública o en alguna otra institución primaria o secundaria sin fines de lucro**
- **Los Perkins Loans se cancelan sobre la base del número de años de enseñanza:**
  - **Cancelación del 15 por ciento anual durante el primer y segundo año**
  - **Cancelación del 20 por ciento durante el tercer y cuarto año**
  - **Cancelación del 30 por ciento durante el quinto año**

Para obtener mayor información, visita al administrador de ayuda financiera de la universidad.

Cancelación o condonación del préstamo

Tu Federal Stafford Loan queda cancelado en caso de muerte o de discapacidad permanente y total de tu hijo. Además, la participación de tu hijo en algunos programas de servicio nacional o comunitario puede hacer que se le condone parte del préstamo. Solicita mayores detalles sobre opciones de cancelación o condonación de préstamo al administrador de ayuda financiera o prestamista.

Resumen de información sobre programas de ayuda estudiantil universitaria bajo la administración del Departamento de Educación de Estados Unidos

Programa	Descripción	Anual/Total	Eligibilidad	Reembolso
Federal Pell Grant	Programa de subvenciones	Varían el mínimo y máximo anual; para 2003–2004, máximo $4,000; sin acumulado	Estudiantes sin primer grado universitario o profesional	No
Federal Supplemental Educational Opportunity Grant, FSEOG	Programa de subvenciones con sede en el campus; fondos otorgados por la institución	$100 mínimo anual; $4,000 máximo anual; sin acumulado (estudiantes de programas aprobados de estudio en el exterior pueden recibir hasta $4,400)	Estudiantes sin primer grado universitario o profesional; primero, estudiantes con gran necesidad financiera; prioridad a beneficiarios del Federal Pell Grant	No
Federal Work-Study, FWS	Programa de empleo con sede en el campus; fondos otorgados por la institución	N/A	Estudiantes universitarios	No
Federal Perkins Loan	Programa de préstamo con sede en el campus; fondos otorgados por la institución	$4,000/año para un máximo de $20,000; otorgados por la institución; estudiantes en el exterior: 5% de interés; pueden ser elegibles para solicitar montos máximos anuales y acumulados que excedan las sumas antes mencionadas hasta un 20%.	Primero, estudiantes con gran necesidad financiera; deben tener aviso de elegibilidad/no elegibilidad para Federal Pell Grant	Sí; comienza 9 meses después de dejar de ser estudiante como mínimo a tiempo parcial; posible aplazamiento, cláusulas de cancelación
Federal Stafford Loan	Federal Family Education Loan; fondos de capital privado con un 8.25% de interés máximo	$2,625/1er año; $3,500/2do año; $5,500/cada año restante a nivel universitario; máximos anuales prorrateados para programas y períodos restantes de estudios; total máximo para estudiante universitario $23,000	Estudiantes inscritos como mínimo a tiempo parcial, deben tener aviso de elegibilidad para Federal Subsidized Stafford, antes de solicitar la Federal Unsubsidized Stafford	Sí; comienza 6 meses después de dejar de ser estudiante como mínimo a tiempo parcial; posible aplazamiento, sin subsidio de interés en préstamos no subsidiados
Additional Unsubsidized Federal Stafford Loan (Préstamo Adicional Federal Stafford No Subsidiado): elegibilidad adicional para estudiantes universitarios independientes y cierto tipo de estudiantes universitarios dependientes	Federal Family Education Loan; fondos de capital privado con un 8.25% de interés máximo	$6625/1er ó 2do año de estudios universitarios; $7,500/cada año restante a nivel universitario; máximos anuales prorrateados para programas o períodos restantes de estudios; total máximo para estudios universitarios $46,000 acumulado en universitario menos los montos concedidos en Subsidized Stafford Loan	Estudiantes independientes y dependientes con padres que no pueden pedir un Federal PLUS Loan; deben tener aviso de elegibilidad para Federal Pell Grant y para el programa Federal Subsidized Stafford antes de aplicar al programa Federal Unsubsidized Stafford	Sí; igual que el Federal Stafford Loan

Programa	Descripción	Anual/Total	Eligibilidad	Reembolso
Federal PLUS Loan	Federal Family Education Loan; fondos de capital privado con un 9% de interés máximo	Sin montos anuales o acumulados, excepto que los padres no pueden pedir prestado más de la diferencia entre los gastos de asistencia y la ayuda financiera estimada	Padres de estudiantes universitarios dependientes elegibles, inscritos como mínimo a tiempo parcial con buen historial crediticio	Sí; comienza 60 días después del último desembolso; posible aplazamiento
Direct Subsidized/Direct Unsubsidized Loan	William D. Ford Federal Direct Loan; fondos otorgados por la institución en las universidades que participan con un 8.25% de interés máximo	$2,625/1er año; $3,500/2do año; $5,500/cada año restante a nivel universitario; máximos anuales prorrateados para programas y períodos restantes de estudios; total máximo para estudiantes universitarios, $23,000	Estudiantes universitarios; inscritos al menos a tiempo parcial; deben tener aviso de elegibilidad para Federal Pell Grant; deben tener aviso de elegibilidad para Direct Subsidized Loan antes de solicitar un Direct Unsubsidized Loan y deben asistir a una institución participante	Sí; comienza 6 meses después de dejar de ser estudiante como mínimo a tiempo parcial; posible aplazamiento, sin subsidio de interés en préstamos no subsidiados
Additional Unsubsidized Loan (Préstamo Adicional No Subsidiado): elegibilidad adicional para estudiantes universitarios independientes y cierto tipo de estudiantes universitarios dependientes	William D. Ford Federal Direct Loan; fondos otorgados por la institución en las universidades que participan con un 8.25% de interés máximo	$6,625/1er ó 2do año para estudios universitarios; $7,500/cada año restante a nivel de universitario; máximos anuales prorrateados para programas o períodos restantes de estudios; total máximo para estudiantes universitarios $46,000, menos montos prestados a través de Direct Loans subsidiados	Estudiantes independientes y dependientes con padres que no pueden pedir un Federal PLUS Loan y deben estar asistiendo a una institución participante	Sí; igual al anterior
Direct Plus Loan (Préstamo Directo PLUS)	William D. Ford Federal Direct Loan; fondos otorgados por la institución en las universidades que participan con un 9% de interés máximo	Sin montos anuales o acumulados, excepto que los padres no pueden pedir prestado más de la diferencia entre los gastos de asistencia y la ayuda financiera estimada	Padres de estudiantes universitarios dependientes, inscritos como mínimo a tiempo parcial, con buen historial crediticio; el estudiante debe asistir a una institución participante	Sí; comienza 60 días después del último desembolso; posible aplazamiento

William D. Ford Federal Direct Loan Program

Este programa incluye préstamos Direct Subsidized y Direct Unsubsidized. Es posible que también los conozcas como Direct Subsidized Stafford Loan o Direct Unsubsidized Stafford Loan. En 1994, el gobierno federal lanzó el William D. Ford Federal Direct Loan Program. Los plazos y condiciones del Direct Loan Program son casi idénticos a los del programa FFEL, excepto por la fuente de fondos, algunos aspectos del proceso de solicitud y los detalles administrativos del proceso de reembolso. La mayoría de las universidades participan en uno u otro de estos programas.

Aunque los programas Federal Stafford y Direct Loan son muy parecidos, vale la pena resaltar una diferencia: al contrario del programa Federal Stafford Loan, no hay solicitud adicional separada; sin embargo, debes llenar y firmar un pagaré antes de que puedas recibir fondos de un Direct Subsidized o Unsubsidized Loan.

Federal Direct Subsidized and Direct Unsubsidized Loan Program

Al igual que el Federal Stafford Loan Program, el Direct Loan Program ofrece también préstamos estudiantiles subsidiados y no subsidiados. Técnicamente, los Direct Subsidized y Direct Unsubsidized Loans son exactamente iguales a los Federal Stafford Loans subsidiados y no subsidiados. Por ejemplo, para ser beneficiario de un Direct Subsidized o Direct Unsubsidized Loan, debes completar y presentar la FAFSA, y los beneficiarios por primera vez deben asistir a una sesión de consejería sobre préstamos antes de recibir fondos.

PROGRAMAS ADMINISTRADOS POR EL DEPARTAMENTO DE SALUD Y SERVICIOS HUMANOS DE ESTADOS UNIDOS

Además de los programas de ayuda estudiantil administrados por el Departamento de Educación de Estados Unidos, son varios los programas de ayuda estudiantil administrados por el Departamento de Salud y Servicios Humanos, HHS (por sus siglas en inglés) para profesiones de la salud y enfermería:

- Nursing Student Loan, NSL (Préstamo para estudiantes de enfermería)
- Health Professions Student Loan, HPSL (Préstamo para estudiantes de profesiones de la salud)

- $ Scholarships for Disadvantaged Students, SDS (Becas para Estudiantes Desfavorecidos)
- $ National Health Service Corps (NHSC) Scholarship (Beca para el Cuerpo de Servicio de Salud Nacional)

A excepción de las NHSC, estos programas son similares a los programas con base en el campus administrados por el Departamento de Educación; por lo tanto, los fondos se asignan a las universidades para que los distribuyan a sus estudiantes elegibles en áreas específicas de cuidados de salud. Las universidades son responsables por la administración y el otorgamiento de fondos de programas según condiciones establecidas por el Departamento de Salud y Servicios Humanos.

Nursing Student Loan Program, NSL

Este programa otorga préstamos de bajo interés a estudiantes que asisten a escuelas aprobadas de enfermería, donde les ofrecen lo siguiente:

- $ Diploma
- $ Título asociado
- $ Grado universitario o equivalente
- $ Posgrado en enfermería

Los préstamos se pueden pedir para inscripción a tiempo completo o a tiempo parcial y los beneficiarios deben ser ciudadanos, nativos de Estados Unidos o residentes permanentes. Las universidades determinan los procedimientos de solicitud y selección. En la mayoría de los casos, los estudiantes de enfermería que llenan la FAFSA y cualquier otra documentación de solicitud, se considerarán automáticamente para este programa siempre que demuestren necesidad.

Las escuelas de enfermería pueden asignar hasta $2,500 por año académico, según la necesidad. Este límite anual aumenta hasta $4,000 durante los dos últimos años de un programa de enfermería. El máximo NSL acumulado es $13,000. El interés NSL es 5 por ciento y el reembolso del capital y de intereses comienza nueve meses después de que tu hijo se gradúe o deje de ser estudiante como mínimo medio tiempo. Los pagos pueden hacerse en forma mensual o trimestral y los prestatarios tienen hasta diez años para reembolsar su NSL.

Health Professions Student Loan Program

El programa Health Professions Student Loan (HPSL) otorga ayuda financiera a estudiantes inscritos en profesiones de áreas específicas de la salud. La ayuda se suministra en forma de préstamos a largo plazo y de bajos intereses. La tasa de interés HPSL es del 5 por ciento durante todo el préstamo. Los préstamos se pueden hacer a estudiantes de tiempo completo que busquen un título universitario o doctorado en ciencias farmacéuticas, odontología, podiatría, optometría o medicina veterinaria.

Las universidades usan tu información como padre para determinar la elegibilidad de tu hijo al programa HPSL, aunque él sea considerado independiente. El máximo HPSL anual que se puede solicitar es igual al costo de matrícula más $2,500. No hay máximo acumulado. El reembolso de capital e intereses comienza un año después de que tu hijo deje de ser estudiante de tiempo completo. Los préstamos deben reembolsarse en un plazo de 10 años en pagos iguales o pagos parciales graduados.

Scholarships for Disadvantaged Students

El programa SDS se desarrolló para ayudar estudiantes desfavorecidos que demuestran interés para seguir una carrera en áreas de la salud. Las universidades participantes reciben fondos anualmente.

Los fondos de SDS pueden usarse para pagar matrículas, otros gastos educativos razonables y gastos razonables de manutención mientras eres estudiante de tiempo completo. La beca no puede exceder el total exigido para estos gastos en un año específico.

La universidad otorga la Scholarship for Disadvantaged Students a estudiantes elegibles en los siguientes programas: doctor en medicina alopática y osteopática, odontología, medicina veterinaria, optometría, y medicina podiátrica; programas de posgrado en psicología clínica o salud pública; programas de pregrado o posgrado en farmacia, higiene dental, tecnología de laboratorio médico, terapia física u ocupacional y tecnología radiológica; y, programas en enfermería conducentes a título asociado, diploma universitario o de posgrado.

National Health Service Corps Scholarships

Este programa está diseñado con el propósito de atraer profesionales de la salud para que trabajen con el National Health Service Corps (NHSC) en áreas donde existe escasez de profesionales médicos de cuidados primarios. Los estudiantes a tiempo completo en las siguientes áreas son elegibles: medicina alopática y osteopática, enfermería obstétrica o enfermería profesional reconocida nacionalmente, y como asistente médico en cuidados primarios. La beca cubre la matrícula y cuotas necesarias y provee un estipendio durante 12 meses. Los beneficiarios de NHSC deben prestar sus servicios, a razón de un año por cada año de beca recibida; mínimo dos años de servicio.

Para mayor información visita la Health and Human Services Bureau of Health Professions (Oficina de servicios de salud y humanitarios de profesiones de la salud), nhsc.bhpr.hrsa.gov.

AYUDA ESTATAL BASADA EN LAS NECESIDADES

La mayoría de programas estatales de ayuda financiera estudiantil se basan en las necesidades y son sólo para estudiantes residentes de cada estado o que asistan a una universidad de dicho estado. En algunos estados, hay tratados de reciprocidad que permiten a los estudiantes usar las subvenciones estatales para asistir a una universidad en uno de los estados del acuerdo. En algunos casos, la ayuda estatal se da en forma de apoyo financiero o subvenciones directas a las universidades, pero no se asignan a un estudiante específico.

Las condiciones de la ayuda estudiantil basada en las necesidades varían de un estado a otro, al igual que el tipo y forma de ayuda ofrecida. Un estado puede ofrecer subvenciones, préstamos o programas de trabajo con requisitos únicos de elegibilidad. Para información actualizada sobre estos programas, montos ofrecidos, requisitos de elegibilidad, fechas límite y procedimientos de solicitud, comunícate con el organismo estatal correspondiente.

Leveraging Educational Assistance Partnership Program, LEAP (Programa para la Promoción de Asociaciones de Ayuda Educativa)

En este programa, los fondos federales se asignan a los estados para promover la creación y ampliación de ayuda por subvención o becas estatales para estudios superiores. El estado debe asignar los fondos correspondientes.

Las condiciones específicas de elegibilidad para los programas LEAP se establecen a nivel estatal; las leyes federales autorizan a los organismos estatales para que extiendan la elegibilidad a estudiantes universitarios y, si se desea, a estudiantes de posgrado y de menos de medio tiempo. Sin embargo, los beneficiarios deben cumplir condiciones federales de elegibilidad estudiantil y demostrar una gran necesidad financiera según lo determina el estado.

Tu hijo debe hacer su solicitud en el organismo estatal que le corresponde, ya sea directamente o a través de la universidad. La máxima subvención anual LEAP es de $5,000. Los organismos estatales pueden estipular menores montos máximos de ayuda. Los estados que asignan sus propios fondos al programa pueden ofrecer una subvención máxima mayor.

AYUDA BASADA EN LAS NECESIDADES PROVISTA POR FUENTES INSTITUCIONALES Y PRIVADAS

El dinero para la mayoría de programas de ayuda estudiantil basada en las necesidades viene de fuentes federales o estatales, o de una combinación de las dos, pero también son muchas las universidades que destinan parte de sus propios recursos para ayuda estudiantil. Esta ayuda puede basarse en el mérito o las necesidades, o en una combinación de ambas, y puede otorgarse en forma de subvenciones, préstamos o empleo. Es frecuente que las universidades reciban contribuciones de

Las organizaciones privadas también tienen fondos disponibles para estudiantes y pueden aplicar criterios de necesidad, estándares por méritos, o una combinación de ambos. Las fuentes potenciales de subvenciones o préstamos privados incluyen clubes comunitarios de servicios, fundaciones privadas, empleadores, grupos de iglesia y asociaciones étnicas.

donantes privados o empresariales bajo restricciones específicas de uso. Puede haber una gran variedad de pequeños programas con condiciones variables o un gran paquete de fondos discrecionales que el administrador de ayudas u otros miembros del equipo administrativo o docente de la institución pueden otorgar.

Los fondos discrecionales pueden tener condiciones estrictas de necesidad o pueden reservase para situaciones de emergencia inesperadas cuando el estudiante ya es beneficiario de la ayuda original. En algunas universidades, la ayuda institucional puede otorgarse con los mismos criterios de la ayuda federal con base en el campus. No dejes de considerar este tipo de fondos de la universidad o de sus departamentos académicos individuales.

Capítulo 6

Recursos de ayuda no basada en las necesidades

La ayuda no basada en las necesidades también se conoce como ayuda basada en el mérito. Las condiciones varían dependiendo del programa y por lo general, son competitivas. Los beneficiarios se escogen de acuerdo a su talento en habilidades particulares. La ayuda basada en el mérito también puede conseguirse con base en la participación en el servicio comunitario, aptitudes de liderazgo y en campos de estudio.

A diferencia de la ayuda basada en las necesidades, donde el gobierno federal proporciona la mayoría de fondos, existen muchas fuentes y medios que puedes utilizar para obtener ayuda no basada en las necesidades. Esta ayuda puede ser federal, estatal e institucional y se encuentra en forma de becas privadas, subvenciones y préstamos.

Los programas de ayuda para profesionales de la salud se basan técnicamente en las necesidades y aplican el concepto del uso de ayuda financiera para motivar a los estudiantes a capacitarse en carreras en áreas de alta demanda. Algunos programas federales y estatales están dirigidos a estudiantes en áreas específicas de estudio.

Cualquiera que sea el medio que escojas, la mejor fuente de información sobre cómo solicitar ayuda no basada en las necesidades es la propia fuente. Por ejemplo:

- $ Visita, escribe o llama por teléfono a la universidad a la cual tu hijo pretende asistir para conocer más acerca de los diferentes programas disponibles basados en el mérito.
- $ Busca en Internet y en la sección de referencias de la biblioteca local de páginas Web y libros que ofrezcan listas de programas de becas y subvenciones.
- $ Solicita información acerca de becas al consejero vocacional de la escuela de secundaria de tu hijo.

- $ Pregúntale al consejero vocacional sobre solicitudes para becas privadas.

Sin importar la fuente, la ayuda no basada en las necesidades con frecuencia afecta tu elegibilidad para ayuda basada en las necesidades. No obstante, la forma como influye en otra ayuda es diferente según la universidad. Por ejemplo, puede reducir el monto de los préstamos que puedes pedir o se puede emplear para cubrir la diferencia, si existe, entre la cantidad de ayuda basada en las necesidades que se te ofrece y tu necesidad real. Aunque algunas universidades podrían reducir subvenciones basadas en las necesidades si recibes otras subvenciones no basadas en las necesidades, la Federal Pell Grant nunca se reduce.

No importa la fuente o tipo de ayuda obtenida, se debe informar a la oficina de ayuda financiera sobre cualquier asistencia externa que tu hijo reciba. Esta obligación se aplica incluso si resultas beneficiario de una beca adicional después de recibir notificación formal de la universidad sobre la ayuda que desea ofrecerte. El administrador de ayuda financiera debe tener en cuenta esta asistencia al otorgar ayuda federal.

BECAS

Con frecuencia la palabra beca causa confusión. La definición de beca es "dinero gratuito donado a un estudiante para que cubra los gastos educativos". La beca puede basarse en el historial académico de tu hijo o en otros méritos, tales como sus habilidades deportivas, su talento en artes, música, liderazgo, servicio a la comunidad o escritura, o sus buenas cualidades ciudadanas. No obstante, mucha gente, incluso los funcionarios de entidades de ayuda financiera universitaria y los patrocinadores de programas, emplean la palabra para referirse a todas las formas de ayuda donada a los estudiantes, incluso becas para profesionales y subvenciones. A continuación, encontrarás algunas definiciones para que entiendas las diferencias de significado cuando encuentres otros términos:

- $ *Becas y subvenciones:* Donación que se emplea para pagar los gastos educativos.
- $ *Becas basadas en las necesidades:* Donación basada en las necesidades demostradas. La necesidad, según la definen las universidades y el gobierno federal, es la diferencia entre el costo de asistir a la universidad y el EFC.

Entre las fuentes de ayuda financiera están los organismos privados, fundaciones, corporaciones, clubes, organizaciones fraternales y de servicio, asociaciones cívicas, sindicatos y grupos religiosos. Estos patrocinadores ofrecen subvenciones, becas y préstamos a bajo interés. Algunos empleadores también proporcionan beneficios de reembolso de matrícula para los empleados y sus dependientes.

$ *Becas basadas en el mérito:* Ayuda financiera basada en criterios diferentes a la necesidad financiera, tal como especialidad académica, objetivos profesionales, notas, puntajes de pruebas, habilidades deportivas, pasatiempos, talentos, lugar de residencia o de nacimiento, identidad étnica, vinculación religiosa, servicio de seguridad militar o pública de un estudiante o un padre, discapacidad, membresía sindical, historia laboral, servicio comunal o afiliaciones a clubes.

$ *Premios:* Dinero otorgado en reconocimiento de un logro sobresaliente. Con frecuencia los premios se entregan a ganadores de competencias.

$ *Pasantías:* Período de tiempo definido durante el cual se trabaja en el campo de interés del estudiante en práctica bajo la supervisión del personal profesional de una organización anfitriona. Con frecuencia, los estudiantes en práctica trabajan tiempo parcial o durante el verano. Algunas pasantías ofrecen estipendios en forma de un salario por hora o una asignación fija.

Consulta la siguiente lista sobre becas por méritos:

$ Aprovecha cualquier beca para la cual tu hijo sea automáticamente elegible basado en beneficios del empleador, servicio militar, asociación o membresía a una iglesia, otras afiliaciones o atributos del estudiante o sus padres (tales como antecedentes étnicos o nacionalidad). Las exenciones de matrícula por sindicatos o empresas son los ejemplos más comunes de este tipo de otorgamiento.

$ Solicita otras ayudas con proceso de selección, en las que tu hijo podría ser elegible con base en las características y afiliaciones antes indicadas.

$ Averigua si el estado donde vives tiene un programa de becas por méritos.

$ Infórmate sobre competencias nacionales de becas. Por lo general, los consejeros vocacionales de tu escuela te pueden dar información sobre estas becas. Los siguientes son ejemplos de estas becas: National Merit Scholarship (Beca Nacional al Mérito), Coca-Cola Scholarship (Beca Coca-Cola), Aid Association for Lutherans (Asociación de Ayuda para Luteranos), Intel Science Talent Search (Búsqueda Intel de Talentos Científicos) y U.S. Senate Youth Program (Programa del Senado de Estados Unidos para la Juventud).

- Comunícate con un sitio de reclutamiento de servicio militar o un consejero de una escuela de secundaria para obtener información sobre las becas del Reserve Officers' Training Corps, ROTC (Cuerpo de Entrenamiento de Oficiales de Reserva) ofrecidas por el Ejército, la Armada, la Infantería de Marina y la Fuerza Aérea. Las becas ROTC completas cubren todos los gastos de matrícula, cuotas y textos. La aceptación de una beca ROTC implica el compromiso de tomar un curso de ciencia militar y servir como oficial en la sede de servicio patrocinadora. La competencia es dura y se puede dar preferencia a estudiantes de ciertos campos de estudio, tales como las ciencias de ingeniería. Los procedimientos de solicitud varían de acuerdo con el servicio.
- Infórmate sobre becas comunitarias. Por lo general, los consejeros vocacionales de las escuelas de secundaria tienen una lista de estas becas y es común que se anuncien en los periódicos locales. Las más comunes son asignadas por organizaciones de servicio tales como American Legion, Rotary International y el club femenino local.
- Ten en cuenta las universidades que ofrecen sus propias becas por méritos a estudiantes talentosos para que se inscriban en ellas. Esta es una buena opción si tu hijo tiene un buen nivel académico (por ejemplo, un National Merit Commended Scholar (Estudiante Reconocido por su Mérito a Nivel Nacional) u otro reconocimiento mayor) o es muy talentoso en el área deportiva o de las artes del espectáculo/creativas.

Existen muchas becas disponibles para estudiantes hispanos. En el Apéndice al final de este libro, se encuentra una lista de becas para estudiantes hispanos y su información de contacto.

AYUDA UNIVERSITARIA POR DONACIÓN

Las becas universitarias basadas en las necesidades, con frecuencia forman parte de un paquete de ayuda financiera estudiantil. La mayoría de universidades otorgan tanto becas basadas en las necesidades como en el mérito, aunque un pequeño número de universidades (entre las que se destacan las de la Ivy League) ofrecen exclusivamente becas basadas en las necesidades. Las universidades pueden ofrecer becas basadas en los méritos a estudiantes de primer año con talentos académicos específicos, talentos en las artes creativas o del espectáculo, logros o actividades especiales y una amplia variedad de circunstancias particulares. Algunas incluyen: padres con profesiones específicas, residentes de áreas geográficas particulares, cónyuges, hijos y hermanos de otros estudiantes y estudiantes con discapacidades.

En las oficinas de ayuda financiera de las universidades puedes informarte acerca de las becas basadas en las necesidades que te pueden ofrecer. Por lo general, la oficina de admisiones es la principal fuente de información sobre cualquier beca basada en los méritos que la universidad ofrece. Algunas universidades, cuentan con información sobre becas en sus sitios Web. Por lo general, las universidades privadas cuentan con programas de ayuda financiera más grandes, mientras que las universidades públicas usualmente son menos costosas, en especial para estudiantes del mismo estado.

Becas deportivas

Si tu hijo está interesado en el béisbol, baloncesto, navegación a remos, deportes a campo traviesa, esgrima, hockey sobre césped, fútbol americano, golf, gimnasia, lacrosse, navegación a vela, esquí, fútbol, softball, natación y buceo, tenis, atletismo, voleibol o lucha, hay muchos dólares en becas disponibles. Pero tú y tu hijo deben planificar con anticipación si deseas obtener el pago de tu matrícula a cambio de sus habilidades competitivas.

Al inicio del penúltimo año de la secundaria de tu hijo, pídele al consejero vocacional que te indique el número y combinación necesaria de cursos académicos que se deben tomar y, que te informe de los puntajes mínimos del SAT y del ACT que se deben conseguir para practicar deportes en la universidad. Pregunta también sobre los

Las universidades tienen diferentes requisitos en cuanto a formatos de solicitud de ayuda financiera necesarios. Todas las universidades exigen la FAFSA para los estudiantes que soliciten ayuda federal. El otro formato que se requiere con mayor frecuencia es el PROFILE, formato de ayuda financiera del College Scholarship Service. Verifica con las universidades en las que está interesado tu hijo sobre los formatos necesarios.

requisitos académicos, ya que tu hijo debe tener la certificación del NCAA Initial-Eligibity Clearinghouse (Centro de Intercambio de Información sobre Elegibilidad Inicial de la NCAA). Este proceso debe comenzar al final del undécimo año de la secundaria, cuando se debe presentar un Student Release Form (Formulario de Autorización del Estudiante) (disponible en las oficinas de consejería). Puedes informarte sobre los requisitos con el consejero o en Internet, www.ncaa.org.

Pero antes de todo, piensa si deseas y necesitas una beca deportiva para tu hijo. A decir verdad, recibir una beca de éstas da prestigio pero algunos deportistas comparan la beca deportiva con un trabajo en el que se espera que se rinda. Las reuniones, entrenamiento, las prácticas, los partidos y (no debes olvidar) el estudio, restan tiempo que se puede dedicar a la vida social y al ocio. Por otro lado, como las becas completas disponibles son muy pocas, lo más probable es que tu hijo reciba una beca parcial o un contrato renovable de un año. Si la beca no se renueva, puede que tengas que solicitar ayuda financiera. Pregúntate, como unidad familiar, si estás listo para las exigencias y funciones asociadas a una beca deportiva.

Tipos de becas deportivas

Las universidades ofrecen dos tipos básicos de becas deportivas:

1. **Subvención institucional, que es un acuerdo entre el deportista y la universidad**
2. **Subvención de liga, que también liga a la universidad con el deportista**

La diferencia es que el deportista que firma una subvención institucional puede cambiar de parecer y firmar con otro equipo. El deportista que firma un contrato con una liga no puede renegociar otro contrato con una universidad que ofrezca subvenciones de liga. A continuación, encontrarás las diferentes formas en que se ofrece una beca:

- $ Cuatro años completos. También se conocen como becas completas y pagan alojamiento, comida, matrícula y libros. Debido al alto costo que implica otorgar becas, las ligas están descartándolas por todo el país y las sustituyen con el contrato renovable de un año o la beca parcial.
- $ Contrato renovable de un año completo. Este tipo de beca, que básicamente ha reemplazado la subvención de cuatro años, se renueva en forma automática al final de cada año académico por cuatro años, si se cumple con las condiciones del contrato. El seleccionador probablemente le dirá a tu hijo, de buena fe, que la intención es ofrecer una beca de cuatro años, pero que legalmente sólo está autorizado a ofrecer una subvención de un año. Deben preguntarle a él y, a otros jugadores, cuál ha sido el récord de renovación de becas para deportistas que cumplen con los requerimientos deportivos, académicos y sociales.
- $ Subvención de prueba de un año (completa o parcial). Acuerdo verbal entre tu hijo y la universidad. La renovación depende del rendimiento académico y deportivo.
- $ Beca parcial. La subvención parcial cubre parte de los gastos universitarios. Ofrece alojamiento y comida, pero no matrícula y libros, o sólo la matrícula; pero existe la probabilidad de que negocies una beca completa después de terminar el primer año de universidad.
- $ Exención de cuotas para estudiantes fuera del estado. Se otorga a estudiantes fuera del estado para que asistan a la universidad al mismo costo que un estudiante que vive dentro del estado.

Cómo encontrar y obtener becas deportivas

A continuación, se señalan cuatro pasos a seguir para que tu hijo obtenga esta beca:

1. **Comunícate formalmente con la universidad.** Una vez tu hijo tenga una lista de las universidades donde quiere estudiar, consigue el nombre del entrenador jefe y haz que tu hijo escriba una carta a las veinte mejores universidades de la lista. Luego, haz un currículum vitae verificable de los logros deportivos y

académicos de tu hijo. Recopila en video, 10 a 15 minutos de momentos destacados de su desempeño deportivo (con su número de camiseta anotado), consigue cartas de recomendación del entrenador de secundaria y del entrenador fuera de temporada e incluye el calendario de la temporada.

2. **Haz de la entrevista un éxito total.** Recuérdale a tu hijo la importancia de mostrar confianza en si mismo con un firme apretón de manos. Asimismo, destaca la importancia de mantener un contacto visual y de una buena presentación personal cuando se reúna con el seleccionador o entrenador. Según afirman los seleccionadores, la actitud más efectiva es la confianza calmada, el respeto, la sinceridad y el entusiasmo.

3. **Haz buenas preguntas.** No temas hacer preguntas al entrevistador para obtener respuestas a las siguientes preguntas: ¿Califica mi hijo deportiva y académicamente? Si lo aceptan, ¿cuáles serían los parámetros de la beca? ¿Para qué puesto se considera a mi hijo elegible? Está bien hacer preguntas al seleccionador para aclarar el interés que tiene en tu hijo.

4. **Seguimiento.** La persistencia vale la pena al buscar una beca deportiva y escoger el momento oportuno puede significarlo todo. Existen cuatro buenos momentos cuando sirve mucho una carta de seguimiento de un entrenador o de tu hijo. Éstos pueden ser antes de la temporada de mayores, durante o justo después de la temporada de mayores, justo antes o después de las fechas de inscripción (asociaciones nacionales o afiliadas a la liga), y al finalizar el verano en caso de ofertas de becas que se hayan retirado o rechazado.

Pídele recomendaciones al entrenador o entrenadores asistentes de tu hijo, o infórmate sobre la liga o institución a través del periódico o la televisión, pregúntale al consejero de tu hijo, revisa libros guía, libros de referencia e Internet; pregúntale a los ex-alumnos, o asiste a una prueba o visita de campus. Escríbele a la NCAA y solicita una guía de reclutamiento para el deporte elegido por tu hijo.

Para resumir, observa objetivamente las aptitudes deportivas y académicas de tu hijo. Evalúa las aptitudes que necesita para mejorar y haz que mantenga vivo el deseo de mejorar. Desarrolla en tu hijo las habilidades de liderazgo y haz que se esfuerce por conseguir la excelencia con sus logros individuales.

BECAS ESTATALES Y LOCALES

Cada gobierno estatal ha establecido uno o más programas de ayuda financiera para estudiantes calificados. Por lo general, sólo los residentes legales del estado son elegibles para dichos programas. Sin embargo, algunos están disponibles para estudiantes que vienen de otro estado y que asisten a universidades dentro del estado. Los estados pueden ofrecer además programas de pasantías o de trabajo y estudio, becas y subvenciones para posgrados o préstamos a bajo interés, además de programas de subvenciones y préstamos condonables.

Muchos estados están intentando incentivar a los estudiantes para que ingresen en áreas ocupacionales específicas porque presentan escasez de personal capacitado, como por ejemplo, educación, cumplimiento de la ley, terapia ocupacional, terapia física, ciencia, enfermería y medicina. Para atraer estudiantes hacia estas áreas, cada vez más estados proporcionan ayuda a través de préstamos especiales comprometiendo a los estudiantes a trabajar en estas áreas después de graduados. Si tu hijo acepta dicha ayuda financiera, es importante confirmar si existe una obligación de servicio como parte de la beca.

Si estás interesado en saber más sobre los programas patrocinados por el estado, la oficina de educación superior estatal puede suministrarte información. Por lo general, en la oficina de orientación de la secundaria de tu hijo o en una oficina de ayuda financiera universitaria de tu estado encontrarás disponibles catálogos y formularios de solicitud para programas de becas estatales. Cada día con mayor frecuencia, los organismos gubernamentales estatales colocan la información de becas estatales en sus sitios Web. La página de ayuda financiera de sitios universitarios administrados por el estado casi siempre tiene una lista de becas patrocinadas por el estado y programas de ayuda financiera.

A menudo las empresas, clubes de servicio comunitario y organizaciones locales patrocinan programas de becas para residentes de una ciudad o condado específico. Estos pueden ser atractivos para quien busca una beca, puesto que tienen más probabilidades de ganar que con las becas otorgadas entre un grupo más amplio de solicitantes. Sin embargo, como la red de información a nivel local es irregular, con frecuencia resulta difícil enterarse de estas opciones. Algunas de las mejores fuentes de información sobre estos programas locales son las oficinas de orientación de la secundaria, las oficinas de ayuda financiera universitaria comunitaria, las oficinas administrativas de distrito de escuelas secundarias y las bibliotecas públicas.

AYUDA PRIVADA

Cada año, donantes privados entregan miles de millones de dólares a los estudiantes y sus familias para ayudarles con los gastos de educación universitaria. El año pasado, los patrocinadores no-institucionales y no-gubernamentales aportaron más de $3,000 millones en asistencia financiera para ayudar a estudiantes universitarios a pagar sus gastos. Las fundaciones, organizaciones fraternales y étnicas, clubes de servicio comunitario, iglesias y grupos religiosos, filántropos, empresas y grupos industriales, sindicatos y asociaciones de empleados públicos, grupos de veteranos, consorcios y legados conforman, en conjunto, una gran red de posibles fuentes financieras.

También puedes averiguar en las oficinas locales de organizaciones que tradicionalmente patrocinan becas, tales como el International Kiwanis Club (Club Kiwanis Internacional), Benevolent and Protective Order of Elks (Orden Benevolente y Protectora de Elks), Lions Club International (Club Internacional de Leones) o National Association of American Business Clubs, AMBUCS (Asociación Nacional de Clubes de Negocios Estadounidenses).

Siempre vale la pena que cualquier estudiante potencial averigüe sobre estas becas; lo cual, es especialmente importante para estudiantes que no califican para ayuda financiera basada en las necesidades y para estudiantes y familias que deseen complementar la ayuda que reciben de fuentes gubernamentales o universitarias. Es bueno que los estudiantes con habilidades, logros o clasificaciones especiales, (por ejemplo, membresías a la iglesia u organizaciones cívicas, antecedentes étnicos específicos, padres que han servido a las fuerzas armadas), que cumplan con los criterios de uno o más patrocinadores de becas privadas, soliciten también ayuda privada.

Algunos factores que pueden afectar la elegibilidad para dichas becas están fuera de tu control, tales como la herencia étnica y el estatus de tus padres. Otros factores, tales como el mérito académico, científico, tecnológico, deportivo, artístico o creativo no se consiguen fácil o rápidamente, a menos que tu hijo haya estado comprometido previamente con un esfuerzo particular. Sin embargo, la elegibilidad para muchos programas está bajo tu control si planeas con anticipación. Por ejemplo, tu hijo puede iniciar o mantener la membresía actual en una iglesia u organización cívica, participar en esfuerzos de servicio voluntario o avanzar en un área de interés, como la radio-afición, el golf, la cría de animales, la escritura, etc. Cualquiera de éstas podría brindarle a tu hijo una ventaja para una beca u oportunidad de subvención, en particular.

Los criterios de elegibilidad para becas, subvenciones y premios privados varían ampliamente e incluyen tanto la necesidad financiera, como las características personales y méritos. El número y los montos de las becas disponibles de patrocinadores individuales puede variar cada año, dependiendo del número de beneficiarios, contribuciones de fondos y otros factores. Sin embargo, prácticamente cualquier persona puede encontrar una beca que se ajuste a sus circunstancias individuales.

Becas: Un enfoque estratégico

Antes de entrar en la odisea de las becas, ten en mente estas perspectivas, estrategias y observaciones generales sobre las becas:

- $ **Comienza temprano.** Te recomendamos especialmente que empieces a participar en los concursos de becas desde la escuela secundaria. Existen incluso varios programas que incluyen competencias separadas para los grados 7 a 9. Varias de las competencias de becas más grandes permiten que los estudiantes que no han ganado un gran premio, participen cada año mientras sean elegibles. La sola experiencia resulta valiosa para que tu hijo participe como estudiante de noveno o de décimo año.
- $ **Haz un análisis de las becas.** Debes iniciar tu búsqueda de becas privadas antes de la primavera del undécimo año de secundaria de tu hijo. Un buen punto de partida es contar con una base de datos confiable sobre becas, como la del muy respetado sitio Web www.petersons.com. Entre abril y septiembre recomendamos que realices la búsqueda y averigües dónde se ofrecen becas. Es bueno reunir las solicitudes de becas entre septiembre y noviembre. Entre diciembre y comienzos de marzo deberías preparar y entregar las solicitudes a los patrocinadores de las becas.

- $ **Comienza a prepararte por anticipado.** Te aconsejamos empezar a prepararte con bastante anticipación para que tengas éxito en los concursos nacionales de becas, antes de las fechas límite. Es posible que en áreas como la redacción y las artes, debas presentar grandes carpetas de trabajo. Varios programas de matemáticas y ciencias involucran proyectos complejos, que requieren de mucho tiempo. Los estudiantes que esperan obtener honores en concursos de oratoria pública, por lo general, se benefician de la práctica repetida. La preparación temprana es definitiva para un solicitante competitivo.
- $ **Enfoque "siempre listos".** Prepárate para cualquier oportunidad que pueda presentarse. Si tu hijo está en el duodécimo año, es buena idea mantener un archivo de documentos que se requieren con frecuencia. Si tienes copias de papeles y documentos, puedes duplicarlos con facilidad y enviarlos como parte de formularios de solicitud de beca, sin perder tiempo valioso. Guarda copias, por lo menos, de tres recomendaciones (el rector o vice rector, el consejero vocacional y uno o más maestros) sobre los logros académicos y no-académicos de tu hijo, como también de sus cualidades personales. Guarda copia de todo ensayo general escrito para solicitud de ingreso a la universidad, que pueda volver a utilizarse para la solicitud de una beca. Si tu hijo tiene numerosos logros sobresalientes en un área específica (tales como, victorias en debates, premios deportivos o artículos publicados en periódicos), enuméralos y descríbelos en una página, que puedes adicionar a los formularios de becas. Si tu hijo está interesado en participar en competencias de redacción, ten copias impresas a la mano de su mejor trabajo. Las fechas límites de los programas no siempre caen en momentos convenientes. El tiempo es dinero, dinero en becas.
- $ **Consigue y estudia registros de ganadores en el pasado.** Los ganadores de becas en redacción u oratoria pública, con frecuencia sacan provecho al estudiar los trabajos de anteriores de ganadores de concursos. Por lo general, se pueden obtener ejemplos al escribir directamente a los administradores del concurso.

- $ **Hazte amigo del consejero vocacional.** Haz que tu hijo converse con su consejero desde el comienzo del año escolar y solicítale colaboración en sus esfuerzos para participar y ganar competencias. Ten copias de toda la información que la escuela reciba sobre oportunidades de becas en las áreas académicas y de estudios universitarios que desea tu hijo.
- $ **Efecto de "utilidad múltiple".** Participar en competencias por becas, no requiere de tanto trabajo como parece. Los estudiantes pueden hacer que sus esfuerzos intelectuales y creativos les sirvan para otras cosas. Puede resultar que varios concursos de un área específica, como ciencias, oratoria, artes o composición escrita, tengan requisitos similares y el trabajo de preparación para un concurso puede adaptarse para otros.
- $ **El síndrome "éxito tras éxito".** Existe un efecto acumulativo definitivo al ganar premios en competencias. El éxito en competencias de desempeño constituye un excelente trampolín para una nueva competencia.
- $ **Utiliza sólo material original.** El plagio es la forma más rápida de ser eliminado de un programa. Asegúrate de que tu hijo entregue un trabajo de autoría propia y que informe los créditos en caso de haber recurrido a otras fuentes.
- $ **Lee con cuidado todo el material del concurso.** Aunque parezca obvio, numerosos funcionarios han señalado que muchos estudiantes no ponen atención a las reglas del concurso. Asegúrate de obtener una copia del folleto más reciente para tener información de primera mano sobre las fechas límite, procedimientos correctos de registro y criterios para becas. No creas todo lo que te digan sobre las reglas del concurso, incluso si se trata de un amigo bien intencionado o un consejero escolar.

BENEFICIOS EDUCATIVOS PARA VETERANOS

El Departamento de Asuntos de los Veteranos y el Departamento de Defensa administran varios programas de ayuda para los veteranos y sus dependientes.

El Survivors and Dependents Educational Assistance Program, DEAP (Programa de Ayuda Educativa para Sobrevivientes y sus Dependientes), ofrece beneficios a los hijos y esposas de veteranos que murieron o quedaron discapacitados permanentemente, como consecuencia de una lesión sufrida en cumplimiento del servicio militar. Bajo el DEAP, las personas dependientes entre los 18 y 26 años pueden recibir un estipendio (dividida proporcionalmente para inscripciones de menos de tiempo completo) al finalizar cada mes de estudio. Este estipendio mensual del Departamento de Asuntos de los Veteranos ayuda a cubrir los gastos educativos y personales de tu hijo mientras esté inscrito en una escuela de estudios superiores. No olvides que el administrador de ayuda financiera debe considerar estos beneficios como un recurso, cuando se determina la elegibilidad de tu hijo para ayuda federal, estatal e institucional.

Los beneficios para los veteranos se pagan a los estudiantes en los siguientes tipos de programas de educación:

$ Programas de estudios universitarios y de posgrado

$ Programas de capacitación cooperativa

$ Programas de estudio independiente acreditado que llevan a un título universitario

$ Cursos que llevan a un certificado o diploma de escuelas empresariales, técnicas o vocacionales

$ Programas de prácticas o capacitación laborales ofrecidos por una empresa o un sindicato

$ Cursos de cooperativas agrarias

$ Programas de estudio en el exterior que llevan a título universitario

Puedes obtener información adicional en cuanto a éstos y otros beneficios para veteranos en la oficina más cercana del Departamento de Asuntos de los Veteranos, VA (por sus siglas en inglés) o en si sitio Web, www.va.gov. También puedes llamar o escribir a la oficina VA más cercana y solicitar panfletos y folletos.

REHABILITACIÓN VOCACIONAL PARA DISCAPACITADOS

El acceso a oportunidades educativas para individuos con discapacidades se garantiza a través de leyes federales que rigen la rehabilitación vocacional. A cada estado se le otorga una asignación federal sobre una base de igualdad, para ayudar a las personas con discapacidad que tengan potencial de empleo, pero cuyas limitaciones crean barreras.

Los programas de rehabilitación vocacional también proporcionan servicios globales bajo un plan escrito de rehabilitación individualizado. El plan puede incluir evaluación, capacitación vocacional, dispositivos especiales requeridos para el empleo, ubicación laboral y servicios de seguimiento. Algunos estados ofrecen programas de asistencia educativa a estudiantes discapacitados por medio de organismos que, a menudo, se conocen como Offices of Vocational Rehabilitation, OVR (Oficinas de Rehabilitación Vocacional). Los estudiantes con discapacidad pueden participar en cualquiera de los programas de ayuda financiera federal, y cuentan además, con ayuda por medio de programas de rehabilitación vocacional para pagar gastos únicos causados por la discapacidad. Los estudiantes elegibles también pueden recibir fondos para matrícula, cuotas, libros y materiales y becas para manutención y transporte.

Si tu hijo es discapacitado, comunícate con tu departamento estatal de rehabilitación vocacional para obtener mayor información. Igualmente, puedes obtener información sobre la ayuda y procesos de adjudicación por medio de HEATH, un centro de intercambio de información financiado por el Departamento de Educación de Estados Unidos y administrado por el American Council on Education, ACE (Consejo de Educación de Estados Unidos). Información de contacto:

HEATH
One Dupont Circle, NW, Suite 800,
Washington, D.C. 20036-1193
Teléfono: 202-939-9320 ó 800-544-3284 (llamada gratuita)

BECAS FRAUDULENTAS: QUÉ SON Y DE QUÉ TE DEBES CUIDAR

La ayuda privada puede incidir en la capacidad de tu hijo para asistir a una universidad durante un año en particular. Desafortunadamente, para los que buscan becas, la ayuda del sector privado existe prácticamente sin patrones o reglas. Se trata de una mezcla de programas individuales con sus propios criterios de otorgamiento, cronogramas, procedimientos de solicitud y procesos de toma de decisiones. Todo esto hace que no sea nada fácil comprender el funcionamiento y beneficiarse efectivamente de las becas privadas.

La combinación de una gran urgencia de dinero, tiempo limitado y este sistema complejo ha creado oportunidad para el fraude. De cada diez estudiantes que reciben una beca legítima, uno es víctima de un plan fraudulento o estafa cometidos por medio de supuestas fundaciones, patrocinadores de becas o servicios de búsqueda de becas que aparentan ser legítimos.

Estos negocios fraudulentos colocan su publicidad en periódicos de los campus, distribuyen volantes, envían cartas y postales, entregan números telefónicos gratuitos e incluso tienen sitios Web en Internet. Los fraudes más obvios operan como servicios de búsqueda de becas o centros de intercambio de información de becas. Otro fraude menos obvio, es una empresa establecida como patrocinador de becas. Se llena los bolsillos con el dinero que recibe de cuotas y gastos varios que pagan miles de esperanzados estudiantes en busca de becas y devuelve poco a cambio, si es que devuelve algo, en proporción con el monto que recolecta. Algunos de estos fraudes son altamente perjudiciales, puesto que se logra acceso a crédito o cuentas corrientes personales con la intención de usurpar fondos.

Un fraude típico, es cuando una firma envía cantidades extraordinarias de correo (en algunos casos, más de un millón de postales al año) a estudiantes de secundaria y universitarios, ofreciéndoles una beca o lista de becas estudiantiles. Igualmente, ofrecen líneas telefónicas gratuitas y cuando los 'beneficiarios' llaman, telemercadistas de gran poder de convencimiento, les informan que la compañía ya no está ofreciendo dichas becas pero que por una suma, que oscila entre $10 y $400, podrán obtener una subvención de por lo menos $1,000 o, se les devolverá su dinero. Quienes pagan, normalmente no reciben nada, y en ocasiones reciben una lista de fuentes de ayuda financiera más o menos igual a la que puedes encontrar en bibliotecas, librerías o en Internet. Los 'afortunados' beneficiarios deben, entonces, solicitar la ayuda por su propia cuenta. Muchos de los programas son concursos, préstamos o programas de trabajo y estudio en lugar de donaciones. Algunos ya no existen, ya han cumplido sus fechas límite o tienen exigencias de elegibilidad que los estudiantes no pueden cumplir. Quienes solicitan la devolución de su dinero, deben demostrar que solicitaron la ayuda por escrito a cada una de las fuentes del listado, y que recibieron una carta de rechazo de cada una de ellas. Con frecuencia, incluso quienes pueden conseguir este tipo de pruebas 'casi imposibles de reunir', no reciben la devolución de su dinero. En el peor de los casos, les solicitan a los estudiantes su número de cuenta corriente o tarjeta de crédito para sustraer los fondos sin autorización.

Sin embargo, existen servicios legítimos de búsqueda de becas, pero no pueden garantizar que un estudiante recibirá una beca. Es mejor que te encargues personalmente de tus trámites, recurriendo a una fuente confiable de información de becas, en lugar de desperdiciar tiempo y dinero con un servicio de búsqueda que promete becas. La Federal Trade Commission, FTC (Comisión Federal de Comercio) advierte que tienes que estar alerta para detectar cualquiera de estos seis signos que indican fraude:

1. **"Te garantizamos la beca o devolvemos tu dinero".** Ningún servicio puede garantizar que obtendrás una subvención o beca, y las garantías de reembolso de dinero a menudo tienen condiciones imposibles de cumplir. Revisa las políticas escritas de reembolso de tal servicio antes de pagar una cuota. Generalmente, los servicios fraudulentos de búsqueda de becas piden a los solicitantes cartas de rechazo de cada patrocinador de la lista que suministran. Si ya no existe un patrocinador, si no ofrece becas o si tiene una fecha límite de inscripción, resulta casi imposible obtener las cartas de rechazo.
2. **"El servicio de beca se encargará de todo".** Lamentablemente, sólo tu hijo y tú pueden llenar los formularios de información personal, escribir ensayos y entregar las referencias que muchas becas requieren.
3. **"La solicitud de beca costará algo de dinero".** Sé cauteloso con respecto a cualquier cargo relacionado con servicios de información de beca o solicitudes de becas individuales, en especial por montos significativos. Algunos patrocinadores legítimos de becas cobran para cubrir gastos de tramitación. Sin

La FTC advierte a estudiantes y padres que estén alertas para detectar servicios fraudulentos de búsqueda que prometen hacer todo por ti. Como afirma Jodie Bernstein, director de Bureau of Consumer Protection (Oficina de protección al consumidor) de la FTC, "Los servicios fraudulentos de búsqueda de becas son una variación más del fraude promocional 'acabas de ganar un premio de . . .', dirigido a un público en particular: estudiantes y padres con ganas de poder pagar una educación universitaria. Los pícaros garantizan a los estudiantes y a sus familias dinero gratis . . . afirmándoles que todo lo que tienen que hacer para reclamarlo es pagar una módica cuota".

embargo, los verdaderos patrocinadores de becas deben ofrecer dinero y no obtenerlo por cuotas de solicitud. Antes de que envíes dinero para solicitar una beca, investiga al patrocinador.

4. **"No podrás obtener esta información en ninguna otra parte".** Se encuentran disponibles directorios de becas de otros editores en cualquier librería grande, biblioteca pública u oficina de orientación de escuela secundaria. Además, hay muchos servicios buenos y gratuitos en Internet con bases de datos sobre becas.

5. **"Eres finalista en un concurso en el que no te has inscrito"** o "Has sido seleccionado por una fundación nacional para recibir una beca". La mayoría de los programas de beca legítimos casi nunca buscan solicitantes en particular, y gran parte de los patrocinadores te contactará sólo en respuesta a una solicitud, porque generalmente no tienen el presupuesto ni están autorizados para hacer algo más que esto. Si piensas que hay alguna posibilidad de que puedas haber sido seleccionado para recibir una beca, antes de enviar el dinero investiga primero para asegurarte de que el patrocinador o programa sea legítimo.

6. **"El servicio de becas te pide tu número de tarjeta de crédito o cuenta corriente por adelantado".** Nunca entregues tu número de tarjeta de crédito o cuenta corriente por teléfono al representante de una organización que no conozcas. Un programa legítimo de becas basado en las necesidades no pide tu número de cuenta corriente. Busca primero información por escrito. No es necesario contar con tu firma en un cheque para realizar una operación inescrupulosa. Es una treta para organizar situaciones en las que se vacía la cuenta de la víctima con giros no autorizados.

Además de los seis signos de la FTC, te damos otras guías que debes tener en cuenta cuando consideres un programa de becas:

- $ A menudo, las operaciones de becas fraudulentas usan nombres que parecen oficiales, con palabras como federal, nacional, administración, división, federación y fundación. Sus nombres son por lo general, ligeramente distintos a los de una organización legítima, sea gubernamental o privada. No te dejes engañar por un nombre que parece prestigioso u oficial, por un sello que parece oficial o por una dirección de Pennsylvania Avenue, Washington, D.C.
- $ Si te ganas una beca, recibirás una notificación oficial por escrito y a través del correo, no por teléfono. Si el patrocinador llama para informarte, la llamada vendrá seguida de una carta por correo. Si te piden dinero por teléfono, probablemente la operación es fraudulenta.
- $ Desconfía si la dirección de alguna organización es una casilla de correos o una dirección residencial. Si un programa de becas de buena fe usa un número de casilla de oficina postal, generalmente, éste incluirá una dirección y un número telefónico en su membrete.
- $ Desconfía de los números telefónicos con código de área 900. Estos pueden cobrarte varios dólares por minuto por una llamada que podría ser una larga grabación que sólo entrega una lista de direcciones o nombres.
- $ Una operación deshonesta puede presionar a un solicitante al decirle que los premios se entregan “por orden de llegada”. Algunos programas de becas dan preferencia a las primera solicitudes que cumplan los requisitos. Sin embargo, si por teléfono te han dicho que debes responder con prontitud, pero que no obtendrás noticias de los resultados en varios meses, es posible que algo no marche bien.
- $ Pon atención a las aprobaciones. Las operaciones fraudulentas afirman tener la aprobación de entidades con nombres muy parecidos a los de organizaciones bien reconocidas, bien sean privadas o gubernamentales. La Better Business Bureau, BBB (Oficina de Buenas Prácticas Comerciales) y las agencias gubernamentales no dan aprobaciones.

No pagues dinero por una beca a una organización de la que nunca has escuchado hablar o cuya legitimidad no puedas verificar. Si ya has pagado a dichas organizaciones y tienes una razón para dudar de su autenticidad, llama a tu banco para detener el pago de tu cheque, si es posible, o llama a tu compañía de tarjetas de crédito y diles que piensas que fuiste víctima de un fraude al consumidor.

Hay muchas becas excelentes disponibles para estudiantes calificados, dispuestos a invertir tiempo y dinero en buscarlas y solicitarlas. Sin embargo, ten cuidado al usar servicios de búsqueda de becas y cuando debas pagar dinero, y analiza detenidamente a todo patrocinador de programas de becas.

Comunícate con las siguientes entidades para orientación sobre cómo reconocer, reportar y detener un posible fraude de becas:

The Federal Trade Commission
600 Pennsylvania Avenue, NW
Washington, D.C. 20580
www.ftc.gov

The National Fraud Information Center
www.fraud.org
(800) 876-7060

The Council of Better Business Bureaus
4200 Wilson Boulevard, Suite 800
Arlington, Virginia 22203-1838
(703) 276-0100 (llama para obtener el teléfono de tu BBB local y de la oficina Better Business Bureau en el área donde se encuentra la organización en cuestión)
www.bbb.org (aquí encontrarás un directorio de oficinas locales y formularios de quejas)

Capítulo 7

101 Consejos de los profesionales

Obtener ayuda financiera es un proceso complicado, y poder hablar con personas que tienen que ver a diario con el tema hace que se eliminen muchos temores. Por esto, Peterson's entrevistó recientemente a profesionales de la educación para saber cuáles son los aspectos más importantes que las familias necesitan saber sobre la ayuda financiera. En este capítulo reunimos los 101 consejos más importantes para que te familiarices con el pensamiento de los funcionarios de ayuda financiera y con otros que, como tú, también están solicitando ayuda financiera.

PARA PADRES: PREPARACIÓN Y BÚSQUEDA DE INFORMACIÓN

1. **Habla con tu hijo sobre tu capacidad y tu disposición para pagar sus estudios universitarios.** Mantén abiertos los canales de comunicación sobre finanzas. Los padres e hijos que no analizan las finanzas como parte del proceso de selección de una universidad, con frecuencia pasan un momento difícil cuando se dan cuenta de que no pueden costear la primera opción de universidad escogida por el hijo. Debes ser sincero y realista sobre las limitaciones financieras de tu familia, así como sobre tus expectativas respecto al papel que tendrá tu hijo en el proceso y en el financiamiento de sus estudios.

2. **Averigua cuánto cuesta "realmente" la universidad.** Una cifra que aparece continuamente en los medios de comunicación es $30,000 al año, pero al igual que el costo de un automóvil depende de la marca y el modelo, los gastos de

universidad pueden variar considerablemente. Si tu hijo asiste a una universidad comunitaria local y reside en tu casa, tus gastos directos para todo el año académico pueden ascender a sólo algunos miles de dólares al año. En universidades públicas subvencionadas por el estado, el costo total de educación al año fluctuará entre $10,000 y $17,000, en tanto que el año en una universidad Ivy League puede costar fácilmente $37,000 (estos costos cubren el año académico de nueve meses e incluyen matrícula, cuotas, libros y materiales, transporte, alojamiento y alimentación).

3. **Todo el mundo debería solicitar ayuda financiera.** Son tantos los diversos factores que determinan tu elegibilidad para ayuda financiera, que nadie puede asegurarte de una vez, si eres o no elegible. El ingreso y los activos familiares no son los únicos aspectos que determinan la elegibilidad para la ayuda basada en la necesidad; el tamaño del grupo familiar y el número de hijos en la universidad son aspectos igualmente importantes.
4. **Los padres deben asegurarse de que sus hijos participen y entiendan el proceso de ayuda financiera.** En la mayoría de las escuelas, el estudiante es el primer punto de contacto para los asuntos administrativos y, en muchas ocasiones, el proceso de ayuda financiera es el primer paso para que tu hijo entienda cómo manejar sus asuntos financieros.
5. **Los padres deben llenar un ejemplo de la FAFSA cuando sus hijos ingresen al undécimo año de la secundaria.** Esta solicitud te da una idea de lo que será tu EFC; así, seleccionarás mejor las universidades al alcance de tus posibilidades financieras. Puedes hacerlo en la mayoría de los centros de orientación vocacional de las escuelas secundarias o en Internet con la ayuda de las Need Analysis Calculators (Calculadoras de Análisis Financiero).
6. **Si no has comenzado a ahorrar para la universidad, comienza a hacerlo ahora.** Puedes utilizar el dinero que ahorres en una cuenta bancaria para la universidad. Mejor aún, este ahorro puede convertirse en un recurso continuo dentro del

presupuesto familiar, que puedes utilizar para el pago de préstamos o como un plan de pagos mensuales cuando tu hijo esté en la universidad.

7. **Invierte en un Qualified State Tuition Plan, QSTP (Plan Estatal Calificado de Matrículas), más conocido como Plan I-529 (derivado del Código I-529 del Internal Revenue Service, IRS).** El I-529 tiene dos tipos de planes: el Prepaid College Tuition Plan (Plan de Pago Anticipado de Matrículas Universitarias), que permite a los inversionistas destinar fondos en un plan estatal que congela el costo actual de la matrícula a la tasa actual y lo protege contra la inflación de la misma en el futuro. El segundo, es el College Investment Plan (Plan de Inversión Universitario), que permite a los inversionistas (patrocinadores) invertir en un plan I-529 en cualquier momento que deseen. Si bien el plan no te garantiza que puedas cubrir los gastos de matrícula, puedes obtener muchos beneficios si participas en un plan de inversión universitario patrocinado por el estado, entre ellos, deducciones en la declaración de renta estatal, ingresos federales exentos de impuestos, ahorros por impuesto diferido y además, no estás obligado a declarar este activo como un activo del estudiante en la FAFSA. Muchos estados ofrecen beneficios tributarios a nivel estatal, así como beneficios exentos de impuestos cuando se usan estos fondos para estudiantes universitarios. Puedes excluir los Prepaid Tuition Plans de la FAFSA, pero no el College Investment Plan.
8. **Pregunta a tu(s) empleador(es), sindicato y cualquier club comunitario al que pertenezcas, si ofrecen ayuda financiera a estudiantes.**
9. **Averigua por los servicios de búsqueda de becas.** Si tu hijo es un estudiante excepcional y consideras que puede calificar para reconocimiento de beca académica, existen muchos servicios gratuitos de búsqueda de becas, como la página Web de Peterson's (www.petersons.com). No necesitas pagar por dicha asistencia.

10. **Averigua sobre los préstamos PLUS.** Si tienes suficientes recursos para financiar los gastos universitarios de tu hijo, pero te preocupa no tener suficiente dinero efectivo disponible para todos los gastos, el gobierno federal ha creado un programa de préstamo no basado en la necesidad denominado Parent Loan for Undergraduate Students, PLUS. Todas las familias pueden beneficiarse de este programa sin importar su ingreso actual. Aunque es importante recordar que este programa es un préstamo, está disponible para todos los padres sin importar su ingreso; además, en este momento, cuenta con una tasa de interés históricamente baja (4.86 por ciento). A través del programa de préstamos PLUS, puedes pedir prestado hasta el total de los gastos educativos menos cualquier ayuda financiera otorgada.
11. **Reduce la cantidad registrada como ahorros de tu hijo.** Si has puesto recursos significativos a nombre de tu hijo para aliviar tu carga de impuesto sobre la renta, ten en cuenta que esto puede reducir la elegibilidad para ayuda financiera de tu hijo. En los cálculos para elegibilidad de ayuda financiera, los ahorros de tu hijo están sujetos a impuestos con una tasa mucho más alta que los ahorros declarados por los padres. Si tú o tu hijo han destinado fondos para los gastos universitarios, piensa que puedes utilizarlos en gastos universitarios necesarios, como tal vez un nuevo vehículo o el pago anticipado de matrícula y cuotas, antes de llenar el formulario de análisis de necesidad. Esto puede significar una gran diferencia, particularmente si dichos gastos se reducen de los ahorros de tu hijo.
12. **Ten cuidado al escuchar a vecinos y amigos que te aconsejan qué hacer o que te dicen que sucederá.** A no ser que veas su declaración de renta o estados bancarios, no sabes realmente nada sobre sus finanzas. Sólo puedes ver cómo gastan su dinero.

PARA ESTUDIANTES: PREPARACIÓN Y HALLAZGO DE HECHOS

13. **Escucha a tus padres cuando hablen contigo sobre finanzas.** ¡La ayuda financiera puede significar grandes cantidades de dinero!
14. **Considera tu educación como una inversión que se te retribuirá muchas veces a lo largo de tu vida.** Tanto hombres como mujeres se benefician de la educación superior. Si tienes un título universitario, puedes ganar hasta $2.1 millones de dólares más en el curso de tu vida. Sin embargo, nunca ganarás lo mismo si no completas tus estudios universitarios; ¡no renuncies!
15. **Piensa qué puedes hacer para prepararte ahora.** Si tienes un trabajo, comienza a ahorrar parte de tu salario para la universidad.
16. **No permitas que el costo de la universidad estropee tus planes de educación.** Puedes contar con ayuda financiera y dinero proveniente de un gran número de fuentes.
17. **Comienza una búsqueda estrecha y personal.** La fuente más probable de becas para los estudiantes está geográficamente cerca a tu casa. La única y mejor fuente para identificar las oportunidades de becas es la oficina de orientación de tu escuela secundaria.
18. **Las bibliotecas públicas cuentan con libros de recursos para ayudarte a averiguar sobre becas.**
19. **Es crucial comenzar temprano.** Comienza la búsqueda al inicio del undécimo año de la escuela secundaria. Inicia el proceso de investigación sobre ayuda financiera al mismo tiempo que inicias el proceso de selección de universidad.
20. **Confirma con el consejero de tu escuela secundaria que has llenado los formularios correctos en tu undécimo año, de manera que puedas solicitar ayuda financiera al finalizar tu duodécimo año.** Por ejemplo, para solicitar ayuda al National Merit Scholarship Program

debes haber completado los exámenes PSAT en tu undécimo año de la secundaria. Muchos estados tienen programas de becas para estudiantes destacados de secundaria, pero la administración estatal de becas debe recibir las cartas de recomendación mientras el estudiante está en el undécimo año de la secundaria.

21. **Infórmate con tu consejero sobre las ventajas de tomar pruebas o clases que tengan crédito universitario, mientras estás en la escuela secundaria.** Esto te ayudará a ahorrar dinero más adelante.

22. **El College-Level Examination Program, CLEP (Programa de Evaluación de Nivel Universitario) permite a los estudiantes demostrar sus conocimientos a nivel universitario.** A su vez, esto permite a las universidades eximir al estudiante de ciertos cursos (lo que te permite ahorrar dinero); también permite que los estudiantes pasen directamente a cursos avanzados y completen sus estudios más pronto (ahorras aún más dinero), y exime a los estudiantes de prerequisitos o cursos introductorios (¡todavía puedes ahorras más!).

23. **El programa Advanced Placement, AP (Nivelación anticipada) permite a los estudiantes experimentar estudios universitarios mientras están en la secundaria.** Muchas universidades otorgan créditos o nivelación anticipada a estudiantes que reciben calificaciones suficientes en los exámenes AP.

24. **Mercadear tu imagen es probablemente el aspecto más importante para recibir una beca al mérito.** Son demasiados los estudiantes que dependen solamente de sus calificaciones para obtener becas universitarias al mérito. Al igual que muchas universidades buscan más allá de los puntajes de las prueba de admisión, para las becas al mérito se establecen otros criterios. Este tipo de becas se concede generalmente a estudiantes que demuestran excelencia en la escuela y que han contribuido a otras áreas de interés. Las universidades buscan estudiantes que se han fijado desafíos

académicos, sin dejar de llevar también una vida aparte de voluntariado, publicaciones o dirigir investigaciones.

25. **Promuévete.** Muchos donantes de becas locales le piden a las escuelas secundarias que sean ellas las que escojan a los estudiantes. Allí está el punto central de tus actividades de búsqueda y auto-promoción.

26. **No esperes que la ayuda financiera te otorgue tu trabajo.** Solicita un trabajo de tiempo parcial en un campus local mientras aún estás en secundaria, incluso si no piensas asistir allí. Al igual que todos los empleadores, los departamentos universitarios prefieren contratar a empleados experimentados. Los trabajos otorgados como ayuda sobre la base de la necesidad, a menudo corresponden a una pequeña proporción de los trabajos del campus.

27. **Haz una carpeta para cada universidad a medida que reduces tus opciones.** En esa carpeta, guarda la información sobre el costo, el tipo de ayuda ofrecida, fechas límite y cualquier beca especial que ofrezca la universidad. Puedes obtener la información en los folletos o en la página Web de la universidad.

28. **Examina los servicios gratuitos automatizados de becas disponibles en la mayoría de las páginas Web de universidades.**

29. **Pide hablar con el asistente de ayuda financiera cuando visites los campus.** Los funcionarios de admisión tienen la información básica sobre la ayuda financiera, pero seguramente querrás más detalles. Si no puedes ir en persona, llama y solicita una cita telefónica. Si puedes, consigue el nombre en la página Web de la universidad y pide hablar con una persona en particular. Los cargos de los funcionarios encargados de la ayuda financiera varían, pero es muy probable que se trate de un "consejero", "director asistente/asociado" o "funcionario", que es quien realmente evalúa las solicitudes. Guarda un registro de las personas con quién hablaste en cada universidad; pide su nombre, o incluso, su tarjeta de presentación.

30. **Haz tus preguntas directa y coherentemente.** No te dejes enredar por la jerga de ayuda financiera.
31. **Averigua si tu solicitud/necesidad de ayuda afecta la probabilidad de que seas admitido.** De ser así, ¿cómo?
32. **Averigua si la universidad ofrece ayuda por mérito.** Si lo hace, ¿cuántas becas por mérito da? ¿Cómo se determinan? y ¿Quién selecciona a los beneficiarios?
33. **Si estás pensando en solicitar la Early Decision/Early Action (Decisión temprana/Acción temprana), pregunta si las políticas/oportunidades de ayuda serían diferentes.** Algunas instituciones no ofrecen becas por mérito ni mejores paquetes basados en la necesidad a quienes solicitan ayuda en forma temprana. (Nota: Básicamente, este es un proceso privado de la universidad.)
34. **Pregunta cómo podría cambiar tu paquete de ayuda si cuentas con $3,000 de ayuda externa.** Puedes usar cualquier monto al hacer esta pregunta, pero usa siempre el mismo monto en cada universidad. Así, conseguirás las respuestas precisas sobre cómo la ayuda externa podría afectar tu paquete.
35. **Lee todo lo que recibas de la universidad.** No leer ni entender las fechas de vencimiento, las multas y las políticas institucionales no te exime de las obligaciones que contiene la información suministrada.
36. **Estudia las guías administrativas, catálogos y horarios de clase.** Los estudiantes que entienden el funcionamiento de su universidad tienen una ventaja competitiva en cada área, desde la ayuda financiera hasta la selección del curso. Aprovecha cada atajo tecnológico posible, desde el archivo electrónico de ayuda financiera hasta el registro temprano de cursos en la Web.
37. **Habla con estudiantes de segundo año de la universidad.** Ellos sabrán cómo sacar el mejor provecho de las reglas y excepciones administrativas, desde los posibles desembolsos tempranos para estudio en el exterior hasta el registro temprano de cursos para estudiantes que trabajan.

EL PROCESO DE SOLICITUD DE AYUDA FINANCIERA

38. **No te intimides por los formularios de ayuda financiera.** Si necesitas ayuda, haz una cita con un consejero vocacional de la escuela secundaria. Si el consejero no puede ayudarte, él puede ponerte en contacto con alguien que sí pueda hacerlo.

39. **No esperes a ser admitido para presentar la FAFSA o los documentos PROFILE. Solicita la ayuda financiera tan pronto como tus padres tengan cálculos de ingresos para el año fiscal exigido para completar los formularios.** Por ejemplo, si comienzas la universidad en agosto o septiembre de 2004, debes tener toda tu información de ingresos financieros de 2003 lista para enero o febrero de 2004. Solicita la asistencia de ayuda financiera en base a la necesidad lo más pronto posible, aún si tienes que usar las cifras de ingresos estimadas. Puedes hacer esto incluso si no has solicitado admisión en una universidad en particular.

40. **No olvides las fechas límite.** Todas las universidades tienen ayuda por subvención disponible para estudiantes elegibles, pero muchas tienen fondos limitados. Los estudiantes que están atentos a las fechas límite tienen una ventaja sobre aquéllos que no lo hacen. Aunque tengas que calcular tus cifras en la FAFSA o las solicitudes institucionales, no dejes de estar pendiente de las fechas. Cuanto antes presentes tu solicitud, mayor será la oportunidad de recibir la ayuda. Igualmente, debes presentar tus declaraciones de renta lo más temprano que puedas en el año.

41. **Establece fechas para llenar los formularios y, si es necesario, haz las correcciones posteriormente.** Un estudiante necesitado puede perder miles de dólares disponibles en subvenciones cada año, si las solicita después de la fecha de prioridad publicada. (Siempre podrás corregir los datos en los formularios, pero lo que no puedes corregir son las fechas límite no cumplidas.)

42. **La ayuda financiera es un evento anual.** Debes volver a solicitarla todos los años.

43. **Completa tu FAFSA.** Para aquellos estudiantes que nunca antes han solicitado ayuda, la metodología básica para solicitar la asistencia de ayuda financiera es la FAFSA. Este documento puede llenarse en Internet en www.fafsa.ed.gov o por escrito con un formulario impreso. El proceso de solicitud es gratuito y la información puede estar disponible para todas las universidades en las que estés interesado. La FAFSA es el documento básico para determinar tu elegibilidad para ayuda financiera federal basada en la necesidad y, frecuentemente, se usa tanto para la ayuda financiera estatal como para las becas institucionales.

44. **La FAFSA debe presentarse cada año después del 1° de enero.**

45. **Tanto estudiantes como padres deben registrarse en el Departamento de Educación de Estados Unidos para obtener los números PIN.** Así, cada miembro de la familia puede firmar la FAFSA en Internet; esto acelerará el proceso FAFSA. Visita www.fafsa.ed.gov.

46. **Si también estás solicitando un préstamo bancario, es importante que sepas la fecha posible de tu graduación en la universidad.** La fecha esperada de graduación se refiere a la fecha en la que esperas graduarte de la universidad (no de la escuela secundaria). Por ejemplo, la mayoría de estudiantes de primer año que inician su programa universitario en el otoño de 2004, esperan graduarse en el 2008. ¿Por qué los prestamistas quieren saber esta fecha? Muchos préstamos (federales y alternativos) son diferidos, es decir, los pagos no se inician mientras el estudiante está en la universidad. Los prestamistas usan la fecha esperada de graduación para determinar el estatus diferido de los beneficiarios. De manera que si usas tu fecha de graduación de la secundaria en lugar de tu fecha esperada de graduación de la universidad, pueden pedirte que comiences a reembolsar tu préstamo estudiantil inmediatamente.

47. **Para los préstamos del banco, calcula el costo total de tu préstamo.** Hay muchas calculadoras disponibles en Internet, que no sólo pueden indicarte cuál será tu pago, sino también cuánto pagarás de interés a lo largo de la vida del préstamo. (Visita www.petersons.com)

48. **Pide el préstamo a través del mismo prestamista cada año.** Esto evita que tengas que pagar a múltiples entidades cuando comienza el reembolso. También sirve para simplificar la administración de tus préstamos.

49. **Al pedir prestado a través de un banco, no tengas miedo de llamar al prestamista, sin importar las circunstancias.** Ellos quieren que tengas éxito en el manejo y reembolso de tu préstamo estudiantil, por lo tanto, les interesa escucharte.

50. **La expectativa normal del proceso de análisis de necesidad es que los padres tienen la responsabilidad financiera primaria de ayudar a sus hijos a pagar la universidad.** Aún si tus padres sienten que su obligación financiera hacia ti acaba cuando vas a la universidad, el sistema de análisis de necesidad que evalúa el EFC no deja que esto suceda. Por consiguiente, declarar tu estatus como independiente no es una opción. Es casi imposible que seas un estudiante independiente inmediatamente después de terminar la escuela secundaria. Sólo un grupo de individuos muy cerrado, como huérfanos o estudiantes ya padres, que proveen el sustento de su propia descendencia, califica como estudiantes independientes.

51. **Siempre informa a la oficina de ayuda financiera de la universidad sobre cualquier otorgamiento.** Si una organización de la comunidad local te ha otorgado una beca, tu elegibilidad para ayuda financiera de la universidad probablemente se verá afectada. En la mayoría de los casos, todo tipo de recursos disponible para ti, bien sea que provenga de tus padres o de una beca que obtuviste de una entidad externa, se tendrá en cuenta para otorgar ayuda financiera basada en la necesidad. Pide que, si es necesario reducir la ayuda, se haga de las becas de auto-ayuda (préstamo o valores de trabajo).

52. **¡Vuelve a solicitar la ayuda! El hecho de que no califiques para ayuda un año, no significa que no calificarás en los años siguientes.** El estudiante y las situaciones familiares cambian; por consiguiente, podría cambiar tu estatus de elegibilidad.

53. **Si te negaron la ayuda cuando iniciaste tus estudios y ahora tienes un hermano o hermana que asiste a la universidad, ya tienes dos razones muy importantes para volver a solicitar ayuda financiera.** Primero, los resultados de cálculos de análisis de necesidad son substancialmente diferentes cuando hay dos o más miembros del grupo familiar en la universidad que cuando hay un solo hijo en la universidad. Segundo, las reglamentaciones cambian frecuentemente y es posible que ahora seas elegible para un nuevo programa o para programas de ayuda financiera modificados.

54. **Llena completamente tus documentos de solicitud de ayuda.** Los espacios en blanco enloquecen a los funcionarios de ayuda financiera; si la respuesta es cero, escríbelo y no dejes espacios en blanco.

55. **Cuando tus padres estén completando los formularios de ayuda financiera, recuerda hacerles llenar tu nombre en la casilla "student's name", la fecha de tu nacimiento en la casilla "student's birth date", y tu número de seguro social en la casilla "student's Social Security number" para que no se confundan y coloquen la información de ellos en la sección del estudiante. Muchas personas cometen errores en esta sección de la FAFSA. Estos errores pueden demorar la ayuda que una universidad puede otorgarte y también puede impedir que recibas alguna ayuda de la universidad.**

56. **Si es posible, usa declaraciones federales de impuesto sobre la renta totalmente llenas al completar tu FAFSA.** Sin embargo, si no tienes las declaraciones de impuesto sobre la renta antes de las fechas

límite en tu estado o institución, calcula tu ingreso y completa el formulario. Después, puedes hacer cambios a la información de la solicitud; lo que no puedes cambiar es la fecha de solicitud si la presentaste tarde.

57. **Guarda copias de todos los documentos que usas para completar los formularios cuando solicites la ayuda.** Tu universidad puede pedir documentación para verificar la información que tú y sus padres proporcionan.
58. **Haz todo a tiempo.** Mira la fecha límite en los documentos para estar seguro de cumplir con la fecha límite correcta de cada universidad a la que estés postulando. Haz una lista de verificación, registra la fecha cuando enviaste los documentos y guarda copias de todo. Haz todo lo que puedas electrónicamente. Si tienes preguntas sobre lo que se requiere o si has recibido algo, pregunta; no asumas nada.
59. **Al enviar por correo artículos que tienen una fecha límite, pide a la oficina de correo un Certificado de envío.** Este recibo normalmente será válido para la institución, en caso que tus documentos lleguen tarde o se extravíen en el correo.
60. **¡Sé proactivo! Ponte en contacto con la oficina de ayuda financiera en la universidad seleccionada para estar seguro de que tus documentos estén completos y de que no falta nada.** Verifica y vuelve a verificar constantemente.
61. **Si tienes circunstancias especiales que quieras que la oficina de ayuda financiera sepa, envía una carta adjunta a tu solicitud.** La ayuda financiera se basa en cifras; si hay gastos extras que quieras que se tengan en cuenta, asegúrate de que la oficina las tenga en cuenta; ¡es mejor usar menos palabras y más cifras!
62. **Informa a tu consejero de ayuda financiera sobre cualquier circunstancia o gasto extraordinario.** Algunos ejemplos son los gastos médicos extraordinarios; gastos de cuidados a ancianos, discapacitados o personas con necesidades

especiales; gastos por el cuidado de niños (algunas instituciones tienen en cuenta gastos en la educación privada para áreas en donde las escuelas secundarias públicas tienen un bajo rendimiento académico); bancarrotas e impuestos atrasados, grandes pagos únicos; despidos, jubilaciones y renuncias; así como también gastos de asistencia para viajes, libros y materiales o gastos de alojamiento.

PARA PADRES Y ESTUDIANTES: ES LA HORA DE LA DECISIÓN: EVALÚA LOS OTORGAMIENTOS DE AYUDA FINANCIERA

63. **Entiende en qué se diferencian la ayuda basada en la NECESIDAD y la ayuda por MÉRITO.** La ayuda basada en la necesidad se centra en la necesidad financiera de la familia. La ayuda por mérito se basa en las calificaciones del estudiante, puntajes de pruebas y otros atributos del estudiante que la universidad desea premiar (beca) para que asistas y hagas tus estudios.
64. **Usa la información de ayuda financiera para evaluar las universidades a las que deseas postular, pero no la uses para excluir una universidad a la que realmente quieras asistir.**
65. **Ten entre las opciones una universidad con seguridad "financiera".** Ésta es una universidad donde te admiten y que puedes pagar, sin importar los resultados de otras solicitudes en otras universidades. Así, tienes vía libre para presentarte en universidades que pueden parecer estar fuera de tus posibilidades financieras.
66. **Conoce el proceso de las universidades para otorgar fondos.** Muchas universidades públicas fuera del estado solamente otorgan préstamos y programas de trabajo a estudiantes que vienen de fuera del estado, sin importar qué tan grande sea la necesidad no satisfecha. Por el contrario, la mayoría de las universidades privadas satisfacen toda la

necesidad y no llenan el vacío. En consecuencia, si deseas asistir a una universidad fuera del estado, en la mayoría de los casos, puede resultar más barato una universidad privada de altos costos que las instituciones públicas de bajos costos.

67. **Si necesitas pedir prestado, recuerda que los términos y condiciones de los préstamos educativos pueden variar.** Asegúrate de entender los términos y condiciones, al igual que los costos (es decir, tasa de interés, las cuotas del préstamo y el programa de reembolso) que tiene cada préstamo.

68. **Existe una gran variedad de préstamos que pueden otorgarse como parte de un paquete de ayuda financiera.** En algunos casos, el interés aumenta mientras el estudiante asiste a la universidad. Si el interés aumenta, piensa en ir pagando el interés para reducir tus pagos cuando empieces a reembolsar el préstamo.

69. **Existen requisitos adicionales que debes cumplir si es la primera vez que aceptas un préstamo como parte de un paquete de ayuda financiera.** Los estudiantes deben tener una asesoría sobre préstamos para "prestatario por primera vez", bien sea personalmente o en Internet, dependiendo de la institución. Los estudiantes también deben firmar un pagaré. No cumplir con estos detalles tardará el desembolso del préstamo.

70. **Los préstamos del banco y los préstamos federales Direct (como parte de un paquete de ayuda financiera) incluyen una cuota del 3 por ciento para cubrir los cargos por originación.** Por lo tanto, si te otorgan un préstamo de $1,000, recibirás realmente $970. El cargo por originación se cobra cada vez que recibes un préstamo. Cuando reembolses el préstamo, debes reembolsar la totalidad de la cantidad prestada, en este caso, $1,000. Es importante que calcules el dinero que necesitas para la universidad. Nota: Es posible que algunos prestamistas no cobren cuota de cargos por originación.

71. **Elabora una tabla que tenga las cuotas que te ha cobrado la universidad (por concepto de matrícula, cuotas, alojamiento y comida).** Suma tus gastos estimados de transporte y resta cualquier ayuda por donación y préstamo estudiantil ofrecidos para ayudarte a pagar tus gastos reales de universidad. Compara estas cifras básicas para determinar cuál es la ayuda más atractiva. Cuidado: Algunas universidades colocarán los préstamos a los padres como parte de la ayuda que otorgan, no los cuentes como ayuda todavía; tampoco cuentes ninguna ayuda de trabajo y estudio, ya que estos fondos normalmente se pagan directamente al estudiante a medida que ellos los ganan.

72. **Compara las diferentes filosofías de empaque y los criterios para otorgar ayuda de cada universidad que estés considerando.** Si tú (el estudiante) has sido aceptado como estudiante en varias universidades muy selectivas y has recibido numerosos paquetes de ayuda financiera y estás intentando decidir a cuál asistir, compara las filosofías de empaque. Para esto, una metodología eficaz es calcular cuáles serán los gastos que pagarás de tu bolsillo, qué parte del paquete otorgado vendrá en forma de subvenciones o becas en comparación con los préstamos. No dejes de evaluar tus posibilidades para renovar tu beca o subvención. Si tienes claro las diferencias en costos y el proceso de renovación de becas y subvenciones, puedes comparar cada una de ellas. Finalmente, debes sopesar el valor del paquete otorgado con la educación que recibirás de la institución.

73. **Existe una gran cantidad de préstamos disponibles para ayudar a las familias en su búsqueda de educación superior.** Todas las universidades tienen programas de préstamos federales disponibles tanto para estudiantes como para padres. Además de los préstamos federales, es posible que haya préstamos privados institucionales o alternativos disponibles. A menudo, las universidades tienen préstamos no publicitados para los estudiantes más necesitados o para emergencias. Debes pedir la

información completa sobre préstamos a la oficina de ayuda financiera de la universidad. La mayoría de los préstamos pueden diferirse hasta que el estudiante ya no esté inscrito por lo menos a tiempo parcial. Con frecuencia, los consejeros de ayuda financiera recomiendan préstamos para el estudiante, más que préstamos para padres debido a las opciones de reembolso y tasas de interés más favorables.

74. **Si hay una diferencia considerable entre las ofertas de tus universidades seleccionadas, consulta la información que tienes sobre cada universidad; quizás una beca se basa en el mérito y otra en la necesidad.**

DEBEN ENTENDER EL PROCESO DE APELACIÓN PARA LAS CARTAS DE OTORGAMIENTO DE AYUDA FINANCIERA

75. **Si piensas que la beca de ayuda no es suficiente, informa a la oficina de ayuda inmediatamente para expresar tus inquietudes y pedir que "reconsideren" la beca.** Comienza con la oficina de ayuda en la universidad donde más quieres estudiar. Si puedes llegar a un acuerdo con ellos, estás listo. Si no, continúa con tu segunda opción y así sucesivamente. No intentes hacer el juego de ofertas y contraofertas, en muy raras ocasiones funciona.

76. **Siempre intenta primero ponerte en contacto directamente con la oficina de ayuda financiera, no con la oficina de admisiones, tampoco con un ex-alumno, ni con el presidente de la institución.** Si tienes problema para hacer este contacto, continúa intentándolo, tal vez se trate de un momento muy ocupado. Sin embargo, si no puedes contactar a nadie en una semana, habla con la oficina de admisiones para ver si ellos te pueden ayudar a hacer el contacto.

77. **Otra razón para presentar una apelación, es que algunas universidades privadas cuentan con una política de apelación, mediante la cual afirman estar**

en capacidad de hacer ofertas tan atractivas como las de cualquier universidad similar.

78. **Ten a mano copias de todos tus documentos cuando hables con el funcionario de ayudas.** Si has actualizado información, por ejemplo, una declaración de renta más reciente, también debes tenerla disponible.

79. **Si tú o tus padres se han quedado desempleados después de llenar la FAFSA, es importante que la oficina de ayuda financiera lo sepa. Deberás solicitar un análisis adicional para ayuda financiera por pérdida de ingresos.** Es normal que la institución requiera documentación para verificar tu ingreso actual. La mayoría de las instituciones tienen políticas estándar que permiten el uso de ingresos proyectados. Es de esperar que esto te signifique un aumento en tu ayuda financiera.

80. **Si tienes una deuda considerable en tu tarjeta de crédito, ten en cuenta que el proceso de análisis de necesidad no considera la deuda por tarjeta de crédito en los cálculos típicos.** Lo mejor que puedes hacer es completar la FAFSA y ponerte en contacto con la oficina de ayuda financiera de la universidad para explicar tu situación. Las diferentes instituciones tienen políticas diferentes para responder a estas situaciones.

81. **Incluye información sobre los "mejores" otorgamientos, pero asegúrate primero de que realmente sean mejores y de que tengan condiciones similares.** No envíes una beca por mérito a una universidad que sólo proporciona ayuda basada en la necesidad.

82. **No esperes una respuesta inmediata, pero pregunta cuándo podrías esperar una decisión y cómo te la comunicarán.** En la hipótesis de que te comunicas con la oficina oportunamente, debes esperar una respuesta a tu solicitud de ayuda antes de la fecha que la universidad ha establecido para responder. Si no has obtenido respuesta para esa fecha, solicita que te prorroguen el plazo para darte respuesta.

83. **Prepárate también para hablar sobre opciones financieras.** Sin embargo, aborda este tema sólo después de estar seguro de que ya no hay más ayuda disponible.

84. **Toma la solicitud como un ejercicio para encontrar información, no como una negociación.** Analiza siempre a la persona con quien hables. Los funcionarios de ayuda tienen familias e hijos en la universidad, facturas que pagar y decisiones que tomar. ¡Ellos no van a reaccionar bien si insistes que necesitas una casa de vacaciones! Te valoran y se esforzarán para que ingreses a su universidad. Sin embargo, están limitados por políticas federales e institucionales, tal y como tú estás limitado por el dinero que tu familia está dispuesta a pagar por tu educación. Si no puedes llegar a un acuerdo que te convenga, continúa con tu segunda opción universitaria.

EL FLUJO DE EFECTIVO Y AHORROS

85. **Trabajo disponible en el campus.** La mayoría de las universidades emplean a un número considerable de sus propios estudiantes porque piensan que están motivados, son confiables e inteligentes.

86. **La remuneración por el trabajo en el campus es muy valiosa, sobre todo para los estudiantes nuevos.** Para el estudiante-empleado que trabaja en el campus y se convierte en alguien que conoce realmente la universidad desde adentro, los contactos en el campus, las tutorías y el conocimiento de su estructura organizativa son beneficios invaluables.

87. **Asegúrate de llegar al campus con "instrumentos financieros" que te permitan aprovechar los descuentos y las decisiones oportunas.** Puedes aprovechar los descuentos disponibles por medio de cuentas corrientes locales, transferencias electrónicas de ayuda financiera y tarjetas de crédito.

88. **Muchos dueños y arrendatarios de apartamentos te harán descuento, si pagas por anticipado todo un semestre.**

89. **Compra libros oportunamente, cómpralos directamente a otros estudiantes y búscalos en las librerías locales.** Puedes pedir prestado muchos libros en las bibliotecas locales y guardarlos durante todo el semestre.

90. **Pregunta si tu universidad proporciona alquiler de libros en lugar de tener que comprarlos.** El alquiler es generalmente menos caro que comprarlos. Si los compras, ten en cuenta la política de devolución. Normalmente hay una fecha límite para devolverlos y solicitar el reembolso. ¿Hay una escala móvil para el reembolso de libros devueltos? Entre más temprano devuelvas un libro, mayor será tu oportunidad de reembolso.

91. **¿La librería te volverá a comprar los libros al final del semestre?** ¿Cómo valoran los libros devueltos? ¿Tienen en cuenta la condición del libro? Estas preguntas te permiten saber cómo reembolsar la mayor cantidad de dinero según la forma de reventa que puedas utilizar.

92. **Ten cuidado con el uso de tarjetas de crédito.** Ésta es la forma más común cómo los estudiantes universitarios pueden iniciar una mala historia crediticia. Sólo necesitas un retardo de noventa días para estropear tú informe crediticio. Estos incidentes se quedan en tu informe durante años y pueden impedirte que obtengas otros tipos de crédito en el futuro, como préstamos para automóvil, préstamos alternativos para educación y préstamos hipotecarios. Las verificaciones de crédito con frecuencia se hacen antes de arrendar un apartamento y algunos empleadores las exigen antes de contratarte. Muchos prestamistas prefieren prestarle a alguien sin crédito que a alguien con mal crédito.

93. **Asegúrate de conocer las fechas de vencimiento para la matrícula y las multas por no pagar en esas fechas.** Muchas instituciones cobran cuotas de retardo por los pagos hechos después de cierta fecha o también por registrarse después de cierta fecha. Si pagas y te registras a tiempo, puedes ahorrar dinero.

94. **Si pagas la matrícula con tarjeta de crédito, ten en cuenta cualquier costo adicional cobrado por la universidad o una entidad de servicio externa para cubrir los costos incurridos al aceptar las tarjetas de crédito.** La cuota puede variar de 1 a 3 por ciento del monto cobrado y es adicional al interés que se te carga en la factura de tu tarjeta de crédito.

95. **Si pagas la matrícula con tarjeta de crédito a fin de recibir millas para viajeros frecuentes, compara el interés que pagas por utilizar la tarjeta de crédito frente al valor de las millas gratuitas.** Si decides cancelar $5,000 de matrícula con tarjeta de crédito y pagas en un año una tasa de interés de 1.25 por ciento mensual, tendrás que pagar aproximadamente $406 por interés. ¿Vale la pena pagar $406 por las millas para viajero frecuente?

96. **Lee y entiende cualquier contrato que vayas a firmar para vivienda en el campus.** ¿Se aplican multas si cambias de parecer respecto al lugar donde quieres vivir? ¿Tienes que mantener cierta carga de créditos para que seas elegible para alojamiento en el campus? ¿Te permiten cambiar de cuarto sin multarte?

97. **Una porción de los gastos de matrícula puede tomarse como crédito de impuestos para los padres o contingente de los estudiantes sobre el ingreso y el método de pago.** El Crédito impositivo Hope Scholarship permite deducciones por cada estudiante para los dos primeros años de educación superior, mientras que el Crédito impositivo Lifetime Learning se usa sobre la base de la declaración de impuestos y cubre un cronograma y programación de cursos más amplios. Las subvenciones, becas y ayuda de empleo-educación exentas de impuestos que se usan para cubrir gastos educativos, no son elegibles para ninguno de estos créditos impositivos. Si deseas aprovechar cualquiera de estos créditos, comunícate con la persona que prepara tu declaración de impuestos.

98. **No olvides las sanciones a tu ayuda financiera por retirarte de clases.** Estas sanciones son adicionales a las que se imponen en la matrícula. Si un estudiante beneficiario de ayuda financiera (federal) Título IV se retira de todas las clases antes de que haya transcurrido el 60 por ciento del semestre, se le puede exigir el reembolso de una parte o toda la ayuda financiera Título IV. Esto se determina mediante una fórmula federal. Pide la opinión de un consejero de ayuda financiera antes de retirarte de clases, específicamente en lo que respecta al Título IV.

PARA PADRES Y ESTUDIANTES: ASPECTOS QUE SE DEBEN TENER EN CUENTA

99. **Evita ofertas de dineros garantizados en los que el estudiante debe pagar para recibir el servicio.** Nunca pagues por ningún servicio que puedas encontrar gratuitamente, bien sea como estudiante o como padre.

100. **Los seminarios "gratis" sobre ayuda financiera no siempre son gratuitos.** Con frecuencia, estas invitaciones las hacen promotores que buscan honorarios exagerados por sus consejos.

101. **Las normas federales protegen la confidencialidad del estudiante.** Si los padres o un tutor legal necesitan información financiera sobre un estudiante (por ejemplo, el saldo de su cuenta o los pagos realizados), infórmate sobre la política de la institución referente a la confidencialidad de los estudiantes. En algunas universidades, los estudiantes pueden convenir que otra persona tenga acceso a su información financiera. Conocer anticipadamente tales políticas te facilitará hacer los pagos correspondientes y recibir la información necesaria.

AGRADECIMIENTOS

Agradecimientos especiales a las siguientes personas por la ayuda prestada en la creación de esta lista de consejos:

Dr. Lawrence Burt, director de servicios financieros estudiantiles, University of Texas Austin

Brenda Dillon, vicepresidente, gerente de producto del programa federal, Key Education Resources

Heather Domeier, directora asistente de los servicios financieros estudiantiles de Rice University

Audrey Hill, consejera vocacional de Col. Zadock Macgruder High School, Rockville, Maryland

John Nametz, director de ayuda basada en la necesidad de University of Arizona

Stephen Rouff, director asociado de ayuda financiera (retirado) de Rutgers University

Myra Baas Smith, directora universitaria de ayuda financiera de Yale University

Dr. Lawrence Waters, decano de servicios de admisión e inscripción de Ball State University

Kathy Wyler, administradora de University of Wisconsin–Parkside

Capítulo 8

Veinte preguntas que deberías hacer al realizar la visita al campus

¿Cuántas veces después de salir del consultorio del médico, dices: "Olvidé preguntarle sobre..."? Igual le pasa a muchas familias que recuerdan las preguntas que deberían hacer sobre la ayuda financiera universitaria sólo después de que ha finalizado su visita al campus. Este capítulo te servirá para hacer las preguntas adecuadas antes de que salgas del campus con tu hijo.

Las respuestas que recibas de los funcionarios de la oficina de ayuda financiera te permitirán decidir cuál universidad es la que mejor se ajusta a tu hijo desde un punto de vista financiero. Además, pon mucha atención a la forma cómo los funcionarios responden a tus preguntas de seguimiento. Busca respuestas que te ofrezcan información y soluciones. Por ejemplo, ¿los funcionarios de la universidad te dan detalles que satisfacen tus inquietudes? ¿se toman el tiempo para analizar y resolver las preguntas? Las cuestiones relacionadas con ayuda financiera con frecuencia son complejas; utiliza las respuestas como punto de referencia para decidir si la universidad está "orientada a la familia" en lo que respecta a ayuda financiera.

Debes ser un "padre pensante", toma nota de toda pregunta que se te venga en mente cuando estés leyendo las preguntas recomendadas. Lo mejor que pueden hacer los padres y los estudiantes es enfocar el proceso de solicitud de ayuda financiera con el mismo cuidado que cuando solicitan admisión.

En el Apéndice se repiten las preguntas. Cuando visites las universidades, desprende este apéndice del libro y úsalo como referencia cuando te reúnas con un director de ayuda financiera.

FLEXIBILIDAD DE LA UNIVERSIDAD

La primera clase de preguntas tiene que ver con la flexibilidad de la oficina de ayuda financiera de la universidad. Los padres deben saber cómo los tratará cada universidad, en especial si las circunstancias financieras se complican. Por ejemplo, ¿cómo responde la oficina de ayuda financiera a las necesidades individuales de una familia? ¿El personal será sensible, oportuno y de ayuda cuando necesites orientación o asistencia inmediata? ¿Una gran universidad estatal pública podrá ayudarte tan rápido como una privada? ¿En la actualidad existen políticas de ayuda financiera establecidas que demuestren una "actitud" de voluntad y ayuda?

¿Es práctica común hacer ajustes de gastos individuales de asistencia cuando los estudiantes y las familias lo soliciten?

Esta debería ser la primera pregunta que se hiciera para determinar la flexibilidad de la universidad. Todas las universidades establecen un "gasto fijo de asistencia" (también conocido como presupuesto) que aplican a diferentes tipos de estudiantes. Por lo general, incluye matrícula, cuotas, alojamiento y comida, gastos estimados de libros y otros gastos misceláneos. A los estudiantes que no residen en el campus se les asigna un presupuesto diferente al de los residentes. Los gastos por libros pueden ser bastante superiores para una especialización en ingeniería que los de una especialización en filosofía. Es posible que un estudiante que no reside en el campus requiera un incremento en gastos de transporte si vive muy lejos de la universidad. Incluso, algunas universidades pueden reducir tu aporte esperado de la familia (es decir, cuánto tienes que pagar) si estás pagando matrícula en escuela privada para tus hijos menores.

En pocas palabras, pregunta si la oficina de ayuda financiera consideraría gastos adicionales, razonables, permisibles y documentados que estén por fuera de la norma. Si la respuesta es "sí" o si la universidad tiene intención de revisar tu archivo y tomar en cuenta estos gastos, ponle una A+ en flexibilidad.

¿Cuál es la política de la universidad en cuanto a "ingresos anuales proyectados"?

Incluso si no prevés una pérdida de ingresos, de todos modos pregunta sobre el ingreso anual proyectado. Nunca se sabe lo que puede pasar en el curso de los siguientes cuatro o cinco años.

El ingreso anual proyectado es un término que emplean las oficinas de ayuda cuando solicitas una nueva evaluación de tu condición financiera en función de una pérdida de ingresos. Por ejemplo, en el momento cuando se llenó la solicitud de ayuda financiera, ambos padres estaban empleados; pero después, uno de ellos perdió su trabajo y se produjo una gran reducción de ingresos (por ejemplo, pérdidas en la bolsa de valores o una discapacidad a largo plazo). Pregunta en la oficina de ayuda financiera si es posible que revisen el análisis de ayuda financiera original y el resultado final de aporte esperado de la familia, y que empleen las ganancias "anuales proyectadas" en lugar de las ganancias del año anterior, que ya no espera recibir la familia. No todas las universidades tendrán en cuenta este tipo de solicitudes, pero los reglamentos federales permiten estas consideraciones. En este caso, debes estar preparado para comprobar (documentar) tu pérdida de ingresos/renta y ofrecer cálculos razonables de futuras ganancias.

POLÍTICAS

Las políticas de ayuda financiera pueden ser tan diferentes como el día y la noche, incluso dentro del mismo sistema universitario. Cada universidad puede tener sus propias políticas y procedimientos institucionales con los que te debes familiarizar. Por ejemplo, la University of Wisconsin-Madison puede tener varias políticas de ayuda estudiantil que no tiene la University of Wisconsin-Milwaukee. Es importante que sepas esto, en especial si estás averiguando en más de una universidad dentro del mismo sistema estatal. Esta sección se centrará en asuntos muy importantes sobre las políticas universitarias que debes entender para tener éxito en la obtención de ayuda financiera.

¿Cuál es la carga académica mínima requerida para mantener las subvenciones?

Por lo general, las universidades deben rendir cuentas a tres autoridades: el gobierno federal, el gobierno estatal y al auditor de la universidad, y ajustarán un otorgamiento para ayuda federal y estatal, según se requiera. En algunos casos, las becas institucionales se pueden reducir o cancelar si tu hijo renuncia a algunos cursos. Ten cuidado. Debes analizar las reducciones de trabajo académico con un consejero de ayuda financiera.

La mayoría de universidades exige que los estudiantes universitarios tengan una carga académica de 12 créditos, de tiempo completo en un período académico, para recibir un otorgamiento de ayuda financiera "completa". Sin embargo, muchos estudiantes reducen su carga académica para conservar su promedio de calificaciones, con la idea de que al tomar menos créditos puedan tener mejores calificaciones. Otros estudiantes se retiran de un curso con el que tienen dificultades, sin darse cuenta que podrían poner en riesgo la posibilidad de elegibilidad para ayuda financiera. Debes conocer las políticas de la universidad y preguntar qué requisitos tienen antes de que tu hijo inicie clases. Además, los estudiantes que sólo reciben fondos por méritos podrían tener sanciones. De hecho, muchas universidades tienen políticas más estrictas para los otorgamientos por mérito académico que para otras formas de subvenciones.

¿Cuál es la política de la universidad en cuanto a las excepciones para la carga mínima de créditos sobre la base de razones de salud o académicas?

Si durante la inscripción, tu hijo desarrolla problemas médicos graves o enfrenta serias dificultades académicas, ¿la oficina de ayuda financiera será consciente de estas circunstancias al revisar tu caso para una posible reducción de la ayuda? Desde el comienzo, debes conocer qué tipo de apoyo personal puedes esperar si enfrentas deterioros de salud o académicos. Prepárate para documentar tu apelación con registros médicos, si se trata de la salud. Si el problema es académico, pídele consejo y apoyo a un orientador académico. Algunas veces, es útil que el orientador académico hable con el consejero de ayuda financiera para desarrollar un plan que resuelva esta nueva situación.

¿Puedes entrevistarte con un consejero de ayuda financiera el mismo día que visitas la universidad?

En tus visitas a la universidad, probablemente asistas a sesiones de orientación presentadas por representantes del personal de admisiones. Además, puedes hablar con un profesor o entrenador deportivo. Pero, ¿has hecho cita para hablar con un consejero de ayuda financiera? La mayoría de los padres no lo hacen; sin embargo, el "padre pensante" sí. Debes presentarte a un consejero de ayuda financiera al inicio del ciclo de admisiones y del ciclo de ayuda financiera para que la oficina de ayuda financiera te conozca a ti y tus necesidades. Cuando hables con el consejero, confirma las fechas prioritarias de registro para todas las solicitudes de ayuda financiera requeridas.

Si tienes mucho que contar, el momento adecuado es la primera cita. Intenta crear una relación de confianza con el consejero de ayuda financiera. Esta es tu oportunidad para tantear qué clase de persona es el consejero de ayuda financiera. ¿Qué tanta experiencia tiene? ¿Será él la persona asignada para tratar contigo y con tu hijo durante todo el año? ¿Escucha y comprende tus inquietudes y problemas? ¿Puede explicarte cómo solicitar ayuda adicional? ¿Qué busca la institución al hacer ajustes en el otorgamiento? ¿El consejero conoce algún fondo institucional discrecional en caso que requieras fondos adicionales?

Cuando estés en la oficina de ayuda financiera, pídele al consejero que revise contigo el registro de tu hijo y explícale cómo se determinó tu aporte esperado de la familia. Puede haber errores; asegúrate de que se emplee la información correcta en el proceso de análisis de necesidad. Si ha habido cambios financieros o médicos desde que presentaste tu solicitud, infórmalo al consejero, ya que en esta cita se pueden hacer ajustes. El punto clave es establecer una relación con el consejero de ayuda financiera tan pronto como sea posible. Tu primera visita al campus es una oportunidad ideal.

La mayoría de oficinas de ayuda financiera (si no todas) apartan fondos discrecionales cada año para aumentar los otorgamientos de ayuda a estudiantes que apelen su paquete de ayuda. Sin embargo, estos fondos no se dan a conocer públicamente y son limitados; por eso, pregunta sobre de su disponibilidad.

ASUNTOS FAMILIARES

En términos financieros, estudiar en la universidad es posible para cualquiera que esté interesado en asistir, sin importar su raza o estatus económico. Pero, cuando los padres se divorcian, es común que te pregunten "¿Quién va a pagar?" Es importante que sepas cuál de los esposos debe presentar la solicitud de ayuda financiera y exactamente cuál solicitud debe llenarse y quién la va a llenar. Además, si tú o tu ex cónyuge se ha vuelto a casar, no te olvides de leer las instrucciones de ayuda financiera para determinar qué información puede requerirse para padrastros.

¿Tienen en cuenta el ingreso de los padrastros cuando analizan una solicitud de ayuda?

Muchos estudiantes provienen de familias divorciadas que pueden tener muchas situaciones financieras muy complejas. La metodología federal de análisis de necesidades exige incluir información de los padrastros al llenar la FAFSA. No hay ninguna otra opción, y si no reportas el ingreso de los padrastros, habrá demoras en el procesamiento de la solicitud de tu hijo. Es mejor apelar después que retardar la revisión inicial de la ayuda. Es posible que un consejero de ayuda financiera "pase por alto" el ingreso del padrastro si tú apelas (una razón valida podría ser la corta duración del matrimonio). No es seguro, pero algunas veces es posible.

Informa el ingreso de los padrastros cuando solicites ayuda financiera federal y verifica los requisitos para tu solicitud de ayuda estatal. Para acceder a otorgamiento institucional de una universidad privada, es posible que también debas llenar la CSS PROFILE. En tu visita al campus, vuelve a revisar cuáles solicitudes de ayuda financiera debes completar.

Tienen en cuenta el ingreso del ex cónyuge en la solicitud de ayuda financiera?

Esta es una pregunta importante, ya que muchas universidades exigen esta información. Si la universidad exige una solicitud CSS PROFILE además de la FAFSA, se te exigirá reportar mucha más información financiera familiar que en la FAFSA. La CSS PROFILE es una solicitud de ayuda financiera que muchas universidades emplean para otorgar ayuda no federal a los estudiantes. Es un servicio del College Board

(Consejo Universitario). Una CSS PROFILE es una solicitud de ayuda financiera complementaria que se emplea para determinar la mejor forma de conceder fondos de otorgamiento institucional basado en la necesidad. No olvides leer con mucho cuidado todos los requisitos de solicitud de ayuda financiera. Aunque no parezca justo, las universidades que otorgan bastantes fondos institucionales requieren tanta información financiera como sea posible, con el fin de garantizar que los estudiantes más necesitados reciban consideración prioritaria.

OBTENCIÓN DE DINERO

Analiza, analiza y analiza. Tu trabajo comienza verdaderamente después de que tu hijo recibe la oferta de otorgamiento de ayuda financiera (también conocida como "paquete") de la universidad. Debes tener ojo crítico en lo que se le "otorga" a tu hijo. Un otorgamiento de ayuda financiera puede estar conformado por becas, subvenciones, préstamos y trabajos. Pero, ¿qué pasaría si tu hijo sólo recibe un préstamo? ¿deberías considerarlo realmente como un otorgamiento? Y, ¿la universidad paga los gastos completos de tu hijo o se espera que tú pagues una parte? Este capítulo te ayudará a realizar el trabajo de detective que requieres para tener más dinero en tu billetera.

¿Cuánta ayuda dan a una familia a la que le determinan que no tiene el aporte esperado de la familia?

La respuesta que esperas aquí es el monto de otorgamiento total (dinero gratis) que te otorgan para reducir la cuenta de matrícula. No te confundas con la respuesta "básica", que podría tener una combinación de subvención, préstamo y trabajo. Entre menor sea el aporte esperado de la familia, mayor debería ser el otorgamiento de ayuda. Sin embargo, esto no significa que cada universidad le de a tu hijo el mismo monto de ayuda, incluso las universidades públicas ofrecen una mezcla de auto-ayuda (préstamo o trabajo) en el paquete de ayuda. Debes comparar el monto total de otorgamiento contra el monto total de auto-ayuda, lo mismo que el gasto total y las cuotas facturadas en cada universidad. Algunas universidades tienen más fondos de ayuda institucional que otras y te ofrecerán un paquete de ayuda para tu hijo de acuerdo con estos fondos. El mejor trato es el paquete de ayuda que cubre la mayor parte del total de gastos institucionales con subvenciones y ayudas en becas. En otras palabras, lo que salga de tu bolsillo debe ser mínimo. Es verdad que existen muchas otras consideraciones al escoger una universidad, pero si el gasto es un elemento importante en la decisión, debes saber cuál va a ser tu pago básico.

¿Se quedan necesidades sin cubrir en el paquete de ayuda financiera?

De acuerdo con el Advisory Committee on Student Financial Assistance (Comité Consejero de Ayuda Financiera Estudiantil), las familias con bajos ingresos de estudiantes graduados de secundaria que son aceptados en la universidad, enfrentan una necesidad anual no satisfecha de $3,800 por gastos universitarios que no cubre la ayuda estudiantil, incluidos préstamos de trabajo y estudio y préstamos estudiantiles.

La mayoría de universidades tratarán de convencerte de que cubren la totalidad de los gastos de asistencia al otorgar la ayuda estudiantil; pero la mayoría no lo hacen. ¿De qué está compuesto el paquete de ayuda financiera? ¿Qué es un otorgamiento "completo" para la universidad? Debes conocer el porcentaje de subvención y auto-ayuda (préstamo o trabajo).

Si una universidad está muy interesada en tu hijo, es posible que quiera recurrir a los fondos discrecionales para hacer más llevaderos los gastos de universidad de tu hijo.

Si la universidad no satisface por completo las necesidades, lo que se conoce algunas veces como "lagunas", pregunta si se espera que tomes más de un préstamo cada año. Si te ofrecen más de un préstamo, actúa con cuidado y piensa: ¿ésta es la mejor oferta de la universidad? o ¿puede ser mejor? Este sería el momento adecuado para sentarte con el consejero de ayuda financiera para encontrar la forma de no solicitar préstamos a más de una fuente, si es posible.

¿Cuál es el monto promedio de deuda que tienen los estudiantes ya graduados? y ¿cuál es el tiempo promedio que les toma graduarse?

Otros factores que se deben tener en cuenta al comparar las ofertas de ayuda universitaria son el monto total esperado de la deuda de acuerdo al aporte esperado de la familia y el tiempo necesario para graduarse, puesto que esto podría extender el préstamo. La deuda promedio por el préstamo a un estudiante universitario en una universidad pública es de $15,000 a $17,000 una vez que se gradúa, y la mayoría de los estudiantes emplean cinco años para graduarse. Debes averiguar si la universidad hace todos los esfuerzos por minimizar los préstamos para los estudiantes y los padres. La mayoría de universidades aumentan anualmente el monto del préstamo en un paquete de ayuda estudiantil, a medida que se incrementa la elegibilidad para programas de préstamo. Si este es el caso, ¿la universidad también reducirá su otorgamiento por subvención anualmente?

¿El otorgamiento para estudiantes de primer año permanece constante para los otros tres años?

Algunas veces, la mejor opción financiera es la de la universidad que te ofrece un otorgamiento constante durante todos los cuatro años de estudios. No te sorprendas si la subvención para el primer año de tu hijo se reduce gradualmente cada año, especialmente si esperas que tu ingreso permanezca relativamente igual. Debes tener presente que la mayoría de los gastos universitarios aumentan cada año. Si las subvenciones disminuyen, pídele a la universidad que te explique claramente su política de asignación de subvención universitaria.

¿Qué pasa si tu hijo demora cinco años en graduarse? ¿Se eliminarán las ayudas institucionales en el quinto año, incluso si se mantiene un promedio general de calificaciones excepcional? Esta situación ocurre con mayor frecuencia de lo que se podría esperar. Averigua si la universidad te deja ver las cartas de otorgamiento típicas para estudiantes que recibieron ayuda por un período de cuatro años y para estudiantes que recibieron ayuda por un período de cinco años.

MANTÉN BAJOS LOS GASTOS

Existe una estrategia sencilla que puedes tener en cuenta al tratar de reducir los gastos universitarios: asiste a cursos de verano. Históricamente, se consideraba los estudios de verano como un período de recuperación. Pero, en la actualidad, algunos de los estudiantes más talentosos toman clases de verano para acortar su carrera académica y ahorrar dinero.

¿Se brinda ayuda para estudios en el verano?

Una buena forma de reducir los gastos universitarios es que tu hijo tome clases de verano, antes de que comiencen las clases de otoño. Pregunta si la universidad ofrece algún tipo de ayuda para gastos de verano. Si tu hijo puede encontrar la forma de tomar de 3 a 6 créditos por verano, los gastos universitarios pueden reducirse hasta en un 25 por ciento. Aunque la mayoría de universidades otorgan préstamos de verano, es posible que recibas alguna ayuda pequeña para el verano. Tu hijo también podría ahorrar dinero en libros, ya que en esa época del año se encuentran más libros usados. También ahorrarás dinero en gastos de alojamiento y comida si tu hijo vive en tu casa. Es posible que haya una universidad cerca de tu casa que tenga precisamente el curso requerido durante el verano.

CONOCE LAS BECAS

Muchos padres y estudiantes no se dan cuenta que el ganar una beca no institucional puede tener un efecto negativo en su otorgamiento de ayuda financiera. La buena noticia es que tu hijo ganó la beca; la mala, es que es posible que tu hijo no la pueda aceptar. En general, un estudiante que recibe ayuda basada en la necesidad no puede recibir más ayuda que los gastos de asistencia a la universidad menos el estimado de aporte esperado de la familia, sin importar cuánto dinero haya ganado en becas. En este capítulo te decimos qué debes observar si el otorgamiento de ayuda institucional de tu hijo es ajustado debido a que obtuviste una beca.

¿Una beca externa reducirá mi otorgamiento, en especial mis subvenciones o becas institucionales?

Cada universidad tiene políticas diferentes respecto a la ayuda financiera cuando se recibe una beca externa. Por ejemplo, si la ayuda financiera de la universidad es de $10,000 y de ese monto, $6,000 corresponden a dinero de subvenciones y el resto a auto-ayuda, ¿qué sucede con tu otorgamiento general si tu hijo recibe una beca externa? ¿La universidad reemplazará sus subvenciones con la ayuda externa para tu hijo? ¿Se empleará la beca externa para llenar cualquier "laguna" en tus necesidades? Si no es así, ¿se reducirán primero los préstamos? ¿La universidad puede reducir tu aporte esperado de la familia para absorber la beca externa? Muchos padres no tienen el aporte esperado de la familia que la universidad estima. Es entonces cuando se debe pensar en una apelación para no perjudicar los fondos de becas externas.

¿Es renovable mi beca institucional?

Si tu hijo es lo suficientemente afortunado de recibir una beca institucional, debes leer la letra menuda respecto a lo que debes hacer para mantener la beca. Asegúrate de saber la duración de la beca y el promedio general mínimo de calificaciones. ¿La beca es útil sólo para un año? ¿Se incrementará si los gastos de matrícula aumentan? o ¿tiene un monto fijo en dólares? Si la beca no es renovable, pregunta cómo ayudará la universidad a cubrir la diferencia el siguiente año. ¿Se tendrá en cuenta a tu hijo para becas alternativas como estudiante universitario?

¿Puede recuperarse la elegibilidad perdida para la beca?

Algunas veces, los estudiantes pueden perder su beca después de un período de estudios universitarios si no mantienen un promedio general mínimo de calificaciones. Por lo general, existen diferentes requisitos mínimos de calificaciones para recibir ayuda federal, estatal e institucional. Si tu hijo recupera su promedio en el siguiente período, ¿recuperará su beca? Debes estar al tanto de las exigencias de cada fuente de fondos. De no ser así, puede costar miles de dólares tanto a padres como a estudiantes. Es muy importante estar informado sobre los requisitos para becas de cada universidad. Determina qué proceso de apelación existe si tu hijo tiene problemas en mantener la beca.

Si tu hijo gana una beca para una especialización específica, como inglés, y cambia de especialización, puede perder la beca.

UNIVERSIDADES FUERA DEL ESTADO

Existen muchas reglas para determinar si tu hijo puede ganar el estatus de residencia estatal para fines de matrícula. Asimismo, muchos estados participan en acuerdos de reciprocidad para fines de matrícula. Las dos opciones pueden ahorrarte dinero. Es importante reunir todo lo necesario para saber cómo aprovechar ambas oportunidades.

¿Cuánto se demora uno en volverse residente estatal? ¿Tienen acuerdos de reciprocidad para matrícula?

¿De verdad quieres ahorrar mucho dinero de matrícula? Averigua qué se requiere para establecer el estatus de residencia estatal en la visita al campus. Infórmate sobre los requisitos para pagar solamente matrícula dentro del estado. Por lo general, en la oficina del secretario de admisiones o en la tesorería encontrarás la mejor información al respecto. Ha habido muchos estudiantes que han ganado estatus estatal mientras asisten a la universidad primero como estudiantes de otro estado. Por lo general, existen comités de residencia que escuchan las apelaciones de las familias. No te dé miedo preguntar qué debes hacer. Asegúrate de leer al respecto en el catálogo de la universidad.

Los acuerdos de reciprocidad son acuerdos de descuento en matrícula entre estados, instituciones e incluso regiones. Por ejemplo, el estado de Maryland no tiene programa universitario de grado en ingeniería de fibras textiles, pero el Georgia Institute of Technology sí, y un residente de Maryland que se especialice en este campo puede asistir a Georgia Tech como residente estatal. Al no tener que pagar la tarifa para matrícula fuera del estado, tu hijo ahorrará más de $30,000 en cuatro años. Otro ejemplo es la Western Interstate Commission for Higher Education (Comisión Occidental Interestatal para Estudios Superiores) que tiene acuerdos para permitir que estudiantes que no encuentran programas de estudios en su campo en el estado donde viven, puedan pagar la tarifa para matrícula estatal en una universidad fuera del estado. En la actualidad, doce estados participan en este programa (Alaska, Colorado, Hawaii, Idaho, Montana, Nevada, New Mexico, North Dakota, Oregon, South Dakota, Utah y Wyoming).

ENCONTRAR EMPLEO EN EL CAMPUS

Trabajar en la universidad puede resultar provechoso tanto financiera como personalmente. Muchos estudiantes han podido sobrevivir los años de universidad trabajando en el campus; desarrollan una relación positiva con el personal de la universidad y con otros estudiantes trabajadores. Un estudiante podría tener la suerte de trabajar para un profesor ganador de un premio Nobel en su especialidad de estudio. Sin embargo, para poder tener uno de los cientos de trabajos del campus que están disponibles, tu hijo debe saber cómo evitar las dificultades.

¿Cuántas oportunidades de trabajo hay en el campus?

Pregunta que porcentaje de trabajos en el campus está basado en la necesidad comparado con los que no están basados en la necesidad. En otras palabras, si solicitaste ayuda financiera y te fue negada, ¿aún queda la opción de un trabajo para estudiantes proveniente de familias como la tuya? ¿Qué tipos de trabajos hay? ¿Existen algunos trabajos más orientados a lo académico que otros? ¿Cuál es el pago típico? y ¿cuántas horas se espera que trabaje tu hijo? Es importante preguntar si existe una oficina de empleo en el campus que ayude a los estudiantes a encontrar trabajos. Pregunta si te pueden enviar por correo electrónico listas de trabajos al finalizar el verano para que tu hijo pueda hacer la solicitud y la entrevista antes de iniciar los afanes del otoño. Averigua si la universidad tiene listas de trabajos en su sitio Web. También ten en mente que por lo general los estudiantes universitarios tienen menos tiempo libre que los de secundaria. ¿Se puede esperar que ganes la cantidad que te ofrece la universidad?

¿Mis ganancias de trabajo dentro o fuera del campus afectarán mi elegibilidad para la subvención?

Si tu hijo recibe un empleo federal de trabajo y estudio basado en la necesidad, considera este empleo respecto a un empleo de trabajo y estudio no federal. Los trabajos federales de esta clase no se cuentan como recurso financiero si vuelves a solicitar ayuda financiera. Los no federales sí se consideran y, pueden reducir tu ayuda al siguiente año. En general, un estudiante puede ganar aproximadamente $2,500 por año antes que afecte su elegibilidad para ayuda financiera. Otra ventaja

Investigaciones demuestran que los estudiantes que trabajan en el campus tienen mayor oportunidad de graduarse que los que no lo hacen.

del trabajo y estudio federal, es la oportunidad que tu hijo tendrá de ganar experiencia para su currículum vitae mientras estudia en la universidad. Tu hijo también puede trabajar fuera del campus en un empleo respaldado con los fondos para trabajo y estudio.

PRÉSTAMO

De acuerdo con el "Survey on Planning and Paying for Higher Education" (Estudio sobre Planificación y Pago de la Educación Superior) del Collegiate Funding Services (Servicios de Fondos Universitarios), 1 de cada 5 ex-alumnos universitarios se sorprendió de la suma que debía pagar mensualmente por su préstamo estudiantil. Controla tus necesidades proyectadas de préstamo y evita sorpresas volviéndote un consumidor informado. El estudio afirma que sólo la mitad de los padres con niños entre los 12 y 17 años piensa asumir todos, o parte de, los gastos universitarios de sus hijos. Si tanto padres como estudiantes buscan en todas partes las mejores opciones de préstamo, pagarán menos cuando sea el momento del reembolso de sus préstamos.

¿La universidad establece acuerdos con prestamistas que ofrecen descuentos en préstamos tanto a padres como a estudiantes?

Debes hacer esta pregunta, ya que muchos prestamistas ofrecen grandes descuentos. Históricamente, los prestamistas deducían un cargo por originación de 3 por ciento en cada desembolso de un préstamo para estudiantes o para padres de los mismos. Sin embargo, en la actualidad muchos prestamistas ya no cobran ese cargo y ofrecen grandes descuentos en el interés durante el reembolso. Los descuentos pueden significar miles de dólares durante la vida del préstamo. Solicita una lista de prestamistas en la oficina de ayuda financiera, de modo que el consejero de ayuda financiera te asesore para que puedas seleccionar el mejor préstamo de acuerdo a las necesidades de tu familia.

¿La universidad conformará paquetes de préstamos que se acomoden a programas emergentes de condonación de préstamos?

Están surgiendo leyes que expandirán mucho los programas de condonación de préstamos a cambio de empleo en áreas con escasez de profesionales, tales como la salud y la educación. A medida que tu hijo avance en sus estudios universitarios, no pierdas de vista estos beneficios. La universidad de tu hijo debería ayudarte a conformar un paquete de préstamos de manera que puedas aprovechar lo mejor posible estos importantes beneficios, si coinciden con el campo de estudios particular de tu hijo.

Capítulo 9

Secretos para ahorrar

En este momento, debes estar preguntándote cuál es la mejor forma de ahorrar para la educación de tu hijo y si cuentas con el tiempo necesario para comenzar a ahorrar. Este capítulo te brinda información sobre las formas más comunes de ahorrar. Además, te presenta un plan para comenzar a ahorrar incluso si a tu hijo sólo le falta uno o dos años para asistir a la universidad.

TRES FORMAS DE AHORRAR

Echemos un vistazo a las tres formas más populares de ahorrar y el modo cómo afectan tu aporte esperado de la familia y la elegibilidad de tu hijo para ayuda financiera.

1. I-529

El código 529 (I-529) del IRS también se conoce como Qualified Savings Plans, QSP (Planes de Ahorro Calificado). Los planes de ahorro universitario ofrecen uno de los más grandes beneficios de impuestos que existen. El dinero en estas cuentas aumenta completamente exento de impuesto federal siempre que se gaste para educación superior, y las contribuciones son deducibles de impuestos en muchos estados.

Si tu familia tiene un ingreso muy alto y no eres elegible para una cuenta de ahorro educativo, ESA (por su siglas en inglés), los I-529 (QSP) son una gran opción. No existen límites de ingresos, puedes hacer contribuciones de hasta $11,000 al año sin originar el impuesto por donaciones, y los límites de contribución vitalicia pueden exceder los $200,000 en algunos estados. Los padres de medianos ingresos también se pueden beneficiar de la capitalización de impuestos exenta de impuestos.

Las suspensiones de impuestos federales para I-529 vencerán al finalizar el año 2010, salvo si el Congreso las renueva. De otro modo, se supone que los retiros del I-529 se revertirán a estar sujetos de impuestos a la tasa federal del estudiante.

Sin embargo, existen algunos inconvenientes. Muchos planes de ahorro I-529 ofrecen opciones limitadas de inversión, en tanto que algunos planes imponen altas cuotas o te exigen pagar una comisión. Además, si no gastas el dinero de tu cuenta en educación superior, pagarás impuestos más una multa del 10 por ciento sobre las ganancias.

Puesto que la inversión en el plan le pertenece al padre (como patrocinador), entonces se considera como activo tuyo y no de tu hijo en la FAFSA. Si un abuelo u otra tercera parte establece un 529-QSP a nombre de un nieto en particular, entonces es propiedad del abuelo y no se reporta en la FAFSA.

Planes de matrícula con pago anticipado

Los planes de matrícula con pago anticipado constituyen otra forma de I-529 que te permite comprar contratos o unidades de educación a precios actuales y, que pueden emplearse para matrícula en el futuro. En otras palabras, puedes asegurar los gastos universitarios del futuro a precios de hoy. Puesto que las cuotas de matrícula vienen creciendo desde 1980 dos o tres veces más rápidamente que el Índice de Precios al Consumidor, ésta es una buena forma de ahorrar.

Las ganancias en cuentas con pago anticipado están exentas del impuesto a la renta federal y las contribuciones son deducibles de impuestos en muchos estados. Por lo general, los planes con pago anticipado son patrocinados por estados individuales y están diseñados para pagar la educación en universidades públicas dentro del estado. La mayoría de estos planes aún se limitan sólo a residentes del estado, pero muchos se están volviendo más competitivos con planes de ahorro I-529 mediante el pago de una tasa de interés mínima en contratos de pago anticipado, lo cual garantiza alguna ganancia incluso en el caso improbable de que los precios de matrícula no suban.

Recuerda que, a diferencia de los planes de ahorro I-529, los planes de pago anticipado reducen la elegibilidad para ayuda financiera dólar por dólar.

Más de 280 universidades privadas en la actualidad se han vinculado a un consorcio de universidades llamado Tuition Plan (Plan de Matrícula). Los padres pueden comprar contratos de pago anticipado que sirven para matricularse en cualquiera de las universidades del consorcio. Si tu hijo no ingresa a ninguna de las universidades de la red, puedes conseguir un reembolso completo con intereses. De acuerdo con la Tax Relief Act (Ley de Desgravación de Impuestos) de 2001, los retiros de planes de pago anticipado de universidades privadas están exentos de impuestos federales desde 2004. Llama al 877-874-0740 (llamada gratuita) para obtener más detalles sobre el Tuition Plan.

Ventajas y desventajas de los planes I-529

Tanto los planes de pago anticipado como los planes de ahorro tienen sus ventajas. Si faltan más de cinco años para que tu hijo vaya a la universidad y crees en la capacidad del mercado de valores para producir ganancias estables, tu inversión podría estar mucho mejor en un plan de ahorros. Un plan de ahorro te permitiría escoger inversiones más dinámicas y podrías hacerlo mientras tu hijo es joven, lo que reduce los riesgos de tu inversión a medida que tu hijo se hace mayor. Si no quieres tomar riesgos o si te da miedo el mercado de valores, los planes de pago anticipado pueden ser una mejor forma de ahorro para ti.

2. Coverdell Education Savings Accounts, ESA

Anteriormente conocidas como Education Individual Retirement Account, IRA (Cuenta de Jubilación Individual para Educación), las Coverdell Education Savings Accounts (Cuentas de Ahorros de Educación Coverdell) son una forma atractiva de ahorro para educación, en especial para familias en los grupos de altos impuestos. El aporte ESA máximo anual es de $2,000 por hijo y el límite de elegibilidad de ingresos para parejas casadas que deseen abrir una cuenta es de $220,000 por año.

Si tu ingreso bruto ajustado (IBA) está entre $190,000 y $220,000, el monto que puedes aportar se reduce gradualmente. Tu familia no tendrá multa por contribuir al mismo tiempo en una ESA y en un I-529 el mismo año a nombre del mismo beneficiario.

Los aportes ESA aumentan exentos de impuestos y no son deducibles de impuestos. Aunque se pueden emplear retiros para gastos educativos

Si crees que tendrás que depender de la ayuda financiera, asegúrate de no ahorrar nada a nombre de tu hijo. En lugar de abrir una ESA, invierte dinero para la universidad bajo tu propio nombre en un fondo indexado o administrado por impuestos, los cuales reducen al mínimo las ganancias sujetas a impuestos.

calificados, puedes invertir tus aportes en lo que desees. Además de emplear dinero ESA para pagar la universidad, puedes utilizarlo para pagar la matrícula en la escuela primaria y secundaria, tutorías, computadoras y otros gastos.

Sin embargo, si estás contando con la ayuda financiera, las ESA pueden ser un arma de doble filo, pues se presume que el dinero de estas cuentas es un activo del estudiante según las fórmulas de ayuda financiera federal. Se espera que tu aporte provenga en una mayor parte de los activos de tu hijo (35 por ciento al año) que de tus activos (hasta 5.6 por ciento). Entre más activos tenga tu hijo, más probable es que reciba menos ayuda.

3. Custodial Account

Las Custodial Accounts (Cuentas de Custodia) también se conocen como cuentas Uniform Transfers to Minors Act, UTMA (cuentas por Ley de Transferencia Uniforme a Menores) o cuentas Uniform Gifts to Minors Act, UGMA (cuentas por Ley de Donación Uniforme a Menores). Estas cuentas se consideran activos generadores de ingresos del estudiante y para tu hijo pueden significar un monto mayor en la elegibilidad para ayuda financiera que el ahorro hecho en impuestos.

A diferencia del dinero proveniente de un plan I-529 o una ESA, el dinero de una UGMA o una UTMA no debe emplearse exclusivamente para fines educativos. Ya que tu hijo obtiene el control de la cuenta cuando cumple los 18 años de edad, no podrás decir nada si él gasta el dinero en algo diferente a la universidad. Muchos planes I-529 permiten transferencias de cuentas de custodia, pero cualquier inversión en una UGMA o UTMA debe liquidarse antes de hacer la transferencia, ya que sólo aceptan efectivo.

Si tienes una cuenta de custodia, pero vas a solicitar ayuda financiera, debes "gastar" la cuenta antes de que tu hijo vaya a la universidad. Es legal que gastes los activos en cualquier cosa que beneficie a tu hijo, incluida una matrícula en universidad privada, un curso de preparatoria SAT o una computadora. Sin embargo, si tu hijo es muy joven (mucho menos de 14 años) y sólo tienes invertida una pequeña cantidad, no toques ningún fondo en la cuenta. Los beneficios de impuestos en cuentas de custodia son modestos y no vale la pena molestarse en transferir pequeñas cantidades a un plan 529. En lugar de eso, invierte sólo el monto permitido como ingreso exento de impuestos, que corresponde hasta $750 por año.

Si tu hijo no ha cumplido 14 años, los primeros $750 de intereses, dividendos o ingreso por ganancias de capital están exentos de impuestos. Los siguientes $750 están sujetos a impuestos a la tasa del 10 por ciento de impuesto para tu hijo. Cualquier ganancia por encima de dicho monto está sujeta a impuestos a tu tasa de impuesto. Si tu hijo tiene 14 años o más, todo ingreso en la cuenta está sujeto a impuestos a la tasa de tu hijo.

¿A qué debes estar atento?

Si tu hijo ingresará a la universidad en septiembre de 2004, los ingresos y activos de tu familia en 2003 serán la base para las decisiones de ayuda financiera para el año académico 2004-2005. Debes planificar una estrategia para cualquier retiro de la universidad, si piensas que vas a solicitar ayuda financiera. A continuación, encontrarás algunos consejos para que le saques el mejor provecho a tus activos:

- **Mantén los ingresos familiares tan bajos como sea posible.** Los ingresos son un factor que pesa mucho en la evaluación de necesidad. Hasta el 47 por ciento del ingreso de los padres se considera elegible para pagar los gastos universitarios. Intenta no incurrir en ganancias de capital en el año impositivo anterior al de la utilización de la ayuda financiera.

Si en tu familia hay más de un hijo en la universidad al mismo tiempo, debes convertir en dinero todas las ganancias de capital antes de que tu primer hijo vaya a la universidad.

- **Revisa regularmente tu estrategia general de inversión.** El plan universitario que escojas debe considerar la edad de tu hijo, los costos anticipados de matrícula y la posibilidad de que tu hijo necesite o no la ayuda financiera.
- **No pongas en peligro lo que necesitas ahorrar para la jubilación.** Tu hijo puede obtener muchos recursos para pagar la universidad, pero nadie te va a dar una beca para tu jubilación.

Las fórmulas de ayuda financiera no tienen en cuenta los ahorros de IRA y 401(k), por lo que tu ahorro para jubilación siempre debe tener prioridad.

NUNCA ES TARDE PARA AHORRAR

No todos comienzan a apartar dinero para la educación de sus hijos desde el momento en que éstos nacen. Si estás atrasado en tus metas de ahorro, los gastos que se acercan pueden atemorizarte. Pero eso no significa que no debas ahorrar dinero. Poco a poco se llega lejos. Si ahorras sólo $400 por mes durante un año, casi reúnes los gastos de matrícula de un año en una universidad pública. La misma estrategia de ahorro cubriría más de cuatro años de libros y materiales escolares para tu hijo, que en promedio ascienden a $850 por año.

Si tu hijo califica para préstamos estudiantiles subsidiados, es posible que tu meta no sea ahorrar para la universidad, sino para ayudarle a tu hijo con el reembolso de estos préstamos cuando llegue la avalancha de intereses y pagos mensuales después de la graduación. Revisa tus gastos de los últimos seis meses para ver cuánto gastas en un mes determinado en comparación con los ingresos familiares. Una vez que identifiques en qué gastas el dinero, busca qué gastos puedes reducir. Luego, establece un plan de ahorros regular y deduce automáticamente el dinero de tu cuenta corriente cada mes.

Pon el dinero en una cuenta de mercado monetario o fondo triple A de bonos del estado, si tu hijo va a necesitar los ahorros universitarios en menos de cinco años. Con tan poco tiempo, la especulación en el mercado de valores no es una opción. Piensa en la posibilidad de invertir en una cartera conservadora de valores y bonos si faltan más de cinco años para que tu hijo ingrese a la universidad. Recuerda que no debes poner ningún dinero a nombre de tu hijo, ya que se considerará como activo de tu hijo cuando solicite ayuda financiera.

Préstamos

Aunque tu hijo califique para ayuda financiera, aún es posible que tengas que depender de préstamos para cubrir los gastos universitarios. Incluso los paquetes de ayuda financiera más generosos incluyen algunos préstamos. Los préstamos más deseables se otorgan con ayuda financiera a nombre de tu hijo y los subsidia el gobierno.

Como se analizó en el Capítulo 3, los Perkins Loans y los Stafford Loans subsidiados no acumulan intereses mientras tu hijo esté en la universidad, y los pagos no se inician sino hasta después de su graduación. Tu hijo puede recibir un Stafford Loan no subsidiado sólo si solicitó ayuda financiera y no calificó para el Stafford Loan subsidiado. Los Stafford Loans no subsidiados acumulan intereses mientras tu hijo está en la universidad, pero tienen tasas de interés más favorables que las de los bancos comerciales. Los PLUS Loans para padres también son más favorables que los préstamos bancarios. Considera primero un préstamo sobre capital de vivienda y luego averigua por un préstamo bancario alternativo diseñado específicamente para educación si tu hijo no califica para un préstamo subsidiado por el gobierno o necesita más dinero para pagar los gastos universitarios.

Ayúdale a tu hijo a ahorrar para la universidad

De acuerdo con el National Center for Education Statistics (Centro Nacional de Estadísticas Educativas), cerca del 51 por ciento de los estudiantes universitarios se consideran financieramente independientes de sus padres. Esta es una cifra sorprendente si se tiene en cuenta el costo de una universidad en la actualidad. Muchos padres sencillamente no pueden pagarlo. Otros deciden que es responsabilidad de su hijo pagar por sus propios medios. Cualquiera que sea la razón, existen muchas maneras de apoyar los esfuerzos de tu hijo para ir a la universidad.

Asegúrate de que tu hijo aproveche las siguientes herramientas de ahorro con ventajas de impuestos, que son útiles para estudiantes universitarios independientes.

Hope Credit (Crédito Hope)

El Crédito Hope ofrece un crédito impositivo de hasta $1,500 por estudiante, sujeto a topes de ingreso anual para gastos educativos. Este crédito se limita a los dos primeros años de estudios universitarios.

Lifetime Learning Credit (Crédito Lifetime Learning)

Este tipo de crédito ofrece un crédito impositivo de hasta $1,000 por familia (o hijo, si es él quien va a pagar las cuentas) para el tercer y cuarto años de universidad. Está sujeto a topes de ingresos y se estipula que el crédito máximo Lifetime Learning es $2,000.

Planes I-529

Los planes de ahorro I-529 son útiles para jóvenes que buscan la manera de aprovechar al máximo el dinero que ganan cortando césped y como regalo de cumpleaños. Las ganancias en una cuenta de este tipo quedaron exoneradas de impuestos desde 2002, asumiendo que el dinero se emplea para fines educativos. Cabe señalar que los padres o tutores legales deben ayudar con la apertura de estas cuentas.

Asegúrate de hacer que tu hijo participe en el proceso de pago, mientras buscas formas de conseguir dinero para la universidad. Los estudiantes universitarios en potencia deben saber que es posible que se gradúen gracias a préstamos estudiantiles y que las buenas calificaciones, los puntajes SAT y los ensayos personales ingeniosos pueden tener gran impacto sobre el precio real de la universidad.

Tu hijo debe estar preparado para ahorrar responsablemente durante sus años universitarios. Eso podría significar tener un trabajo a tiempo parcial durante el año escolar y un trabajo a tiempo completo durante las vacaciones de verano e invierno. El Bureau of Labor Statistics (Oficina de Estadísticas Laborales) informa que el 56 por ciento de los estudiantes en edades entre los 16 y los 24 años trabajan, ya sea tiempo completo o parcial. El dinero ganado que se ahorra durante los años universitarios puede aliviar en gran medida el estrés asociado con la deuda después de la graduación. Tu hijo puede adquirir habilidades ahorrativas que le ayudarán toda su vida, y puede comenzar a reembolsar los préstamos tan pronto como se gradúe.

AmeriCorps

AmeriCorps es un programa de servicio nacional que dura un año y brinda oportunidad a estudiantes en edad universitaria para ganar dinero extra, e incluso obtener créditos universitarios. Los miembros del programa orientan a jóvenes bajo riesgo, ayudan en la construcción de viviendas accesibles, realizan pruebas de salud y ayudan a grupos sin ánimo de lucro en toda la nación. Más allá de los beneficios de servir a una comunidad que lo necesita, los miembros de AmeriCorps reciben un otorgamiento de $4,725 para educación, después de un año de servicio, que pueden emplear para pagar la matrícula o reintegrar préstamos estudiantiles. El programa les brinda la oportunidad de reducir cerca de $10,000 en sus cuentas de matrícula ganando hasta dos otorgamientos.

AmeriCorps inscribe a más de 50,000 personas al año y es el único programa estadounidense de servicios de esta naturaleza. Sus variados programas tienen diferentes requisitos y fechas límite. Algunos, como Teach for America (Enseñanza para Estados Unidos), se llevan a cabo en el calendario escolar y requieren de un título universitario. Otros, simplemente exigen que los solicitantes sean ciudadanos estadounidenses mayores de 17 años.

Cuando los miembros de AmeriCorps completan un mínimo de 1,700 horas en un año o menos (un período de servicio a tiempo completo), la beca es de ellos. Algunos miembros pueden ser elegibles para recibir un otorgamiento parcial si su período de servicio es menor.

Tu hijo puede solicitar indulgencia de morosidad en préstamos estudiantiles mientras presta sus servicios en AmeriCorps, de manera que no necesitaría hacer ningún pago en ese lapso. Se seguirían acumulando intereses, pero si tu hijo califica para indulgencia de morosidad y completa su tiempo de servicio, AmeriCorps paga una parte o la totalidad de los intereses causados sobre estos préstamos.

Algunas universidades, como la University of Vermont y la Northeastern University en Boston, Massachusetts, ofrecen acreditación de cursos o becas por participar en el programa. Lo mismo hacen muchas universidades de posgrado, entre otras, Brandeis University, en Waltham, Massachusetts; George Washington University, en Washington, D.C. y Clark University, en Worcester, Massachusetts.

Visita AmeriCorps Alums en Internet, www.americorpsalums.org, para tener una lista completa de las universidades que ofrecen becas e incentivos. Muchas universidades ofrecen incentivos a miembros de AmeriCorps, ya sea adaptando el otorgamiento para educación, ofreciendo becas u acreditando cursos por aprendizaje experimental a alumnos de AmeriCorps.

El otorgamiento para educación por servicio en AmeriCorps está sujeto a impuestos en el año que se emplea, pero tu hijo puede aprovechar la Hope Scholarship o los créditos Lifetime Learning, cuando se emplea el otorgamiento, lo que permite una importante exención de impuestos.

Trabajos de verano

Existen numerosas formas creativas para que tu hijo adolescente gane dinero durante el verano. Abundan oportunidades interesantes de trabajo para adultos jóvenes emprendedores, incluidos puestos como guías turísticos en parques nacionales, operarios de juegos en parques de diversiones y salvavidas.

Anima a tu hijo para que comience a buscar un empleo de verano solicitando trabajos de temporada. Por ejemplo, el National Park Service (Servicio de Parques Nacionales), contrata cerca de 3,000 trabajadores de temporada todos los veranos para manejar sus 370 parques en todo el país, en Guam, Puerto Rico y las Islas Vírgenes. Muchos pagan un pequeño estipendio de varios cientos de dólares por mes, con alojamiento y comida incluidos, haciendo de esto más una experiencia de aventura que una oportunidad para hacer dinero. Miles de posibles trabajadores llenan su solicitud cada año en los parques más populares, entre ellos, Yellowstone y el Gran Cañón, por lo tanto la solicitud de tu hijo debe ser competitiva.

También hay oportunidades de trabajo de verano en centros y ranchos vacacionales turísticos. En el Home Ranch de 1,500 acres, cerca de Steamboat Springs, Colorado, por ejemplo, pueden hacer su solicitud trabajadores de temporada de 18 años o más. El personal de verano comparte una variedad de cabinas y dormitorios y gana cerca de $1,200 mensuales. Los trabajos incluyen guías de caminatas, vaqueros, asistentes de oficina, guías de pesca con moscas, panaderos e incluso amas de llaves.

Otra opción para estudiantes mayores de 18 años que buscan empleo de verano son los cruceros. Este es un trabajo físicamente exigente, con muchas horas de trabajo y poca paga, dicen los que conocen. Para adolescentes que tengan 15 años o más, los parques de diversiones crean una atmósfera de campo, con baja renta y alojamiento en el sitio. Los parques de diversión contratan durante los meses de verano y la mayoría necesita operarios de quioscos, salvavidas autorizados, guardianes, personal de seguridad, auxiliares de quioscos en concesión y operarios para recorridos. Algunos, entre ellos, Six Flags Great Adventure en Jackson, New Jersey, incluso contratan vigilantes y porteros de safaris. Además del salario por hora (que comienza por sobre el salario mínimo), los empleados reciben entrada gratis al parque, descuentos del 40 por ciento en mercancía del parque, cinco pases de cortesía y se les incentiva a participar en ligas de béisbol, barbacoas y bingos.

El trabajo de salvavidas es otra opción para trabajar en verano. La paga es buena, pero el trabajo exige certificación de salvavidas y resucitación cardiopulmonar, RCP, y obviamente, Primeros Auxilios. Aunque puede haber demanda de trabajos de playa, las empresas administradoras de apartamentos tienden a pagar mejor; ofrecen empleos a salvavidas en piscinas de complejos de apartamentos en temporadas que van desde el Memorial Day (Día del Soldado Muerto) hasta el Labor Day (Día del Trabajo). Los salvavidas pueden ganar entre $5,000 y $8,000 durante los meses de verano, dependiendo donde trabajen. Los operarios de piscinas entrenados para manejar personal, operar las bombas y controlar los niveles de químicos en las piscinas, pueden ganar otros $3,000 por verano.

Six Flags otorga más de $10,000 en becas cada año para empleados meritorios.

Capítulo 10

Otras formas de recortar los gastos universitarios

Cuando se trata de pagar la universidad, el ingenio es tan útil como los recursos. La eliminación del respaldo federal para los fondos de subvención creó un ambiente en el que los préstamos son la forma más común de ayuda financiera. El préstamo significa el pago diferido de algo que quieres en este momento. La forma más rápida y, desafortunadamente, más fácil de obtener dinero para educación es simplemente firmar en la última línea de un formulario de préstamo. Sin embargo, puede resultar costosa, por lo que debes buscar otros recursos y formas para reducir tus gastos.

Las siguientes estrategias tal vez no sean las mejores, o no estén disponibles para todo el mundo, pero te ofrecen opciones que puedes considerar:

- $ Reducir tu presupuesto universitario
- $ Obtener un crédito universitario sobre una base acelerada (reducción del tiempo que tu hijo permanece en la universidad)
- $ Obtener crédito universitario por fuera del aula tradicional de clases
- $ Uso de alternativas de pago
- $ Créditos impositivos
- $ Combinar los estudios de educación superior con un empleo relacionado con tus estudios
- $ Servicio nacional y comunitario

REDUCCIÓN DE TU PRESUPUESTO

Aumentar recursos es una forma de satisfacer tus necesidades, pero también lo puedes hacer mediante la reducción de tu presupuesto.

El paquete de ayuda que ofrece una universidad se basa en la definición de gasto que tenga, lo que implica presunciones y promedios. La naturaleza estándar del presupuesto significa que está diseñado para satisfacer las necesidades promedio de un estudiante. Es posible que tu hijo gaste más o menos de lo que le permite el presupuesto, pero esta variación individual no afecta el monto de la ayuda ofrecida por la universidad. Un presupuesto estándar asume que limitas tus gastos razonablemente. No se espera que tu hijo viva en condiciones inferiores al nivel de pobreza, pero sí se espera que acepte ciertos sacrificios para obtener una educación. Para determinar si estos gastos estándar se pueden reducir, debes analizarlos en conjunto con las expectativas de tu hijo para vivir con recursos limitados.

En términos generales, si tu hijo gasta más de lo que le permite el presupuesto estándar, tendrás dificultades para pagar la universidad. Por otro lado, si tiende a economizar, es probable que termines con menos deuda. Igualmente, si reembolsas parte de tu préstamo antes de su vencimiento real con dineros ahorrados, puedes disminuir los intereses y así reducir el monto de las cuotas mensuales de reembolso.

Puesto que es necesaria mucha disciplina para no gastar el dinero, tal vez prefieras aceptar un monto menor de préstamo que puedes pedir prestado de otra forma. Antes de tomar esta decisión, considera la fuente del préstamo y la disponibilidad continua del mismo. Si rechazas parte o la totalidad de un Federal Perkins Loan, que te ofrece las mejores condiciones de aplazamiento y cancelación, el monto que rechazas se ofrecerá a otro estudiante necesitado. Si más adelante en el curso del año, te das cuenta que realmente necesitas el Federal Perkins Loan, ya no tendrás disponible estos fondos dentro de ese programa y, por lo tanto, es posible que tengas que aceptar un préstamo que no tenga esas condiciones favorables.

Los programas FFEL y Direct Loan no tienen las mismas limitaciones que el Federal Perkins Loan. En el caso de los programas FFEL, a no ser que el prestamista tenga restricciones sobre el número de solicitudes que puede aceptar de un estudiante en un año determinado, puedes solicitar fondos adicionales posteriormente, siempre que seas elegible. Ten en mente las fechas límite, puesto que los fondos normalmente se desembolsan mientras tu hijo aún está en la universidad. Tanto tú como tu hijo deben sopesar su tendencia a gastar dinero, su propensión al ahorro y la fuente del préstamo antes de decidir rechazarlo o aplazar su solicitud.

Matrícula

Con la excepción de descartar las universidades costosas, no puedes controlar la tarifa de matrícula que determinan las universidades. El costo de la matrícula varía entre universidades y también puede variar entre los programas de estudio dentro de una universidad. El costo de la matrícula no siempre es un indicador de calidad o prestigio, por lo que te aconsejamos no descartar las universidades de bajos costos que también ofrecen los programas de estudio que tu hijo quiere.

La mayoría de los programas de cuatro años incluyen cierto número de cursos de artes liberales que son requisito para graduarse, aunque no necesariamente afectan en forma directa la especialidad. Es posible que tu hijo pueda tomar ciertos cursos preparatorios en una universidad de menor costo y luego solicitar la transferencia a una universidad con altos costos para tomar los cursos más avanzados en el programa de estudios que está interesado.

Es posible que un estudiante de transferencia experimente otros gastos, que no son monetarios, tales como adaptarse a una nueva universidad y su ambiente. Si tu hijo decide primero asistir a una universidad de bajos costos para ahorrar dinero y después solicitar transferencia a una universidad de costos superiores, considera cuidadosamente si todos los cursos que ha tomado en la primera universidad son compatibles con los requisitos de la segunda universidad. De lo contrario, puedes terminar perdiendo dinero por tener que quedarse en la universidad más tiempo o por repetir cursos.

Si tu hijo piensa cambiarse a otra universidad, es probable que se encuentre con fechas límites y procedimientos completamente diferentes. Igualmente, podrías contar con otras formas de ayuda y el proceso de solicitud puede diferir significativamente. Es importante obtener información completa antes de hacer la transferencia para lograr una transición fácil.

Puesto que se benefician de las recaudaciones tributarias, las universidades públicas generalmente cobran matrículas más bajas, en especial a estudiantes residentes del estado. Normalmente, en las universidades públicas los estudiantes no residentes del estado tienen una tarifa más alta de matrícula. La distinción entre estudiantes residentes y estudiantes no residentes en las universidades públicas parece ser un asunto bastante sencillo, pero a decir verdad, puede resultar algo complicado. Algunos estados requieren un tiempo mínimo de residencia para poder aprovechar la tarifa de matrícula dentro del estado. Los estudiantes del ejército asignados a un lugar específico, estudiantes con propiedades en otro estado o distrito, y estudiantes extranjeros que han permanecido en este país como residentes por un breve período, pueden descubrir que algunas universidades o estados verán con reserva las ofertas de tarifas de matrículas para estudiantes residentes. Las preguntas en los formularios de solicitud sobre tus direcciones durante un período de tiempo, el estado donde tu hijo obtuvo la licencia de conducir y el lugar de registro de votación de tu hijo, sirven para que las universidades determinen el estado de residencia. Puesto que la diferencia entre la matrícula para residente y no residente puede significar cientos, incluso miles de dólares al año, debes solicitar a las universidades que estás considerando que te aclaren este asunto.

Instituto de enseñanza para la comunidad

Las universidades de dos años normalmente se financian con impuestos locales o estatales; por lo tanto, la matrícula es menos costosa que en las universidades de cuatro años (casi la mitad del precio de una universidad pública de cuatro años y 85 por ciento menos que una universidad privada de cuatro años). Tu hijo puede inscribirse en un instituto de enseñanza para la comunidad durante uno o dos años y puede tomar cursos introductorios y cursos que son requisitos previos, a un costo significativamente más bajo, y luego solicitar transferencia a una universidad de cuatro años para tomar los cursos de su carrera universitaria. Otra forma en que esto te ayudará a ahorrar dinero, es el gasto por alojamiento y comida, ya que tu hijo puede vivir en casa y trasladarse a un instituto de enseñanza para la comunidad local. Antes de inscribir a tu hijo en un instituto de enseñanza para la comunidad, comunícate con la universidad de cuatro años que tu hijo prefiere, ya que no todos los cursos del instituto de enseñanza para la comunidad se pueden transferir.

REDUCCIÓN DEL PROGRAMA DE ESTUDIOS

Tu hijo puede obtener un título o certificado en un plazo menor que el plazo normal. Por ejemplo, podría considerar tomar un curso adicional por período académico. Si lo hace durante cierto tiempo, es más fácil que pueda graduarse antes de lo previsto. Algunas universidades no cobran más por inscribirse en cursos adicionales a la carga académica mínima de la universidad de tiempo completo, en tanto que otras cobran por hora crédito. Sin embargo, a pesar de los cargos adicionales por cursos extras, los ahorros en otros gastos pueden ser considerables.

Los cursos de verano constituyen otra alternativa. Aunque es posible que la ayuda financiera esté disponible durante el verano, debes informarte si al recibir ayuda durante el verano disminuye el monto de ayuda que puedas tener durante el resto del año o programa de estudios.

Acreditación universitaria por exámenes

Otra alternativa que puede tomar tu hijo para reducir los gastos, es obtener acreditación por exámenes, así reduce el plazo exigido para recibir un título o certificado. En esta sección se describen diversos programas de alcance nacional:, AP, CLEP, PEP (Excelsior College en New York), y DANTES. Aunque debes pagar una cuota por el examen, las pruebas pueden ofrecerte soluciones más directas que se traducen en ahorros para la educación de tu hijo.

Sé consciente que las universidades consideran de forma diferente los créditos obtenidos por examen, de manera que debes averiguar si la universidad también cobra una cuota para determinar la acreditación correspondiente en el registro académico de tu hijo. También es común que las universidades establezcan un número mínimo de créditos que debes cursar en el campus a fin de que un estudiante se gradúe en esa universidad. Otras, simplemente limitan el número de créditos que puedes obtener por examen. Si tu hijo solicita transferencia, es posible que la nueva universidad no acepte los créditos concedidos por la universidad anterior si los obtuvo por examen. Esto puede darse particularmente si haces transferencia de una universidad de dos años a una universidad de cuatro años, puesto que las universidades de dos años tradicionalmente tienen una política más liberal respecto a la acreditación por examen.

Advanced Placement Program

Las universidades establecen sus propias políticas respecto del uso de los puntajes AP para garantizar una ubicación apropiada o acreditar el ingreso de estudiantes de primer año. El College Board te puede facilitar una lista de las universidades participantes. Sin embargo, puedes obtener una mejor respuesta a las preguntas específicas sobre las políticas AP de los funcionarios de la universidad donde tu hijo está solicitando la acreditación.

Este programa ofrece a los estudiantes de secundaria la oportunidad de completar los estudios a nivel universitario en materias que van desde biología, español hasta literatura inglesa. Al terminar el año, los estudiantes toman un examen que se administra a nivel nacional para esa materia. Si tu hijo obtiene un puntaje lo suficientemente alto, puede obtener crédito académico universitario. Se sabe de estudiantes que han tomado tantos exámenes AP, que no ha sido necesario que cursen su primer año de universidad. El valor monetario de los créditos potenciales AP es fácil de determinar: calcula el valor de un año de matrícula, alojamiento y comida. Entre más cara una universidad, mayor la cantidad de dinero que ahorrarás si tu hijo puede saltarse un año de estudios a través del programa AP.

College-Level Examination Program

Las ofertas College-Level Examination Program, CLEP operan con la premisa de que el logro de nivel universitario no sólo puede obtenerse en el aula sino también a través del estudio independiente y la experiencia. Si tu hijo tiene aficiones, talentos o intereses con un alto nivel de habilidad, podrías pensar en convertir ese interés en acreditación universitaria a través del programa CLEP.

Existen dos tipos de exámenes CLEP:

1. **Los Exámenes generales**
2. **Los Exámenes por materias**

Los Exámenes generales miden el logro de nivelación universitaria en cinco áreas básicas de las artes liberales: composición inglesa, humanidades, matemática, ciencias naturales, y sociología e historia. Estos exámenes evalúan temas que normalmente se cubren en los primeros dos años de universidad y que normalmente se consideran parte del requisito de estudios generales o liberales. Los Exámenes generales no tratan de medir el conocimiento especializado de una disciplina en particular ni se basan en un plan de estudios o curso de estudios determinado. Más bien, se diseñan para evaluar la habilidad general que puede adquirirse de varias maneras, a través de la lectura personal, empleo, televisión, radio, clases para adultos o trabajo avanzado en la escuela secundaria.

Los Exámenes por materias miden el logro en cursos universitarios específicos y se usan para conceder la exención y acreditación de estos cursos. Se ofrecen veintinueve Exámenes por materias en áreas que van desde el gobierno de Estados Unidos a la macroeconomía, y de la literatura inglesa a los sistemas de información y aplicaciones informáticas. Aunque no hay ningún plan de estudios establecido por materias, se han diseñado textos y libros de repaso como ayuda para que te prepares para los exámenes.

Excelsior College Examinations (Exámenes Excelsior College)

Tu hijo realmente puede obtener un título asociado o universitario en ciertas áreas de concentración a través del Excelsior College de la Universidad estatal de New York (anteriormente conocido como Regents College). El programa, anteriormente conocido como Proficiency Examination Program, PEP (Programa de Examen de Nivel de Conocimientos), combina varios elementos (prueba de habilidad, cursos por correspondencia, experiencia adquirida, cursos militares, e instrucción universitaria real) para medir el progreso con miras a obtener un título. El programa mismo no ofrece ningún curso, pero evalúa el conocimiento a nivel universitario y evalúa el número de créditos que tu hijo ha acumulado a través de diversos métodos aceptables. Se otorga un título cuando se han cumplido los requisitos.

Aproximadamente 1,000 universidades, aceptan créditos otorgados por el programa Excelsior College como créditos de transferencia. Muchas universidades también usan las pruebas para realizar su propia evaluación de conocimientos a nivel universitario de un estudiante y otorgar crédito. Estos exámenes se ofrecen gratuitamente a miembros del ejército americano a través del DANTES Examinations Program.

Los Excelsior College Examinations equiparan la materia enseñada en cursos de universidades estándar y miden el conocimiento en áreas específicas. Cuatro áreas generales de prueba son:

- Artes y ciencias
- Enfermería
- Negocios
- Educación

Se puede acreditar desde el conocimiento introductorio hasta el conocimiento de nivel superior, dependiendo del contenido de la prueba. Excelsior College desarrolla y administra las pruebas, y se realizan en Prometric Testing Centers (Centros de prueba Prometric) en todo Estados Unidos y Canadá. Existen guías de estudio detalladas para cada prueba, que contienen una descripción del contenido, bibliografía y ejemplos de preguntas.

Defense Activity for Non-Traditional Education Support, DANTES (Actividad de Protección para la Subvención de Educación no tradicional)

El programa DANTES permite a los estudiantes validar su asimilación de conocimiento y aptitudes que normalmente se adquirirían en cursos universitarios, pero que se han adquirido a través del estudio independiente, la experiencia práctica en el trabajo y las experiencias de vida. Mil cuatrocientas universidades en Estados Unidos acreditan estudiantes que reciben puntajes bastante altos en más de treinta y cinco DANTES Standardized Tests, DSST (Pruebas estandarizadas DANTES) en áreas como negocios, humanidades, sociología, matemáticas, física y tecnología aplicada. Las pruebas se administran principalmente a miembros actuales o anteriores de las Fuerzas Armadas. Los ciudadanos civiles también pueden presentar exámenes DSST, por una cuota, durante todo el año en universidades de todo Estados Unidos y alrededor del mundo. Antes de registrarse para un examen, verifica si la universidad de tu hijo acepta la acreditación DSST para los puntajes mínimos de aprobación.

ALTERNATIVAS DE PAGO

Los gastos institucionales a menudo se dividen según los períodos (semestres o trimestres), de manera que la parte del EFC que se usa para gastos universitarios pueda extenderse a dos o más pagos en lugar de uno. Es posible que el EFC no sea tan agobiante, si entiendes que no necesitas hacer un pago único.

Una vez que se han determinado los verdaderos gastos, y se han investigado y establecido todos los recursos, aún cuentas con opciones para ayudarte con tu Expected Family Contribution. La mayoría de las universidades te permiten solicitar ayuda financiera para gastos universitarios, como matrícula, cuotas, alojamiento y alimentación. Si realmente no has recibido la ayuda, muchas universidades te permiten aplazar el pago hasta que tengas disponibles los fondos. Si tienes suficiente ayuda para cubrir todos o la mayoría de los gastos universitarios, el EFC realmente se usa para gastos indirectos universitarios, como los libros y materiales, gastos de transporte y gastos personales. Si tu hijo vive en tu casa o fuera del campus, los gastos universitarios indirectos incluirían las comidas diarias y quizás, arriendo mensual o hipoteca.

Planes de pago

Si la ayuda financiera disponible es muy poca o no la tienes, aún puedes contar con planes de pago normalmente disponibles. Los planes de pago son administrados por la propia universidad o por una entidad externa que cobra una cuota nominal. Generalmente, los pagos comienzan unos meses antes del inicio del año universitario y continúan durante los siguientes doce meses o más. En esencia, este es un plan de cuotas que por lo general tiene un menor interés. Puede ser preferible tomar dicho plan a un préstamo y, puede ser suficiente para evitar que solicites los Unsubsidized Federal Stafford, Direct Unsubsidized o PLUS Loans. Para obtener mayor información, comunícate con la oficina administrativa la universidad.

Planes de ahorro

Un creciente número de estados ha aprobado planes de ahorro a través de la venta de bonos. Los instrumentos de ahorros podrían ser bonos sin cupón o bonos de obligación general. Las condiciones varían de acuerdo al estado; comunícate con tu organismo estatal para obtener mayor información. Según la ley federal de impuestos, si has comprado bonos de ahorro de Estados Unidos Serie EE el o después del 1° de enero de 1990, puedes excluir de la declaración de renta, la totalidad o parte del interés ganado por estos bonos, con ciertas limitaciones si estás pagando gastos educativos específicos (por ejemplo, matrícula y cuotas para ti, tu cónyuge o personas a tu cargo).

Home Equity Loan o Line of Credit (Línea de crédito)

Muchas familias pagan algunos de sus gastos universitarios mediante la solicitud de un préstamo que respaldan con su casa. Normalmente, puedes solicitar una línea de crédito sobre capital de vivienda (qué te permite pedir prestado cuando lo necesites, no todo de una vez como con un préstamo) a una tasa considerablemente menor que cualquier otro tipo de préstamo. Además, estas opciones pueden ser deducibles; no obstante, siempre debes verificar con un asesor tributario para estar seguro.

CRÉDITOS IMPOSITIVOS

Hope Scholarship

El gobierno federal también ofrece ciertos créditos impositivos a estudiantes que cumplen con los requisitos para ellos. En realidad, Hope Scholarship es un crédito impositivo, no una beca. Los créditos impositivos se substraen del impuesto por pagar, en lugar de reducirlo de las rentas impositivas como una deducción de impuestos. Debes presentar una declaración de renta e impuestos por pagar para aprovechar este tipo de crédito. El crédito Hope no es reembolsable si no pagas los impuestos o debes menos en impuestos que el monto máximo del crédito impositivo Hope para el cual eres elegible.

Una familia puede solicitar un crédito impositivo hasta por $1,500 por año impositivo para cada hijo, durante los primeros dos años de estudios universitarios. Puedes solicitar hasta 100 por ciento de los primeros $1,000 de tus gastos educativos elegibles y el 50 por ciento de los próximos $1,000, para un crédito máximo de $1,500. El monto real del crédito depende de tu ingreso, el monto autorizado de matrícula y cuotas pagadas, y el monto de ciertas becas y subvenciones que se substraen de la matrícula.

Eres elegible para el beneficio máximo con un ingreso bruto ajustado (IBA) hasta $50,000 para contribuyente soltero o, $100,000 para contribuyentes casados. El monto del crédito se retira paulatinamente entre $40,000 y $50,000 para contribuyentes solteros y, entre $80,000 y $100,000 para contribuyentes casados. Tu hijo debe estar matriculado por lo menos a tiempo parcial en un programa elegible conducente a título o certificado, en una universidad elegible, durante el año calendario. Para solicitar el crédito impositivo Hope, debes completar el formulario 8863 del IRS.

Lifetime Learning Tax Credit (Crédito impositivo Lifetime Learning)

Al igual que la Hope Scholarship, el Lifetime Learning es un crédito impositivo disponible para individuos que presentan una declaración de renta y tienen impuestos por pagar. Esto significa que el monto del crédito se substrae de tu pasivo tributario real. El crédito Lifetime Learning no es reembolsable.

Como contribuyente, puedes solicitar un crédito impositivo hasta por $1,000 para cada hijo de tu familia, por año impositivo y por declaración de renta. El crédito no se limita a dos años de estudio, como la Hope, sino que cubre un número ilimitado de años. Puedes solicitar hasta 20 por ciento de los primeros $5,000 de gastos elegibles para gastos pagados después del 30 de junio de 1998, y antes del 1° de enero de 2003; y hasta 20 por ciento de los $10,000 de gastos elegibles por gastos pagados después del 1° de enero de 2003.

El monto real del crédito depende de tu ingreso, el monto de matrícula autorizado y cuotas pagadas, y el monto de ciertas becas y subvenciones substraídas de la matrícula. Éste es un crédito familiar (por ejemplo, $1,000 por familia). Para ser elegible, debes presentar una declaración de renta e impuestos por pagar. Eres elegible para el beneficio máximo con un IBA hasta por $40,000 en el caso de contribuyentes solteros u, $80,000 en el caso de contribuyentes casados. El monto del crédito se retira paulatinamente entre $40,000 y $50,000 para contribuyentes solteros y, entre $80,000 y $100,000 para contribuyentes casados. Para solicitar el crédito impositivo Lifetime Learning debes completar el formulario 8863 del IRS.

SERVICIO NACIONAL Y COMUNITARIO, AMERICORPS

La National and Community Service Trust Act (ley de fideicomiso National and Community Service) de 1993 estableció la Corporation for National Service (Corporación de Servicio Nacional), que ofrece oportunidades educativas a través del servicio a las comunidades estadounidenses. Cada estado tiene una comisión para servicio nacional a través de la cual se reclutan los participantes y se organizan los programas de servicio. La Corporation es la organización madre de los dos programas AmeriCorps:

- $ AmeriCorps—National Civilian and Community Corps, NCCC (Cuerpo Comunitario y Civil Nacional)
- $ AmeriCorps—VISTA

Los programas de AmeriCorps están diseñados para premiar con beneficios educativos a individuos que prestan servicios comunitarios a fin de cubrir necesidades específicas en áreas de educación, servicios humanos, seguridad pública y medio ambiente.

Tu hijo puede prestar servicios antes, durante o después de sus estudios universitarios. Debe completar dos años de servicio a tiempo completo o dos años de servicio a medio tiempo en un programa aceptado, para obtener un otorgamiento educativo.

Actualmente, si terminas satisfactoriamente un año de servicio a tiempo completo, obtienes un premio de $4,725. Si tu hijo ya tiene préstamos estudiantiles, puede ser elegible para un aplazamiento del préstamo. Los premios pueden usarse para gastos pasados, presentes o futuros, inclusive en programas universitarios de dos o cuatro años, programas de capacitación y programas de posgrado y profesionales. Puedes encontrar información adicional sobre el programa AmeriCorps en Internet en www.cns.gov.

SERVICIO MILITAR

El ejército ofrece diversas maneras para que tu hijo pueda alcanzar sus metas educativas. Los programas educativos militares benefician a hombres y a mujeres que sirven en las fuerzas armadas del país. Los participantes pueden recibir educación mientras prestan servicio en el ejército o, pueden servir primero en el ejército y luego concentrarse en la educación universitaria. Algunos programas ofrecen sólo una de estas opciones, en tanto que otros las combinan.

Beneficios educativos para veteranos

En la versión actual, los beneficios educativos para veteranos se autorizan para individuos que han ingresado al Ejército, la Armada, la Fuerzas Aérea, la Infantería de Marina o la Guardia Costera el o después del 1° de julio de 1985. Autorizado bajo el Montgomery G.I. Bill (decreto ley Montgomery G.I.), el programa difiere de acuerdo a si el estudiante está en el servicio activo o es reservista.

Beneficios por servicio activo

Los beneficios por servicio activo pueden usarse después de un mínimo de dos años de servicio, con el fin de obtener una educación universitaria mientras se presta servicio, y pueden reembolsarse después de terminar el servicio. Para ser elegible, tu hijo debe tener un diploma de escuela secundaria o su equivalente antes de completar el período de servicio activo requerido. El estudiante aporta $100 mensual a manera de reducción del pago durante los primeros doce meses de servicio activo. Si tu hijo se retira del servicio, debe haber sido dado de baja honorablemente y debe haber prestado servicio continuamente durante tres años o dos años seguidos de cuatro años en las Reservas Seleccionadas. Los beneficios deben usarse dentro de un plazo de diez años después de la baja. Después de servir un mínimo dos años, tu hijo tiene derecho a un beneficio educativo de $23,400 por treinta y seis meses para estudio de tiempo completo. Después de tres o más años de servicio, aumenta a $28,800.

Beneficios por servicio en las Reservas Seleccionadas de acuerdo al Montgomery G.I. Bill

Mientras estés en las Reservas Seleccionadas (la Reserva del Ejército, la Reserva de la Armada, la Reserva de la Fuerza Aérea, la Reserva de Infantería de Marina, la Reserva de la Guardia Costera, la Guardia del Ejército Nacional y la Guardia Nacional Aérea), puedes aprovechar los

Puedes encontrar mayor información sobre beneficios para veteranos en www.gibill.va.gov.

beneficios educativos autorizados conforme al decreto ley Montgomery G.I. El compromiso de servicio debe ser mínimo de seis años, y debes reunir ciertos requisitos de elegibilidad, como tener diploma de secundaria o su equivalente. Tu hijo no será elegible si ya tiene título universitario. Estos beneficios sólo están disponibles durante el período de servicio de tu hijo en las Reservas Seleccionadas. Los beneficios se pueden pagar hasta en treinta y seis meses.

Ayuda financiera del Ejército y de la Reserva del Ejército

Al reclutarse en el Ejército o en la Reserva del Ejército, tu hijo puede obtener el dinero para pagar su educación o puede solicitar que el Ejército reembolse sus préstamos estudiantiles. A continuación, encontrarás un resumen de los programas patrocinados por el Ejército. Otras ramas militares también ofrecen ayuda para programas similares. Tu hijo debe comunicarse con el reclutador de la rama que le interesa para obtener mayor información.

Army College Fund

Si tu hijo obtiene un puntaje mínimo de 50 en la Armed Forces Qualification Test, AFQT (Prueba de Calificación de la Fuerzas Armadas), puede escoger una especialidad del Ejército que proporcione los beneficios del Army College Fund (Fondo Universitario del Ejército) hasta $50,000 para la universidad, cuando se combina con los beneficios del Montgomery G.I. Bill. Si tu hijo se recluta por dos años en uno de los trabajos que ofrece el Army College Fund, recibirá la ayuda financiera para la universidad después de su período de servicio activo. Un reclutamiento de tres años proporciona un beneficio mayor y la posibilidad de escoger especialidades de trabajo. Si tu hijo se recluta por cuatro años en uno de los trabajos que califican para esta opción, recibe el mayor beneficio financiero posible. En todos los casos, él aporta $100 mensualmente al Montgomery G.I. Bill Fund (Fondo del decreto ley Montgomery G.I.) durante el primer año de reclutamiento, para un aporte total de $1,200.

Los beneficios de los Army College Funds se pagan directamente a tu hijo cada mes, de acuerdo al número de meses y al monto recibido por mes conforme al estatus de inscripción. Otras becas, subvenciones y ayudas no afectan los beneficios del ejército. Los beneficios pueden utilizarse dentro de un plazo de diez años a partir de la fecha de baja.

Specialized Training for Army Reserve Readiness, STARR (Entrenamiento Especializado de Preparación de Reservas del Ejército)

En conformidad con este programa, la Reserva del Ejército paga un máximo de $6,000 en concepto de matrícula, libros y gastos educativos aledaños por hasta dos años para entrenamiento en especialidades médicas seleccionadas en la universidad local de tu hijo. Cabe señalar que este programa no cubre los gastos de residencia. Si tu hijo ha prestado servicio militar anteriormente, también puede ser elegible para un bono.

Debido a la escasez de cargos de entrenamiento, la Reserva del Ejército paga el estudio en los siguientes puestos:

$ Especialista de laboratorio dental

$ Técnico médico de urgencias o paramédico (sin bono)

$ Enfermero práctico con licencia

$ Especialista de quirófano

$ Especialista en radiología

$ Especialista farmacéutico

$ Especialista en terapia respiratoria

Antes de reclutarlo, el reclutador de Reserva de Ejército local ayudará a tu hijo a seleccionar y presentarse en una universidad estatal certificada u otra institución educativa en la especialidad médica escogida.

Después de solicitar y recibir la licencia correspondiente para la especialidad médica escogida, tu hijo debe completar cuatro semanas en las instalaciones médicas del Ejército. Como

Si tu hijo no tiene experiencia militar previa, debe tener entrenamiento básico durante el verano previo a reclutarse. También debe participar en instrucciones pagas, un fin de semana cada mes durante el año académico.

especialista médico totalmente capacitado, buscará una carrera médica civil al tiempo que termina su obligación con las Reservas de las Fuerzas Armadas de Estados Unidos. También puede participar en el Montgomery G.I. Bill o en programas de reembolso de préstamos.

Army Loan Repayment Program (Programa de Reembolso de Préstamos del Ejército)

Si tu hijo es un estudiante calificado que ha asistido a la universidad gracias a préstamos estudiantiles federales concedidos después del 1° de octubre de 1975, puede escoger el programa de reembolso de préstamos en el momento de inscribirse en el ejército por un período mínimo de tres años en cualquier especialidad laboral. Sin embargo, si tu hijo escoge la opción de reembolso, no podrá beneficiarse del Montgomery G.I. Bill. Por cada año de servicio activo, la deuda de tu hijo se reduce en un tercio o $1,500, cualquiera que sea mayor, hasta un máximo de $65,000. Para ser elegible en este programa, el préstamo no debe estar en mora.

Además del reembolso de préstamos adquiridos antes de entrar a prestar servicio, este programa reembolsa los préstamos estudiantiles adquiridos durante el tiempo de servicio. Los préstamos considerados para reembolso son:

- $ Federal Stafford Loans subsidiados y no subsidiados y Direct/Subsidized y Unsubsidized Loans.
- $ Federal Perkins Loans o National Direct Student Loans, NDSL (Préstamos Estudiantiles Directos Nacionales)
- $ Federal PLUS y Federal Direct PLUS Loans
- $ Federal Supplemental Loans for Students, FSLS (Préstamo Federal Complementario para Estudiantes)
- $ Federal Consolidation and Direct Consolidation Loans (Préstamo Federal de Consolidación y Préstamo Directo de Consolidación) a nombre del soldado

Para ser considerado en el Loan Repayment Program del Ejército, tu hijo debe tener diploma de secundaria, no haber prestado servicio militar anteriormente y haber obtenido un puntaje mínimo de 50 en el AFQT.

Army Reserve Student Loan Repayment Program (Programa de Reembolso de Préstamo Estudiantil de la Reserva del Ejército)

Los mismos préstamos estudiantiles con financiación federal que se consideran para el reembolso completo si te reclutas en el servicio activo, se consideran para reembolso parcial si te reclutas en la Reserva del Ejército. Por cada año de servicio satisfactorio, la Reserva del Ejército paga 15 por ciento del préstamo o $1,500 por año, cualquiera que sea mayor, hasta $10,000. Según la especialidad militar ocupacional, algunos soldados pueden ser considerados para el reembolso del 15 por ciento o $3,000 por año, hasta $20,000.

Aunque la opción de reembolso del préstamo debe seleccionarse al momento de reclutamiento, la Reserva del Ejército reembolsa los préstamos adquiridos luego del reclutamiento. El reembolso se inicia una vez que tu hijo ha completado un año de servicio después de adquirido el préstamo y de volverse diestro en un oficio.

Para obtener mayor información, visita el sitio web del Ejército www.goarmy.com o comunícate con tu reclutador del Ejército más cercano.

Servicemember Opportunity College/Community College of the Air Force

El personal reclutado también puede recibir un título a través del Community College of the Air Force (CCAF) o la Servicemember Opportunity College (SOC) del Ejército, la Armada, la Infantería de Marina o la Guardia Costera. Estas redes permiten que los miembros reclutados opten por un título a través de una serie de acuerdos con un sinnúmero de universidades. Las universidades participantes ofrecen programas académicos flexibles que tienen en cuenta el estilo de vida único de los miembros del servicio, que tienen restricciones de tiempo y un patrón de reasignación frecuente.

A fin de aprovechar una de estas oportunidades, tu hijo debe ser un servidor estacionado en una base cercana a un campus universitario que haya provisto la programación necesaria para el personal militar fuera de servicio. Cada base tiene un funcionario académico que puede ayudarte si tu hijo quiere inscribirse en una universidad local o tomar cursos por correspondencia.

La ayuda para matrícula se encuentra disponible en forma de descuentos para miembros del servicio y sus familias que quieren continuar su educación a través de este medio. El Ejército cubre entre el 75 y el 90 por ciento del costo de matrícula. Tu hijo puede aprovechar este programa mientras presta servicio y continuar recibiendo los beneficios conforme al G.I. Bill cuando se retire. Los miembros del servicio y sus familias pueden inscribirse en programas de título asociado, universitario y de posgrado a través de la SOC.

Existen otras opciones militares, tales como cursos exentos de matrícula que ofrece la Armada para el personal naval en servicio y acreditación ofrecida por algunas instituciones por experiencia militar, como el U.S. Coast Guard Institute. Para obtener mayor información, tu hijo y su consejero universitario deben comunicarse con un reclutador militar.

Con sede en las afueras de la base Maxwell Air Force Base en Montgomery, Alabama, la CCAF es la comunidad con campus múltiples más grande del mundo. La CCAF permite que miembros de la Fuerza Aérea obtengan un título acreditado de Asociado en ciencias aplicadas en más de 60 programas educativos directamente relacionados con trabajos en la Fuerza Aérea en áreas de mantenimiento de aeronaves y misiles, electrónica y telecomunicaciones, salud aliada, logística y recursos, y servicios públicos y de apoyo. El personal reclutado debe completar su programa que lleva a título antes de la baja, ascenso o retiro. La Fuerza Aérea recientemente extendió sus programas CCAF a otras ramas militares.

Tuition Assistance Program, TA (Programa de Ayuda para Matrícula)

Este programa brinda ayuda financiera para programas voluntarios educativos fuera de servicio como soporte para alcanzar las metas profesionales y de autodesarrollo del soldado. Todos los soldados en servicio activo y en servicio seleccionado de reserva cuentan con la autorización para participar en el programa. Esta ayuda está disponible para cursos que se ofrecen en Internet, por correspondencia o a través de otros medios no tradicionales. Éstos deben ser ofrecidos por universidades acreditadas por entidades de acreditación reconocidas por el Departamento de Educación de EE.UU. Los soldados reciben un total máximo de hasta $3,500 con una tasa del 75 por ciento de los costos de matrícula o hasta $187.50 por hora semestral, cualquiera que sea menor.

Capítulo 11

Si lo hubiera sabido...

Solicitar ayuda financiera puede parecer muy difícil, especialmente cuando las familias no pueden pedir consejo a alguien que haya pasado ya por el proceso. Para ayudarte a eliminar cualquier temor, Peterson's entrevistó a cinco familias que han pasado por el proceso de ayuda financiera. Estas familias no sólo comparten contigo sus experiencias, buenas y malas, sino que te cuentan qué harían diferente si pudieran iniciar el proceso nuevamente. Si otras familias aprovechan su experiencia, podrán usar de manera más efectiva el sistema de ayuda financiera. Hemos cambiado los apellidos de las familias por respeto a su confidencialidad.

LA FAMILIA RODRÍGUEZ

Diana Rodríguez puede por fin ver la luz al final del túnel. Tiene tres hijas, dos se han graduado de la universidad y la tercera comienza en su segundo año universitario. Pero lo sorprendente en la historia de esta mujer viuda es que aunque vive con un ingreso fijo, envió a sus tres hijas a la universidad sin recibir el beneficio de ninguna ayuda financiera. ¿Cómo lo logró? Enviándolas a universidades estatales. La Sra. Rodríguez admite que no buscó ayuda financiera durante mucho tiempo. "Simplemente pensé que no sería elegible si tenía casa propia y dinero en el banco".

Los consejeros que sus hijas tuvieron en la secundaria tampoco les ofrecieron mucha orientación sobre ayuda financiera. En lugar de esto, ayudaron a las chicas a eliminar posibles universidades en función de lo que la Sra. Rodríguez podía gastar de sus ingresos. Ella pensó que entre las universidades sugeridas por estos consejeros, los gastos de asistencia más razonables eran los de las universidades públicas. Entonces, en lugar de dejar que sus hijas obtuvieran préstamos, las animó para que buscaran ingreso a universidades públicas de Texas, su estado natal. Como resultado, sus dos hijas mayores se inscribieron en Texas Tech y Claudia, la menor, fue admitida en University of Texas en Austin.

Sin embargo, Claudia prefería University of Hartford en Connecticut. Aunque Hartford le envió una carta de aceptación, los gastos de matrícula, alojamiento y comida, y cuotas en la universidad privada fuera de su estado, eran mayores de lo que podía costear la familia. Consciente del gran deseo de su hija por ingresar a Hartford, su madre se contactó por teléfono con la oficina de ayuda financiera de la universidad y explicó la situación; además pidió posteriormente a su contador que enviara a la universidad una carta de seguimiento a la conversación telefónica. Sin embargo, esta carta fue probablemente un error, ya que pudo dar a la universidad la impresión de que la familia no necesitaba ayuda financiera si podía tener un contador a su servicio. Finalmente, Claudia decidió asistir a University of Texas en Austin para que su madre y ella no tuvieran que solicitar préstamos. "Todos tenemos decepciones en la vida", dijo la Sra. Rodríguez, "pero las superamos". Al reconsiderar su experiencia, lamenta no haber comprendido el proceso de ayuda financiera, lo que significa que ella y sus hijas se vieron limitadas en la selección de universidades. Si pudiera volver atrás, haría tres cosas en forma diferente:

Primero, no dejaría que sus hijas esperaran hasta el duodécimo año de la secundaria para buscar posibles universidades. El número de posibles universidades que pudieron analizar fue muy limitado. Hoy, la Sra. Rodríguez dice que comenzaría la búsqueda a comienzos del undécimo año de la secundaria, a fin de explorar una gama más amplia de universidades.

Segundo, La Sra. Rodríguez llevaría a cada una de sus hijas a visitar las posibles universidades antes de que enviaran solicitudes de admisión, pues todas esperaron hasta ser aceptadas para visitarlas.

Finalmente, la Sra. Rodríguez ahora se da cuenta de lo poco que sabía sobre el proceso de ayuda financiera. "Debí haber visitado las universidades y haber hablado con alguien sobre nuestras opciones", señala.

LA FAMILIA VERACRUZ

La mayoría de los estudiantes esperan que sean sus padres quienes obtengan ayuda financiera, pero, ¿qué sucede cuando los padres son inmigrantes que no hablan mucho inglés? Marisol Veracruz dice, "Tuve que hacer todo por mi cuenta".

Marisol comenzó a pensar en ayuda financiera a mediados del undécimo año de la secundaria. "Mis padres tienen ingresos reducidos y dos de nosotros íbamos a asistir a la universidad al mismo tiempo (ella tiene un hermano mellizo), así que sabía que tendríamos necesidad financiera". Marisol pasó mucho tiempo en la oficina del consejero vocacional de su escuela, informándose bien sobre este tema importante. Gracias al consejero, descubrió el Equal Opportunity Fund, EOF (Fondo para la Igualdad de Oportunidades) de su estado natal de New Jersey. Esta fuente proporciona dinero para subvenciones de residentes desfavorecidos del estado, que puedan demostrar necesidad financiera y motivación para seguir estudios superiores.

Cuando tenía alguna pregunta, Marisol también acudía a las oficinas de ayuda financiera de las universidades y quedó sorprendida con las subvenciones que le concedieron Montclair State y Rutgers University de New Jersey. "No pensé que fuera a obtener toda esa ayuda monetaria", dice. Escogió Rutgers y en su segundo año volvió a sorprenderse, esta vez por el monto de su paquete de ayuda. Además del EOF, de un Perkins Loan y de un Stafford Loan subsidiado, el paquete de ayuda para Marisol Veracruz incluía asignación de trabajo y estudio. "Obtengo $2,000 anuales en trabajo y estudio que me han sido de gran ayuda", agrega. Usa una parte del dinero proveniente de trabajo y estudio para pagar sus cuentas mensuales, pero ahorra la mayor parte para reembolsar los préstamos después de graduarse. Marisol ya ha pasado dos veces por el proceso de solicitud. "Hasta ahora todo ha salido bastante bien", dice. Aunque no dudó en formular preguntas a los funcionarios de ayuda financiera y a su consejero vocacional en la secundaria, hoy cree que el proceso hubiera sido más fácil si sus padres hablaran un mejor inglés. "Podrían haberme brindado más apoyo, haberme dado más consejos", dice Marisol.

Ella ofrece dos consejos para las familias que van a solicitar ayuda:

$ "Entre más pronto puedan iniciar el proceso, mejor. Si esperan hasta el ultimo año de la secundaria, se sentirán acosadísimos".

$ Mantengan toda la documentación en archivos separados para cada universidad cuando estén enviando correspondencia con solicitudes de ayuda financiera. “Así pude ir verificando ‘a medida que pasaban los días’ si iba por el camino correcto”.

LA FAMILIA GÓMEZ

Teresa, la hija de Verónica Gómez obtuvo elevados puntajes en el SAT, tenía muy buenas calificaciones, y realizó muchas actividades extracurriculares en su secundaria pública en Florida. La Sra. Gómez señala, “Hizo todo lo que se suponía que debía hacer para obtener toda la ayuda posible y esperábamos que toda la ayuda que necesitaba le llegaría sin problemas”.

Al comienzo, la familia Gómez estuvo encantada cuando Teresa recibió subvenciones por mérito de University of Tampa y de Ekerd College sobre la base de la solicitud de admisión y del registro académico. Sin embargo, los $3,000 anuales de subvención no eran suficientes, pues los gastos de matrícula, alojamiento y comida, cuotas y transporte eran de casi $30,000 al año. Verónica Gómez dice que cuando se considera un gasto tan alto: “Uno no piensa tanto en lo que la universidad ofrece, sino en el dinero que te falta pagarle”.

La familia Gómez hizo luego lo más lógico, solicitar ayuda basada en la necesidad. La Sra. y su marido estaban orgullosos de haber ahorrado $45,000 para los estudios universitarios de su hija. En lugar de colocar su dinero en una cuenta familiar de ahorros, les habían aconsejado abrir una cuenta de ahorros a nombre de su hija. Con el tiempo, los intereses y los dividendos de Teresa generarían reducciones en impuestos. Desafortunadamente, cuando la Sra. Gómez entregó la Free Application for Federal Student Aid, FAFSA, el sistema de análisis de necesidad calculó un aporte de la estudiante a partir de activos y determinó un aporte esperado de la familia que ascendía a $15,750, ó 35 por ciento de los ahorros/activos en la cuenta a nombre de Teresa, se tuvieron en cuenta en el EFC. Su aporte como estudiante, más el aporte que se esperaba de sus padres, hizo que el EFC estuviera al nivel de los COA. Como resultado, la familia Gómez no demostró necesidad financiera y, por tanto, no se le otorgó ayuda basada en la necesidad.

Todos los funcionarios de ayuda financiera con los que hablaron les dieron la misma respuesta: "Si hubieran colocado el dinero de Teresa en una cuenta a nombre de los padres, no se habría esperado aporte por activos y hubieran sido elegibles para recibir $15,000 por ayuda basada en la necesidad". Finalmente, la familia Gómez solicitó un Parent Loan for Undergraduate Students, PLUS, a fin de enviar a su hija a la universidad. En lugar de mostrar resentimiento por lo sucedido, Verónica Gómez dice, "Todos los padres deben dar una educación a sus hijos, de modo que los padres deben aportar parte de su dinero para la demostrarles a sus hijos el valor de la educación universitaria. Sin embargo, ahora sé cómo planificar y lo que debo hacer en el proceso de solicitud de ayuda financiera para el año próximo".

Verónica tiene varias recomendaciones para reducir costos:

- $ No acumules un gran activo a nombre del estudiante, que pueda tenerse en cuenta en la FAFSA. Guarda este dinero en la cuenta de los padres.
- $ Haz un cálculo de prueba de la FAFSA antes de entregarla para evaluación al centro de procesamiento. Que no te queden dudas sobre la forma cómo las partidas serán calculadas en la Metodología Federal.
- $ Paga los gastos de asistencia de tu hijo a partir de su cuenta de ahorros, pues con esto se reducirá el aporte esperado del estudiante al llenar formularios de renovación cada año.

LA FAMILIA VÁSQUEZ

Tomás, el hijo de Viviana Vásquez, fue favorecido con paquetes de ayuda de diez universidades diferentes. Cuando los miembros de la familia se sentaron a comparar los otorgamientos, pronto se dieron cuenta que debían organizarse. "No puedes simplemente mirar las cifras e ir pasando documentos", dice Viviana, "debes ingresarlos a la computadora y analizar la universidad, la matrícula, el alojamiento y la comida".

Los Vásquez viven en California y al comienzo estaban impresionados ante el gran paquete de ayuda ofrecido por una reconocida universidad privada de Massachusetts. "Sin embargo, señala la Sra. Vásquez, al comienzo la gente no considera todos los gastos adicionales que acompañan los estudios universitarios y se asume que la cantidad de dinero que indica la universidad en la guía será el costo real y no suman todos los otros gastos no previsibles". Estos gastos a menudo olvidados incluyen viajes a casa para vacaciones y visitas, fin de semana con los padres y gastos médicos. La Sra. Vásquez dice al respecto, "Cuando consideres estos gastos, debes tener en cuenta que la cuestión sería muy diferente si tu hijo asiste a la universidad que está a 10 minutos de casa".

El Sr. y la Sra. Vásquez habían pasado hace diez años por el proceso de ayuda financiera con otros dos hijos, pero cuando llegó el momento de solicitar ayuda para Jorge, se dieron cuenta de que las cosas habían cambiado radicalmente. "Más formularios que llenar, más preguntas que responder, quieren saber hasta los montos que tus hijos tienen en sus cuentas de ahorros". No hacen que el proceso de ayuda financiera sea fácil de comprender para toda la gente. La familia Vásquez se dio cuenta de la importancia de entender bien las preguntas de los formularios y decidió contratar un asesor en ayuda financiera.

Cuando llegó el momento de comparar los paquetes de ayuda, la Sra. Vásquez creó una hoja de cálculo en la computadora de su casa con tres columnas: gastos (matrícula, alojamiento y comida, y transporte), ayuda (préstamos subsidiados y no subsidiados, oportunidad de trabajo y estudio y becas), y necesidades no satisfechas. "No es nada del otro mundo", dice la Sra. Vásquez, a quien le sirvió la hoja de cálculo para ayudar a su hijo a elegir Villanova University. "Ni siquiera tiene que ser en computadora, se puede hacer con papel y lápiz".

Viviana Vásquez tiene los siguientes consejos para los padres:

- $ No vale la pena contratar a un asesor financiero. En cambio, ella recomienda organizarse haciendo carpetas para cada universidad de interés.
- $ Visitar la oficina de ayuda financiera de cada una de estas universidades.
- $ Anotar todas las impresiones e información relacionadas con cada institución luego de la primera visita, "de lo contrario empieza uno a confundir quién dijo que y qué fue lo que dijo".

LA FAMILIA HERRERA

Cuando se trata de encontrar ayuda financiera, se puede pensar que Víctor Herrera tiene una ventaja sobre la mayoría de las familias porque es contador de profesión. Sin embargo, las cosas le resultaron al contrario. "No sabía qué esperar", dice al recordar cuando solicitó ayuda financiera para su hijastra. Pero no pasó mucho tiempo antes de que aprendiera a "olvidar al gobierno a menos que te encuentres en condiciones de pobreza, excepto cuando se trate de préstamos".

La experiencia de Herrera le demostró que las familias de clase media que tienen casa propia y ganan un buen salario no obtienen mucha ayuda federal. Su hijastra consideró por igual universidades públicas y privadas, sin tener una sola como favorita. La decisión final en cuanto a universidad quedó pendiente del paquete de ayuda financiera que recibiera. Como contador, el Sr. Herrera sabía de muchas familias que habían solicitado elevados préstamos para que sus hijos ingresaran a la universidad. "Pero no quería que mi hijastra ni yo nos viéramos con la carga de una cuantiosa deuda", recuerda. Por esto, se dedicó a buscar dinero de becas privadas para su hijastra. De los 15 programas de becas privadas y estatales a los cuales ella solicitó ayuda, sólo obtuvo una subvención, que el Sr. Herrera describe como una beca estatal desconocida ganada al azar. "Probablemente, hay muchas más becas disponibles de lo que sabe la gente", dice, lamentando lo difícil que le fue ubicar programas legítimos de becas.

Los Herrera tuvieron que recurrir primero a ayuda financiera institucional. Al darse cuenta que su hijastra tendría más oportunidad de obtener dinero de beca en universidades pequeñas y poco conocidas, pusieron manos a la obra. Enviaron solicitudes a cuatro universidades pequeñas en Massachusetts, entre ellas, Regis College. Después de recibidas las cartas de aceptación, Herrera se comunicó por teléfono con las oficinas de ayuda financiera para negociar paquetes de ayuda. "Si la universidad quiere admitir a tu hijo, te encontrará una solución", dice Herrera.

En las tres o cuatro llamadas que hizo le pareció que el personal de la universidad era muy amable y, como la institución es pequeña, cada vez habló con las mismas dos personas, entre ellas, el director de ayuda financiera de la universidad. Finalmente, el Sr. Herrera negoció con la institución un paquete de ayuda muy favorable. Regis ofreció a su hijastra dos subvenciones basadas en su rendimiento académico, una oportunidad de trabajo y estudio con empleo fuera del campus y un Stafford Loan subsidiado. Herrera recuerda que, “El primer año la ayuda cubrió 50 por ciento de los gastos, incluidos los gastos por concepto de matrícula, alojamiento y comida”; los gastos restantes se hicieron más manejables con un plan mensual de pagos.

Herrera está a punto de comenzar de nuevo el proceso con su hijo, quien está en undécimo año de secundaria. ¿Qué va a hacer ahora de diferente? “Estoy comenzando con mayor anticipación, buscando universidades que cumplan las expectativas del chico”. Además, espera lograr mejores paquetes de ayuda financiera y aconseja a su hijo postularse en más instituciones y visitar los diferentes campus para tener entrevistas personales.

Sus recomendaciones para otras familias son sencillas:

- $ “Identifiquen las universidades especiales que se encuentran a la cabeza de la lista de cualquier estudiante”. Hay cientos de pequeñas universidades que las familias pasan por alto porque no son las más populares o prestigiosas, pero no se dan cuenta de que son las más dispuestas a hacer concesiones para que el costo de la educación superior esté al alcance de las familias de clase media.
- $ Busquen universidades que tengan estudiantes provenientes de minorías y que tengan subvenciones para otras razas.
- $ Busquen universidades que deseen estudiantes provenientes de diferentes ubicaciones geográficas para enriquecer su actual población estudiantil.

Apéndices

Glosario

Academia militar: Las cinco instituciones de estudios superiores administradas por las diferentes ramas del ejército: U.S. Military Academy, U.S. Air Force Academy, U.S. Naval Academy, U.S. Coast Guard Academy y U.S. Merchant Marine Academy.

Activos: Dinero disponible en cuentas corrientes o de ahorro; fideicomisos, acciones, bonos y otros títulos valores; bien raíz (sin incluir vivienda), propiedad que genera ingresos, equipos empresariales e inventario empresarial, que se consideran para fijar el Expected Family Contribution (EFC) según la fórmula regular.

Activos empresariales: Propiedad utilizada en la actividad comercial o empresarial, como bien raíz, existencias, edificaciones, maquinaria y otros equipos, patentes, derechos de franquicia y derechos de autor que se tienen en cuenta para determinar el Expected Family Contribution (EFC) según la fórmula regular.

Administrador de ayuda financiera: Individuo responsable de organizar y comunicar la información sobre programas de préstamos, subvenciones, becas y empleo para asesorar, otorgar, informar, aconsejar y supervisar todo lo relacionado con la ayuda financiera. Debe atender los diversos tipos de población involucrados y, como administrador, interpreta las políticas y reglamentaciones federales, estatales e institucionales; además, está en capacidad de analizar al estudiante y sus necesidades de empleo para hacer los cambios pertinentes.

Advanced Placement, AP (Nivelación anticipada): Serie de exámenes que demuestran el conocimiento de un estudiante en un área de estudio, para la cual algunas instituciones de estudios superiores ofrecen crédito.

AmeriCorps: *Ver National and Community Service.*

Análisis de necesidad: Sistema para evaluar y calcular la capacidad de pago de un estudiante para sufragar gastos educativos. Tiene dos componentes básicos: (a) cálculo de la capacidad de pago de la familia del solicitante para ayudar a sufragar los gastos educativos y (b) cálculo preciso de la cuantía de los gastos educativos.

Año académico (AY, por sus siglas en inglés): Medición del trabajo académico que debe lograr un estudiante. La universidad determina su propio año académico pero las regulaciones federales establecen estándares mínimos para determinar las becas de ayuda financiera. Por ejemplo, el año académico debe incluir por lo menos 30 semanas de instrucción en las que se espera que un estudiante de tiempo completo haya cumplido por lo menos 24 horas-crédito durante el semestre o trimestre, 36 horas-crédito trimestrales ó 900 horas-reloj.

Año base: Para fines de análisis de necesidad, el año base corresponde al año calendario de doce meses que precede al año de otorgamiento; por ejemplo, 2001 es el año base para el año de otorgamiento 2002–2003.

Año de otorgamiento: Período entre el 1° de julio de un año y el 30 de junio del siguiente año.

Año escolar: *Ver Año académico.*

Aplazamiento (de un préstamo): Condición mediante la cual no es necesario efectuar pago de capital y no se acumulan intereses para Federal Perkins Loans, Federal Subsidized Stafford y Direct Subsidized. El período de reembolso se extiende por el tiempo de duración del aplazamiento.

Auxilio de auto-ayuda: Fondos provistos a través del trabajo y esfuerzo del estudiante, que incluyen ahorros de ganancias anteriores, ingresos por ganancias actuales o préstamo a reembolsar con futuras ganancias.

Avance académico satisfactorio: Progreso requerido de un beneficiario de ayuda financiera en estudios u otras actividades aceptables para lograr un objetivo educativo específico.

Ayuda de acuerdo a la necesidad: Ayuda para estudiantes que, por circunstancias financieras, no pueden asumir sus gastos educativos superiores.

Ayuda financiera: Término general que describe cualquier fuente de ayuda estudiantil externa al estudiante o su familia. Fondos otorgados a un estudiante para ayudar a sufragar sus gastos de educación superior. Generalmente se otorgan sobre un criterio de ayuda de necesidad financiera e incluyen becas, subvenciones, préstamos y empleo.

Ayuda no basada en la necesidad: Ayuda determinada con base en criterios diferentes a la necesidad, como habilidades académicas, musicales o deportivas. También hace referencia a programas de ayuda estudiantil en los que no se tiene en cuenta el EFC en la ecuación de necesidad.

Ayuda por donación: Fondos educativos como subvenciones o becas que no requieren el reembolso proveniente de ganancias actuales o futuras.

Ayuda por mérito: Ayuda estudiantil otorgada por el logro o talento de un estudiante en un área particular (académica, deportiva o musical).

Beca: Forma de ayuda financiera que no requiere reembolso o empleo; generalmente, se otorga a estudiantes que demuestran o exhiben su potencial de distinción, especialmente en cuanto a desempeño académico.

Beca departamental: Auxilio de asistencia por donación específicamente diseñado para un beneficiario en un departamento académico particular dentro de la institución.

Beca militar: Beca del Reserve Officer Training Corps, ROTC (Cuerpo de Entrenamiento de Oficiales de Reservas) disponible para el Ejército, la Armada y la Fuerza Aérea en diferentes universidades de Estados Unidos. Estas becas cubren matrícula y cuotas, libros y materiales, y una partida para manutención.

Beneficios educativos: Fondos, principalmente federales, destinados a cierto tipo de estudiantes (veteranos, hijos de veteranos fallecidos u otros beneficiarios de pensiones por fallecimiento y estudiantes con discapacidades físicas), para ayudarles a financiar sus estudios superiores sin importar su capacidad de demostrar necesidad en el sentido tradicional.

Beneficios educativos para veteranos: Programas de ayuda para educación o capacitación dirigido a veteranos elegibles o sus dependientes.

Cancelación (de un préstamo): Condición existente cuando el beneficiario de un préstamo federal para estudiantes ha cumplido con los requisitos que permiten cancelar o amortizar parte del capital y sus intereses adeudados.

Capacidad de aprovechamiento: Las instituciones de estudios superiores no otorgan ayuda federal a estudiantes que no posean diploma de secundaria o equivalente, a no ser que se demuestre que éste puede sacar provecho de los estudios ofrecidos.

Capital (de un préstamo): Cantidad de dinero prestada sin incluir intereses u otros cargos, a no ser que se hayan capitalizado.

Capitalización (de intereses): Pagos de intereses diferidos y agregados al capital del préstamo.

Carta de otorgamiento: Medio de notificación a los solicitantes aceptados de ayuda financiera sobre la ayuda ofrecida. La carta de otorgamiento normalmente contiene información sobre el tipo de ayuda ofrecida y el monto de la misma, al igual que información específica del programa, las responsabilidades del estudiante y las condiciones que regulan dicho otorgamiento. Generalmente, permite que el estudiante acepte o decline la ayuda ofrecida.

Certificado: Reconocimiento formal de término exitoso de un programa o curso de estudios particular realizado especialmente en una escuela universitaria vocacional, universitaria de oficios o escuela semisuperior.

Certificado de Ayuda Financiera (FAT, por sus siglas en inglés): Contiene la historia de la ayuda financiera del estudiante para observar ciertos aspectos de elegibilidad del estudiante. Esta información se reporta en los SAR y los ISIR; las universidades pueden consultar electrónicamente dicho historial a través del National Student Loan Data System, NSLDS (Sistema Nacional de Información sobre Préstamos Estudiantiles). En algunos casos, la universidad puede solicitar un FAT impreso.

Ciudadano: Persona que debe lealtad a Estados Unidos. La mayoría de los programas de ayuda financiera federal y estatal se consideran programas de asistencia nacional y se encuentran disponibles sólo para ciudadanos, ciudadanos residentes en el exterior, residentes permanentes en Estados Unidos y personas que no se encuentran en el país temporalmente. Los ciudadanos de la República de las Islas Marshall, los Estados Federados de Micronesia y la República de Palau son sólo elegibles para la Federal Pell Grant, la FSEOG y FWS.

CLEP: *Ver College-Level Examination Board Program.*

COA: *Ver Gastos de asistencia.*

College-Level Examination Board Program, CLEP (Programa de Evaluación de Nivel Universitario): Serie de exámenes que demuestran el nivel de conocimiento de un estudiante en un área determinada para la cual algunas instituciones de estudios superiores ofrecen crédito.

Confirmación de información SAR: Informe de ayuda estudiantil de una página, no corregible, que contiene sólo la primera parte. Los estudiantes que diligencian electrónicamente las solicitudes o que corrigen electrónicamente la información del solicitante a través de la universidad, reciben esta confirmación.

Consultor de ayuda financiera: Aquella persona que, por una tarifa determinada, presta una variedad de servicios a los estudiantes, entre ellos el diligenciamiento de la FAFSA y otras ayudas financieras, el cálculo del EFC y de la necesidad financiera.

Contribución del estudiante: Cálculo cuantitativo de la capacidad del estudiante para ayudar a pagar sus gastos de estudios superiores durante un año determinado.

Crédito (u hora-crédito): Unidad de medición que algunas instituciones asignan para cumplir con los requisitos de un curso.

Crédito académico: Unidad de medición dada por la institución a un estudiante cuando cumple los requisitos de un curso o asignatura como estipula la institución.

Criterios de elegibilidad: Condiciones específicas que debe cumplir un estudiante para ser beneficiario de una ayuda financiera. En todos los programas es indispensable demostrar necesidad; pero adicionalmente, los criterios generales de elegibilidad para ayuda financiera federal incluyen, entre otros, estatus de ciudadanía y registro de servicio militar obligatorio. Ciertos programas pueden tener otros requisitos específicos adicionales.

Cronograma de reembolso: Plan de pagos que debe entregársele al prestatario cuando ha terminado, por lo menos, la mitad de sus estudios; debe estipular el capital y los intereses para cada cuota, junto con el número de pagos necesarios para el pago total del préstamo. Debe incluir, además, la tasa de interés, fecha de vencimiento del primer pago y frecuencia de los pagos.

DANTES: *Ver Defense Activity for Non-Traditional Education Support.*

Declaración de objetivo educativo: Declaración firmada por el estudiante beneficiario de ayuda financiera en la que se compromete a utilizar la totalidad de los fondos otorgados, exclusivamente en gastos educativos o relacionados con su educación. Se incluye como parte de la FAFSA.

Defense Activity for Non-Traditional Education Support, DANTES (Actividad de Protección para la Subvención de Educación no Tradicional): Serie de exámenes patrocinados por el ejército para otorgar reconocimiento universitario a hombres y mujeres que prestan servicio militar, y a otros no militares, por el conocimiento y habilidades que han adquirido.

Departamento de Educación de Estados Unidos (ED, por sus siglas en inglés): Dependencia del gobierno federal que administra las asistencias educativas a estudiantes inscritos en uno de los siguientes programas de educación superior: Federal Pell Grant, Federal Perkins Loan, Federal Supplemental Educational Opportunity Grant (FSEOG), Federal Work-Study (FWS), Federal Family Education Loan (FFEL) y William D. Ford Direct Stafford Loans.

Departamento de Salud y Servicios Humanos de Estados Unidos (HHS, por sus siglas en inglés): Dependencia del gobierno federal que provee ayuda a futuros profesionales de la atención de la salud. Entre los programas que administra el HHS están el Nursing Student Loan, Health Professions Student Loan y Scholarships for Disadvantaged Students Program.

Dependiente legal: Hijo biológico o adoptado, o persona para quien el solicitante ha sido nombrado tutor legal y para la cual el solicitante asume más de la mitad de su manutención. Adicionalmente, una persona que vive con el solicitante y recibe al menos la mitad de su sustento, y continuará recibiendo dicho sustento durante el año de auxilio otorgado.

Descuento de protección de ingresos: Deducción contra ingresos para los gastos básicos de manutención familiar que se basa en cálculos de consumo y otros gastos estimados por la Bureau of Labor Statistics (Oficina de Estadísticas Laborales) para una familia con bajo estándar de vida.

Desembolso: Proceso por el cual los fondos de ayuda financiera se ponen a disposición de los estudiantes para cubrir sus gastos educativos y de manutención.

Direct Loan (Préstamo Directo) (subsidiado y no subsidiado): Préstamos a largo plazo y con bajo interés administrados por el Departamento de Educación y las instituciones. Tasa de interés variable que no excede el 8.25 por ciento. Los Direct Loans no subsidiados pueden utilizarse en reemplazo de los EFC.

Dotación: Fondos obtenidos y poseídos por una institución superior que se invierten de manera que sus utilidades puedan utilizarse para diversos fines, como construcciones, investigaciones y ayuda financiera.

Ecuación de necesidad: *Ver Ecuación de necesidad financiera.*

Ecuación de necesidad financiera: La necesidad financiera es igual a los gastos de asistencia menos la Expected Family Contribution (COA – EFC = Necesidad).

ED: *Ver Departamento de Educación de Estados Unidos.*

EFC: *Ver Expected Family Contribution.*

Empaquetar: Proceso para combinar diversos tipos de ayudas estudiantil, tales como subvenciones, préstamos, becas y empleo, con miras a completar el monto total de las necesidades del estudiantes.

Empleo: Respecto a la ayuda financiera, el empleo constituye la oportunidad para que el estudiante devengue un dinero que le permita ayudarse a pagar su educación. El Federal Work-Study Program es uno de los programas que le permite al estudiante trabajar para sufragar sus gastos educativos.

Estatus de inscripción: Para las instituciones que trabajan por semestres o trimestres y otros períodos académicos o mediciones de progreso por horas-crédito, el estatus de ingreso equivale a la carga de hora-crédito de los estudiantes de acuerdo a su dedicación de tiempo completo, tercera parte del tiempo, medio tiempo o menos de medio tiempo.

Estudiante a tiempo completo: En general, es aquel que toma mínimo 12 horas académicas por semestre o trimestre en un período académico, 24 horas-semestre o 36 horas-trimestre al año en instituciones que usan créditos en lugar de períodos, o 24 horas-reloj semanales en las instituciones que miden el avance en horas-reloj.

Estudiante a tiempo parcial: Según lo determine la institución educativa, es aquel estudiante que no asiste al programa con una dedicación de tiempo completo.

Estudiante de fuera del estado: Según definición de las instituciones públicas, es aquel estudiante que no tiene residencia legal en el estado o distrito local legal que supervisa legal y fiscalmente a tales instituciones. Estos estudiantes generalmente pagan matrículas más elevadas que los residentes legales. Consulte también estudiantes no residentes.

Estudiante extranjero: Estudiante que pertenece, o debe lealtad, a otro país. Dichos estudiantes no son elegibles para programas básicos federales. Sin embargo, de acuerdo a ciertas categorías de estudiantes no-ciudadanos que deben lealtad permanente a Estados Unidos, algunos son elegibles para ayuda estudiantil.

Estudiante independiente: Estudiante que: (a) tendrá 24 años de edad al 31 de diciembre del año académico para el que está solicitando ayuda financiera; o (b) es huérfano o está bajo custodia de un tribunal; (c) es veterano; (d) está casado o es estudiante universitario o de posgrado; (e) tiene dependientes legales diferentes a su cónyuge; o (f) presenta documentación de circunstancias inusuales que demuestran su independencia del administrador de ayudas financieras estudiantiles.

Estudiante que no reside en el campus: Estudiante que no vive en el campus; normalmente hace referencia al estudiante que vive en casa con sus padres, pero igualmente se refiere a cualquier estudiante que vive lejos del campus.

Estudiante regular: Estudiante inscrito o aceptado para inscribirse en una institución de estudios superiores a fin de obtener un grado, certificado u otra credencial educativa reconocida ofrecidos por una institución.

Estudiante universitario: Estudiante aún sin título universitario o grado universitario.

Expectativas de auto-ayuda: Presunción de que un estudiante tiene la obligación de ayudar a pagar parte de sus estudios.

Expected Family Contribution, EFC (Aporte Esperado de la familia): Cantidad que se espera que un estudiante y su familia paguen por gastos de asistencia estudiantil según el cálculo hecho con la fórmula ordenada por el congreso, conocida como Metodología Federal. El EFC se usa para determinar la elegibilidad de un estudiante para programas de ayuda financiera estudiantil.

FAFSA: *Ver Free Application for Federal Student Aid.*

Federal Family Education Loan, FFEL (Préstamo Educativo Familiar Federal): Nombre colectivo para programas de Federal Stafford Loan (subsidiado y no subsidiado), Federal PLUS y Federal Consolidated Loan. Los prestamistas privados suministran los fondos para dichos programas y el gobierno federal respalda los préstamos.

Federal Pell Grant (Beca Federal Pell): Programa de beca federal de educación superior para estudiantes necesitados, que no han recibido aún grado profesional o universitario, y es administrado por el Departamento de Educación de Estados Unidos.

Federal Perkins Loan (Préstamo Federal Perkins): Uno de los programas con sede en el campus con préstamo a largo plazo y bajo interés, para estudiantes universitarios y de posgrado, con una tasa de interés corriente del 5 por ciento.

Federal Stafford Loan (Préstamo Federal Stafford) (subsidiado y no subsidiado): Préstamos a largo plazo y bajo interés administrados por el Departamento de Educación a través de organismos privados de garantía. Antes conocido como Guaranteed Students Loan, GSL (Préstamos Estudiantiles Garantizados); cuenta con una tasa de interés variable no superior al 8.25 por ciento. Los Federal Stafford Loans no subsidiados pueden reemplazar el EFC.

Federal Supplemental Educational Opportunity Grant, FSEOG (Beca Federal Suplementaria para la Oportunidad Educativa): Uno de los programas con sede en el campus, que otorga ayuda financiera a estudiantes que no han completado sus estudios universitarios y que tienen gran necesidad de esta ayuda para continuar sus estudios. La prioridad del auxilio FSEOG son los beneficiarios de la Federal Pell Grant con el EFC más bajo.

Federal Work-Study Program, FWS (Programa Federal de Trabajo y Estudio): Uno de los programas con sede en el campus, que ofrece empleo de tiempo parcial a estudiantes universitarios y de posgrado para sufragar parte de sus gastos educativos.

FFELP: *Ver Federal Family Education Loan Program.*

Filosofía de empaque: Criterios de combinación de los tipos de ayuda de una institución superior para satisfacer la necesidad del estudiante. Varía de una universidad a otra.

FM: *Ver Metodología Federal de Análisis de Necesidad.*

Fórmula: *Ver Fórmula de Análisis de Necesidad.*

Fórmula de Análisis de Necesidad: Define los datos que se usan para calcular el EFC; existen dos fórmulas distintas: regular y simplificada. La fórmula calcula el EFC con la metodología federal de análisis de necesidad.

Free Application for Federal Student Aid, FAFSA (Solicitud Gratuita de Ayuda Federal para Estudiantes): Solicitud de ayuda financiera diligenciada por el estudiante donde reúne información familiar y financiera. Este es el documento base para todos los cálculos de análisis de necesidad financiera federal y correspondencias de bases de datos aplicables al estudiante.

FSEOG: *Ver Federal Supplemental Educational Opportunity Grant.*

Gastos de asistencia (COA, por sus siglas en inglés): En términos generales, incluye la matrícula y cuotas que debe pagar un estudiante, junto con el estimado de las instituciones por concepto de alojamiento y comida, gastos de transporte, libros y materiales, más otros gastos personales. Adicionalmente, pueden incluirse, cuando sea necesario, las cuotas del préstamo estudiantil, el cuidado dependiente, los gastos razonables para programas de educación en el exterior o educación cooperativa, o los gastos relacionados con una discapacidad. Véase también gastos de educación o presupuesto educativo.

Gastos educativos: *Ver Gastos de asistencia.*

Gastos institucionales: Cargos de matrícula, cuotas, alojamiento y alimentación de propiedad de la institución o administrados por ésta, y otros gastos educativos estipulados por la institución.

Gastos no institucionales: Gastos asociados a la asistencia a estudios superiores no calculados por la institución, tales como alojamiento y alimentación fuera del campus, libros, materiales, transporte y gastos varios personales.

Health Professions Student Loan, HPSL (Préstamo para Estudiantes Profesionales de la Salud): Programa de préstamos a largo plazo, con bajo interés, dirigido a estudiantes que cursan estudios en disciplinas específicas de la salud.

HHS: *Ver Departamento de Salud y Servicios Humanos de Estados Unidos.*

Hoja de verificación: Documento que la institución superior envía al estudiante para que él y su familia lo diligencien y devuelvan a la institución, con el fin de obtener documentación de verificación.

Hope Scholarship (Beca Hope): Crédito impositivo para sufragar gastos de educación superior.

Hora-reloj: Unidad de medida que ciertas instituciones dan para cumplir con los requerimientos de un curso.

Incumplimiento (Federal Perkins Loan): Cuando el prestatario de un préstamo no cumple con el pago a tiempo de cuotas vencidas y dicho retraso persiste, sin que medie un pago u otro tipo de acuerdo de pago. El Departamento de Educación considera que la exoneración de un préstamo por quiebra no es incumplimiento.

Incumplimiento (Federal Stafford Loans, Direct, Federal PLUS, o Direct PLUS): Cuando la Secretaría de Educación, o la entidad de garantía correspondiente, determina que el prestatario ya no tiene la intención de reembolsar su deuda, por incumplimiento en el pago de una cuota vencida o de cualquier otro plazo del pagaré. El Departamento de Educación considera que la exoneración de un préstamo por quiebra no es incumplimiento.

Indulgencia de morosidad: Período que permite la interrupción temporal del reembolso de préstamos con una extensión del plazo de los pagos, o con aceptación de pagos de menor cantidad a la acordada previamente.

Ingreso anual proyectado: Ingreso previsto para el primer año calendario del año de otorgamiento, que puede bien ser otro período de doce meses.

Ingreso bruto ajustado (IBA): Todo ingreso sujeto a impuestos como aparece en una declaración de impuesto sobre la renta de Estados Unidos.

Ingreso disponible ajustado: Parte del ingreso familiar que queda luego de deducir impuestos locales, estatales y federales, manutención y con otros factores utilizados en la Metodología Federal de Análisis de Necesidad.

Ingreso sujeto a impuestos: Ingreso percibido de salarios, mensualidades, propinas e intereses, dividendos o utilidades comerciales o agrarias, o ingresos por renta o propiedad.

Ingresos exentos de impuestos: Todo ingreso recibido y no reportado ante el Internal Revenue Service (Servicio de Impuestos Internos), o reportado pero exento de impuestos. Dicho ingreso incluiría, pero sin limitarse a ello, cualquier porción exenta de impuestos por beneficios del seguro social, crédito sobre ingresos percibidos, pagos del seguro social, ganancias de capital exentas de impuestos, intereses sobre bonos exentos de impuestos, exclusión de dividendos y otorgamiento militares y otros gastos de manutención y alojamiento.

Ingresos: Cantidad de dinero recibida de: salarios, intereses, dividendos, ventas o renta de propiedad o por servicios prestados, utilidades comerciales o agrarias, algunos programas de bienestar, pensiones de manutención, tales como beneficios del seguro social sujetos o no a impuestos, y manutención de hijos.

Inscripción: Cumplimiento de los requisitos de registro, diferentes al pago de matrícula y cuotas, en la institución donde asiste, o asistirá, el estudiante. Un estudiante universitario por correspondencia debe ser aceptado para ingresar, y para que se le considere inscrito debe completar y entregar una lección.

Institución elegible: Institución de educación superior, escuela universitaria vocacional, vocacional superior, o institución privada de educación superior que cumple con todos los criterios para participar en los programas de ayuda federal estudiantil

Institutional Student Information Record, ISIR (Registro Institucional de Información Estudiantil): Documento de resultados o información que recibe la universidad como parte del proceso de intercambio electrónico de información. Contiene la información de la FAFSA diligenciada por el estudiante, independientemente de que se halla diligenciado electrónicamente o en papel. Es la versión electrónica del SAR.

ISIR: *Ver Institutional Student Information Record.*

Leyes de confidencialidad: Leyes colectivas que protegen al individuo de la divulgación de información específica sin previo consentimiento escrito.

Lifetime Learning Tax Credit (Crédito impositivo Lifetime Learning): Crédito federal impositivo para sufragar los gastos educativos superiores.

Metodología: Hace referencia al sistema utilizado para calcular el Expected Family Contribution, también conocida como Metodología Federal de Análisis de Necesidad.

Metodología Federal (FM, por sus siglas en inglés): *Ver Metodología Federal de Análisis de Necesidad.*

Metodología Federal de Análisis de Necesidad: Método estandarizado que determina la capacidad de pago de un estudiante para sufragar sus gastos de educación superior; conocido también como Metodología Federal (FM). Fórmula única para determinar el EFC para Pell Grants, programas con sede en el campus, programas FFEL y Federal Direct Lending Programs. La fórmula está definida por la ley.

Montgomery GI Bill (Decreto de ley Montgomery G.I.): Programa para ayudar al personal del ejército a sufragar los gastos de educación superior. También se le conoce como Nuevo Decreto GI.

National and Community Service (Servicio Nacional y Comunitario) (AmeriCorps): Programa creado por medio de la Ley de Fideicomiso para el National and Community Service de 1993, para premiar con beneficios educativos, cancelación de la deuda a quienes ofrecen servicios comunitarios.

National Health Service Corps Scholarship, NHSC (Beca para el Cuerpo de Servicio de Salud Nacional): Programa de becas para estudiantes que adelantan estudios a tiempo completo en ciertas disciplinas de la salud y que, al terminar sus estudios, desean trabajar como profesionales de atención primaria en áreas marginadas.

National Student Loan Data System, NSLDS (Sistema Nacional de Información sobre Préstamos Estudiantiles): Base de datos nacional de información de préstamos del Título IV y subvenciones federales seleccionadas.

Necesidad: *Ver Necesidad financiera.*

Necesidad financiera: Diferencia entre los gastos de asistencia fijados por la institución y la capacidad de pago familiar, es decir, el Expected Family Contribution. La capacidad de pago está representada por el Expected Family Contribution tanto para la ayuda federal basada en la necesidad como para muchos programas estatales e institucionales.

Necesidad no satisfecha: Diferencia entre el gasto total de asistencia en una institución determinada y los recursos totales disponibles para el estudiante.

No-ciudadano elegible: Aquella persona que aunque no es ciudadano estadounidense, califica para la ayuda financiera federal estudiantil en una de las siguientes categorías: 1) Residente permanente de Estados Unidos acreditado con una Tarjeta de Recepción de Registro de Extranjería (Formulario I-151, I-551, generalmente conocido como tarjeta verde (green card)) u otra prueba de admisión para residencia permanente; 2) Residente permanente condicional (I-151C); 3) Persona con permanencia legal en Estados Unidos para otros propósitos no temporales con Registro de Entradas y Salidas (Formulario I-94) del Bureau of Citizenship and Immigration Service, BCIS (Oficina de Ciudadanía y Servicios de Inmigración) sellado como refugiado, asilado, bajo libertad indefinida bajo palabra o bajo libertad humanitaria bajo palabra, o inmigrante cubano-haitiano; 5) Residentes permanentes de la República de Palau o ciudadano de la República de las Islas Marshall y los Estados Federados de Micronesia. Los no-ciudadanos no elegibles para la ayuda financiera federal estudiantil son quienes tienen visa de estudiante, visa de intercambio por visita, visas serie G o quienes sólo tienen una notificación de aprobación para postular a residencia permanente.

Notificación: *Ver Carta de otorgamiento y Notificación de ayuda financiera.*

Notificación de ayuda financiera: Carta de la institución superior que notifica al estudiante si ha sido favorecido o no con una ayuda. En caso afirmativo, la notificación describe, además, el paquete de ayuda financiera a recibir. Los organismos estatales y las organizaciones privadas deben enviar notificaciones de ayuda financiera tanto a los estudiantes como a la institución superior. Ver también *Carta de otorgamiento.*

Nursing Student Loan, NSL (Préstamo para Estudiantes de Enfermería): Préstamos para estudiantes de enfermería que cursan estudios en instituciones de enfermería aprobadas que ofrecen diploma o título asociado, universitario o de posgrado en enfermería.

Otorgamiento de ayuda financiera: Oferta de ayuda financiera o en especie para un estudiante de una institución de estudios superiores en una de las siguientes formas de ayuda financiera: préstamo reembolsable, subvención no reembolsable o beca y empleo estudiantil.

Otorgamiento especial: Pago que el gobierno federal provee a prestamistas para que eleven las tasas de interés al valor comercial, y que actúa como incentivo para que las instituciones prestamistas ofrezcan subvenciones para programas de Federal Family Education Loan.

Otorgamiento excesivo: Situación en la que los recursos combinados del estudiante, como el EFC y ayuda financiera, sobrepasan los gastos de asistencia. Excepto ciertos casos, no se permite el otorgamiento excesivo para estudiantes que reciben fondos de ayuda financiera federal estudiantil.

Pagaré: Documento legal que obliga legalmente a un prestatario al reembolso de las obligaciones y a cumplir con otros términos y condiciones que rigen un programa de préstamos.

Paquete de ayuda financiera: El otorgamiento de ayuda financiera a un estudiante comprende una combinación de formas de ayuda financiera como préstamos, subvenciones o becas y empleo.

Período de gracia: Período que comienza a partir del momento que el beneficiario de un préstamo deja su estatus como estudiante, al menos a medio tiempo, y finaliza cuando se inicia el período de reembolso. En este período, generalmente no se hacen pagos a capital y no se generan intereses acumulados.

Planes de inversión: Programas de ahorro educativo, generalmente patrocinados por instituciones bancarias comerciales.

Planes de pago de matrícula: Estrategia que permite sufragar los gastos actuales de educación superior en el futuro.

Prestamista comercial: Banco comercial, corporación de ahorros y préstamos, unión crediticia, caja de ahorros, compañía fiduciaria o caja de ahorros mutuos que puede actuar como prestamista para un Programa Federal Family Education Loan (FFEL).

Préstamo: Avance de fondos respaldados por un pagaré que el beneficiario se compromete a reembolsar en cantidades específicas, según las condiciones prescritas.

Préstamo de consolidación: Préstamo que permite a un prestatario con diferentes tipos de préstamos, la oportunidad de obtener un único préstamo con una tasa de interés y un plan de amortización. Préstamos como el Federal Perkins Loan, el Stafford (subsidiado o no subsidiado), Direct Loan, Health Education Assistance Loans, HEAL (Préstamos de Asistencia Educativa para la Salud), Health Professions Students Loan y Loans for Disadvantaged Students pueden combinarse para efectos de consolidación, sujetos a ciertos requisitos de elegibilidad. Un préstamo de consolidación cancela los préstamos existentes; el prestatario asume el reembolso del préstamo consolidado.

Presupuesto estudiantil: *Ver Gastos de asistencia.*

Procesador FAFSA: Organización contratada por el Departamento de Educación encargada de suministrar los medios a fin de que un estudiante solicite ayuda federal estudiantil. El procesador FAFSA ingresa electrónicamente al sistema la información FAFSA del estudiante y la transmite al Central Processing System (Sistema Central de Procesamiento).

Programa de ayuda social: Programa que cuenta con fondos suficientes para asegurar que todos los solicitantes elegibles tengan la garantía de recibir el máximo auxilio autorizado. En la medida que el estudiante cumpla con todos los requisitos de elegibilidad y se inscriba en un programa e institución elegibles, recibirá el auxilio que se le ha asignado.

Programa de reembolso de préstamo: Programa especial disponible para estudiantes calificados que han asistido a la universidad, cubiertos por préstamos estudiantiles federales, y que luego se vinculan al Ejército por un período mínimo de tres años en un cargo de su especialidad.

Programa elegible: Programa de educación o capacitación conducente a obtener un título o certificado de una universidad participante en uno o más programas de ayuda federal estudiantil. El estudiante debe inscribirse en un programa elegible de una universidad elegible para recibir la ayuda estudiantil federal.

Programas con sede en el campus: Término generalmente aplicado a los programas de ayuda estudiantil federal del Departamento de Educación de Estados Unidos administrados directamente por instituciones de educación superior. Incluye la Federal Supplemental Educational Opportunity Grant (FSEOG), Federal Work-Study Program (FWS) y programas de Federal Perkins Loan.

Programas para profesionales de la salud: Programas de ayuda federal estudiantil, administrados por el Departamento de Salud y Servicios Humanos de Estados Unidos (HHS). Dirigido a estudiantes que cursan estudios en ciencias de la salud.

Programas Título IV: Programas de ayuda federal para estudiantes autorizados bajo el Título IV de la Ley de Educación Superior de 1965, en su enmienda. Incluye la Federal Pell Grant, Federal Supplemental Educational Opportunity Grant (FSEOG), Federal Work-Study Program (FWS), Federal Perkins Loan, Federal Stafford Loan, Federal PLUS Loan, Federal Direct Loan, Federal Direct PLUS Loan y LEAP.

Prueba simplificada de necesidades: Método alterno para calcular el Expected Family Contribution (EFC) en familias con ingresos brutos ajustados de menos de $50,000, que han presentado, o pueden presentar, un formulario IRS 1040A ó 1040EZ, o que no necesitan presentar declaración de impuesto sobre la renta. No se considera ningún activo.

Reautorización: Proceso de revisión por parte del congreso para refinar los programas federales autorizados y asegurarse de que continúen satisfaciendo las necesidades de la población a la que se dirigen.

Recursos: Incluyen, pero sin limitarse a ello, todo (a) fondo que el estudiante tenga derecho a recibir por conducto de una Federal Pell Grant (b) exoneración de matrícula y cuotas; (c) subvenciones, como las partidas de manutención para FSEOG y ROTC; (d) becas, incluso becas deportivas y ROTC; (e) becas o auxilios no universitarios según necesidad; (f) programas de seguros para educación; (g) préstamos a largo plazo otorgados por la institución, entre ellos, Direct Loans y Federal Perkins Loans; (h) ingresos percibidos por empleo con base en la necesidad; (i) beneficios de veteranos; y (j) cualquier parte de otros préstamos a largo plazo, como Stafford Loans (GSL), FPLUS, Direct Loans PLUS, préstamos respaldados por el estado o préstamos privados. No substituye el EFC.

Rehabilitación vocacional: Programas administrados por los departamentos estatales de servicios de rehabilitación vocacional, dirigido a individuos con discapacidad mental o física que representa un impedimento substancial para trabajar.

Renovación FAFSA: Tipo de solicitud FAFSA similar al SAR con las mismas preguntas de la solicitud FAFSA. La renovación FAFSA lleva impresas las respuestas que el estudiante consignó el año anterior para la información que probablemente no cambie de un año a otro.

Requisitos de residencia: Criterios que los estudiantes deben cumplir para tener estatus de residente en un estado o distrito; se utiliza en ciertos casos para determinar el monto de la matrícula.

Reserve Officer Training Corps Scholarship Program: *Ver ROTC Scholarship Program.*

Residente legal: Persona que ha cumplido los requisitos estatales o del distrito local para recibir el estatus de residente; también puede referirse al estudiante no-ciudadano de Estados Unidos pero elegible para recibir ayuda financiera federal. Ver *No-ciudadano elegible* y *Requisitos de residencia.*

ROTC Scholarship Program (Programa de Becas ROTC): Beca competitiva que asume el costo de matrícula, cuotas, libros y un estipendio mensual de manutención, así como otros beneficios a cambio de su participación en entrenamientos y clases durante el año académico, o en campamentos militares de verano y, al término de sus estudios, servicio de tiempo completo en el Ejército, por lo menos durante cuatro años.

Sanción por pago anticipado: Cargo que el prestamista fija a los prestatarios responsables del reembolso, por el pago en menor tiempo del máximo estipulado en el pagaré. Los programas de préstamo federal no contemplan sanciones por pago anticipado.

SAR: *Ver Student Aid Report.*

Scholarships for Disadvantaged Students, SDS (Becas para Estudiantes Desfavorecidos): Programa federal de becas dirigido a estudiantes desfavorecidos inscritos en ciertas disciplinas para profesionales de la salud.

Servicios de búsqueda de beca: Organizaciones que ayudan a los estudiantes en la búsqueda de fondos de ayuda financiera poco conocidos y sin aprovechar. Las familias interesadas deben primero investigar cuidadosamente la empresa que ofrece dichos servicios.

Specialized Training for Army Reserve Readiness, STARR (Entrenamiento Especializado de Preparación de Reservas del Ejército): Programa educativo patrocinado por la Reserva del Ejército por medio del cual las Reservas sufragan todos los gastos educativos de los reservistas que reciben instrucción en especialidades médicas específicas en universidades locales.

Student Aid Report, SAR (Informe de Ayuda para el Estudiante): Notificación oficial enviada al estudiante una vez que el Central Processing System, CPS recibe un registro del solicitud vía FAFSA para el estudiante. El SAR contiene la información resumida del solicitante, muestra el Expected Family Contribution (EFC) para el estudiante y brinda información adicional referente a la solicitud del estudiante. En ciertos casos, puede ser necesario presentar el SAR en la oficina de ayuda financiera de la universidad donde el estudiante pretende realizar estudios, bajo solicitud expresa de la universidad. Ver *Institutional Student Information Record (ISIR).*

Subsidio: Dinero que utiliza el gobierno federal para que un estudiante se inscriba en uno de los programas de ayuda para estudiantes. Básicamente, hace referencia a los pagos gubernamentales a prestamistas a propósito del interés intra-escolar sobre Federal Stafford Loans.

Subvención: Ayuda financiera que no requiere reembolso; generalmente otorgada con base en la necesidad y probablemente combinada con algunas capacidades o características que posee el estudiante. Ver también *Ayuda por donación.*

Tasa de interés variable: Tasa de interés de un préstamo ajustada a intervalos regulares sobre una base mensual, trimestral o anual. Los Federal Stafford Loans (subsidiados y no subsidiados), Federal PLUS Loans, Direct Loans (subsidiados y no subsidiados) y Direct PLUS Loans tienen tasas variables fijadas anualmente.

Título asociado: Título obtenido al completar exitosamente algunos cursos de estudios en una universidad que ofrece estudios de dos años.

Título universitario: Título otorgado al completar exitosamente el plan de estudios universitarios en una universidad o institución de educación superior de cuatro años. También se denomina grado universitario.

Transferibilidad: Atributo de ciertos programas que permite al estudiante elegible recibir fondos de cualquier institución elegible sin limitarse a una en particular. Válido para Federal Pell Grants y otras becas estatales disponibles en instituciones superiores, entre ellas, las ubicadas fuera del estado y que otorgan los fondos.

Verificación: Proceso de verificación de la información registrada en la solicitud FAFSA por comparación de documentos específicos con los datos contenidos en un documento procesado electrónicamente: Student Aid Report (SAR) o ISIR. Las universidades deben verificar la información de los estudiantes seleccionados a través del Central Processing System, CPS de acuerdo con los procedimientos establecidos por la ley. Igualmente, las universidades deben seleccionar los solicitantes adicionales que deben someterse al proceso de verificación.

Veterano (para determinar dependencia): Aquel que ha prestado servicio activo en el Ejército, la Armada, la Fuerza Aérea, la Infantería de Marina, la Guardia Costera, o que ha sido cadete o guardia marina de una de las academias militares (excepto la Guardia Costera), y que no ha sido dado de baja por deshonra. Se considera que los veteranos son independientes. No se precisa un tiempo mínimo de servicio militar.

William D. Ford Federal Direct Loan (Programa Federal de Préstamo Directo William D. Ford): Nombre colectivo para designar los programas de Direct Loan (subsidiado y no subsidiado), Direct PLUS y Direct Consolidation Loan. Los fondos de préstamos para estos fondos provienen del gobierno federal y están disponibles para estudiantes y padres, a través de instituciones superiores que forman parte del programa. Excepto, en caso de ciertas opciones de reembolso, los términos y condiciones de los préstamos bajo programas de préstamos directo son idénticos a los que aplican para el programa FFEL.

BECAS PARA HISPANOS Y OTRAS MINORÍAS

AGA FOUNDATION FOR DIGESTIVE HEALTH AND NUTRITION (FUNDACIÓN AGA PARA LA SALUD DIGESTIVA Y NUTRICIÓN)

www.fdhn.org

American Gastroenterological Association Student Research Fellowship Underrepresented Minorities Award (Beca para Minorías con Menos Representación de Investigación Estudiantil de la Asociación Gastroenterológica Estadounidense)

Apoyo financiero para estudiantes de minorías con poca representación para pasar el tiempo realizando investigaciones en las áreas de enfermedades digestivas o nutrición.

Áreas académicas o profesionales Ciencia alimentaria o nutrición; ciencias de la salud o médicas.

Ortorgamiento Beca de investigación para usarse en el primer, segundo, penúltimo, último año de universidad o como graduado; no renovable. *Número:* hasta 7. *Monto:* $2,000 a $3,000.

Requisitos de elegibilidad El postulante debe ser hispano, nativo americano/de Alaska o negro (no hispano) y debe estar inscrito o espera inscribirse en una institución o universidad que ofrece carreras de dos o cuatro años. Disponible para ciudadanos estadounidenses y canadienses.

Plazo de solicitud 5 de marzo.

Contacta: Desta Wallace, Research Awards Manager
AGA Foundation for Digestive Health and Nutrition
4930 Del Ray Avenue
Bethesda, MD 20814
Teléfono: 301-222-4005
Fax: 301-222-4010
E-mail: desta@gastro.org

AMERICAN ARCHITECTURAL FOUNDATION (FUNDACIÓN ESTADOUNIDENSE DE ARQUITECTURA)

www.archfoundation.org

American Institute of Architects Minority/Disadvantaged Scholarship (Beca para Estudiantes de Minorías o de Escasos Recursos del Instituto Estadounidense de Arquitectos)

Beca para estudiantes nominados por una empresa de arquitectos, maestro, decano u organización cívica. Co-subvencionada por el American Institute of Architects, AIA y la American Architectural Foundation, AAF.

Área académica o profesional Arquitectura.

Ortorgamiento Beca para usarse en el primer año de universidad; renovable. *Número:* 20. *Monto:* $500 a $2,500.

Requisitos de elegibilidad El postulante debe ser hispano, nativo americano/de Alaska, asiático o de las islas del Pacífico o negro (no hispano) y debe estar inscrito o espera inscribirse a tiempo completo en una institución o universidad que ofrece carreras de cuatro años. Los postulantes deben ser estudiantes de duodécimo año y de primer año de universidad. Disponible para ciudadanos estadounidenses.

Plazo de solicitud 15 de enero.

Contacta: Mary Felber, Director of Scholarship Programs
American Architectural Foundation
1735 New York Avenue, NW
Washington, DC 20006-5292
Teléfono: 202-626-7511
Fax: 202-626-7509
E-mail: mfelber@archfoundation.org

AMERICAN CHEMICAL SOCIETY (SOCIEDAD ESTADOUNIDENSE DE QUÍMICA)

www.chemistry.org

American Chemical Society Scholars Program (Programa de Becas de la Sociedad Estadounidense de Química)

Áreas académicas o profesionales Bioquímica, ingeniería química, química, tecnología química o cualquier ciencia química o ingeniería química; ciencia de los materiales, ingeniería y metalurgia; ciencias naturales.

Ortorgamiento Beca para usarse en el primer, segundo o penúltimo año de universidad; renovable. *Número:* 100 a 200. *Monto:* $2,500 a $3,000.

Requisitos de elegibilidad El postulante debe ser hispano, nativo americano/de Alaska o negro (no hispano) y debe estar inscrito o espera inscribirse a tiempo completo en una universidad que ofrece carreras de dos o cuatro años o en una institución técnica. El postulante debe tener un GPA de 3.0 ó superior. Disponible para ciudadanos estadounidenses o residente permanente.

Plazo de solicitud 15 de febrero.

Contacta:
Robert Hughes, Manager
American Chemical Society
1155 L Street, NW
Washington, DC 20036
Teléfono: 202-872-6048
Fax: 202-776-8003
E-mail: scholars@acs.org

AMERICAN INSTITUTE FOR FOREIGN STUDY (INSTITUTO AMERICANO PARA ESTUDIOS EXTRANJEROS)

www.aifsabroad.com

American Institute for Foreign Study Minority Scholarships, AIFS (Becas para Minorías del Instituto Americano para Estudios Extranjeros)

Beca para estudiantes que postulan a un programa de estudio en el extranjero de la AIFS. Los postulantes deben demostrar necesidad financiera, capacidad de liderazgo y logro académico y cumplir con los requisitos del programa.

Ortorgamiento Una beca completa y becas para los tres mejores siguientes cada semestre. Ésta es para usarse en el segundo, penúltimo o último año de universidad; no renovable. *Número:* 8. *Monto:* $2,000 a $11,500.

Requisitos de elegibilidad El postulante debe ser hispano, nativo americano/de Alaska, asiático o de las islas del Pacífico o negro (no hispano); debe tener 17 años; debe estar inscrito o espera inscribirse a tiempo completo en una institución o universidad que ofrece carreras de cuatro años y debe tener interés en liderazgo. El postulante debe tener un GPA de 3.0 ó superior. Disponible para ciudadanos estadounidenses y para aquellos que no son ciudadanos estadounidenses.

Plazo de solicitud 15 de abril (otoño); 15 de octubre (primavera).

Contacta: David Mauro, Admissions Counselor
American Institute for Foreign Study
River Plaza, 9 West Broad Street
Stamford, CT 06902-3788
Teléfono: 800-727-2437 Ext. 5163
Fax: 203-399-5598
E-mail: college.info@aifs.com

AMERICAN INSTITUTE OF CERTIFIED PUBLIC ACCOUNTANTS (INSTITUTO ESTADOUNIDENSE DE CONTADORES PÚBLICOS AUTORIZADOS)

www.aicpa.org

Becas para estudiantes de minorías de contabilidad

Se entregan becas a estudiantes de minorías que tienen especialidades declaradas en contabilidad.

Área académica o profesional Contabilidad.

Ortorgamiento Beca para usarse en el penúltimo, último año de universidad o como graduado; no renovable. *Monto:* hasta $5,000.

Requisitos de elegibilidad El postulante debe ser hispano, nativo americano/de Alaska, asiático o de las islas del Pacífico o negro (no hispano) con un GPA total de 3.3. El estudiante debe estar inscrito o espera inscribirse a tiempo completo como estudiante universitario o ser graduado de una institución o universidad que ofrece carreras de cuatro años. Los postulantes deben haber completado satisfactoriamente al menos 30 horas semestrales (o equivalente), incluidas al menos 6 horas semestrales en contabilidad. Disponible para ciudadanos estadounidenses.

Plazo de solicitud 1° de julio.

Contacta: Scholarship Coordinator
American Institute of Certified Public Accountants
1211 Avenue of the Americas
New York, NY 10036-8775
Teléfono: 212-596-6270
E-mail: educat@aicpa.org

AMERICAN INSTITUTE OF CHEMICAL ENGINEERS (INSTITUTO ESTADOUNIDENSE DE INGENIEROS QUÍMICOS)

www.aiche.org

Beca para minorías para estudiantes universitarios

Beca que se entrega por una vez para estudiantes universitarios que se encuentran estudiando ingeniería química. Debe nominarse y ser miembro estudiantil nacional del American Institute of Chemical Engineers, AICHE al momento de la postulación.

Área académica o profesional Ingeniería química.

Ortorgamiento Beca para usarse en el primer, segundo, penúltimo o último año de universidad; no renovable. *Número:* hasta 10. *Monto:* $1,000.

Requisitos de elegibilidad El postulante debe ser hispano, nativo americano/de Alaska, asiático o de las islas del Pacífico o negro (no hispano) y debe estar inscrito o espera inscribirse en una institución o universidad que ofrece carreras de cuatro años.

Plazo de solicitud 15 de abril.

Contacta: Awards Administrator
American Institute of Chemical Engineers
Three Park Avenue
New York, NY 10016-5991
Teléfono: 212-591-7478
Fax: 212-591-8882
E-mail: awards@aiche.org

MINORITY SCHOLARSHIP AWARDS FOR INCOMING COLLEGE FRESHMEN (BECAS PARA MINORÍAS PARA ESTUDIANTES QUE INGRESAN A PRIMER AÑO DE UNIVERSIDAD)

Las becas son para graduados de la escuela secundaria que planean estudiar cursos para obtener un título en ingeniería química. Los postulante deben nominarse.

Área académica o profesional Ingeniería química.

Ortorgamiento Beca para usarse en el primer año de universidad; no renovable. *Número:* hasta 10. *Monto:* $1,000.

Requisitos de elegibilidad El postulante debe ser hispano, nativo americano/de Alaska, asiático o de las islas del Pacífico o negro (no hispano); debe ser estudiante de escuela secundaria y que planee inscribirse en una institución o universidad.

Plazo de solicitud 15 de abril.

Contacta: Awards Administrator
American Institute of Chemical Engineers
Three Park Avenue
New York, NY 10016-5991
Teléfono: 212-591-7478
Fax: 212-591-8882
E-mail: awards@aiche.org

AMERICAN METEOROLOGICAL SOCIETY (SOCIEDAD METEOROLÓGICA ESTADOUNIDENSE)

www.ametsoc.org/AMS

American Meteorological Society/Industry Minority Scholarships (Becas para Minorías de la Sociedad Meteorológica Estadounidense)

Becas de dos años para estudiantes de minorías que ingresan a su primer año de universidad. Deben planear seguir carreras en ciencias atmosféricas y oceánicas e hidrológicas relacionadas.

Áreas académicas o profesionales Meteorología o ciencia atmosférica.

Ortorgamiento Beca para usarse en el primer o segundo año de universidad; no renovable. *Número:* variable. *Monto:* $3,000.

Requisitos de elegibilidad El postulante debe ser hispano, nativo americano/de Alaska, asiático o de las islas del Pacífico o negro (no hispano); debe ser estudiante de escuela secundaria y que planee inscribirse a tiempo completo en una institución o universidad que ofrece carreras de cuatro años. Disponible para ciudadanos estadounidenses o residentes permanentes.

Plazo de solicitud 20 de febrero.

Contacta: Donna Fernandez, Fellowship/Scholarship Coordinator
American Meteorological Society
45 Beacon Street
Boston, MA 02108-3693
Teléfono: 617-227-2426 Ext. 246
Fax: 617-742-8718
E-mail: dfernand@ametsoc.org

AMERICAN PHYSICAL SOCIETY (SOCIEDAD ESTADOUNIDENSE DE FÍSICA)

www.aps.org/educ/com/index.html

Corporate Sponsored Scholarships for Minority Undergraduate Students Who Major in Physics (Becas Subvencionadas por Empresas para Estudiantes Universitarios de Minorías con Especialidades en Física)

Beca que se entrega por una vez para estudiantes de duodécimo año, de primer y de segundo año de universidad que planeen ingresar a una especialidad en física.

Áreas académicas o profesionales Ciencias físicas y matemáticas.

Ortorgamiento Beca para usarse en el primer o segundo año de universidad; no renovable. *Monto:* $2,000 a $3,000.

Requisitos de elegibilidad El postulante debe ser hispano, nativo americano/de Alaska o negro (no hispano) y debe estar inscrito o espera inscribirse a tiempo completo en una institución o universidad que ofrece carreras de dos o cuatro años. Debe ser ciudadano estadounidense o residente legal.

Plazo de solicitud 1° de febrero.

Contacta: Arlene Knowles, Scholarship Administrator
American Physical Society
One Physics Ellipse
College Park, MD 20740
Teléfono: 301-209-3232
Fax: 301-209-0865
E-mail: knowles@aps.org

AMERICAN PHYSICAL SOCIETY (SOCIEDAD ESTADOUNIDENSE DE FISIOLOGÍA)

www.the-aps.org

American Physiological Society Minority Travel Fellowships (Becas de Investigación para Viaje para Minorías de la Sociedad Estadounidense de Fisiología)

Beca de viaje para estudiantes de fisiología de parte de grupos de minorías para asistir a la reunión de Biología experimental o a la conferencia de la American Physiological Society. Disponible para estudiantes universitarios avanzados y graduados.

Áreas académicas o profesionales Ciencias animales o veterinaria; biología; ciencias de la salud y médicas; ciencias físicas y matemática.

Ortorgamiento Beca para usarse en el primer, segundo, penúltimo, último año de universidad, como graduado o en posgrado; no renovable. *Número:* 30 a 40. *Monto:* $1,000 a $1,500.

Requisitos de elegibilidad El postulante debe ser hispano, nativo americano/de Alaska o negro (no hispano) y debe estar inscrito o espera inscribirse a tiempo completo en una institución o universidad que ofrece carreras de dos o cuatro años. El postulante o uno de los padres del postulante debe ser miembro de la American Physiological Society. Disponible para ciudadanos estadounidenses.

Plazo de solicitud Comuníquese con la American Physiological Society (APS) o revise su sitio Web para ver los plazos.

Contacta: Mrs. Brooke Bruthers, Award Coordinator
American Physiological Society
9650 Rockville Pike
Bethesda, MD 20814-3991
Teléfono: 301-634-7132
Fax: 301-634-7098
E-mail: bbruthers@the-aps.org

AMERICAN POLITICAL SCIENCE ASSOCIATION (ASOCIACIÓN ESTADOUNIDENSE DE CIENCIAS POLÍTICAS)

www.apsanet.org

American Political Science Association Minority Fellows Program (Programa de Becas de Investigación para Minorías de la Asociación Estadounidense de Ciencias Políticas)

Beca que se entrega por una vez para estudiantes de minorías que ingresan por primera vez a un programa de doctorado en ciencias políticas. Los postulantes deben demostrar interés en enseñanza y tienen que tener potencial de investigación en ciencias políticas.

Área académica o profesional Ciencias políticas.

Ortorgamiento Beca de investigación para usarse en el último año de universidad o como graduado; no renovable. *Número:* 6. *Monto:* $4,000.

Requisitos de elegibilidad El postulante debe ser hispano, nativo americano/de Alaska o negro (no hispano) y debe estar inscrito o espera inscribirse en una institución o universidad. El postulante debe tener un GPA de 3.0 ó superior. Los postulantes deben ser ciudadanos estadounidenses y tener necesidad financiera.

Plazo de solicitud 1° de noviembre.

Contacta: Linda Lopez, Director
American Political Science Association
1527 New Hampshire Avenue, NW
Washington, DC 20036-1206
E-mail: apsa@apsanet.org

AMERICAN SOCIETY OF RADIOLOGIC TECHNOLOGISTS EDUCATION AND RESEARCH FOUNDATION (FUNDACIÓN PARA LA EDUCACIÓN E INVESTIGACIÓN DE LA SOCIEDAD ESTADOUNIDENSE DE TÉCNICOS EN RADIOLOGÍA)

www.asrt.org

Royce Osborn Minority Student Scholarship (Beca para Estudiantes de Minorías Royce Osborn)

Beca para minorías para estudiantes de certificación o universitarios. Para postular, deben haber completado al menos un semestre en ciencias radiológicas.

Áreas académicas o profesionales Ciencias de la salud y médicas.

Ortorgamiento Beca para usarse en el primer, segundo o penúltimo año de universidad; no renovable. *Número:* 5. *Monto:* $4,000.

Requisitos de elegibilidad El postulante debe ser hispano, nativo americano/de Alaska, asiático o de las islas del Pacífico, o negro (no hispano) y debe estar inscrito o espera inscribirse a tiempo completo o a tiempo parcial en una universidad que ofrece carreras de dos o cuatro años o en una institución técnica. Tiene que existir el factor de la necesidad financiera. Los requisitos incluyen tener un GPA de 3.0 ó superior, una recomendación y un ensayo de 250 a 300 palabras. Disponible para ciudadanos estadounidenses.

Plazo de solicitud 1° de febrero.

Contacta: Phelosha Collaros, Development Specialist
American Society of Radiologic Technologists
Education and Research Foundation
15000 Central Avenue, SE
Albuquerque, NM 87123-3917
Teléfono: 505-298-4500 Ext. 1233
Fax: 505-298-5063
E-mail: pcollaros@asrt.org

ARKANSAS DEPARTMENT OF HIGHER EDUCATION (DEPARTAMENTO DE EDUCACIÓN SUPERIOR DEL ESTADO DE ARKANSAS)

www.arscholarships.com

Arkansas Minority Teacher Scholars Program (Programa de Becas para Maestros de Minorías del Estado de Arkansas)

Beca para postulantes de minorías que hayan completado al menos 60 horas semestrales y que estén inscritos a tiempo completo en un programa de educación para maestros en el estado de Arkansas.

Área académica o profesional Educación.

Ortorgamiento Préstamo que puede ser condonado para ser usado en el penúltimo o último año de universidad; renovable. *Número:* hasta 100. *Monto:* hasta $5,000. La beca puede renovarse por un año.

Requisitos de elegibilidad El postulante debe residir y estudiar en el estado de Arkansas y tener un GPA mínimo de 2.5. Debe enseñar durante tres a cinco años en el estado de Arkansas para reembolsar los fondos que recibió de la beca y aprobar el examen PPST. El postulante debe ser hispano, nativo americano/de Alaska, asiático o de las islas del Pacífico o negro (no hispano) y debe estar inscrito o espera inscribirse a tiempo completo en una institución o universidad que ofrece carreras de cuatro años. Disponible para ciudadanos estadounidenses.

Plazo de solicitud 1° de junio.

Contacta: Lillian Williams, Assistant Coordinator
Arkansas Department of Higher Education
114 East Capitol
Little Rock, AR 72201
Teléfono: 501-371-2050
Fax: 501-371-2001

ASPEN INSTITUTE (INSTITUTO ASPEN)

www.nonprofitresearch.org/

William Randolph Hearst Endowed Scholarship for Minority Students (Beca Donada por William Randolph Hearst para Estudiantes de Minorías)

Becas para estudiantes de minorías que demuestren aptitudes de investigación destacadas, una base en ciencias sociales o humanidades y excelentes aptitudes de redacción y comunicación.

Áreas académicas o profesionales Humanidades; ciencias sociales.

Ortorgamiento Beca para usarse en el primer, segundo, penúltimo, último año de universidad o como graduado; no renovable. *Monto:* $2,500 a $5,000.

Requisitos de elegibilidad El postulante debe ser hispano, nativo americano/de Alaska, asiático o de las islas del Pacífico o negro (no hispano) y debe estar inscrito o espera inscribirse en una institución o universidad. Disponible para ciudadanos estadounidenses.

Plazo de solicitud 14 de marzo. (No hay solicitud. Envíe una carta de interés, currículum vitae, certificado de calificaciones, una carta del funcionario de ayuda financiera adecuado de la universidad que certifique una necesidad financiera demostrada y dos cartas de referencia.)

Contacta: Aspen Institute
One Dupont Circle, NW, Suite 700
Washington, DC 20036

BROWN FOUNDATION FOR EDUCATIONAL EQUITY, EXCELLENCE, AND RESEARCH (FUNDACIÓN BROWN PARA LA EQUIDAD, EXCELENCIA E INVESTIGACIÓN EDUCACIONAL)

http://brownvboard.org/foundatn/sclrbroc.htm

Brown Scholar (Beca Brown)

Beca para estudiantes universitarios que ingresar a su penúltimo año de universidad que son admitidos en un programa de educación para maestros en una universidad que ofrece carreras de cuatro años.

Área académica o profesional Educación.

Ortorgamiento Beca para usarse en el penúltimo o último año de universidad; renovable.

Requisitos de elegibilidad El postulante debe ser hispano, nativo americano/de Alaska, asiático o de las islas del Pacífico o negro (no hispano) y debe estar inscrito o espera inscribirse a tiempo completo o a tiempo parcial en una institución o universidad que ofrece carreras de cuatro años. El postulante debe tener un GPA de 3.0 ó superior. Disponible para ciudadanos estadounidenses.

Plazo de solicitud 1° de abril.

Contacta: Chelsey Smith, Staff/Administrative Assistant
Brown Foundation for Educational Equity, Excellence, and Research
PO Box 4862
Topeka, KS 66604
Teléfono: 785-235-3939
Fax: 785-235-1001
E-mail: brownfound@juno.com

CALIFORNIA ADOLESCENT NUTRITION AND FITNESS (CANFIT) PROGRAM (PROGRAMA DE NUTRICIÓN Y CONDICIÓN FÍSICA ADOLESCENTE DEL ESTADO DE CALIFORNIA (CANFIT))

www.canfit.org

California Adolescent Nutrition and Fitness (CANFit) Program Scholarship (Beca del Programa de Nutrición y Condición Física Adolescente del Estado de California)

Beca para estudiantes de minorías universitarios y de posgrado.

Áreas académicas o profesionales Ciencia alimentaria o nutrición; servicio de alimento u hospitalidad; ciencias de la salud y médicas; relacionadas con el deporte.

Ortorgamiento Beca para usarse en el penúltimo, último año de universidad, como graduado o en posgrado; no renovable. *Número:* 10 a 15. *Monto:* $500 a $1,500.

Requisitos de elegibilidad El postulante debe ser hispano, nativo americano/de Alaska, asiático o de las islas del Pacífico o negro (no hispano); debe estar inscrito o espera inscribirse a tiempo completo o a tiempo parcial en una institución o universidad que ofrece carreras de cuatro años y ser residente y estudiar en el estado de California. El postulante debe tener un GPA de 2.5 ó superior. Disponible para ciudadanos estadounidenses.

Plazo de solicitud 31 de marzo.

Contacta: Leena Kamat, Office Manager
California Adolescent Nutrition and Fitness (CANFit) Program
2140 Shattuck Avenue, Suite 610
Berkeley, CA 94704
Teléfono: 510-644-1533
Fax: 510-644-1535
E-mail: info@canfit.org

CALIFORNIA TEACHERS ASSOCIATION, CTA (ASOCIACIÓN DE MAESTROS DE CALIFORNIA)

www.cta.org

Martin Luther King, Jr. Memorial Scholarship (Beca en Memoria de Martin Luther King, Jr.)

Para miembros de minorías étnicas de la California Teachers Association, sus hijos dependientes y miembros de minorías étnicas de la Student California Teachers Association (Asociación Estudiantil de Maestros de California) que desean seguir un título o credenciales en educación pública.

Área académica o profesional Educación.

Ortorgamiento Beca para usarse en el primer, segundo, penúltimo, último año de universidad o como graduado; no renovable. *Monto:* $500 a $5,000.

Requisitos de elegibilidad El postulante debe ser hispano, nativo americano/de Alaska, asiático o de las islas del Pacífico o negro (no hispano) y debe estar inscrito o espera inscribirse a tiempo completo en una institución o universidad que ofrece carreras de dos o cuatro años. El postulante o uno de los padres del postulante debe ser miembro de la California Teachers Association. Disponible para ciudadanos estadounidenses y para aquellos que no son ciudadanos estadounidenses.

Plazo de solicitud 15 de marzo.

Contacta: Human Rights Department
California Teachers Association (CTA)
PO Box 921
Burlingame, CA 94011-0921
Teléfono: 650-697-1400
E-mail: scholarships@cta.org

CASUALTY ACTUARIAL SOCIETY/SOCIETY OF ACTUARIES JOINT COMMITTEE ON MINORITY RECRUITING (SOCIEDAD ACTUARIAL DE SEGUROS CONTRA ACCIDENTES O COMITÉ CONJUNTO DE LA SOCIEDAD DE ACTUARIOS PARA RECLUTAR A MINORÍAS)

www.BeAnActuary.org

Actuarial Scholarships for Minority Students (Becas actuariales para estudiantes de minorías)

Beca para estudiantes que planean carreras en ciencia actuarial o matemática. Los postulantes deben haber presentado el ACT Assessment (Evaluación ACT) o el SAT.

Área académica o profesional Servicios de negocios o al consumidor.

Ortorgamiento Beca para usarse en el primer, segundo, penúltimo, último año de universidad o como graduado; no renovable. El número y monto de becas varía según el mérito y la necesidad financiera. *Número:* 20 a 40. *Monto:* $500 a $3,000.

Requisitos de elegibilidad El postulante debe ser hispano, nativo americano/de Alaska o negro (no hispano) y debe estar inscrito o espera inscribirse a tiempo completo o tiempo parcial en una institución o universidad que ofrece carreras de dos o cuatro años. Debe ser ciudadano estadounidense o residente permanente.

Plazo de solicitud 1° de mayo.

Contacta: Frank Lupo, Minority Scholarship Coordinator
Casualty Actuarial Society/Society of Actuaries Joint Committee on Minority Recruiting
475 North Martingale Road, Suite 800
Schaumburg, IL 60173-2226
Teléfono: 703-276-3100
E-mail: flupo@casact.org

COMTO-BOSTON CHAPTER (CONFERENCIA DE FUNCIONARIOS DE TRANSPORTE DE MINORÍAS DE LA DELEGACIÓN DE BOSTON)

www.comto.org/local_boston.htm

COMTO Boston/Garrett A. Morgan Scholarship (Beca Boston/Garrett A. Morgan de COMTO)

Cinco becas subvencionadas por empresas específicamente para estudiantes de ingeniería y cinco becas de delegación local para estudiantes de duodécimo año que se gradúan y que siguen carreras tanto en transporte como campos no relacionados con él.

Áreas académicas o profesionales Arquitectura; dibujo; educación; ingeniería civil; ingeniería eléctrica o electrónica; ingeniería mecánica; ingeniería o tecnología; tecnologías relacionadas con la ingeniería; tecnología en topografía, cartografía o ciencia de información geográfica; topografía; transporte.

Ortorgamiento Beca para usarse en el primer o segundo año de universidad; no renovable. *Número:* hasta 10. *Monto:* $1,000 a $5,000.

Requisitos de elegibilidad El postulante debe ser hispano, nativo americano/de Alaska, asiático o de las islas del Pacífico o negro (no hispano) y debe estar inscrito o espera inscribirse a tiempo completo en una universidad que ofrece carreras de cuatro años o en una institución técnica. El postulante debe tener un GPA de 2.5 ó superior. Disponible para ciudadanos estadounidenses.

Plazo de solicitud 31 de marzo.

Contacta: Virginia Turner, Scholarship Chairperson
COMTO-Boston Chapter
Scholarship Program
PO Box 1173
Boston, MA 02117-1173
Teléfono: 617-248-2878
Fax: 617-248-2904
E-mail: virginia.turner@state.ma.us

DOW JONES NEWSPAPER FUND (FONDO DEL DOW JONES NEWSPAPER)

http://djnewspaperfund.dowjones.com

Dow Jones Newspaper Fund Minority Business Reporting Program (Programa de Informe de Negocios para Minorías de Dow Jones Newspaper Fund)

Pasantía y beca de periodismo de negocios que se entrega una vez para estudiantes de segundo y de penúltimo año de universidad de minorías que vuelven a sus estudios universitarios.

Ortorgamiento Beca para usarse en el segundo o penúltimo año de universidad; no renovable. *Número:* 12. *Monto:* $1,000.

Requisitos de elegibilidad El postulante debe ser hispano, nativo americano/de Alaska, asiático o de las islas del Pacífico o negro (no hispano) y debe estar inscrito o espera inscribirse a tiempo completo en una institución que ofrece carreras de dos o cuatro años. Disponible para ciudadanos estadounidenses.

Plazo de solicitud 1° de noviembre.

Contacta: Jan Maressa, Office Manager
Dow Jones Newspaper Fund
PO Box 300
Princeton, NJ 08543-0300
Teléfono: 609-452-2820
Fax: 609-520-5804

EATON CORPORATION (CORPORACIÓN EATON)

www.eaton.com

Eaton Corporation Multicultural Scholars Program (Programa de Becas Multiculturales de la Corporación Eaton)

Beca para minorías que son estudiantes universitarios a tiempo completo de primer o segundo año en una universidad que ofrece carreras de cuatro años.

Áreas académicas o profesionales Ciencias de la computación o procesamiento de datos; ingeniería eléctrica o electrónica; ingeniería mecánica; ingeniería o tecnología; tecnologías relacionadas con la ingeniería.

Ortorgamiento Beca para usarse en el primer o segundo año de universidad; renovable. *Número:* hasta 50. *Monto:* $500 a $3,000.

Requisitos de elegibilidad El postulante debe ser hispano, nativo americano/de Alaska, asiático o de las islas del Pacífico o negro (no hispano) y debe estar inscrito o espera inscribirse en una institución o universidad. El postulante debe tener un GPA de 3.0 ó superior.

Plazo de solicitud 31 de diciembre.

Contacta: Mildred Neumann, Scholarship Coordinator
Eaton Corporation
Eaton Center
1111 Superior Avenue
Cleveland, OH 44114
Teléfono: 216-523-4354
Fax: 216-479-7354
E-mail: mildredneumann@eaton.com

FISHER BROADCASTING COMPANY

www.fisherbroadcasting.com/

Fisher Broadcasting, Inc., Scholarship for Minorities (Fisher Broadcasting, Inc., Beca para minorías)

Beca para estudiantes de minorías que están inscritos en un plan de estudios de transmisión, periodismo o mercadeo. Para residentes del estado de Washington, Oregon, Montana, Idaho y Georgia que asisten a escuelas dentro del estado o fuera de él o para estudiantes fuera del estado que asisten a instituciones en Washington, Oregon, Montana, Idaho o Georgia.

Áreas académicas o profesionales Comunicaciones, ingeniería o tecnología; periodismo; periodismo fotográfico; transmisión de televisión o radio.

Ortorgamiento Beca para usarse en el segundo, penúltimo o último año de universidad; no renovable. *Número:* 2 a 4. *Monto:* $1,000 a $10,000.

Requisitos de elegibilidad El postulante debe ser hispano, nativo americano/de Alaska, asiático o de las islas del Pacífico, negro (no hispano) y debe estar inscrito o espera inscribirse a tiempo completo en una universidad que ofrece carreras de dos o cuatro años o en una institución técnica. El postulante debe tener un GPA de 2.5 ó superior. Disponible para ciudadanos estadounidenses.

Plazo de solicitud 30 de abril.

Contacta: Laura Boyd, Vice President, Human Resources
Fisher Broadcasting Company
600 University Street
Suite 1525
Seattle, WA 98101-3185
Teléfono: 206-404-7000
Fax: 206-404-6811
E-mail: laurab@fsci.com

FLORIDA DEPARTMENT OF EDUCATION (DEPARTAMENTO DE EDUCACIÓN DEL ESTADO DE FLORIDA)

www.floridastudentfinancialaid.org

Rosewood Family Scholarship Fund (Fondo para beca Rosewood Family)

Beca para estudiantes de minorías elegibles para que asistan a una institución de educación superior pública de Florida a tiempo completo. Se le da preferencia a descendientes directos de familias Rosewood afroamericanas que se vieron afectados por los incidentes de enero de 1923.

Ortorgamiento Beca para usarse en el primer, segundo, penúltimo o último año de universidad; renovable. *Número:* hasta 25. *Monto:* hasta $4,000.

Requisitos de elegibilidad El postulante debe ser hispano, nativo americano/de Alaska, asiático o de las islas del Pacífico, o negro (no hispano) y debe estar inscrito o espera inscribirse a tiempo completo en una universidad que ofrece carreras de dos o cuatro años o en una institución técnica y estudiar en el estado de Florida. Disponible para ciudadanos estadounidenses.

Plazo de solicitud 1° de abril.

Contacta: Scholarship Information
Florida Department of Education
Office of Student Financial Assistance
1940 North Monroe, Suite 70
Tallahassee, FL 32303-4759
Teléfono: 888-827-2004
E-mail: osfa@fldoe.org

FOUNDATION OF THE NATIONAL STUDENT NURSES' ASSOCIATION (FUNDACIÓN DE LA ASOCIACIÓN NACIONAL DE ESTUDIANTES DE ENFERMERÍA)

www.nsna.org

Breakthrough to Nursing Scholarships for Racial/Ethnic Minorities (Adelanto para becas de enfermería para minorías raciales o étnicas)

Disponible para estudiantes de minorías que están inscritos en programas de enfermería o pre-enfermería. Becas basadas en la necesidad económica, escolaridad y actividades relacionadas con la salud.

Área académica o profesional Enfermería.

Ortorgamiento Beca para usarse en el primer, segundo, penúltimo o último año de universidad; no renovable. *Número:* 5. *Monto:* $1,000 a $2,000.

Requisitos de elegibilidad El postulante debe ser hispano, nativo americano/de Alaska, asiático o de las islas del Pacífico o negro (no hispano) y debe estar inscrito o espera inscribirse en una institución o universidad. Disponible para ciudadanos estadounidenses.

Plazo de solicitud 31 de enero. Postulación disponible en el sitio Web o envía un sobre franqueado con dirección con dos estampillas junto con la solicitud de postulación. Arancel de postulación de $10.

Contacta: Solicitud disponible en el sitio Web
E-mail: receptionist@nsna.org

FREEDOM FORUM (FORO POR LA LIBERTAD)

www.freedomforum.org

Chips Quinn Scholars Program (Programa de becas Chips Quinn)

Beca para estudiantes de color que están en penúltimo o último año de universidad o se graduaron recientemente. Deben tener un interés definido en periodismo escrito como carrera. La beca requiere una pasantía pagada. Los postulantes deben ser nominados por sus universidades, por editores de periódicos o mediante solicitación directa con cartas de apoyo de aprobación.

Área académica o profesional Periodismo.

Ortorgamiento Beca para usarse en el penúltimo o último año de universidad; no renovable. *Monto:* $1,000.

Requisitos de elegibilidad El postulante debe ser hispano, nativo americano/de Alaska, asiático o de las islas del Pacífico o negro (no hispano) y debe estar inscrito o espera inscribirse en una institución o universidad que ofrece carreras de cuatro años.

Plazo de solicitud 15 de enero.

Contacta: Karen Catone, Director
Freedom Forum
1101 Wilson Boulevard
Arlington, VA 22209
Teléfono: 703-284-2863
Fax: 703-284-3543
E-mail: chipsquinnscholars@freedomforum.org

GEM CONSORTIUM (CONSORCIO DE GEM)

www.gemfellowship.org

GEM MS Engineering Fellowship (Beca de ingeniería de GEM MS)

Beca para estudiantes universitarios de penúltimo, último año o aquellos que tienen un título universitario en una disciplina de ingeniería acreditada. Incluye pasantía de verano.

Áreas académicas o profesionales Agricultura; arquitectura; biología; ciencias de la computación o procesamiento de datos; ciencia de los materiales; ciencia nuclear; ingeniería civil; ingeniería eléctrica o electrónica; ingeniería mecánica; ingeniería o tecnología; ingeniería química; ingeniería y metalurgia.

Ortorgamiento Beca para usarse en el penúltimo, último año de universidad o como graduado; renovable. *Número:* 200. *Monto:* \$20,000 a \$40,000.

Requisitos de elegibilidad El postulante debe ser hispano, nativo americano/de Alaska o negro (no hispano) y debe estar inscrito o espera inscribirse a tiempo completo en una institución o universidad que ofrece carreras de cuatro años. Disponible para ciudadanos estadounidenses.

Plazo de solicitud 1° de diciembre.

Contacta: Saundra D. Johnson, Executive Director
GEM Consortium
PO Box 537
Notre Dame, IN 46556-0537
Teléfono: 574-631-7771
Fax: 574-287-1486
E-mail: gem.1@nd.edu

GEM Ph.D. Science Fellowship (Beca de Investigación de Ciencias para Doctorado GEM)

Beca para estudiantes universitarios de penúltimo o último año, o graduados o aquellos que tienen un título universitario en una disciplina acreditada de ciencias o ingeniería. Deben asistir a una universidad miembro del programa de beca de investigación para doctorado GEM. Incluye pasantía de verano.

Áreas académicas o profesionales Ciencias naturales (biología; geología; ciencia de la meteorología o atmosférica; ciencias físicas y matemáticas).

Ortorgamiento Beca de investigación para usarse en el penúltimo, último año de universidad o como graduado; renovable. *Número:* 20 a 30. *Monto:* $60,000.

Requisitos de elegibilidad El postulante debe ser hispano, nativo americano/de Alaska o negro (no hispano) y debe estar inscrito o espera inscribirse a tiempo completo en una institución o universidad que ofrece carreras de cuatro años. El postulante debe tener un GPA de 3.0 ó superior. Disponible para ciudadanos estadounidenses.

Plazo de solicitud 1° de diciembre.

Contacta: Saundra D. Johnson, Executive Director
GEM Consortium
PO Box 537
Notre Dame, IN 46556-0537
Teléfono: 574-631-7771
Fax: 574-287-1486
E-mail: gem.1@nd.edu

GENERAL BOARD OF GLOBAL MINISTRIES (JUNTA GENERAL DE MINISTERIOS GLOBALES)

www.gbgm-umc.org

National Leadership Development Grants (Subvención Nacional de Desarrollo de Liderazgo)

Beca para miembros de grupos étnicos y raciales minoritarios de la Iglesia Metodista Unida que aspiran tener estudios universitarios.

Ortorgamiento Subvención para usarse en el primer, segundo, penúltimo o último año de universidad; renovable. *Número:* 75. *Monto:* $500 a $5,000.

Requisitos de elegibilidad El postulante debe ser metodista, hispano, nativo americano/de Alaska, asiático o de las islas del Pacífico, o negro (no hispano),y debe estar inscrito o espera inscribirse a tiempo completo en una universidad que ofrece carreras de dos o cuatro años o en una institución técnica. Debe ser ciudadano estadounidense, residente extranjero o residir en Estados Unidos como refugiado.

Plazo de solicitud 31 de mayo.

Contacta: Scholarship Office
General Board of Global Ministries
475 Riverside Drive
Room 1351
New York, NY 10115
Teléfono: 212-870-3787
Fax: 212-870-3932
E-mail: scholars@gbgm-umc.org

HBCU-CENTRAL.COM

www.hbcu-central.com/

HBCU-Central.com Minority Scholarship Program (Programa de Becas para Minorías de HBCU-Central.com)

Destinada a minorías que elijan asistir a Universidades históricamente para gente de color. Los beneficiarios se seleccionan de acuerdo a sus ensayos, calificaciones y necesidades financieras.

Ortorgamiento Beca para usarse en el primer, segundo, penúltimo o último año de universidad; no renovable. *Número:* 3 a 10. *Monto:* $1,000 a $2,500.

Requisitos de elegibilidad El postulante debe ser hispano, nativo americano/de Alaska, asiático o de las islas del Pacífico o negro (no hispano) y debe estar inscrito o espera inscribirse a tiempo completo en una institución o una universidad que ofrece carreras de cuatro años. Disponible para ciudadanos estadounidenses.

Plazo de solicitud Continuo.

Contacta: William Moss, Scholarship Administrator
HBCU-Central.com
7846 Grandlin Park
Suite AA
Blacklick, OH 43004
Teléfono: 614-284-3007
Fax: 215-893-5398
E-mail: wrmoss@hbcu-central.com

HISPANIC SCHOLARSHIP FUND (FONDO DE BECAS PARA HISPANOS)

www.hsf.net

New Horizons Scholars Program (Programa de Becas New Horizons)

Becas disponibles para estudiantes hispanos y afroamericanos que estén infectados con hepatitis C o quienes dependan de alguien infectado con hepatitis C.

Ortorgamiento Beca para usarse en el primer, segundo, penúltimo o último año de universidad; no renovable.

Requisitos de elegibilidad El postulante debe ser hispano o negro (no hispano) y debe estar inscrito o espera inscribirse como estudiante a tiempo completo en una universidad o institución que ofrece carreras de dos o cuatro años. El postulante debe tener un GPA de 3.0 ó superior. Disponible para ciudadanos estadounidenses.

Plazo de solicitud 21 de marzo.

Contacta: Solicitud disponible en el sitio Web

ILLINOIS STUDENT ASSISTANCE COMMISSION, ISAC (COMISIÓN DE ASISTENCIA PARA ESTUDIANTES DE ILLINOIS)

www.isac-online.org

Minority Teachers of Illinois Scholarship Program (Maestros de Minorías del Programa de Becas de Illinois)

Beca para estudiantes de minorías que planean enseñar en una escuela preescolar, primaria o secundaria.

Áreas académicas o profesionales Educación; educación especial.

Ortorgamiento Préstamo perdonable para usarse en el primer, segundo, penúltimo, último año de universidad, como graduado o en posgrado; renovable. *Número:* 450-550. *Monto:* $4,000 a $5,000.

Requisitos de elegibilidad El postulante debe ser hispano, nativo americano/de Alaska, asiático o de las islas del Pacífico o negro (no hispano); debe estar inscrito o espera inscribirse a tiempo completo en una institución o universidad que ofrece carreras de cuatro años; debe ser residente y estudiar en el estado de Illinois. El postulante debe tener un GPA de 2.5 ó superior. Disponible para ciudadanos estadounidenses y para aquellos que no son ciudadanos estadounidenses.

Plazo de solicitud 1° de mayo.

Contacta: David Barinholtz, Client Information
Illinois Student Assistance Commission (ISAC)
1755 Lake Cook Road
Deerfield, IL 60015-5209
Teléfono: 847-948-8500 Ext. 2385
E-mail: cssupport@isac.org

INSTITUTE FOR INTERNATIONAL PUBLIC POLICY (IIPP) (INSTITUTO PARA LA POLICÍA PÚBLICA INTERNACIONAL)

www.ed.gov/offices/OPE/HEP/legps/iipp.html

Institute for International Public Policy Fellowship Program (Programa de Beca de Investigación del Instituto para la Policía Pública Internacional)

El Programa de Beca de Investigación IIPP le proporciona a los estudiantes de minorías con poca representación la educación y capacitación necesaria para ingresar, avanzar y realizar una profesión en relaciones internacionales.

Áreas académicas o profesionales Estudios regionales interdisciplinarios o étnicos; economía; idioma extranjero; humanidades; estudios internacionales; estudios sobre paz y conflictos; ciencias políticas; ciencias sociales.

Ortorgamiento Beca de investigación para usarse en el segundo año de universidad; no renovable. *Número:* 20 a 30. *Monto:* $35,000 a $50,000.

Requisitos de elegibilidad El postulante debe ser hispano, nativo americano/de Alaska, asiático o de las islas del Pacífico o negro (no hispano) y debe estar inscrito o espera inscribirse a tiempo completo en una institución o universidad que ofrece carreras de cuatro años. Debe tener un GPA de 3.2. Disponible para ciudadanos estadounidenses y para aquellos que no son ciudadanos estadounidenses.

Plazo de solicitud 1° de marzo.

Contacta: Helen Ezenwa, Program Manager
Institute for International Public Policy (IIPP)
2750 Prosperity Avenue
Suite 600
Fairfax, VA 22031
Fax: 703-205-7645
E-mail: helen.ezenwa@uncfsp.org

INSTITUTE OF CHINA STUDIES (INSTITUTO DE ESTUDIOS DE CHINA)

Institute of Chinese Studies Awards (Beca del Instituto de Estudios de China)

Beca renovable para estudiantes de minorías que ya se encuentran en la universidad.

Áreas académicas o profesionales Debe ser en estudios de China, incluyendo mandarín, historia u otros estudios relacionados. Estudios regionales interdisciplinarios o étnicos.

Ortorgamiento Beca para usarse en el primer, segundo, penúltimo o último año de universidad; renovable. Los estudiantes que hayan completado 30 y 15 horas de estudios son elegibles para una beca de $1,000 y de $500, respectivamente.

Número: 10. *Monto:* hasta $1,000.

Requisitos de elegibilidad El postulante debe ser hispano, nativo americano/de Alaska, asiático o de las islas del Pacífico o negro (no hispano) y debe estar inscrito o espera inscribirse a tiempo completo en una institución o universidad que ofrece carreras de cuatro años. El postulante debe tener un GPA de 3.0 ó superior. Disponible para ciudadanos estadounidenses.

Plazo de solicitud Continuo.

Contacta: Dr. Harry Kiang, President
Institute of China Studies
7341 North Kolmar Street
Lincolnwood, IL 60712
Teléfono: 847-677-0982

JACKIE ROBINSON FOUNDATION (BECA DE LA FUNDACIÓN JACKIE ROBINSON)

www.jackierobinson.org

Jackie Robinson Scholarship (Beca Jackie Robinson)

Beca para estudiantes de minorías de duodécimo año que hayan sido aceptados en una universidad acreditada que ofrece carreras de cuatro años.

Ortorgamiento Beca para usarse en el primer año de universidad; renovable. *Número:* 50 a 60. *Monto:* hasta $6,000.

Requisitos de elegibilidad El postulante debe ser hispano, nativo americano/de Alaska, asiático o de las islas del Pacífico o negro (no hispano); debe ser estudiante de escuela secundaria y planea inscribirse a tiempo completo en una universidad que ofrece carreras de cuatro años. Debe acreditar necesidad financiera, potencial de liderazgo y un alto nivel de logros académicos. Disponible para ciudadanos estadounidenses.

Plazo de solicitud 1° de abril.

Contacta: Scholarship Program
Jackie Robinson Foundation
3 West 35th Street, 11th Floor
New York, NY 10001-2204
Teléfono: 212-290-8600
Fax: 212-290-8081

KANSAS BOARD OF REGENTS (JUNTA DE REGENTES DE KANSAS)

www.kansasregents.org

Ethnic Minority Scholarship Program (Programa de Becas de Minorías Étnicas)

Este programa fue diseñado para asistir a los estudiantes de minorías étnica académicamente competitivos con necesidades financieras.

Ortorgamiento Beca para usarse en el primer, segundo, penúltimo o último año de universidad; renovable. *Número:* 200 a 250. *Monto:* $1,850.

Requisitos de elegibilidad El postulante debe ser hispano, nativo americano/de Alaska, asiático o de las islas del Pacífico o negro (no hispano); debe estar inscrito o espera inscribirse a tiempo completo en una institución o universidad que ofrece carreras de cuatro años; debe ser residente y estudiar en el estado de Kansas. El postulante debe tener un GPA de 3.0 ó superior. Disponible para ciudadanos estadounidenses.

Plazo de solicitud 1° de mayo.

Contacta: Diane Lindeman, Director of Student Financial Assistance
Kansas Board of Regents
1000 Southwest Jackson, Suite 520
Topeka, KS 66612-1368
Teléfono: 785-296-3517
Fax: 785-296-0983
E-mail: dlindeman@ksbor.org

MISSOURI DEPARTMENT OF ELEMENTARY AND SECONDARY EDUCATION (DEPARTAMENTO DE EDUCACIÓN PRIMARIA Y SECUNDARIA DEL ESTADO DE MISSOURI)

www.dese.state.mo.us

Missouri Minority Teaching Scholarship (Beca de Enseñanza para Minorías del Estado de Missouri)

Beca para residentes de minorías del estado de Missouri que se encuentren en programas de enseñanza. Los beneficiarios deben comprometerse a enseñar durante cinco años en una escuela primaria o secundaria pública de Missouri. Los graduados deben enseñar matemáticas o ciencias o la beca debe ser reembolsada.

Área académica o profesional Educación.

Ortorgamiento Beca para usarse en el primer, segundo, penúltimo, último año de universidad o como graduado; renovable. *Número:* 100. *Monto:* $3,000.

Requisitos de elegibilidad El postulante debe ser de origen hispano, africano, chino, indio o japonés; nativo americano/de Alaska, asiático o de las islas del Pacífico o negro (no hispano); debe estar inscrito o espera inscribirse a tiempo completo en una institución o universidad que ofrece carreras de dos o cuatro años; debe ser residente y estudiar en el estado de Missouri. El postulante debe tener un GPA de 3.5 ó superior. Disponible para ciudadanos estadounidenses.

Plazo de solicitud 15 de febrero.

Contacta: Laura Harrison, Administrative Assistant II
Missouri Department of Elementary and Secondary Education
PO Box 480
Jefferson City, MO 65102-0480
Teléfono: 573-751-1668
Fax: 573-526-3580
E-mail: lharriso@mail.dese.state.mo.us

NAMEPA NATIONAL SCHOLARSHIP FOUNDATION (FUNDACIÓN DE BECA NACIONAL NAMEPA)

www.namepa.org

National Association of Minority Engineering Program Administrators National Scholarship Fund (Asociación Nacional del Fondo Nacional de Becas para Administradores del Programa de Ingeniería de la Minoridad)

NAMEPA ofrece becas únicas para estudiantes que hayan demostrado potencial e interés en continuar un título universitario en ingeniería.

Áreas académicas o profesionales Aviación o aeroespacial; ciencias de la computación o procesamiento de datos; ciencia de los materiales, ingeniería civil; ingeniería eléctrica o electrónica; ingeniería mecánica; ingeniería o tecnología; ingeniería química; ingeniería y metalurgia; tecnología relacionada con la ingeniería.

Ortorgamiento Beca para usarse en el primer o penúltimo año de universidad; no renovable. *Número:* 10 a 50. *Monto:* $1,000 a $5,000.

Requisitos de elegibilidad El postulante debe ser nativo americano/de Alaska o negro (no hispano) o hispano y debe estar inscrito o espera inscribirse a tiempo completo en una institución o universidad que ofrece carreras de dos o cuatro años. El postulante debe tener un GPA mínimo de 3.0 y un puntaje superior a 25 en ACT Assessment (Evaluación ACT) o superior a 1000 en SAT. Disponible para ciudadanos estadounidenses y para aquellos que no son ciudadanos estadounidenses.

Plazo de solicitud 30 de marzo.

Contacta: Latisha Moore, Administrative Assistant
NAMEPA National Scholarship Foundation
1133 West Morse Boulevard, Suite 201
Winter Park, FL 32789
Teléfono: 407-647-8839
Fax: 407-629-2502
E-mail: namepa@namepa.org

PLAYWRIGHTS' CENTER (CENTRO DE DRAMATURGOS)

www.pwcenter.org

Many Voices Residency Program (Programa Many Voices Residency)

El Programa Many Voices del Playwrights' Center enriquece el teatro estadounidense al ofrecer residencias de dramaturgia a artistas de color.

Áreas académicas o profesionales Literatura, inglés, redacción.

Ortorgamiento Subvención para usarse en el primer, segundo, penúltimo, último año de universidad, como graduado o en posgrado; no renovable. *Número:* 7. *Monto:* $1,200 a $2,000.

Requisitos de elegibilidad El postulante debe ser hispano, nativo americano/de Alaska, asiático o de las islas del Pacífico o negro (no hispano) y debe estar inscrito o espera inscribirse a tiempo completo o a tiempo parcial en una institución o universidad que ofrece carreras de cuatro años y ser residente y estudiar en el estado de Minnesota y estar interesado en la redacción. Disponible para ciudadanos estadounidenses.

Plazo de solicitud 31 de julio.

Contacta: Kristen Gandrow, Director of Playwright Services
Playwrights' Center
2301 Franklin Avenue, E
Minneapolis, MN 55406-1099
Teléfono: 612-332-7481
Fax: 612-332-6037
E-mail: info@pwcenter.org

PRESBYTERIAN CHURCH (USA) (IGLESIA PRESBITERIANA DE ESTADOS UNIDOS)

www.pcusa.org/financialaid

Student Opportunity Scholarship-Presbyterian Church (U.S.A.) (Beca de Oportunidad para Estudiantes – Iglesia Presbiteriana (Estados Unidos))

Disponible para estudiantes de duodécimo año de escuela secundaria que estén a punto de graduarse. Los postulantes deben ser miembros de una minoría racial y miembros comulgantes de una iglesia presbiteriana de Estados Unidos.

Ortorgamiento Beca para usarse en el primer, segundo, penúltimo o último año de universidad; renovable. *Número:* hasta 200. *Monto:* $100 a $1,000.

Requisitos de elegibilidad El postulante debe ser presbiteriano, hispano, nativo americano/de Alaska, asiático o de las islas del Pacífico, o negro (no hispano), debe ser estudiante de escuela secundaria y planea inscribirse a tiempo completo en una universidad que ofrece carreras de dos o cuatro años o en una institución técnica. El postulante debe tener un GPA de 2.5 ó superior. Disponible para ciudadanos estadounidenses.

Plazo de solicitud 1° de mayo.

Contacta: Kathy Smith, Program Assistant, Undergraduate Grants
Presbyterian Church (USA)
100 Witherspoon Street
Louisville, KY 40202-1396
Teléfono: 888-728-7228 Ext. 5745
Fax: 502-569-8766
E-mail: ksmith@ctr.pcusa.org

RADIO-TELEVISION NEWS DIRECTORS ASSOCIATION AND FOUNDATION (FUNDACIÓN Y ASOCIACIÓN DE DIRECTORES DE NOTICIAS DE TELEVISIÓN Y RADIO)

www.rtndf.org

Carole Simpson Scholarship (Beca Carole Simpson)

Beca para estudiantes universitarios de minorías de segundo, penúltimo y último año de universidad inscritos en un programa de periodismo electrónico.

Áreas académicas o profesionales Comunicaciones; periodismo; transmisión de televisión o radio.

Ortorgamiento Beca para usarse en el segundo, penúltimo, último año de universidad o graduado; no renovable. *Número:* 1. *Monto:* $2,000.

Requisitos de elegibilidad El postulante debe ser hispano, nativo americano/de Alaska, asiático o de las islas del Pacífico o negro (no hispano); debe estar inscrito o espera inscribirse a tiempo completo en una institución o universidad que ofrece carreras de cuatro años y debe tener interés en fotografía, fotogrametría, filmación de video o redacción. Debe enviar ejemplos de aptitudes de reportajes o producción. Disponible para ciudadanos estadounidenses y para aquellos que no son ciudadanos estadounidenses.

Plazo de solicitud 5 de mayo.

Contacta: Karen Jackson-Buillitt, Project Coordinator
Radio-Television News Directors Association and Foundation
1600 K Street, NW, Suite 700
Washington, DC 20006
Teléfono: 202-467-5218
Fax: 202-223-4007
E-mail: karenb@rtndf.org

Ed Bradley Scholarship (Beca Ed Bradley)

Beca que se entrega por una vez para estudiantes universitarios de minorías de segundo, penúltimo y último año de universidad inscritos en un programa de periodismo electrónico.

Áreas académicas o profesionales Comunicaciones; periodismo; transmisión de televisión o radio.

Ortorgamiento Beca para usarse en el segundo, penúltimo, último año de universidad o graduado; no renovable. *Número:* 1. *Monto:* $10,000.

Requisitos de elegibilidad El postulante debe ser hispano, nativo americano/de Alaska, asiático o de las islas del Pacífico o negro (no hispano) y debe estar inscrito o espera inscribirse a tiempo completo en una institución o universidad que ofrece carreras de cuatro años. Disponible para ciudadanos estadounidenses y para aquellos que no son ciudadanos estadounidenses.

Plazo de solicitud 5 de mayo.

Ken Kashiwahara Scholarship (Beca Ken Kashiwahara)

Beca que se entrega por una vez para estudiantes universitarios de minorías de segundo, penúltimo o último año de universidad cuyo objetivo sea el periodismo electrónico.

Áreas académicas o profesionales Comunicaciones; periodismo; transmisión de televisión o radio.

Ortorgamiento Beca para usarse en el segundo, penúltimo, último año de universidad o graduado; no renovable. *Número:* 1. *Monto:* $2,500.

Requisitos de elegibilidad El postulante debe ser hispano, nativo americano/de Alaska, asiático o de las islas del Pacífico o negro (no hispano) y debe estar inscrito o espera inscribirse a tiempo completo en una institución o universidad que ofrece carreras de cuatro años. Debe enviar ejemplos donde se muestren las aptitudes de reportajes o producción. Disponible para ciudadanos estadounidenses y para aquellos que no son ciudadanos estadounidenses.

Plazo de solicitud 5 de mayo.

Mike Reynolds $1,000 Scholarship (Beca de $1,000 Mike Reynolds)

Se le da preferencia a estudiantes universitarios de minorías que demuestren necesidad de asistencia financiera. Debe incluir un resumen de sus trabajos realizados relacionados con los medios de comunicación y explicar la contribución que haya hecho para financiar su propia educación.

Áreas académicas o profesionales Comunicaciones; periodismo; transmisión de televisión o radio.

Ortorgamiento Beca para usarse en el segundo, penúltimo, último año de universidad o graduado; no renovable. *Número:* 1. *Monto:* $1,000.

Requisitos de elegibilidad El postulante debe ser hispano, nativo americano/de Alaska, asiático o de las islas del Pacífico o negro (no hispano) y debe estar inscrito o espera inscribirse a tiempo completo en una institución o una universidad que ofrece carreras de cuatro años. Disponible para ciudadanos estadounidenses y para aquellos que no son ciudadanos estadounidenses.

Plazo de solicitud 5 de mayo.

N.S. Bienstock Fellowship (Beca de Investigación Bienstock N.S.)

Beca para periodistas de minorías prometedores en la administración de noticias de televisión o radio.

Áreas académicas o profesionales Comunicaciones; periodismo; transmisión de televisión o radio.

Beca de investigación otorgada para usarse en el primer, segundo, penúltimo, último año de universidad o como graduado; no renovable. *Número:* 1. *Monto:* $2,500.

Requisitos de elegibilidad El postulante debe ser hispano, nativo americano/de Alaska, asiático o de las islas del Pacífico o negro (no hispano) y debe estar inscrito o espera inscribirse en una institución o universidad que ofrece carreras de cuatro años.

Plazo de solicitud 5 de mayo.

Contacta: Awards and Events Assistant
Radio-Television News Directors Association and Foundation
1600 K Street, NW, Suite 700
Washington, DC 20006
Teléfono: 202-467-5218
Fax: 202-223-4007

RHODE ISLAND FOUNDATION (FUNDACIÓN DE RHODE ISLAND)

Raymond H. Trott Scholarship (Beca de Raymond H. Trott)

Beca para estudiantes de minorías que sea residente de Rhode Island y que esté en su último año en una universidad acreditada.

Área académica o profesional Operaciones bancarias.

Ortorgamiento Beca para usarse en el último año de universidad; no renovable. *Número:* 1. *Monto:* $1,000.

Requisitos de elegibilidad Debe planear continuar una profesión en operaciones bancarias.

El postulante debe ser hispano, nativo americano/de Alaska, asiático o de las islas del Pacífico o negro (no hispano) y debe estar inscrito o espera inscribirse a tiempo completo en una institución o universidad que ofrece carreras de cuatro años y ser residente del estado de Rhode Island. Disponible para ciudadanos estadounidenses.

Plazo de solicitud 13 de junio.

RDW Group, Inc. Minority Scholarship for Communications (Beca RDW Group, Inc. para Minorías para Comunicaciones)

Beca que se entrega una vez para proporcionar apoyo a estudiantes de minorías que desean continuar un curso de estudio en comunicaciones en un nivel de graduado o universitario.

Área académica o profesional Comunicaciones.

Ortorgamiento Beca para usarse en el primer, segundo, penúltimo, último año de universidad o como graduado; no renovable. *Número:* 1. *Monto:* $2,000.

Requisitos de elegibilidad El postulante debe ser hispano, nativo americano/de Alaska, asiático o de las islas del Pacífico, o negro (no hispano) y debe estar inscrito o espera inscribirse en una institución o universidad y ser residente del estado de Rhode Island.

Plazo de solicitud 13 de junio.

Contacta: Libby Monahan, Scholarship Coordinator
Rhode Island Foundation
One Union Station
Providence, RI 02903
Teléfono: 401-274-4564
Fax: 401-272-1359
E-mail: libbym@rifoundation.org

SOCIETY OF ACTUARIES (SOCIEDAD DE ACTUARIOS)

www.soa.org o www.beanactuary.org

Actuarial Scholarships for Minority Students (Becas actuariales para estudiantes de minorías)

Beca para estudiantes de minorías en un nivel de graduado o universitario que busca una carrera actuarial. Monto basado en el mérito y necesidades individuales.

Área académica o profesional Carrera actuarial.

Ortorgamiento Beca para usarse en el primer, segundo, penúltimo, último año de universidad o como graduado; no renovable. *Monto:* El beneficiario recibe $500 adicionales por cada examen actuarial aprobado.

Requisitos de elegibilidad El postulante debe ser hispano, nativo americano/de Alaska, negro (no hispano) o hispano y estar inscrito o espera inscribirse en una institución o universidad. Debe ser ciudadano estadounidense o residente permanente.

Plazo de solicitud 1° de mayo.

Contacta: Minority Scholarship Coordinator
Society of Actuaries
475 North Martingale Road, Suite 800
Schaumberg, IL 60173-2226
Teléfono: 847-706-3500
E-mail: flupo@casct.org

SOCIETY OF PROFESSIONAL JOURNALISTS, LOS ANGELES CHAPTER (SOCIEDAD DE PERIODISTAS PROFESIONALES, DELEGACIÓN DE LOS ANGELES)

www.spj.org/losangeles

Ken Inouye Scholarship (Beca Ken Inouye)

Becas para estudiantes que hayan completado su segundo año de universidad y estén inscritos o hayan sido aceptados en un programa de periodismo.

Área académica o profesional Periodismo.

Ortorgamiento Beca para usarse en el penúltimo, último año de universidad o como graduado; no renovable. *Monto:* $1,000.

Requisitos de elegibilidad El postulante debe ser nativo americano/de Alaska, asiático o de las islas del Pacífico, negro (no hispano) o hispano, y debe estar inscrito o espera inscribirse a tiempo completo en una institución o universidad que ofrece carreras de cuatro años en el condado de Los Angeles, Ventura u Orange. Disponible para ciudadanos estadounidenses.

Plazo de solicitud 15 de marzo.

Contacta: Society of Professional Journalists, Los Angeles Chapter
c/o Department of Journalism, California State University, Long Beach
1250 Bellflower
Long Beach, CA 90840

STATE STUDENT ASSISTANCE COMMISSION OF INDIANA (SSACI) (COMISIÓN DE ASISTENCIA A ESTUDIANTES DEL ESTADO DE INDIANA)

www.ssaci.in.gov

Programa de Beca de Servicios de Educación Especial y Maestros de Minorías del Estado de Indiana

Destinada a estudiantes negros o hispanos que buscan certificación en enseñanza, certificación de educación especial o certificación de terapia física u ocupacional.

Áreas académicas o profesionales Educación; Educación especial; Rehabilitación o Terapia física.

Ortorgamiento Beca para usarse en el primer, segundo, penúltimo o último año de universidad; no renovable. *Número:* 330 a 370. *Monto:* $1,000 a $4,000.

Requisitos de elegibilidad Debe ser ciudadano estadounidense y residente del estado de Indiana. Debe enseñar en una escuela primaria o secundaria acreditada del estado de Indiana después de graduarse. El postulante debe ser hispano o negro (no hispano) y debe estar inscrito o tener planes de inscribirse como un estudiante a tiempo completo en una universidad o institución que ofrece carreras de cuatro años. Se exige un GPA mínimo de 2.0.

Plazo de solicitud Continuo.

Contacta: Ms. Yvonne Heflin, Director, Special Programs
State Student Assistance Commission of Indiana
(SSACI)
150 West Market Street, Suite 500
Indianapolis, IN 46204-2805
Teléfono: 317-232-2350
Fax: 317-232-3260
E-mail: grants@ssaci.state.un.is

TENNESSEE STUDENT ASSISTANCE CORPORATION (CORPORACIÓN DE ASISTENCIA A ESTUDIANTES DEL ESTADO DE TENNESSEE)

www.state.tn.us/tsac

Minority Teaching Fellows Program/Tennessee (Programa de Becas de Investigación para Minorías de Enseñanza/Tennesse)

Préstamo perdonable a residentes de minorías del estado de Tennessee que continúen carreras en educación. Debe enseñar un año por cada año de beca o reembolsarlo como préstamo.

Áreas académicas o profesionales Educación; educación especial.

Ortorgamiento Préstamo perdonable para usarse en el primer, segundo, penúltimo o último año de universidad; renovable. *Número:* 19 a 29. *Monto:* $5,000.

Requisitos de elegibilidad El postulante de escuela secundaria debe tener un GPA mínimo de 2.75, debe estar en el cuarto superior de la clase o un puntaje de 18 en ACT Assessment. El postulante a la universidad debe tener un GPA mínimo de 2.50. El postulante debe ser hispano, nativo americano/de Alaska, asiático o de las islas del Pacífico o negro (no hispano); debe estar inscrito o espera inscribirse a tiempo completo en una institución o universidad que ofrece carreras de cuatro años; debe ser residente y estudiar en el estado de Tennessee. Disponible para ciudadanos estadounidenses.

Plazo de solicitud 15 de abril.

Contacta: Kathy Stripling, Scholarship Coordinator
Tennessee Student Assistance Corporation
404 James Robertson Parkway, Suite 1950,
Parkway Towers
Nashville, TN 37243-0820
Teléfono: 615-741-1346
Fax: 615-741-6101
E-mail: kathy.stripling@state.tn.us

TEXAS DEPARTMENT OF TRANSPORTATION (DEPARTAMENTO DE TRANSPORTE DEL ESTADO DE TEXAS)

www.dot.state.tx.us

Programa de Subvención Condicional

Subvención que proporciona asistencia financiera de educación a mujeres de minorías para planes de títulos aprobados.

Áreas académicas o profesionales Ciencias de la computación o procesamiento de datos; ingeniería civil.

Ortorgamiento Subvención para usarse en el primer, segundo, penúltimo o último año de universidad; renovable. *Número:* 25. *Monto:* hasta $6,000.

Requisitos de elegibilidad La postulante debe ser hispana, nativa americana/de Alaska, asiática o de las islas del Pacífico o negra (no hispana) y debe estar inscrita o espera inscribirse a tiempo completo en una institución que ofrece carreras de cuatro años; debe ser mujer; y ser residente y estudiar en el estado de Texas. La postulante debe tener un GPA de 2.5 ó superior. Disponible para ciudadanas estadounidenses.

Plazo de solicitud 1° de marzo.

Contacta: Minnie Brown, Program Coordinator
Texas Department of Transportation
125 East 11th Street
Austin, TX 78701-2483
Teléfono: 512-416-4979
Fax: 512-416-4980
E-mail: mbrown2@dot.state.tx.us

UNITED METHODIST CHURCH (IGLESIA METODISTA UNIDA)

www.umc.org/

United Methodist Church Ethnic Scholarship (Beca Étnica de la Iglesia Metodista Unida)

Becas para estudiantes de minorías que continúan un título universitario. Beca que se entrega por una vez, pero es renovable mediante una solicitud cada año.

Áreas académicas o profesionales cualquier título, especialidad o carrera universitaria.

Ortorgamiento Beca para usarse en el primer, segundo, penúltimo o último año de universidad. *Número:* 430 a 500. *Monto:* $800 a $1,000.

Requisitos de elegibilidad El postulante debe ser un miembro certificado de la Iglesia Metodista Unida por un año. El postulante debe ser hispano, nativo americano/de Alaska, asiático o de las islas del Pacífico o negro (no hispano) y debe estar inscrito o espera inscribirse a tiempo completo en una institución o universidad que ofrece carreras de dos o cuatro años. El postulante debe tener un GPA de 2.5 ó superior. Disponible para ciudadanos estadounidenses y para aquellos que no son ciudadanos canadienses.

Plazo de solicitud 1° de mayo.

Contacta: Patti J. Zimmerman, Scholarships Administrator
United Methodist Church
PO Box 340007
Nashville, TN 37203-0007
Teléfono: 615-340-7344
E-mail: pzimmer@gbhem.org

United Methodist Church Hispanic, Asian, and Native American Scholarship (Beca de la Iglesia Metodista Unida Hispana, Asiática y Nativa Americana)

Beca para miembros de Iglesia Metodista Unida que sean estudiantes universitarios de penúltimo, último año o graduados.

Ortorgamiento Beca para usarse en el penúltimo, último año de universidad o como graduado; no renovable. *Número:* 200 a 250. *Monto:* $1,000 a $3,000.

Requisitos de elegibilidad Prueba de membresía y carta del pastor. Se exige un GPA mínimo de 2.8. El postulante debe ser metodista, hispano, nativo americano/de Alaska, asiático o de las islas del Pacífico y debe estar inscrito o espera inscribirse a tiempo completo en una institución o universidad que ofrece carreras de cuatro años. Disponible para ciudadanos estadounidenses.

Plazo de solicitud 1° de abril.

Contacta: Patti J. Zimmerman, Scholarships Administrator
United Methodist Church
PO Box 340007
Nashville, TN 37203-0007
Teléfono: 615-340-7344
E-mail: pzimmer@gbhem.org

WORLDSTUDIO FOUNDATION (FUNDACIÓN WORLDSTUDIO)

www.umc.org/

Special Animation and Illustration Scholarship (Beca de Ilustración y Animación Especiales)

Becas para estudiantes de minorías y de escasos recursos que estén estudiando ilustración y animación en universidades estadounidense. Los beneficiarios se seleccionan de acuerdo con su capacidad y necesidad y por su compromiso demostrado para restituirlo a una gran comunidad a través de su trabajo.

Áreas académicas o profesionales Ilustración y animación.

Ortorgamiento Beca para usarse en el primer, segundo, penúltimo, último año de universidad o como graduado; no renovable. *Número:* 25. *Monto:* $1,500.

Requisitos de elegibilidad El postulante debe ser hispano, nativo americano/de Alaska, asiático o de las islas del Pacífico, o negro (no hispano), y debe estar inscrito o espera inscribirse a tiempo completo en una universidad que ofrece carreras de dos o cuatro años o en una institución técnica. El postulante debe tener un GPA de 2.5 ó superior. Disponible para ciudadanos estadounidenses y para aquellos que no son ciudadanos estadounidenses.

Plazo de solicitud 14 de febrero.

Contacta: Roben Stikeman, Associate Director
Worldstudio Foundation
200 Varick Street, Suite 507
New York, NY 10014
Teléfono: 212-366-1317 Ext. 18
Fax: 212-807-0024
E-mail: scholarships@worldstudio.org

DIRECTORIO DE LA LÍNEA DIRECTA

INFORMACIÓN DEL DEPARTAMENTO DE EDUCACIÓN DE ESTADOS UNIDOS

Presentar la Free Application for Federal Student Aid, FAFSA
www.fafsa.ed.gov

- Enviar una nueva FAFSA
- Enviar una FAFSA renovada
- Corregir una FAFSA o Student Aid Report, SAR
- Solicitar un PIN (Número de identificación personal)

Línea de Ayuda de la FAFSA

- Preguntas sobre la FAFSA
- Estado de la FAFSA

(800) 433-3243

Centro de Información de Ayuda Financiera para Estudiantes
www.studentaid.ed.gov

- Códigos de universidades del Título IV
- Duplicado del SAR

(319) 337-5665

Ayuda Financiera para Estudiantes
www.ed.gov/offices/OPE/Students/

- Lista de códigos de universidades
- Guía para estudiantes
- Guía para préstamos no cumplidos

Ayuda Financiera para Funcionarios de Ayuda Profesional
http://ifap.ed.gov

- Cartas a colegas
- Reglamentos
- Publicaciones de SFZ
- Enlaces a información de capacitación y conferencias

Información de Direct Loans
www.ed.gov/DirectLoan

- Guías y boletines de Direct Loans
- Calculadores de presupuesto y reembolso interactivos
- Información de cuentas de préstamos para prestatarios
- Preguntas más frecuentes
- Enlaces a universidades con préstamos directos

Proyecto EASI (Acceso Fácil para Estudiantes e Instituciones)
http://easi.ed.gov

- Herramientas y recursos para planificar, postular y pagar la educación después de la escuela secundaria
- Acceso futuro de ayuda financiera para estudiantes

William D. Ford Direct Loan Program (Programa de Préstamo Directo William D. Ford)
www.dlservicer.ed.gov

Origen del préstamo: (800) 848-0979

INFORMACIÓN GENERAL DEL GOBIERNO DE ESTADOS UNIDOS

Departamento de Hacienda de Estados Unidos
www.savingsbonds.gov

Administración de Beneficios para Veteranos
www.va.gov

www.gibill.va.gov/education/C35pam.htm

(800) 827-1000

Federal Information Exchange, Inc. para Becas para Minorías
www.fie.com

- Servicio de recuperación de base de datos para universidades y estudiantes

(301) 975-0103

Servicio Selectivo
(847) 688-6888

Administración del Seguro Social
www.ssa.gov

(800) 772-1213

FUENTES GENERALES DE BECAS UNIVERSITARIAS

Planificación Universitaria y Búsqueda de Becas
www.collegenet.com

Servicio de Becas Universitarias
www.collegeboard.com

- Para inscribirse para el PROFILE

(800) 778-6888

Fastweb (parte de monster.com)
www.fastweb.com

FreSch! Servicios de Información
www.freschinfo.com

National Achievement Scholarship Corporation (Sociedad para la Beca Nacional al Mérito)
www.nationalmerit.org

Peterson's
www.petersons.com

Scholarship Resource Network Express (Red Expres de Recursos para Becas)
www.srnexpress.com

CALCULADORES DE NECESIDAD FINANCIERA UNIVERSITARIA

College Board (Consejo Universitario)
www.collegeboard.com

College Smart
www.collegesmart.com

Peterson's
www.petersons.com

UBICADORES DE NIVELACIÓN O DE ADMISIÓN UNIVERSITARIA

College Board
www.collegeboard.com

- Permite desarrollar tu perfil para buscar más de 3,000 universidades.

College Edge
www.collegeedge.com

- Hace coincidir el perfil del estudiante con las universidades para selección.

College Express
www.collegeexpress.com

- Le da a la familia un recorrido del campus de las universidades para selección.

CollegeNET
www.collegenet.com

- Hace coincidir el perfil del estudiante y permite que haya una postulación por Internet.

College View
www.collegeview.com

- Le da a la familia la posibilidad de visitar y ver las oficinas de la universidad.

Peterson's
www.petersons.com

- Proporciona información acerca de más de 3,000 universidades. También incluye información sobre institutos de capacitación profesional, educación a distancia y más.

UBICADOR DE BECAS Y RECURSOS PARA HISPANOS

American Association of Hispanic Certified Public Accountants (Asociación Estadounidense de Contadores Públicos Hispanos Autorizados)
www.college-financial-aid-com/scholarships/hispanic.htm

American Association of Hispanic CPA's Scholarships (Becas de la Asociación Estadounidense de Contadores Públicos Hispanos Autorizados)
www.castldrive.com/scholarships.html

Congressional Hispanic Caucus Institute (Instituto del Grupo Hispano del Congreso)
www.chci.org

Gates Millennium Scholars Program (Programa de Becas Gates Milennium)
www.gmsp.org

GE and GM League of United Latin American Citizens (LULAC) Scholarship Funds (Fondos para la Beca de la Liga de los Ciudadanos Unidos Latinoamericanos de GE y GM).
www.LNESC.org
www.lulac.org/Programs/Scholar.html
(202) 833-6130

Hispanic Certified Public Accountants Scholarships (Becas de Contadores Hispanos Públicos Autorizados)
www.aahcpa.org/scholar.htm

Hispanic Scholarships for Undergraduates (Becas Hispanas para Estudiantes Universitarios)
www.elmhurst.edu/-bio/arriola/Hablamos/scholarships.html

Hispanic Heritage Youth Awards (Beca para Jóvenes de Origen Hispano)
www.hispanicawards.org

Hispanic College Fund (Fondo de Becas Universitarias Hispanas)
www.hispanicfund.org

Hispanic Designers, Inc. (va dirigida a talentos en la industria cultural y del diseño)
www.hispanicdesigners.org

Hispanic College Fund. Inc. (First in My Family Scholarship Program) (Programa de Beca El Primero en Mi Familia)
www.hispanicfund.org

Hispanic MBA's (NSHMBA) (MBA para Hispanos)
www.nshmba.org/infocenter/scholarships.asp

Hispanic Scholarship Fund (Fondo de Becas Hispanas)
www.hsf.net

Hispanic Scholarships for Latino Students (Becas Hispanas para Estudiantes Latinos)
www.lasculturas.com/lib/libScholarships.php

Joel Garcia Memorial Scholarship (Beca en Memoria de Joel Garcia)
www.ccnma.org

Lowrider Magazine Scholarship Fund (Fondo de Beca de la Lowrider Magazine)
www.lowridermagazine.com

Mexican American Grocers Assoc. Foundation Scholarships (for sales merchandising and marketing in the grocery industry) (Becas de la Fundación (para técnica mercantil de ventas y mercadeo en la industria de abarrotes))
www.maga.org/pages.educational programs.htm

National Association of Hispanic Journalist (Asociación Nacional de Periodistas Hispanos)
www.nahg.org/student.html

National Association of Hispanic Publications (Asociación Nacional de Publicaciones Hispanas)
www.nahponline.org/scholarships.html

Peterson's
www.petersons.com

PRÉSTAMOS

Bank of America
www.bankofamerica.com/studentbanking
(800) 344-8382

Chase Education
www.chase.com
(888) 272-5543

Citibank Student Loan Corporation
www.citibank.com/student
(800) 967-2400

Educaid
www.educaid.com
(800) 776-2344

The Educational Resource Institute (TERI)
www.teri.org
(800) 255-8374

MISCELÁNEO

Academic Common Market (Mercado Académico Común)
www.sreb.org/programs/acm/acmindex.asp
(410) 974-2971

ACT
www.act.org
(319) 337-1200

American Legion Education Assistance Program (Programa de Ayuda Educacional de la American Legion)

www.legion.org

(317) 630-1200

California Student Aid Comisión (Comisión de Ayuda para Estudiantes del Estado de California)

(916) 445-0880

CollegeTown

www.ctown.com

(703) 934-2025

The Foundation Center

Servicio al cliente: 800/424-9836

Llamada del estado de NY: 212/620-4230

National Association of College Admissions Counselors, NACAC (Asociación Nacional de Consejeros para el Ingreso Universitario)

www.nacac.com

(800) 822-6285

National Association of Student Financial Aid Administrators, NASFAA (Asociación Nacional de Administradores de Ayuda Financiera a Estudiantes)

www.nasfaa.org

(202) 785-0453

CALENDARIO DE CUENTA REGRESIVA PARA AYUDA FINANCIERA ESTUDIANTIL

Undécimo año, otoño

Ahora es el momento para pensar seriamente en las universidades que te interesan. Acude a tu oficina de orientación para que te ayuden a limitar tu selección. Si todo sale bien, para la primavera tendrás entre cinco o diez buenas alternativas en tu lista. Siempre es buena idea visitar las universidades, recuerda que es allí donde permanecerás los próximos cuatro años, visita el campus cuanto antes.

- Regístrate para el PSAT.
- Averigua sobre las reuniones nocturnas de ayuda financiera en tu localidad. Asegúrate de asistir a estas invaluables sesiones, especialmente si es la primera vez que en tu familia alguien va a la universidad. Trata de aprenderte la jerga de ayuda financiera. Consigue la literatura disponible y empieza a familiarizarte con los diversos programas.
- Presenta el PSAT/NMSQT en noviembre.
- Busca en Internet. Existen muchos motores de búsqueda gratuitos que son extraordinarios para la búsqueda de becas. Es ahora cuando debes averiguar si podrías calificar para becas.
- Haz que tus padres averigüen con sus empleadores, iglesias y fraternidades las posibles oportunidades de becas.
- Verifica en tu oficina de orientación los requisitos y fechas límite para otorgamientos locales.

Undécimo año, invierno

- Sigue buscando becas. Recuerda que esto es algo que puedes controlar. Entre más te esfuerces, mayores oportunidades de éxito tendrás.
- Regístrate y estudia para el SAT (I y II). La mayoría de los programas de becas controlados por universidades toman el SAT como un criterio determinante en el proceso de decisión. Definitivamente, el SAT no es un examen para el que puedas

prepararte trasnochando la noche anterior. Invierte en una guía completa de preparación para el examen. Con una guía de estudio podrás darte cuenta de tus debilidades y fortalezas en las áreas de matemáticas y expresión verbal. Empieza a programar tiempo extra para estudiar las áreas que te resultan difíciles.

Undécimo año, primavera

- $ Receso de primavera: excelente oportunidad para visitar universidades. ¿Tienes una lista de las 10 mejores? Comienza a limitar tu lista.
- $ Revisa los requisitos para becas locales. ¿Qué puedes hacer ahora y durante el verano para mejorar tus oportunidades?
- $ Preséntate a los SAT.
- $ Busca un trabajo de verano, especialmente uno que pueda ajustarse dentro de tus planes universitarios.

Meses de verano

- $ ¡Ya es hora de visitar universidades, en marcha! Comienza a preguntarte: ¿Es aquí donde me veo graduándome? ¿Puedo ajustarme a las estaciones, la ciudad que rodea al campus, la distancia a casa y el tamaño de la universidad?

Duodécimo año, otoño

- $ ¿Puedes limitar tu lista a cinco opciones? Una vez que te concentres en tus cinco opciones, haz una lista de los requisitos de cada universidad para admisiones y ayuda financiera. Asegúrate de que tu lista resalte las fechas límite.
- $ ¿Cuáles universidades requieren la solicitud Profile? Muchas universidades privadas utilizan este formulario para la ayuda financiera. Necesitas llenar este detallado formulario a fines de septiembre o principios de octubre.

- Presenta tus solicitudes de beca antes de la fecha límite publicada. Recuerda que tienes tres opciones: fuentes por tus padres (empleador, religión y fraternidad), escuela secundaria (otorgamientos locales de la PTA (por sus siglas en inglés), Kiwanis y el Lions Club), y los motores de búsqueda de Internet.
- Si piensas volver a presentar el SAT, asegúrate de registrarte ahora.
- Tanto tú como tus padres deben asistir a la reunión nocturna de presentación de ayuda financiera. Algunas de estas sesiones ofrecen ayuda para llenar los formularios, en tanto que otras ofrecen una visión más amplia del proceso. Comunícate con el presentador (por lo general, se trata de un profesional universitario) para asegurarte de obtener la información necesaria.

Duodécimo año, invierno

- Consigue un formulario del Free Application for Federal Student Aid (FAFSA). Este es un formulario clave de ayuda financiera para todas las universidades del país. Recuerda estar pendiente de las fechas límite, pero no lo presentes antes del 1° de enero. Asegúrate de guardar una copia del formulario, bien sea que lo llenes electrónicamente o en formato impreso. ¿Tienes preguntas? Comunícate con tu oficina local de ayuda financiera. Igualmente, ten en cuenta que algunos estados tienen programas de convocatoria especiales en enero y febrero.
- Por lo general, a medida que comienzan a llegar las cartas de admisión, inmediatamente siguen las cartas de otorgamiento. La pregunta clave para los padres es: ¿Cuál es la base? Recuerda, la ayuda para una universidad estatal menos costosa será menor que para una universidad privada más costosa. Pero, ¿qué deberás pagar? Este asunto puede resultar confuso. Trata de estar pendiente de las ayudas financieras (becas y subvenciones), préstamos estudiantiles y préstamos a padres. La universidad con precios más económicos (matrícula, cuotas, alojamiento y comida) puede no ser la más económica al considerar el paquete de ayuda.

Duodécimo año, primavera

- $ ¿Aún no sabes adónde ir? ¿El paquete de ayuda financiera de tus mejores opciones no es suficiente? Comunícate con la oficina de ayuda financiera al respecto. Aunque a las universidades no les gusta el regateo, normalmente están dispuestas a reconsiderar, en especial si se trata de excelentes estudiantes.
- $ Hacia el 1° de mayo debes haber tomado una decisión definitiva. Informa a la universidad y averigua cuál es el próximo paso a seguir. Avisa a las otras universidades que no vas a aceptar sus ofertas de admisión y ayuda financiera.

Verano

- $ Ya es hora de sacar cuentas. Padres, consigan información de los gastos estimados en la universidad. Deduzcan el paquete de ayuda y luego planifiquen cómo pagar los diversos gastos. Comunícate con la oficina de ayuda financiera de la universidad en busca del mejor programa de préstamos a padres.

No olvides: ¡Debes volver a solicitar ayuda cada año!

20 preguntas que debes hacer cuando realices la visita al campus

¿Es práctica común hacer ajustes de gastos individuales de asistencia si los estudiantes y las familias lo solicitan?

¿Cuál es la política de la universidad en cuanto a "ingresos anuales proyectados"?

¿Cuál es la carga académica mínima requerida para mantener las subvenciones?

¿Cuál es la política de la universidad sobre excepciones para una carga mínima de créditos basada en razones de salud o académicas?

¿Puedo entrevistarme con un consejero de ayuda financiera hoy?

¿Tienen en cuenta el ingreso de los padrastros o madrastras cuando analizan una solicitud de ayuda?

¿Tienen en cuenta el ingreso del ex-cónyuge en la solicitud de ayuda financiera?

¿Cuánta ayuda otorgan a una familia a la que le determinan que no tiene el aporte esperado de la familia?

¿Se quedan necesidades sin cubrir en el paquete de ayuda financiera?

¿Cuál es el monto promedio de deuda que tienen estudiantes ya graduados? Y, ¿cuál es el tiempo promedio que les toma graduarse?

¿La subvención para estudiantes de primer año permanece constante durante los tres años restantes?

¿Se brinda ayuda para cursos de verano?

¿Una beca externa reducirá mi ayuda, en especial mis subvenciones o becas institucionales?

¿Es renovable mi beca institucional?

¿Puede recuperarse la elegibilidad perdida para la beca?

¿Cuánto se demora uno en volverse residente estatal? ¿Tienen acuerdos de reciprocidad para matrícula?

¿Cuántas oportunidades de trabajo hay en el campus?

¿Mis ganancias de trabajo dentro o fuera del campus afectarán mi elegibilidad para la subvención?

¿La universidad establece acuerdos con prestamistas que ofrecen descuentos en préstamos tanto a padres como a estudiantes?

¿La universidad conformará paquetes de préstamos que se acomoden a programas emergentes de condonación de préstamos?

NOTAS